INTERNATIONAL ENERGY AGENCY
AGENCE INTERNATIONALE DE L'ENERGIE

ENERGY STATISTICS OF OECD COUNTRIES

1992 - 1993

STATISTIQUES DE L'ENERGIE DES PAYS DE L'OCDE

OECD
OCDE

PARIS 1995

INTERNATIONAL ENERGY AGENCY

2, RUE ANDRÉ-PASCAL, 75775 PARIS CEDEX 16, FRANCE

The International Energy Agency (IEA) is an autonomous body which was established in November 1974 within the framework of the Organisation for Economic Co-operation and Development (OECD) to implement an international energy programme.

It carries out a comprehensive programme of energy co-operation among twenty-three* of the OECD's twenty-five Member countries. The basic aims of the IEA include:

i) co-operation among IEA participating countries to reduce excessive dependence on oil through energy conservation, development of alternative energy sources and energy research and development;

ii) an information system on the international oil market as well as consultation with oil companies;

iii) co-operation with oil producing and other oil consuming countries with a view to developing a stable international energy trade as well as the rational management and use of world energy resources in the interest of all countries;

iv) a plan to prepare participating countries against the risk of a major disruption of oil supplies and to share available oil in the event of an emergency.

* IEA participating countries are: Australia, Austria, Belgium, Canada, Denmark, Finland, France, Germany, Greece, Ireland, Italy, Japan, Luxembourg, the Netherlands, New Zealand, Norway (by special agreement), Portugal, Spain, Sweden, Switzerland, Turkey, the United Kingdom, the United States. The Commission of the European Communities takes part in the work of the IEA.

ORGANISATION FOR ECONOMIC CO-OPERATION AND DEVELOPMENT

Pursuant to Article 1 of the Convention signed in Paris on 14th December 1960, and which came into force on 30th September 1961, the Organisation for Economic Co-operation and Development (OECD) shall promote policies designed:

— to achieve the highest sustainable economic growth and employment and a rising standard of living in Member countries, while maintaining financial stability, and thus to contribute to the development of the world economy;

— to contribute to sound economic expansion in Member as well as non-member countries in the process of economic development; and

— to contribute to the expansion of world trade on a multilateral, non-discriminatory basis in accordance with international obligations.

The original Member countries of the OECD are Austria, Belgium, Canada, Denmark, France, Germany, Greece, Iceland, Ireland, Italy, Luxembourg, the Netherlands, Norway, Portugal, Spain, Sweden, Switzerland, Turkey, the United Kingdom and the United States. The following countries became Members subsequently through accession at the dates indicated hereafter: Japan (28th April 1964), Finland (28th January 1969), Australia (7th June 1971), New Zealand (29th May 1973) and Mexico (18th May 1994). The Commission of the European Communities takes part in the work of the OECD (Article 13 of the OECD Convention).

AGENCE INTERNATIONALE DE L'ÉNERGIE
2, RUE ANDRÉ-PASCAL 75775 PARIS CEDEX 16, FRANCE

L'Agence Internationale de l'Énergie (AIE) est un organe autonome institué en novembre 1974 dans le cadre de l'Organisation de Coopération et de Développement Économiques (OCDE) afin de mettre en œuvre un programme international de l'énergie.

Elle applique un programme général de coopération entre vingt-trois* des vingt-cinq pays Membres de l'OCDE. Les objectifs fondamentaux de l'AIE sont les suivants :

i)   réaliser une coopération entre les pays participants de l'AIE, en vue de réduire leur dépendance excessive à l'égard du pétrole grâce à des économies d'énergie, le développement de sources d'énergie de remplacement, ainsi que la recherche et le développement dans le domaine de l'énergie ;

ii)   l'établissement d'un système d'information sur le marché international du pétrole, ainsi que des consultations avec les compagnies pétrolières ;

iii)   une coopération avec les pays producteurs de pétrole et les autres pays consommateurs de pétrole en vue de développer un commerce international stable de l'énergie et de réaliser une gestion et une utilisation rationnelle des ressources énergétiques dans le monde, dans l'intérêt de tous les pays ;

iv)   l'élaboration d'un plan destiné à préparer les pays participants à l'éventualité d'un bouleversement important des approvisionnements pétroliers et de partager le pétrole disponible en cas de crise.

* Pays participants de l'AIE : Allemagne, Australie, Autriche, Belgique, Canada, Danemark, Espagne, États-Unis, Finlande, France, Grèce, Irlande, Italie, Japon, Luxembourg, Norvège (en vertu d'un accord spécial), Nouvelle-Zélande, Pays-Bas, Portugal, Royaume-Uni, Suède, Suisse et Turquie. La Commission des Communautés européennes participe aux travaux de l'AIE.

ORGANISATION DE COOPÉRATION
ET DE DÉVELOPPEMENT ÉCONOMIQUES

En vertu de l'article 1er de la Convention signée le 14 décembre 1960, à Paris, et entrée en vigueur le 30 septembre 1961, l'Organisation de Coopération et de Développement Économiques (OCDE) a pour objectif de promouvoir des politiques visant :

—   à réaliser la plus forte expansion de l'économie et de l'emploi et une progression du niveau de vie dans les pays Membres, tout en maintenant la stabilité financière, et à contribuer ainsi au développement de l'économie mondiale ;

—   à contribuer à une saine expansion économique dans les pays Membres, ainsi que les pays non membres, en voie de développement économique ;

—   à contribuer à l'expansion du commerce mondial sur une base multilatérale et non discriminatoire conformément aux obligations internationales.

Les pays Membres originaires de l'OCDE sont : l'Allemagne, l'Autriche, la Belgique, le Canada, le Danemark, l'Espagne, les États-Unis, la France, la Grèce, l'Irlande, l'Islande, l'Italie, le Luxembourg, la Norvège, les Pays-Bas, le Portugal, le Royaume-Uni, la Suède, la Suisse et la Turquie. Les pays suivants sont ultérieurement devenus Membres par adhésion aux dates indiquées ci-après : le Japon (28 avril 1964), la Finlande (28 janvier 1969), l'Australie (7 juin 1971), la Nouvelle-Zélande (29 mai 1973) et le Mexique (18 mai 1994). La Commission des Communautés européennes participe aux travaux de l'OCDE (article 13 de la Convention de l'OCDE).

TABLE OF CONTENTS

TABLE DES MATIERES

I. INTRODUCTION

This publication is intended for those involved in analytical and policy work related to international energy issues. It provides detailed statistics on production, trade and consumption for each source of energy in the OECD in a common format (definitional and methodological) for all Member countries.

The data shown in this publication are based on information provided in four annual OECD questionnaires: Oil, Natural Gas, Solid Fuels, Wastes and Manufactured Gases, and Electricity and Heat completed by the national administrations of the OECD Member governments.

While every effort is made to ensure the accuracy of the data, quality is not homogeneous throughout the publication. Country notes and individual country data should be consulted when using regional aggregates. In general, data are likely to be more accurate for production, trade and total consumption than for individual sectors in final consumption which often need to be estimated by administrations.

OECD regional statistics now include Mexico (from 1971 onwards) following Mexico's accession to the OECD on 18th May 1994.

For historical data please refer to *Energy Statistics of OECD Countries 1960-1969, 1970-1979,* and *1980-1989,* which were published in 1991.

A companion volume - *Energy Balances of OECD Countries 1992 to 1993* - presents corresponding data in comprehensive balances expressed in a common unit, million tonnes of oil equivalent (Mtoe), with 1 toe = 10^7 kcal = 41.868 gigajoules.

Complete supply and consumption data from 1960 to 1993 are available on diskettes suitable for use on IBM-compatible personal computers and on magnetic tapes from the main sales outlets listed in the back of the book.

Enquiries about data or methodology should be addressed to Karen Tréanton (33-1) 45-24-94-46.

Note	**See multilingual pullout on back cover.**
Achtung	**Aufklappbaren Text auf der letzten Umschlagseite.**
Attenzione	**Riferirsi al glossario poliglotta alla fine del libro.**
Nota	**Véase el glosario plurilingüe al final del libro.**
Примеч.	**Смотрите многоязычный словарь в конце книги.**

II.   GENERAL NOTES

The tables include all "commercial" sources of energy, both primary (hard coal, brown coal/lignite, peat, natural gas, crude oil, NGL, hydro, geothermal/solar, wind, tide etc. and nuclear power) and secondary (coal products, manufactured gases, petroleum products and electricity).   Data are given for various sources of combustible renewables and waste such as solid biomass and animal products, gas/liquids from biomass, municipal waste and industrial waste, as well as for heat (produced in Combined Heat and Power stations and in Heat plants) under the heading *heat*.

Each table is divided into three main parts; the first shows *supply* elements; the second gives the *transformation* and *energy* sectors; the third shows *final consumption* broken down into the various end-use sectors.

A. Supply

The first part of the basic energy balance shows the following elements of supply:

	Production
+	*Inputs from other sources*
+	*Imports*
-	*Exports*
-	*International marine bunkers*
±	*Stock changes*
=	*Domestic supply*

1.   Production

Production refers to the quantities of fuels extracted or produced, calculated after any operation for removal of inert matter or impurities (e.g. sulphur from natural gas).   Indigenous production in the heat column represents the quantity of heat from heat pumps that is extracted from the ambient environment.

2.   Inputs from Other Sources

All inputs of origin other than primary energy sources explicitly recognised in the tables are listed under inputs *from other sources*, e.g. under crude oil: inputs of origin other than crude oil and NGL such as hydrogen, synthetic crude oil (including mineral oil extracted from bituminous minerals such as shales, bituminous sand, etc.); under additives: benzol, alcohol and methanol produced from natural gas; under refinery feedstocks: backflows from the petrochemical industry used as refinery feedstocks; under hard coal: recovered slurries, middlings, recuperated coal dust and other low-grade coal products that cannot be classified according to type of coal from which they are obtained; under gas works gas: natural gas, refinery gas, and LPG, that are treated or mixed in gas works (i.e. gas works gas produced from sources other than coal).

3.   Imports and Exports

Imports and exports comprise amounts having crossed the national territorial boundaries of the country whether or not customs clearance has taken place.

a)   Oil and Gas

Quantities of crude oil and oil products imported or exported under processing agreements (i.e. refining on account) are included.   Quantities of oil in transit are excluded. Crude oil, NGL and natural gas are reported as coming from the country of origin; refinery feedstocks and oil products are reported as coming from the country of last consignment.

Re-exports of oil imported for processing within bonded areas are shown as an export of product from the processing country to the final destination.

b) Solid Fuels

Imports and exports comprise the amount of fuels obtained from or supplied to other countries, whether or not there is an economic or customs union between the relevant countries. Solid fuels in transit should not be included.

c) Electricity

Amounts are considered as imported or exported when they have crossed the national territorial boundaries of the country.

4. International Marine Bunkers

International marine bunkers cover those quantities delivered to sea-going ships of all flags, including warships. Consumption by ships engaged in transport in inland and coastal waters and by fishing vessels in all waters is not included. See definition of the transport [C.2] and agriculture [C.3] sectors below.

5. Stock Changes

Stock changes reflect the difference between opening stock levels at the first day of the year and closing levels on the last day of the year of stocks on national territory held by producers, importers, energy transformation industries and large consumers. Oil and gas stock changes in pipelines are not taken into account. With the exception of large users mentioned above, changes in final users' stocks are not taken into account. A stock build is shown as a negative number, and a stock draw as a positive number.

6. Domestic Supply

Domestic supply is defined as production + supply from other sources + imports - exports - international marine bunkers ± stock changes.

7. Transfers

Transfers comprise *interproduct transfers* and *products transferred*.

Interproduct transfers result from reclassification of products either because their specification has changed or because they are blended into another product, e.g. kerosene may be reclassified as gasoil after blending with the latter in order to meet its winter diesel specification. The net balance of *interproduct transfers* is zero.

Products transferred is intended for petroleum products imported for further processing in refineries. For example, fuel oil imported for upgrading in a refinery is transferred to the feedstocks category.

For petroleum products, this row also includes primary product receipts which cover indigenous or imported crude oil and indigenous NGL which are *used directly* without being processed in an oil refinery (for example, crude oil used for electricity production).

8. Statistical Difference

In principle, the figure for domestic supply should equal the sum of transfers, distribution losses, deliveries to final consumption, and use for transformation and consumption within the energy sector. However, in practice this is rarely the case and the difference is shown as *statistical difference*. This arises because the data for the individual components of supply are often derived from different data sources by the national administration. Furthermore, the inclusion of changes in some large consumers' stocks in the supply part of the balance introduces distortions which also contribute to the statistical difference.

B. Transformation and Energy Sectors

The *transformation sector* comprises the conversion of primary forms of energy to secondary and further transformation, e.g. coking coal to coke, crude oil to petroleum products, heavy fuel oil to electricity.

The *energy sector* comprises the amount of fuels used by the energy producing industries, e.g. for heating, lighting and operation of all equipment used in the extraction process, for traction and for distribution.

The following categories are distinguished in the *transformation* and *energy* sectors.

1. Transformation Sector

- *Electricity plants* (refers to plants which are designed to produce electricity only). If one or more units of the plant is a CHP unit (and the inputs and outputs can not be distinguished on a unit basis) then the whole plant is designated as a CHP plant. Both public[1] and autoproducer[2] plants are included here.

- *Combined heat and power plants* (refers to plants which are designed to produce both heat and electricity). UNIPEDE refers to these as co-generation power stations. If possible, fuel inputs and electricity/heat outputs are on a unit basis rather than on a plant basis. However, if data are not available on a unit basis, the convention for defining a CHP plant noted above should be adopted. Both public and autoproducer plants are included here. *Note that for autoproducer's CHP plants, all fuel inputs to electricity production are taken into account, while only the part of fuel inputs to heat **sold** is shown. Fuel inputs for the production of heat consumed within the*

*autoproducer's establishment are **not** included here but are included with figures for the final consumption of fuels in the appropriate consuming sector.*

- *Heat plants* (refers to plants [including heat pumps and electric boilers] designed to produce heat only and who sell heat to a third party [e.g. residential, commercial or industrial consumers] under the provisions of a contract). Both public and autoproducer plants are included here.

- *Transformation to solids* (covers the use of fuels for the manufacture of patent fuels, coke and BKB).

- *Transformation to gases* (covers the quantities of fuels used for the production of town, blast furnace and coke oven gases). The production of pig-iron from iron ore in blast furnaces uses fuels for supporting the blast furnace charge and providing heat and carbon for the reduction of the iron ore. Some of the carbon is absorbed into the pig-iron. Accounting for the calorific content of the fuels entering the process is therefore a complex matter as transformation (into blast furnace gas), consumption (heat of combustion) and non-energy use (retention of carbon in pig-iron) occur simultaneously. In the 1992/1993 annual questionnaires, member countries were asked for the first time, to report in the transformation sector all fuels entering blast furnaces. Using these data and basing itself on studies of blast furnace behavior, the Secretariat has reallocated the calorific content of the fuels between the three categories of use as follows: 30% to transformation, 65% to consumption (shown in the industry branch - iron and steel) and 5% to non-energy use. Due to data availability, this model was applied selectively. See Country Notes.

- *Petroleum refineries* (covers the use of hydrocarbons for the manufacture of finished petroleum products).

- *Liquefaction* includes diverse liquefaction processes, such as coal liquefaction into oil in Germany, and natural gas to gasoline in New Zealand.

- *Other transformation sector* (includes backflows returned from the petrochemical sector and non-specified transformation).

---

1 Public supply undertakings generate electricity and/or heat for sale to third parties, *as their primary activity.* They may be privately or publicly owned. Note that the sale need not take place through the public grid.

2 Autoproducer undertakings generate electricity and/or heat, wholly or partly for their own use as an activity which supports their primary activity. They may be privately or publicly owned.

2. Energy Sector

Energy producing industry's own use includes energy consumed by transformation industries for heating, pumping, traction and lighting purposes [ISIC[3] Divisions 10, 11, 12, 23 and 40]:

- *Coal mines* (hard coal and lignite);

- *Oil and gas extraction* (flared gas is not included);

- *Petroleum refineries*;

- *Electricity, CHP and heat plants*;

- *Pumped storage* (electricity consumed in hydro-electric plants);

- *Other energy sector* (including own consumption in patent fuel plants, coke ovens, gas works, BKB and lignite coke plants as well as the non-specified energy sector's use).

3. Distribution losses

Distribution losses include losses in gas distribution, electricity transmission, and coal transport.

C. Final Consumption

The term *final consumption* (equal to the sum of end-use sectors' consumption) implies that energy used for transformation and for own use of the energy producing industries is excluded. Final consumption reflects for the most part deliveries to consumers (see note on stock changes in paragraph A.5 above).

In final consumption, petrochemical feedstocks are covered under **industry** as an *of which* item under chemical industry for those oil products that are principally used for energy purposes. Separated from these are the other oil products that are mainly used for non-energy purposes (see non-energy use in paragraph C.4 below), which are shown in the rows for non-

energy uses and included only in **total final consumption**. Backflows from the petrochemical industry are not included in final consumption (see paragraphs A.2 and B.1 above).

1. Industry Sector

Consumption of the *industry sector* is specified in the following sub-sectors (energy used for transport by industry is not included here but reported under transport):

- *Iron and steel industry* [ISIC Group 271 and Class 2731];

- *Chemical industry* [ISIC Division 24];
  of which: petrochemical feedstocks. The petrochemical industry includes cracking and reforming processes for the purpose of producing ethylene, propylene, butylene, synthesis gas, aromatics, butadene and other hydrocarbon-based raw materials in processes such as steam cracking, aromatics plants and steam reforming. [Part of ISIC Group 241]; See feedstocks under paragraph C.4 below. (Non-energy use).

- *Non-ferrous metals* basic industries [ISIC Group 272 and Class 2732];

- *Non-metallic mineral* products such as glass, ceramic, cement, etc. [ISIC Division 26];

- *Transport equipment* [ISIC No. Divisions 34 and 35];

- *Machinery.* Fabricated metal products, machinery and equipment other than transport equipment [ISIC Divisions 28, 29, 30, 31 and 32];

- *Mining (excluding fuels) and quarrying* [ISIC Divisions 13 and 14];

- *Food processing, beverages and tobacco* [ISIC Divisions 15 and 16];

- *Pulp, paper and printing* [ISIC Divisions 21 and 22];

- *Wood and wood products* (other than pulp and paper) [ISIC Division 20];

---

3 International Standard Classification of All Economic Activities, Series M, No. 4/Rev. 3, United Nations, New York, 1990.

- *Construction* [ISIC Division 45];

- *Textiles and leather* [ISIC Divisions 17, 18 and 19];

- *Non-specified* (any manufacturing industry not included above) [ISIC Divisions 25, 33, 36 and 37];

Note: Most countries have difficulties supplying an industrial breakdown for all fuels. In this case, the *non-specified* industry row has been used. *Regional aggregates of industrial consumption should therefore be used with caution.* Please see Country Notes.

2. Transport Sector

Consumption in the *Transport sector* covers all transport activity regardless of the economic sector to which it is contributing [ISIC Divisions 60, 61 and 62], and is divided into the following sub-sectors:

- *International Civil Aviation*: Deliveries of aviation fuels to international civil aviation. For many countries this excludes fuel used by domestically owned carriers for their international departures;

- *Domestic Air Transport*: Deliveries of aviation fuels to all domestic air transport, commercial, private, agricultural, military, etc. It also includes use for purposes other than flying, e.g. bench testing of engines, but not airline use of fuel for road transport. For many countries this also includes fuel used by domestically owned carriers for outbound international traffic;

- *Road transport*: All fuels used in road vehicles (including military) as well as agricultural and industrial highway use. Excludes motor gasoline used in stationary engines, and diesel oil for use in tractors that are not for highway use;

- *Railways*: All quantities used in rail traffic, including industrial railways;

- *Internal and coastal navigation* (including small craft and coastal vessels not purchasing their bunker requirements under international marine bunker contracts). Fuel used for ocean, coastal and inland fishing should be included in agriculture;

- *Pipeline transport*: Energy used for transport of materials by pipeline;

- *Non-specified*.

3. Other Sectors

- *Agriculture*: Defined as all deliveries to users classified as agriculture, hunting and forestry by the ISIC, and therefore includes energy consumed by such users whether for traction (excluding agricultural highway use), power or heating (agricultural and domestic). Also includes fuels used for ocean, coastal and inland fishing. ISIC Divisions 01, 02 and 05;

- *Commercial and public services*: All activities coming into ISIC Divisions 41, 50, 51, 52, 55, 63, 64, 65, 66, 70, 71, 72, 73, 74, 75, 80, 85, 90, 91, 93 and 99;

- *Residential*: All consumption by households;

- *Non-specified*: Includes all fuel use not elsewhere specified (e.g. military fuel consumption with the exception of transport fuels in the domestic air and road sectors and consumption in the above-designated categories for which separate figures have not been provided).

4. Non-energy use

Non-energy use covers use of *other* petroleum products such as white spirit, paraffin waxes, lubricants, bitumen and other products (see paragraph III.21-22 below). They are shown separately by final consumption sector under the heading *non-energy use* and are included in total final consumption. It is assumed that the use of these products is exclusively non-energy use. It should be noted that petroleum coke is shown as *non-energy use* only when there is evidence of such use, otherwise it is shown under energy use in industry or other sectors.

Feedstocks for petrochemical industry are accounted for in industry under chemical industry (row 31) and shown separately under: *of which: feedstocks* (row 32). This covers all oil and gas, including naphtha except the *other petroleum products* listed below in paragraph III.22.

III. NOTES ON ENERGY SOURCES

Solid Fuels

The heading *coal mines* refers only to coal which is used directly within the coal industry. It excludes coal burned in pithead power stations (included under *transformation* - electric plants) and free allocations to miners and their families (considered as part of household consumption and therefore included under *other sectors* - residential).

1. Coking Coal

Coking coal refers to coal with a quality that allows the production of a coke suitable to support a blast furnace charge. Its gross calorific value is greater than 23 865 kJ/kg (5 700 kcal/kg) on an ash-free but moist basis.

2. Steam Coal (Other Bituminous Coal and Anthracite)

Steam coal is coal used for steam raising and space heating purposes and includes all anthracite coals and bituminous coals not included under coking coal. Its gross calorific value is greater than 23 865 kJ/kg (5 700 kcal/kg), but usually lower than that of coking coal.

3. Sub-Bituminous Coal

Non-agglomerating coals with a gross calorific value between 17 435 kJ/kg (4 165 kcal/kg) and 23 865 kJ/kg (5 700 kcal/kg) containing more than 31 per cent volatile matter on a dry mineral matter free basis.

4. Lignite

Lignite is a non-agglomerating coal with a gross calorific value of less than 17 435 kJ/kg (4 165 kcal/kg), and greater than 31 per cent volatile matter on a dry mineral matter free basis.

5. Peat

Combustible soft, porous or compressed, fossil sedimentary deposit of plant origin with high water content (up to 90 per cent in the raw state), easily cut, of light to dark brown colour.

6. Coke Oven Coke and Gas Coke

Coke oven coke is the solid product obtained from the carbonisation of coal, principally coking coal, at high temperature. It is low in moisture content and volatile matter. Also included are semi-coke, a solid product obtained from the carbonisation of coal at a low temperature, lignite coke and semi-coke made from lignite. The heading *other energy sector* represents consumption at the coking plants themselves. Consumption in the iron and steel industry does not include coke converted into blast furnace gas. To obtain the total consumption of coke oven coke in the iron and steel industry, the quantities converted into blast furnace gas have to be added (these are shown under *transformation* - for gases).

Gas coke is a by-product of hard coal used for the production of town gas in gas works. Gas coke is used for heating purposes. *Other energy sector* data represent consumption of gas coke at gas works.

7. Patent Fuel and Brown Coal/Peat Briquettes (BKB)

Patent fuel is a composition fuel manufactured from coal fines with the addition of a binding agent (pitch). The amount of patent fuel produced is, therefore, slightly higher than the actual amount of coal consumed in the transformation process. Consumption of patent fuels during the patent fuel manufacturing process is shown under *other energy sector*.

BKB are composition fuels manufactured from brown coal, produced by briquetting under high pressure. These figures include peat briquettes, dried lignite, fines and dust and brown coal breeze. The heading *other energy sector* includes consumption by briquetting plants.

Crude Oil, NGL, Refinery Feedstocks

Petroleum refineries under *transformation* shows inputs of crude oil, NGL, refinery feedstocks, additives and other hydrocarbons into the refining process.

8. Crude Oil

Crude oil is a mineral oil consisting of a mixture of hydrocarbons of natural origin, being yellow to black in colour, of variable density and viscosity. It also includes lease condensate (separator liquids) which are recovered from gaseous hydrocarbons in lease separation facilities.

Other hydrocarbons, including synthetic crude oil, mineral oils extracted from bituminous minerals such as shales, bituminous sand, etc., and oils from coal liquefaction are included in the row *from other sources*. See paragraph A.2 above.

Imports and production of emulsified oils (e.g. orimulsion) are included here. As these oils do not need further processing in a refinery, they are transferred to *other petroleum products* for consumption. Please consult individual country notes for exceptions to this treatment.

9. Natural Gas Liquids (NGL)

NGLs are the liquid or liquefied hydrocarbons produced in the manufacture, purification and stabilisation of natural gas. These are those portions of natural gas which are recovered as liquids in separators, field facilities, or gas processing plants. NGLs include but are not limited to ethane, propane, butane, pentane, natural gasoline and condensate. They may also include small quantities of non-hydrocarbons.

10. Refinery Feedstocks

A refinery feedstock is a product or a combination of products derived from crude oil and destined for further processing other than blending in the refining industry. It is transformed into one or more components and/or finished products. This definition covers those finished products imported for refinery intake and those returned from the petro-chemical industry to the refining industry.

11. Additives

Additives are non-hydrocarbon substances added or blended with a product to modify its properties, for example, to improve its combustion characteristics e.g. alcohols and ethers (MTBE, methyl tertiary-butyl ether) and chemical alloys such as tetraethyl lead. However, ethanol is not included here, but under Gas/Liquids from Biomass.

Petroleum Products

Petroleum products are any oil-based products which can be obtained by distillation and are normally used outside the refining industry. The exception to this are those finished products which are classified as refinery feedstocks above.

Production of the petroleum products shows gross refinery output for each product.

Refinery fuel (row *petroleum refineries*, under *energy sector*) represents consumption of petroleum products, both intermediate and finished, within refineries, e.g. for heating, lighting, traction, etc.

12. Refinery Gas (not liquefied)

Refinery gas is defined as non-condensible gas obtained during distillation of crude oil or treatment of oil products (e.g. cracking) in refineries. It consists mainly of hydrogen, methane, ethane and olefins. It also includes gases which are returned from the petrochemical industry. Refinery gas production refers to gross production. Own consumption is shown separately under *petroleum refineries* in the *energy* sector.

13. Liquefied Petroleum Gases (LPG) and Ethane

These are the light hydrocarbons fraction of the paraffin series, derived from refinery processes, crude oil stabilisation plants and natural gas processing plants comprising propane (C_3H_8) and butane (C_4H_{10}) or a combination of the two. They are normally liquefied under pressure for transportation and storage.

Ethane is a naturally gaseous straight-chain hydrocarbon (C_2H_6). It is a colourless paraffinic gas which is extracted from natural gas and refinery gas streams.

14. Motor Gasoline

This is light hydrocarbon oil for use in internal combustion engines such as motor vehicles, excluding aircraft. Motor gasoline is distilled between 35 °C and 215 °C and is used as a fuel for land based spark ignition engines. Motor gasoline may include additives (such as ethanol), oxygenates and octane enhancers, including lead compounds such as TEL (Tetraethyl lead) and TML (tetramethyl lead).

15. Aviation Gasoline

Aviation gasoline is motor spirit prepared especially for aviation piston engines, with an octane number suited to the engine, a freezing point of -60 °C, and a distillation range usually within the limits of 30 °C and 180 °C.

16. Jet Fuel

This category comprises both gasoline and kerosene type jet fuels meeting specifications for use in aviation turbine power units.

a) *Gasoline type jet fuel*

This includes all light hydrocarbon oils for use in aviation turbine power units. They distil between 100 °C and 250 °C. It is obtained by blending kerosenes and gasoline or naphthas in such a way that the aromatic content does not exceed 25 per cent in volume, and the vapour pressure is between 13.7 kPa and 20.6 kPa. Additives can be included to improve fuel stability and combustibility.

b) *Kerosene type jet fuel*

This is medium distillate used for aviation turbine power units. It has the same distillation characteristics and flash point as kerosene (between 150 °C and 300 °C but not generally above 250 °C). In addition, it has particular specifications (such as freezing point) which are established by the International Air Transport Association (IATA).

17. Kerosene

Kerosene comprises refined petroleum distillate intermediate in volatility between gasoline and gas/diesel oil. It is a medium oil distilling between 150 °C and 300 °C.

18. Gas/Diesel Oil (Distillate Fuel Oil)

Gas/diesel oil includes heavy gas oils. Gas oils are obtained from the lowest fraction from atmospheric distillation of crude oil, while heavy gas oils are obtained by vacuum redistillation of the residual from atmospheric distillation. Gas/diesel oil distils between 180 °C and 380 °C. Several grades are available depending on uses: diesel oil for diesel compression ignition (cars, trucks, marine, etc.), light heating oil for industrial and commercial uses, and other gas oil including heavy gas oils which distil between 380 °C and 540 °C and which are used as petrochemical feedstocks.

19. Heavy Fuel Oil (Residual)

This heading defines oils that make up the distillation residue. It comprises all residual fuel oils (including those obtained by blending). Its kinematic viscosity is above 10 cST at 80 °C. The flash point is always above 50 °C and the density is always more than 900 kg/l.

20. Naphtha

Naphtha is a feedstock destined for either the petrochemical industry (e.g. ethylene manufacture or aromatics production) or for gasoline production by reforming or isomerisation within the refinery. Naphtha comprises material in the 30 °C and 210 °C distillation range or part of this range. Naphtha imported for blending is shown as an import of naphtha, then shown in the transfers row as a negative entry for naphtha and a positive entry for the corresponding finished product (e.g. gasoline).

21. Petroleum Coke

Petroleum coke is defined as a black solid residue, obtained mainly by cracking and carbonising of residue feedstocks, tar and pitches in processes such as delayed coking or fluid coking. It consists mainly of carbon (90 to 95 per cent) and has a low ash content.

It is used as a feedstock in coke ovens for the steel industry, for heating purposes, for electrode manufacture and for production of chemicals. The two most important qualities are "green coke" and "calcinated coke". This category also includes "catalyst coke" deposited on the catalyst during refining processes: this coke is not recoverable and is usually burned as refinery fuel.

22. Other Petroleum Products

The category *other petroleum products* groups together white spirit and SBP, lubricants, bitumen, paraffin waxes and others.

a)   ***White Spirit and SBP***: White spirit and SBP are refined distillate intermediates with a distillation in the naphtha/kerosene range.

They are sub-divided as:

i)   **Industrial Spirit (SBP)**: Light oils distilling between 30 °C and 200 °C, with a temperature difference between 5 per cent volume and 90 per cent volume distillation points, including losses, of not more than 60 °C. In other words, SBP is a light oil of narrower cut than motor spirit. There are 7 or 8 grades of industrial spirit, depending on the position of the cut in the distillation range defined above.

ii)   **White Spirit**: Industrial spirit with a flash point above 30 °C. The distillation range of white spirit is 135 °C to 200 °C.

b)   ***Lubricants***: Lubricants are hydrocarbons produced from distillate or residue; they are mainly used to reduce friction between bearing surfaces. This category includes all finished grades of lubricating oil, from spindle oil to cylinder oil, and those used in greases, including motor oils and all grades of lubricating oil base stocks.

c)   ***Bitumen***: Solid, semi-solid or viscous hydrocarbon with a colloidal structure, being brown to black in colour, obtained as a residue in the distillation of crude oil, vacuum distillation of oil residues from atmospheric distillation. Bitumen is often referred to as asphalt and is primarily used for surfacing of roads and for roofing material. This category includes fluidized and cut back bitumen.

d) ***Paraffin Waxes***: Saturated aliphatic hydrocarbons (with the general formula C_nH_{2n+2}). These waxes are residues extracted when dewaxing lubricant oils and they have a crystalline structure with carbon number greater than 12. Their main characteristics are as follows: they are colourless, odourless and translucent, with a melting point above 45 °C.

e) ***Others***: Includes the petroleum products not classified above, for example: tar, sulphur, and grease. This category also includes aromatics (e.g. BTX or benzene, toluene and xylene) and olefins (e.g. propylene) produced within refineries.

Gases

The figures for these four categories of gas are all expressed in terajoules based on **gross calorific values**.

23. Natural Gas

Natural gas comprises gases, occurring in underground deposits, whether liquefied or gaseous, consisting mainly of methane. It includes both "non-associated" gas originating from fields producing only hydrocarbons in gaseous form, and "associated" gas produced in association with crude oil as well as methane recovered from coal mines (colliery gas).

Production is measured after purification and extraction of NGL and sulphur, and excludes re-injected gas, quantities vented or flared. It includes gas consumed by gas processing plants and gas transported by pipeline.

24. Gas Works Gas

Gas works gas covers all types of gas produced in public utility or private plants, whose main purpose is manufacture, transport and distribution of gas. It includes gas produced by carbonisation (including gas produced by coke ovens and transferred to gas works), by total gasification with or without enrichment with oil products, by cracking of natural gas, and by reforming and simple mixing of gases and/or air. This heading also includes substitute natural gas, which is a high calorific value gas manufactured by chemical conversion of a hydrocarbon fossil fuel.

25. Coke Oven Gas

Coke oven gas is obtained as a by-product of the manufacture of coke oven coke for the production of iron and steel.

26. Blast Furnace Gas

Blast furnace gas is produced during the combustion of coke in blast furnaces in the iron and steel industry. It is recovered and used as a fuel partly within the plant and partly in other steel industry processes or in power stations equipped to burn it. Also included here is oxygen steel furnace gas which is obtained as a by-product of the production of steel in an oxygen furnace and is recovered on leaving the furnace. The gas is also known as converter gas or LD gas.

Combustible Renewables and Waste

The figures for these four categories of gas are all expressed in terajoules based on **net calorific values**.

27. Solid Biomass and Animal Products

Biomass is defined as any plant matter used directly as fuel or converted into other forms before combustion. Included are wood, vegetal waste (including wood waste and crops used for energy production), animal materials/wastes and sulphite lyes, also known as "black liquor" (an alkaline spent liquor from the digesters in the production of sulphate or soda pulp during the manufacture of paper where the energy content derives from the lignin removed from the wood pulp).

28. Gas/Liquids from Biomass

Biomass gases are derived principally from the anaerobic fermentation of biomass and solid wastes and combusted to produce heat and/or power. Included in this category are landfill gas and sludge gas (sewage gas and gas from animal slurries). Bio-additives such as ethanol are also included in this category.

29. Municipal Waste

Municipal waste consists of products that are combusted directly to produce heat and/or power and comprises wastes produced by the residential, commercial and public services sectors that are collected by local authorities for disposal in a central location. Hospital waste is included in this category.

30. Industrial Waste

Industrial waste consists of solid and liquid products combusted directly (usually in specialised plants, e.g. tyres) to produce heat and/or power.

Electricity and Heat

31. Electricity

Gross electricity production is measured at the terminals of all alternator sets in a station; it therefore includes the energy taken by station auxiliaries and losses in transformers that are considered integral parts of the station.

The difference between gross and net production is generally calculated as 7 per cent for conventional thermal stations, 1 per cent for hydro stations, and 6 per cent for nuclear, geothermal and solar stations. Hydro stations' production includes production from pumped storage plants.

32. Heat

In recent years, the production of heat for sale has been increasing in importance. To reflect this, quantities of heat for sale are being recorded in the transformation sector under the rows CHP plants and heat plants. The use of fuels for heat consumed locally is recorded under the sectors in which the fuel use occurs.

IV. COUNTRY NOTES

General Notes:

The notes given below refer to data for the years 1960 to 1993 and cover the summary tables at the back of the book, as well as the information on diskettes. Prior to 1974, separate series for public and autoproduced electricity are not available. The figures for the quantities of fuels used for the generation of electricity and heat and the corresponding outputs in CHP and heat plants should be used with caution. Despite estimates introduced by the Secretariat, inputs and outputs are not always consistent. Please refer to notes below under *Electricity and Heat*.

1. Australia

All data refer to the fiscal year, July 1991 to June 1992 for 1992.

Solid Fuels: No data are available prior to 1974 for the use of coke oven gas and blast furnace gas in coke ovens. The use of coke oven coke in coke ovens for 1960 to 1973 has been estimated by the Secretariat. Lignite inputs to public CHP plants were estimated by the Secretariat, based on the responses to the annual electricity questionnaire. From 1990, consumption of lignite in the pulp and paper industry and coke oven coke in the chemicals industry has ceased. Non-specified industry consumption of combustible renewables and waste includes all *other sectors'* consumption for 1960 to 1969. The IEA blast furnace model has been applied for 1986 to 1993 following revisions to inputs and outputs made by the Australian Administration.

Oil: Between 1969 and 1970 there are breaks in the series for supply and consumption data due to lack of information prior to 1970. For the period 1970 to 1973, Secretariat estimates have been based on available published sources. Separate series for kerosene consumption in commercial and public services prior to 1974 are not available; the consumption has been included in the residential category. Prior to 1974, refinery gas is reported net of consumption in refineries. Negative refinery losses are caused by differences in treatment of transfers between refineries. Starting in 1990, imports of heavy fuel oil have been estimated by the Australian Administration.

Gas: Liquefied natural gas exports to Japan are estimated by the national administration. Prior to 1986, natural gas inputs to blast furnaces were included in the iron and steel sector. Prior to 1991, natural gas data included ethane.

Electricity and Heat: Prior to 1974, consumption in the energy sector has been included with industry. Consumption in coke ovens has been estimated by the Australian Administration from 1974. Fuels used for generation by autoproducers are for single-fuel-fired units only. The use of fuel in multi-fired units, operated by autoproducers, is included with industry consumption. Inputs and outputs from autoproducer CHP plants are not available prior to 1992. The breakdown of production by fuel at autoproducer CHP plants has been estimated by the Secretariat for 1992 and 1993. Prior to 1992, the generation of electricity and/or heat from the use of combustible renewables and waste (i.e. comprising solid biomass and animal products, gas/liquids from biomass, municipal waste and industrial waste) is included in solid biomass and animal products. Heat output is not available for 1992 and 1993. The direct use of solar energy is included from 1974.

2. Austria

Solid Fuels: Steam coal includes hard coal briquettes. "Trockenkohle" is included with BKB because of its high calorific value of 20 900 kJ/kg. Own use of blast furnace gas in the energy sector is available from 1983. There is no gas works gas production from coal or coal products after 1982. Fuel use in the industry sector for 1993 was estimated based on 1992 percentages. Industrial waste includes firewood.

Oil: From 1978, data for the consumption of heavy fuel oil in the industry sector include gas/diesel oil. *Other petroleum products* include paraffin waxes and petroleum coke from 1978.

Electricity and Heat: Consumption in petroleum refineries includes gas works' consumption prior to 1991. Starting in 1991, consumption in petroleum refineries includes consumption by patent fuel plants, coke ovens and BKB plants. Consumption in the iron and steel industry includes consumption at coke ovens prior to 1991. Consumption in commerce and public services includes small industries and offices in the tertiary sector, and electric energy in the field of electricity supply, district heating and water supply prior to 1991. Starting in 1991, consumption by small industries and small offices of the tertiary sector are included in non-specified *other sectors* while consumption of electric energy in the field of electricity supply, district heating and water supply are included in *other energy sector*. The breakdown of electricity consumption in the energy and industry sectors has been estimated by the Secretariat for 1993. Inputs to public electricity plants include inputs to public CHP plants prior to 1992. Inputs to electricity plants of autoproducers are not available for 1992 and 1993. Output of electricity from CHP plants is included in electricity plants. Output of heat from heat plants became available in 1981, while inputs of fuels to heat plants became available in 1989. For heat, own use is included in distribution losses and the residential sector includes commerce and public services. Autoproducer CHP heat production is available from 1992. The breakdown of heat consumption in industry (except chemical) has been estimated by the Secretariat for 1993. Break in series exist between 1991 and 1992 for heat consumption in industry. The heat production

split for each category of combustible fuel has been estimated by the Secretariat based on fuel input in annual fuel questionnaires submitted by the Austrian Administration for 1992 and 1993.

3. Belgium

Solid Fuels: Sub-bituminous coal data refer to recovered coal products. Production of steam coal ceased on 31 August 1992. Data for solid biomass and animal products, gas/liquids from biomass, industrial waste and municipal waste used for electricity and heat generation are available from 1983.

Oil: Prior to 1975, the production of refinery gas has been reported net of consumption in refineries. LPG and gas/diesel oil consumption in the commercial and public services sector are included with the residential sector prior to 1976. Gas/diesel oil consumption in the construction sector is included with non-metallic mineral products prior to 1981. *Other petroleum products* are included with naphtha prior to 1967. The break in series for heavy fuel oil between 1975 and 1976 is due to a change in classification between the industrial and commercial sectors. Oil consumption by public CHP plants has been estimated by the Secretariat for 1991 to 1993.

Electricity and Heat: Electricity production by autoproducer CHP plants is included in production from electricity plants. Electricity production in public CHP plants is included in production from electricity plants prior to 1982. Output of heat from CHP plants is not available prior to 1973. Breaks in series exist between 1991 and 1992 for heat consumption in chemical and non-specified industry.

4. Canada

Solid Fuels: Due to the unavailability of data, non-energy use of hard coal and coke oven coke is included with final consumption sectors prior to 1978. The category solid biomass and animal products has been revised from 1960 to 1992 based on data supplied by the Canadian Administration.

Oil: For kerosene, gas/diesel oil and heavy fuel oil, several breaks in series exist for detailed industrial consumption prior to 1980. As of 1982, gas/diesel oil consumed by fleets in the wholesale/retail service industry is reported in the commercial and public services sector. Prior to 1982, it was included in the road sector. From 1980, all consumption data are based on a single survey. However, from 1988 onwards, data for several industrial sub-sectors are no longer available. Separate consumption data for agriculture (including forestry) are available from 1983 for kerosene, from 1973 for gas/diesel oil and from 1978 for heavy fuel oil. For previous years agricultural consumption is included with residential. Deliveries to international marine bunkers are included with internal navigation prior to 1978. Transfers for naphtha and *other petroleum products* include purchases by reporting companies of feedstock and other additives from non-reporting companies. The reporting of LPG supply data changed starting in 1989. Production data, as well as products transferred, will therefore show changes in series between 1988 and 1989. LPG includes pentanes plus for all years, and ethane prior to 1991. Liquefaction represents synthetic crude oil produced from tar sands. From 1990, a different methodology was adopted by the Canadian Administration for the reporting of synthetic crude oil.

Gas: Natural gas consumption in agriculture is included with industrial consumption prior to 1978. From 1960 to 1977, consumption in the non-specified category of industry includes natural gas used as fuel in oil refineries. In 1976 and 1977, consumption of natural gas in the chemical industry is for feedstock use only, feedstock use in earlier years is not available. Starting in 1990, natural gas liquefaction represents the amounts of natural gas used for the production of hydrogen for the upgrading of synthetic crude oil. Prior to 1990, the amounts of hydrogen used in this process were included in the consumption of the oil and gas extraction sector. In 1992, consumption of natural gas in public CHP plants includes use in three new co-generation facilities in the province of Ontario.

Electricity and Heat: Consumption of electricity in coal mines is not available between 1982 and 1986, and consumption in oil and gas extraction is not available prior to 1987. Breaks in series occur between 1973 and 1974 in agriculture and between 1987 and 1988 in the industry sector. Electricity used for pumped storage has been estimated by the Secretariat from 1991 onwards. Heat production includes heat produced by nuclear power stations for distribution to other consumers. Secretariat estimates have been made for certain inputs to CHP production based on output. However, incompatibility of data for inputs to and output from thermal production of autoproducers may result in variable efficiency rates. Inputs of fuels to heat plants are not available for 1979 to 1987. Prior to 1992, the generation of electricity and/or heat from the use of combustible renewables and waste (i.e. comprising solid biomass and animal products, gas/liquids from biomass, municipal waste and industrial waste) is included in solid biomass and animal products.

5. Denmark

During 1993 and 1994, the Danish Administration undertook a major review of national electricity and heat statistics which is reflected in the quality of the data for 1993. As a result of the review there may be breaks in series between 1992 and 1993. Data for 1992 and for prior years are currently being reviewed by the Danish Administration.

Solid Fuels: Data for combustible renewables and waste are available from 1970. New series became available in 1988 for commercial and public services and industry non-specified use of combustible renewables and waste and there is a break in series between 1989 and 1990 in heat plants, agriculture and residential. Autoproducers' use of steam coal has been estimated by the Secretariat.

Oil: Prior to 1975, production of refinery gas is reported net of consumption in refineries. From 1974 to 1979, the consumption of heavy fuel oil for electricity generated by autoproducers has been estimated by the Secretariat. Prior to 1975, all consumption of oil in the commercial and public services sector has been included with residential consumption. As of 1987, data for paraffin waxes are no longer available. Following revisions in methodology, motor gasoline consumption in the commercial and residential sectors has been placed in the road transport sector as of 1988. Consumption of LPG in the industry sector has been estimated by the Danish Energy Agency in 1991. Prior to 1992, gas/diesel oil and heavy fuel oil consumption for fishing is included in inland waterways while after this date it is reported in the agriculture sector. Consumption data are based on a detailed survey sent to companies in Denmark every other year. For non-survey years, the consumption figures are estimated by the Danish Energy Agency.

Gas: Since 1989, data for natural gas consumption in the non-ferrous metals sub-sector are no longer available, while the decrease in consumption observed in the machinery sub-sector is due to incomplete coverage of the sector. From 1991 onwards, there was a reclassification of gas consumption between commerce and public services, and non-specified *other sectors*.

Electricity and Heat: Data for electricity and heat do not include Greenland and the Faroe Islands. Output of heat is not available prior to 1976. Breaks in series occur between 1989 and 1990 for heat, as data then became available for public heat plants. Heat produced in heat plants for sale by autoproducers is only reported from 1993; heat produced in CHP plants for sale by autoproducers is available from 1991. Prior to 1993, output from the use of combustible renewables and waste to generate electricity and/or heat (i.e. comprising solid biomass and animal products, gas/liquids from biomass, municipal waste and industrial waste) is included in solid biomass and animal products.

6.   Finland

Solid Fuels: There is a break in series in the industry sector's use of combustible renewables and waste in 1981 as data prior to this were estimated by the Secretariat. From 1984 onwards, these estimates were made by the Finnish Administration. The residential/agriculture breakdown of combustible renewables and waste is available from 1975. Peat consumption in tonnes for electricity and heat production has been estimated by the Secretariat assuming a net calorific value of 0.2 toe/tonne for years prior to 1992. The IEA blast furnace model has been applied for 1993.

Oil: No information is available on quantities of oil used by autoproducers or at heat plants prior to 1970. Data on petroleum coke are available only from 1985 as these data were previously not collected by the Finnish Administration.

Gas: Prior to 1989, natural gas consumption in the residential and agricultural sectors has been estimated by the Finnish Administration.

Electricity and Heat: Prior to 1978, consumption of liquid fuels and natural gas by public CHP plants has been included with the consumption of these fuels by electricity and heat plants. Electricity consumption in machinery includes consumption in transport equipment from 1990. There is a break in series in 1992 for electricity consumption in the transport sector. Electricity production from combustible renewables and waste is not available between 1974 and 1976. Prior to 1992, the generation of electricity and/or heat from the use of combustible renewables and waste (i.e. comprising solid biomass and animal products, gas/liquids from biomass, municipal waste and industrial waste) is included in peat. Consumption of heat in non-specified *other sectors* includes consumption in transport, agriculture, commercial and public services.

7.   France

Solid Fuels: Breaks in series for industrial consumption occur between 1970 and 1971 when a more detailed industry breakdown became available. Breaks in series in the industry sector between 1982 and 1983 are due to a reclassification of sectors by the French Administration. From 1986, industry consumption (except for the iron and steel industry) has been estimated by the Secretariat. Prior to 1985, consumption of colliery gas is included with autoproducers' use of coke oven gas. From 1985, coke oven coke inputs to blast furnaces have been estimated by the Secretariat based on blast furnace gas production. No data are available for coking coal stock changes prior to 1982. No data are available on combustible renewables and waste prior to 1966. From 1966 to 1969, the only data available relate to the quantities used for electricity generation.

Oil: From 1980, motor gasoline used for inland waterways and coastal shipping is separated from road consumption. Due to a change in classification of naphtha between 1969 and 1970, there is a break in series for feedstocks consumption data in the chemical industry. The separation of petroleum coke consumption into energy and non-energy use is not available prior to 1982. From 1988, ethane is included in NGL production. The separation of consumption of oil products by the tertiary sector between residential and commerce and public services has been estimated by the Secretariat.

Gas: Distribution losses include the statistical difference.

Electricity and Heat: There are significant breaks in series in 1965, when more detailed consumption data became available. The industrial classifications used by the French Administration were changed in 1986. Consumption of electricity for oil and gas extraction includes that used in oil refineries starting in 1988. Non-specified *other sectors* consumption includes exports to Monaco prior to 1992. A large part of consumption in the category *other energy sector* covers consumption in uranium treatment plants. This consumption was not available prior to 1980. Data on heat sold to third parties are not available. Electricity production by autoproducers is not available by type of plant. Accordingly, data on electricity production in autoproducer CHP plants are included in electricity plants.

8.   Germany

German data include the new federal states of Germany from 1970 onwards.

Solid Fuels: Figures for quantities used for non-energy purposes became available from 1970. Prior to this, non-energy uses are included with consumption in the respective final consumption sectors. The IEA blast furnace model has been applied for 1992 and 1993. Fuel inputs to blast furnaces have been estimated by the Secretariat for 1992 and 1993. Information on peat (submitted in Terajoules) was converted to tonnes assuming a net calorific value of 0.2 toe/tonne. For lignite and BKB, the industrial sector breakdown is not available for 1991 and 1992. Fuels used in autoproducer heat plants are not available prior to 1992. Fuels used in public heat plants are not available for 1992 and 1993. Fuels used in public CHP and autoproducer CHP are included with public electricity and autoproducer electricity plants respectively for 1992 and 1993.

Oil: Prior to 1976, consumption of refinery gas in the chemical industry is included with refineries' own consumption. Irregularities in the time series for supply data exist for several products between 1979 and 1980 due to a change in the source of the data. Industry consumption detail has improved since 1985 due to changes in the national reporting system. Prior to 1993, inputs of heavy fuel oil to blast furnaces were included in the iron and steel industry.

Gas: Due to changes in the national reporting system for natural gas, the series show a break between 1967

and 1968. Prior to 1970, refineries' own use and distribution losses are included with the consumption of natural gas for oil and gas extraction. Consumption of natural gas has been based on *Arbeitsgemeinshaft Energiebilanzen*. The breakdown of natural gas consumption into commerce and public services, residential and agricultural sectors is available only since 1984.

Electricity and Heat: Between 1971 and 1980, consumption in coal mines included consumption in coke ovens and BKB plants. All data relating to heat output are included with CHP heat. Heat production, which is not available prior to 1970, has been estimated by the Secretariat from 1989 onwards. Prior to 1989, sizeable distribution losses may have been deducted from total heat production, thus understating the level of production reported. However, this should not affect the consumption data. Heat consumption has been estimated by the Secretariat from 1991. For 1992 and 1993, the breakdown by fuel for heat production has been estimated by the Secretariat based on the input to heat production published in *Energiebilanz der Bundesrepublik Deutschland für das Jahr 1990*.

9.   Greece

Solid Fuels: Exports of steam coal stopped in 1989. From 1970 to 1986, data on combustible renewables and waste were estimated by the Ministry of Agriculture based on the supply and sales of wood to the commercial sector and public services. Data for own use in lignite mines are incomplete referring to one mine only. This mine was not operating from 1987 to 1989.

Oil: Consumption of NGL for the production of electricity in the oil and gas extraction industry is shown under oil and gas extraction in the energy sector. Data on feedstocks for cracking in refineries are available as of 1986.

Electricity and Heat: Consumption in the iron and steel industry and in the non-ferrous metals industry prior to 1971 has been estimated by the Secretariat. Inputs of natural gas to autoproducer CHP plants include natural gas consumed for steam generation prior to 1991. A break in series exists between 1991 and 1992 for electricity consumption in the transport sector.

10.   Iceland

Oil: Consumption data prior to 1980 are estimated by the Secretariat.

Electricity and Heat: *Other sectors'* consumption covers the NATO base at Keflavik airport prior to 1987. The residential sector includes agriculture prior to 1986. The industrial classifications used by the Icelandic Administration were changed in 1987. Energy sector consumption of electricity refers mainly to the use of electricity by the geothermal industry to pump geothermal water from underground. Electricity production from geothermal sources in public CHP plants is available from 1992. Heat production from municipal waste is available from 1993. Revisions have been made to the basic energy statistics to incorporate the direct use of geothermal energy from 1960.

11.   Ireland

Solid Fuels: Information on peat (submitted in Terajoules) was converted to tonnes assuming a net calorific value of 0.2 toe/tonne.

Oil: Production and consumption of refinery gas in refineries are estimated by the Secretariat for the period 1982 to 1984.   During the years 1966 to 1974, classification of *other sectors* changes, thus causing breaks in consumption series for that period. For the period 1970 to 1977, separate series for the consumption of kerosene in the commercial, public services and agricultural sectors have been estimated by the Secretariat.   For 1985, 56 000 tonnes of kerosene in *other sectors* non-specified represents imports which appeared in trade statistics, but which were not traceable in the consumption data. Consumption in commercial and public services includes quantities used by state-owned agricultural companies. Consumption of heavy fuel oil in industry and transport for 1986 are Secretariat estimates. Gas/diesel oil consumption in agriculture is available starting in 1986.   Prior to 1986 it was not reported. Consumption data collected for 1993 are based on a detailed survey. Data for historical years back to 1990 were revised by the national administration based on the results of this survey. Owing to these revisions, breaks in series exist between 1989 and 1990 in the detailed consumption data for LPG, kerosene, gas/diesel oil and heavy fuel oil.

Gas: Detailed consumption figures for the use of natural gas in industry and *other sectors* are not available prior to 1986. Consumption of natural gas in gas works stopped in 1985, as natural gas was no longer being converted to town gas.

Electricity and Heat: Electricity consumption by agriculture is included in the residential sector's consumption. Electricity consumption in the iron and steel industry includes non-ferrous metals consumption. Heat production by autoproducers is not available.

12.   Italy

Solid Fuels: From 1980, production of manufactured gases includes a small amount of steel oxygen furnace gas consumed by public electricity plants. Combustible renewables and waste is mainly comprised of three products, of which only vegetal fuels (mostly wood) is a primary product and is therefore included in production. Solid biomass and animal products was estimated by the Secretariat for 1992. Figures for the non-energy use of coal in the chemical industry are not available and have been excluded from the balance altogether. During 1991, all industrial activities were reclassified on the basis of ISTAT/NACE 91. This has implied some transfers of activities which may result in some anomalies between 1991 and earlier years.

Oil: The detailed consumption breakdown is partly estimated by the Secretariat on the basis of the *Bilancio Energetico Nazionale*. Prior to 1970, autoproducers' consumption of heavy fuel oil is included with industry.   Because of a change in classification, some of the aviation fuels and kerosene show breaks in series in 1988.

Gas: The residential sector includes consumption in commercial and public services. Data for distribution losses include some statistical differences as of 1991.

Electricity and Heat: *Other energy sector* includes electricity consumption for blast furnaces; prior to 1989 consumption for uranium extraction was also included. The production of electricity reported in the category *other fuel sources* refers to electricity produced from the regasification of LNG or heat recovered from industrial processes. Data relating to heat produced for sale are not available. However, the

Italian Administration estimates that in 1993 about 10 000 TJ of heat was produced for sale; this is the equivalent of about 0.5 per cent of equivalent heat input to electricity generation. Prior to 1992, the generation of electricity and/or heat from the use of combustible renewables and waste (i.e. comprising solid biomass and animal products, gas/liquids from biomass, municipal waste and industrial waste) is included in industrial waste.

13. Japan

Solid Fuels: Consumption of steam coal at heat plants has been estimated using the annual electricity questionnaire prior to 1992. Data on combustible renewables and waste for 1992 and 1993 have been estimated by the Secretariat based on the electricity questionnaire submission.

Oil: Between 1969 and 1970 there are breaks in series. The classification of fuel use between road transport and internal navigation changed in 1970. Prior to 1981, information on the non-energy use of petroleum coke was not available. Due to improved data collection methods, breaks in series exist for several products between 1981 and 1982.

Gas: For natural gas, consumption is larger than supply (balanced by statistical difference) because gas which is being resold may have been counted twice in consumption data. The magnitude of the double counting is believed to be around 20 000 - 30 000 TJ a year. Consumption of natural gas in public heat plant has been estimated by the national administration.

Electricity and Heat: Data refer to fiscal year (April 1992 to March 1993 for 1992). Quantities of fuels used for autoproducers' electricity generation are Secretariat estimates. Consumption of electricity in non-specified industry includes wood and wood products and construction. Residential heat consumption is included with commerce and public services prior to 1992. Output of heat from heat plants is not available prior to 1972. Electricity and heat production in autoproducer CHP plants is included in autoproducer electricity plants. Electricity and heat produced in public CHP plants are not included in the data series. Heat produced for sale in public heat plants from electric boilers is available from 1977, but

may include the recovery of waste heat. Data on heat produced for sale by autoproducer heat plants are not available.

14. Luxembourg

Oil: For 1978 and 1979, heavy fuel oil consumption by autoproducers of electricity has been estimated by the Secretariat.

Electricity and Heat: Electricity consumption by final consumption sector and for industry sub-sectors has been estimated by the Secretariat based on data published by CEGEDEL. Generation of electricity by autoproducers according to fuel used has been estimated by the Secretariat based on submitted input data for 1989. Prior to 1992, the generation of electricity and/or heat from the use of combustible renewables and waste (i.e. comprising solid biomass and animal products, gas/liquids from biomass, municipal waste and industrial waste) is included in municipal waste.

15. Mexico

Data are available starting in 1971. Data for all years are partly estimated based on the publication *Balance Nacional - Energia*. The Mexican Administration submitted data directly by questionnaire for the first time with 1992 data. As a result, some breaks in series may occur between 1991 and 1992.

Electricity and Heat: Electricity consumption in the energy sector is included in industry (such as chemical as well as non-specified).

16. Netherlands

Solid Fuels: For 1984 to 1986, production "from other sources" of steam coal represents a stock of "smalls" washed for re-use. This stock was exhausted in 1987. A new classification system, instituted in the mid-seventies gives rise to breaks in series for most products between 1975 and 1976. Data on non-energy use are available starting in 1989. For prior years, non-energy use is included with industry consumption.

Oil: Over the years there have been several changes in national oil statistics for the Netherlands. Time series have been only partly revised in accordance with these changes. Consequently, there are still major irregularities in Dutch oil statistics. Prior to 1970, production of refinery gas and heavy fuel oil are reported net of consumption in refineries. Petroleum coke is included with *other petroleum products* for all years except 1978 to 1982. Breaks in series between 1983 and 1984 are due to the introduction of a more comprehensive survey on end-use consumption. However, aggregated consumption data for transport, industry and *other sectors* are not affected. Refinery gas includes chemical gas from 1978. The latter is shown as chemical industry consumption. Naphtha includes aromates for all years except 1981, when they are included with *other petroleum products*. Motor gasoline includes other light oils. For *other sectors*, the non-specified category includes consumption by hospitals, offices, public buildings and commercial companies. This applies only to oil products.

Gas: Significant breaks in series between 1981 to 1982 and 1983 to 1984 reflect the introduction of more comprehensive surveys on end-use consumption. Aggregated consumption data for industry and *other sectors*, however, are not affected. Between 1987 and 1988 a break in series is observed in the *other sectors* (commerce and public services) due to a major reorganisation of three public utility companies. All heat plants were converted to CHP plants in 1990.

Electricity and Heat: Electricity consumption in agriculture is included with that of commercial and public services prior to 1979. Commercial and public services sector electricity consumption includes small users. Electricity production in public CHP plants is included with public electricity plants prior to 1982. Information on heat output from CHP plants and heat plants, prior to 1982, is not available. Fuel inputs to heat plants are not available prior to 1982. Heat production by fuel in heat plants prior to 1987 is estimated by the Secretariat based on fuel inputs submitted by the Netherlands' Administration. Heat produced for sale by autoproducers is not available. Prior to 1992, the generation of electricity and/or heat from the use of combustible renewables and waste (i.e. comprising solid biomass and animal products, gas/liquids from biomass, municipal waste and industrial waste) is included in municipal waste.

17. New Zealand

A reorganisation of government departments during 1987 leading to cessation of certain data series, has resulted in several breaks in series between 1987 and 1988.

Solid Fuels: No information is available for the consumption of coking coal prior to 1987. Apparent breaks in series between 1987 and 1988 in final consumption and the transformation and energy sectors for steam coal and sub-bituminous coal, result from the latest coal analysis survey and the reclassification of some coal mines. These classification differences continue at present. From 1987, a full industry breakdown of steam coal and sub-bituminous coal ceased. In 1987 there was a large reduction in lignite consumption in the industry sector. However, as no data are available to separate this amount from residential, commercial and public consumption, all final consumption of lignite has been allocated to *other sectors* non-specified for this year. Beginning in 1985, the Secretariat has estimated industry consumption of combustible renewables and waste. Black liquor has been included with combustible renewables and waste starting in 1990. Peat, although produced in New Zealand, is not used as a fuel. It is used for agricultural purposes only.

Oil: There is a change in classification for gas/diesel oil and heavy fuel oil between industry and *other sectors* in 1970. Gas/diesel oil consumption for road and rail transport is not separately identifiable, and is reported as non-specified transport consumption. Liquefaction of other hydrocarbons shown as crude oil represents gasoline production from natural gas. From 1991 onwards a different methodology was adopted for the reporting of synthetic gasoline. The increase in the 1991 other hydrocarbons reflects the total production of methanol. Before 1991, only the amounts of methanol for conversion to synthetic gasoline were reported in this category.

Gas: Consumption within the industry sector is based on surveys conducted during the period 1981 to 1986. Subsequently, as the survey was discontinued, a break in series occurred in 1987. Main aggregates in transformation, energy, transport, industry and *other sectors* are estimated by the national administration.

Electricity and Heat: Data refer to fiscal year (April 1992 to March 1993 for 1992).   Electricity production by autoproducers from natural gas and from oil has been estimated by the Secretariat for the years 1970 to 1973.   The classifications used by the Administration of New Zealand were changed in 1991.   Electricity consumption in paper, pulp and printing is included in wood and wood products prior to 1991.   Data for 1993 have been estimated by the New Zealand Administration.

18.   Norway

Solid Fuels: The detailed breakdown of industry consumption starts in 1971 for hard coal and in 1972 for coke oven coke.   Distribution losses of blast furnace gas for 1960 to 1971 have been estimated by the Secretariat.

Oil: A detailed consumption breakdown for gas/diesel oil and heavy fuel oil is available from 1976. Quantities of gas/diesel oil for electricity generation from 1970 to 1975 have been estimated by the Secretariat.   Since 1986, imports of refinery feedstocks are reported under the relevant petroleum product imports.   Consumption of lubricants is reported in the industry sector as no further detail is available. Consumption of *other products* in 1987 includes deliveries to civil stocks for wartime purposes.   The amount, which is approximately 500 000 tonnes, is not included in national oil statistics.   As of 1990, the Norwegian Administration has revised the transformation sector series.   Breaks will be observed between 1989 and 1990 until the historical data are revised.

Electricity and Heat: Information on the quantities of fuel used in heat plants is not available prior to 1983. Heat production is not available prior to 1983.   Breaks in series in public and autoproducer electricity plants between 1989 and 1990 are due to a revision of data by the Norwegian Administration.   Breakdown of heat consumption by industry sub-sector was expanded in 1992.   Prior to 1992, the generation of electricity and/or heat from the use of combustible renewables and waste (i.e. comprising solid biomass and animal products, gas/liquids from biomass, municipal waste and industrial waste) is included in solid biomass and animal products.

19.   Portugal

Solid Fuels: Own use of coke oven gas for 1989 has been estimated by the Secretariat.

Oil: Prior to 1969, production of refinery gas is reported net of consumption in refineries.   Prior to 1970, figures for consumption of gas/diesel oil in the transport sector include part of the *other sectors* consumption.   Up until 1984, statistics of petroleum coke were included with coke oven coke data.   Since then, they have been reported with *other petroleum products* statistics.   The negative production for *other petroleum products* in 1990 refers to unfinished products transferred during blending operations within the refinery process.   The gross production of secondary products includes those transferred quantities.

Electricity and Heat: Production of electricity in public CHP plants is not available prior to 1980.

20.   Spain

Solid Fuels: Figures for the consumption of coking coal in coke ovens are not available prior to 1980. Data on final consumption of combustible renewables and waste are available from 1980 onwards.   From 1970 to 1979 the only data available on combustible renewables and waste reflect inputs to electricity generation.

Oil: Detailed consumption data prior to 1981 are partly estimated on the basis of national statistics covering consumption in the Spanish mainland. However, a reclassification of Spanish national statistics between 1976 and 1977 has resulted in a break in series for *other sectors* for gas/diesel oil and heavy fuel oil.   For LPG and heavy fuel oil, consumption specifications are less detailed prior to 1973.   Data for feedstock are not available in 1981. Due to the availability of more detailed consumption data, there is a break in series in 1981 for petroleum coke.

Gas: The increase in consumption of natural gas in the agricultural sector, which occurred in 1988, reflects a substitution of naphthas for the production of fertilizers.

Electricity and Heat: Information on heat production is not available prior to 1987. Electricity production from wind is included with hydro from 1992 onwards. Prior to 1987, electricity production in public CHP plants is included with production from public electricity plants. Electricity production in public CHP plants ceased in 1991. Breaks in series exist for autoproducer electricity production in electricity plants and CHP plants between 1989 and 1990. Data on heat consumption are not available. Prior to 1992, the generation of electricity and/or heat from the use of combustible renewables and waste (i.e. comprising solid biomass and animal products, gas/liquids from biomass, municipal waste and industrial waste) is included in solid biomass and animal products.

21. Sweden

Solid Fuels: Data on non-energy use are available from 1973. Prior to this they are included with final consumption. For 1960 to 1974 the split between energy sector use of blast furnace gas in coke ovens and distribution losses has been estimated. Starting in 1989, coking coal imports can no longer be separated from steam coal. The imports have been estimated by the Secretariat using exporters' data. Steam coal production is coal recovered during the quarrying of clay.

Oil: Please note the many classification changes between 1969 and 1970. For example, prior to 1970, petroleum coke is included with *other petroleum products*. Due to more detailed reporting, there are breaks in consumption series between 1985 and 1986 for heavy fuel oil. Kerosene consumption in the road sector is discontinued in 1984 due to product re-classification. The negative consumption figure for feedstocks reflects the treatment of intra/inter refinery transfers of semi-finished products in national statistics, which reveals anomalies when used in overall balances.

Electricity and Heat: Production by autoproducers is included with public electricity plants for oil. Consumption of electricity for distribution of district heat is included with *other energy sector*. Prior to 1992, the generation of electricity and/or heat from the use of combustible renewables and waste (i.e. comprising solid biomass and animal products, gas/liquids from biomass, municipal waste and industrial waste) is included in solid biomass and animal products. Heat produced in CHP plants is not available prior to 1974; heat produced in heat plants is included in CHP plants prior to 1987. There is a break in series for heat consumption between 1983 and 1984. Consumption of heat in the industry and residential sectors has been estimated by the Swedish Administration for 1991. Information on heat for sale produced in heat pumps and electric boilers is available starting in 1992. In Sweden, heat produced in heat pumps is sold to third parties (as district heat) and is therefore included in transformation. Inputs to heat pumps include heat recovered from industry and from ambient sources (including sewage and seawater). Ambient heat is shown as the indigenous production of heat. The electricity used to drive heat pumps is considered to be transformed and appears as output in the transformation sector rather than as electricity used in the energy sector. Fuel inputs to the heat that is recovered by the heat pump are reported in the appropriate industry sub-sector (i.e. chemical and paper, pulp and printing). Consumption by industry of the heat produced by heat pumps has been estimated by the Secretariat based on fuel inputs submitted by the Swedish Administration (2/3 in paper, pulp and printing and 1/3 in chemical). Heat produced for sale by autoproducer heat plants is reported starting in 1992.

23. Switzerland

Solid Fuels: From 1985, industrial consumption of gas works gas is reported in non-specified industry to prevent the disclosure of commercially confidential data. Prior to 1978, combustible renewables and waste includes only wood consumed in residential, agriculture and commercial and public services. From 1978, it also includes industry consumption of wood and industrial waste and public utilities (CHP) consumption of municipal wastes.

Oil: Gross production of refinery gas is not available for 1967 to 1969. Non-specified industry consumption (small manufacturers and producers) of gas/diesel oil is estimated.

Gas: The break in series for natural gas between 1977 and 1978 is the result of the introduction of a new survey by industry type. Starting in 1978, natural gas imports are net of re-exports.

Electricity and Heat: Prior to 1978, data on heat output from CHP plants are not available. Heat production includes heat produced by nuclear power stations and distributed to other consumers. Electricity consumption in the transport equipment industry is included with machinery.

23. Turkey

Oil: International marine bunkers are included with exports for 1978, 1980 to 1981, and 1983 to 1984. As of 1978, the commercial sector is included with industry, while public services are included with transport sub-sector. Non-metallic mineral products industry consumption is included with non-ferrous metals sector. The end-use classification of gas/diesel oil and heavy fuel oil were changed in the Turkish national statistics between 1977 and 1978. Consequently, breaks in detailed consumption series appear between these two years. Data on *other petroleum products* are not available for 1960.

Gas: Data on natural gas consumption in the chemical industry (for fertilizers) and in non-specified industry (dye industry) are available starting in 1988. The large distribution losses in 1989 are due to an increase in natural gas consumption in the industry and residential sectors.

Electricity and Heat: Between 1972 and 1973 there are significant breaks in electricity consumption data. Consumption in the industry sub-sector, machinery, includes transport equipment. Consumption in the wood and wood products sub-sector includes that of the paper, pulp and printing industry. Direct use of geothermal heat in 1993 has been estimated by the Secretariat. Information for prior years is not available.

24. United Kingdom

Solid Fuels: Consumption shown for the commercial and public services sector includes consumption of some of the non-specified sector. Own use in coal mines in the energy sector refers only to deep mines operated by British Coal. The consumption of substitute natural gas is included with natural gas. Its production is included with gas works gas. From 1984 onwards there is no sectoral breakdown of industrial consumption of coke oven gas except for the iron and steel industry. Prior to 1978, some of the hard coal inputs to autoproducers are included with the respective industry sectors (mainly non-ferrous metals and paper). There is a break in series for all

manufactured gases between 1979 and 1980. Data for coke oven gas (1988 to 1993) and for combustible renewables and waste (1989 to 1993) were revised by the U.K. Administration.

Oil: Petroleum coke is included with *other petroleum products* prior to 1979. Trade data for petroleum coke are included with *other petroleum products* from 1970. From 1980, NGL includes condensates. For earlier years condensates are included with crude oil. The product breakdown for transfers is estimated. Stock changes of refinery feedstocks and NGLs are reported separately from 1985; before that they are included with crude oil. Stock changes in public utilities are included from 1985. Prior to 1990, LPG includes ethane. Oil consumption in public CHP plants is not available for the years 1990 to 1993.

Gas: Prior to 1985, stock changes for natural gas are included with distribution losses. The consumption of natural gas in the commercial sector is included with non-specified *other sectors* while the public administration sector is shown separately. Natural gas consumption includes substitute natural gas made at gas works and piped into the natural gas distribution system. Consumption of natural gas is thus somewhat larger than supply. Non-energy use of natural gas is not separately identifiable. From 1992 onwards, distribution losses are included in the statistical difference. Consumption in the wood and wood products sector is not available after 1991. Data in the non-specified industry sub-sector refer to sales by independent gas suppliers unallocated by category. For reasons of confidentiality, inputs of natural gas for public electricity generation are included with autoproducers for 1990 and 1991. Prior to 1992 deliveries of natural gas to autoproducer CHP were included in the industry sector. For 1993, consumption of natural gas in coal mines is based on a revised estimation method and is therefore not compatible with historical data.

Electricity and Heat: From 1984 onwards, non-specified industries' consumption includes wood and wood products, and unallocated consumption. Electricity consumption in coal mines includes consumption in patent fuel plants. Gas works' consumption includes electricity use in the transmission/distribution of public supply gas. The reorganisation, and subsequent privatisation, of the electricity supply industry in 1990 results in some breaks in series between 1989 and 1990. Consumption in the machinery sub-sector includes transport equipment from 1989 onwards. Consumption in the non-metallic mineral products sub-sector includes mining and quarrying. Prior to 1988, electricity output from CHP plants is included with public electricity plants. Production of electricity and heat by CHP plants has been estimated by the Secretariat for 1991. Inputs and output from natural gas for public electricity production are included in autoproducer electricity for 1990 and 1991. Information on production of electricity by autoproducer CHP plants is not available prior to 1992 and production of heat in autoproducer CHP plants is not available prior to 1993. This results in a break in series for heat consumption between 1992 and 1993. Prior to 1992, the generation of electricity and/or heat from the use of combustible renewables and waste (i.e. comprising solid biomass and animal products, gas/liquids from biomass, municipal waste and industrial waste) is included in solid biomass and animal products.

25. United States

Solid Fuels: The gas works gas balance for 1960 has been estimated by the Secretariat. Data on gas works gas production from 1973 are not available for reasons of commercial confidentiality. Coke oven coke inputs to blast furnaces are Secretariat estimates. Imports and *other sectors* consumption of steam coal include sub-bituminous coal, coking coal and lignite. Exports of steam coal include sub-bituminous coal. The separation of steam coal and sub-bituminous coal inputs to public power plants has been estimated by the Secretariat until 1990. Blast furnace gas and coke oven gas consumption was estimated by the Secretariat for 1991 to 1993. Blast furnace gas and coke oven gas consumption was estimated by the Secretariat for 1991 to 1993. Blast furnace gas production from 1987 to 1993 and coke oven gas production from 1991 to 1993 were revised by the Secretariat based on American Iron and Steel Institute (AISI) statistics.

Oil: Detailed breakdown of industry consumption is not available for oil products. However, data by industry are published for heavy fuel oil for the period 1971 to 1982. Data for Puerto Rico, Guam, the U.S. Virgin Islands and the Hawaiian Free Trade Zone are not included prior to 1976. Direct use of crude oil, i.e. crude oil used as pipeline fuel oil on production sites, is not available prior to 1973. Imports and exports of NGL are reported as LPG trade prior to 1978. The split of motor gasoline in agriculture and industry is estimated by the Secretariat prior to 1982. Gas/diesel oil consumption in agriculture prior to 1980 is also estimated by the Secretariat: it was included with

industry prior to 1970. The drop in use of naphtha in the petrochemical industry beginning in 1978 is due to a reclassification of the product. Consumption of LPG in the chemical and petrochemical sub-sectors in 1983 to 1985 is a Secretariat estimate. LPG includes pentanes plus (mainly natural gasoline) for all years, and ethane prior to 1990. Data on naphtha are not available for the years 1960 to 1962. International marine bunkers of heavy fuel oil show a large increase in 1990 due to a change in the data collection and reporting methodology of the U.S. Administration. International marine bunkers for 1993 have been estimated by the U.S. Administration. From 1992 onwards, the individual components of NGL and LPG have been converted using their respective gravities rather than an average gravity, resulting in a break in series. In 1993, the U.S. Administration made several adjustments to its collection system for oil statistics in order to accommodate the revisions to the Clean Air Act of 1990. As a result, data for oxygenates (i.e. fuel ethanol, MTBE, etc.) were collected in 1993 and reported in the additives category, or in the case of ethanol, in the gas/liquids from biomass category.

Gas: A detailed breakdown of industry consumption is not available for natural gas. Data on natural gas use in the road sector were collected for the first time in 1991 and are not available for previous years.

Electricity and Heat: Data for electricity absorbed by pumping and electricity production from pumped storage plants, became available starting in 1987. Electricity produced by autoproducers is available from 1989. Prior to this date, no data for the total electricity production by U.S. autoproducers are available. For the United States, autoproducers include small and independent power producers, which under IEA definitions are considered public producers. Production from these small and independent power producers accounts for about 25 per cent of reported production of electricity by autoproducers in the United States. Electricity production in public CHP plants is available from 1991. Heat produced in public heat plants is available from 1992. Data for heat produced in public CHP plants is available, but the corresponding amounts of electricity produced are not available prior to 1991. The consumption of heat sold in the industry sector is available from 1991 and in the energy sector from 1993. Prior to 1991, total consumption of heat sold referred to consumption in the commercial and public service sector. No data are available for heat sold that is consumed in the residential and agriculture sectors.

V. GEOGRAPHICAL COVERAGE

- Denmark includes Greenland and the Danish Faroes.

- German data include the new federal states of Germany from 1970 onwards.

- Japan includes Okinawa.

- The Netherlands excludes Surinam and the Netherlands Antilles.

- Portugal includes the Azores and Madeira.

- Spain includes the Canary Islands.

- United States includes Puerto Rico, Guam, the Virgin Islands and the Hawaiian Free Trade Zone.

- EU includes Austria, Belgium, Denmark, France, Finland, Germany, Greece, Ireland, Italy, Luxembourg, Netherlands, Portugal, Spain, Sweden and the United Kingdom. Please note that in the interest of having comparable data, all these countries are included for all years despite different entry dates into the European Union.

- OECD regional statistics now include Mexico (from 1971 onwards) following Mexico's accession to the OECD on 18th May 1994.

I. INTRODUCTION

Ce recueil s'adresse aux lecteurs qui participent aux travaux d'analyse et d'étude des questions de fond concernant la situation énergétique internationale. Il fournit, pour chaque source d'énergie, des statistiques détaillées sur la production, les échanges et la consommation dans la zone de l'OCDE selon une présentation unifiée (définitions et méthode), pour l'ensemble des pays Membres.

Les données publiées dans cet ouvrage sont fondées sur les informations recueillies dans quatre questionnaires annuels de l'OCDE : Pétrole, Gaz naturel, Combustibles solides, Déchets et Gaz manufacturés, et Electricité et chaleur, remplis par les administrations nationales des pays Membres de l'OCDE.

Bien que tout ait été mis en oeuvre pour assurer l'exactitude de ces données, la qualité des chiffres de cette publication n'est pas toujours homogène. Il convient, lors de l'utilisation des agrégats régionaux, de consulter également les notes relatives aux différents pays et les données par pays. D'une façon générale, les chiffres sont sans doute plus exacts en ce qui concerne la production, les échanges et la consommation totale que pour la consommation finale dans les différents secteurs, qui doit souvent être estimée par les administrations.

Les statistiques régionales de l'OCDE comprennent désormais le Mexique (à partir de 1971), par suite de l'adhésion de ce pays à l'OCDE le 18 mai 1994.

Le lecteur trouvera des données rétrospectives dans les publications *Statistiques de l'énergie des pays de l'OCDE 1960-1969*, *1970-1979* et *1980-1989*, parues en 1991.

Un recueil complémentaire - *Bilans énergétiques des pays de l'OCDE 1992 à 1993* - contient des données correspondantes sous la forme de bilans globaux exprimés dans une unité commune, à savoir en millions de tonnes d'équivalent pétrole (Mtep), sur la base de 1 tep = 10^7 kcal = 41.868 gigajoules.

Des données complètes sur l'offre et la demande sont disponibles, pour les années 1960 à 1993, sur disquettes exploitables par des ordinateurs personnels compatibles IBM et sur bandes magnétiques, aux principaux points de vente dont la liste figure à la fin de cet ouvrage.

Les demandes de renseignements sur les données ou la méthodologie doivent être adressées à Karen Tréanton (33-1) 45-24-94-46.

Attention	**Voir le dépliant en plusieurs langues à la fin du présent recueil.**
Achtung	**Aufklappbaren Text auf den letzten Umschlagseite.**
Attenzione	**Riferirsi al glossario poliglotta alla fine del libro.**
Nota	**Véase el glosario plurilingüe al final del libro.**
Примеч.	**Смотрите многоязычный словарь в конце книги.**

II. NOTES GENERALES

Les tableaux couvrent l'ensemble des sources "commerciales" d'énergie, c'est-à-dire à la fois les sources primaires (houille, lignite, tourbe, gaz naturel, pétrole brut, liquides de gaz naturel (LGN) et énergies hydraulique, géothermique/solaire, éolienne, marémotrice, etc. et nucléaire) et les sources secondaires (dérivés du charbon, gaz manufacturés, produits pétroliers et électricité). Des données sont indiquées pour diverses sources d'énergies renouvelables combustibles et de déchets, telles que la biomasse solide et les produits d'origine animale, les gaz/liquides tirés de la biomasse, les déchets urbains et les déchets industriels, ainsi que pour la chaleur (produite dans les installations de cogénération chaleur/électricité et les centrales calogènes) sous la rubrique *chaleur*.

Chaque tableau est divisé en trois parties principales: la première récapitule les éléments de *l'approvisionnement*, la deuxième présente les secteurs *transformation* et *énergie*, et la troisième indique la *consommation finale* ventilée entre les divers secteurs d'utilisation finale.

A. Approvisionnement

La première partie du bilan énergétique de base fournit les éléments suivants de l'approvisionnement:

    Production

+   *Apports d'autres sources*
+   *Importations*
-   *Exportations*
-   *Soutages maritimes internationaux*

±   *Variations des stocks*
=   *Approvisionnement intérieur*

1. Production

La *production* comprend les quantités de combustibles extraites ou produites, après extraction des matières inertes ou des impuretés (par exemple, après extraction du soufre contenu dans le gaz naturel). La production nationale figurant à la colonne chaleur correspond à la quantité de chaleur extraite du milieu ambiant au moyen de pompes à chaleur.

2. Apports d'autres sources

La rubrique *apports d'autres sources* couvre tous les apports de produits dont l'origine ne correspond pas explicitement aux définitions des sources d'énergie primaire figurant dans les tableaux ; par exemple, sous pétrole brut : les produits provenant d'autres sources que le pétrole brut ou les LGN, comme l'hydrogène, le pétrole brut de synthèse (y compris les huiles minérales extraites de minéraux bitumineux tels que les schistes, les sables asphaltiques, etc.) ; sous additifs : le benzol, l'alcool et le méthanol produits à partir du gaz naturel ; sous produits d'alimentation des raffineries ; les quantités renvoyées par l'industrie pétrochimique et utilisées comme produits d'alimentation des raffineries ; sous houille : les schlamms et les mixtes, la poussière récupérée et d'autres produits charbonniers de basse qualité, qui ne sont pas classables d'après le type de charbon d'origine ; sous gaz d'usine à gaz : le gaz naturel, le gaz de raffinerie et le GPL, traités ou mélangés dans les usines à gaz (c'est-à-dire, gaz d'usine à gaz produit à partir d'autres sources que le charbon).

3. Importations et exportations

La rubrique *importations et exportations* désigne les quantités de produits ayant franchi les frontières du territoire national, que le dédouanement ait été effectué ou non.

a) *Pétrole et gaz*

Cette rubrique comprend les quantités de pétrole brut et de produits pétroliers importées ou exportées au titre d'accords de traitement (à savoir, raffinage à façon). Les quantités de pétrole en transit ne sont pas prises en compte. Le pétrole brut, les LGN et le gaz naturel sont indiqués comme provenant de leur pays d'origine. Pour les produits d'alimentation des raffineries et les produits pétroliers, en revanche, c'est le dernier pays de provenance qui est pris en compte.

Les réexportations de pétrole importé pour raffinage en zone franche sont comptabilisées dans les exportations de produits pétroliers par le pays de raffinage vers le pays de destination finale.

b) *Combustibles solides*

Les *importations et exportations* comprennent les quantités de combustibles obtenues d'autres pays ou fournies à d'autres pays, qu'il existe ou non une union économique ou douanière entre les pays en question. Les combustibles solides en transit ne sont pas pris en compte.

c) *Electricité*

Les quantités sont considérées comme importées ou exportées lorsqu'elles ont franchi les limites territoriales du pays.

4. Soutages maritimes internationaux

Les *soutages maritimes internationaux* correspondent aux quantités fournies aux navires de haute mer, y compris les navires de guerre, quel que soit leur pavillon. La consommation des navires assurant le transport par cabotage ou navigation intérieure et des navires de pêche n'est pas comprise. Voir ci-dessous la définition des secteurs des transports [C.2] et de l'agriculture [C.3].

5. Variations des stocks

Les *variations des stocks* expriment la différence enregistrée entre le premier jour et le dernier jour de l'année dans le niveau des stocks détenus sur le territoire national par les producteurs, les importateurs, les entreprises de transformation de l'énergie et les gros consommateurs. Les variations des quantités de pétrole et de gaz stockées dans les oléoducs et les gazoducs ne sont pas prises en compte. Sauf chez les gros consommateurs susmentionnés, les variations des stocks des utilisateurs finals ne sont pas comptabilisées. Une augmentation des stocks est indiquée par un chiffre négatif, tandis qu'une diminution apparaît sous la forme d'un chiffre positif.

6. Approvisionnement intérieur

L'*approvisionnement intérieur* est ainsi défini : production + apports d'autres sources + importations - exportations - soutages maritimes internationaux ± variations des stocks.

7. Transferts

La rubrique *transferts* comprend les lignes *transferts entre produits* et *produits transférés*.

Les *transferts entre produits* visent les produits dont le classement a changé soit parce que leurs spécifications ont été modifiées soit parce qu'ils ont été mélangés pour former un autre produit. Ainsi, le kérosène peut être reclassé comme gazole après mélange avec ce dernier produit pour obtenir un gazole conforme aux spécifications hivernales. Le solde net des *transferts entre produits* est nul.

Les *produits transférés* sont des produits pétroliers importés pour subir un traitement complémentaire dans des raffineries. Par exemple : le fioul importé pour conversion dans une raffinerie est transféré dans la catégorie des produits d'alimentation.

Dans le cas des produits pétroliers, cette ligne comprend également les produits primaires reçus. Il s'agit du pétrole brut national ou importé et de LGN d'origine nationale qui sont *utilisés directement* sans être passés par une raffinerie de pétrole (par exemple, le pétrole brut utilisé pour la production d'électricité).

8. Ecart statistique

En principe, le chiffre obtenu pour l'approvisionnement intérieur devrait correspondre à la somme des transferts, des pertes de distribution, des livraisons destinées à la consommation finale et des quantités utilisées pour la transformation et la consommation dans le secteur de l'énergie. Cependant, c'est rarement le cas dans la pratique et la différence qui apparaît est appelée *écart statistique*. En effet, les données relatives aux différentes composantes de l'approvisionnement sont souvent tirées par l'administration nationale de sources différentes. En outre, la prise en compte des variations des stocks de certains gros consommateurs dans la partie approvisionnement du bilan crée des distorsions qui contribuent à l'écart statistique.

B. Secteurs transformation et énergie

Le *secteur transformation* englobe les activités de transformation des formes d'énergie primaire en énergie secondaire, et de transformation ultérieure, par exemple la transformation du charbon à coke en coke, du pétrole brut en produits pétroliers, du fioul lourd en électricité.

Le *secteur énergie* englobe les quantités de combustibles utilisées par les industries productrices d'énergie, par exemple pour le chauffage, l'éclairage et le fonctionnement de tous les équipements intervenant dans le processus d'extraction, ou encore pour la traction et la distribution.

Dans les secteurs *transformation* et *énergie* on distingue les catégories suivantes :

1. Secteur Transformation

- *Centrales électriques* (désigne les centrales conçues pour produire uniquement de l'électricité). Si une unité ou plus de la centrale est une installation de cogénération (et que l'on ne peut pas comptabiliser séparément, sur une base unitaire, les combustibles utilisés et la production), elle est considerée comme une centrale de cogénération. Tant les centrales publiques[1] que les installations des autoproducteurs[2] entrent dans cette rubrique.

- *Centrales de cogénération chaleur/électricité* (désigne les centrales conçues pour produire de la chaleur et de l'électricité). L'UNIPEDE les appelle "installations de production combinée d'énergie électrique et de chaleur". Dans la mesure du possible, les consommations de combustibles et les productions de chaleur/électricité doivent être exprimées sur la base des unité plutôt que des centrales. Cependant, à défaut de données disponibles exprimées sur une base unitaire, il convient d'adopter la convention indiquée ci-dessus pour la définition d'une centrale de cogénération. *On notera que, dans le cas des installations de cogénération chaleur/électricité des autoproducteurs, sont comptabilisés tous les combustibles utilisés pour la production d'électricité, tandis qu'une partie seulement des combustibles utilisés pour la production de chaleur **vendue** est indiquée. Les combustibles utilisés pour la production de la chaleur destinée à la consommation interne des autoproducteurs **ne sont pas** comptabilisés dans cette rubrique mais dans les données concernant la consommation finale de combustibles du secteur de consommation approprié.*

---

1 La production publique désigne les installations dont la *principale activité* est la production d'électricité et/ou de chaleur pour la vente à des tiers. Elles peuvent appartenir au secteur privé ou public. Il convient de noter que les ventes ne se font pas nécessairement par l'intermédiaire du réseau public.

2 L'autoproduction désigne les installations qui produisent de l'électricité et/ou de la chaleur, en totalité ou en partie pour leur consommation propre, en tant qu'activité qui contribue à leur activité principale. Elles peuvent appartenir au secteur privé ou public.

- *Centrales calogènes* (désigne les installations [pompes à chaleur et chaudières électriques comprises] conçues pour produire uniquement de la chaleur et qui en vendent à des tiers [par exemple, consommateurs des secteurs résidentiel, commercial ou industriel] selon les termes d'un contrat). Cette rubrique comprend aussi bien les centrales publiques que les installations des autoproducteurs.

- *Transformation en solides* (couvrant les combustibles utilisés pour l'élaboration d'agglomérés, de coke et de briquettes de lignite [BKB]).

- *Transformation en gaz* (couvrant les quantités de combustibles utilisées pour la production de gaz de ville, de gaz de haut-fourneau et de gaz de cokerie). Dans la production de fonte brute à partir de minerai de fer dans les hauts-fourneaux, les combustibles sont utilisés pour la charge des hauts-fourneaux et pour l'apport de chaleur et de carbone nécessaires à la réduction du minerai. Une partie du carbone est absorbée dans la fonte brute. Comptabiliser le pouvoir calorifique des combustibles qui entrent dans ce procédé est donc une tâche complexe, car la transformation (en gaz de haut-fourneau), la consommation (chaleur de la combustion) et l'utilisation non énergétique (rétention de carbone dans la fonte brute) interviennent simultanément. Dans les questionnaires annuels de 1992/1993, il a été demandé pour la première fois aux pays Membres de notifier dans le secteur transformation tous les combustibles entrant dans les hauts-fourneaux. A l'aide de ces données et sur la base d'études du fonctionnement des hauts-fourneaux, le Secrétariat a réaffecté le pouvoir calorifique des combustibles correspondant aux trois catégories d'utilisation dans les proportions suivantes: 30 pour cent imputés à la transformation, 65 pour cent à la consommation (indiquée dans le sous-secteur industriel Sidérurgie) et 5 pour cent à l'utilisation non énergétique. Ce modèle a été appliqué de façon sélective, en fonction des données disponibles. Se reporter aux notes relatives aux différents pays.

- *Raffineries de pétrole* (couvrant les hydrocarbures utilisés pour l'élaboration de produits pétroliers finis).

- La *liquéfaction* comprend divers procédés de liquéfaction, notamment la liquéfaction de charbon en hydrocarbure liquide en Allemagne et de gaz naturel en essence en Nouvelle-Zélande.

- *Secteur transformation - autres* (comprenant les produits retournés aux raffineries par l'industrie pétrochimique et autres transformations non spécifiées).

2.   Secteur énergie

La consommation propre du secteur de la production d'énergie comprend l'énergie consommée par les industries de transformation pour la chauffe, le pompage, la traction et l'éclairage [Divisions 10, 11, 12, 23, et 40 de la CITI[3]] :

- *mines de charbon* (houille et lignite) ;

- *extraction de pétrole et de gaz* (le gaz brûlé à la torche n'est pas compris) ;

- *raffineries de pétrole* ;

- *centrales électriques, centrales de cogénération et centrales calogènes* ;

- *énergie absorbée par le pompage* (électricité consommée dans les centrales hydrauliques) ;

- *secteur énergie-autres* (comprennent la consommation propre des fabriques d'agglomérés, des cokeries, des usines à gaz, des fabriques de briquettes et de coke de lignite, ainsi que les utilisations non spécifiées du secteur énergie).

3.   Pertes de distribution

Les *pertes de distribution* incluent les pertes enregistrées lors de la distribution du gaz, du transport de l'électricité et du transport du charbon.

---

3 Classification internationale type par industrie de toutes les branches d'activité économique, Série M, No. 4/Rév. 3, Nations Unies, New York, 1990.

C. Consommation finale

Le terme *consommation finale* (qui correspond à la somme des consommations des secteurs d'utilisation finale) signifie que l'énergie utilisée pour la transformation et pour la consommation propre des industries productrices d'énergie est exclue. La consommation finale recouvre la majeure partie des livraisons aux consommateurs (voir la note sur les variations des stocks au paragraphe A.5 ci-dessus).

Dans la consommation finale, les produits d'alimentation de l'industrie pétrochimique sont inclus dans le secteur **industrie** dans une sous-catégorie de la rubrique *industrie chimique* pour les produits pétroliers qui sont utilisés essentiellement à des fins énergétiques. En revanche, les produits pétroliers qui sont principalement utilisés à des fins non énergétiques (voir utilisations non énergétiques au paragraphe C.4 ci-après), sont indiqués sous les rubriques *utilisations non énergétiques* et inclus uniquement dans la **consommation finale totale**. Les retours de produits de l'industrie pétrochimique ne sont pas pris en compte dans la consommation finale (voir paragraphes A.2 et B.1 ci-dessus).

1. Secteur industrie

La consommation du *secteur industrie* est répartie entre les sous-secteurs suivants (l'énergie utilisée par l'industrie pour le transport n'est pas prise en compte ici mais figure dans la rubrique transports) :

- *Sidérurgie* [Groupe 271 et Classe 2731 de la CITI] ;

- *Industrie chimique* [Division 24 de la CITI] ; *dont* : produits d'alimentation de l'industrie pétrochimique. L'industrie pétrochimique comprend les opérations de craquage et de reformage destinées à la production de l'éthylène, du propylène, du butylène, du gaz de synthèse, des aromatiques, du butadiène et d'autres matières premières à base d'hydrocarbures [partie du Groupe 241 de la CITI] ; Voir produits d'alimentation, dans le paragraphe C.4 ci-après (Utilisations non énergétiques) ;

- Industries de base des *métaux non ferreux* [Groupe 272 et Classe 2732 de la CITI] ;

- *Produits minéraux non métalliques* tels que verre, céramiques, ciment, etc. [Division 26 de la CITI] ;

- *Matériel de transport* [Divisions 34 et 35 de la CITI] ;

- *Construction mécanique*. Fabrication d'ouvrages en métaux, de machines et de matériels à l'exclusion du matériel de transport [Divisions 28, 29, 30, 31 et 32 de la CITI] ;

- *Industries extractives (à l'exception des combustibles)* [Divisions 13 et 14 de la CITI] ;

- *Produits alimentaires, boissons et tabacs* [Divisions 15 et 16 de la CITI] ;

- *Imprimerie, pâtes à papier et papier* [Divisions 21 et 22 de la CITI] ;

- *Bois et produits dérivés* (à exclusion de la pâte à papier et du papier) [Division 20 de la CITI] ;

- *Construction* [Division 45 de la CITI] ;

- *Textiles et cuir* [Divisions 17, 18 et 19 de la CITI] ;

- *Non spécifiés* (tout autre secteur industriel non spécifié précédemment) [Divisions 25, 33, 36 et 37 de la CITI].

Note : La plupart des pays éprouvent des difficultés pour fournir une ventilation par branche d'activité pour tous les combustibles. Dans ce cas, la rubrique *non spécifiés* a été utilisée. *Les agrégats régionaux de la consommation industrielle doivent donc être employés avec précaution*. Voir les Notes relatives aux différents pays.

2. Secteur transports

La consommation dans le *secteur transports* couvre toutes les activités de transport quel que soit le secteur économique concerné [Divisions 60, 61 et 62 de la CITI], et elle est ventilée entre les différents sous-secteurs suivants :

- *Aviation civile internationale* : Livraisons de carburants aviation à l'aviation civile internationale. Pour nombre de pays, cette rubrique ne comprend pas les quantités de carburant utilisées par des transporteurs nationaux pour leurs vols internationaux ;

- *Transport aérien intérieur* : Livraisons de carburants aviation pour toutes les activités de transport aérien intérieur, à savoir commerciales, privées, agricoles, militaires, etc. Comprend également les quantités utilisées à des fins autres que le vol proprement dit, par exemple, l'essai de moteurs au banc, mais non le carburant utilisé par les compagnies aériennes pour le transport routier. Pour nombre de pays, cette rubrique ne comprend pas les quantités de carburant utilisées par des transporteurs nationaux pour leurs vols internationaux ;

- *Transport routier* : La totalité des carburants utilisés dans les véhicules routiers (militaires compris) ainsi que le carburant consommé par les transports agricoles et industriels sur route. Ne tient pas compte de l'essence moteur employée dans les moteurs fixes, ni du gazole utilisé par les tracteurs ailleurs que sur route ;

- *Transport ferroviaire* : Toutes les quantités utilisées par le trafic ferroviaire, y compris par les chemins de fer industriels ;

- *Navigation intérieure et cabotage* (y compris la consommation des petites embarcations et des bateaux de cabotage n'achetant pas leur soutage aux termes de contrats de soutages maritimes internationaux). Le carburant utilisé pour la pêche en haute mer, le long du littoral et dans les eaux intérieures doit être comptabilisé dans le secteur agriculture ;

- *Transport par conduites* : L'énergie utilisée pour le transport de substances par conduites ;

- *Non spécifiés*.

3. Autres secteurs

- *Agriculture* : Cette rubrique couvre, par définition, toutes les livraisons aux usagers classés dans les rubriques agriculture, chasse et sylviculture de la CITI, et comprend donc les produits énergétiques consommés par ces usagers que ce soit pour la

traction automobile (à l'exception des carburants utilisés par les engins agricoles sur route), pour la production d'énergie ou le chauffage (dans les secteurs agricole ou résidentiel). Elle comprend aussi les carburants utilisés pour la pêche en haute mer, le long du littoral et dans les eaux intérieures. Divisions 01, 02 et 05 de la CITI ;

- *Commerce et services publics* : Cette rubrique recouvre toutes les activités qui relèvent des Divisions 41, 50, 51, 52, 55, 63, 64, 65, 66, 70, 71, 72, 73, 74, 75, 80, 85, 90, 91, 93 et 99 ;

- *Résidentiel* : Cette rubrique couvre toutes les quantités consommées par les ménages ;

- *Non spécifiés* : Cette rubrique couvre toutes les quantités de combustibles consommées qui n'ont pas été précisées ailleurs (par exemple, la consommation de combustibles pour les activités militaires, à l'exclusion des carburants dans les secteurs du transport routier et du transport aérien intérieur, et la consommation dans les catégories précitées pour lesquelles des données ventilées n'ont pas été fournies).

4. Utilisations non énergétiques

Les utilisations non énergétiques comprennent la consommation des *autres* produits pétroliers, notamment white spirit, paraffines, lubrifiants, bitume et produits divers (voir paragraphe III.21-22 ci-après). Ces produits se trouvent ventilés à part, par secteur d'utilisation finale, sous la rubrique *utilisations non énergétiques,* et sont pris en compte dans la consommation finale totale. Il est présumé que l'usage de ces produits est strictement non énergétique. Il convient de noter que le coke de pétrole ne figure sous la rubrique *utilisations non énergétiques* que si cette utilisation est avérée, autrement, ce produit est comptabilisé dans les utilisations énergétiques dans l'industrie ou les autres secteurs.

Les chiffres concernant les produits d'alimentation de l'industrie pétrochimique sont comptabilisés dans le secteur de l'industrie, au titre de l'industrie chimique (ligne 31) et figurent séparément à la rubrique *dont : produits d'alimentation* (ligne 32). Sont compris dans cette rubrique tous les produits pétroliers, y compris le naphta, sauf les *autres produits pétroliers* énumérés ci-après au paragraphe III.22.

III. NOTES CONCERNANT LES SOURCES D'ENERGIE

Combustibles solides

La rubrique *mines de charbon* ne comprend que le charbon utilisé directement par les charbonnages. Elle exclut le charbon consommé par les centrales électriques minières (y compris dans la rubrique *transformation* -centrales électriques) et les quantités de charbon allouées gratuitement aux mineurs et à leurs familles (considérées comme consommation des ménages et classées de ce fait dans la rubrique *autres secteurs* - résidentiel).

1. Charbon à coke

On appelle charbon à coke un charbon d'une qualité permettant la production d'un coke susceptible d'être utilisé dans les hauts-fourneaux. Son pouvoir calorifique supérieur dépasse 23 865 kJ/kg (5 700 kcal/kg), valeur mesurée pour un combustible exempt de cendres, mais humide.

2. Charbon vapeur (autres charbons bitumineux et anthracite)

On appelle charbon vapeur le charbon utilisé pour la production de vapeur et pour le chauffage des locaux; cette catégorie comprend tous les charbons anthraciteux et bitumineux autres que les charbons à coke. Son pouvoir calorifique supérieur dépasse 23 865 kJ/kg (5 700 kcal/kg), mais est généralement inférieur à celui du charbon à coke.

3. Charbons sous-bitumineux

On appelle charbons sous-bitumineux les charbons non agglutinants d'un pouvoir calorifique supérieur compris entre 17 435 kJ/kg (4 165 kcal/kg) et 23 865 kJ/kg (5 700 kcal/kg), contenant plus de 31 pour cent de matières volatiles sur produit sec exempt de matières minérales.

4. Lignite

Le lignite est un charbon non agglutinant dont le pouvoir calorifique supérieur n'atteint pas 17 435 kJ/kg (4 165 kcal/kg), et qui contient plus de 31 pour cent de matières volatiles sur produit sec exempt de matières minérales.

5. Tourbe

Sédiment fossile d'origine végétale poreux ou comprimé, combustible à haute teneur en eau (jusqu'à 90 pour cent sur brut), facilement rayé, de couleur brun clair à brun foncé.

6. Coke de four à coke (coke de cokerie) et coke d'usine à gaz

Le coke de cokerie est un produit solide obtenu par carbonisation à haute température du charbon, et surtout du charbon à coke ; la teneur en eau et en matières volatiles est faible. Le semi-coke, produit solide obtenu par carbonisation à basse température, le coke et le semi-coke de lignite sont également inclus dans cette rubrique. La rubrique *secteur énergie-autres* représente la consommation interne des cokeries. La consommation de l'industrie sidérurgique ne comprend pas le coke transformé en gaz de haut-fourneau. Pour obtenir la consommation totale de coke de cokerie de l'industrie sidérurgique, il faut ajouter les quantités de coke transformées en gaz de haut-fourneau (elles apparaissent sous la rubrique *transformation* à la ligne transformation en gaz).

Le coke d'usine à gaz est un sous-produit de la houille utilisée pour la production de gaz de ville dans les usines à gaz. Il est principalement utilisé pour le chauffage. La rubrique *secteur énergie-autres* couvre la consommation de coke de gaz dans les usines à gaz.

7. Agglomérés et briquettes de lignite (et de tourbe) (BKB)

Les agglomérés sont des combustibles composites fabriqués à partir de fines de charbon par moulage avec adjonction d'un liant tel que le brai. La quantité d'agglomérés produite est donc légèrement supérieure au tonnage de houille effectivement utilisé à cet effet. La consommation d'agglomérés durant le processus de fabrication des agglomérés apparaît sous la rubrique *secteur énergie-autres*.

Les briquettes de lignite (BKB) sont des combustibles composites fabriqués à partir du lignite, et agglomérés sous haute pression. Ces données couvrent les briquettes de tourbe, le lignite séché, la poussière de lignite et les fines de lignite. La consommation des usines de briquettes est comprise dans la rubrique *secteur énergie-autres*.

Pétrole brut, liquides de gaz naturel et produits d'alimentation des raffineries

Sous le titre *transformation*, la rubrique *raffineries de pétrole* indique les quantités de pétrole brut, de LGN, de produits d'alimentation des raffineries, d'additifs et d'autres hydrocarbures qui sont utilisées dans le processus de raffinage.

8. Pétrole brut

C'est une huile minérale, constituée d'un mélange d'hydrocarbures d'origine naturelle. Sa couleur va du jaune au noir, sa densité et sa viscosité sont variables. Cette catégorie comprend aussi les condensats (provenant des séparateurs) directement récupérés sur les périmètres d'exploitation des hydrocarbures gazeux dans les installations de séparation des phases liquide et gazeuse.

Les autres hydrocarbures, notamment le pétrole brut synthétique, les huiles minérales extraites des roches bitumineuses telles que schistes, sables asphaltiques, etc. et les huiles issues de la liquéfaction du charbon figurent à la ligne *autres sources*. Voir paragraphe A.2 ci-dessus.

Les importations et la production d'huiles émulsionnées (par exemple, l'Orimulsion) sont prises en compte. Etant donné que ces huiles ne demandent pas de traitement ultérieur en raffinerie, elles sont transférées à la rubrique *autres produits pétroliers* pour ce qui est de la consommation. Il convient de se reporter aux notes relatives à certains pays pour prendre connaissance des exceptions à ce transfert.

9. Liquides de gaz naturel (LGN)

Les LGN sont des hydrocarbures liquides ou liquéfiés obtenus pendant le traitement, la purification et la stabilisation du gaz naturel. Il s'agit des fractions de gaz naturel qui sont récupérées sous forme liquide dans les installations de séparation, dans les installations sur les gisements ou dans les usines de traitement du gaz. Les LGN comprennent l'éthane, le propane, le butane, le pentane, l'essence naturelle et les condensats, sans que la liste soit limitative. Ils peuvent aussi inclure certaines quantités de substances autres que des hydrocarbures.

10. Produits d'alimentation des raffineries

C'est un produit ou une combinaison de produits dérivés du pétrole brut et destinés à subir un traitement ultérieur autre qu'un mélange dans l'industrie du raffinage. Il est transformé en un ou plusieurs constituants et/ou produits finis. Cette définition recouvre les produits finis qui sont importés pour la consommation des raffineries et ceux qui sont renvoyés par l'industrie pétrochimique aux raffineries.

11. Additifs

Les additifs sont des substances autres que des hydrocarbures qui sont ajoutées ou mélangées à un produit afin de modifier ses propriétés, pour améliorer par exemple ses caractéristiques lors de la combustion, comme les alcools et les éthers (MTBE ou méthyl tertio-butyl éther), ou des substances telles que le plomb tétraéthyle. Cependant, cette rubrique ne couvre pas l'éthanol, qui apparaît à la rubrique Gaz/liquides tirés de la biomasse.

Produits pétroliers

Ce sont tous les produits dérivés du pétrole qui peuvent être obtenus par distillation et qui sont, en général, utilisés en dehors de l'industrie du raffinage. Les produits finis classés comme produits d'alimentation des raffineries (voir ci-dessus) n'entrent pas dans cette catégorie.

Les données sur la *production* de produits pétroliers font apparaître, pour chaque produit, la production brute des raffineries.

La consommation de combustibles des raffineries (figurant dans le *secteur énergie*, ligne *raffineries de pétrole*) représente leur consommation de produits pétroliers, qu'il s'agisse de produits intermédiaires ou de produits finis, utilisés par example pour le chauffage, l'éclairage, la traction, etc.

12. Gaz de raffinerie (non liquéfiés)

Cette catégorie couvre, par définition, les gaz non condensables obtenus dans les raffineries lors de la distillation du pétrole brut ou du traitement des produits pétroliers (par craquage, par exemple). Il s'agit principalement d'hydrogène, de méthane, d'éthane et d'oléfines. Sont compris également les gaz retournés aux raffineries par l'industrie pétrochimique. La production de gaz de raffinerie correspond à la production brute. La consommation propre des raffineries est comptabilisée séparément à la ligne *raffineries de pétrole* dans la rubrique *secteur énergie*.

13. Gaz de pétrole liquéfiés (GPL) et éthane

Il s'agit des fractions légères d'hydrocarbures paraffiniques qui s'obtiennent lors du raffinage ainsi que dans les installations de stabilisation du pétrole brut et de traitement du gaz naturel. Ce sont le propane (C_3H_8) et le butane (C_4H_{10}) ou un mélange de ces deux hydrocarbures. Ils sont généralement liquéfiés sous pression pour le transport et le stockage.

L'éthane (C_2H_6) est un hydrocarbure à chaîne droite, gazeux à l'état naturel. C'est un gaz paraffinique incolore que l'on extrait du gaz naturel et des gaz de raffinerie.

14. Essence moteur

C'est un hydrocarbure léger utilisé dans les moteurs à combustion interne, tels que ceux des véhicules à moteur, à l'exception des aéronefs. L'essence moteur est distillée entre 35°C et 215°C et utilisée comme carburant pour les moteurs terrestres à allumage commandé. L'essence moteur peut contenir des additifs (comme l'éthanol), des composés oxygénés et des additifs améliorant l'indice d'octane, notamment des composés plombés comme le PTE (plomb tétraéthyle) et le PTM (plomb tétraméthyle).

15. Essence aviation

Il s'agit d'une essence spécialement préparée pour les moteurs à pistons des avions, avec un indice d'octane adapté au moteur, un point de congélation de -60°C et un intervalle de distillation habituellement compris entre 30°C et 180°C.

16. Carburéacteurs

Cette catégorie comprend les carburéacteurs type essence et les carburéacteurs type kérosène, qui répondent aux spécifications d'utilisation pour les turbomoteurs pour avion.

Carburéacteur type essence

Cette catégorie comprend tous les hydrocarbures légers utilisés dans les turbomoteurs pour avion. Ils distillent entre 100°C et 250°C. Ils sont obtenus par mélange de kérosène et d'essence ou de naphtas, de manière à ce que la teneur en aromatiques soit égale ou inférieure à 25 pour cent en volume, et que la pression de vapeur se situe entre 13.7 kPa et 20.6 kPa. Des additifs peuvent être ajoutés afin d'accroître la stabilité et la combustibilité du carburant.

Carburéacteur type kérosène

C'est un distillat moyen utilisé dans les turbomoteurs pour avion, qui répond aux mêmes caractéristiques de distillation et présente le même point d'éclair que le kérosène (entre 150°C et 300°C, mais ne dépassant pas 250°C en général). De plus, il est conforme à des spécifications particulières (concernant notamment le point de congélation), définies par l'Association du transport aérien international (IATA).

17. Kérosène

Le kérosène comprend les distillats de pétrole raffiné dont la volatilité est comprise entre celle de l'essence et celle du gazole/carburant diesel. C'est une huile moyenne qui distille entre 150°C et 300°C.

18. Gazole/carburant diesel (Distillat de coupe intermédiaire)

Les gazoles/carburants diesel sont des huiles lourdes. Les gazoles sont extraits de la dernière fraction issue de la distillation atmosphérique du pétrole brut, tandis que les gazoles lourds sont obtenus par redistillation sous vide du résidu de la distillation atmosphérique. Le gazole/carburant diesel distille entre 180°C et 380°C. Plusieurs qualités sont disponibles, selon l'utilisation : gazole pour moteur diesel à allumage par compression (automobiles, poids lourds, bateaux, etc.), fioul léger pour le chauffage des locaux industriels et commerciaux, et autres gazoles, y compris les huiles lourdes distillant entre 380°C et 540°C utilisées comme produit d'alimentation dans l'industrie pétrochimique

19. Fioul lourd (résiduel)

Ce sont les huiles lourdes constituant le résidu de distillation. La définition englobe tous les fiouls résiduels (y compris ceux obtenus par mélange). La viscosité cinétique est supérieure à 10 cST à 80°C. Le

point d'éclair est toujours supérieur à 50°C, et la densité est toujours supérieure à 900 kg/l.

20. Naphtas

Les naphtas sont un produit d'alimentation des raffineries destiné soit à l'industrie pétrochimique (par exemple, fabrication d'éthylène ou production de composés aromatiques) soit à la production d'essence par reformage ou isomérisation dans la raffinerie. Les naphtas correspondent aux fractions distillant entre 30°C et 210°C ou sur une partie de cette plage de température. Les naphtas importés pour mélange doivent être indiqués dans les importations, puis repris à la ligne *transferts*, affectés d'un signe négatif pour les naphtas, et d'un signe positif pour les produits finis correspondants (par exemple, essence).

21. Coke de pétrole

Le coke de pétrole est un résidu solide noir brillant, obtenu principalement par craquage et carbonisation de résidus de produits d'alimentation, de goudrons et de poix, dans des procédés tels que la cokéfaction différée ou la cokéfaction fluide. Il se compose essentiellement de carbone (90 à 95 pour cent) et brûle en laissant peu de cendres. Il est employé comme produit d'alimentation dans les cokeries des usines sidérurgiques, pour la chauffe, pour la fabrication d'électrodes et pour la production de substances chimiques. Les deux qualités les plus importantes de coke sont le coke de pétrole et le coke de pétrole calciné. Cette catégorie comprend également le coke de catalyse, qui se dépose sur le catalyseur pendant les opérations de raffinage ; ce coke n'est pas récupérable, et il est en général brûlé comme combustible dans les raffineries.

22. Autres produits pétroliers

La catégorie *autres produits pétroliers* regroupe les white spirit et SBP, les lubrifiants, le bitume, les paraffines et d'autres produits.

a) *White spirit et essences spéciales (SBP)* : Ce sont des distillats intermédiaires raffinés, dont l'intervalle de distillation se situe entre celui des naphtas et celui du kérosène.

Ils se subdivisent en :

i) **Essences spéciales (SBP)** : Huiles légères distillant entre 30°C et 200°C et dont l'écart de température entre les points de distillation de 5 pour cent et 90 pour cent en volume, y compris les pertes, est inférieur ou égal à 60°C. En d'autres termes, il s'agit d'une huile légère, de coupe plus étroite que celle des essences moteur. On distingue 7 ou 8 qualités d'essences spéciales, selon la position de la coupe dans l'intervalle de distillation défini plus haut.

ii) **White spirit** : Essence industrielle dont le point d'éclair est supérieur à 30°C. L'intervalle de distillation du white spirit est compris entre 135°C et 200°C.

b) *Lubrifiants* : Les lubrifiants sont des hydrocarbures obtenus à partir de distillats ou de résidus ; ils sont principalement utilisés pour réduire les frottements entre surfaces d'appui. Cette catégorie comprend tous les grades d'huiles lubrifiantes, depuis les spindles jusqu'aux huiles à cylindres, et les huiles entrant dans les graisses, y compris les huiles moteur et tous les grades d'huiles de base pour lubrifiants.

c) *Bitume* : Hydrocarbure solide, semi-solide ou visqueux, à structure colloïdale, de couleur brune à noire ; c'est un résidu de la distillation du pétrole brut obtenu par distillation sous vide des huiles résiduelles de distillation atmosphérique. Le bitume est aussi souvent appelé asphalte, et il est principalement employé pour le revêtement des routes et pour les matériaux de toiture. Cette catégorie couvre le bitume fluidisé et le cutback.

d) *Paraffines* : Hydrocarbures aliphatiques saturés (dont la formule générale est C_nH_{2n+2}). Les paraffines sont des résidus du déparaffinage des huiles lubrifiantes ; elles présentent une structure cristalline, avec $C > 12$. Leurs principales caractéristiques sont les suivantes : incolores, inodores et translucides, point de fusion supérieur à 45°C.

e) *Autres* : Tous les produits pétroliers qui ne sont pas classés ci-dessus, par exemple, le goudron, le soufre et la graisse. Cette catégorie comprend également les composés aromatiques (par exemple, BTX ou benzène, toluène et xylènes) et les oléfines (par exemple, propylène) produits dans les raffineries.

Gaz

Les chiffres relatifs à ces quatre catégories sont tous exprimés en térajoules, sur la base du **pouvoir calorifique supérieur**.

23. Gaz naturel

Le gaz naturel est constitué de gaz, méthane essentiellement, sous forme liquide ou gazeuse, extraits de gisements naturels souterrains. Il peut s'agir aussi bien de gaz "non associé" provenant de gisements qui produisent uniquement des hydrocarbures sous forme gazeuse, que de gaz "associé" obtenu en même temps que le pétrole brut, ou de méthane récupéré dans les mines de charbon (grisou).

24. Gaz d'usine à gaz

Cette catégorie couvre tous les types de gaz produits dans les usines des entreprises publiques ou privées ayant pour principal objet la production, le transport et la distribution de gaz. Cette catégorie comprend le gaz produit par carbonisation (y compris le gaz produit dans les fours à coke et transféré aux usines à gaz), par gazéification totale avec ou sans enrichissement au moyen de produits pétroliers, par craquage du gaz naturel ou par reformage et simple mélange avec d'autres gaz et/ou de l'air. Cette rubrique recouvre également le gaz naturel de substitution dont le pouvoir calorifique est élevé, et qui est produit par conversion chimique d'hydrocarbures.

25. Gaz de cokerie

Le gaz de cokerie est un sous-produit de la fabrication du coke de cokerie utilisé en sidérurgie.

26. Gaz de haut-fourneau

Le gaz de haut-fourneau est obtenu lors de la combustion du coke dans les hauts-fourneaux de l'industrie sidérurgique. Il est récupéré et utilisé comme combustible, en partie dans l'usine même, et en partie pour d'autres procédés de l'industrie sidérurgique, ou encore dans des centrales électriques dotées d'équipements adaptés pour en brûler. Cette rubrique comprend également le gaz obtenu comme sous-produit lors de l'élaboration de l'acier dans les fours à oxygène ou convertisseurs basiques avec soufflage d'oxygène, qui est récupéré à la sortie du gueulard. Ce gaz est également appelé gaz de convertisseur ou gaz LD.

Energies renouvelables combustibles et déchets

Les données concernant ces quatre catégories de gaz sont toutes exprimées en térajoules, sur la base du **pouvoir calorifique inférieur**.

27. Biomasse solide et produits d'origine animale

La biomasse est, par définition, toute matière végétale utilisée directement comme combustible ou transformée avant de la brûler sous une autre forme. Elle comprend le bois, les déchets végétaux (y compris les déchets de bois et les cultures destinées à la production d'énergie), les matières/déchets d'origine animale et les lessives sulfitiques (résidus de fabrication de la pâte à papier), également appelées "liqueur noire"(liqueur alcaline de rejet des digesteurs lors de la production de pâte au sulfate ou à la soude dans le procédé d'élaboration du papier, dont le contenu énergétique provient de la lignine extraite de la pâte chimique).

28. Gaz/liquides tirés de la biomasse

Ce sont les gaz qui sont produits principalement par fermentation anaérobie de biomasse et de déchets solides et brûlés pour produire de la chaleur et/ou de l'énergie électrique. Cette catégorie comprend les gaz de décharges et les gaz de digestion des boues (gaz issus des eaux usées et des lisiers). Les additifs tirés de la biomasse (ou bio-additifs) comme l'éthanol entrent également dans cette catégorie.

29. Déchets urbains et assimilés

Les déchets urbains correspondent aux produits brûlés directement pour produire de la chaleur et/ou de

l'énergie électrique, dont notamment les déchets des secteurs résidentiel et commercial ainsi que du secteur des services publics, qui sont recueillis par les autorités municipales pour leur élimination dans des installations centralisées. Les déchets hospitaliers entrent dans cette catégorie.

30. Déchets industriels

Il s'agit de produits liquides et solides brûlés directement (généralement dans des installations spécialisées, par exemple pour les pneumatiques) pour produire de la chaleur et/ou l'énergie électrique.

Electricité et chaleur

31. Electricité

La production brute d'électricité est mesurée aux bornes de tous les groupes d'alternateurs d'une centrale. Elle comprend donc l'énergie absorbée par les équipements auxiliaires et les pertes dans les transformateurs qui sont considérés comme faisant partie intégrante de la centrale.

La différence entre production nette et brute est généralement évaluée à 7 pour cent dans les centrales thermiques classiques, à 1 pour cent dans les centrales hydro-électriques et à 6 pour cent dans les centrales nucléaires, géothermiques ou solaires. La production hydraulique comprend la production des centrales à accumulation par pompage.

32. Chaleur

La production de chaleur destinée à la vente acquiert une importance grandissante depuis quelques années. Pour tenir compte de cette évolution, les quantités de chaleur destinée à la vente sont indiquées, dans le secteur transformation, aux lignes "installations de cogénération"et "centrales calogènes". Les quantités de combustibles utilisées pour produire de la chaleur consommée localement sont notifiées dans les secteurs où cette consommation a lieu.

IV. NOTES RELATIVES AUX DIFFERENTS PAYS

Notes générales :

Les notes qui suivent renvoient aux données pour les années de 1960 à 1993 ; elles concernent les tableaux récapitulatifs figurant à la fin de cet ouvrage, ainsi que les données sur disquettes. Pour les données précédant 1974, on ne dispose pas de séries à part concernant la production d'électricité des centrales publiques d'électricité et celle des autoproducteurs. Les données sur les quantités de combustibles utilisés pour la production d'électricité et de chaleur, et sur les productions correspondantes dans les centrales de cogénération chaleur/électricité et les centrales calogènes, devraient être utilisées avec précaution. Malgré les estimations introduites par le Secrétariat, les données sur la consommation et la production ne sont pas toujours compatibles. Le lecteur est invité à se reporter aux notes figurant ci-dessous, sous le titre *Electricité et chaleur*.

1.   Allemagne

Les données relatives à l'Allemagne tiennent compte des nouveaux Länder de l'Allemagne à partir de 1970.

Combustibles solides : Les données concernant les quantités employées pour des utilisations non énergétiques sont disponibles à partir de 1970. Avant cette date, les utilisations non énergétiques sont comptabilisées avec les données concernant les secteurs de consommation finale respectifs. Le modèle de l'AIE relatif au fonctionnement des hauts-fourneaux a été appliqué pour 1992 et 1993. Les données sur les combustibles utilisés dans les hauts-fourneaux ont été estimées par le Secrétariat pour 1992 et 1993. Les données sur la tourbe (communiquées en térajoules) ont été converties en tonnes en retenant pour hypothèse un pouvoir calorifique inférieur de 0.2 tep/tonne. S'agissant du lignite et des BKB, il n'existe pas de ventilation du secteur industriel pour 1991 et 1992. Les quantités de combustibles utilisées dans les centrales calogènes des autoproducteurs ne sont disponibles qu'à partir de 1992. Les données correspondantes pour les centrales calogènes publiques ne sont pas disponibles pour 1992 et 1993. Les combustibles consommés pour la cogénération en 1992 et 1993 sont respectivement imputés aux centrales publiques d'électricité dans le cas de la cogénération publique et aux installations de production d'électricité des autoproducteurs lorsqu'il s'agit de l'autoproduction de chaleur/électricité.

Pétrole : Avant 1976, la consommation de gaz de raffinerie dans l'industrie chimique est incluse dans la consommation propre des raffineries. En raison d'un changement de source des données, les séries chronologiques concernant l'approvisionnement de plusieurs produits comportent des irrégularités entre 1979 et 1980. Le degré de détail des données sur la consommation industrielle s'est amélioré depuis 1985 par suite de changements dans le système national de notification. Avant 1993, les quantités de fioul lourd consommées dans les hauts-fourneaux étaient comptabilisées avec les données concernant l'industrie sidérurgique.

Gaz : En raison de modifications du système national de notification en ce qui concerne le gaz naturel, la série comporte une rupture entre 1967 et 1968. Avant 1970, la consommation propre des raffineries et les pertes de distribution sont comptabilisées avec la consommation de gaz naturel lors de l'extraction du pétrole et du gaz. La consommation de gaz naturel est fondée sur les données de l'*Arbeitsgemeinschaft Energiebilanzen*. La ventilation de la consommation de gaz naturel entre les secteurs commercial, services publics, agricole et résidentiel n'est disponible qu'à partir de 1984.

Electricité et chaleur : Entre 1971 et 1980, la consommation des mines de charbon comprend la consommation des fours à coke et des usines de briquettes de lignite. Toutes les données relatives à la production de chaleur sont comptabilisées avec celles concernant la chaleur produite par les centrales de cogénération chaleur/électricité. Les données sur la production de chaleur, qui ne sont pas disponibles avant 1970, ont été estimées par le Secrétariat pour 1989 et les années suivantes. En ce qui concerne la chaleur, il se peut que les données sur la production totale avant 1989 soient inférieures à la réalité par suite de la soustraction qui a pu être faite de quantités considérables au titre de pertes de distribution, ce qui ne devrait pas, cependant, influer sur les données relatives à la consommation. La consommation de chaleur à partir de 1991 a été estimée par le Secrétariat. Pour 1992 et 1993, la ventilation de la production de chaleur par combustible a été estimée par le Secrétariat sur la base des données sur la consommation de combustibles pour la production de chaleur publiées dans *Energiebilanz der Bundesrepublik Deutschland für das Jahr 1990*.

2.   Australie

Toutes les données correspondent à l'exercice budgétaire qui va de juillet 1991 à juin 1992 pour l'année 1992.

Combustibles solides : Avant 1974, on ne dispose pas de données concernant la consommation de gaz de cokerie ou de gaz de haut-fourneau dans les fours à coke. Pour les années 1960 à 1973, les quantités de coke de cokerie utilisées dans les fours à coke ont été estimées par le Secrétariat. Les quantités de lignite utilisées dans les centrales publiques de cogénération chaleur/électricité ont été estimées par le Secrétariat,

sur la base des réponses reçues pour le questionnaire annuel concernant l'électricité. L'industrie des pâtes et papiers ne consomme plus de lignite depuis 1990. L'industrie chimique ne consomme plus de coke de cokerie depuis cette même date. La consommation correspondant à la rubrique industrie-non spécifiés d'énergies renouvelables combustibles et de déchets comprend la totalité de la consommation des *autres secteurs* de 1960 à 1969. Le modèle de l'AIE relatif au fonctionnement des hauts-fourneaux a été appliqué pour les années 1986 à 1993 après que l'administration australienne ait révisé les données correspondant aux combustibles utilisés et à la production.

Pétrole : En raison du manque d'informations pour la période antérieure à 1970, il existe, entre 1969 et 1970, des ruptures dans les séries de données relatives aux approvisionnements et à la consommation. Les données concernant les années 1970 à 1973 sont des estimations du Secrétariat calculées à partir des sources publiées disponibles. Il n'existe pas de séries distinctes de données sur la consommation de kérosène dans le secteur du commerce et dans celui des services publics avant 1974 ; la consommation correspondante a été comptabilisée dans la consommation du secteur résidentiel. Avant cette date également, les quantités de gaz de raffinerie indiquées sont nettes, hors consommation dans les raffineries. Les pertes en raffinerie, affectées d'un signe négatif, proviennent de différences de traitement des transferts entre raffineries. A partir de 1990, les importations de fioul lourd ont été estimées par l'administration australienne.

Gaz : Les chiffres indiqués pour les exportations de gaz naturel liquéfié vers le Japon ont été estimés par l'administration nationale. Avant 1986, la consommation de gaz naturel des hauts-fourneaux était comptabilisée avec celle de la sidérurgie. Avant 1991, les données sur le gaz naturel tiennent compte de l'éthane.

Electricité et chaleur : Avant 1974, la consommation du secteur de l'énergie était comptabilisée avec celle de l'industrie. A partir de 1974, la consommation des fours à coke a été estimée par l'administration australienne. Dans le cas de l'électricité produite par des autoproducteurs, les quantités de combustibles utilisées ne concernent que les installations admettant un seul combustible. La consommation des installations pluricombustibles exploitées par des autoproducteurs est comptabilisée avec celle de l'industrie. Les consommations et les productions des installations de cogénération chaleur/électricité des autoproducteurs ne sont pas disponibles pour la période précédant 1992. Pour 1992 et 1993, la ventilation par combustible de la production des installations de cogénération des autoproducteurs a été estimée par le Secrétariat. Avant 1992, la production d'électricité et/ou de chaleur à partir d'énergies renouvelables combustibles et de déchets (à savoir, la biomasse solide et les produits d'origine animale, les gaz/liquides tirés de la biomasse, les déchets urbains et les déchets industriels) est comptabilisée avec la biomasse solide et les produits d'origine animale. On ne dispose pas de données sur la production de chaleur pour 1992 et 1993. L'utilisation directe de l'énergie solaire est prise en compte à partir de 1974.

3. Autriche

Combustibles solides : Le charbon vapeur comprend les briquettes de houille. Le "Trockenkohle" est regroupé avec les briquettes de lignite (BKB) en raison de son pouvoir calorifique élevé de 20 900 kJ/kg. Les données relatives à la consommation propre de gaz de haut-fourneau dans le secteur de l'énergie sont disponibles à partir de 1983. Après 1982, le gaz d'usine à gaz n'a plus été produit à partir de charbon ou de produits charbonniers. La consommation de combustibles du secteur industriel en 1993 a été estimée sur la base de données de 1992 exprimées en pourcentages. Le bois de feu entre dans la catégorie des déchets industriels.

Pétrole : A partir de 1978, les données relatives à la consommation de fioul lourd dans l'industrie comprennent la consommation de gazole/carburant diesel. A partir de 1978, les données relatives aux *autres produits pétroliers* comprennent les paraffines et le coke de pétrole.

Electricité et chaleur : Avant 1991, la consommation des raffineries de pétrole comprend également la consommation des usines à gaz, tandis qu'à compter de cette date, elle englobe la consommation des fabriques d'agglomérés, des cokeries et des fabriques de briquettes de lignite (BKB). La consommation de l'industrie sidérurgique comprend la consommation des fours à coke avant 1991. De même, jusqu'en 1991, la consommation du secteur du commerce et des services publics comprend les petites entreprises et les bureaux du secteur tertiaire, et l'énergie électrique utilisée pour la fourniture d'électricité, le chauffage urbain et la distribution d'eau. A partir de 1991, la consommation des petites entreprises et des bureaux du secteur tertiaire est incluse dans les *autres secteurs* non spécifiés, tandis que l'énergie électrique consommée par la fourniture d'électricité, le chauffage urbain et la distribution d'eau figure dans la rubrique *secteur énergie-autres*. La ventilation de la consommation d'électricité dans les secteurs énergie et industrie a été estimée par le Secrétariat pour 1993. Avant 1992, les consommations des installations publiques de cogénération chaleur/électricité sont comprises dans celles des centrales publiques d'électricité. Pour 1992 et 1993, on ne dispose pas de données sur les consommations des installations de production d'électricité des autoproducteurs. La production d'électricité des centrales de cogénération est comptabilisée avec celle des centrales électriques. C'est depuis 1981 que l'on dispose de données sur la production de chaleur des centrales calogènes, alors que les données sur les combustibles utilisés dans ces centrales sont disponibles à partir de 1989. S'agissant de la chaleur, la consommation propre est comptabilisée avec les pertes de distribution, et le secteur résidentiel comprend le commerce et les services publics. Les données sur la production de chaleur dans les installations de cogénération des autoproducteurs sont disponbiles à partir de 1992. La ventilation de la consommation de chaleur dans l'industrie (à l'exclusion de l'industrie chimique) a été estimée par le Secrétariat pour 1993. La série de données sur la consommation de chaleur dans l'industrie comporte une rupture entre 1991 et 1992. La répartition de la production de chaleur entre les différentes catégories des combustibles classiques et assimilés a été estimée par le Secrétariat sur la base des quantités de combustibles utilisées figurant dans les questionnaires annuels sur les combustibles présentés par l'administration autrichienne pour les années 1992 et 1993.

4. Belgique

Combustibles solides : Les données concernant le charbon sous-bitumineux concernent les produits de récupération du charbon. La production de charbon vapeur a cessé le 31 août 1992. Les données sur la biomasse solide et les produits d'origine animale, les gaz/liquides tirés de la biomasse, ainsi que sur les déchets industriels et urbains utilisés pour la production de chaleur et d'électricité sont disponibles à partir de 1983.

Pétrole : Avant 1975, les données relatives à la production de gaz de raffinerie sont indiquées déduction faite de la consommation des raffineries. Avant 1976, la consommation de GPL et de gazole/carburant diesel dans le secteur du commerce et des services publics est comptabilisée avec la consommation du secteur résidentiel. Avant 1981, la consommation de gazole/carburant diesel du secteur de la construction est comptabilisée avec celle du secteur des produits minéraux non métalliques. Avant 1967, les *autres produits pétroliers* sont regroupés avec le naphta. La rupture constatée entre 1975 et 1976 dans la série chronologique concernant le fioul lourd provient d'une modification de classification entre secteurs industriel et commercial. Les données relatives à la consommation de pétrole des centrales publiques de cogénération chaleur/électricité ont été estimées par le Secrétariat pour la période de 1991 à 1993.

Electricité et chaleur : La production d'électricité des installations de cogénération chaleur/électricité des autoproducteurs est comptabilisée avec celle des centrales électriques. Avant 1982, la production d'électricité des centrales publiques de cogénération est comptabilisée avec celle des centrales électriques. Les données relatives à la chaleur produite par les centrales de cogénération chaleur/électricité ne sont pas disponibles avant 1973. Les séries chronologiques de données sur la consommation de chaleur dans l'industrie chimique et dans la rubrique industrie-non spécifiés comportent des ruptures entre 1991 et 1992.

5. Canada

Combustibles solides : Pour la période antérieure à 1978, en raison de l'absence de données, les utilisations non énergétiques de la houille et du coke de cokerie sont comptabilisées dans les différents secteurs d'utilisation finale. Pour la période comprise entre 1960 et 1992, la catégorie de la biomasse solide et des produits d'origine animale a fait l'objet d'une révision, sur la base des données communiquées par l'administration canadienne.

Pétrole : Avant 1980, il existe plusieurs ruptures des séries concernant les détails de la consommation industrielle pour le kérosène, le gazole/carburant diesel et le fioul lourd. A partir de 1982, la consommation de gazole/carburant diesel des parcs automobiles du

secteur des services de distribution en gros et au détail est comptabilisée dans le secteur du commerce et des services publics. Avant 1982, elle entrait dans la catégorie du transport routier. A partir de 1980, toutes les données relatives à la consommation sont fondées sur une même enquête. Toutefois, à partir de 1988, les données concernant plusieurs sous-secteurs industriels ne sont plus disponibles. Des données distinctes relatives à la consommation du secteur de l'agriculture (y compris la foresterie) sont disponibles à partir de 1983 pour le kérosène, à partir de 1973 pour le gazole/carburant diesel, et à partir de 1978 pour le fioul lourd. Pour les années antérieures, la consommation du secteur de l'agriculture est comptabilisée avec celle du secteur résidentiel. Avant 1978, les livraisons destinées aux soutages maritimes internationaux sont comptabilisées avec les données sur la navigation intérieure. Les transferts de naphta et *d'autres produits pétroliers* tiennent compte des quantités de produits d'alimentation et autres additifs achetées par les compagnies qui communiquent des données aux compagnies qui ne le font pas. La notification des données sur les approvisionnements en GPL a changé à partir de 1989. Les données concernant la production, ainsi que celles sur les transferts de produits, s'en verront modifiées dans les séries comprises entre 1988 et 1989. Le GPL comprend les "pentanes plus" pour toutes les années, et l'éthane avant 1991. La liquéfaction correspond à la production de pétrole brut synthétique à partir de sables asphaltiques. A partir de 1990, l'administration canadienne a adopté une méthode différente pour la notification concernant le pétrole brut synthétique.

Gaz : Avant 1978, la consommation de gaz naturel du secteur de l'agriculture est comptabilisée avec la consommation industrielle. Entre 1960 et 1977, la consommation du secteur industrie, catégorie non spécifiés, comprend le gaz naturel utilisé comme combustible dans les raffineries de pétrole. En 1976 et 1977, la consommation de gaz naturel de l'industrie chimique ne concerne que les produits d'alimentation ; des données sur cette consommation ne sont pas disponibles pour les années antérieures. A partir de 1990, la liquéfaction du gaz naturel concerne les quantités de gaz naturel utilisées pour produire de l'hydrogène destiné à la valorisation du pétrole brut synthétique. Avant 1990, les quantités d'hydrogène entrant dans ce procédé étaient comptabilisées dans la rubrique consommation du secteur de l'extraction du pétrole et du gaz. En 1992, la consommation de gaz naturel dans les centrales publiques de cogénération chaleur/électricité comprend celle de trois nouvelles installations de cogénération dans la province de l'Ontario.

Electricité et chaleur : On ne dispose pas de données sur la consommation d'électricité dans les mines de charbon entre 1982 et 1986, ni sur la consommation du secteur de l'extraction du pétrole et du gaz avant 1987. Des ruptures de séries se produisent entre 1973 et 1974 dans le secteur de l'agriculture et entre 1987 et 1988 dans le secteur de l'industrie. L'électricité absorbée pour l'accumulation par pompage a été estimée par le Secrétariat pour 1991 et les années suivantes. La production de chaleur comprend les quantités produites dans des centrales nucléaires et destinées à la distribution à d'autres consommateurs. Le Secrétariat s'est fondé sur la production pour estimer certaines quantités de combustibles utilisées dans les centrales de cogénération chaleur/électricité. Cependant, les données sur les combustibles utilisés et la production thermique chez les autoproducteurs n'étant pas compatibles, les coefficients de rendement résultants pourraient être variables. On ne dispose pas de données sur les combustibles utilisés dans les installations calogènes pour les années 1979 à 1987. Avant 1992, la production d'électricité et/ou de chaleur à partir d'énergies renouvelables combustibles et de déchets (à savoir, biomasse solide et produits d'origine animale, gaz/liquides tirés de la biomasse, déchets urbains et déchets industriels) est comptabilisée avec la biomasse solide et les produits d'origine animale.

6.   Danemark

En 1993 et 1994, l'administration danoise à procédé à un examen de fond des statistiques nationales sur la chaleur et l'électricité, ce dont témoigne la qualité des données pour 1993. Cet examen risque d'entraîner des ruptures des séries de données entre 1992 et 1993. Les données concernant 1992 et la période antérieure sont actuellement réexaminées par l'administration danoise.

Combustibles solides : Des données sur les énergies renouvelables combustibles et les déchets sont disponibles à partir de 1970. Depuis 1988, on dispose de nouvelles séries concernant la consommation d'énergies renouvelables combustibles et de déchets du secteur du commerce et des services publics ainsi que celle de l'industrie dans la catégorie non spécifiés ; par ailleurs, il existe une rupture entre 1989 et 1990 dans

les séries de données sur les centrales calogènes, l'agriculture et le secteur résidentiel. Le Secrétariat a estimé les quantités de charbon vapeur utilisées par les autoproducteurs.

Pétrole : Avant 1975, les données sur la production de gaz de raffinerie sont indiquées déduction faite de la consommation des raffineries. Entre 1974 et 1979, la consommation de fioul lourd par les autoproducteurs pour la production d'électricité a été estimée par le Secrétariat. Avant 1975, la totalité de la consommation de pétrole du secteur du commerce et des services publics était comptabilisée avec celle du secteur résidentiel. Depuis 1987, les données sur les paraffines ne sont plus disponibles. La méthode de classification ayant été modifiée, la consommation d'essence des secteurs résidentiel et commercial est comptabilisée dans le secteur du transport routier depuis 1988. Pour l'année 1991, la consommation de GPL du secteur industriel a été estimée par l'Agence danoise de l'énergie. Avant 1992, la consommation de gazole/carburant diesel et de fioul lourd pour la pêche entre dans la rubrique navigation intérieure, alors qu'après cette date elle est indiquée dans le secteur de l'agriculture. Les données relatives à la consommation sont fondées sur une enquête détaillée effectuée auprès d'entreprises danoises une année sur deux. Pour les années non couvertes par l'enquête, l'Agence danoise de l'énergie fournit des estimations de la consommation.

Gaz : Depuis 1989, les données sur la consommation de gaz naturel dans l'industrie des métaux non ferreux ne sont plus disponibles. Par ailleurs, la baisse de consommation observée dans le sous-secteur de la construction mécanique est due à des données incomplètes. A partir de 1991, une nouvelle classification de la consommation de gaz a été adoptée entre le commerce et les services publics, et les *autres secteurs* non spécifiés.

Electricité et chaleur : Les données sur l'électricité et la chaleur ne tiennent pas compte du Groenland ni des Iles Féroé. On ne dispose pas de données sur la production de chaleur avant 1976. Entre 1989 et 1990, il existe des ruptures dans les séries de données concernant la chaleur, car c'est depuis que l'on dispose de données sur les centrales calogènes publiques. La chaleur produite dans les centrales calogènes par les autoproducteurs pour la vente n'est indiquée qu'à partir de 1993 ; la chaleur produite par les autoproducteurs dans des installations de cogénération chaleur/électricité figure parmi les données à partir de 1991. Avant 1993, la production d'électricité et/ou de chaleur au moyen d'énergies renouvelables combustibles et de déchets (à savoir, biomasse solide et produits d'origine animale, gaz/liquides tirés de la biomasse, déchets urbains et déchets industriels) est comptabilisée dans la rubrique biomasse solide et produits d'origine animale.

7. Espagne

Combustibles solides : Avant 1980, on ne dispose pas de données sur la consommation de charbon à coke dans les fours à coke. Des données sur la consommation finale d'énergies renouvelables combustibles et de déchets sont disponibles à partir de 1980. Entre 1970 et 1979, les seules données disponibles sur les énergies renouvelables combustibles et les déchets concernent les quantités utilisées pour la production d'électricité.

Pétrole : Avant 1981, les données détaillées relatives à la consommation sont estimées en partie d'après les statistiques nationales qui couvrent la consommation en Espagne continentale. A la suite d'une nouvelle classification des statistiques nationales espagnoles entre 1976 et 1977, il s'est produit une rupture dans les séries concernant les *autres secteurs* pour le gazole/carburant diesel et le fioul lourd. Avant 1973, les spécifications relatives à la consommation de GPL et de fioul lourd sont moins détaillées. On ne dispose pas de données sur les produits d'alimentation pour 1981. Il s'est produit une rupture de série en 1981 pour le coke de pétrole, en raison de la mise à disposition de données plus détaillées sur la consommation.

Gaz : L'accroissement de la consommation de gaz naturel dans le secteur de l'agriculture, intervenu en 1988, traduit le remplacement des naphtas pour la production d'engrais.

Electricité et chaleur : On ne dispose pas de données sur la production de chaleur avant 1987. A partir de l'année 1992, la production d'électricité d'origine éolienne est regroupée avec celles des centrales hydrauliques. Avant 1987, la production d'électricité des centrales publiques de cogénération chaleur/électricité est comptabilisée avec celle des centrales électriques publiques. La production d'électricité dans des centrales publiques de cogénération a cessé en 1991. Il existe des ruptures de série entre 1989 et 1990

dans les données sur la production d'électricité assurée par des autoproducteurs dans des installations de production d'électricité et de cogénération. On ne dispose pas de données sur la consommation de chaleur. Avant 1992, la production d'électricité et/ou de chaleur à partir d'énergies renouvelables combustibles et de déchets (à savoir, biomasse solide et produits d'origine animale, gaz/liquides tirés de la biomasse, déchets urbains et déchets industriels) est indiquée dans la rubrique biomasse solide et produits d'origine animale.

8. Etats-Unis

Combustibles solides : Pour l'année 1960, le bilan relatif au gaz d'usine à gaz a été estimé par le Secrétariat. Les données étant confidentielles, il n'est pas possible de connaître la production des usines à gaz à partir de 1973. Le Secrétariat a estimé les quantités de coke de cokerie utilisées dans les hauts-fourneaux. Les importations et la consommation dans les *autres secteurs* de charbon vapeur comprennent le charbon sous-bitumineux, le charbon à coke et le lignite. Les exportations de charbon vapeur comprennent le charbon sous-bitumineux. La ventilation entre les quantités de charbon vapeur et de charbon sous-bitumineux utilisées dans les centrales publiques d'électricité a été estimée par le Secrétariat jusqu'en 1990. Les consommations de gaz de haut-fourneau et de gaz de cokerie ont été estimées par le Secrétariat pour les années 1991 à 1993. Les données sur la production de gaz de haut-fourneau entre 1987 et 1993 et celle de gaz de cokerie entre 1991 et 1993 ont fait l'objet d'une révision, effectuée par le Secrétariat sur la base des statistiques de l'American Iron and Steel Institute (AISI).

Pétrole : La ventilation détaillée de la consommation de produits pétroliers dans l'industrie n'est pas disponible. Toutefois, des données par branche d'activité ont été publiées en ce qui concerne le fioul lourd pour la période comprise entre 1971 et 1982. Avant 1976, les données concernant Porto Rico, Guam, les Iles Vierges et la zone franche d'Hawaï ne sont pas prises en compte. Les données relatives à l'utilisation directe du pétrole brut, à savoir le pétrole brut utilisé comme combustible pour les oléoducs sur les lieux de production, ne sont pas disponibles pour la période antérieure à 1973. Avant 1978, les importations et exportations de LGN sont comptabilisées comme échanges de GPL. Pour la période antérieure à 1982, la ventilation des consommations d'essence entre le secteur de l'agriculture et celui de l'industrie a été estimée par le Secrétariat. La consommation de gazole/carburant diesel dans le secteur de l'agriculture avant 1980 est également estimée par le Secrétariat : avant 1970, cette consommation figure avec celle de l'industrie. La chute de consommation de naphta dans l'industrie pétrochimique à partir de 1978 provient d'une nouvelle classification de ce produit. La consommation de GPL dans la chimie et la pétrochimie a été estimée par le Secrétariat pour les années 1983 à 1985. Les GPL comprennent les pentanes plus (principalement l'essence naturelle) pour toutes les années, et l'éthane avant 1990. Les données concernant les naphtas ne sont pas disponibles pour les années 1960 à 1962. Les soutages maritimes internationaux de fioul lourd accusent une forte hausse en 1990 par suite d'un changement adopté par l'administration des Etats-Unis concernant le recueil des données et la méthode de notification. Pour 1993, les soutages maritimes internationaux ont été estimés par l'administration des Etats-Unis. A partir de 1992, les différents composants des LGN et des GPL ont été convertis en utilisant leurs densités respectives au lieu d'une densité moyenne, ce qui a entraîné une rupture dans les séries de données. En 1993, l'administration des Etats-Unis a adapté à plusieurs reprises son système de recueil des statistiques sur le pétrole afin de prendre en compte les remaniements apportés à la Loi sur la pureté de l'air (Clean Air Act) de 1990. De ce fait, les données concernant les composés oxygénés (à savoir, l'éthanol utilisé comme carburant, le MTBE, etc.) ont été recueillies en 1993 et notifiées dans la catégorie des additifs, ou bien, pour l'éthanol, dans la catégorie des gaz/liquides tirés de la biomasse.

Gaz : Il n'existe pas de ventilation détaillée disponible concernant la consommation de gaz naturel dans l'industrie. Les données relatives à l'utilisation de gaz naturel dans le secteur du transport routier ont été recueillies pour la première fois en 1991 et ne sont donc pas disponibles pour les années précédentes.

Electricité et chaleur : Les données sur l'électricité consommée pour le pompage et sur la production d'électricité des centrales à accumulation par pompage sont disponibles à partir de l'année 1987. Les données sur l'électricité produite par les autoproducteurs sont disponibles à partir de 1989. Avant cette date, il n'existe aucune donnée sur la production totale d'électricité des autoproducteurs aux Etats-Unis. Dans

ce pays, la rubrique des autoproducteurs comprend les petits producteurs indépendants d'électricité qui, selon les définitions de l'AIE, entrent dans la catégorie des compagnies publiques d'électricité. La production de ces petits producteurs indépendants d'électricité représente 25 pour cent environ de la production notifiée des autoproducteurs aux Etats-Unis. Les données sur la production d'électricité des centrales publiques de cogénération chaleur/électricité sont disponibles à partir de 1991. Les données sur la production de chaleur dans les centrales calogènes publiques sont disponibles à partir de 1992. On dispose de données sur la chaleur produite dans des installations publiques de cogénération chaleur/électricité, mais les quantités correspondantes d'électricité produite ne sont pas disponibles pour la période antérieure à 1991. Il existe des données sur la consommation de chaleur vendue dans le secteur industriel à partir de 1991, et dans le secteur de l'énergie depuis 1993. Avant 1991, la consommation totale de chaleur vendue correspond à la consommation dans le secteur du commerce et des services publics. Il n'existe pas de données sur la chaleur vendue qui est consommée dans le secteur résidentiel et dans celui de l'agriculture.

9. Finlande

Combustibles solides : Il existe une rupture en 1981 dans la série de données concernant la consommation d'énergies renouvelables combustibles et de déchets dans le secteur de l'industrie, car avant cette date les données étaient estimées par le Secrétariat. A partir de 1984, ces estimations ont été effectuées par l'administration finlandaise. La ventilation entre secteur résidentiel/agriculture, pour les énergies renouvelables combustibles et les déchets, est disponible à partir de 1975. La consommation de tourbe, exprimée en tonnes, pour la production d'électricité et de chaleur a été estimée par le Secrétariat à partir de l'hypothèse d'un pouvoir calorifique inférieur de 0.2 tep/tonne pour les années antérieures à 1992. Le modèle de l'AIE relatif au fonctionnement des hauts-fourneaux a été appliqué pour l'année 1993.

Pétrole : Aucune information n'est disponible sur les quantités de produits pétroliers utilisées avant 1970 par les autoproducteurs ou les installations calogènes. Les données concernant le coke de pétrole ne sont disponibles que depuis 1985 car avant cette date elles n'étaient pas collectées par l'administration finlandaise.

Gaz : Pour la période antérieure à 1989, les données concernant la consommation de gaz naturel dans le secteur résidentiel et dans celui de l'agriculture ont été estimées par l'administration finlandaise.

Electricité et chaleur : Avant 1978, les données sur la consommation de combustibles liquides et de gaz naturel dans les centrales publiques de cogénération chaleur/électricité sont regroupées avec la consommation de ces combustibles dans les centrales électriques et calogènes. La consommation d'électricité du sous-secteur de la construction mécanique comprend celle du sous-secteur du matériel de transport à compter de 1990. Il existe une rupture en 1992 dans la série de données concernant la consommation d'électricité du secteur des transports. Les données sur la production d'électricité à partir d'énergies renouvelables combustibles et de déchets ne sont pas disponibles pour les années comprises entre 1974 et 1976. Avant 1992, la production d'électricité et/ou de chaleur au moyen d'énergies renouvelables combustibles et de déchets (à savoir, biomasse solide et produits d'origine animale, gaz/liquides tirés de la biomasse, déchets urbains et déchets industriels) est comptabilisée avec la tourbe. La consommation de chaleur dans les *autres secteurs* non spécifiés comprend la consommation pour les transports, l'agriculture, le commerce et les services publics.

10. France

Combustibles solides : En ce qui concerne la consommation du secteur industriel, des ruptures de séries se produisent entre 1970 et 1971, car une ventilation plus détaillée des données relatives à l'industrie est disponible depuis lors. Les ruptures de séries dans le secteur de l'industrie entre 1982 et 1983 sont dues à une nouvelle classification des branches d'activité adoptée par l'administration française. A partir de 1986, la consommation de l'industrie (à l'exception de la sidérurgie) a été estimée par le Secrétariat. Avant 1985, la consommation de gaz de houillère est comptabilisée avec celle de gaz de cokerie des autoproducteurs. A partir de 1985, les quantités de coke de cokerie consommées dans les hauts-fourneaux ont été estimées par le Secrétariat d'après la production de gaz de haut-fourneau. Avant 1982, il n'existe pas de données disponibles sur les variations des stocks de charbon à coke. Les données sur les énergies renouvelables combustibles et les déchets ne sont pas disponibles pour la période antérieure à 1966. Entre

cette date et 1969, les seules données disponibles concernent les quantités utilisées pour la production d'électricité.

Pétrole : A partir de 1980, l'essence moteur utilisée pour la navigation intérieure et le cabotage est indiquée à part, et non plus avec la consommation pour le transport routier. En raison d'une modification de la classification des naphtas entre 1969 et 1970, il existe une rupture de série dans les données relatives à la consommation de produits d'alimentation de l'industrie chimique. La ventilation de la consommation de coke de pétrole entre utilisations énergétiques et non énergétiques n'est pas disponible avant 1982. A partir de 1988, l'éthane est pris en compte dans la production de LGN. La ventilation de la consommation de produits pétroliers du secteur tertiaire entre secteur résidentiel, commerce et services publics a été estimée par le Secrétariat.

Gaz : Les pertes de distribution comprennent aussi les écarts statistiques.

Electricité et chaleur : Il existe d'importantes ruptures de séries en 1965, car des données plus précises sur la consommation sont disponibles depuis cette année-là. Les classifications des branches d'activité utilisées par l'administration française ont été modifées en 1986. La consommation d'électricité pour l'extraction de pétrole et de gaz comprend celle des raffineries de pétrole à partir de 1988. La consommation des *autres secteurs* non spécifiés comprend les exportations à destination de Monaco avant 1992. Une grande partie de la consommation figurant dans la catégorie *secteur énergie - autres* couvre la consommation des usines de traitement d'uranium. Les données concernant cette consommation n'étaient pas disponibles avant 1980. Il n'existe pas de données sur la chaleur vendue a des tiers. Les données sur la production d'électricité des autoproducteurs ne sont pas ventilées par type d'installation. En conséquence, la production d'électricité des installations de cogénération chaleur/électricité des autoproducteurs est comptabilisée avec celle des centrales électriques.

11. Grèce

Combustibles solides : Les exportations de charbon vapeur ont cessé en 1989. Les données sur les énergies renouvelables combustibles et les déchets pour la période comprise entre 1970 et 1986 ont été estimées par le Ministère de l'Agriculture à partir des données sur l'approvisionnement en bois et les ventes destinées au secteur du commerce et des services publics. Les données sur la consommation propre des mines de lignite sont incomplètes en ce qui concerne une seule mine, qui n'a pas été exploitée entre 1987 et 1989.

Pétrole : La consommation de LGN pour la production d'électricité dans l'industrie de l'extraction du pétrole et du gaz figure, dans le secteur de l'énergie, à la rubrique extraction du pétrole et du gaz. Les données relatives aux produits d'alimentation utilisés pour le craquage dans les raffineries sont disponibles à partir de 1986.

Electricité et chaleur : Pour la période antérieure à 1971, la consommation de l'industrie sidérurgique et de l'industrie des métaux non ferreux a été estimée par le Secrétariat. Les quantités de gaz naturel utilisées dans les installations de cogénération chaleur/électricité des autoproducteurs comprennent aussi la consommation de gaz naturel pour la production de vapeur avant 1991. Il existe une rupture entre 1991 et 1992 dans la série de données concernant la consommation d'électricité du secteur des transports.

12. Irlande

Combustibles solides : Les informations concernant la tourbe (données exprimées en térajoules) ont été converties en tonnes en prenant pour hypothèse un pouvoir calorifique inférieur de 0.2 tep/tonne.

Pétrole : Pour la période de 1982 à 1984, la production et la consommation de gaz de raffinerie dans les raffineries ont été estimées par le Secrétariat. La classification de la consommation des *autres secteurs* a changé au cours des années 1966 à 1974, ce qui a provoqué des ruptures de séries dans cette période. Pour la période de 1970 à 1977, la ventilation de la consommation de kérosène entre les secteurs de l'agriculture et celui du commerce et des services publics a été estimée par le Secrétariat. En 1985, 56 000 tonnes de kérosène figurant dans les *autres secteurs* non spécifiés représentent des importations qui apparaissaient dans les statistiques sur les échanges, mais que l'on ne retrouvait pas dans les données relatives à la consommation. La consommation du secteur du commerce et des services publics comprend les quantités utilisées par les

établissements agricoles appartenant à l'Etat. La consommation de fioul lourd dans l'industrie et les transports a été estimée par le Secrétariat pour l'année 1986. Les données sur la consommation de gazole/carburant diesel dans l'agriculture sont disponibles à partir de 1986. Avant 1986, la consommation correspondante ne figurait pas dans les statistiques. Les données sur la consommation recueillies pour l'année 1993 sont fondées sur une enquête détaillée. Les données concernant les années antérieures jusqu'à 1990 ont été révisées par l'administration nationale sur la base des résultats de cette enquête. En raison de ces révisions, il existe des ruptures, entre 1989 et 1990, dans les séries de données détaillées sur la consommation de GPL, de kérosène, de gazole/carburant diesel et de fioul lourd.

Gaz : La ventilation détaillée de la consommation de gaz naturel dans l'industrie et les *autres secteurs* n'est pas disponible pour la période antérieure à 1986. Les usines à gaz ont cessé de consommer du gaz naturel en 1985, car le gaz naturel n'a plus été transformé en gaz de ville.

Electricité et chaleur : La consommation d'électricité du secteur de l'agriculture est regroupée avec celle du secteur résidentiel. La consommation d'électricité dans la sidérurgie comprend celle de l'industrie des métaux non ferreux. On ne dispose pas de données sur la production de chaleur des autoproducteurs.

13. Islande

Pétrole : Pour la période antérieure à 1980, les données relatives à la consommation ont été estimées par le Secrétariat.

Electricité et chaleur : Avant 1987, la consommation des *autres secteurs* couvre celle de la base de l'OTAN à l'aéroport de Kéflavik. Avant 1986, le secteur résidentiel comprend celui de l'agriculture. Les classifications des branches d'activité de l'industrie utilisées par l'administration islandaise ont été modifiées en 1987. La consommation d'électricité du secteur de l'énergie concerne principalement l'électricité utilisée dans les installations géothermiques pour le pompage des eaux géothermales du sous-sol. Les données sur la production d'électricité d'origine géothermique dans les centrales publiques de cogénération chaleur/électricité sont disponibles à partir de 1992. Les données sur la production de chaleur à partir de déchets urbains sont disponibles à partir de 1993. Les statistiques énergétiques de base ont été révisées pour introduire les données sur l'utilisation directe d'énergie géothermique à partir de 1960.

14. Italie

Combustibles solides : A partir de 1980, la production de gaz manufacturés comprend une faible quantité de gaz de convertisseur à l'oxygène, consommée par des centrales publiques d'électricité. Les énergies renouvelables combustibles et déchets se composent, pour l'essentiel, de trois produits, dont seuls les combustibles végétaux (essentiellement le bois) constituent un produit primaire entrant dans la catégorie de la production. Les données sur la biomasse solide et les produits d'origine animale ont été estimées par le Secrétariat pour 1992. On ne dispose pas de données sur l'utilisation du charbon à des fins non énergétiques dans l'industrie chimique, et elle n'a donc pas été prise en compte dans le bilan global. En 1991, toutes les activités industrielles ont fait l'objet d'une nouvelle classification, d'après le système ISTAT/NACE 91. De ce fait, il se peut que des anomalies apparaissent entre 1991 et les années précédentes par suite de certains transferts d'activités effectués.

Pétrole : La ventilation détaillée de la consommation a été partiellement estimée par le Secrétariat, qui s'est fondé sur le "*Bilancio Energetico Nazionale*" (Bilan énergétique national). Avant 1970, la consommation de fioul lourd des autoproducteurs est regroupée avec celle de l'industrie. En raison d'un changement de classification, il existe des ruptures de séries en 1988 pour certains carburants aviation et pour le kérosène.

Gaz : La consommation du secteur résidentiel comprend celle du secteur du commerce et des services publics. A partir de 1991, les données sur les pertes de distribution comprennent aussi certains écarts statistiques.

Electricité et chaleur : Les données indiquées pour le *secteur énergie-autres* comprennent la consommation d'électricité des hauts-fourneaux ; avant 1989, la consommation pour l'extraction de l'uranium y figure également. La production d'électricité indiquée dans la catégorie *autres sources* concerne l'électricité produite pendant le procédé de regazéification du GNL

ou avec la chaleur récupérée de procédés industriels. On ne dispose pas de données relatives à la production de chaleur destinée à la vente. Or, l'administration italienne estime qu'en 1993 quelque 10 000 TJ de chaleur ont été produits à cette fin ; ce chiffre équivaut à 0.5 pour cent environ de l'apport thermique correspondant pour la production d'électricité. Avant 1992, les données sur la production d'électricité et/ou de chaleur à partir d'énergies renouvelables combustibles et de déchets (à savoir, biomasse solide et produits d'origine animale, gaz/liquides tirés de la biomasse, déchets urbains et déchet industriels) sont regroupées avec les données sur les déchets industriels.

15. Japon

Combustibles solides : Avant 1992, les quantités de charbon vapeur utilisées dans les centrales calogènes ont été estimées à l'aide du questionnaire annuel sur l'électricité. Les données concernant les énergies renouvelables combustibles et les déchets pour 1992 et 1993 sont des estimations du Secrétariat fondées sur les données communiquées dans le questionnaire sur l'électricité.

Pétrole : Il existe des ruptures dans les séries entre 1969 et 1970. La classification de la consommation de combustibles entre transport routier et navigation intérieure a changé en 1970. Avant 1981, les informations concernant les utilisations non énergétiques du coke de pétrole n'étaient pas disponibles. Par suite d'une amélioration des méthodes de recueil de données, il existe des ruptures dans les séries de données concernant plusieurs produits entre 1981 et 1982.

Gaz : En ce qui concerne le gaz naturel, la consommation est supérieure aux approvisionnements (les écarts statistiques permettent de rétablir l'équilibre) parce que le gaz revendu peut avoir été comptabilisé deux fois dans les données sur la consommation. Cette double comptabilisation représente environ, selon les estimations, de 20 000 à 30 000 TJ par an. La consommation de gaz naturel dans les centrales calogènes publiques a été estimée par l'administration nationale.

Electricité et chaleur : Les données correspondent à l'exercice budgétaire (avril 1992 à mars 1993 pour l'année 1992). Les quantités de combustibles utilisées par les autoproducteurs pour la production d'électricité ont été estimées par le Secrétariat. La consommation d'électricité dans la rubrique industrie-non spécifiés comprend la consommation de l'industrie du bois et produits dérivés ainsi que celle de l'industrie de la construction. La consommation de chaleur du secteur résidentiel est regroupée avec celle du commerce et des services publics avant 1992. On ne dispose pas de données sur la production de chaleur des installations calogènes pour la période antérieure à 1972. La production de chaleur et d'électricité des installations de cogénération des autoproducteurs figure dans celle des installations de production d'électricité des autoproducteurs. L'électricité et la chaleur produites dans les installations publiques de cogénération ne sont pas prises en compte dans les séries de données. Pour la chaleur produite pour la vente dans les centrales calogènes publiques au moyen de chaudières électriques, on dispose de données à partir de 1977, mais ces données peuvent être regroupées avec la récupération de chaleur résiduelle. On ne dispose pas de données sur la chaleur produite pour la vente par des autoproducteurs dans des installations calogènes.

16. Luxembourg

Pétrole : Pour 1978 et 1979, les quantités de fioul lourd utilisées par les autoproducteurs d'électricité ont été estimées par le Secrétariat.

Electricité et chaleur : La consommation d'électricité ventilée par secteur de consommation finale et pour chacun des sous-secteurs industriels a été estimée par le Secrétariat sur la base des données publiées par la CEGEDEL. Le Secrétariat a également réalisé les estimations de la ventilation de la production d'électricité assurée par les autoproducteurs, par combustible : à cet effet, il s'est fondé sur les données communiquées pour 1989. Avant 1992, la production d'électricité et/ou de chaleur au moyen d'énergies renouvelables combustibles et de déchets (à savoir, biomasse solide et produits d'origine animale, gaz/liquides tirés de la biomasse, déchets urbains et déchets industriels) est comptabilisée avec les déchets urbains.

17. Mexique

Les données sont disponibles à partir de 1971. Quelle que soit l'année, les données sont en partie estimées à partir de la publication *Balance nacional-Energia.*

L'administration mexicaine a communiqué pour la première fois des données directement à l'aide du questionnaire pour l'année 1992. De ce fait, il existe peut-être quelques ruptures de séries entre 1991 et 1992.

Electricité et chaleur : La consommation d'électricité du secteur de l'énergie est comptabilisée avec celle de l'industrie (par exemple, chimie ainsi qu'industrie-non spécifiés).

18. Norvège

Combustibles solides : La ventilation détaillée de la consommation industrielle de houille commence en 1971 et celle concernant le coke de cokerie est disponible depuis 1972. Les pertes lors de la distribution du gaz de haut-fourneau ont été estimées par le Secrétariat pour la période de 1960 à 1971.

Pétrole : En ce qui concerne le gazole/carburant diesel et le fioul lourd, la ventilation détaillée de la consommation est disponible à partir de 1976. La consommation de gazole/carburant diesel pour la production d'électricité entre 1970 et 1975 a été estimée par le Secrétariat. Depuis 1986, les importations de produits d'alimentation des raffineries sont indiquées à la rubrique correspondante des importations de produits pétroliers. La consommation de lubrifiants figure dans la consommation de l'industrie, car il n'existe pas de ventilation plus détaillée. En 1987, la consommation d'*autres produits* comprend des livraisons destinées aux stocks civils constitués pour faire face aux situations de guerre. Les quantités concernées, soit environ 500 000 tonnes, ne sont pas prises en compte dans les statistiques pétrolières nationales. A partir de 1990, l'administration norvégienne a procédé à une révision de la série concernant le secteur de la transformation. On constatera des ruptures entre 1989 et 1990, dans l'attente de la révision des données rétrospectives correspondantes.

Electricité et chaleur : Les informations relatives aux quantités de combustibles utilisées par les centrales calogènes ne sont pas disponibles pour la période antérieure à 1983. Les données sur la production de chaleur ne sont pas disponibles pour la période précédant 1983. Les ruptures de séries relatives aux centrales électriques publiques et des autoproducteurs, entre 1989 et 1990, sont dues à une révision des données effectuée par l'administration norvégienne. La ventilation de la consommation de chaleur par sous-secteur industriel est plus détaillée à partir de 1992. Avant cette année, la production de chaleur et/ou d'électricité au moyen d'énergies renouvelables combustibles et de déchets (à savoir, biomasse solide et produits d'origine animale, gaz/liquides tirés de la biomasse, déchets urbains et déchets industriels) est comptabilisée avec la biomasse solide et les produits d'origine animale.

19. Nouvelle-Zélande

A la suite d'un remaniement de l'administration en 1987 qui a entraîné la cessation de certaines séries de données, il s'est produit plusieurs ruptures de séries entre 1987 et 1988.

Combustibles solides : Aucune information n'est disponible sur la consommation de charbon à coke avant 1987. Les ruptures apparentes qui se produisent entre 1987 et 1988 dans les séries chronologiques concernant les secteurs de la consommation finale, de la transformation et de l'énergie pour le charbon vapeur et le charbon sous-bitumineux sont la conséquence des dernières enquêtes analytiques sur le charbon et du reclassement de certaines mines de charbon. Ces différences de classification subsistent à l'heure actuelle. De plus, à partir de 1987, la ventilation complète n'est plus disponible pour le secteur de l'industrie en ce qui concerne le charbon vapeur et le charbon sous-bitumineux. La consommation de lignite du secteur de l'industrie a considérablement diminué en 1987. Cependant, on ne dispose pas de données permettant de séparer ces quantités de la consommation du secteur résidentiel, du commerce et des services publics, c'est pourquoi toute la consommation finale de lignite a été attribuée aux *autres secteurs* non spécifiés pour l'année 1987. A partir de 1985, la consommation d'énergies renouvelables combustibles et de déchets de l'industrie a été estimée par le Secrétariat. La liqueur noire est comptabilisée avec les énergies renouvelables combustibles et les déchets à partir de 1990. La tourbe, quoique produite en Nouvelle-Zélande, n'y est pas utilisée comme combustible mais uniquement à des fins agricoles.

Pétrole : En 1970, une modification a été effectuée dans la classification du gazole/carburant diesel et du fioul lourd pour le secteur de l'industrie et les *autres*

secteurs. La consommation de gazole/carburant diesel pour les transports routier et ferroviaire ne peut plus être identifiée séparément, mais elle est comptabilisée dans la consommation non spécifiée des transports. La liquéfaction d'autres hydrocarbures, regroupée avec le pétrole brut, correspond à la production d'essence à partir de gaz naturel. A partir de 1991, une nouvelle méthode a été adoptée pour la présentation de données concernant l'essence de synthèse. L'augmentation en 1991 des chiffres relatifs aux autres hydrocarbures reflète la production totale de méthanol. Avant 1991, seules les quantités de méthanol destinées à la transformation en essence de synthèse étaient indiquées dans cette catégorie.

Gaz : La ventilation de la consommation du secteur de l'industrie est fondée sur des enquêtes effectuées au cours de la période comprise entre 1981 et 1986. Ultérieurement, ces enquêtes n'étant plus réalisées, une nouvelle rupture des séries intervient en 1987. Les principaux agrégats indiqués pour les secteurs de la transformation, de l'énergie, des transports, de l'industrie et pour les *autres secteurs* sont estimés par l'administration nationale.

Electricité et chaleur : Les données correspondent à l'exercice budgétaire (avril 1992 à mars 1993 pour l'année 1992). La production d'électricité par les autoproducteurs à partir de gaz naturel et de produits pétroliers a été estimée par le Secrétariat pour les années 1970 à 1973. Les classifications utilisées par l'administration néo-zélandaise ont changé en 1991. La consommation d'électricité du sous-secteur pâte à papier, papier et imprimerie est comptabilisée avec celle du sous-secteur bois et produits dérivés avant 1991. Les données pour 1993 ont été estimées par l'administration néo-zélandaise.

20. Pays-Bas

Combustibles solides : Pour les années 1984 à 1986, la production "provenant d'autres sources" de charbon vapeur correspond à une réserve de morceaux de petit calibre qui ont subi un lavage pour pouvoir être réutilisés. Le stock correspondant a été épuisé en 1987. Une nouvelle classification, mise en vigueur au milieu des années 70, provoque des ruptures de séries pour la plupart des produits entre 1975 et 1976. Les données concernant les utilisations non énergétiques ne sont disponibles qu'à partir de 1989. Pour les années antérieures, les utilisations non énergétiques sont comprises dans la consommation de l'industrie.

Pétrole : Au fil des années, plusieurs modifications sont intervenues dans les statistiques pétrolières nationales des Pays-Bas. Les séries chronologiques n'ont été que partiellement révisées en fonction de ces modifications. Les statistiques pétrolières des Pays-Bas comportent donc encore des irrégularités importantes. Avant 1970, les productions de gaz de raffinerie et de fioul lourd sont indiquées déduction faite de la consommation des raffineries. Le coke de pétrole est comptabilisé avec les *autres produits pétroliers* pour toutes les années, sauf pour la période comprise entre 1978 et 1982. Des ruptures de séries se produisent entre 1983 et 1984 par suite d'une enquête plus complète sur la consommation des secteurs d'utilisation finale. Toutefois, les données agrégées sur la consommation des secteurs des transports, de l'industrie et des *autres secteurs* n'en sont pas modifiées. A partir de 1978, la consommation de gaz de raffinerie comprend le gaz utilisé par l'industrie chimique, qui est regroupé avec la consommation de l'industrie chimique. Les données pour les naphtas englobent les aromatiques pour toutes les années sauf 1981, où ils sont regroupés avec les *autres produits pétroliers*. L'essence moteur comprend les autres huiles légères. Pour les *autres secteurs*, la catégorie non spécifiés comprend la consommation des hôpitaux, des bureaux, des bâtiments publics et des sociétés commerciales. Ceci n'est valable que dans le cas des produits pétroliers.

Gaz : Les ruptures importantes qui se produisent dans les séries entre 1981 et 1982 ainsi qu'entre 1983 et 1984 découlent des résultats d'enquêtes plus complètes sur la consommation des secteurs d'utilisation finale. Toutefois, les données agrégées sur la consommation de l'industrie et des *autres secteurs* n'en sont pas modifiées. Entre 1987 et 1988, une rupture de séries se produit dans les *autres secteurs* (commerce et services publics) par suite d'une réorganisation importante de trois compagnies publiques de gaz. En 1990, les installations calogènes ont été transformées en centrales de cogénération chaleur/électricité.

Electricité et chaleur : Avant 1979, la consommation d'électricité du secteur de l'agriculture est regroupée avec celle du commerce et des services publics. La consommation d'électricité de ce secteur comprend celle des petits consommateurs. Avant 1982, la production d'électricité des centrales publiques de cogénération chaleur/électricité est comptabilisée avec

celle des centrales électriques publiques. On ne dispose pas de données concernant la production de chaleur des centrales de cogénération chaleur/électricité et des centrales calogènes ni sur les quantités de combustibles utilisés par ces dernières pour la période antérieure à 1982. La ventilation de la production de chaleur par combustible dans les installations calogènes avant 1987 est estimée par le Secrétariat sur la base des données communiquées par l'administration néerlandaise concernant les combustibles utilisés à cet effet. On ne dispose pas de données sur la chaleur produite pour la vente par les autoproducteurs. Avant 1992, la production d'électricité et/ou de chaleur à partir d'énergies renouvelables combustibles et de déchets (à savoir, biomasse solide et produits d'origine animale, gaz/liquides tirés de la biomasse, déchets urbains et déchets industriels) est comptabilisée avec les déchets urbains.

21. Portugal

Combustibles solides : La consommation propre de gaz de cokerie pour l'année 1989 a été estimée par le Secrétariat.

Pétrole : Avant 1969, la production de gaz de raffinerie est indiquée déduction faite de la consommation des raffineries. Avant 1970, les données sur la consommation de gazole/carburant diesel du secteur des transports recouvrent une partie de la consommation des *autres secteurs*. Jusqu'en 1984, les statistiques sur le coke de pétrole étaient regroupées avec les données sur le coke de cokerie. Depuis lors, elles sont comptabilisées avec les statistiques sur les *autres produits pétroliers*. Le chiffre négatif indiqué pour la production d'*autres produits pétroliers* en 1990 s'explique par le fait que des produits non finis ont été transférés au cours d'opérations de mélange en raffinerie. La production brute de produits secondaires englobe ces quantités transférées.

Electricité et chaleur : Les données sur la production d'électricité des centrales publiques de cogénération chaleur/électricité ne sont pas disponibles pour la période antérieure à 1980.

22. Royaume-Uni

Combustibles solides : La consommation du secteur du commerce et des services publics comprend certaines autres consommations non spécifiées. Dans le secteur de l'énergie, la consommation propre des mines de charbon ne concerne que les mines souterraines exploitées par British Coal. La consommation de gaz de synthèse est regroupée avec celle de gaz naturel. Toutefois, la production correspondante figure avec celle de gaz d'usine à gaz. A partir de 1984, il n'existe plus de ventilation par secteur de la consommation de gaz de cokerie dans l'industrie, sauf dans le cas de l'industrie sidérurgique. Avant 1978, une partie des quantités de houille fournies aux autoproducteurs figure dans les sous-secteurs industriels correspondants (principalement, métaux non ferreux et papier). Pour toutes les utilisations du gaz manufacturé, il y a rupture des séries entre 1979 et 1980. Les données sur le gaz de cokerie (1988 à 1993) et sur les énergies renouvelables combustibles et les déchets (1989 à 1993) ont été révisées par l'administration du Royaume-Uni.

Pétrole : Avant 1979, le coke de pétrole figurait avec les *autres produits pétroliers*. A partir de 1970, les données relatives aux échanges de coke de pétrole figurent avec celles des *autres produits pétroliers*. A partir de 1980, les LGN comprennent les condensats. Pour les années antérieures, les condensats sont regroupés avec le pétrole brut. La ventilation des produits est estimée dans le cas des transferts. Depuis 1985, les variations des stocks de produits d'alimentation des raffineries et de LGN sont indiquées séparément. Avant cette année, ces variations des stocks étaient regroupées avec celles du pétrole brut. Les variations des stocks des compagnies publiques d'électricité ou de gaz sont prises en compte depuis 1985. Avant 1990, l'éthane est comptabilisé avec les GPL. Les données concernant la consommation de pétrole dans les centrales publiques de cogénération chaleur/électricité ne sont pas disponibles pour les années 1990 à 1993.

Gaz : Avant 1985, les variations des stocks de gaz naturel étaient regroupées avec les pertes de distribution. La consommation de gaz naturel du secteur commercial figure dans les *autres secteurs* non spécifiés, alors que celle du secteur de l'administration publique est indiquée séparément. La consommation de gaz naturel comprend celle de gaz de synthèse, fabriqué dans les usines à gaz et acheminé par le réseau de distribution de gaz naturel. La consommation de gaz naturel est donc légèrement supérieure à l'approvisionnement. Les utilisations non énergétiques du gaz naturel ne peuvent pas être identifiées séparément. A partir de 1992, les pertes de distribution

sont comptabilisées avec les écarts statistiques. Pour la consommation de l'industrie du bois et des produits dérivés, on ne dispose pas de données après 1991. Les données figurant à la rubrique non spécifiés du secteur de l'industrie correspondent aux ventes effectuées par des fournisseurs indépendants de gaz qui ne sont pas réparties par catégorie. Pour 1990 et 1991, les données étant confidentielles, les quantités de gaz naturel utilisées pour la production d'électricité par les centrales publiques sont regroupées avec la consommation des autoproducteurs. Avant 1992, les livraisons de gaz naturel destinées aux installations de cogénération de chaleur/électricité des autoproducteurs étaient regroupées avec celles du secteur de l'industrie. Pour 1993, la consommation de gaz naturel dans les mines de charbon est calculée à l'aide d'une méthode d'estimation révisée ; elle n'est donc pas compatible avec les données rétrospectives.

Electricité et chaleur : Depuis 1984, la consommation des industries non spécifiées comprend celle de l'industrie du bois et des produits dérivés, de même que la consommation non affectée. La consommation d'électricité des mines de charbon englobe celle des fabriques d'agglomérés. La consommation des usines à gaz comprend l'électricité utilisée pour le transport et la distribution du gaz destiné au public. La réorganisation, puis la privatisation des compagnies d'électricité en 1990 a entraîné certaines ruptures de séries entre 1989 et 1990. A partir de 1989, la consommation du sous-secteur de la construction mécanique comprend celle du sous-secteur du matériel de transport. La consommation du sous-secteur des produits minéraux non métalliques comprend celle des industries extractives. Avant 1988, la production d'électricité des centrales de cogénération de chaleur/électricité est regroupée avec celle des centrales électriques publiques. Pour 1991, les productions de chaleur et d'électricité des centrales de cogénération ont été estimées par le Secrétariat. Les quantités de gaz naturel utilisées et la production d'électricité à partir de gaz naturel dans les centrales publiques sont comptabilisées avec l'électricité produite par les autoproducteurs pour 1990 et 1991. Les données sur la production d'électricité des centrales de cogénération chaleur/électricité des autoproducteurs ne sont pas disponibles avant 1992, et celles concernant la production de chaleur des installations de cogénération des autoproducteurs ne le sont pas avant 1993. De ce fait, il y a des ruptures de série concernant la consommation de chaleur entre 1992 et 1993. Avant 1992, la production d'électricité et/ou de chaleur à partir d'énergies renouvelables combustibles et de déchets (à savoir, biomasse solide et produits d'origine animale, gaz/liquides tirés de la biomasse, déchets urbains et déchets industriels) est regroupée avec la biomasse solide et les produits d'origine animale.

23. Suède

Combustibles solides : Les données relatives aux utilisations non énergétiques sont disponibles à partir de 1973. Avant cette date, ces données étaient regroupées avec celles concernant la consommation finale. Pour la période comprise entre 1960 et 1974, la répartition des quantités de gaz de haut-fourneau utilisées par le secteur de l'énergie dans les fours à coke et des pertes de distribution a été estimée. A partir de 1989, il n'est plus possible de séparer les importations de charbon à coke de celles de charbon vapeur. L'estimation des importations a été faite par le Secrétariat, à partir de données fournies par les exportateurs. La production de charbon vapeur concerne le charbon récupéré lors de l'exploitation de carrières argileuses.

Pétrole : Il convient de noter les nombreuses modifications de classification qui sont intervenues entre 1969 et 1970. Par exemple, avant 1970, le coke de pétrole figurait avec les *autres produits pétroliers*. La notification étant plus détaillée, il s'est produit des ruptures dans les séries de données sur la consommation de fioul lourd entre 1985 et 1986. Les données relatives à la consommation de kérosène dans le sous-secteur du transport routier cessent de figurer à partir de 1984, en raison d'une nouvelle classification de ce produit. Le chiffre négatif indiqué pour la consommation de produits d'alimentation des raffineries reflète le traitement, dans les statistiques nationales, des transferts de produits semi-finis à l'intérieur des raffineries et entre celles-ci, ce qui fait ressortir certaines anomalies lors de l'utilisation de ces chiffres dans les bilans globaux.

Electricité et chaleur : Dans le cas du pétrole, la production des autoproducteurs est regroupée avec celle des centrales électriques publiques. La consommation d'électricité pour la distribution du chauffage urbain figure sous la rubrique *énergie - autres secteurs*. Avant 1992, la production d'électricité et/ou de chaleur à partir d'énergies renouvelables combustibles et de déchets (à savoir, biomasse solide et produits d'origine animale, gaz/liquides tirés de la

biomasse, déchets urbains et déchets industriels) est comptabilisée avec la biomasse solide et les produits d'origine animale. Les données sur la chaleur produite dans les centrales de cogénération chaleur/électricité sont disponibles à partir de 1974 et celles qui concernent la production des centrales calogènes apparaissent à partir de 1987. Il se produit une rupture de série entre 1983 et 1984 pour les données sur la consommation de chaleur. Pour 1991, la consommation de chaleur dans l'industrie et le secteur résidentiel a été estimée par l'administration suédoise. Les données sur la chaleur destinée à la vente, produite au moyen de pompes à chaleur et de chaudières électriques, sont disponibles depuis 1992. En Suède, la chaleur produite au moyen de pompes à chaleur est vendue à des tiers (sous forme de chauffage urbain) et elle figure donc dans le secteur transformation. L'énergie consommée par les pompes à chaleur comprend la chaleur récupérée de procédés industriels et du milieu ambiant (eaux usées et eau de mer comprises). La chaleur ambiante figure à la rubrique production nationale de chaleur. L'électricité utilisée pour actionner les pompes à chaleur est considérée comme étant transformée et apparaît donc dans la production du secteur transformation, au lieu d'être regroupée avec la consommation d'électricité du secteur de l'énergie. Les combustibles utilisés pour produire la chaleur récupérée par la pompe à chaleur sont indiqués dans le sous-secteur correspondant de l'industrie (par exemple, industrie chimique ou pâte à papier, papier et imprimerie). La consommation de chaleur produite par des pompes à chaleur dans l'industrie a été estimée par le Secrétariat d'après les données sur les combustibles utilisés à cet effet qui ont été communiquées par l'administration suédoise (2/3 dans l'industrie de la pâte à papier, du papier et de l'imprimerie et 1/3 dans l'industrie chimique). Les données sur la production de chaleur destinée à la vente des installations calogènes des autoproducteurs apparaissent à partir de 1992.

24. Suisse

Combustibles solides : A partir de 1985, la consommation par l'industrie de gaz d'usine à gaz figure à la rubrique industrie, non spécifiés, les données étant confidentielles. Avant 1978, la consommation d'énergies renouvelables combustibles et de déchets ne porte que sur le bois consommé dans le secteur résidentiel, dans le secteur de l'agriculture, et dans le secteur du commerce et des services publics. A partir de 1978, les chiffres correspondants comprennent aussi la consommation, par l'industrie, de bois et de déchets industriels, de même que la consommation de déchets urbains des centrales publiques de cogénération chaleur/électricité.

Pétrole : On ne dispose pas de données sur la production brute de gaz de raffinerie pour les années 1967 à 1969. Les données sur la consommation de gazole/carburant diesel dans l'industrie, non spécifiés (petits fabricants et petits producteurs), sont des estimations.

Gaz : Des ruptures dans les séries concernant le gaz naturel apparaissent entre 1977 et 1978 parce qu'une enquête par branche d'activité a commencé à être effectuée. A partir de 1978, les réexportations sont déduites des importations de gaz naturel.

Electricité et chaleur : Avant 1978, les données sur la production de chaleur des centrales de cogénération chaleur/électricité ne sont pas disponibles. La production de chaleur comprend la chaleur produite par les centrales nucléaires et distribuée à d'autres consommateurs. La consommation d'électricité du sous-secteur du matériel de transport est comptabilisée avec celle du sous-secteur de la construction mécanique.

25. Turquie

Pétrole : Pour les années 1978, 1980 à 1981, et 1983 à 1984, les soutages maritimes internationaux figurent dans les exportations. A partir de 1978, la consommation du secteur commercial est regroupée avec celle de l'industrie, tandis que celle des services publics est regroupée avec celle du secteur des transports. La consommation du sous-secteur des produits minéraux non métalliques est regroupée avec celle du sous-secteur des métaux non ferreux. Entre 1977 et 1978, la classification par utilisation finale du gazole/carburant diesel et du fioul lourd a été modifiée dans les statistiques nationales turques. En conséquence, il y a des ruptures des séries concernant la consommation détaillée entre ces deux années. Les données relatives aux *autres produits pétroliers* ne sont pas disponibles pour 1960.

Gaz : Les données relatives à la consommation de gaz naturel par l'industrie chimique (pour la fabrication des engrais) et par des industries non spécifiées (fabrication de colorants) sont disponibles à partir de 1988. Les fortes pertes de distribution en 1989 sont dues à un accroissement de la consommation de gaz naturel dans l'industrie et le secteur résidentiel.

Electricité et chaleur : Entre 1972 et 1973, les séries de données sur la consommation d'électricité comportent des ruptures importantes. La consommation du sous-secteur industriel de la construction mécanique comprend celle du sous-secteur du matériel de transport. La consommation du sous-secteur du bois et des produits dérivés comprend celle de l'industrie du papier, de la pâte à papier et de l'imprimerie. L'utilisation directe de chaleur géothermique a été estimée par le Secrétariat pour 1993. On ne dispose pas de données sur les années précédentes.

V. COUVERTURE GEOGRAPHIQUE

- Les données relatives à l'Allemagne tiennent compte des nouveaux Länder à partir de 1970.

- Le Danemark englobe le Groenland et les Iles Féroé danoises.

- L'Espagne englobe les Iles Canaries.

- Les Etats-Unis englobent Porto-Rico, Guam et les Iles Vierges ainsi que la zone franche d'Hawaï.

- Le Japon englobe Okinawa.

- Les Pays-Bas n'englobent ni le Surinam, ni les Antilles néerlandaises.

- Le Portugal englobe les Açores et l'île de Madère.

- L'UE englobe l'Allemagne, l'Autriche, la Belgique, le Danemark, l'Espagne, la Finlande, la France, la Grèce, l'Irlande, l'Italie, le Luxembourg, les Pays-Bas, le Portugal, le Royaume-Uni et la Suède. Il convient de noter que, pour rendre ces données comparables, tous ces pays sont pris en compte pour toutes les années malgré des dates différentes d'entrée dans les l'Union européenne.

- Les statistiques régionales de l'OCDE comprennent désormais le Mexique (à partir de 1971), après l'adhésion de ce pays à l'OCDE le 18 mai 1994.

VI. ANNUAL TABLES

VI. TABLEAUX ANNUELS

1992 - 1993

OECD Total / OCDE Total : 1992

SUPPLY AND CONSUMPTION / APPROVISIONNEMENT ET DEMANDE	Coking Coal / Charbon à coke	Steam Coal / Charbon vapeur	Sub-Bit. Coal / Charbon sous-bit.	Lignite / Lignite	Peat / Tourbe	Oven and Gas Coke / Coke de four/gaz	Pat. Fuel and BKB / Agg./briq. de lignite	Crude Oil / Pétrole brut	NGL / LGN	Feedstocks / Produits d'aliment.	Additives / Additifs
Production	220573	757409	280437	506725	12618	127343	20060	828014	91421	-	144
From Other Sources	-	1350	979	-	-	-	-	103	-	15169	1790
Imports	117825	166134	-	4096	7	9824	954	1092710	13475	64862	192
Exports	-143207	-107335	-14	-79	-338	-8506	-1013	-270158	-13262	-5100	-
Intl. Marine Bunkers	-	-	-	-	-	-	-	-	-	-	-
Stock Changes	-1289	-16811	495	2953	2233	-581	65	-5034	-185	-702	-20
DOMESTIC SUPPLY	**193902**	**800747**	**281897**	**513695**	**14520**	**128080**	**20066**	**1645635**	**91449**	**74229**	**2106**
Transfers	-	-	-	-	-	-	-	-1879	-59353	41000	-
Statistical Differences	-466	1134	-728	-942	-	239	-7	4388	1198	-1829	-21
TRANSFORMATION	**191257**	**708808**	**272333**	**477277**	**9330**	**38947**	**2773**	**1647056**	**29737**	**113400**	**2085**
Electricity Plants	16996	643402	261891	431157	4149	-	1590	17576	217	-	-
CHP Plants	-	60836	10442	-	3351	-	-	-	-	-	-
Heat Plants	-	1416	-	2603	784	5	554	-	-	-	-
Transfer to Gases	1123	581	-	-	-	38715	392	-	-	-	-
Transfer to Solids	173138	2573	-	43517	1046	227	237	-	-	-	-
Petroleum Refineries	-	-	-	-	-	-	-	1632722	29520	113400	2085
Petrochemical Industry	-	-	-	-	-	-	-	-	-	-	-
Liquefaction	-	-	-	-	-	-	-	-	-	-	-
Other Transformation Sector	-	-	-	-	-	-	-	-3242	-	-	-
ENERGY SECTOR	**60**	**1126**	**33**	**1749**	**-**	**363**	**277**	**1057**	**-**	**-**	**-**
Coal Mines	-	993	33	2	-	-	-	-	-	-	-
Oil and Gas Extraction	-	-	-	-	-	-	-	1057	-	-	-
Petroleum Refineries	-	121	-	146	-	-	36	-	-	-	-
Electricity, CHP+Heat plants	-	-	-	-	-	-	-	-	-	-	-
Pumped Storage (Elec.)	-	-	-	-	-	-	-	-	-	-	-
Other Energy Sector	60	12	-	1601	-	363	241	-	-	-	-
Distribution Losses	14	-	-	-	-	7	-	-	-	-	-
FINAL CONSUMPTION	**2105**	**91947**	**8803**	**33727**	**5190**	**89002**	**17009**	**31**	**3557**	**-**	**-**
INDUSTRY SECTOR	**1360**	**77045**	**8285**	**22920**	**3435**	**84230**	**4414**	**31**	**3557**	**-**	**-**
Iron and Steel	805	9003	698	21	-	74959	-	31	3557	-	-
Chemical and Petrochemical	61	9749	2980	6572	7	601	148	-	-	-	-
of which: Feedstocks	-	-	-	-	-	-	-	-	-	-	-
Non-Ferrous Metals	1	1442	1961	394	-	1346	1	-	-	-	-
Non-Metallic Minerals	12	33075	952	317	-	967	8	-	-	-	-
Transport Equipment	-	381	-	-	-	42	2	-	-	-	-
Machinery	4	1147	48	59	-	811	-	-	-	-	-
Mining and Quarrying	-	391	310	3	-	281	-	-	-	-	-
Food and Tobacco	121	2668	420	1624	-	291	150	-	-	-	-
Paper, Pulp and Print	-	4292	-	289	30	43	57	-	-	-	-
Wood and Wood Products	-	116	-	46	-	1	5	-	-	-	-
Construction	272	1057	16	1192	-	7	-	-	-	-	-
Textile and Leather	-	573	-	238	-	5	26	-	-	-	-
Non-specified	84	13151	900	12165	3398	4876	4017	-	-	-	-
TRANSPORT SECTOR	**15**	**28**	**192**	**4**	**-**	**5**	**-**	**-**	**-**	**-**	**-**
International Civil Aviation	-	-	-	-	-	-	-	-	-	-	-
Domestic Air	-	-	-	-	-	-	-	-	-	-	-
Road	-	-	-	-	-	-	-	-	-	-	-
Rail	15	28	-	4	-	5	-	-	-	-	-
Pipeline Transport	-	-	-	-	-	-	-	-	-	-	-
Internal Navigation	-	-	192	-	-	-	-	-	-	-	-
Non-specified	-	-	-	-	-	-	-	-	-	-	-
OTHER SECTORS	**488**	**14605**	**326**	**10746**	**1755**	**2712**	**12343**	**-**	**-**	**-**	**-**
Agriculture	-	205	13	333	94	56	403	-	-	-	-
Commerce and Publ. Serv.	-	2636	70	1863	6	302	2411	-	-	-	-
Residential	488	11314	243	8342	1655	2319	8778	-	-	-	-
Non-specified	-	450	-	208	-	35	751	-	-	-	-
NON-ENERGY USE	**242**	**269**	**-**	**57**	**-**	**2055**	**252**	**-**	**-**	**-**	**-**
in Industry/Transf./Energy	242	269	-	57	-	2055	252	-	-	-	-
in Transport	-	-	-	-	-	-	-	-	-	-	-
in Other Sectors	-	-	-	-	-	-	-	-	-	-	-

Industry sector details shown only where sectorial data are available for most countries.
La ventilation du secteur industriel n'est indiquée que s'il existe des données sectorielles disponibles pour la plupart des pays concernés.

OECD Total / OCDE Total : 1992

SUPPLY AND CONSUMPTION / APPROVISIONNEMENT ET DEMANDE	Oil cont. / *Pétrole cont.* (1000 tonnes)										
	Refinery Gas / *Gaz de raffinerie*	LPG + Ethane / *GPL + éthane*	Motor Gasoline / *Essence moteur*	Aviation Gasoline / *Essence aviation*	Jet Fuel / *Carbu- réacteur*	Kerosene / *Kérosène*	Gas/ Diesel / *Gazole*	Heavy Fuel Oil / *Fioul lourd*	Naphtha / *Naphta*	Pétrol. Coke / *Coke de pétrole*	Other Prod. / *Autres prod.*
Production	67558	43817	541158	1248	113928	31927	469534	269672	59148	49046	119772
From Other Sources	-	-	-	-	-	-	-	-	-	-	-
Imports	-	28484	48412	154	15642	3118	78115	77232	40864	12926	21462
Exports	-	-5986	-47035	-278	-12785	-2814	-74765	-68631	-14841	-15213	-16995
Intl. Marine Bunkers	-	-	-	-	-	-	-16469	-59730	-	-	-365
Stock Changes	-7	194	601	35	530	625	2043	2166	517	-157	833
DOMESTIC SUPPLY	**67551**	**66509**	**543136**	**1159**	**117315**	**32856**	**458458**	**220709**	**85688**	**46602**	**124707**
Transfers	-129	53284	161	3	-194	-2179	-1189	-3486	-7921	-38	-15144
Statistical Differences	-12	-161	32	78	-2263	-421	5014	645	1279	575	-103
TRANSFORMATION	**1150**	**5122**	**398**	**-**	**-**	**274**	**6357**	**113226**	**12801**	**4098**	**2273**
Electricity Plants	69	1003	-	-	-	-	4986	106040	918	1833	2099
CHP Plants	688	20	-	-	-	-	173	5572	-	276	142
Heat Plants	-	61	-	-	-	12	57	934	-	-	-
Transfer to Gases	244	2916	-	-	-	-	3	20	420	-	-
Transfer to Solids	-	-	-	-	-	-	1	24	-	1989	-
Petroleum Refineries	-	-	-	-	-	-	-	-	-	-	-
Petrochemical Industry	149	1122	398	-	-	262	1137	636	11463	-	2
Liquefaction	-	-	-	-	-	-	-	-	-	-	-
Other Transformation Sector	-	-	-	-	-	-	-	-	-	-	30
ENERGY SECTOR	**63594**	**1851**	**112**	**-**	**58**	**14**	**786**	**19419**	**201**	**21223**	**2808**
Coal Mines	-	2	-	-	-	-	405	36	-	-	2
Oil and Gas Extraction	-	398	-	-	-	-	86	58	-	738	-
Petroleum Refineries	63580	1400	108	-	58	13	247	19134	201	20482	2672
Electricity, CHP+Heat plants	-	1	4	-	-	-	45	160	-	-	1
Pumped Storage (Elec.)	-	-	-	-	-	-	-	-	-	-	-
Other Energy Sector	14	50	-	-	1	3	31	-	3	133	
Distribution Losses	-	17	74	-	21	4	52	57	-	-	1
FINAL CONSUMPTION	**2666**	**112642**	**542745**	**1240**	**114779**	**29964**	**455088**	**85166**	**66044**	**21818**	**104378**
INDUSTRY SECTOR	**2666**	**71609**	**3114**	**-**	**20**	**6153**	**50758**	**59565**	**66044**	**8678**	**1634**
Iron and Steel	-	-	-	-	-	-	-	-	-	-	-
Chemical and Petrochemical	-	-	-	-	-	-	-	-	-	-	-
of which: Feedstocks	-	-	-	-	-	-	-	-	-	-	-
Non-Ferrous Metals	-	-	-	-	-	-	-	-	-	-	-
Non-Metallic Minerals	-	-	-	-	-	-	-	-	-	-	-
Transport Equipment	-	-	-	-	-	-	-	-	-	-	-
Machinery	-	-	-	-	-	-	-	-	-	-	-
Mining and Quarrying	-	-	-	-	-	-	-	-	-	-	-
Food and Tobacco	-	-	-	-	-	-	-	-	-	-	-
Paper, Pulp and Print	-	-	-	-	-	-	-	-	-	-	-
Wood and Wood Products	-	-	-	-	-	-	-	-	-	-	-
Construction	-	-	-	-	-	-	-	-	-	-	-
Textile and Leather	-	-	-	-	-	-	-	-	-	-	-
Non-specified	-	-	-	-	-	-	-	-	-	-	-
TRANSPORT SECTOR	**-**	**6467**	**535020**	**1231**	**114756**	**25**	**245046**	**5033**	**-**	**-**	**6**
International Civil Aviation	-	-	-	3	31790	-	-	-	-	-	-
Domestic Air	-	-	-	1228	82966	-	1	-	-	-	-
Road	-	6465	530993	-	-	10	213029	49	-	-	6
Rail	-	2	-	-	-	12	16398	48	-	-	-
Pipeline Transport	-	-	-	-	-	-	11	-	-	-	-
Internal Navigation	-	-	4027	-	-	3	12827	4831	-	-	-
Non-specified	-	-	-	-	-	-	2780	105	-	-	-
OTHER SECTORS	**-**	**34566**	**4611**	**9**	**3**	**23786**	**159284**	**20568**	**-**	**132**	**13**
Agriculture	-	2217	2557	3	-	3206	34705	903	-	15	6
Commerce and Publ. Serv.	-	4668	1828	6	3	4599	55084	14169	-	7	7
Residential	-	26930	226	-	-	15258	66211	2767	-	110	-
Non-specified	-	751	-	-	-	723	3284	2729	-	-	-
NON-ENERGY USE	**-**	**-**	**-**	**-**	**-**	**-**	**-**	**-**	**-**	**13008**	**102725**
in Industry/Transf./Energy	-	-	-	-	-	-	-	-	-	13008	93501
in Transport	-	-	-	-	-	-	-	-	-	-	7295
in Other Sectors	-	-	-	-	-	-	-	-	-	-	1929

INTERNATIONAL ENERGY AGENCY

OECD Total / OCDE Total : 1992

CONSUMPTION / APPROVISIONNEMENT ET DEMANDE	Gas / Gaz (TJ)				Combust. Renew. & Waste / En. Re. Comb. & Déchets (TJ)				Electricity (GWh)	Heat (TJ)
	Natural Gas / Gaz naturel	Gas Works / Usines à gaz	Coke Ovens / Cokeries	Blast Furnaces / Hauts fourneaux	Solid Biomass & Anim. Prod. / Biomasse solide & prod. anim.	Gas/Liquids from Biomass / Gaz/Liquides tirés de biomasse	Municipal Waste / Déchets urbains	Industrial Waste / Déchets industriels	Electricity / Electricité	Heat / Chaleur
Production	34668713	652567	917949	1144500	5306981	52596	398562	296331	7495211	1189970
From Other Sources	-	200733	-	-	-	-	-	-	-	-
Imports	10844597	-	-	-	5490	-	-	2913	214494	-
Exports	-5305204	-198	-	-	-	-	-	-68	-206604	-
Intl. Marine Bunkers	-	-	-	-	-	-	-	-	-	-
Stock Changes	113313	3564	-1	-	2690	-	-	279	-	-
DOMESTIC SUPPLY	**40321419**	**856666**	**917948**	**1144500**	**5315161**	**52596**	**398562**	**299455**	**7503101**	**1189970**
Transfers	-	-	-	-	-	-	-	-	-	-
Statistical Differences	-574930	1633	-20993	36100	650	-	-17	-	-	-
TRANSFORMATION	**7778874**	**655**	**319188**	**609909**	**1542812**	**49835**	**382495**	**188599**	**9623**	**-**
Electricity Plants	5892829	-	149937	365444	332918	36858	265369	35567	-	-
CHP Plants	869223	-	158609	243869	1163755	9696	89784	152114	-	-
Heat Plants	159534	655	511	592	41898	3281	27342	918	9623	-
Transfer to Gases	663559	-	10131	-	-	-	-	-	-	-
Transfer to Solids	1083	-	-	4	4241	-	-	-	-	-
Petroleum Refineries	-	-	-	-	-	-	-	-	-	-
Petrochemical Industry	-	-	-	-	-	-	-	-	-	-
Liquefaction	179924	-	-	-	-	-	-	-	-	-
Other Transformation Sector	12722	-	-	-	-	-	-	-	-	-
ENERGY SECTOR	**3251908**	**18481**	**179410**	**111945**	**2**	**-**	**-**	**-**	**674518**	**43338**
Coal Mines	9255	-	2376	-	-	-	-	-	32780	-
Oil and Gas Extraction	2007766	-	-	-	-	-	-	-	53541	-
Petroleum Refineries	880795	288	5473	-	-	-	-	-	80600	36912
Electricity, CHP+Heat plants	550	-	-	-	2	-	-	-	407850	405
Pumped Storage (Elec.)	-	-	-	-	-	-	-	-	62671	-
Other Energy Sector	353542	18193	171561	111945	-	-	-	-	37076	6021
Distribution Losses	78320	10153	2301	20743	-	-	-	-	483839	119455
FINAL CONSUMPTION	**28637387**	**829010**	**396056**	**438003**	**3772997**	**2761**	**16050**	**110856**	**6335121**	**1027177**
INDUSTRY SECTOR	**13111895**	**235150**	**395336**	**438003**	**1949216**	**455**	**15632**	**16768**	**2619060**	**353255**
Iron and Steel	-	1764	366419	437851	155	-	-	-	266165	3379
Chemical and Petrochemical	-	6723	13458	152	18750	91	638	10317	480798	159818
of which: Feedstocks	-	-	-	-	-	-	-	-	-	-
Non-Ferrous Metals	-	1854	936	-	1994	131	-	20	266261	1536
Non-Metallic Minerals	-	2910	2056	-	18874	-	185	832	124451	366
Transport Equipment	-	528	306	-	-	-	-	-	116494	5639
Machinery	-	2866	4177	-	338	-	16	119	205413	27193
Mining and Quarrying	-	-	1932	-	-	-	-	-	77724	22
Food and Tobacco	-	2685	1296	-	147093	172	27	205	156813	20570
Paper, Pulp and Print	-	185	1260	-	1403847	61	14766	2307	323341	26146
Wood and Wood Products	-	109	18	-	292029	-	-	148	47985	91
Construction	-	2	565	-	-	-	-	10	10689	15
Textile and Leather	-	291	756	-	22988	-	-	120	86746	7913
Non-specified	-	215233	2157	-	43148	-	-	2690	456180	100567
TRANSPORT SECTOR	**854588**	**-**	**-**	**-**	**-**	**-**	**6**	**65**	**85878**	**-**
International Civil Aviation	-	-	-	-	-	-	-	-	-	-
Domestic Air	-	-	-	-	-	-	-	-	-	-
Road	16479	-	-	-	-	-	-	-	-	-
Rail	-	-	-	-	-	-	6	65	73535	-
Pipeline Transport	836609	-	-	-	-	-	-	-	3345	-
Internal Navigation	-	-	-	-	-	-	-	-	-	-
Non-specified	1500	-	-	-	-	-	-	-	8998	-
OTHER SECTORS	**14670494**	**593860**	**720**	**-**	**1823781**	**2306**	**412**	**94023**	**3630183**	**673922**
Agriculture	214124	216	-	-	9415	-	-	-	55340	4843
Commerce and Publ. Serv.	4349648	131474	-	-	3982	311	277	-	1611857	158373
Residential	9639159	462120	720	-	1810384	-	135	94023	1955953	365312
Non-specified	467563	50	-	-	-	1995	-	-	7033	145394
NON-ENERGY USE	**410**	**-**	**-**	**-**	**-**	**-**	**-**	**-**	**-**	**-**
in Industry/Transf./Energy	410	-	-	-	-	-	-	-	-	-
in Transport	-	-	-	-	-	-	-	-	-	-
in Other Sectors	-	-	-	-	-	-	-	-	-	-

OECD Total / OCDE Total : 1993

SUPPLY AND CONSUMPTION / APPROVISIONNEMENT ET DEMANDE	Coal / Charbon (1000 tonnes)							Oil / Pétrole (1000 tonnes)			
	Coking Coal / Charbon à coke	Steam Coal / Charbon vapeur	Sub-Bit. Coal / Charbon sous-bit.	Lignite / Lignite	Peat / Tourbe	Oven and Gas Coke / Coke de four/gaz	Pat. Fuel and BKB / Agg./briq. de lignite	Crude Oil / Pétrole brut	NGL / LGN	Feedstocks / Produits d'aliment.	Additives / Additifs
Production	217405	670920	302091	478325	13306	121163	16823	823704	94958	-	6687
From Other Sources	-	1229	971	-	-	-	-	85	-	16437	1876
Imports	115785	149046	-	3374	36	10279	1026	1140103	14513	66794	1222
Exports	-142294	-86738	-1955	-75	-303	-7969	-1084	-288174	-13273	-6555	-
Intl. Marine Bunkers	-	-	-	-	-	-	-	-	-	-	-
Stock Changes	-2299	57392	2403	1097	809	1085	102	-5070	-340	1334	-1434
DOMESTIC SUPPLY	188597	791849	303510	482721	13848	124558	16867	1670648	95858	78010	8351
Transfers	-	-	-	-	-	-	-	-2053	-60862	43420	473
Statistical Differences	-568	-17731	14983	2768	-	282	-	-73	213	-2312	-450
TRANSFORMATION	186080	689646	310430	455113	9482	38573	1826	1667690	32376	119118	8374
Electricity Plants	18668	618540	296637	414598	4436	-	1146	13564	214	-	-
CHP Plants	-	66828	13793	1208	3272	-	-	-	-	-	-
Heat Plants	-	1407	-	2856	764	11	464	-	-	-	-
Transfer to Gases	1042	565	-	-	-	38478	-	-	-	-	-
Transfer to Solids	166370	2306	-	36451	1010	84	216	-	-	-	-
Petroleum Refineries	-	-	-	-	-	-	-	1657467	32162	119118	8374
Petrochemical Industry	-	-	-	-	-	-	-	-	-	-	-
Liquefaction	-	-	-	-	-	-	-	-3341	-	-	-
Other Transformation Sector	-	-	-	-	-	-	-	-	-	-	-
ENERGY SECTOR	57	784	3	1609	-	309	115	807	-	-	-
Coal Mines	-	553	3	-	-	-	-	-	-	-	-
Oil and Gas Extraction	-	-	-	-	-	-	-	807	-	-	-
Petroleum Refineries	-	129	-	-	-	-	-	-	-	-	-
Electricity, CHP+Heat plants	-	-	-	-	-	-	-	-	-	-	-
Pumped Storage (Elec.)	-	-	-	-	-	-	-	-	-	-	-
Other Energy Sector	57	102	-	1609	-	309	115	-	-	-	-
Distribution Losses	10	-	-	-	-	6	-	-	-	-	-
FINAL CONSUMPTION	1882	83688	8060	28767	4366	85952	14926	25	2833	-	-
INDUSTRY SECTOR	1361	69945	7454	18818	2817	81876	3899	25	2833	-	-
Iron and Steel	856	8469	725	-	-	73073	-	-	-	-	-
Chemical and Petrochemical	3	8256	2832	5861	28	538	134	-	-	-	-
of which: Feedstocks	-	-	-	-	-	-	-	-	-	-	-
Non-Ferrous Metals	2	1261	2030	475	-	1310	-	-	-	-	-
Non-Metallic Minerals	6	30993	772	294	-	913	10	-	-	-	-
Transport Equipment	-	319	-	-	-	39	2	-	-	-	-
Machinery	5	939	83	58	-	672	-	-	-	-	-
Mining and Quarrying	-	306	305	3	-	302	-	-	-	-	-
Food and Tobacco	136	2461	3	1656	-	315	157	-	-	-	-
Paper, Pulp and Print	-	3937	-	250	33	45	50	-	-	-	-
Wood and Wood Products	-	108	-	49	-	-	1	-	-	-	-
Construction	188	920	12	1287	-	54	-	-	-	-	-
Textile and Leather	-	539	-	280	-	8	25	-	-	-	-
Non-specified	165	11437	692	8605	2756	4607	3520	-	-	-	-
TRANSPORT SECTOR	14	23	198	1	-	5	2	-	-	-	-
International Civil Aviation	-	-	-	-	-	-	-	-	-	-	-
Domestic Air	-	-	-	-	-	-	-	-	-	-	-
Road	-	-	-	-	-	-	-	-	-	-	-
Rail	14	23	-	1	-	5	2	-	-	-	-
Pipeline Transport	-	-	-	-	-	-	-	-	-	-	-
Internal Navigation	-	-	198	-	-	-	-	-	-	-	-
Non-specified	-	-	-	-	-	-	-	-	-	-	-
OTHER SECTORS	296	13447	408	9895	1549	2406	10823	-	-	-	-
Agriculture	-	181	17	240	49	52	351	-	-	-	-
Commerce and Publ. Serv.	-	1211	-	1117	15	267	2100	-	-	-	-
Residential	296	11638	139	8374	1485	2068	7904	-	-	-	-
Non-specified	-	417	252	164	-	19	468	-	-	-	-
NON-ENERGY USE	211	273	-	53	-	1665	202	-	-	-	-
in Industry/Transf./Energy	211	273	-	53	-	1665	202	-	-	-	-
in Transport	-	-	-	-	-	-	-	-	-	-	-
in Other Sectors	-	-	-	-	-	-	-	-	-	-	-

Industry sector details shown only where sectorial data are available for most countries.
La ventilation du secteur industriel n'est indiquée que s'il existe des données sectorielles disponibles pour la plupart des pays concernés.

OECD Total / OCDE Total : 1993

SUPPLY AND CONSUMPTION / APPROVISIONNEMENT ET DEMANDE	Oil cont. / Pétrole cont. (1000 tonnes)										
	Refinery Gas / Gaz de raffinerie	LPG + Ethane / GPL + éthane	Motor Gasoline / Essence moteur	Aviation Gasoline / Essence aviation	Jet Fuel / Carbu-réacteur	Kerosene / Kérosène	Gas/ Diesel / Gazole	Heavy Fuel Oil / Fioul lourd	Naphtha / Naphta	Pétrol. Coke / Coke de pétrole	Other Prod. / Autres prod.
Production	67883	44095	557269	1275	116657	33319	487905	263963	57725	51137	122927
From Other Sources	-	-	-	-	-	-	-	-	-	-	-
Imports	-	29652	45554	177	15282	3941	74328	76075	38725	12920	22290
Exports	-	-6299	-50424	-214	-12850	-2124	-83424	-65937	-13523	-18059	-18189
Intl. Marine Bunkers	-	-	-	-	-6	-	-15620	-62622	-	-	-339
Stock Changes	-3	-1206	-2845	-39	93	187	1941	1918	-82	257	268
DOMESTIC SUPPLY	67880	66242	549554	1199	119176	35323	465130	213397	82845	46255	126957
Transfers	-113	54401	730	-2	-42	-3388	1513	-5032	-7428	34	-16160
Statistical Differences	16	-425	91	-27	-1493	-384	4234	-2036	907	-37	-115
TRANSFORMATION	1346	5090	510	-	-	390	6752	108173	13439	4121	2405
Electricity Plants	58	814	-	-	-	-	4998	100859	891	1972	2255
CHP Plants	751	18	-	-	-	-	184	5432	-	209	112
Heat Plants	113	61	-	-	-	11	64	949	-	-	-
Transfer to Gases	277	2962	-	-	-	-	3	367	433	-	-
Transfer to Solids	-	-	-	-	-	-	1	19	-	1940	-
Petroleum Refineries	-	-	-	-	-	-	-	-	-	-	-
Petrochemical Industry	147	1235	510	-	-	379	1502	547	12115	-	2
Liquefaction	-	-	-	-	-	-	-	-	-	-	-
Other Transformation Sector	-	-	-	-	-	-	-	-	-	-	36
ENERGY SECTOR	63488	1672	101	-	69	17	850	20401	144	21708	2850
Coal Mines	-	2	-	-	-	-	416	34	-	-	1
Oil and Gas Extraction	-	421	-	-	-	-	90	49	-	756	-
Petroleum Refineries	63488	1211	97	-	69	17	289	20135	144	20950	2766
Electricity, CHP+Heat plants	-	1	4	-	-	-	40	154	-	-	2
Pumped Storage (Elec.)	-	-	-	-	-	-	-	-	-	-	-
Other Energy Sector	-	37	-	-	-	-	15	29	-	2	81
Distribution Losses	-	17	81	-	12	1	48	58	-	-	1
FINAL CONSUMPTION	2949	113439	549683	1170	117560	31143	463227	77697	62741	20423	105426
INDUSTRY SECTOR	2949	72051	3081	-	17	5688	51751	56722	62741	8759	1048
Iron and Steel	-	-	-	-	-	-	-	-	-	-	-
Chemical and Petrochemical	-	-	-	-	-	-	-	-	-	-	-
of which: Feedstocks	-	-	-	-	-	-	-	-	-	-	-
Non-Ferrous Metals	-	-	-	-	-	-	-	-	-	-	-
Non-Metallic Minerals	-	-	-	-	-	-	-	-	-	-	-
Transport Equipment	-	-	-	-	-	-	-	-	-	-	-
Machinery	-	-	-	-	-	-	-	-	-	-	-
Mining and Quarrying	-	-	-	-	-	-	-	-	-	-	-
Food and Tobacco	-	-	-	-	-	-	-	-	-	-	-
Paper, Pulp and Print	-	-	-	-	-	-	-	-	-	-	-
Wood and Wood Products	-	-	-	-	-	-	-	-	-	-	-
Construction	-	-	-	-	-	-	-	-	-	-	-
Textile and Leather	-	-	-	-	-	-	-	-	-	-	-
Non-specified	-	-	-	-	-	-	-	-	-	-	-
TRANSPORT SECTOR	-	6038	541964	1168	117535	22	252201	5055	-	-	5
International Civil Aviation	-	-	-	4	34198	-	-	-	-	-	-
Domestic Air	-	-	-	1164	83337	-	1	-	-	-	-
Road	-	6033	537861	-	-	8	220334	41	-	-	5
Rail	-	5	-	-	-	12	16540	46	-	-	-
Pipeline Transport	-	-	-	-	-	-	7	-	-	-	-
Internal Navigation	-	-	4103	-	-	2	12427	4809	-	-	-
Non-specified	-	-	-	-	-	-	2892	159	-	-	-
OTHER SECTORS	-	35350	4638	2	8	25433	159275	15862	-	124	12
Agriculture	-	2188	2571	2	1	3098	34639	904	-	16	5
Commerce and Publ. Serv.	-	4477	1846	-	7	4980	54395	9871	-	8	7
Residential	-	27927	221	-	-	16375	67972	2564	-	99	-
Non-specified	-	758	-	-	-	980	2269	2523	-	1	-
NON-ENERGY USE	-	-	-	-	-	-	-	58	-	11540	104361
in Industry/Transf./Energy	-	-	-	-	-	-	-	58	-	11540	94932
in Transport	-	-	-	-	-	-	-	-	-	-	7454
in Other Sectors	-	-	-	-	-	-	-	-	-	-	1975

OECD Total / OCDE Total : 1993

CONSUMPTION *APPROVISIONNEMENT ET DEMANDE*	Gas / *Gaz* (TJ)				Combust. Renew. & Waste / *En. Re. Comb. & Déchets* (TJ)				(GWh)	(TJ)
	Natural Gas *Gaz naturel*	Gas Works *Usines à gaz*	Coke Ovens *Cokeries*	Blast Furnaces *Hauts fourneaux*	Solid Biomass & Anim. Prod. *Biomasse solide & prod. anim.*	Gas/Liquids from Biomass *Gaz/Liquides tirés de biomasse*	Municipal Waste *Déchets urbains*	Industrial Waste *Déchets industriels*	Electricity *Electricité*	Heat *Chaleur*
Production	36196673	612553	873315	1194047	5471287	153652	412602	295246	7657454	1245069
From Other Sources	-	262085	-	-	-	-	-	-	-	-
Imports	11095778	-	-	-	5550	844	-	2657	220526	-
Exports	-5475255	-180	-	-	-	-	-	-20	-213787	-
Intl. Marine Bunkers	-	-	-	-	-	-	-	-	-	-
Stock Changes	221478	2484	2	-	1345	1089	-	150	-	-
DOMESTIC SUPPLY	**42038674**	**876942**	**873317**	**1194047**	**5478182**	**155585**	**412602**	**298033**	**7664193**	**1245069**
Transfers	-	-	-	-	-	-82475	-	-	-	-
Statistical Differences	-777762	-191	-18664	-6440	538	-2150	-78	-	-	-
TRANSFORMATION	**8091035**	**25**	**302719**	**628282**	**1576811**	**67137**	**396972**	**195471**	**9128**	**-**
Electricity Plants	6064872	-	139541	368728	295144	41861	275185	63934	-	-
CHP Plants	928037	-	152067	258990	1230866	11167	94397	130345	-	-
Heat Plants	224573	25	566	564	46096	2622	27390	1192	9128	-
Transfer to Gases	677168	-	10545	-	-	-	-	-	-	-
Transfer to Solids	1683	-	-	-	4705	-	-	-	-	-
Petroleum Refineries	-	-	-	-	-	11487	-	-	-	-
Petrochemical Industry	-	-	-	-	-	-	-	-	-	-
Liquefaction	182308	-	-	-	-	-	-	-	-	-
Other Transformation Sector	12394	-	-	-	-	-	-	-	-	-
ENERGY SECTOR	**3249638**	**16072**	**163253**	**112006**	**-**	**-**	**-**	**-**	**669812**	**43787**
Coal Mines	7761	-	1620	-	-	-	-	-	31096	-
Oil and Gas Extraction	2033467	-	-	-	-	-	-	-	53870	-
Petroleum Refineries	907102	-	2232	-	-	-	-	-	83016	37514
Electricity, CHP+Heat plants	500	-	-	-	-	-	-	-	406293	251
Pumped Storage (Elec.)	-	-	-	-	-	-	-	-	64166	-
Other Energy Sector	300808	16072	159401	112006	-	-	-	-	31371	6022
Distribution Losses	50641	10201	1965	18982	-	-	-	-	509902	144341
FINAL CONSUMPTION	**29869598**	**850453**	**386716**	**428337**	**3901909**	**3823**	**15552**	**102562**	**6475351**	**1056941**
INDUSTRY SECTOR	**13581294**	**255847**	**385731**	**428216**	**2049254**	**564**	**15212**	**19120**	**2626124**	**351586**
Iron and Steel	-	1891	359353	428056	202	-	-	-	263312	3404
Chemical and Petrochemical	-	7641	10520	160	19526	55	245	11722	480362	151131
of which: Feedstocks	-	-	-	-	-	-	-	-	-	-
Non-Ferrous Metals	-	1512	270	-	1864	149	-	30	268748	1521
Non-Metallic Minerals	-	740	5976	-	18160	-	172	1128	119816	392
Transport Equipment	-	132	180	-	18	-	6	-	113554	5862
Machinery	-	1221	3961	-	302	-	15	110	207463	27844
Mining and Quarrying	-	-	2091	-	47	-	-	-	75774	25
Food and Tobacco	-	1448	1152	-	173249	284	4	243	159989	21557
Paper, Pulp and Print	-	111	450	-	1449828	65	14770	1972	330338	27645
Wood and Wood Products	-	36	-	-	316675	-	-	125	50840	101
Construction	-	2	554	-	-	-	-	10	10414	15
Textile and Leather	-	254	252	-	22744	-	-	120	86007	8291
Non-specified	-	240859	972	-	46639	11	-	3660	459507	103798
TRANSPORT SECTOR	**904899**	**-**	**-**	**-**	**371**	**-**	**7**	**65**	**87323**	**-**
International Civil Aviation	-	-	-	-	-	-	-	-	-	-
Domestic Air	-	-	-	-	-	-	-	-	-	-
Road	17271	-	-	-	-	-	-	-	74398	-
Rail	-	-	-	-	371	-	7	65	-	-
Pipeline Transport	886059	-	-	-	-	-	-	-	3545	-
Internal Navigation	-	-	-	-	-	-	-	-	-	-
Non-specified	1569	-	-	-	-	-	-	-	9380	-
OTHER SECTORS	**15382938**	**594605**	**936**	**-**	**1852284**	**3259**	**333**	**83377**	**3761904**	**705355**
Agriculture	231080	108	-	-	9211	5	-	-	55849	5244
Commerce and Publ. Serv.	4483589	134141	-	-	4250	940	240	-	1661761	168649
Residential	10182955	460306	936	-	1838823	7	93	83377	2037472	385906
Non-specified	485314	50	-	-	-	2307	-	-	6822	145556
NON-ENERGY USE	**467**	**1**	**49**	**121**	**-**	**-**	**-**	**-**	**-**	**-**
in Industry/Transf./Energy	467	1	49	121	-	-	-	-	-	-
in Transport	-	-	-	-	-	-	-	-	-	-
in Other Sectors	-	-	-	-	-	-	-	-	-	-

North America / Amérique du Nord : 1992

SUPPLY AND CONSUMPTION	Coal / _Charbon_ (1000 tonnes)							Oil / _Pétrole_ (1000 tonnes)			
	Coking Coal	Steam Coal	Sub-Bit. Coal	Lignite	Peat	Oven and Gas Coke	Pat. Fuel and BKB	Crude Oil	NGL	Feedstocks	Additives
APPROVISIONNEMENT ET DEMANDE	_Charbon à coke_	_Charbon vapeur_	_Charbon sous-bit._	_Lignite_	_Tourbe_	_Coke de four/gaz_	_Agg./briq. de lignite_	_Pétrole brut_	_LGN_	_Produits d'aliment._	_Additifs_
Production	106508	521913	256273	91730	11	26981	-	578517	80370	-	-
From Other Sources	-	-	-	-	-	-	-	-	-	-	-
Imports	5482	11435	-	-	-	2054	-	351570	4772	22646	-
Exports	-76274	-44082	-	-55	-	-682	-	-110002	-9713	-	-
Intl. Marine Bunkers	-	-	-	-	-	-	-	-	-	-	-
Stock Changes	1272	-5428	-349	258	-	595	-	-126	-134	82	-
DOMESTIC SUPPLY	**36988**	**483838**	**255924**	**91933**	**11**	**28948**	**-**	**819959**	**75295**	**22728**	**-**
Transfers	-	-	-	-	-	-	-	-	-53853	12542	-
Statistical Differences	-187	1942	-696	-941	-	-26	-	1865	1191	-	-
TRANSFORMATION	**36801**	**456257**	**251240**	**84514**	**11**	**8615**	**-**	**820977**	**22633**	**35270**	**-**
Electricity Plants	-	417351	240878	84514	11	-	-	-	-	-	-
CHP Plants	-	38906	10362	-	-	-	-	-	-	-	-
Heat Plants	-	-	-	-	-	-	-	-	-	-	-
Transfer to Gases	-	-	-	-	-	8615	-	-	-	-	-
Transfer to Solids	36801	-	-	-	-	-	-	-	-	-	-
Petroleum Refineries	-	-	-	-	-	-	-	823060	22633	35270	-
Petrochemical Industry	-	-	-	-	-	-	-	-	-	-	-
Liquefaction	-	-	-	-	-	-	-	-2083	-	-	-
Other Transformation Sector	-	-	-	-	-	-	-	-	-	-	-
ENERGY SECTOR	**-**	**615**	**-**	**-**	**-**	**-**	**-**	**847**	**-**	**-**	**-**
Coal Mines	-	494	-	-	-	-	-	-	-	-	-
Oil and Gas Extraction	-	-	-	-	-	-	-	847	-	-	-
Petroleum Refineries	-	121	-	-	-	-	-	-	-	-	-
Electricity, CHP+Heat plants	-	-	-	-	-	-	-	-	-	-	-
Pumped Storage (Elec.)	-	-	-	-	-	-	-	-	-	-	-
Other Energy Sector	-	-	-	-	-	-	-	-	-	-	-
Distribution Losses	-	-	-	-	-	-	-	-	-	-	-
FINAL CONSUMPTION	**-**	**28908**	**3988**	**6478**	**-**	**20307**	**-**	**-**	**-**	**-**	**-**
INDUSTRY SECTOR	**-**	**25207**	**3950**	**6465**	**-**	**20251**	**-**	**-**	**-**	**-**	**-**
Iron and Steel	-	596	-	-	-	18116	-	-	-	-	-
Chemical and Petrochemical	-	2547	2976	6178	-	-	-	-	-	-	-
of which: Feedstocks	-	-	-	-	-	-	-	-	-	-	-
Non-Ferrous Metals	-	371	-	-	-	94	-	-	-	-	-
Non-Metallic Minerals	-	10329	509	2	-	74	-	-	-	-	-
Transport Equipment	-	-	-	-	-	-	-	-	-	-	-
Machinery	-	691	48	-	-	-	-	-	-	-	-
Mining and Quarrying	-	45	-	-	-	259	-	-	-	-	-
Food and Tobacco	-	484	417	54	-	-	-	-	-	-	-
Paper, Pulp and Print	-	168	-	96	-	-	-	-	-	-	-
Wood and Wood Products	-	-	-	-	-	-	-	-	-	-	-
Construction	-	-	-	-	-	-	-	-	-	-	-
Textile and Leather	-	-	-	-	-	-	-	-	-	-	-
Non-specified	-	9976	-	135	-	1708	-	-	-	-	-
TRANSPORT SECTOR	**-**	**-**	**-**	**-**	**-**	**-**	**-**	**-**	**-**	**-**	**-**
International Civil Aviation	-	-	-	-	-	-	-	-	-	-	-
Domestic Air	-	-	-	-	-	-	-	-	-	-	-
Road	-	-	-	-	-	-	-	-	-	-	-
Rail	-	-	-	-	-	-	-	-	-	-	-
Pipeline Transport	-	-	-	-	-	-	-	-	-	-	-
Internal Navigation	-	-	-	-	-	-	-	-	-	-	-
Non-specified	-	-	-	-	-	-	-	-	-	-	-
OTHER SECTORS	**-**	**3542**	**38**	**13**	**-**	**-**	**-**	**-**	**-**	**-**	**-**
Agriculture	-	-	-	-	-	-	-	-	-	-	-
Commerce and Publ. Serv.	-	1297	-	-	-	-	-	-	-	-	-
Residential	-	2245	38	13	-	-	-	-	-	-	-
Non-specified	-	-	-	-	-	-	-	-	-	-	-
NON-ENERGY USE	**-**	**159**	**-**	**-**	**-**	**56**	**-**	**-**	**-**	**-**	**-**
in Industry/Transf./Energy	-	159	-	-	-	56	-	-	-	-	-
in Transport	-	-	-	-	-	-	-	-	-	-	-
in Other Sectors	-	-	-	-	-	-	-	-	-	-	-

Industry sector details shown only where sectorial data are available for most countries.
La ventilation du secteur industriel n'est indiquée que s'il existe des données sectorielles disponibles pour la plupart des pays concernés.

North America / Amérique du Nord : 1992

SUPPLY AND CONSUMPTION / *APPROVISIONNEMENT ET DEMANDE*	Oil cont. / *Pétrole cont.* (1000 tonnes)										
	Refinery Gas / *Gaz de raffinerie*	LPG + Ethane / *GPL + éthane*	Motor Gasoline / *Essence moteur*	Aviation Gasoline / *Essence aviation*	Jet Fuel / *Carbu-réacteur*	Kerosene / *Kérosène*	Gas/Diesel / *Gazole*	Heavy Fuel Oil / *Fioul lourd*	Naphtha / *Naphta*	Pétrol. Coke / *Coke de pétrole*	Other Prod. / *Autres prod.*
Production	38083	21846	348240	977	72648	5014	185930	86771	13253	41768	64322
From Other Sources	-	-	-	-	-	-	-	-	-	-	-
Imports	-	1159	17140	19	3285	193	9014	24846	866	1238	9965
Exports	-	-607	-8100	-5	-3096	-458	-16984	-13443	-430	-14427	-3027
Intl. Marine Bunkers	-	-	-	-	-	-	-7255	-26623	-	-	-
Stock Changes	-9	351	812	9	561	232	1096	1766	-7	2	679
DOMESTIC SUPPLY	**38074**	**22749**	**358092**	**1000**	**73398**	**4981**	**171801**	**73317**	**13682**	**28581**	**71939**
Transfers	-81	49976	4948	4	69	-1807	1136	621	-721	-33	-11577
Statistical Differences	32	-13	-127	-7	-61	49	149	-289	65	62	-186
TRANSFORMATION	-	**246**	-	-	-	-	**2309**	**38376**	-	**905**	-
Electricity Plants	-	-	-	-	-	-	2309	38329	-	905	-
CHP Plants	-	-	-	-	-	-	-	47	-	-	-
Heat Plants	-	-	-	-	-	-	-	-	-	-	-
Transfer to Gases	-	246	-	-	-	-	-	-	-	-	-
Transfer to Solids	-	-	-	-	-	-	-	-	-	-	-
Petroleum Refineries	-	-	-	-	-	-	-	-	-	-	-
Petrochemical Industry	-	-	-	-	-	-	-	-	-	-	-
Liquefaction	-	-	-	-	-	-	-	-	-	-	-
Other Transformation Sector	-	-	-	-	-	-	-	-	-	-	-
ENERGY SECTOR	**37381**	**1135**	**103**	-	**57**	-	**122**	**5765**	**6**	**16968**	**202**
Coal Mines	-	-	-	-	-	-	-	-	-	-	-
Oil and Gas Extraction	-	-	-	-	-	-	-	-	-	738	-
Petroleum Refineries	37381	1135	103	-	57	-	122	5765	6	16230	202
Electricity, CHP+Heat plants	-	-	-	-	-	-	-	-	-	-	-
Pumped Storage (Elec.)	-	-	-	-	-	-	-	-	-	-	-
Other Energy Sector	-	-	-	-	-	-	-	-	-	-	-
Distribution Losses	-	-	-	-	-	-	-	-	-	-	-
FINAL CONSUMPTION	**644**	**71331**	**362810**	**997**	**73349**	**3223**	**170655**	**29508**	**13020**	**10737**	**59974**
INDUSTRY SECTOR	**644**	**54132**	**2171**	-	-	**212**	**19192**	**19532**	**13020**	**297**	**1234**
Iron and Steel	-	-	-	-	-	-	-	-	-	-	-
Chemical and Petrochemical	-	-	-	-	-	-	-	-	-	-	-
of which: Feedstocks	-	-	-	-	-	-	-	-	-	-	-
Non-Ferrous Metals	-	-	-	-	-	-	-	-	-	-	-
Non-Metallic Minerals	-	-	-	-	-	-	-	-	-	-	-
Transport Equipment	-	-	-	-	-	-	-	-	-	-	-
Machinery	-	-	-	-	-	-	-	-	-	-	-
Mining and Quarrying	-	-	-	-	-	-	-	-	-	-	-
Food and Tobacco	-	-	-	-	-	-	-	-	-	-	-
Paper, Pulp and Print	-	-	-	-	-	-	-	-	-	-	-
Wood and Wood Products	-	-	-	-	-	-	-	-	-	-	-
Construction	-	-	-	-	-	-	-	-	-	-	-
Textile and Leather	-	-	-	-	-	-	-	-	-	-	-
Non-specified	-	-	-	-	-	-	-	-	-	-	-
TRANSPORT SECTOR	-	**1282**	**356619**	**997**	**73349**	-	**98054**	**1391**	-	-	-
International Civil Aviation	-	-	-	-	2784	-	-	-	-	-	-
Domestic Air	-	-	-	997	70565	-	-	-	-	-	-
Road	-	1282	352987	-	-	-	82763	-	-	-	-
Rail	-	-	-	-	-	-	12311	-	-	-	-
Pipeline Transport	-	-	-	-	-	-	11	-	-	-	-
Internal Navigation	-	-	3632	-	-	-	870	1391	-	-	-
Non-specified	-	-	-	-	-	-	2099	-	-	-	-
OTHER SECTORS	-	**15917**	**4020**	-	-	**3011**	**53409**	**8585**	-	-	-
Agriculture	-	1692	2223	-	-	205	15411	16	-	-	-
Commerce and Publ. Serv.	-	1682	1797	-	-	357	13789	6131	-	-	-
Residential	-	11889	-	-	-	1807	22835	38	-	-	-
Non-specified	-	654	-	-	-	642	1374	2400	-	-	-
NON-ENERGY USE	-	-	-	-	-	-	-	-	-	**10440**	**58740**
in Industry/Transf./Energy	-	-	-	-	-	-	-	-	-	10440	53065
in Transport	-	-	-	-	-	-	-	-	-	-	4856
in Other Sectors	-	-	-	-	-	-	-	-	-	-	819

North America / Amérique du Nord : 1992

CONSUMPTION *APPROVISIONNEMENT ET DEMANDE*	Gas / *Gaz* (TJ)				Combust. Renew. & Waste / *En. Re. Comb. & Déchets* (TJ)				(GWh)	(TJ)
	Natural Gas *Gaz naturel*	Gas Works *Usines à gaz*	Coke Ovens *Cokeries*	Blast Furnaces *Hauts fourneaux*	Solid Biomass & Anim. Prod. *Biomasse solide & prod. anim.*	Gas/Liquids from Biomass *Gaz/Liquides tirés de biomasse*	Municipal Waste *Déchets urbains*	Industrial Waste *Déchets industriels*	Electricity *Electricité*	Heat *Chaleur*
Production	25425443	-	195727	240911	3832517	36571	236331	165816	3934443	394008
From Other Sources	-	-	-	-	-	-	-	-	-	-
Imports	2409660	-	-	-	-	-	-	-	44671	-
Exports	-2427581	-	-	-	-	-	-	-	-42424	-
Intl. Marine Bunkers	-	-	-	-	-	-	-	-	-	-
Stock Changes	352327	-	-	-	-	-	-	-	-	-
DOMESTIC SUPPLY	**25759849**	**-**	**195727**	**240911**	**3832517**	**36571**	**236331**	**165816**	**3936690**	**394008**
Transfers	-	-	-	-	-	-	-	-	-	-
Statistical Differences	-613961	-	1838	2364	-465	-	-	-	-	-
TRANSFORMATION	**3386225**	**-**	**166051**	**213337**	**1338215**	**36571**	**236331**	**165816**	**-**	**-**
Electricity Plants	3150738	-	14042	17844	226053	27967	191636	18790	-	-
CHP Plants	127839	-	152009	195493	1112162	8604	44695	147026	-	-
Heat Plants	-	-	-	-	-	-	-	-	-	-
Transfer to Gases	-	-	-	-	-	-	-	-	-	-
Transfer to Solids	-	-	-	-	-	-	-	-	-	-
Petroleum Refineries	-	-	-	-	-	-	-	-	-	-
Petrochemical Industry	-	-	-	-	-	-	-	-	-	-
Liquefaction	94965	-	-	-	-	-	-	-	-	-
Other Transformation Sector	12683	-	-	-	-	-	-	-	-	-
ENERGY SECTOR	**2656532**	**-**	**-**	**-**	**-**	**-**	**-**	**-**	**348908**	**36912**
Coal Mines	4161	-	-	-	-	-	-	-	14565	-
Oil and Gas Extraction	1520584	-	-	-	-	-	-	-	46466	-
Petroleum Refineries	827872	-	-	-	-	-	-	-	48633	36912
Electricity, CHP+Heat plants	-	-	-	-	-	-	-	-	215741	-
Pumped Storage (Elec.)	-	-	-	-	-	-	-	-	23503	-
Other Energy Sector	303915	-	-	-	-	-	-	-	-	-
Distribution Losses	-	-	-	-	-	-	-	-	291654	41368
FINAL CONSUMPTION	**19103131**	**-**	**31514**	**29938**	**2493837**	**-**	**-**	**-**	**3296128**	**315728**
INDUSTRY SECTOR	**9076788**	**-**	**31514**	**29938**	**1464986**	**-**	**-**	**-**	**1205129**	**251976**
Iron and Steel	-	-	31514	29938	-	-	-	-	71934	337
Chemical and Petrochemical	-	-	-	-	-	-	-	-	238766	138544
of which: Feedstocks	-	-	-	-	-	-	-	-	-	-
Non-Ferrous Metals	-	-	-	-	-	-	-	-	138964	1536
Non-Metallic Minerals	-	-	-	-	-	-	-	-	36610	351
Transport Equipment	-	-	-	-	-	-	-	-	35609	5126
Machinery	-	-	-	-	-	-	-	-	103530	6920
Mining and Quarrying	-	-	-	-	-	-	-	-	52996	-
Food and Tobacco	-	-	-	-	69890	-	-	-	59015	19635
Paper, Pulp and Print	-	-	-	-	1179216	-	-	-	180670	23223
Wood and Wood Products	-	-	-	-	215880	-	-	-	26437	-
Construction	-	-	-	-	-	-	-	-	330	-
Textile and Leather	-	-	-	-	-	-	-	-	37464	7809
Non-specified	-	-	-	-	-	-	-	-	222804	48495
TRANSPORT SECTOR	**834533**	**-**	**-**	**-**	**-**	**-**	**-**	**-**	**8285**	**-**
International Civil Aviation	-	-	-	-	-	-	-	-	-	-
Domestic Air	-	-	-	-	-	-	-	-	-	-
Road	3427	-	-	-	-	-	-	-	-	-
Rail	-	-	-	-	-	-	-	-	5693	-
Pipeline Transport	831106	-	-	-	-	-	-	-	2592	-
Internal Navigation	-	-	-	-	-	-	-	-	-	-
Non-specified	-	-	-	-	-	-	-	-	-	-
OTHER SECTORS	**9191810**	**-**	**-**	**-**	**1028851**	**-**	**-**	**-**	**2082714**	**63752**
Agriculture	25134	-	-	-	-	-	-	-	15153	91
Commerce and Publ. Serv.	3465210	-	-	-	-	-	-	-	976498	63661
Residential	5701466	-	-	-	1028851	-	-	-	1091063	-
Non-specified	-	-	-	-	-	-	-	-	-	-
NON-ENERGY USE	**-**	**-**	**-**	**-**	**-**	**-**	**-**	**-**	**-**	**-**
in Industry/Transf./Energy	-	-	-	-	-	-	-	-	-	-
in Transport	-	-	-	-	-	-	-	-	-	-
in Other Sectors	-	-	-	-	-	-	-	-	-	-

North America / Amérique du Nord : 1993

SUPPLY AND CONSUMPTION / *APPROVISIONNEMENT ET DEMANDE*	Coal / *Charbon* (1000 tonnes)							Oil / *Pétrole* (1000 tonnes)			
	Coking Coal / *Charbon à coke*	Steam Coal / *Charbon vapeur*	Sub-Bit. Coal / *Charbon sous-bit.*	Lignite / *Lignite*	Peat / *Tourbe*	Oven and Gas Coke / *Coke de four/gaz*	Pat. Fuel and BKB / *Agg./briq. de lignite*	Crude Oil / *Pétrole brut*	NGL / *LGN*	Feedstocks / *Produits d'aliment.*	Additives / *Additifs*
Production	100782	463289	277952	91283	24	26629	-	563012	82463	-	6544
From Other Sources	-	-	-	-	-	-	-	-	-	-	-
Imports	4702	10349	-	-	-	2445	-	389372	5675	26635	870
Exports	-68999	-24902	-1932	-29	-	-1065	-	-113314	-9315	-	-
Intl. Marine Bunkers	-	-	-	-	-	-	-	-	-	-	-
Stock Changes	-733	46106	2273	-2474	-	286	-	-2634	-371	828	-1456
DOMESTIC SUPPLY	**35752**	**494842**	**278293**	**88780**	**24**	**28295**	**-**	**836436**	**78452**	**27463**	**5958**
Transfers	-	-	-	-	-	-	-	-	-55176	12383	473
Statistical Differences	-227	-17723	14948	2740	-	68	-	-3576	971	-1	-352
TRANSFORMATION	**35525**	**448473**	**289908**	**85442**	**24**	**8858**	**-**	**832257**	**24247**	**39845**	**6079**
Electricity Plants	-	404700	276128	84234	24	-	-	-	-	-	-
CHP Plants	-	43773	13780	1208	-	-	-	-	-	-	-
Heat Plants	-	-	-	-	-	-	-	-	-	-	-
Transfer to Gases	-	-	-	-	-	8858	-	-	-	-	-
Transfer to Solids	35525	-	-	-	-	-	-	-	-	-	-
Petroleum Refineries	-	-	-	-	-	-	-	834488	24247	39845	6079
Petrochemical Industry	-	-	-	-	-	-	-	-	-	-	-
Liquefaction	-	-	-	-	-	-	-	-2231	-	-	-
Other Transformation Sector	-	-	-	-	-	-	-	-	-	-	-
ENERGY SECTOR	**-**	**277**	**-**	**-**	**-**	**-**	**-**	**603**	**-**	**-**	**-**
Coal Mines	-	148	-	-	-	-	-	-	-	-	-
Oil and Gas Extraction	-	-	-	-	-	-	-	603	-	-	-
Petroleum Refineries	-	129	-	-	-	-	-	-	-	-	-
Electricity, CHP+Heat plants	-	-	-	-	-	-	-	-	-	-	-
Pumped Storage (Elec.)	-	-	-	-	-	-	-	-	-	-	-
Other Energy Sector	-	-	-	-	-	-	-	-	-	-	-
Distribution Losses	-	-	-	-	-	-	-	-	-	-	-
FINAL CONSUMPTION	**-**	**28369**	**3333**	**6078**	**-**	**19505**	**-**	**-**	**-**	**-**	**-**
INDUSTRY SECTOR	**-**	**25805**	**3290**	**6072**	**-**	**19454**	**-**	**-**	**-**	**-**	**-**
Iron and Steel	-	451	-	-	-	17396	-	-	-	-	-
Chemical and Petrochemical	-	2686	2828	5546	-	-	-	-	-	-	-
of which: Feedstocks	-	-	-	-	-	-	-	-	-	-	-
Non-Ferrous Metals	-	306	-	-	-	85	-	-	-	-	-
Non-Metallic Minerals	-	11186	379	2	-	10	-	-	-	-	-
Transport Equipment	-	-	-	-	-	-	-	-	-	-	-
Machinery	-	631	83	-	-	-	-	-	-	-	-
Mining and Quarrying	-	22	-	-	-	283	-	-	-	-	-
Food and Tobacco	-	464	-	46	-	-	-	-	-	-	-
Paper, Pulp and Print	-	138	-	82	-	-	-	-	-	-	-
Wood and Wood Products	-	-	-	-	-	-	-	-	-	-	-
Construction	-	-	-	-	-	-	-	-	-	-	-
Textile and Leather	-	-	-	-	-	-	-	-	-	-	-
Non-specified	-	9921	-	396	-	1680	-	-	-	-	-
TRANSPORT SECTOR	**-**	**-**	**-**	**-**	**-**	**-**	**-**	**-**	**-**	**-**	**-**
International Civil Aviation	-	-	-	-	-	-	-	-	-	-	-
Domestic Air	-	-	-	-	-	-	-	-	-	-	-
Road	-	-	-	-	-	-	-	-	-	-	-
Rail	-	-	-	-	-	-	-	-	-	-	-
Pipeline Transport	-	-	-	-	-	-	-	-	-	-	-
Internal Navigation	-	-	-	-	-	-	-	-	-	-	-
Non-specified	-	-	-	-	-	-	-	-	-	-	-
OTHER SECTORS	**-**	**2391**	**43**	**6**	**-**	**-**	**-**	**-**	**-**	**-**	**-**
Agriculture	-	-	-	-	-	-	-	-	-	-	-
Commerce and Publ. Serv.	-	125	-	-	-	-	-	-	-	-	-
Residential	-	2266	43	6	-	-	-	-	-	-	-
Non-specified	-	-	-	-	-	-	-	-	-	-	-
NON-ENERGY USE	**-**	**173**	**-**	**-**	**-**	**51**	**-**	**-**	**-**	**-**	**-**
in Industry/Transf./Energy	-	173	-	-	-	51	-	-	-	-	-
in Transport	-	-	-	-	-	-	-	-	-	-	-
in Other Sectors	-	-	-	-	-	-	-	-	-	-	-

Industry sector details shown only where sectorial data are available for most countries.
La ventilation du secteur industriel n'est indiquée que s'il existe des données sectorielles disponibles pour la plupart des pays concernés.

North America / Amérique du Nord : 1993

SUPPLY AND CONSUMPTION / APPROVISIONNEMENT ET DEMANDE	Oil cont. / *Pétrole cont.* (1000 tonnes)										
	Refinery Gas / *Gaz de raffinerie*	LPG + Ethane / *GPL + éthane*	Motor Gasoline / *Essence moteur*	Aviation Gasoline / *Essence aviation*	Jet Fuel / *Carbu-réacteur*	Kerosene / *Kérosène*	Gas/Diesel / *Gazole*	Heavy Fuel Oil / *Fioul lourd*	Naphtha / *Naphta*	Pétrol. Coke / *Coke de pétrole*	Other Prod. / *Autres prod.*
Production	37669	21798	360192	962	73643	5719	194807	83919	11902	43391	66291
From Other Sources	-	-	-	-	-	-	-	-	-	-	-
Imports	-	1411	14396	18	3715	143	7667	24296	905	1265	10321
Exports	-	-584	-9117	-10	-3576	-255	-21106	-10281	-429	-17212	-3471
Intl. Marine Bunkers	-	-	-	-	-	-	-7243	-26618	-	-	-
Stock Changes	-3	-1320	-1358	-29	412	178	234	1239	-25	206	138
DOMESTIC SUPPLY	**37666**	**21305**	**364113**	**941**	**74194**	**5785**	**174359**	**72555**	**12353**	**27650**	**73279**
Transfers	-8	51199	5613	10	104	-1819	1591	631	-287	9	-10896
Statistical Differences	-6	199	-161	-9	-43	34	6	-1413	70	75	3
TRANSFORMATION	**-**	**240**	**-**	**-**	**-**	**-**	**2260**	**39778**	**-**	**1105**	**-**
Electricity Plants	-	-	-	-	-	-	2260	39732	-	1105	-
CHP Plants	-	-	-	-	-	-	-	46	-	-	-
Heat Plants	-	-	-	-	-	-	-	-	-	-	-
Transfer to Gases	-	240	-	-	-	-	-	-	-	-	-
Transfer to Solids	-	-	-	-	-	-	-	-	-	-	-
Petroleum Refineries	-	-	-	-	-	-	-	-	-	-	-
Petrochemical Industry	-	-	-	-	-	-	-	-	-	-	-
Liquefaction	-	-	-	-	-	-	-	-	-	-	-
Other Transformation Sector	-	-	-	-	-	-	-	-	-	-	-
ENERGY SECTOR	**36592**	**947**	**97**	**-**	**69**	**2**	**129**	**5916**	**3**	**17395**	**265**
Coal Mines	-	-	-	-	-	-	-	-	-	-	-
Oil and Gas Extraction	-	-	-	-	-	-	-	-	-	756	-
Petroleum Refineries	36592	947	97	-	69	2	129	5916	3	16639	265
Electricity, CHP+Heat plants	-	-	-	-	-	-	-	-	-	-	-
Pumped Storage (Elec.)	-	-	-	-	-	-	-	-	-	-	-
Other Energy Sector	-	-	-	-	-	-	-	-	-	-	-
Distribution Losses	-	-	-	-	-	-	-	-	-	-	-
FINAL CONSUMPTION	**1060**	**71516**	**369468**	**942**	**74186**	**3998**	**173567**	**26079**	**12133**	**9234**	**62121**
INDUSTRY SECTOR	**1060**	**54131**	**2209**	**-**	**-**	**253**	**19527**	**17614**	**12133**	**177**	**1016**
Iron and Steel	-	-	-	-	-	-	-	-	-	-	-
Chemical and Petrochemical	-	-	-	-	-	-	-	-	-	-	-
of which: Feedstocks	-	-	-	-	-	-	-	-	-	-	-
Non-Ferrous Metals	-	-	-	-	-	-	-	-	-	-	-
Non-Metallic Minerals	-	-	-	-	-	-	-	-	-	-	-
Transport Equipment	-	-	-	-	-	-	-	-	-	-	-
Machinery	-	-	-	-	-	-	-	-	-	-	-
Mining and Quarrying	-	-	-	-	-	-	-	-	-	-	-
Food and Tobacco	-	-	-	-	-	-	-	-	-	-	-
Paper, Pulp and Print	-	-	-	-	-	-	-	-	-	-	-
Wood and Wood Products	-	-	-	-	-	-	-	-	-	-	-
Construction	-	-	-	-	-	-	-	-	-	-	-
Textile and Leather	-	-	-	-	-	-	-	-	-	-	-
Non-specified	-	-	-	-	-	-	-	-	-	-	-
TRANSPORT SECTOR	**-**	**1340**	**363169**	**942**	**74186**	**-**	**100400**	**1115**	**-**	**-**	**-**
International Civil Aviation	-	-	-	-	2833	-	-	-	-	-	-
Domestic Air	-	-	-	942	71353	-	-	-	-	-	-
Road	-	1340	359474	-	-	-	84890	-	-	-	-
Rail	-	-	-	-	-	-	12531	-	-	-	-
Pipeline Transport	-	-	-	-	-	-	7	-	-	-	-
Internal Navigation	-	-	3695	-	-	-	828	1115	-	-	-
Non-specified	-	-	-	-	-	-	2144	-	-	-	-
OTHER SECTORS	**-**	**16045**	**4090**	**-**	**-**	**3745**	**53640**	**7350**	**-**	**-**	**-**
Agriculture	-	1642	2261	-	-	189	15130	18	-	-	-
Commerce and Publ. Serv.	-	1660	1829	-	-	447	14147	5053	-	-	-
Residential	-	12104	-	-	-	2226	24060	34	-	-	-
Non-specified	-	639	-	-	-	883	303	2245	-	-	-
NON-ENERGY USE	**-**	**-**	**-**	**-**	**-**	**-**	**-**	**-**	**-**	**9057**	**61105**
in Industry/Transf./Energy	-	-	-	-	-	-	-	-	-	9057	55115
in Transport	-	-	-	-	-	-	-	-	-	-	4933
in Other Sectors	-	-	-	-	-	-	-	-	-	-	1057

North America / Amérique du Nord : 1993

CONSUMPTION *APPROVISIONNEMENT ET DEMANDE*	Gas / *Gaz* (TJ)				Combust. Renew. & Waste / *En. Re. Comb. & Déchets* (TJ)				(GWh)	(TJ)
	Natural Gas *Gaz naturel*	Gas Works *Usines à gaz*	Coke Ovens *Cokeries*	Blast Furnaces *Hauts fourneaux*	Solid Biomass & Anim. Prod. *Biomasse solide & prod. anim.*	Gas/Liquids from Biomass *Gaz/Liquides tirés de biomasse*	Municipal Waste *Déchets urbains*	Industrial Waste *Déchets industriels*	Electricity *Electricité*	Heat *Chaleur*
Production	26445247	-	180878	247765	3945049	134505	240650	173307	4065233	415656
From Other Sources	-	-	-	-	-	-	-	-	-	-
Imports	2603556	-	-	-	-	844	-	-	45352	-
Exports	-2547750	-	-	-	-	-	-	-	-45128	-
Intl. Marine Bunkers	-	-	-	-	-	-	-	-	-	-
Stock Changes	291755	-	-	-	-	1089	-	-	-	-
DOMESTIC SUPPLY	**26792808**	**-**	**180878**	**247765**	**3945049**	**136438**	**240650**	**173307**	**4065457**	**415656**
Transfers	-	-	-	-	-	-82475	-	-	-	-
Statistical Differences	-823280	-	-	-	-616	-2150	-	-	-	-
TRANSFORMATION	**3315926**	**-**	**149190**	**216805**	**1358506**	**51813**	**240650**	**173307**	**-**	**-**
Electricity Plants	3079890	-	6531	9134	189630	31498	197532	47124	-	-
CHP Plants	126349	-	142659	207671	1168876	8828	43118	126183	-	-
Heat Plants	-	-	-	-	-	-	-	-	-	-
Transfer to Gases	-	-	-	-	-	-	-	-	-	-
Transfer to Solids	-	-	-	-	-	-	-	-	-	-
Petroleum Refineries	-	-	-	-	-	11487	-	-	-	-
Petrochemical Industry	-	-	-	-	-	-	-	-	-	-
Liquefaction	97371	-	-	-	-	-	-	-	-	-
Other Transformation Sector	12316	-	-	-	-	-	-	-	-	-
ENERGY SECTOR	**2638367**	**-**	**1694**	**-**	**-**	**-**	**-**	**-**	**351891**	**37514**
Coal Mines	4377	-	-	-	-	-	-	-	14085	-
Oil and Gas Extraction	1540301	-	-	-	-	-	-	-	46614	-
Petroleum Refineries	848212	-	-	-	-	-	-	-	49447	37514
Electricity, CHP+Heat plants	-	-	-	-	-	-	-	-	217921	-
Pumped Storage (Elec.)	-	-	-	-	-	-	-	-	23824	-
Other Energy Sector	245477	-	1694	-	-	-	-	-	-	-
Distribution Losses	-	-	-	-	-	-	-	-	306102	65181
FINAL CONSUMPTION	**20015235**	**-**	**29994**	**30960**	**2585927**	**-**	**-**	**-**	**3407464**	**312961**
INDUSTRY SECTOR	**9489597**	**-**	**29994**	**30960**	**1534914**	**-**	**-**	**-**	**1222349**	**246401**
Iron and Steel	-	-	29994	30960	-	-	-	-	73893	346
Chemical and Petrochemical	-	-	-	-	-	-	-	-	236489	129365
of which: Feedstocks	-	-	-	-	-	-	-	-	-	-
Non-Ferrous Metals	-	-	-	-	-	-	-	-	139367	1493
Non-Metallic Minerals	-	-	-	-	-	-	-	-	37409	359
Transport Equipment	-	-	-	-	-	-	-	-	36152	5204
Machinery	-	-	-	-	-	-	-	-	105674	7096
Mining and Quarrying	-	-	-	-	-	-	-	-	51112	-
Food and Tobacco	-	-	-	-	80633	-	-	-	60070	20030
Paper, Pulp and Print	-	-	-	-	1213298	-	-	-	184050	23261
Wood and Wood Products	-	-	-	-	240983	-	-	-	27917	-
Construction	-	-	-	-	-	-	-	-	365	-
Textile and Leather	-	-	-	-	-	-	-	-	38678	8084
Non-specified	-	-	-	-	-	-	-	-	231173	51163
TRANSPORT SECTOR	**883255**	**-**	**-**	**-**	**-**	**-**	**-**	**-**	**8634**	**-**
International Civil Aviation	-	-	-	-	-	-	-	-	-	-
Domestic Air	-	-	-	-	-	-	-	-	-	-
Road	4046	-	-	-	-	-	-	-	-	-
Rail	-	-	-	-	-	-	-	-	5814	-
Pipeline Transport	879209	-	-	-	-	-	-	-	2820	-
Internal Navigation	-	-	-	-	-	-	-	-	-	-
Non-specified	-	-	-	-	-	-	-	-	-	-
OTHER SECTORS	**9642383**	**-**	**-**	**-**	**1051013**	**-**	**-**	**-**	**2176481**	**66560**
Agriculture	31207	-	-	-	-	-	-	-	15400	180
Commerce and Publ. Serv.	3591320	-	-	-	-	-	-	-	1009313	66380
Residential	6019856	-	-	-	1051013	-	-	-	1151768	-
Non-specified	-	-	-	-	-	-	-	-	-	-
NON-ENERGY USE	**-**	**-**	**-**	**-**	**-**	**-**	**-**	**-**	**-**	**-**
in Industry/Transf./Energy	-	-	-	-	-	-	-	-	-	-
in Transport	-	-	-	-	-	-	-	-	-	-
in Other Sectors	-	-	-	-	-	-	-	-	-	-

Pacific / Pacifique : 1992

SUPPLY AND CONSUMPTION / APPROVISIONNEMENT ET DEMANDE	Coal / Charbon (1000 tonnes)							Oil / Pétrole (1000 tonnes)			
	Coking Coal / Charbon à coke	Steam Coal / Charbon vapeur	Sub-Bit. Coal / Charbon sous-bit.	Lignite / Lignite	Peat / Tourbe	Oven and Gas Coke / Coke de four/gaz	Pat. Fuel and BKB / Agg./briq. de lignite	Crude Oil / Pétrole brut	NGL / LGN	Feedstocks / Produits d'aliment.	Additives / Additifs
Production	71594	94075	19828	50902	-	48749	833	27422	2259	-	-
From Other Sources	-	-	-	-	-	-	-	-	-	4879	132
Imports	64468	44654	-	-	-	-	-	219381	5448	5187	-
Exports	-66219	-57739	-	-	-	-3623	-82	-7921	-	-146	-
Intl. Marine Bunkers	-	-	-	-	-	-	-	-	-	-	-
Stock Changes	462	-1539	300	43	-	183	-85	1061	-	-857	-
DOMESTIC SUPPLY	70305	79451	20128	50945	-	45309	666	239943	7707	9063	132
Transfers	-	-	-	-	-	-	-	-588	-2256	48	-
Statistical Differences	-	-1685	-	1	-	142	-	1888	-15	-1331	-
TRANSFORMATION	70244	58381	15778	50675	-	13888	91	241230	1879	7780	132
Electricity Plants	-	58240	15778	48665	-	-	91	17576	217	-	-
CHP Plants	-	-	-	-	-	-	-	-	-	-	-
Heat Plants	-	29	-	-	-	-	-	-	-	-	-
Transfer to Gases	1042	-	-	-	-	13888	-	-	-	-	-
Transfer to Solids	69202	112	-	2010	-	-	-	-	-	-	-
Petroleum Refineries	-	-	-	-	-	-	-	224813	1662	7780	132
Petrochemical Industry	-	-	-	-	-	-	-	-	-	-	-
Liquefaction	-	-	-	-	-	-	-	-1159	-	-	-
Other Transformation Sector	-	-	-	-	-	-	-	-	-	-	-
ENERGY SECTOR	-	219	-	-	-	110	-	2	-	-	-
Coal Mines	-	219	-	-	-	-	-	-	-	-	-
Oil and Gas Extraction	-	-	-	-	-	-	-	2	-	-	-
Petroleum Refineries	-	-	-	-	-	-	-	-	-	-	-
Electricity, CHP+Heat plants	-	-	-	-	-	-	-	-	-	-	-
Pumped Storage (Elec.)	-	-	-	-	-	-	-	-	-	-	-
Other Energy Sector	-	-	-	-	-	110	-	-	-	-	-
Distribution Losses	-	-	-	-	-	-	-	-	-	-	-
FINAL CONSUMPTION	61	19166	4350	271	-	31453	575	11	3557	-	-
INDUSTRY SECTOR	61	18958	4051	164	-	31292	373	11	3557	-	-
Iron and Steel	-	2290	698	-	-	27547	-	-	-	-	-
Chemical and Petrochemical	61	2663	-	-	-	125	148	11	3557	-	-
of which: Feedstocks	-	-	-	-	-	-	-	-	3557	-	-
Non-Ferrous Metals	-	495	1961	-	-	474	-	-	-	-	-
Non-Metallic Minerals	-	9817	186	2	-	306	8	-	-	-	-
Transport Equipment	-	-	-	-	-	-	2	-	-	-	-
Machinery	-	1	-	-	-	-	-	-	-	-	-
Mining and Quarrying	-	14	310	-	-	10	-	-	-	-	-
Food and Tobacco	-	418	3	-	-	-	150	-	-	-	-
Paper, Pulp and Print	-	2219	-	-	-	-	39	-	-	-	-
Wood and Wood Products	-	20	-	46	-	-	-	-	-	-	-
Construction	-	-	-	-	-	-	-	-	-	-	-
Textile and Leather	-	21	-	-	-	-	26	-	-	-	-
Non-specified	-	1000	893	116	-	2830	-	-	-	-	-
TRANSPORT SECTOR	-	1	192	-	-	-	-	-	-	-	-
International Civil Aviation	-	-	-	-	-	-	-	-	-	-	-
Domestic Air	-	-	-	-	-	-	-	-	-	-	-
Road	-	-	-	-	-	-	-	-	-	-	-
Rail	-	1	-	-	-	-	-	-	-	-	-
Pipeline Transport	-	-	-	-	-	-	-	-	-	-	-
Internal Navigation	-	-	192	-	-	-	-	-	-	-	-
Non-specified	-	-	-	-	-	-	-	-	-	-	-
OTHER SECTORS	-	207	107	107	-	-	202	-	-	-	-
Agriculture	-	2	13	-	-	-	-	-	-	-	-
Commerce and Publ. Serv.	-	110	70	-	-	-	82	-	-	-	-
Residential	-	95	24	45	-	-	120	-	-	-	-
Non-specified	-	-	-	62	-	-	-	-	-	-	-
NON-ENERGY USE	-	-	-	-	-	161	-	-	-	-	-
in Industry/Transf./Energy	-	-	-	-	-	161	-	-	-	-	-
in Transport	-	-	-	-	-	-	-	-	-	-	-
in Other Sectors	-	-	-	-	-	-	-	-	-	-	-

Pacific / Pacifique : 1992

SUPPLY AND CONSUMPTION *APPROVISIONNEMENT ET DEMANDE*	Oil cont. / *Pétrole cont.* (1000 tonnes)										
	Refinery Gas *Gaz de raffinerie*	LPG + Ethane *GPL + éthane*	Motor Gasoline *Essence moteur*	Aviation Gasoline *Essence aviation*	Jet Fuel *Carbu-réacteur*	Kerosene *Kérosène*	Gas/Diesel *Gazole*	Heavy Fuel Oil *Fioul lourd*	Naphtha *Naphta*	Pétrol. Coke *Coke de pétrole*	Other Prod. *Autres prod.*
Production	9038	5364	48444	108	8451	21398	66984	46548	11992	816	12610
From Other Sources	-	-	-	-	-	-	-	-	-	-	-
Imports	-	15311	1196	15	3242	1916	2948	7820	15238	4886	419
Exports	-	-897	-581	-112	-366	-529	-2668	-3423	-461	-96	-925
Intl. Marine Bunkers	-	-	-	-	-	-	-550	-6174	-	-	-49
Stock Changes	-	-264	-120	18	-38	274	447	320	237	-1	-214
DOMESTIC SUPPLY	**9038**	**19514**	**48939**	**29**	**11289**	**23059**	**67161**	**45091**	**27006**	**5605**	**11841**
Transfers	-	2256	59	-	-5	4	1	20	-	-	461
Statistical Differences	-51	82	34	70	-326	-485	142	-760	-199	-48	588
TRANSFORMATION	**214**	**3911**	**-**	**-**	**-**	**12**	**1064**	**26859**	**5651**	**1737**	**812**
Electricity Plants	-	993	-	-	-	-	1064	26817	909	908	812
CHP Plants	-	-	-	-	-	-	-	-	-	-	-
Heat Plants	-	6	-	-	-	12	-	18	-	-	-
Transfer to Gases	214	2512	-	-	-	-	-	-	263	-	-
Transfer to Solids	-	-	-	-	-	-	-	24	-	829	-
Petroleum Refineries	-	-	-	-	-	-	-	-	-	-	-
Petrochemical Industry	-	400	-	-	-	-	-	-	4479	-	-
Liquefaction	-	-	-	-	-	-	-	-	-	-	-
Other Transformation Sector	-	-	-	-	-	-	-	-	-	-	-
ENERGY SECTOR	**8765**	**44**	**-**	**-**	**-**	**7**	**365**	**2540**	**105**	**550**	**110**
Coal Mines	-	-	-	-	-	-	296	1	-	-	-
Oil and Gas Extraction	-	37	-	-	-	-	5	-	-	-	-
Petroleum Refineries	8765	6	-	-	-	7	26	2383	105	550	110
Electricity, CHP+Heat plants	-	1	-	-	-	-	38	156	-	-	-
Pumped Storage (Elec.)	-	-	-	-	-	-	-	-	-	-	-
Other Energy Sector	-	-	-	-	-	-	-	-	-	-	-
Distribution Losses	-	-	-	-	-	-	-	-	-	-	-
FINAL CONSUMPTION	**8**	**17897**	**49032**	**99**	**10958**	**22559**	**65875**	**14952**	**21051**	**3270**	**11968**
INDUSTRY SECTOR	**8**	**7232**	**29**	**-**	**-**	**4804**	**15734**	**8304**	**21051**	**2602**	**19**
Iron and Steel	-	632	2	-	-	288	629	930	-	108	-
Chemical and Petrochemical	8	2599	-	-	-	260	1300	717	20903	601	1
of which: Feedstocks	-	2570	-	-	-	-	-	-	20903	-	-
Non-Ferrous Metals	-	238	-	-	-	164	791	1101	18	62	4
Non-Metallic Minerals	-	224	-	-	-	97	891	1618	-	446	13
Transport Equipment	-	4	-	-	-	-	2	-	-	-	-
Machinery	-	449	-	-	-	362	885	7	-	-	-
Mining and Quarrying	-	3	-	-	-	29	898	93	-	-	1
Food and Tobacco	-	61	2	-	-	-	1713	525	-	-	-
Paper, Pulp and Print	-	68	-	-	-	33	281	1882	-	159	-
Wood and Wood Products	-	4	-	-	-	-	19	16	-	-	-
Construction	-	1	3	-	-	1010	4552	11	-	-	-
Textile and Leather	-	129	-	-	-	15	685	971	-	30	-
Non-specified	-	2820	22	-	-	2546	3088	433	130	1196	-
TRANSPORT SECTOR	**-**	**2923**	**48916**	**90**	**10955**	**3**	**37526**	**2160**	**-**	**-**	**-**
International Civil Aviation	-	-	-	-	6432	-	-	-	-	-	-
Domestic Air	-	-	-	90	4523	-	1	-	-	-	-
Road	-	2923	48916	-	-	3	30104	49	-	-	-
Rail	-	-	-	-	-	-	1081	-	-	-	-
Pipeline Transport	-	-	-	-	-	-	-	-	-	-	-
Internal Navigation	-	-	-	-	-	-	5689	2006	-	-	-
Non-specified	-	-	-	-	-	-	651	105	-	-	-
OTHER SECTORS	**-**	**7742**	**87**	**9**	**3**	**17752**	**12615**	**4488**	**-**	**-**	**-**
Agriculture	-	18	55	3	-	2767	4948	102	-	-	-
Commerce and Publ. Serv.	-	1836	31	6	3	4181	7614	4386	-	-	-
Residential	-	5888	1	-	-	10804	53	-	-	-	-
Non-specified	-	-	-	-	-	-	-	-	-	-	-
NON-ENERGY USE	**-**	**-**	**-**	**-**	**-**	**-**	**-**	**-**	**-**	**668**	**11949**
in Industry/Transf./Energy	-	-	-	-	-	-	-	-	-	668	11003
in Transport	-	-	-	-	-	-	-	-	-	-	223
in Other Sectors	-	-	-	-	-	-	-	-	-	-	723

Pacific / Pacifique : 1992

Column groups: Gas / *Gaz* (TJ) — Natural Gas, Gas Works, Coke Ovens, Blast Furnaces. Combust. Renew. & Waste / *En. Re. Comb. & Déchets* (TJ) — Solid Biomass & Anim. Prod., Gas/Liquids from Biomass, Municipal Waste, Industrial Waste. Electricity (GWh). Heat (TJ).

CONSUMPTION / *APPROVISIONNEMENT ET DEMANDE*	Natural Gas / *Gaz naturel*	Gas Works / *Usines à gaz*	Coke Ovens / *Cokeries*	Blast Furnaces / *Hauts fourneaux*	Solid Biomass & Anim. Prod. / *Biomasse solide & prod. anim.*	Gas/Liquids from Biomass / *Gaz/Liquides tirés de biomasse*	Municipal Waste / *Déchets urbains*	Industrial Waste / *Déchets industriels*	Electricity / *Electricité* (GWh)	Heat / *Chaleur* (TJ)
Production	1201277	587135	315732	372557	276119	59	13666	7920	1086209	13680
From Other Sources	-	173982	-	-	-	-	-	-	-	-
Imports	2124285	-	-	-	-	-	-	-	-	-
Exports	-235400	-	-	-	-	-	-	-	-	-
Intl. Marine Bunkers	-	-	-	-	-	-	-	-	-	-
Stock Changes	-13514	-	-	-	-	-	-	-	-	-
DOMESTIC SUPPLY	**3076648**	**761117**	**315732**	**372557**	**276119**	**59**	**13666**	**7920**	**1086209**	**13680**
Transfers	-	-	-	-	-	-	-	-	-	-
Statistical Differences	33468	1657	-21678	37661	-	-	-	-	-	-
TRANSFORMATION	**2471444**	**-**	**82070**	**189647**	**78567**	**59**	**13389**	**350**	**1019**	**-**
Electricity Plants	1791974	-	75156	189647	78567	59	13389	350	-	-
CHP Plants	-	-	-	-	-	-	-	-	-	-
Heat Plants	8402	-	-	-	-	-	-	-	-	-
Transfer to Gases	586109	-	6914	-	-	-	-	-	1019	-
Transfer to Solids	-	-	-	-	-	-	-	-	-	-
Petroleum Refineries	-	-	-	-	-	-	-	-	-	-
Petrochemical Industry	-	-	-	-	-	-	-	-	-	-
Liquefaction	84959	-	-	-	-	-	-	-	-	-
Other Transformation Sector	-	-	-	-	-	-	-	-	-	-
ENERGY SECTOR	**117948**	**16932**	**40817**	**59113**	**-**	**-**	**-**	**-**	**87094**	**262**
Coal Mines	-	-	-	-	-	-	-	-	216	-
Oil and Gas Extraction	106791	-	-	-	-	-	-	-	3835	-
Petroleum Refineries	11157	-	-	-	-	-	-	-	944	-
Electricity, CHP+Heat plants	-	-	-	-	-	-	-	-	8244	-
Pumped Storage (Elec.)	-	-	-	-	-	-	-	-	62090	262
Other Energy Sector	-	16932	40817	59113	-	-	-	-	11765	-
Distribution Losses	-	8642	-	-	-	-	-	-	47221	2675
FINAL CONSUMPTION	**520724**	**737200**	**171167**	**161458**	**197552**	**-**	**277**	**7570**	**950875**	**10743**
INDUSTRY SECTOR	**368869**	**220769**	**171167**	**161458**	**117378**	**-**	**-**	**7570**	**511419**	**-**
Iron and Steel	52107	-	169401	161458	147	-	-	-	85029	-
Chemical and Petrochemical	70227	5682	-	-	-	-	-	-	60940	-
of which: Feedstocks	17029	-	-	-	-	-	-	7537	-	-
Non-Ferrous Metals	99931	-	-	-	1789	-	-	-	41818	-
Non-Metallic Minerals	50620	-	-	-	736	-	-	-	22738	-
Transport Equipment	6298	6	-	-	-	-	-	-	26727	-
Machinery	6902	2	-	-	-	-	-	-	38660	-
Mining and Quarrying	1199	-	1766	-	-	-	-	-	8072	-
Food and Tobacco	25199	93	-	-	63587	-	-	-	19325	-
Paper, Pulp and Print	17219	-	-	-	7763	-	-	33	38077	-
Wood and Wood Products	1258	-	-	-	22256	-	-	-	1407	-
Construction	244	-	-	-	-	-	-	-	108	-
Textile and Leather	6289	-	-	-	21100	-	-	-	9464	-
Non-specified	31376	214986	-	-	-	-	-	-	159054	-
TRANSPORT SECTOR	**8163**	**-**	**-**	**-**	**-**	**-**	**-**	**-**	**22713**	**-**
International Civil Aviation	-	-	-	-	-	-	-	-	-	-
Domestic Air	-	-	-	-	-	-	-	-	-	-
Road	3069	-	-	-	-	-	-	-	-	-
Rail	-	-	-	-	-	-	-	-	22460	-
Pipeline Transport	4584	-	-	-	-	-	-	-	3	-
Internal Navigation	-	-	-	-	-	-	-	-	-	-
Non-specified	510	-	-	-	-	-	-	-	250	-
OTHER SECTORS	**143282**	**516431**	**-**	**-**	**80174**	**-**	**277**	**-**	**416743**	**10743**
Agriculture	52	-	-	-	-	-	-	-	-	-
Commerce and Publ. Serv.	42259	115677	-	-	701	-	-	-	4920	-
Residential	97430	400754	-	-	79473	-	277	-	163298	9380
Non-specified	3541	-	-	-	-	-	-	-	248525	1363
NON-ENERGY USE	**410**	**-**	**-**	**-**	**-**	**-**	**-**	**-**	**-**	**-**
in Industry/Transf./Energy	410	-	-	-	-	-	-	-	-	-
in Transport	-	-	-	-	-	-	-	-	-	-
in Other Sectors	-	-	-	-	-	-	-	-	-	-

Pacific / Pacifique : 1993

SUPPLY AND CONSUMPTION	Coal / *Charbon* (1000 tonnes)							Oil / *Pétrole* (1000 tonnes)			
	Coking Coal	Steam Coal	Sub-Bit. Coal	Lignite	Peat	Oven and Gas Coke	Pat. Fuel and BKB	Crude Oil	NGL	Feedstocks	Additives
APPROVISIONNEMENT ET DEMANDE	*Charbon à coke*	*Charbon vapeur*	*Charbon sous-bit.*	*Lignite*	*Tourbe*	*Coke de four/gaz*	*Agg./briq. de lignite*	*Pétrole brut*	*LGN*	*Produits d'aliment.*	*Additifs*
Production	79118	87806	19745	47824	-	47916	629	27058	2400	-	-
From Other Sources	-	-	-	-	-	-	-	-	-	4863	131
Imports	64972	46433	-	-	-	-	-	226033	5021	6242	-
Exports	-73199	-55986	-7	-	-	-3476	-61	-8857	-	-286	-
Intl. Marine Bunkers	-	-	-	-	-	-	-	-	-	-	-
Stock Changes	-238	3993	212	53	-	582	50	-2354	-	164	-
DOMESTIC SUPPLY	**70653**	**82246**	**19950**	**47877**	**-**	**45022**	**618**	**241880**	**7421**	**10983**	**131**
Transfers	-	-	-	-	-	-	-	-636	-2375	-	-
Statistical Differences	-	-1277	-	1	-	-1	-	1264	-37	-2373	-
TRANSFORMATION	**70650**	**64317**	**15498**	**47597**	**-**	**14017**	**65**	**242494**	**2176**	**8610**	**131**
Electricity Plants	-	64142	15498	46333	-	-	65	13564	214	-	-
CHP Plants	-	-	-	-	-	-	-	-	-	-	-
Heat Plants	-	47	-	-	-	-	-	-	-	-	-
Transfer to Gases	1005	15	-	-	-	14017	-	-	-	-	-
Transfer to Solids	69645	113	-	1264	-	-	-	-	-	-	-
Petroleum Refineries	-	-	-	-	-	-	-	230040	1962	8610	131
Petrochemical Industry	-	-	-	-	-	-	-	-	-	-	-
Liquefaction	-	-	-	-	-	-	-	-1110	-	-	-
Other Transformation Sector	-	-	-	-	-	-	-	-	-	-	-
ENERGY SECTOR	**-**	**199**	**-**	**-**	**-**	**104**	**-**	**4**	**-**	**-**	**-**
Coal Mines	-	199	-	-	-	-	-	-	-	-	-
Oil and Gas Extraction	-	-	-	-	-	-	-	4	-	-	-
Petroleum Refineries	-	-	-	-	-	-	-	-	-	-	-
Electricity, CHP+Heat plants	-	-	-	-	-	-	-	-	-	-	-
Pumped Storage (Elec.)	-	-	-	-	-	-	-	-	-	-	-
Other Energy Sector	-	-	-	-	-	104	-	-	-	-	-
Distribution Losses	-	-	-	-	-	-	-	-	-	-	-
FINAL CONSUMPTION	**3**	**16453**	**4452**	**281**	**-**	**30900**	**553**	**10**	**2833**	**-**	**-**
INDUSTRY SECTOR	**3**	**16272**	**3983**	**170**	**-**	**30742**	**356**	**10**	**2833**	**-**	**-**
Iron and Steel	-	2128	725	-	-	27246	-	-	-	-	-
Chemical and Petrochemical	3	1730	-	-	-	118	134	10	2833	-	-
of which: Feedstocks	-	-	-	-	-	-	-	-	*2833*	-	-
Non-Ferrous Metals	-	494	2030	-	-	419	-	-	-	-	-
Non-Metallic Minerals	-	9225	233	2	-	294	6	-	-	-	-
Transport Equipment	-	-	-	-	-	-	2	-	-	-	-
Machinery	-	-	-	-	-	-	-	-	-	-	-
Mining and Quarrying	-	16	305	-	-	8	-	-	-	-	-
Food and Tobacco	-	384	3	-	-	-	157	-	-	-	-
Paper, Pulp and Print	-	2017	-	-	-	-	32	-	-	-	-
Wood and Wood Products	-	22	-	49	-	-	-	-	-	-	-
Construction	-	-	-	-	-	-	-	-	-	-	-
Textile and Leather	-	23	-	-	-	-	25	-	-	-	-
Non-specified	-	233	687	119	-	2657	-	-	-	-	-
TRANSPORT SECTOR	**-**	**1**	**198**	**-**	**-**	**-**	**-**	**-**	**-**	**-**	**-**
International Civil Aviation	-	-	-	-	-	-	-	-	-	-	-
Domestic Air	-	-	-	-	-	-	-	-	-	-	-
Road	-	-	-	-	-	-	-	-	-	-	-
Rail	-	1	-	-	-	-	-	-	-	-	-
Pipeline Transport	-	-	-	-	-	-	-	-	-	-	-
Internal Navigation	-	-	198	-	-	-	-	-	-	-	-
Non-specified	-	-	-	-	-	-	-	-	-	-	-
OTHER SECTORS	**-**	**180**	**271**	**111**	**-**	**-**	**197**	**-**	**-**	**-**	**-**
Agriculture	-	3	12	-	-	-	-	-	-	-	-
Commerce and Publ. Serv.	-	88	-	-	-	-	77	-	-	-	-
Residential	-	78	7	70	-	-	120	-	-	-	-
Non-specified	-	11	252	41	-	-	-	-	-	-	-
NON-ENERGY USE	**-**	**-**	**-**	**-**	**-**	**158**	**-**	**-**	**-**	**-**	**-**
in Industry/Transf./Energy	-	-	-	-	-	158	-	-	-	-	-
in Transport	-	-	-	-	-	-	-	-	-	-	-
in Other Sectors	-	-	-	-	-	-	-	-	-	-	-

Pacific / Pacifique : 1993

SUPPLY AND CONSUMPTION / APPROVISIONNEMENT ET DEMANDE	Oil cont. / *Pétrole cont.* (1000 tonnes)										
	Refinery Gas / *Gaz de raffinerie*	LPG + Ethane / *GPL + éthane*	Motor Gasoline / *Essence moteur*	Aviation Gasoline / *Essence aviation*	Jet Fuel / *Carbu-réacteur*	Kerosene / *Kérosène*	Gas/ Diesel / *Gazole*	Heavy Fuel Oil / *Fioul lourd*	Naphtha / *Naphta*	Pétrol. Coke / *Coke de pétrole*	Other Prod. / *Autres prod.*
Production	9268	5373	50124	133	9123	22188	68712	46507	13054	1109	12836
From Other Sources	-	-	-	-	-	-	-	-	-	-	-
Imports	-	15294	1036	19	2764	1684	2761	5496	14212	5468	262
Exports	-	-850	-1091	-49	-483	-305	-2712	-3863	-163	-112	-1083
Intl. Marine Bunkers	-	-	-	-	-	-	-594	-7147	-	-	-32
Stock Changes	-	106	-46	-3	-51	120	-217	-161	69	-16	-32
DOMESTIC SUPPLY	**9268**	**19923**	**50023**	**100**	**11353**	**23687**	**67950**	**40832**	**27172**	**6449**	**11951**
Transfers	-	2375	94	-	-5	4	2	1	-	-	540
Statistical Differences	-35	-34	-458	-8	31	-679	305	-632	-196	-244	580
TRANSFORMATION	**248**	**3808**	**-**	**-**	**-**	**11**	**1056**	**25026**	**5616**	**1714**	**838**
Electricity Plants	-	813	-	-	-	-	1056	24989	886	853	838
CHP Plants	-	-	-	-	-	-	-	-	-	-	-
Heat Plants	-	6	-	-	-	11	-	18	-	-	-
Transfer to Gases	248	2581	-	-	-	-	-	-	275	-	-
Transfer to Solids	-	-	-	-	-	-	-	19	-	861	-
Petroleum Refineries	-	-	-	-	-	-	-	-	-	-	-
Petrochemical Industry	-	408	-	-	-	-	-	-	4455	-	-
Liquefaction	-	-	-	-	-	-	-	-	-	-	-
Other Transformation Sector	-	-	-	-	-	-	-	-	-	-	-
ENERGY SECTOR	**8977**	**43**	**-**	**-**	**-**	**10**	**400**	**2699**	**83**	**536**	**108**
Coal Mines	-	-	-	-	-	-	308	1	-	-	-
Oil and Gas Extraction	-	31	-	-	-	-	6	-	-	-	-
Petroleum Refineries	8977	11	-	-	-	10	53	2546	83	536	108
Electricity, CHP+Heat plants	-	1	-	-	-	-	33	152	-	-	-
Pumped Storage (Elec.)	-	-	-	-	-	-	-	-	-	-	-
Other Energy Sector	-	-	-	-	-	-	-	-	-	-	-
Distribution Losses	-	-	-	-	-	-	-	-	-	-	-
FINAL CONSUMPTION	**8**	**18413**	**49659**	**92**	**11379**	**22991**	**66801**	**12476**	**21277**	**3955**	**12125**
INDUSTRY SECTOR	**8**	**8190**	**11**	**-**	**-**	**4388**	**16061**	**8336**	**21277**	**3258**	**27**
Iron and Steel	-	605	1	-	-	302	536	940	-	163	-
Chemical and Petrochemical	8	2688	-	-	-	252	984	953	21159	689	-
of which: Feedstocks	-	2657	-	-	-	-	-	-	21159	-	-
Non-Ferrous Metals	-	240	-	-	-	159	887	1041	19	60	6
Non-Metallic Minerals	-	223	-	-	-	93	886	1526	-	761	19
Transport Equipment	-	4	-	-	-	-	2	-	-	-	-
Machinery	-	440	-	-	-	346	809	7	-	-	-
Mining and Quarrying	-	3	-	-	-	44	958	110	-	-	2
Food and Tobacco	-	69	1	-	-	-	1786	486	-	-	-
Paper, Pulp and Print	-	68	-	-	-	58	395	2014	-	147	-
Wood and Wood Products	-	5	-	-	-	-	20	17	-	-	-
Construction	-	1	6	-	-	991	4904	10	-	-	-
Textile and Leather	-	128	-	-	-	13	810	1085	-	30	-
Non-specified	-	3716	3	-	-	2130	3084	147	99	1408	-
TRANSPORT SECTOR	**-**	**2360**	**49579**	**90**	**11371**	**2**	**37523**	**2478**	**-**	**-**	**-**
International Civil Aviation	-	-	-	-	6591	-	-	-	-	-	-
Domestic Air	-	-	-	90	4780	-	1	-	-	-	-
Road	-	2360	49579	-	-	2	30526	41	-	-	-
Rail	-	-	-	-	-	-	1028	-	-	-	-
Pipeline Transport	-	-	-	-	-	-	-	-	-	-	-
Internal Navigation	-	-	-	-	-	-	5220	2290	-	-	-
Non-specified	-	-	-	-	-	-	748	147	-	-	-
OTHER SECTORS	**-**	**7863**	**69**	**2**	**8**	**18601**	**13217**	**1662**	**-**	**-**	**-**
Agriculture	-	19	51	2	1	2708	5323	77	-	-	-
Commerce and Publ. Serv.	-	1861	17	-	7	4483	7840	1585	-	-	-
Residential	-	5983	1	-	-	11410	54	-	-	-	-
Non-specified	-	-	-	-	-	-	-	-	-	-	-
NON-ENERGY USE	**-**	**-**	**-**	**-**	**-**	**-**	**-**	**-**	**-**	**697**	**12098**
in Industry/Transf./Energy	-	-	-	-	-	-	-	-	-	697	11290
in Transport	-	-	-	-	-	-	-	-	-	-	214
in Other Sectors	-	-	-	-	-	-	-	-	-	-	594

Pacific / Pacifique : 1993

CONSUMPTION / APPROVISIONNEMENT ET DEMANDE	Gas / Gaz (TJ)				Combust. Renew. & Waste / En. Re. Comb. & Déchets (TJ)				(GWh)	(TJ)
	Natural Gas / Gaz naturel	Gas Works / Usines à gaz	Coke Ovens / Cokeries	Blast Furnaces / Hauts fourneaux	Solid Biomass & Anim. Prod. / Biomasse solide & prod. anim.	Gas/Liquids from Biomass / Gaz/Liquides tirés de biomasse	Municipal Waste / Déchets urbains	Industrial Waste / Déchets industriels	Electricity / Electricité	Heat / Chaleur
Production	1265539	575299	312958	426897	292753	54	14424	8785	1104080	14498
From Other Sources	-	235687	-	-	-	-	-	-	-	-
Imports	2134762	-	-	-	-	-	-	-	-	-
Exports	-276600	-	-	-	-	-	-	-	-	-
Intl. Marine Bunkers	-	-	-	-	-	-	-	-	-	-
Stock Changes	-7393	-	-	-	-	-	-	-	-	-
DOMESTIC SUPPLY	**3116308**	**810986**	**312958**	**426897**	**292753**	**54**	**14424**	**8785**	**1104080**	**14498**
Transfers	-	-	-	-	-	-	-	-	-	-
Statistical Differences	26303	-245	-20247	-2910	-	-	-	-	-	-
TRANSFORMATION	**2480553**	**-**	**89406**	**206566**	**77042**	**54**	**14184**	**350**	**990**	**-**
Electricity Plants	1763245	-	82001	206566	77042	54	14184	350	-	-
CHP Plants	-	-	-	-	-	-	-	-	-	-
Heat Plants	9252	-	-	-	-	-	-	-	990	-
Transfer to Gases	623119	-	7405	-	-	-	-	-	-	-
Transfer to Solids	-	-	-	-	-	-	-	-	-	-
Petroleum Refineries	-	-	-	-	-	-	-	-	-	-
Petrochemical Industry	-	-	-	-	-	-	-	-	-	-
Liquefaction	84937	-	-	-	-	-	-	-	-	-
Other Transformation Sector	-	-	-	-	-	-	-	-	-	-
ENERGY SECTOR	**131418**	**15826**	**37778**	**60821**	**-**	**-**	**-**	**-**	**91876**	**106**
Coal Mines	-	-	-	-	-	-	-	-	4009	-
Oil and Gas Extraction	120120	-	-	-	-	-	-	-	935	-
Petroleum Refineries	11298	-	-	-	-	-	-	-	8791	-
Electricity, CHP+Heat plants	-	-	-	-	-	-	-	-	61961	106
Pumped Storage (Elec.)	-	-	-	-	-	-	-	-	15964	-
Other Energy Sector	-	15826	37778	60821	-	-	-	-	216	-
Distribution Losses	-	8968	-	-	-	-	-	-	47928	2490
FINAL CONSUMPTION	**530640**	**785947**	**165527**	**156600**	**215711**	**-**	**240**	**8435**	**963286**	**11902**
INDUSTRY SECTOR	**372202**	**247626**	**165527**	**156600**	**132292**	**-**	**-**	**8435**	**509752**	**-**
Iron and Steel	52727	-	163583	156600	58	-	-	-	84840	-
Chemical and Petrochemical	67911	7018	-	-	-	-	-	8392	60058	-
of which: Feedstocks	*16398*	-	-	-	-	-	-	-	-	-
Non-Ferrous Metals	104101	-	-	-	1855	-	-	-	42700	-
Non-Metallic Minerals	50976	-	-	-	671	-	-	-	22318	-
Transport Equipment	5931	6	-	-	-	-	-	-	25505	-
Machinery	7125	4	-	-	-	-	-	-	38929	-
Mining and Quarrying	1121	-	1944	-	-	-	-	-	8125	-
Food and Tobacco	25615	37	-	-	77275	-	-	43	19945	-
Paper, Pulp and Print	18031	-	-	-	8583	-	-	-	37953	-
Wood and Wood Products	1121	-	-	-	22450	-	-	-	1451	-
Construction	247	-	-	-	-	-	-	-	52	-
Textile and Leather	6770	-	-	-	21400	-	-	-	8713	-
Non-specified	30526	240561	-	-	-	-	-	-	159163	-
TRANSPORT SECTOR	**9078**	**-**	**-**	**-**	**-**	**-**	**-**	**-**	**22897**	**-**
International Civil Aviation	-	-	-	-	-	-	-	-	-	-
Domestic Air	-	-	-	-	-	-	-	-	-	-
Road	3155	-	-	-	-	-	-	-	22633	-
Rail	-	-	-	-	-	-	-	-	3	-
Pipeline Transport	5395	-	-	-	-	-	-	-	-	-
Internal Navigation	-	-	-	-	-	-	-	-	-	-
Non-specified	528	-	-	-	-	-	-	-	261	-
OTHER SECTORS	**148893**	**538321**	**-**	**-**	**83419**	**-**	**240**	**-**	**430637**	**11902**
Agriculture	53	-	-	-	-	-	-	-	4842	-
Commerce and Publ. Serv.	43973	120950	-	-	691	-	240	-	169928	10519
Residential	102079	417371	-	-	82728	-	-	-	255867	1383
Non-specified	2788	-	-	-	-	-	-	-	-	-
NON-ENERGY USE	**467**	**-**	**-**	**-**	**-**	**-**	**-**	**-**	**-**	**-**
in Industry/Transf./Energy	467	-	-	-	-	-	-	-	-	-
in Transport	-	-	-	-	-	-	-	-	-	-
in Other Sectors	-	-	-	-	-	-	-	-	-	-

OECD Europe / OCDE Europe : 1992

SUPPLY AND CONSUMPTION / APPROVISIONNEMENT ET DEMANDE	Coal / Charbon (1000 tonnes)							Oil / Pétrole (1000 tonnes)			
	Coking Coal / Charbon à coke	Steam Coal / Charbon vapeur	Sub-Bit. Coal / Charbon sous-bit.	Lignite / Lignite	Peat / Tourbe	Oven and Gas Coke / Coke de four/gaz	Pat. Fuel and BKB / Agg./briq. de lignite	Crude Oil / Pétrole brut	NGL / LGN	Feedstocks / Produits d'aliment.	Additives / Additifs
Production	42471	141421	4336	364093	12607	51613	19227	222075	8792	-	144
From Other Sources	-	1350	979	-	-	-	-	103	-	10290	1658
Imports	47875	110045	-	4096	7	7770	954	521759	3255	37029	192
Exports	-714	-5514	-14	-24	-338	-4201	-931	-152235	-3549	-4954	-
Intl. Marine Bunkers	-	-	-	-	-	-	-	-	-	-	-
Stock Changes	-3023	-9844	544	2652	2233	-1359	150	-5969	-51	73	-20
DOMESTIC SUPPLY	**86609**	**237458**	**5845**	**370817**	**14509**	**53823**	**19400**	**585733**	**8447**	**42438**	**1974**
Transfers	-	-	-	-	-	-	-	-1291	-3244	28410	-
Statistical Differences	-279	877	-32	-2	-	123	-7	635	22	-498	-21
TRANSFORMATION	**84212**	**194170**	**5315**	**342088**	**9319**	**16444**	**2682**	**584849**	**5225**	**70350**	**1953**
Electricity Plants	16996	167811	5235	297978	4138	-	1499	-	-	-	-
CHP Plants	-	21930	80	-	3351	-	-	-	-	-	-
Heat Plants	-	1387	-	2603	784	5	554	-	-	-	-
Transfer to Gases	81	581	-	-	-	16212	392	-	-	-	-
Transfer to Solids	67135	2461	-	41507	1046	227	237	-	-	-	-
Petroleum Refineries	-	-	-	-	-	-	-	584849	5225	70350	1953
Petrochemical Industry	-	-	-	-	-	-	-	-	-	-	-
Liquefaction	-	-	-	-	-	-	-	-	-	-	-
Other Transformation Sector	-	-	-	-	-	-	-	-	-	-	-
ENERGY SECTOR	**60**	**292**	**33**	**1749**	**-**	**253**	**277**	**208**	**-**	**-**	**-**
Coal Mines	-	280	33	2	-	-	-	-	-	-	-
Oil and Gas Extraction	-	-	-	-	-	-	-	208	-	-	-
Petroleum Refineries	-	-	-	146	-	-	36	-	-	-	-
Electricity, CHP+Heat plants	-	-	-	-	-	-	-	-	-	-	-
Pumped Storage (Elec.)	-	-	-	-	-	-	-	-	-	-	-
Other Energy Sector	60	12	-	1601	-	253	241	-	-	-	-
Distribution Losses	14	-	-	-	-	7	-	-	-	-	-
FINAL CONSUMPTION	**2044**	**43873**	**465**	**26978**	**5190**	**37242**	**16434**	**20**	**-**	**-**	**-**
INDUSTRY SECTOR	**1299**	**32880**	**284**	**16291**	**3435**	**32687**	**4041**	**20**	**-**	**-**	**-**
Iron and Steel	805	6117	-	21	-	29296	-	-	-	-	-
Chemical and Petrochemical	-	4539	4	394	7	476	-	20	-	-	-
of which: Feedstocks	-	-	-	-	-	-	-	-	-	-	-
Non-Ferrous Metals	1	576	-	394	-	778	1	-	-	-	-
Non-Metallic Minerals	12	12929	257	313	-	587	-	-	-	-	-
Transport Equipment	-	381	-	-	-	42	-	-	-	-	-
Machinery	4	455	-	59	-	811	-	-	-	-	-
Mining and Quarrying	-	332	-	3	-	12	-	-	-	-	-
Food and Tobacco	121	1766	-	1570	-	291	-	-	-	-	-
Paper, Pulp and Print	-	1905	-	193	30	43	18	-	-	-	-
Wood and Wood Products	-	96	-	-	-	1	5	-	-	-	-
Construction	272	1057	16	1192	-	7	-	-	-	-	-
Textile and Leather	-	552	-	238	-	5	-	-	-	-	-
Non-specified	84	2175	7	11914	3398	338	4017	-	-	-	-
TRANSPORT SECTOR	**15**	**27**	**-**	**4**	**-**	**5**	**-**	**-**	**-**	**-**	**-**
International Civil Aviation	-	-	-	-	-	-	-	-	-	-	-
Domestic Air	-	-	-	-	-	-	-	-	-	-	-
Road	-	-	-	-	-	-	-	-	-	-	-
Rail	15	27	-	4	-	5	-	-	-	-	-
Pipeline Transport	-	-	-	-	-	-	-	-	-	-	-
Internal Navigation	-	-	-	-	-	-	-	-	-	-	-
Non-specified	-	-	-	-	-	-	-	-	-	-	-
OTHER SECTORS	**488**	**10856**	**181**	**10626**	**1755**	**2712**	**12141**	**-**	**-**	**-**	**-**
Agriculture	-	203	-	333	94	56	403	-	-	-	-
Commerce and Publ. Serv.	-	1229	-	1863	6	302	2329	-	-	-	-
Residential	488	8974	181	8284	1655	2319	8658	-	-	-	-
Non-specified	-	450	-	146	-	35	751	-	-	-	-
NON-ENERGY USE	**242**	**110**	**-**	**57**	**-**	**1838**	**252**	**-**	**-**	**-**	**-**
in Industry/Transf./Energy	242	110	-	57	-	1838	252	-	-	-	-
in Transport	-	-	-	-	-	-	-	-	-	-	-
in Other Sectors	-	-	-	-	-	-	-	-	-	-	-

OECD Europe / OCDE Europe : 1992

SUPPLY AND CONSUMPTION / APPROVISIONNEMENT ET DEMANDE	Oil cont. / *Pétrole cont.* (1000 tonnes)										
	Refinery Gas / *Gaz de raffinerie*	LPG + Ethane / *GPL + éthane*	Motor Gasoline / *Essence moteur*	Aviation Gasoline / *Essence aviation*	Jet Fuel / *Carbu-réacteur*	Kerosene / *Kérosène*	Gas/ Diesel / *Gazole*	Heavy Fuel Oil / *Fioul lourd*	Naphtha / *Naphta*	Pétrol. Coke / *Coke de pétrole*	Other Prod. / *Autres prod.*
Production	20437	16607	144474	163	32829	5515	216620	136353	33903	6462	42840
From Other Sources	-	-	-	-	-	-	-	-	-	-	-
Imports	-	12014	30076	120	9115	1009	66153	44566	24760	6802	11078
Exports	-	-4482	-38354	-161	-9323	-1827	-55113	-51765	-13950	-690	-13043
Intl. Marine Bunkers	-	-	-	-	-	-	-8664	-26933	-	-	-316
Stock Changes	2	107	-91	8	7	119	500	80	287	-158	368
DOMESTIC SUPPLY	**20439**	**24246**	**136105**	**130**	**32628**	**4816**	**219496**	**102301**	**45000**	**12416**	**40927**
Transfers	-48	1052	-4846	-1	-258	-376	-2326	-4127	-7200	-5	-4028
Statistical Differences	7	-230	125	15	-1876	15	4723	1694	1413	561	-505
TRANSFORMATION	**936**	**965**	**398**	**-**	**-**	**262**	**2984**	**47991**	**7150**	**1456**	**1461**
Electricity Plants	69	10	-	-	-	-	1613	40894	9	20	1287
CHP Plants	688	20	-	-	-	-	173	5525	-	276	142
Heat Plants	-	55	-	-	-	-	57	916	-	-	-
Transfer to Gases	30	158	-	-	-	-	3	20	157	-	-
Transfer to Solids	-	-	-	-	-	-	1	-	-	1160	-
Petroleum Refineries	-	-	-	-	-	-	-	-	-	-	-
Petrochemical Industry	149	722	398	-	-	262	1137	636	6984	-	2
Liquefaction	-	-	-	-	-	-	-	-	-	-	-
Other Transformation Sector	-	-	-	-	-	-	-	-	-	-	30
ENERGY SECTOR	**17448**	**672**	**9**	**-**	**1**	**7**	**299**	**11114**	**90**	**3705**	**2496**
Coal Mines	-	2	-	-	-	-	109	35	-	-	2
Oil and Gas Extraction	-	361	-	-	-	-	81	58	-	-	-
Petroleum Refineries	17434	259	5	-	1	6	99	10986	90	3702	2360
Electricity, CHP+Heat plants	-	-	4	-	-	-	7	4	-	-	1
Pumped Storage (Elec.)	-	-	-	-	-	-	-	-	-	-	-
Other Energy Sector	14	50	-	-	-	1	3	31	-	3	133
Distribution Losses	-	17	74	-	21	4	52	57	-	-	1
FINAL CONSUMPTION	**2014**	**23414**	**130903**	**144**	**30472**	**4182**	**218558**	**40706**	**31973**	**7811**	**32436**
INDUSTRY SECTOR	**2014**	**10245**	**914**	**-**	**20**	**1137**	**15832**	**31729**	**31973**	**5779**	**381**
Iron and Steel	-	293	-	-	-	-	464	3465	-	71	-
Chemical and Petrochemical	1940	6766	812	-	-	571	5243	7815	31970	257	281
of which: Feedstocks	*890*	*6415*	*812*	-	-	*548*	*3942*	*2521*	*31039*	-	-
Non-Ferrous Metals	-	278	-	-	-	-	470	1283	-	66	-
Non-Metallic Minerals	-	708	2	-	-	7	777	4224	-	4207	-
Transport Equipment	-	83	-	-	-	-	478	403	-	-	-
Machinery	-	294	53	-	20	14	1824	1294	-	84	-
Mining and Quarrying	-	6	-	-	-	1	681	427	-	18	-
Food and Tobacco	4	384	1	-	-	2	1658	4635	-	-	-
Paper, Pulp and Print	51	114	-	-	-	-	362	2869	-	8	-
Wood and Wood Products	-	11	1	-	-	-	373	231	-	-	-
Construction	-	35	5	-	-	1	2002	460	-	-	-
Textile and Leather	-	79	-	-	-	-	447	1953	-	39	-
Non-specified	19	1194	40	-	-	541	1053	2670	3	1029	100
TRANSPORT SECTOR	**-**	**2262**	**129485**	**144**	**30452**	**22**	**109466**	**1482**	**-**	**-**	**6**
International Civil Aviation	-	-	-	3	22574	-	-	-	-	-	-
Domestic Air	-	-	-	141	7878	-	-	-	-	-	-
Road	-	2260	129090	-	-	7	100162	-	-	-	6
Rail	-	2	-	-	-	12	3006	48	-	-	-
Pipeline Transport	-	-	-	-	-	-	-	-	-	-	-
Internal Navigation	-	-	395	-	-	3	6268	1434	-	-	-
Non-specified	-	-	-	-	-	-	30	-	-	-	-
OTHER SECTORS	**-**	**10907**	**504**	**-**	**-**	**3023**	**93260**	**7495**	**-**	**132**	**13**
Agriculture	-	507	279	-	-	234	14346	785	-	15	6
Commerce and Publ. Serv.	-	1150	-	-	-	61	33681	3652	-	7	7
Residential	-	9153	225	-	-	2647	43323	2729	-	110	-
Non-specified	-	97	-	-	-	81	1910	329	-	-	-
NON-ENERGY USE	**-**	**-**	**-**	**-**	**-**	**-**	**-**	**-**	**-**	**1900**	**32036**
in Industry/Transf./Energy	-	-	-	-	-	-	-	-	-	1900	29433
in Transport	-	-	-	-	-	-	-	-	-	-	2216
in Other Sectors	-	-	-	-	-	-	-	-	-	-	387

INTERNATIONAL ENERGY AGENCY

OECD Europe / OCDE Europe : 1992

CONSUMPTION / APPROVISIONNEMENT ET DEMANDE	Gas / Gaz (TJ)				Combust. Renew. & Waste / En. Re. Comb. & Déchets (TJ)				(GWh)	(TJ)
	Natural Gas / Gaz naturel	Gas Works / Usines à gaz	Coke Ovens / Cokeries	Blast Furnaces / Hauts fourneaux	Solid Biomass & Anim. Prod. / Biomasse solide & prod. anim.	Gas/Liquids from Biomass / Gaz/Liquides tirés de biomasse	Municipal Waste / Déchets urbains	Industrial Waste / Déchets industriels	Electricity / Electricité	Heat / Chaleur
Production	8041993	65432	406490	531032	1198345	15966	148565	122595	2474559	782282
From Other Sources	-	26751	-	-	-	-	-	-	-	-
Imports	6310652	-	-	-	5490	-	-	2913	169823	-
Exports	-2642223	-198	-	-	-	-	-	-68	-164180	-
Intl. Marine Bunkers	-	-	-	-	-	-	-	-	-	-
Stock Changes	-225500	3564	-1	-	2690	-	-	279	-	-
DOMESTIC SUPPLY	11484922	95549	406489	531032	1206525	15966	148565	125719	2480202	782282
Transfers	-	-	-	-	-	-	-	-	-	-
Statistical Differences	5563	-24	-1153	-3925	1115	-	-	-17	-	-
TRANSFORMATION	1921205	655	71067	206925	126030	13205	132775	22433	8604	-
Electricity Plants	950117	-	60739	157953	28298	8832	60344	16427	-	-
CHP Plants	741384	-	6600	48376	51593	1092	45089	5088	-	-
Heat Plants	151132	655	511	592	41898	3281	27342	918	8604	-
Transfer to Gases	77450	-	3217	-	-	-	-	-	-	-
Transfer to Solids	1083	-	-	4	4241	-	-	-	-	-
Petroleum Refineries	-	-	-	-	-	-	-	-	-	-
Petrochemical Industry	-	-	-	-	-	-	-	-	-	-
Liquefaction	-	-	-	-	-	-	-	-	-	-
Other Transformation Sector	39	-	-	-	-	-	-	-	-	-
ENERGY SECTOR	477428	1549	138593	52832	2	-	-	-	238516	6164
Coal Mines	5094	-	2376	-	-	-	-	-	14380	-
Oil and Gas Extraction	380391	-	-	-	-	-	-	-	6131	-
Petroleum Refineries	41766	288	5473	-	-	-	-	-	23723	-
Electricity, CHP+Heat plants	550	-	-	-	2	-	-	-	130019	143
Pumped Storage (Elec.)	-	-	-	-	-	-	-	-	27403	-
Other Energy Sector	49627	1261	130744	52832	-	-	-	-	36860	6021
Distribution Losses	78320	1511	2301	20743	-	-	-	-	144964	75412
FINAL CONSUMPTION	9013532	91810	193375	246607	1081608	2761	15773	103286	2088118	700706
INDUSTRY SECTOR	3666238	14381	192655	246607	366852	455	15632	9198	902512	101279
Iron and Steel	358970	1764	165504	246455	8	-	-	-	109202	3042
Chemical and Petrochemical	1309086	1041	13458	152	18750	91	638	2780	181092	21274
of which: Feedstocks	559405	-	-	-	-	-	-	-	-	-
Non-Ferrous Metals	84082	1854	936	-	205	131	-	20	85479	-
Non-Metallic Minerals	499326	2910	2056	-	18138	-	185	832	65103	15
Transport Equipment	117145	522	306	-	-	-	-	-	54158	513
Machinery	293796	2864	4177	-	338	-	16	119	63223	20273
Mining and Quarrying	25706	-	166	-	-	-	-	-	16656	22
Food and Tobacco	402766	2592	1296	-	13616	172	27	172	78473	935
Paper, Pulp and Print	270324	185	1260	-	216868	61	14766	2307	104594	2923
Wood and Wood Products	7028	109	18	-	53893	-	-	148	20141	91
Construction	10650	2	565	-	-	-	-	10	10251	15
Textile and Leather	123307	291	756	-	1888	-	-	120	39818	104
Non-specified	164052	247	2157	-	43148	-	-	2690	74322	52072
TRANSPORT SECTOR	11892	-	-	-	-	-	6	65	54880	-
International Civil Aviation	-	-	-	-	-	-	-	-	-	-
Domestic Air	-	-	-	-	-	-	-	-	-	-
Road	9983	-	-	-	-	-	-	-	-	-
Rail	-	-	-	-	-	-	-	-	-	-
Pipeline Transport	919	-	-	-	-	-	6	65	45382	-
Internal Navigation	-	-	-	-	-	-	-	-	750	-
Non-specified	990	-	-	-	-	-	-	-	8748	-
OTHER SECTORS	5335402	77429	720	-	714756	2306	135	94023	1130726	599427
Agriculture	188938	216	-	-	9415	-	-	-	35267	4752
Commerce and Publ. Serv.	842179	15797	-	-	3281	311	-	-	472061	85332
Residential	3840263	61366	720	-	702060	-	135	94023	616365	363949
Non-specified	464022	50	-	-	-	1995	-	-	7033	145394
NON-ENERGY USE	-	-	-	-	-	-	-	-	-	-
in Industry/Transf./Energy	-	-	-	-	-	-	-	-	-	-
in Transport	-	-	-	-	-	-	-	-	-	-
in Other Sectors	-	-	-	-	-	-	-	-	-	-

OECD Europe / OCDE Europe : 1993

SUPPLY AND CONSUMPTION / APPROVISIONNEMENT ET DEMANDE	Coal / Charbon (1000 tonnes)							Oil / Pétrole (1000 tonnes)			
	Coking Coal / Charbon à coke	Steam Coal / Charbon vapeur	Sub-Bit. Coal / Charbon sous-bit.	Lignite / Lignite	Peat / Tourbe	Oven and Gas Coke / Coke de four/gaz	Pat. Fuel and BKB / Agg./briq. de lignite	Crude Oil / Pétrole brut	NGL / LGN	Feedstocks / Produits d'aliment.	Additives / Additifs
Production	37505	119825	4394	339218	13282	46618	16194	233634	10095	-	143
From Other Sources	-	1229	971	-	-	-	-	85	-	11574	1745
Imports	46111	92264	-	3374	36	7834	1026	524698	3817	33917	352
Exports	-96	-5850	-16	-46	-303	-3428	-1023	-166003	-3958	-6269	-
Intl. Marine Bunkers	-	-	-	-	-	-	-	-	-	-	-
Stock Changes	-1328	7293	-82	3518	809	217	52	-82	31	342	22
DOMESTIC SUPPLY	**82192**	**214761**	**5267**	**346064**	**13824**	**51241**	**16249**	**592332**	**9985**	**39564**	**2262**
Transfers	-	-	-	-	-	-	-	-1417	-3311	31037	-
Statistical Differences	-341	1269	35	27	-	215	-	2239	-721	62	-98
TRANSFORMATION	**79905**	**176856**	**5024**	**322074**	**9458**	**15698**	**1761**	**592939**	**5953**	**70663**	**2164**
Electricity Plants	18668	149698	5011	284031	4412	-	1081	-	-	-	-
CHP Plants	-	23055	13	-	3272	-	-	-	-	-	-
Heat Plants	-	1360	-	2856	764	11	464	-	-	-	-
Transfer to Gases	37	550	-	-	-	15603	-	-	-	-	-
Transfer to Solids	61200	2193	-	35187	1010	84	216	-	-	-	-
Petroleum Refineries	-	-	-	-	-	-	-	592939	5953	70663	2164
Petrochemical Industry	-	-	-	-	-	-	-	-	-	-	-
Liquefaction	-	-	-	-	-	-	-	-	-	-	-
Other Transformation Sector	-	-	-	-	-	-	-	-	-	-	-
ENERGY SECTOR	**57**	**308**	**3**	**1609**	**-**	**205**	**115**	**200**	**-**	**-**	**-**
Coal Mines	-	206	3	-	-	-	-	-	-	-	-
Oil and Gas Extraction	-	-	-	-	-	-	-	200	-	-	-
Petroleum Refineries	-	-	-	-	-	-	-	-	-	-	-
Electricity, CHP+Heat plants	-	-	-	-	-	-	-	-	-	-	-
Pumped Storage (Elec.)	-	-	-	-	-	-	-	-	-	-	-
Other Energy Sector	57	102	-	1609	-	205	115	-	-	-	-
Distribution Losses	10	-	-	-	-	6	-	-	-	-	-
FINAL CONSUMPTION	**1879**	**38866**	**275**	**22408**	**4366**	**35547**	**14373**	**15**	**-**	**-**	**-**
INDUSTRY SECTOR	**1358**	**27868**	**181**	**12576**	**2817**	**31680**	**3543**	**15**	**-**	**-**	**-**
Iron and Steel	856	5890	-	-	-	28431	-	-	-	-	-
Chemical and Petrochemical	-	3840	4	315	28	420	-	15	-	-	-
of which: Feedstocks	-	-	-	-	-	-	-	-	-	-	-
Non-Ferrous Metals	2	461	-	475	-	806	-	-	-	-	-
Non-Metallic Minerals	6	10582	160	290	-	609	4	-	-	-	-
Transport Equipment	-	319	-	-	-	39	-	-	-	-	-
Machinery	5	308	-	58	-	672	-	-	-	-	-
Mining and Quarrying	-	268	-	3	-	11	-	-	-	-	-
Food and Tobacco	136	1613	-	1610	-	315	-	-	-	-	-
Paper, Pulp and Print	-	1782	-	168	33	45	18	-	-	-	-
Wood and Wood Products	-	86	-	-	-	-	1	-	-	-	-
Construction	188	920	12	1287	-	54	-	-	-	-	-
Textile and Leather	-	516	-	280	-	8	-	-	-	-	-
Non-specified	165	1283	5	8090	2756	270	3520	-	-	-	-
TRANSPORT SECTOR	**14**	**22**	**-**	**1**	**-**	**5**	**2**	**-**	**-**	**-**	**-**
International Civil Aviation	-	-	-	-	-	-	-	-	-	-	-
Domestic Air	-	-	-	-	-	-	-	-	-	-	-
Road	-	-	-	-	-	-	-	-	-	-	-
Rail	14	22	-	1	-	5	2	-	-	-	-
Pipeline Transport	-	-	-	-	-	-	-	-	-	-	-
Internal Navigation	-	-	-	-	-	-	-	-	-	-	-
Non-specified	-	-	-	-	-	-	-	-	-	-	-
OTHER SECTORS	**296**	**10876**	**94**	**9778**	**1549**	**2406**	**10626**	**-**	**-**	**-**	**-**
Agriculture	-	178	5	240	49	52	351	-	-	-	-
Commerce and Publ. Serv.	-	998	-	1117	15	267	2023	-	-	-	-
Residential	296	9294	89	8298	1485	2068	7784	-	-	-	-
Non-specified	-	406	-	123	-	19	468	-	-	-	-
NON-ENERGY USE	**211**	**100**	**-**	**53**	**-**	**1456**	**202**	**-**	**-**	**-**	**-**
in Industry/Transf./Energy	211	100	-	53	-	1456	202	-	-	-	-
in Transport	-	-	-	-	-	-	-	-	-	-	-
in Other Sectors	-	-	-	-	-	-	-	-	-	-	-

OECD Europe / OCDE Europe : 1993

SUPPLY AND CONSUMPTION / APPROVISIONNEMENT ET DEMANDE	Refinery Gas / Gaz de raffinerie	LPG + Ethane / GPL + éthane	Motor Gasoline / Essence moteur	Aviation Gasoline / Essence aviation	Jet Fuel / Carbu-réacteur	Kerosene / Kérosène	Gas/Diesel / Gazole	Heavy Fuel Oil / Fioul lourd	Naphtha / Naphta	Pétrol. Coke / Coke de pétrole	Other Prod. / Autres prod.
Production	20946	16924	146953	180	33891	5412	224386	133537	32769	6637	43800
From Other Sources	-	-	-	-	-	-	-	-	-	-	-
Imports	-	12947	30122	140	8803	2114	63900	46283	23608	6187	11707
Exports	-	-4865	-40216	-155	-8791	-1564	-59606	-51793	-12931	-735	-13635
Intl. Marine Bunkers	-	-	-	-	-6	-	-7783	-28857	-	-	-307
Stock Changes	-	8	-1441	-7	-268	-111	1924	840	-126	67	162
DOMESTIC SUPPLY	20946	25014	135418	158	33629	5851	222821	100010	43320	12156	41727
Transfers	-105	827	-4977	-12	-141	-1573	-80	-5664	-7141	25	-5804
Statistical Differences	57	-590	710	-10	-1481	261	3923	9	1033	132	-698
TRANSFORMATION	1098	1042	510	-	-	379	3436	43369	7823	1302	1567
Electricity Plants	58	1	-	-	-	-	1682	36138	5	14	1417
CHP Plants	751	18	-	-	-	-	184	5386	-	209	112
Heat Plants	113	55	-	-	-	-	64	931	-	-	-
Transfer to Gases	29	141	-	-	-	-	3	367	158	-	-
Transfer to Solids	-	-	-	-	-	-	1	-	-	1079	-
Petroleum Refineries	-	-	-	-	-	-	-	-	-	-	-
Petrochemical Industry	147	827	510	-	-	379	1502	547	7660	-	2
Liquefaction	-	-	-	-	-	-	-	-	-	-	-
Other Transformation Sector	-	-	-	-	-	-	-	-	-	-	36
ENERGY SECTOR	17919	682	4	-	-	5	321	11786	58	3777	2477
Coal Mines	-	2	-	-	-	-	108	33	-	-	1
Oil and Gas Extraction	-	390	-	-	-	-	84	49	-	-	-
Petroleum Refineries	17919	253	-	-	-	5	107	11673	58	3775	2393
Electricity, CHP+Heat plants	-	-	4	-	-	-	7	2	-	-	2
Pumped Storage (Elec.)	-	-	-	-	-	-	-	-	-	-	-
Other Energy Sector	-	37	-	-	-	-	15	29	-	2	81
Distribution Losses	-	17	81	-	12	1	48	58	-	-	1
FINAL CONSUMPTION	1881	23510	130556	136	31995	4154	222859	39142	29331	7234	31180
INDUSTRY SECTOR	1881	9730	861	-	17	1047	16163	30772	29331	5324	5
Iron and Steel	-	205	-	-	-	-	481	3314	-	92	-
Chemical and Petrochemical	1870	6377	793	-	1	462	4228	7948	29331	225	5
of which: Feedstocks	868	5961	582	-	-	436	3924	2190	28270	-	-
Non-Ferrous Metals	-	255	-	-	-	-	492	1113	-	60	-
Non-Metallic Minerals	-	662	-	-	-	5	875	4052	-	3922	-
Transport Equipment	-	89	-	-	-	-	436	355	-	-	-
Machinery	-	286	39	-	16	11	1626	1163	-	84	-
Mining and Quarrying	-	5	-	-	-	1	608	388	-	20	-
Food and Tobacco	4	413	1	-	-	1	1575	4307	-	2	-
Paper, Pulp and Print	7	120	-	-	-	-	326	2658	-	4	-
Wood and Wood Products	-	19	-	-	-	-	219	239	-	-	-
Construction	-	40	8	-	-	-	2569	407	-	-	-
Textile and Leather	-	58	-	-	-	-	431	1854	-	-	-
Non-specified	-	1201	20	-	-	567	2297	2974	-	915	-
TRANSPORT SECTOR	-	2338	129216	136	31978	20	114278	1462	-	-	5
International Civil Aviation	-	-	-	4	24774	-	-	-	-	-	-
Domestic Air	-	-	-	132	7204	-	-	-	-	-	-
Road	-	2333	128808	-	-	6	104918	-	-	-	5
Rail	-	5	-	-	-	12	2981	46	-	-	-
Pipeline Transport	-	-	-	-	-	-	-	-	-	-	-
Internal Navigation	-	-	408	-	-	2	6379	1404	-	-	-
Non-specified	-	-	-	-	-	-	-	12	-	-	-
OTHER SECTORS	-	11442	479	-	-	3087	92418	6850	-	124	12
Agriculture	-	527	259	-	-	201	14186	809	-	16	5
Commerce and Publ. Serv.	-	956	-	-	-	50	32408	3233	-	8	7
Residential	-	9840	220	-	-	2739	43858	2530	-	99	-
Non-specified	-	119	-	-	-	97	1966	278	-	1	-
NON-ENERGY USE	-	-	-	-	-	-	-	58	-	1786	31158
in Industry/Transf./Energy	-	-	-	-	-	-	-	58	-	1786	28527
in Transport	-	-	-	-	-	-	-	-	-	-	2307
in Other Sectors	-	-	-	-	-	-	-	-	-	-	324

Oil cont. / *Pétrole cont.* (1000 tonnes)

OECD Europe / OCDE Europe : 1993

CONSUMPTION / APPROVISIONNEMENT ET DEMANDE	Gas / Gaz (TJ)				Combust. Renew. & Waste / En. Re. Comb. & Déchets (TJ)				(GWh)	(TJ)
	Natural Gas / Gaz naturel	Gas Works / Usines à gaz	Coke Ovens / Cokeries	Blast Furnaces / Hauts fourneaux	Solid Biomass & Anim. Prod. / Biomasse solide & prod. anim.	Gas/Liquids from Biomass / Gaz/Liquides tirés de biomasse	Municipal Waste / Déchets urbains	Industrial Waste / Déchets industriels	Electricity / Electricité	Heat / Chaleur
Production	8485887	37254	379479	519385	1233485	19093	157528	113154	2488141	814915
From Other Sources	-	26398	-	-	-	-	-	-	-	-
Imports	6357460	-	-	-	5550	-	-	2657	175174	-
Exports	-2650905	-180	-	-	-	-	-	-20	-168659	-
Intl. Marine Bunkers	-	-	-	-	-	-	-	-	-	-
Stock Changes	-62884	2484	2	-	1345	-	-	150	-	-
DOMESTIC SUPPLY	**12129558**	**65956**	**379481**	**519385**	**1240380**	**19093**	**157528**	**115941**	**2494656**	**814915**
Transfers	-	-	-	-	-	-	-	-	-	-
Statistical Differences	19215	54	1583	-3530	1154	-	-78	-	-	-
TRANSFORMATION	**2294556**	**25**	**64123**	**204911**	**141263**	**15270**	**142138**	**21814**	**8138**	**-**
Electricity Plants	1221737	-	51009	153028	28472	10309	63469	16460	-	-
CHP Plants	801688	-	9408	51319	61990	2339	51279	4162	-	-
Heat Plants	215321	25	566	564	46096	2622	27390	1192	8138	-
Transfer to Gases	54049	-	3140	-	-	-	-	-	-	-
Transfer to Solids	1683	-	-	-	4705	-	-	-	-	-
Petroleum Refineries	-	-	-	-	-	-	-	-	-	-
Petrochemical Industry	-	-	-	-	-	-	-	-	-	-
Liquefaction	-	-	-	-	-	-	-	-	-	-
Other Transformation Sector	78	-	-	-	-	-	-	-	-	-
ENERGY SECTOR	**479853**	**246**	**123781**	**51185**	**-**	**-**	**-**	**-**	**226045**	**6167**
Coal Mines	3384	-	1620	-	-	-	-	-	13002	-
Oil and Gas Extraction	373046	-	-	-	-	-	-	-	6321	-
Petroleum Refineries	47592	-	2232	-	-	-	-	-	24778	-
Electricity, CHP+Heat plants	500	-	-	-	-	-	-	-	126411	145
Pumped Storage (Elec.)	-	-	-	-	-	-	-	-	24378	-
Other Energy Sector	55331	246	119929	51185	-	-	-	-	31155	6022
Distribution Losses	50641	1233	1965	18982	-	-	-	-	155872	76670
FINAL CONSUMPTION	**9323723**	**64506**	**191195**	**240777**	**1100271**	**3823**	**15312**	**94127**	**2104601**	**732078**
INDUSTRY SECTOR	**3719495**	**8221**	**190210**	**240656**	**382048**	**564**	**15212**	**10685**	**894023**	**105185**
Iron and Steel	346037	1891	165776	240496	144	-	-	-	104579	3058
Chemical and Petrochemical	1300801	623	10520	160	19526	55	245	3330	183815	21766
of which: Feedstocks	*508232*	-	-	-	-	-	-	-	-	-
Non-Ferrous Metals	80533	1512	270	-	9	149	-	30	86681	28
Non-Metallic Minerals	500048	740	5976	-	17489	-	172	1128	60089	33
Transport Equipment	109462	126	180	-	18	-	6	-	51897	658
Machinery	275934	1217	3961	-	302	-	15	110	62860	20748
Mining and Quarrying	26297	-	147	-	47	-	-	-	16537	25
Food and Tobacco	400635	1411	1152	-	15341	284	4	200	79974	1527
Paper, Pulp and Print	281044	111	450	-	227947	65	14770	1972	108335	4384
Wood and Wood Products	6666	36	-	-	53242	-	-	125	21472	101
Construction	11516	2	554	-	-	-	-	10	9997	15
Textile and Leather	135051	254	252	-	1344	-	-	120	38616	207
Non-specified	245471	298	972	-	46639	11	-	3660	69171	52635
TRANSPORT SECTOR	**12566**	**-**	**-**	**-**	**371**	**-**	**7**	**65**	**55792**	**-**
International Civil Aviation	-	-	-	-	-	-	-	-	-	-
Domestic Air	-	-	-	-	-	-	-	-	-	-
Road	10070	-	-	-	-	-	-	-	-	-
Rail	-	-	-	-	371	-	7	65	45951	-
Pipeline Transport	1455	-	-	-	-	-	-	-	722	-
Internal Navigation	-	-	-	-	-	-	-	-	-	-
Non-specified	1041	-	-	-	-	-	-	-	9119	-
OTHER SECTORS	**5591662**	**56284**	**936**	**-**	**717852**	**3259**	**93**	**83377**	**1154786**	**626893**
Agriculture	199820	108	-	-	9211	5	-	-	35607	5064
Commerce and Publ. Serv.	848296	13191	-	-	3559	940	-	-	482520	91750
Residential	4061020	42935	936	-	705082	7	93	83377	629837	384523
Non-specified	482526	50	-	-	-	2307	-	-	6822	145556
NON-ENERGY USE	**-**	**1**	**49**	**121**	**-**	**-**	**-**	**-**	**-**	**-**
in Industry/Transf./Energy	-	1	49	121	-	-	-	-	-	-
in Transport	-	-	-	-	-	-	-	-	-	-
in Other Sectors	-	-	-	-	-	-	-	-	-	-

IEA / AIE : 1992

SUPPLY AND CONSUMPTION / APPROVISIONNEMENT ET DEMANDE	Coal / Charbon (1000 tonnes)							Oil / Pétrole (1000 tonnes)			
	Coking Coal / Charbon à coke	Steam Coal / Charbon vapeur	Sub-Bit. Coal / Charbon sous-bit.	Lignite / Lignite	Peat / Tourbe	Oven and Gas Coke / Coke de four/gaz	Pat. Fuel and BKB / Agg./briq. de lignite	Crude Oil / Pétrole brut	NGL / LGN	Feedstocks / Produits d'aliment.	Additives / Additifs
Production	218968	757409	275938	506725	12618	125310	20060	687829	76099	-	144
From Other Sources	-	1350	979	-	-	-	-	103	-	15169	1790
Imports	117179	166096	-	4096	7	9639	954	1092710	13475	64862	192
Exports	-143207	-107335	-14	-79	-338	-8506	-1013	-197993	-13262	-5100	-
Intl. Marine Bunkers	-	-	-	-	-	-	-	-	-	-	-
Stock Changes	-1764	-16811	1002	2953	2233	-763	65	-5172	-185	-702	-20
DOMESTIC SUPPLY	**191176**	**800709**	**277905**	**513695**	**14520**	**125680**	**20066**	**1577477**	**76127**	**74229**	**2106**
Transfers	-	-	-	-	-	-	-	-1879	-46958	41000	-
Statistical Differences	-306	1134	-985	-942	-	239	-7	5680	1198	-1829	-21
TRANSFORMATION	**188703**	**708808**	**268084**	**477277**	**9330**	**38947**	**2773**	**1580190**	**26810**	**113400**	**2085**
Electricity Plants	16996	643402	257642	431157	4149	-	1590	17576	217	-	-
CHP Plants	-	60836	10442	-	3351	-	-	-	-	-	-
Heat Plants	-	1416	-	2603	784	5	554	-	-	-	-
Transfer to Gases	1123	581	-	-	-	38715	392	-	-	-	-
Transfer to Solids	170584	2573	-	43517	1046	227	237	-	-	-	-
Petroleum Refineries	-	-	-	-	-	-	-	1565856	26593	113400	2085
Petrochemical Industry	-	-	-	-	-	-	-	-	-	-	-
Liquefaction	-	-	-	-	-	-	-	-3242	-	-	-
Other Transformation Sector	-	-	-	-	-	-	-	-	-	-	-
ENERGY SECTOR	**60**	**1126**	**33**	**1749**	**-**	**363**	**277**	**1057**	**-**	**-**	**-**
Coal Mines	-	993	33	2	-	-	-	-	-	-	-
Oil and Gas Extraction	-	-	-	-	-	-	-	1057	-	-	-
Petroleum Refineries	-	121	-	146	-	-	36	-	-	-	-
Electricity, CHP+Heat plants	-	-	-	-	-	-	-	-	-	-	-
Pumped Storage (Elec.)	-	-	-	-	-	-	-	-	-	-	-
Other Energy Sector	60	12	-	1601	-	363	241	-	-	-	-
Distribution Losses	14	-	-	-	-	7	-	-	-	-	-
FINAL CONSUMPTION	**2093**	**91909**	**8803**	**33727**	**5190**	**86602**	**17009**	**31**	**3557**	**-**	**-**
INDUSTRY SECTOR	**1348**	**77007**	**8285**	**22920**	**3435**	**81848**	**4414**	**31**	**3557**	**-**	**-**
Iron and Steel	805	8965	698	21	-	72756	-	-	-	-	-
Chemical and Petrochemical	61	9749	2980	6572	7	601	148	-	-	-	-
of which: Feedstocks	-	-	-	-	-	-	-	-	-	-	-
Non-Ferrous Metals	1	1442	1961	394	-	1346	1	-	-	-	-
Non-Metallic Minerals	-	33075	952	317	-	967	8	-	-	-	-
Transport Equipment	-	381	-	-	-	42	2	-	-	-	-
Machinery	4	1147	48	59	-	811	-	-	-	-	-
Mining and Quarrying	-	391	310	3	-	136	-	-	-	-	-
Food and Tobacco	121	2668	420	1624	-	291	150	-	-	-	-
Paper, Pulp and Print	-	4292	-	289	30	43	57	-	-	-	-
Wood and Wood Products	-	116	-	46	-	1	5	-	-	-	-
Construction	272	1057	16	1192	-	7	-	-	-	-	-
Textile and Leather	-	573	-	238	-	5	26	-	-	-	-
Non-specified	84	13151	900	12165	3398	4842	4017	-	-	-	-
TRANSPORT SECTOR	**15**	**28**	**192**	**4**	**-**	**5**	**-**	**-**	**-**	**-**	**-**
International Civil Aviation	-	-	-	-	-	-	-	-	-	-	-
Domestic Air	-	-	-	-	-	-	-	-	-	-	-
Road	-	-	-	-	-	-	-	-	-	-	-
Rail	15	28	-	4	-	5	-	-	-	-	-
Pipeline Transport	-	-	-	-	-	-	-	-	-	-	-
Internal Navigation	-	-	192	-	-	-	-	-	-	-	-
Non-specified	-	-	-	-	-	-	-	-	-	-	-
OTHER SECTORS	**488**	**14605**	**326**	**10746**	**1755**	**2712**	**12343**	**-**	**-**	**-**	**-**
Agriculture	-	205	13	333	94	56	403	-	-	-	-
Commerce and Publ. Serv.	-	2636	70	1863	6	302	2411	-	-	-	-
Residential	488	11314	243	8342	1655	2319	8778	-	-	-	-
Non-specified	-	450	-	208	-	35	751	-	-	-	-
NON-ENERGY USE	**242**	**269**	**-**	**57**	**-**	**2037**	**252**	**-**	**-**	**-**	**-**
in Industry/Transf./Energy	242	269	-	57	-	2037	252	-	-	-	-
in Transport	-	-	-	-	-	-	-	-	-	-	-
in Other Sectors	-	-	-	-	-	-	-	-	-	-	-

Industry sector details shown only where sectorial data are available for most countries.
La ventilation du secteur industriel n'est indiquée que s'il existe des données sectorielles disponibles pour la plupart des pays concernés.

IEA / AIE : 1992

SUPPLY AND CONSUMPTION / APPROVISIONNEMENT ET DEMANDE	Oil cont. / *Pétrole cont.* (1000 tonnes)										
	Refinery Gas / *Gaz de raffinerie*	LPG + Ethane / *GPL + éthane*	Motor Gasoline / *Essence moteur*	Aviation Gasoline / *Essence aviation*	Jet Fuel / *Carbu-réacteur*	Kerosene / *Kérosène*	Gas/Diesel / *Gazole*	Heavy Fuel Oil / *Fioul lourd*	Naphtha / *Naphta*	Pétrol. Coke / *Coke de pétrole*	Other Prod. / *Autres prod.*
Production	66430	42511	524815	1248	111305	30956	454360	244130	57806	48967	117195
From Other Sources	-	-	-	-	-	-	-	-	-	-	-
Imports	-	27549	44451	152	15565	3118	77805	74190	40864	12871	21432
Exports	-	-5385	-46070	-278	-12073	-2814	-72857	-67758	-14841	-15213	-16995
Intl. Marine Bunkers	-	-	-	-	-	-	-16451	-59329	-	-	-365
Stock Changes	-7	174	493	35	498	625	1916	2296	517	-157	833
DOMESTIC SUPPLY	**66423**	**64849**	**523689**	**1157**	**115295**	**31885**	**444773**	**193529**	**84346**	**46468**	**122100**
Transfers	-129	43886	-2836	3	-194	-2179	-1189	-3486	-7921	-38	-15144
Statistical Differences	-12	-161	-8	78	-2263	-417	5013	610	1279	575	-103
TRANSFORMATION	**1150**	**5122**	**398**	**-**	**-**	**274**	**6074**	**98402**	**12801**	**4098**	**2273**
Electricity Plants	69	1003	-	-	-	-	4703	91216	918	1833	2099
CHP Plants	688	20	-	-	-	-	173	5572	-	276	142
Heat Plants	-	61	-	-	-	12	57	934	-	-	-
Transfer to Gases	244	2916	-	-	-	-	3	20	420	-	-
Transfer to Solids	-	-	-	-	-	-	1	24	-	1989	-
Petroleum Refineries	-	-	-	-	-	-	-	-	-	-	-
Petrochemical Industry	149	1122	398	-	-	262	1137	636	11463	-	2
Liquefaction	-	-	-	-	-	-	-	-	-	-	-
Other Transformation Sector	-	-	-	-	-	-	-	-	-	-	30
ENERGY SECTOR	**62466**	**1851**	**112**	**-**	**58**	**14**	**786**	**16419**	**201**	**21223**	**2808**
Coal Mines	-	2	-	-	-	-	405	36	-	-	2
Oil and Gas Extraction	-	398	-	-	-	-	86	58	-	738	-
Petroleum Refineries	62452	1400	108	-	58	13	247	16134	201	20482	2672
Electricity, CHP+Heat plants	-	1	4	-	-	-	45	160	-	-	1
Pumped Storage (Elec.)	-	-	-	-	-	-	-	-	-	-	-
Other Energy Sector	14	50	-	-	-	1	3	31	-	3	133
Distribution Losses	-	17	74	-	21	4	52	57	-	-	1
FINAL CONSUMPTION	**2666**	**101584**	**520261**	**1238**	**112759**	**28997**	**441685**	**75775**	**64702**	**21684**	**101771**
INDUSTRY SECTOR	**2666**	**68206**	**3114**	**-**	**20**	**6105**	**49065**	**53409**	**64702**	**8678**	**1634**
Iron and Steel	-	-	-	-	-	-	-	-	-	-	-
Chemical and Petrochemical	-	-	-	-	-	-	-	-	-	-	-
of which: Feedstocks	-	-	-	-	-	-	-	-	-	-	-
Non-Ferrous Metals	-	-	-	-	-	-	-	-	-	-	-
Non-Metallic Minerals	-	-	-	-	-	-	-	-	-	-	-
Transport Equipment	-	-	-	-	-	-	-	-	-	-	-
Machinery	-	-	-	-	-	-	-	-	-	-	-
Mining and Quarrying	-	-	-	-	-	-	-	-	-	-	-
Food and Tobacco	-	-	-	-	-	-	-	-	-	-	-
Paper, Pulp and Print	-	-	-	-	-	-	-	-	-	-	-
Wood and Wood Products	-	-	-	-	-	-	-	-	-	-	-
Construction	-	-	-	-	-	-	-	-	-	-	-
Textile and Leather	-	-	-	-	-	-	-	-	-	-	-
Non-specified	-	-	-	-	-	-	-	-	-	-	-
TRANSPORT SECTOR	**-**	**6099**	**512536**	**1229**	**112736**	**25**	**236537**	**5025**	**-**	**-**	**6**
International Civil Aviation	-	-	-	3	29777	-	-	-	-	-	-
Domestic Air	-	-	-	1226	82959	-	1	-	-	-	-
Road	-	6097	508509	-	-	10	204531	49	-	-	6
Rail	-	2	-	-	-	12	16398	48	-	-	-
Pipeline Transport	-	-	-	-	-	-	11	-	-	-	-
Internal Navigation	-	-	4027	-	-	3	12816	4823	-	-	-
Non-specified	-	-	-	-	-	-	2780	105	-	-	-
OTHER SECTORS	**-**	**27279**	**4611**	**9**	**3**	**22867**	**156083**	**17341**	**-**	**132**	**13**
Agriculture	-	2195	2557	3	-	3109	32949	851	-	15	6
Commerce and Publ. Serv.	-	4668	1828	6	3	4599	55044	13397	-	7	7
Residential	-	20319	226	-	-	15078	66197	2764	-	110	-
Non-specified	-	97	-	-	-	81	1893	329	-	-	-
NON-ENERGY USE	**-**	**-**	**-**	**-**	**-**	**-**	**-**	**-**	**-**	**12874**	**100118**
in Industry/Transf./Energy	-	-	-	-	-	-	-	-	-	12874	90901
in Transport	-	-	-	-	-	-	-	-	-	-	7288
in Other Sectors	-	-	-	-	-	-	-	-	-	-	1929

IEA / AIE : 1992

CONSUMPTION APPROVISIONNEMENT ET DEMANDE	Gas / Gaz (TJ)				Combust. Renew. & Waste / En. Re. Comb. & Déchets (TJ)				Electricity (GWh)	Heat (TJ)
	Natural Gas Gaz naturel	Gas Works Usines à gaz	Coke Ovens Cokeries	Blast Furnaces Hauts fourneaux	Solid Biomass & Anim. Prod. Biomasse solide & prod. anim.	Gas/Liquids from Biomass Gaz/Liquides tirés de biomasse	Municipal Waste Déchets urbains	Industrial Waste Déchets industriels	Electricity Electricité	Heat Chaleur
Production	33520451	652567	917949	1144500	4936583	52596	398562	296331	7369012	1181771
From Other Sources	-	200733	-	-	-	-	-	-	-	-
Imports	10732135	-	-	-	5490	-	-	2913	213504	-
Exports	-5305204	-198	-	-	-	-	-	-68	-204563	-
Intl. Marine Bunkers	-	-	-	-	-	-	-	-	-	-
Stock Changes	121389	3564	-1	-	2690	-	-	279		-
DOMESTIC SUPPLY	**39068771**	**856666**	**917948**	**1144500**	**4944763**	**52596**	**398562**	**299455**	**7377953**	**1181771**
Transfers										
Statistical Differences	-570278	1633	-20993	36100	1115	-	-17	-	-	-
TRANSFORMATION	**7604857**	**655**	**319188**	**609909**	**1542812**	**49835**	**382495**	**188599**	**9455**	**-**
Electricity Plants	5718812	-	149937	365444	332918	36858	265369	35567	-	-
CHP Plants	869223	-	158609	243869	1163755	9696	89784	152114	-	-
Heat Plants	159534	655	511	592	41898	3281	27342	918	9455	-
Transfer to Gases	663559	-	10131	-	-	-	-	-	-	-
Transfer to Solids	1083	-	-	4	4241	-	-	-	-	-
Petroleum Refineries	-	-	-	-	-	-	-	-	-	-
Petrochemical Industry	-	-	-	-	-	-	-	-	-	-
Liquefaction	179924	-	-	-	-	-	-	-	-	-
Other Transformation Sector	12722	-	-	-	-	-	-	-	-	-
ENERGY SECTOR	**2947993**	**18481**	**179410**	**111945**	**2**	**-**	**-**	**-**	**668359**	**43338**
Coal Mines	9255	-	2376	-	-	-	-	-	32780	-
Oil and Gas Extraction	2007766	-	-	-	-	-	-	-	53541	-
Petroleum Refineries	880795	288	5473	-	-	-	-	-	80600	36912
Electricity, CHP+Heat plants	550	-	-	-	2	-	-	-	401800	405
Pumped Storage (Elec.)	-	-	-	-	-	-	-	-	62671	-
Other Energy Sector	49627	18193	171561	111945	-	-	-	-	36967	6021
Distribution Losses	78320	10153	2301	20743	-	-	-	-	466457	118709
FINAL CONSUMPTION	**27867323**	**829010**	**396056**	**438003**	**3403064**	**2761**	**16050**	**110856**	**6233682**	**1019724**
INDUSTRY SECTOR	**12388086**	**235150**	**395336**	**438003**	**1879326**	**455**	**15632**	**16768**	**2563723**	**353255**
Iron and Steel	-	1764	366419	437851	155	-	-	-	259002	3379
Chemical and Petrochemical	-	6723	13458	152	18750	91	638	10317	475382	159818
of which: Feedstocks	-	-	-	-	-	-	-	-	-	-
Non-Ferrous Metals	-	1854	936	-	1994	131	-	20	264659	1536
Non-Metallic Minerals	-	2910	2056	-	18874	-	185	832	120211	366
Transport Equipment	-	528	306	-	-	-	-	-	116487	5639
Machinery	-	2866	4177	-	338	-	16	119	204695	27193
Mining and Quarrying	-	-	1932	-	-	-	-	-	73461	22
Food and Tobacco	-	2685	1296	-	77203	172	27	205	155861	20570
Paper, Pulp and Print	-	185	1260	-	1403847	61	14766	2307	320958	26146
Wood and Wood Products	-	109	18	-	292029	-	-	148	47977	91
Construction	-	2	565	-	-	-	-	10	10342	15
Textile and Leather	-	291	756	-	22988	-	-	120	86726	7913
Non-specified	-	215233	2157	-	43148	-	-	2690	427962	100567
TRANSPORT SECTOR	**854588**	**-**	**-**	**-**	**-**	**-**	**6**	**65**	**84975**	**-**
International Civil Aviation	-	-	-	-	-	-	-	-	-	-
Domestic Air	-	-	-	-	-	-	-	-	-	-
Road	16479	-	-	-	-	-	-	-	-	-
Rail	-	-	-	-	-	-	-	-	-	-
Pipeline Transport	836609	-	-	-	-	-	6	65	72662	-
Internal Navigation	-	-	-	-	-	-	-	-	3315	-
Non-specified	1500	-	-	-	-	-	-	-	8998	-
OTHER SECTORS	**14624239**	**593860**	**720**	**-**	**1523738**	**2306**	**412**	**94023**	**3584984**	**666469**
Agriculture	214124	216	-	-	9415	-	-	-	49439	4843
Commerce and Publ. Serv.	4349648	131474	-	-	3982	311	277	-	1597233	157627
Residential	9592904	462120	720	-	1510341	-	135	94023	1931360	358605
Non-specified	467563	50	-	-	-	1995	-	-	6952	145394
NON-ENERGY USE	**410**	**-**	**-**	**-**	**-**	**-**	**-**	**-**	**-**	**-**
in Industry/Transf./Energy	410	-	-	-	-	-	-	-	-	-
in Transport	-	-	-	-	-	-	-	-	-	-
in Other Sectors	-	-	-	-	-	-	-	-	-	-

IEA / AIE : 1993

SUPPLY AND CONSUMPTION *APPROVISIONNEMENT ET DEMANDE*	Coal / *Charbon* (1000 tonnes)							Oil / *Pétrole* (1000 tonnes)			
	Coking Coal *Charbon à coke*	Steam Coal *Charbon vapeur*	Sub-Bit. Coal *Charbon sous-bit.*	Lignite *Lignite*	Peat *Tourbe*	Oven and Gas Coke *Coke de four/gaz*	Pat. Fuel and BKB *Agg./briq. de lignite*	Crude Oil *Pétrole brut*	NGL *LGN*	Feedstocks *Produits d'aliment.*	Additives *Additifs*
Production	215695	670920	297186	478325	13306	119221	16823	683605	79806	-	6687
From Other Sources	-	1229	971	-	-	-	-	85	-	16437	1876
Imports	115761	148999	-	3374	36	9656	1026	1140103	14513	66794	1222
Exports	-142289	-86738	-1955	-75	-303	-7969	-1084	-217088	-13273	-6555	-
Intl. Marine Bunkers	-	-	-	-	-	-	-	-	-	-	-
Stock Changes	-3172	57392	1915	1097	809	1231	102	-4938	-340	1334	-1434
DOMESTIC SUPPLY	**185995**	**791802**	**298117**	**482721**	**13848**	**122139**	**16867**	**1601767**	**80706**	**78010**	**8351**
Transfers	-	-	-	-	-	-	-	-2053	-48609	43420	473
Statistical Differences	-411	-17731	14983	2768	-	282	-	587	213	-2312	-450
TRANSFORMATION	**183641**	**689646**	**305037**	**455113**	**9482**	**38573**	**1826**	**1599469**	**29477**	**119118**	**8374**
Electricity Plants	18668	618540	291244	414598	4436	-	1146	13564	214	-	-
CHP Plants	-	66828	13793	1208	3272	-	-	-	-	-	-
Heat Plants	-	1407	-	2856	764	11	464	-	-	-	-
Transfer to Gases	1042	565	-	-	-	38478	-	-	-	-	-
Transfer to Solids	163931	2306	-	36451	1010	84	216	-	-	-	-
Petroleum Refineries	-	-	-	-	-	-	-	1589246	29263	119118	8374
Petrochemical Industry	-	-	-	-	-	-	-	-	-	-	-
Liquefaction	-	-	-	-	-	-	-	-3341	-	-	-
Other Transformation Sector	-	-	-	-	-	-	-	-	-	-	-
ENERGY SECTOR	**57**	**784**	**3**	**1609**	**-**	**309**	**115**	**807**	**-**	**-**	**-**
Coal Mines	-	553	3	-	-	-	-	-	-	-	-
Oil and Gas Extraction	-	-	-	-	-	-	-	807	-	-	-
Petroleum Refineries	-	129	-	-	-	-	-	-	-	-	-
Electricity, CHP+Heat plants	-	-	-	-	-	-	-	-	-	-	-
Pumped Storage (Elec.)	-	-	-	-	-	-	-	-	-	-	-
Other Energy Sector	57	102	-	1609	-	309	115	-	-	-	-
Distribution Losses	10	-	-	-	-	6	-	-	-	-	-
FINAL CONSUMPTION	**1876**	**83641**	**8060**	**28767**	**4366**	**83533**	**14926**	**25**	**2833**	**-**	**-**
INDUSTRY SECTOR	**1355**	**69898**	**7454**	**18818**	**2817**	**79472**	**3899**	**25**	**2833**	**-**	**-**
Iron and Steel	856	8422	725	-	-	70855	-	-	-	-	-
Chemical and Petrochemical	3	8256	2832	5861	28	538	134	-	-	-	-
of which: Feedstocks	-	-	-	-	-	-	-	-	-	-	-
Non-Ferrous Metals	2	1261	2030	475	-	1310	-	-	-	-	-
Non-Metallic Minerals	-	30993	772	294	-	913	10	-	-	-	-
Transport Equipment	-	319	-	-	-	39	2	-	-	-	-
Machinery	5	939	83	58	-	672	-	-	-	-	-
Mining and Quarrying	-	306	305	3	-	150	-	-	-	-	-
Food and Tobacco	136	2461	3	1656	-	315	157	-	-	-	-
Paper, Pulp and Print	-	3937	-	250	33	45	50	-	-	-	-
Wood and Wood Products	-	108	-	49	-	-	1	-	-	-	-
Construction	188	920	12	1287	-	54	-	-	-	-	-
Textile and Leather	-	539	-	280	-	8	25	-	-	-	-
Non-specified	165	11437	692	8605	2756	4573	3520	-	-	-	-
TRANSPORT SECTOR	**14**	**23**	**198**	**1**	**-**	**5**	**2**	**-**	**-**	**-**	**-**
International Civil Aviation	-	-	-	-	-	-	-	-	-	-	-
Domestic Air	-	-	-	-	-	-	-	-	-	-	-
Road	-	-	-	-	-	-	-	-	-	-	-
Rail	14	23	-	1	-	5	2	-	-	-	-
Pipeline Transport	-	-	-	-	-	-	-	-	-	-	-
Internal Navigation	-	-	198	-	-	-	-	-	-	-	-
Non-specified	-	-	-	-	-	-	-	-	-	-	-
OTHER SECTORS	**296**	**13447**	**408**	**9895**	**1549**	**2406**	**10823**	**-**	**-**	**-**	**-**
Agriculture	-	181	17	240	49	52	351	-	-	-	-
Commerce and Publ. Serv.	-	1211	-	1117	15	267	2100	-	-	-	-
Residential	296	11638	139	8374	1485	2068	7904	-	-	-	-
Non-specified	-	417	252	164	-	19	468	-	-	-	-
NON-ENERGY USE	**211**	**273**	**-**	**53**	**-**	**1650**	**202**	**-**	**-**	**-**	**-**
in Industry/Transf./Energy	211	273	-	53	-	1650	202	-	-	-	-
in Transport	-	-	-	-	-	-	-	-	-	-	-
in Other Sectors	-	-	-	-	-	-	-	-	-	-	-

Industry sector details shown only where sectorial data are available for most countries.
La ventilation du secteur industriel n'est indiquée que s'il existe des données sectorielles disponibles pour la plupart des pays concernés.

IEA / AIE : 1993

SUPPLY AND CONSUMPTION *APPROVISIONNEMENT ET DEMANDE*	Oil cont. / *Pétrole cont.* (1000 tonnes)										
	Refinery Gas *Gaz de raffinerie*	LPG + Ethane *GPL + éthane*	Motor Gasoline *Essence moteur*	Aviation Gasoline *Essence aviation*	Jet Fuel *Carbu-réacteur*	Kerosene *Kérosène*	Gas/Diesel *Gazole*	Heavy Fuel Oil *Fioul lourd*	Naphtha *Naphta*	Pétrol. Coke *Coke de pétrole*	Other Prod. *Autres prod.*
Production	66735	42246	540589	1275	113818	32231	473280	237729	56423	51058	120095
From Other Sources	-	-	-	-	-	-	-	-	-	-	-
Imports	-	28705	41563	176	15218	3941	73996	72874	38725	12874	22260
Exports	-	-5741	-48875	-214	-12061	-2124	-81208	-63990	-13523	-18059	-18189
Intl. Marine Bunkers	-	-	-	-	-6	-	-15590	-62221	-	-	-339
Stock Changes	-3	-1256	-3105	-39	87	187	1875	1825	-82	257	268
DOMESTIC SUPPLY	**66732**	**63954**	**530172**	**1198**	**117056**	**34235**	**452353**	**186217**	**81543**	**46130**	**124095**
Transfers	-113	45212	-2334	-2	-42	-3388	1513	-5032	-7428	34	-16160
Statistical Differences	16	-425	44	-27	-1493	-379	4254	-2024	907	-37	-115
TRANSFORMATION	**1346**	**5090**	**510**	**-**	**-**	**390**	**6483**	**93142**	**13439**	**4121**	**2405**
Electricity Plants	58	814	-	-	-	-	4729	85828	891	1972	2255
CHP Plants	751	18	-	-	-	-	184	5432	-	209	112
Heat Plants	113	61	-	-	-	11	64	949	-	-	-
Transfer to Gases	277	2962	-	-	-	-	3	367	433	-	-
Transfer to Solids	-	-	-	-	-	-	1	19	-	1940	-
Petroleum Refineries	-	-	-	-	-	-	-	-	-	-	-
Petrochemical Industry	147	1235	510	-	-	379	1502	547	12115	-	2
Liquefaction	-	-	-	-	-	-	-	-	-	-	-
Other Transformation Sector	-	-	-	-	-	-	-	-	-	-	36
ENERGY SECTOR	**62340**	**1672**	**101**	**-**	**69**	**17**	**850**	**17401**	**144**	**21708**	**2850**
Coal Mines	-	2	-	-	-	-	416	34	-	-	1
Oil and Gas Extraction	-	421	-	-	-	-	90	49	-	756	-
Petroleum Refineries	62340	1211	97	-	69	17	289	17135	144	20950	2766
Electricity, CHP+Heat plants	-	1	4	-	-	-	40	154	-	-	2
Pumped Storage (Elec.)	-	-	-	-	-	-	-	-	-	-	-
Other Energy Sector	-	37	-	-	-	-	15	29	-	2	81
Distribution Losses	-	17	81	-	12	1	48	58	-	-	1
FINAL CONSUMPTION	**2949**	**101962**	**527190**	**1169**	**115440**	**30060**	**450739**	**68560**	**61439**	**20298**	**102564**
INDUSTRY SECTOR	**2949**	**68607**	**3081**	**-**	**17**	**5664**	**50152**	**50653**	**61439**	**8759**	**1048**
Iron and Steel	-	-	-	-	-	-	-	-	-	-	-
Chemical and Petrochemical	-	-	-	-	-	-	-	-	-	-	-
of which: Feedstocks	-	-	-	-	-	-	-	-	-	-	-
Non-Ferrous Metals	-	-	-	-	-	-	-	-	-	-	-
Non-Metallic Minerals	-	-	-	-	-	-	-	-	-	-	-
Transport Equipment	-	-	-	-	-	-	-	-	-	-	-
Machinery	-	-	-	-	-	-	-	-	-	-	-
Mining and Quarrying	-	-	-	-	-	-	-	-	-	-	-
Food and Tobacco	-	-	-	-	-	-	-	-	-	-	-
Paper, Pulp and Print	-	-	-	-	-	-	-	-	-	-	-
Wood and Wood Products	-	-	-	-	-	-	-	-	-	-	-
Construction	-	-	-	-	-	-	-	-	-	-	-
Textile and Leather	-	-	-	-	-	-	-	-	-	-	-
Non-specified	-	-	-	-	-	-	-	-	-	-	-
TRANSPORT SECTOR	**-**	**5666**	**519471**	**1167**	**115415**	**22**	**243480**	**5048**	**-**	**-**	**5**
International Civil Aviation	-	-	-	4	32085	-	-	-	-	-	-
Domestic Air	-	-	-	1163	83330	-	1	-	-	-	-
Road	-	5661	515368	-	-	8	211621	41	-	-	5
Rail	-	5	-	-	-	12	16540	46	-	-	-
Pipeline Transport	-	-	-	-	-	-	7	-	-	-	-
Internal Navigation	-	-	4103	-	-	2	12419	4802	-	-	-
Non-specified	-	-	-	-	-	-	2892	159	-	-	-
OTHER SECTORS	**-**	**27689**	**4638**	**2**	**8**	**24374**	**157107**	**12801**	**-**	**124**	**12**
Agriculture	-	2165	2571	2	1	3019	32842	853	-	16	5
Commerce and Publ. Serv.	-	4477	1846	-	7	4980	54356	9109	-	8	7
Residential	-	20928	221	-	-	16278	67959	2561	-	99	-
Non-specified	-	119	-	-	-	97	1950	278	-	1	-
NON-ENERGY USE	**-**	**-**	**-**	**-**	**-**	**-**	**-**	**58**	**-**	**11415**	**101499**
in Industry/Transf./Energy	-	-	-	-	-	-	-	58	-	11415	92077
in Transport	-	-	-	-	-	-	-	-	-	-	7447
in Other Sectors	-	-	-	-	-	-	-	-	-	-	1975

IEA / AIE : 1993

CONSUMPTION *APPROVISIONNEMENT ET DEMANDE*	Gas / *Gaz* (TJ)				Combust. Renew. & Waste / *En. Re. Comb. & Déchets* (TJ)				(GWh)	(TJ)
	Natural Gas *Gaz naturel*	Gas Works *Usines à gaz*	Coke Ovens *Cokeries*	Blast Furnaces *Hauts fourneaux*	Solid Biomass & Anim. Prod. *Biomasse solide & prod. anim.*	Gas/Liquids from Biomass *Gaz/Liquides tirés de biomasse*	Municipal Waste *Déchets urbains*	Industrial Waste *Déchets industriels*	Electricity *Electricité*	Heat *Chaleur*
Production	35072927	612553	873315	1194047	5088157	153652	412602	295246	7526161	1237323
From Other Sources	-	262085	-	-	-	-	-	-	-	-
Imports	11052314	-	-	-	5550	844	-	2657	219617	-
Exports	-5473036	-180	-	-	-	-	-	-20	-211772	-
Intl. Marine Bunkers	-	-	-	-	-	-	-	-	-	-
Stock Changes	212537	2484	2	-	1345	1089	-	150	-	-
DOMESTIC SUPPLY	**40864742**	**876942**	**873317**	**1194047**	**5095052**	**155585**	**412602**	**298033**	**7534006**	**1237323**
Transfers	-	-	-	-	-	-82475	-	-	-	-
Statistical Differences	-777762	-191	-18664	-6440	1154	-2150	-78	-	-	-
TRANSFORMATION	**7920628**	**25**	**302719**	**628282**	**1576811**	**67137**	**396972**	**195471**	**8962**	**-**
Electricity Plants	5894465	-	139541	368728	295144	41861	275185	63934	-	-
CHP Plants	928037	-	152067	258990	1230866	11167	94397	130345	-	-
Heat Plants	224573	25	566	564	46096	2622	27390	1192	8962	-
Transfer to Gases	677168	-	10545	-	-	-	-	-	-	-
Transfer to Solids	1683	-	-	-	4705	-	-	-	-	-
Petroleum Refineries	-	-	-	-	-	11487	-	-	-	-
Petrochemical Industry	-	-	-	-	-	-	-	-	-	-
Liquefaction	182308	-	-	-	-	-	-	-	-	-
Other Transformation Sector	12394	-	-	-	-	-	-	-	-	-
ENERGY SECTOR	**3004161**	**16072**	**163253**	**112006**	**-**	**-**	**-**	**-**	**663616**	**43787**
Coal Mines	7761	-	1620	-	-	-	-	-	31096	-
Oil and Gas Extraction	2033467	-	-	-	-	-	-	-	53870	-
Petroleum Refineries	907102	-	2232	-	-	-	-	-	83016	37514
Electricity, CHP+Heat plants	500	-	-	-	-	-	-	-	400203	251
Pumped Storage (Elec.)	-	-	-	-	-	-	-	-	64166	-
Other Energy Sector	55331	16072	159401	112006	-	-	-	-	31265	6022
Distribution Losses	50641	10201	1965	18982	-	-	-	-	492369	143644
FINAL CONSUMPTION	**29111550**	**850453**	**386716**	**428337**	**3519395**	**3823**	**15552**	**102562**	**6369059**	**1049892**
INDUSTRY SECTOR	**12872818**	**255847**	**385731**	**428216**	**1968621**	**564**	**15212**	**19120**	**2568302**	**351586**
Iron and Steel	-	1891	359353	428056	202	-	-	-	255876	3404
Chemical and Petrochemical	-	7641	10520	160	19526	55	245	11722	473661	151131
of which: Feedstocks	-	-	-	-	-	-	-	-	-	-
Non-Ferrous Metals	-	1512	270	-	1864	149	-	30	266967	1521
Non-Metallic Minerals	-	740	5976	-	18160	-	172	1128	115424	392
Transport Equipment	-	132	180	-	18	-	6	-	113547	5862
Machinery	-	1221	3961	-	302	-	15	110	206742	27844
Mining and Quarrying	-	-	2091	-	47	-	-	-	71457	25
Food and Tobacco	-	1448	1152	-	92616	284	4	243	159020	21557
Paper, Pulp and Print	-	111	450	-	1449828	65	14770	1972	327890	27645
Wood and Wood Products	-	36	-	-	316675	-	-	125	50833	101
Construction	-	2	554	-	-	-	-	10	10031	15
Textile and Leather	-	254	252	-	22744	-	-	120	85988	8291
Non-specified	-	240859	972	-	46639	11	-	3660	430866	103798
TRANSPORT SECTOR	**904899**	**-**	**-**	**-**	**371**	**-**	**7**	**65**	**86400**	**-**
International Civil Aviation	-	-	-	-	-	-	-	-	-	-
Domestic Air	-	-	-	-	-	-	-	-	-	-
Road	17271	-	-	-	-	-	-	-	73504	-
Rail	-	-	-	-	371	-	7	65	3516	-
Pipeline Transport	886059	-	-	-	-	-	-	-	-	-
Internal Navigation	-	-	-	-	-	-	-	-	9380	-
Non-specified	1569	-	-	-	-	-	-	-		-
OTHER SECTORS	**15333366**	**594605**	**936**	**-**	**1550403**	**3259**	**333**	**83377**	**3714357**	**698306**
Agriculture	231080	108	-	-	9211	5	-	-	49698	5244
Commerce and Publ. Serv.	4483589	134141	-	-	4250	940	240	-	1646515	167944
Residential	10133383	460306	936	-	1536942	7	93	83377	2011402	379562
Non-specified	485314	50	-	-	-	2307	-	-	6742	145556
NON-ENERGY USE	**467**	**1**	**49**	**121**	**-**	**-**	**-**	**-**	**-**	**-**
in Industry/Transf./Energy	467	1	49	121	-	-	-	-	-	-
in Transport	-	-	-	-	-	-	-	-	-	-
in Other Sectors	-	-	-	-	-	-	-	-	-	-

INTERNATIONAL ENERGY AGENCY

European Union / Union Européenne : 1992

SUPPLY AND CONSUMPTION *APPROVISIONNEMENT ET DEMANDE*	Coal / *Charbon* (1000 tonnes)							Oil / *Pétrole* (1000 tonnes)			
	Coking Coal *Charbon à coke*	Steam Coal *Charbon vapeur*	Sub-Bit. Coal *Charbon sous-bit.*	Lignite *Lignite*	Peat *Tourbe*	Oven and Gas Coke *Coke de four/gaz*	Pat. Fuel and BKB *Agg./briq. de lignite*	Crude Oil *Pétrole brut*	NGL *LGN*	Feedstocks *Produits d'aliment.*	Additives *Additifs*
Production	41093	139610	4123	315705	12607	48364	19202	113311	6418	-	144
From Other Sources	-	1350	979	-	-	-	-	103	-	10171	1658
Imports	44301	107388	-	4082	7	7157	936	497333	3255	36924	104
Exports	-714	-5343	-14	-24	-338	-4201	-931	-60773	-2014	-4954	-
Intl. Marine Bunkers	-	-	-	-	-	-	-	-	-	-	-
Stock Changes	-3306	-10124	560	395	2233	-1426	152	-5080	-47	32	-22
DOMESTIC SUPPLY	**81374**	**232881**	**5648**	**320158**	**14509**	**49894**	**19359**	**544894**	**7612**	**42173**	**1884**
Transfers	-	-	-	-	-	-	-	-1291	-2412	27824	-
Statistical Differences	-279	845	-32	-2	-	134	-7	718	25	-498	-21
TRANSFORMATION	**79931**	**192822**	**5315**	**306740**	**9319**	**15383**	**2682**	**544093**	**5225**	**69499**	**1863**
Electricity Plants	16973	166494	5235	262660	4138	-	1499	-	-	-	-
CHP Plants	-	21899	80	-	3351	-	-	-	-	-	-
Heat Plants	-	1387	-	2603	784	5	554	-	-	-	-
Transfer to Gases	-	581	-	-	-	15157	392	-	-	-	-
Transfer to Solids	62958	2461	-	41477	1046	221	237	-	-	-	-
Petroleum Refineries	-	-	-	-	-	-	-	544093	5225	69499	1863
Petrochemical Industry	-	-	-	-	-	-	-	-	-	-	-
Liquefaction	-	-	-	-	-	-	-	-	-	-	-
Other Transformation Sector	-	-	-	-	-	-	-	-	-	-	-
ENERGY SECTOR	**60**	**292**	**33**	**1749**	**-**	**236**	**277**	**208**	**-**	**-**	**-**
Coal Mines	-	280	33	2	-	-	-	-	-	-	-
Oil and Gas Extraction	-	-	-	-	-	-	-	208	-	-	-
Petroleum Refineries	-	-	-	146	-	-	36	-	-	-	-
Electricity, CHP+Heat plants	-	-	-	-	-	-	-	-	-	-	-
Pumped Storage (Elec.)	-	-	-	-	-	-	-	-	-	-	-
Other Energy Sector	60	12	-	1601	-	236	241	-	-	-	-
Distribution Losses	14	-	-	-	-	7	-	-	-	-	-
FINAL CONSUMPTION	**1090**	**40612**	**268**	**11667**	**5190**	**34402**	**16393**	**20**	**-**	**-**	**-**
INDUSTRY SECTOR	**848**	**30747**	**261**	**8909**	**3435**	**30191**	**4041**	**20**	**-**	**-**	**-**
Iron and Steel	805	5663	-	21	-	27203	-	20	-	-	-
Chemical and Petrochemical	-	4451	4	76	7	439	-	-	-	-	-
of which: Feedstocks	-	-	-	-	-	-	-	20	-	-	-
Non-Ferrous Metals	-	574	-	394	-	764	1	-	-	-	-
Non-Metallic Minerals	-	12542	257	313	-	571	-	-	-	-	-
Transport Equipment	-	381	-	-	-	42	-	-	-	-	-
Machinery	-	454	-	16	-	798	-	-	-	-	-
Mining and Quarrying	-	332	-	3	-	12	-	-	-	-	-
Food and Tobacco	-	1742	-	50	-	229	-	-	-	-	-
Paper, Pulp and Print	-	1891	-	193	30	43	18	-	-	-	-
Wood and Wood Products	-	96	-	-	-	1	5	-	-	-	-
Construction	-	-	-	-	-	-	-	-	-	-	-
Textile and Leather	-	547	-	15	-	5	-	-	-	-	-
Non-specified	43	2074	-	7828	3398	84	4017	-	-	-	-
TRANSPORT SECTOR	**-**	**27**	**-**	**2**	**-**	**5**	**-**	**-**	**-**	**-**	**-**
International Civil Aviation	-	-	-	-	-	-	-	-	-	-	-
Domestic Air	-	-	-	-	-	-	-	-	-	-	-
Road	-	-	-	-	-	-	-	-	-	-	-
Rail	-	27	-	2	-	5	-	-	-	-	-
Pipeline Transport	-	-	-	-	-	-	-	-	-	-	-
Internal Navigation	-	-	-	-	-	-	-	-	-	-	-
Non-specified	-	-	-	-	-	-	-	-	-	-	-
OTHER SECTORS	**-**	**9731**	**7**	**2699**	**1755**	**2387**	**12100**	**-**	**-**	**-**	**-**
Agriculture	-	197	-	333	94	56	403	-	-	-	-
Commerce and Publ. Serv.	-	1228	-	1863	6	302	2329	-	-	-	-
Residential	-	7856	7	357	1655	1994	8617	-	-	-	-
Non-specified	-	450	-	146	-	35	751	-	-	-	-
NON-ENERGY USE	**242**	**107**	**-**	**57**	**-**	**1819**	**252**	**-**	**-**	**-**	**-**
in Industry/Transf./Energy	242	107	-	57	-	1819	252	-	-	-	-
in Transport	-	-	-	-	-	-	-	-	-	-	-
in Other Sectors	-	-	-	-	-	-	-	-	-	-	-

European Union / Union Européenne : 1992

SUPPLY AND CONSUMPTION *APPROVISIONNEMENT ET DEMANDE*	Oil cont. / *Pétrole cont.* (1000 tonnes)										
	Refinery Gas *Gaz de raffinerie*	LPG + Ethane *GPL + éthane*	Motor Gasoline *Essence moteur*	Aviation Gasoline *Essence aviation*	Jet Fuel *Carbu-réacteur*	Kerosene *Kérosène*	Gas/Diesel *Gazole*	Heavy Fuel Oil *Fioul lourd*	Naphtha *Naphta*	Pétrol. Coke *Coke de pétrole*	Other Prod. *Autres prod.*
Production	19109	15544	137072	163	31037	5202	202046	125050	31916	6297	41228
From Other Sources	-	-	-	-	-	-	-	-	-	-	-
Imports	-	10620	26427	108	7954	975	60086	43726	24496	6378	10321
Exports	-	-4250	-36488	-161	-8834	-1827	-51241	-48289	-13149	-578	-12919
Intl. Marine Bunkers	-	-	-	-	-	-	-8348	-26612	-	-	-316
Stock Changes	2	108	-235	8	63	148	256	118	301	-162	327
DOMESTIC SUPPLY	**19111**	**22022**	**126776**	**118**	**30220**	**4498**	**202799**	**93993**	**43564**	**11935**	**38641**
Transfers	-48	220	-4856	-1	-258	-365	-2325	-3557	-7186	-5	-4028
Statistical Differences	7	-115	228	17	-1717	20	4315	1159	1354	545	-400
TRANSFORMATION	**936**	**888**	**398**	**-**	**-**	**262**	**2909**	**46641**	**7106**	**1456**	**1458**
Electricity Plants	69	10	-	-	-	-	1598	39684	9	20	1287
CHP Plants	688	20	-	-	-	-	115	5385	-	276	142
Heat Plants	-	55	-	-	-	-	56	916	-	-	-
Transfer to Gases	30	153	-	-	-	-	3	20	157	-	-
Transfer to Solids	-	-	-	-	-	-	1	-	-	1160	-
Petroleum Refineries	-	-	-	-	-	-	-	-	-	-	-
Petrochemical Industry	149	650	398	-	-	262	1136	636	6940	-	-
Liquefaction	-	-	-	-	-	-	-	-	-	-	-
Other Transformation Sector	-	-	-	-	-	-	-	-	-	-	29
ENERGY SECTOR	**16120**	**672**	**5**	**-**	**1**	**7**	**209**	**10366**	**90**	**3705**	**2496**
Coal Mines	-	2	-	-	-	-	105	35	-	-	2
Oil and Gas Extraction	-	361	-	-	-	-	2	58	-	-	-
Petroleum Refineries	16106	259	5	-	1	6	99	10238	90	3702	2360
Electricity, CHP+Heat plants	-	-	-	-	-	-	-	4	-	-	1
Pumped Storage (Elec.)	-	-	-	-	-	-	-	-	-	-	-
Other Energy Sector	14	50	-	-	1	1	3	31	-	3	133
Distribution Losses	-	17	74	-	21	4	52	57	-	-	1
FINAL CONSUMPTION	**2014**	**20550**	**121671**	**134**	**28223**	**3880**	**201619**	**34531**	**30536**	**7314**	**30258**
INDUSTRY SECTOR	**2014**	**9267**	**870**	**-**	**20**	**1131**	**15028**	**27085**	**30536**	**5755**	**381**
Iron and Steel	-	293	-	-	-	-	438	2888	-	71	-
Chemical and Petrochemical	1940	5865	812	-	-	571	5117	7085	30533	257	281
of which: Feedstocks	*890*	*5545*	*812*	-	-	*548*	*3918*	*2521*	*29602*	-	-
Non-Ferrous Metals	-	272	-	-	-	-	421	906	-	66	-
Non-Metallic Minerals	-	668	2	-	-	7	751	4164	-	4201	-
Transport Equipment	-	79	-	-	-	-	464	402	-	-	-
Machinery	-	287	53	-	20	14	1676	1260	-	84	-
Mining and Quarrying	-	6	-	-	-	-	608	336	-	-	-
Food and Tobacco	4	379	1	-	-	2	1555	4345	-	-	-
Paper, Pulp and Print	51	112	-	-	-	-	333	2475	-	8	-
Wood and Wood Products	-	11	1	-	-	-	363	227	-	-	-
Construction	-	35	1	-	-	-	1906	449	-	-	-
Textile and Leather	-	79	-	-	-	-	404	1588	-	39	-
Non-specified	19	1181	-	-	-	537	992	960	3	1029	100
TRANSPORT SECTOR	**-**	**2259**	**120325**	**134**	**28203**	**19**	**101746**	**1268**	**-**	**-**	**6**
International Civil Aviation	-	-	-	3	21154	-	-	-	-	-	-
Domestic Air	-	-	-	131	7049	-	-	-	-	-	-
Road	-	2257	119937	-	-	4	93690	-	-	-	6
Rail	-	2	-	-	-	12	2799	18	-	-	-
Pipeline Transport	-	-	-	-	-	-	-	-	-	-	-
Internal Navigation	-	-	388	-	-	3	5227	1250	-	-	-
Non-specified	-	-	-	-	-	-	30	-	-	-	-
OTHER SECTORS	**-**	**9024**	**476**	**-**	**-**	**2730**	**84845**	**6178**	**-**	**132**	**13**
Agriculture	-	507	251	-	-	234	12012	732	-	15	6
Commerce and Publ. Serv.	-	1150	-	-	-	51	31478	3651	-	7	7
Residential	-	7346	225	-	-	2364	39462	1466	-	110	-
Non-specified	-	21	-	-	-	81	1893	329	-	-	-
NON-ENERGY USE	**-**	**-**	**-**	**-**	**-**	**-**	**-**	**-**	**-**	**1427**	**29858**
in Industry/Transf./Energy	-	-	-	-	-	-	-	-	-	1427	27427
in Transport	-	-	-	-	-	-	-	-	-	-	2044
in Other Sectors	-	-	-	-	-	-	-	-	-	-	387

European Union / Union Européenne : 1992

CONSUMPTION / APPROVISIONNEMENT ET DEMANDE	Gas / Gaz (TJ)				Combust. Renew. & Waste / En. Re. Comb. & Déchets (TJ)				(GWh)	(TJ)
	Natural Gas / Gaz naturel	Gas Works / Usines à gaz	Coke Ovens / Cokeries	Blast Furnaces / Hauts fourneaux	Solid Biomass & Anim. Prod. / Biomasse solide & prod. anim.	Gas/Liquids from Biomass / Gaz/Liquides tirés de biomasse	Municipal Waste / Déchets urbains	Industrial Waste / Déchets industriels	Electricity / Electricité	Heat / Chaleur
Production	6862326	64762	383499	499470	816491	15655	128167	113827	2226048	754816
From Other Sources	-	26521	-	-	-	-	-	-	-	-
Imports	6051255	-	-	-	4900	-	-	2913	148684	-
Exports	-1592297	-198	-	-	-	-	-	-68	-129897	-
Intl. Marine Bunkers	-	-	-	-	-	-	-	-	-	-
Stock Changes	-225461	3564	-1	-	2690	-	-	279	-	-
DOMESTIC SUPPLY	**11095823**	**94649**	**383498**	**499470**	**824081**	**15655**	**128167**	**116951**	**2244835**	**754816**
Transfers	-	-	-	-	-	-	-	-	-	-
Statistical Differences	5560	-24	-1153	-3925	-	-	-	-17	-	-
TRANSFORMATION	**1815844**	**655**	**67401**	**197197**	**124782**	**13205**	**112377**	**22035**	**8053**	**-**
Electricity Plants	849946	-	57073	148276	27239	8832	60344	16427	-	-
CHP Plants	736194	-	6600	48376	51593	1092	26898	5088	-	-
Heat Plants	151132	655	511	541	41709	3281	25135	520	8053	-
Transfer to Gases	77450	-	3217	-	-	-	-	-	-	-
Transfer to Solids	1083	-	-	4	4241	-	-	-	-	-
Petroleum Refineries	-	-	-	-	-	-	-	-	-	-
Petrochemical Industry	-	-	-	-	-	-	-	-	-	-
Liquefaction	-	-	-	-	-	-	-	-	-	-
Other Transformation Sector	39	-	-	-	-	-	-	-	-	-
ENERGY SECTOR	**353870**	**1546**	**134484**	**44114**	**2**	**-**	**-**	**-**	**226460**	**6021**
Coal Mines	5094	-	2376	-	-	-	-	-	13626	-
Oil and Gas Extraction	257383	-	-	-	-	-	-	-	5991	-
Petroleum Refineries	41766	288	5473	-	-	-	-	-	21731	-
Electricity, CHP+Heat plants	-	-	-	-	2	-	-	-	122994	-
Pumped Storage (Elec.)	-	-	-	-	-	-	-	-	25407	-
Other Energy Sector	49627	1258	126635	44114	-	-	-	-	36711	6021
Distribution Losses	77576	1346	2301	20281	-	-	-	-	125057	71357
FINAL CONSUMPTION	**8854093**	**91078**	**178159**	**233953**	**699297**	**2450**	**15773**	**94916**	**1885265**	**677438**
INDUSTRY SECTOR	**3572504**	**14271**	**177439**	**233953**	**344119**	**455**	**15632**	**828**	**811068**	**98205**
Iron and Steel	356900	1764	150288	233801	8	-	-	-	95328	3033
Chemical and Petrochemical	1267983	1041	13458	152	18749	91	638	-	171021	20710
of which: Feedstocks	535314	-	-	-	-	-	-	-	-	-
Non-Ferrous Metals	82677	1854	936	-	205	131	-	-	63789	-
Non-Metallic Minerals	482711	2910	2056	-	18138	-	185	502	58841	15
Transport Equipment	116479	522	306	-	-	-	-	-	53365	466
Machinery	286611	2864	4177	-	338	-	16	9	57081	19753
Mining and Quarrying	25706	-	166	-	-	-	-	-	15483	22
Food and Tobacco	400087	2592	1296	-	13612	172	27	2	72359	510
Paper, Pulp and Print	263881	185	1260	-	201396	61	14766	167	96343	1653
Wood and Wood Products	7028	109	18	-	46645	-	-	148	17313	80
Construction	10536	2	565	-	-	-	-	-	9219	-
Textile and Leather	119801	291	756	-	1888	-	-	-	34577	45
Non-specified	152104	137	2157	-	43140	-	-	-	66349	51918
TRANSPORT SECTOR	**10973**	**-**	**-**	**-**	**-**	**-**	**6**	**65**	**50357**	**-**
International Civil Aviation	-	-	-	-	-	-	-	-	-	-
Domestic Air	-	-	-	-	-	-	-	-	-	-
Road	9983	-	-	-	-	-	-	-	-	-
Rail	-	-	-	-	-	-	6	65	41918	-
Pipeline Transport	-	-	-	-	-	-	-	-	720	-
Internal Navigation	-	-	-	-	-	-	-	-	-	-
Non-specified	990	-	-	-	-	-	-	-	7719	-
OTHER SECTORS	**5270616**	**76807**	**720**	**-**	**355178**	**1995**	**135**	**94023**	**1023840**	**579233**
Agriculture	188327	216	-	-	8535	-	-	-	32567	4729
Commerce and Publ. Serv.	826297	15767	-	-	2931	-	-	-	427024	78070
Residential	3791970	60824	720	-	343712	-	135	94023	557523	351158
Non-specified	464022	-	-	-	-	1995	-	-	6726	145276
NON-ENERGY USE	**-**	**-**	**-**	**-**	**-**	**-**	**-**	**-**	**-**	**-**
in Industry/Transf./Energy	-	-	-	-	-	-	-	-	-	-
in Transport	-	-	-	-	-	-	-	-	-	-
in Other Sectors	-	-	-	-	-	-	-	-	-	-

European Union / Union Européenne : 1993

SUPPLY AND CONSUMPTION / APPROVISIONNEMENT ET DEMANDE	Coking Coal / Charbon à coke	Steam Coal / Charbon vapeur	Sub-Bit. Coal / Charbon sous-bit.	Lignite / Lignite	Peat / Tourbe	Oven and Gas Coke / Coke de four/gaz	Pat. Fuel and BKB / Agg./briq. de lignite	Crude Oil / Pétrole brut	NGL / LGN	Feedstocks / Produits d'aliment.	Additives / Additifs
Production	36222	118052	4308	293932	13282	43520	16183	117888	7478	-	143
From Other Sources	-	1229	971	-	-	-	-	85	-	11461	1745
Imports	42418	89424	-	3374	36	7242	1011	496891	3817	33704	300
Exports	-96	-5623	-16	-46	-303	-3426	-1023	-67362	-2274	-6269	-
Intl. Marine Bunkers	-	-	-	-	-	-	-	-	-	-	-
Stock Changes	-1302	6990	-98	1464	809	189	53	1325	50	293	20
DOMESTIC SUPPLY	**77242**	**210072**	**5165**	**298724**	**13824**	**47525**	**16224**	**548827**	**9071**	**39189**	**2208**
Transfers	-	-	-	-	-	-	-	-1417	-2384	30480	-
Statistical Differences	-341	1313	35	27	-	184	-	2127	-734	62	-98
TRANSFORMATION	**75723**	**175551**	**5024**	**290143**	**9458**	**14659**	**1761**	**549322**	**5953**	**69731**	**2110**
Electricity Plants	18645	148422	5011	252114	4412	-	1081	-	-	-	-
CHP Plants	-	23026	13	-	3272	-	-	-	-	-	-
Heat Plants	-	1360	-	2856	764	11	464	-	-	-	-
Transfer to Gases	-	550	-	-	-	14564	-	-	-	-	-
Transfer to Solids	57078	2193	-	35173	1010	84	216	-	-	-	-
Petroleum Refineries	-	-	-	-	-	-	-	549322	5953	69731	2110
Petrochemical Industry	-	-	-	-	-	-	-	-	-	-	-
Liquefaction	-	-	-	-	-	-	-	-	-	-	-
Other Transformation Sector	-	-	-	-	-	-	-	-	-	-	-
ENERGY SECTOR	**57**	**308**	**3**	**1609**	**-**	**195**	**115**	**200**	**-**	**-**	**-**
Coal Mines	-	206	3	-	-	-	-	-	-	-	-
Oil and Gas Extraction	-	-	-	-	-	-	-	200	-	-	-
Petroleum Refineries	-	-	-	-	-	-	-	-	-	-	-
Electricity, CHP+Heat plants	-	-	-	-	-	-	-	-	-	-	-
Pumped Storage (Elec.)	-	-	-	-	-	-	-	-	-	-	-
Other Energy Sector	57	102	-	1609	-	195	115	-	-	-	-
Distribution Losses	10	-	-	-	-	6	-	-	-	-	-
FINAL CONSUMPTION	**1111**	**35526**	**173**	**6999**	**4366**	**32849**	**14348**	**15**	**-**	**-**	**-**
INDUSTRY SECTOR	**900**	**25812**	**168**	**5161**	**2817**	**29190**	**3543**	**15**	**-**	**-**	**-**
Iron and Steel	856	5375	-	-	-	26355	-	-	-	-	-
Chemical and Petrochemical	-	3751	4	145	28	389	-	15	-	-	-
of which: Feedstocks	-	-	-	-	-	-	-	-	-	-	-
Non-Ferrous Metals	-	460	-	475	-	795	-	-	-	-	-
Non-Metallic Minerals	-	10189	160	290	-	591	4	-	-	-	-
Transport Equipment	-	319	-	-	-	39	-	-	-	-	-
Machinery	-	308	-	13	-	660	-	-	-	-	-
Mining and Quarrying	-	268	-	3	-	11	-	-	-	-	-
Food and Tobacco	-	1590	-	40	-	245	-	-	-	-	-
Paper, Pulp and Print	-	1772	-	168	33	45	18	-	-	-	-
Wood and Wood Products	-	86	-	-	-	-	1	-	-	-	-
Construction	-	-	-	-	-	-	-	-	-	-	-
Textile and Leather	-	509	-	15	-	8	-	-	-	-	-
Non-specified	44	1185	4	4012	2756	52	3520	-	-	-	-
TRANSPORT SECTOR	**-**	**22**	**-**	**1**	**-**	**5**	**2**	**-**	**-**	**-**	**-**
International Civil Aviation	-	-	-	-	-	-	-	-	-	-	-
Domestic Air	-	-	-	-	-	-	-	-	-	-	-
Road	-	-	-	-	-	-	-	-	-	-	-
Rail	-	22	-	1	-	5	2	-	-	-	-
Pipeline Transport	-	-	-	-	-	-	-	-	-	-	-
Internal Navigation	-	-	-	-	-	-	-	-	-	-	-
Non-specified	-	-	-	-	-	-	-	-	-	-	-
OTHER SECTORS	**-**	**9596**	**5**	**1784**	**1549**	**2213**	**10601**	**-**	**-**	**-**	**-**
Agriculture	-	177	5	240	49	52	351	-	-	-	-
Commerce and Publ. Serv.	-	997	-	1117	15	267	2023	-	-	-	-
Residential	-	8016	-	304	1485	1875	7759	-	-	-	-
Non-specified	-	406	-	123	-	19	468	-	-	-	-
NON-ENERGY USE	**211**	**96**	**-**	**53**	**-**	**1441**	**202**	**-**	**-**	**-**	**-**
in Industry/Transf./Energy	211	96	-	53	-	1441	202	-	-	-	-
in Transport	-	-	-	-	-	-	-	-	-	-	-
in Other Sectors	-	-	-	-	-	-	-	-	-	-	-

European Union / Union Européenne : 1993

Oil cont. / *Pétrole cont.* (1000 tonnes)

SUPPLY AND CONSUMPTION / *APPROVISIONNEMENT ET DEMANDE*	Refinery Gas / *Gaz de raffinerie*	LPG + Ethane / *GPL + éthane*	Motor Gasoline / *Essence moteur*	Aviation Gasoline / *Essence aviation*	Jet Fuel / *Carbu-réacteur*	Kerosene / *Kérosène*	Gas/ Diesel / *Gazole*	Heavy Fuel Oil / *Fioul lourd*	Naphtha / *Naphta*	Pétrol. Coke / *Coke de pétrole*	Other Prod. / *Autres prod.*
Production	19511	15794	139101	180	31864	5108	208668	121899	30911	6439	41516
From Other Sources	-	-	-	-	-	-	-	-	-	-	-
Imports	-	11183	26550	133	7816	2064	58206	44916	23408	5736	10818
Exports	-	-4568	-38415	-155	-8258	-1540	-55863	-48107	-12092	-599	-13354
Intl. Marine Bunkers	-	-	-	-	-6	-	-7449	-28518	-	-	-307
Stock Changes	-	14	-1404	-7	-209	-107	1198	912	-107	63	231
DOMESTIC SUPPLY	**19511**	**22423**	**125832**	**151**	**31207**	**5525**	**204760**	**91102**	**42120**	**11639**	**38904**
Transfers	-105	-100	-4977	-12	-141	-1561	1	-5200	-7141	25	-5804
Statistical Differences	57	-343	819	-10	-1455	261	3302	-144	848	136	-639
TRANSFORMATION	**1098**	**965**	**510**	**-**	**-**	**379**	**3381**	**41607**	**7785**	**1302**	**1560**
Electricity Plants	58	1	-	-	-	-	1667	34418	5	14	1417
CHP Plants	751	18	-	-	-	-	146	5344	-	209	112
Heat Plants	113	55	-	-	-	-	63	931	-	-	-
Transfer to Gases	29	136	-	-	-	-	3	367	158	-	-
Transfer to Solids	-	-	-	-	-	-	1	-	-	1079	-
Petroleum Refineries	-	-	-	-	-	-	-	-	-	-	-
Petrochemical Industry	147	755	510	-	-	379	1501	547	7622	-	-
Liquefaction	-	-	-	-	-	-	-	-	-	-	-
Other Transformation Sector	-	-	-	-	-	-	-	-	-	-	31
ENERGY SECTOR	**16484**	**682**	**-**	**-**	**-**	**5**	**230**	**10935**	**58**	**3777**	**2477**
Coal Mines	-	2	-	-	-	-	106	33	-	-	1
Oil and Gas Extraction	-	390	-	-	-	-	2	49	-	-	-
Petroleum Refineries	16484	253	-	-	-	5	107	10822	58	3775	2393
Electricity, CHP+Heat plants	-	-	-	-	-	-	-	2	-	-	2
Pumped Storage (Elec.)	-	-	-	-	-	-	-	-	-	-	-
Other Energy Sector	-	37	-	-	-	-	15	29	-	2	81
Distribution Losses	-	17	81	-	12	1	48	58	-	-	1
FINAL CONSUMPTION	**1881**	**20316**	**121083**	**129**	**29599**	**3840**	**204404**	**33158**	**27984**	**6721**	**28423**
INDUSTRY SECTOR	**1881**	**8651**	**833**	**-**	**17**	**1043**	**15457**	**26286**	**27984**	**5297**	**5**
Iron and Steel	-	205	-	-	-	-	465	2680	-	92	-
Chemical and Petrochemical	1870	5408	793	-	1	462	4131	7212	27984	225	5
of which: Feedstocks	*868*	*5026*	*582*	-	-	*436*	*3905*	*2190*	*26923*	-	-
Non-Ferrous Metals	-	248	-	-	-	-	429	863	-	60	-
Non-Metallic Minerals	-	607	-	-	-	5	828	3887	-	3915	-
Transport Equipment	-	84	-	-	-	-	422	353	-	-	-
Machinery	-	278	39	-	16	11	1503	1144	-	84	-
Mining and Quarrying	-	5	-	-	-	-	591	266	-	-	-
Food and Tobacco	4	407	1	-	-	1	1465	4042	-	2	-
Paper, Pulp and Print	7	117	-	-	-	-	305	2312	-	4	-
Wood and Wood Products	-	19	-	-	-	-	209	236	-	-	-
Construction	-	40	-	-	-	-	2478	407	-	-	-
Textile and Leather	-	58	-	-	-	-	378	1535	-	-	-
Non-specified	-	1175	-	-	-	564	2253	1349	-	915	-
TRANSPORT SECTOR	**-**	**2334**	**119807**	**129**	**29582**	**18**	**105346**	**1232**	**-**	**-**	**5**
International Civil Aviation	-	-	-	4	23253	-	-	-	-	-	-
Domestic Air	-	-	-	125	6329	-	-	-	-	-	-
Road	-	2329	119403	-	-	4	97321	-	-	-	5
Rail	-	5	-	-	-	12	2754	21	-	-	-
Pipeline Transport	-	-	-	-	-	-	-	-	-	-	-
Internal Navigation	-	-	404	-	-	2	5271	1199	-	-	-
Non-specified	-	-	-	-	-	-	-	12	-	-	-
OTHER SECTORS	**-**	**9331**	**443**	**-**	**-**	**2779**	**83601**	**5582**	**-**	**124**	**12**
Agriculture	-	527	223	-	-	200	11446	756	-	16	5
Commerce and Publ. Serv.	-	956	-	-	-	44	30199	3232	-	8	7
Residential	-	7816	220	-	-	2438	40006	1316	-	99	-
Non-specified	-	32	-	-	-	97	1950	278	-	1	-
NON-ENERGY USE	**-**	**-**	**-**	**-**	**-**	**-**	**-**	**58**	**-**	**1300**	**28401**
in Industry/Transf./Energy	-	-	-	-	-	-	-	58	-	1300	25974
in Transport	-	-	-	-	-	-	-	-	-	-	2103
in Other Sectors	-	-	-	-	-	-	-	-	-	-	324

European Union / Union Européenne : 1993

CONSUMPTION / *APPROVISIONNEMENT ET DEMANDE*	Gas / *Gaz* (TJ)				Combust. Renew. & Waste / *En. Re. Comb. & Déchets* (TJ)				(GWh)	(TJ)
	Natural Gas / *Gaz naturel*	Gas Works / *Usines à gaz*	Coke Ovens / *Cokeries*	Blast Furnaces / *Hauts fourneaux*	Solid Biomass & Anim. Prod. / *Biomasse solide & prod. anim.*	Gas/Liquids from Biomass / *Gaz/Liquides tirés de biomasse*	Municipal Waste / *Déchets urbains*	Industrial Waste / *Déchets industriels*	Electricity / *Electricité*	Heat / *Chaleur*
Production	7351441	36919	356175	489280	850988	18782	133625	103028	2228532	787540
From Other Sources	-	26168	-	-	-	-	-	-	-	-
Imports	6073852	-	-	-	4960	-	-	2657	154846	-
Exports	-1640924	-180	-	-	-	-	-	-20	-132975	-
Intl. Marine Bunkers	-	-	-	-	-	-	-	-	-	-
Stock Changes	-62731	2484	2	-	1345	-	-	150	-	-
DOMESTIC SUPPLY	**11721638**	**65391**	**356177**	**489280**	**857293**	**18782**	**133625**	**105815**	**2250403**	**787540**
Transfers	-	-	-	-	-	-	-	-	-	-
Statistical Differences	19216	54	1583	-3530	-	-	4	-	-	-
TRANSFORMATION	**2190346**	**25**	**58988**	**194142**	**139924**	**15270**	**118317**	**21408**	**7573**	**-**
Electricity Plants	1122677	-	45874	142311	27325	10309	63469	16460	-	-
CHP Plants	796538	-	9408	51319	61990	2339	29709	4162	-	-
Heat Plants	215321	25	566	512	45904	2622	25139	786	7573	-
Transfer to Gases	54049	-	3140	-	-	-	-	-	-	-
Transfer to Solids	1683	-	-	-	4705	-	-	-	-	-
Petroleum Refineries	-	-	-	-	-	-	-	-	-	-
Petrochemical Industry	-	-	-	-	-	-	-	-	-	-
Liquefaction	-	-	-	-	-	-	-	-	-	-
Other Transformation Sector	78	-	-	-	-	-	-	-	-	-
ENERGY SECTOR	**362289**	**243**	**119646**	**42305**	**-**	**-**	**-**	**-**	**214044**	**6022**
Coal Mines	3384	-	1620	-	-	-	-	-	12268	-
Oil and Gas Extraction	255982	-	-	-	-	-	-	-	6125	-
Petroleum Refineries	47592	-	2232	-	-	-	-	-	22534	-
Electricity, CHP+Heat plants	-	-	-	-	-	-	-	-	119540	-
Pumped Storage (Elec.)	-	-	-	-	-	-	-	-	22572	-
Other Energy Sector	55331	243	115794	42305	-	-	-	-	31005	6022
Distribution Losses	49292	1135	1965	18616	-	-	-	-	134002	72854
FINAL CONSUMPTION	**9138927**	**64042**	**177161**	**230687**	**717369**	**3512**	**15312**	**84407**	**1894784**	**708664**
INDUSTRY SECTOR	**3608076**	**8111**	**176176**	**230566**	**359227**	**564**	**15212**	**965**	**798824**	**101723**
Iron and Steel	344947	1891	151742	230406	144	-	-	-	89900	3049
Chemical and Petrochemical	1253376	623	10520	160	19526	55	245	-	173672	21091
of which: Feedstocks	*478343*	-	-	-	-	-	-	-	-	-
Non-Ferrous Metals	73922	1512	270	-	9	149	-	-	65318	28
Non-Metallic Minerals	486179	740	5976	-	17489	-	172	798	53641	33
Transport Equipment	108696	126	180	-	18	-	6	-	51110	607
Machinery	269232	1217	3961	-	302	-	15	-	56815	20292
Mining and Quarrying	26297	-	147	-	47	-	-	-	15133	25
Food and Tobacco	396518	1411	1152	-	15337	284	4	-	73621	1075
Paper, Pulp and Print	273341	111	450	-	212377	65	14770	42	98845	2834
Wood and Wood Products	6666	36	-	-	46005	-	-	125	18704	89
Construction	11408	2	554	-	-	-	-	-	8867	-
Textile and Leather	126770	254	252	-	1344	-	-	-	32897	145
Non-specified	230724	188	972	-	46629	11	-	-	60301	52455
TRANSPORT SECTOR	**11111**	**-**	**-**	**-**	**371**	**-**	**7**	**65**	**51266**	**-**
International Civil Aviation	-	-	-	-	-	-	-	-	-	-
Domestic Air	-	-	-	-	-	-	-	-	-	-
Road	10070	-	-	-	-	-	-	-	42531	-
Rail	-	-	-	-	371	-	7	65	693	-
Pipeline Transport	-	-	-	-	-	-	-	-	-	-
Internal Navigation	-	-	-	-	-	-	-	-	-	-
Non-specified	1041	-	-	-	-	-	-	-	8042	-
OTHER SECTORS	**5519740**	**55930**	**936**	**-**	**357771**	**2948**	**93**	**83377**	**1044694**	**606941**
Agriculture	199205	108	-	-	8331	5	-	-	32801	5040
Commerce and Publ. Serv.	832169	13191	-	-	3209	629	-	-	435693	84428
Residential	4005840	42631	936	-	346231	7	93	83377	569709	372053
Non-specified	482526	-	-	-	-	2307	-	-	6491	145420
NON-ENERGY USE	**-**	**1**	**49**	**121**	**-**	**-**	**-**	**-**	**-**	**-**
in Industry/Transf./Energy	-	1	49	121	-	-	-	-	-	-
in Transport	-	-	-	-	-	-	-	-	-	-
in Other Sectors	-	-	-	-	-	-	-	-	-	-

Australia / Australie : 1992

SUPPLY AND CONSUMPTION *APPROVISIONNEMENT ET DEMANDE*	Coal / *Charbon* (1000 tonnes)							Oil / *Pétrole* (1000 tonnes)			
	Coking Coal *Charbon à coke*	Steam Coal *Charbon vapeur*	Sub-Bit. Coal *Charbon sous-bit.*	Lignite *Lignite*	Peat *Tourbe*	Oven and Gas Coke *Coke de four/gaz*	Pat. Fuel and BKB *Agg./briq. de lignite*	Crude Oil *Pétrole brut*	NGL *LGN*	Feedstocks *Produits d'aliment.*	Additives *Additifs*
Production	70821	86309	18000	50723	-	4250	721	24825	2102	-	-
From Other Sources	-	-	-	-	-	-	-	-	-	-	-
Imports	-	-	-	-	-	-	-	7980	-	5110	-
Exports	-65461	-57739	-	-	-	-724	-82	-7035	-	-146	-
Intl. Marine Bunkers	-	-	-	-	-	-	-	-	-	-	-
Stock Changes	477	-1548	-	-	-	29	-85	-2	-	-122	-
DOMESTIC SUPPLY	**5837**	**27022**	**18000**	**50723**	**-**	**3555**	**554**	**25768**	**2102**	**4842**	**-**
Transfers	-	-	-	-	-	-	-	-	-2102	-	-
Statistical Differences	-	-	-	-	-	-	-	2163	-	-1307	-
TRANSFORMATION	**5837**	**24405**	**15347**	**50675**	**-**	**968**	**91**	**27929**	**-**	**3535**	**-**
Electricity Plants	-	24405	15347	48665	-	-	91	1	-	-	-
CHP Plants	-	-	-	-	-	-	-	-	-	-	-
Heat Plants	-	-	-	-	-	-	-	-	-	-	-
Transfer to Gases	-	-	-	-	-	968	-	-	-	-	-
Transfer to Solids	5837	-	-	2010	-	-	-	-	-	-	-
Petroleum Refineries	-	-	-	-	-	-	-	27928	-	3535	-
Petrochemical Industry	-	-	-	-	-	-	-	-	-	-	-
Liquefaction	-	-	-	-	-	-	-	-	-	-	-
Other Transformation Sector	-	-	-	-	-	-	-	-	-	-	-
ENERGY SECTOR	**-**	**-**	**-**	**-**	**-**	**-**	**-**	**2**	**-**	**-**	**-**
Coal Mines	-	-	-	-	-	-	-	-	-	-	-
Oil and Gas Extraction	-	-	-	-	-	-	-	2	-	-	-
Petroleum Refineries	-	-	-	-	-	-	-	-	-	-	-
Electricity, CHP+Heat plants	-	-	-	-	-	-	-	-	-	-	-
Pumped Storage (Elec.)	-	-	-	-	-	-	-	-	-	-	•
Other Energy Sector	-	-	-	-	-	-	-	-	-	-	-
Distribution Losses	-	-	-	-	-	-	-	-	-	-	-
FINAL CONSUMPTION	**-**	**2617**	**2653**	**48**	**-**	**2587**	**463**	**-**	**-**	**-**	**-**
INDUSTRY SECTOR	**-**	**2509**	**2460**	**48**	**-**	**2426**	**373**	**-**	**-**	**-**	**-**
Iron and Steel	-	412	-	-	-	2214	-	-	-	-	-
Chemical and Petrochemical	-	133	-	-	-	-	148	-	-	-	-
of which: Feedstocks	-	-	-	-	-	-	-	-	-	-	-
Non-Ferrous Metals	-	495	1961	-	-	198	-	-	-	-	-
Non-Metallic Minerals	-	682	186	2	-	4	8	-	-	-	-
Transport Equipment	-	-	-	-	-	-	2	-	-	-	-
Machinery	-	1	-	-	-	-	-	-	-	-	-
Mining and Quarrying	-	14	310	-	-	10	-	-	-	-	-
Food and Tobacco	-	418	3	-	-	-	150	-	-	-	-
Paper, Pulp and Print	-	313	-	-	-	-	39	-	-	-	-
Wood and Wood Products	-	20	-	46	-	-	-	-	-	-	-
Construction	-	-	-	-	-	-	-	-	-	-	-
Textile and Leather	-	21	-	-	-	-	26	-	-	-	-
Non-specified	-	-	-	-	-	-	-	-	-	-	-
TRANSPORT SECTOR	**-**	**1**	**192**	**-**	**-**	**-**	**-**	**-**	**-**	**-**	**-**
International Civil Aviation	-	-	-	-	-	-	-	-	-	-	-
Domestic Air	-	-	-	-	-	-	-	-	-	-	-
Road	-	-	-	-	-	-	-	-	-	-	-
Rail	-	1	-	-	-	-	-	-	-	-	-
Pipeline Transport	-	-	-	-	-	-	-	-	-	-	-
Internal Navigation	-	-	192	-	-	-	-	-	-	-	-
Non-specified	-	-	-	-	-	-	-	-	-	-	-
OTHER SECTORS	**-**	**107**	**1**	**-**	**-**	**-**	**90**	**-**	**-**	**-**	**-**
Agriculture	-	-	-	-	-	-	-	-	-	-	-
Commerce and Publ. Serv.	-	102	1	-	-	-	82	-	-	-	-
Residential	-	5	-	-	-	-	8	-	-	-	-
Non-specified	-	-	-	-	-	-	-	-	-	-	-
NON-ENERGY USE	**-**	**-**	**-**	**-**	**-**	**161**	**-**	**-**	**-**	**-**	**-**
in Industry/Transf./Energy	-	-	-	-	-	161	-	-	-	-	-
in Transport	-	-	-	-	-	-	-	-	-	-	-
in Other Sectors	-	-	-	-	-	-	-	-	-	-	-

Australia / Australie : 1992

SUPPLY AND CONSUMPTION *APPROVISIONNEMENT ET DEMANDE*	Oil cont. / *Pétrole cont.* (1000 tonnes)										
	Refinery Gas *Gaz de raffinerie*	LPG + Ethane *GPL + éthane*	Motor Gasoline *Essence moteur*	Aviation Gasoline *Essence aviation*	Jet Fuel *Carbu-réacteur*	Kerosene *Kérosène*	Gas/Diesel *Gazole*	Heavy Fuel Oil *Fioul lourd*	Naphtha *Naphta*	Pétrol. Coke *Coke de pétrole*	Other Prod. *Autres prod.*
Production	1079	640	12640	99	3043	230	8794	2645	199	516	2105
From Other Sources	-	-	-	-	-	-	-	-	-	-	-
Imports	-	25	149	-	82	10	329	905	-	602	207
Exports	-	-866	-507	-112	-197	-107	-702	-988	-	-	-611
Intl. Marine Bunkers	-	-	-	-	-	-	-98	-536	-	-	-
Stock Changes	-	49	33	16	-7	-4	193	44	10	-	-117
DOMESTIC SUPPLY	**1079**	**-152**	**12315**	**3**	**2921**	**129**	**8516**	**2070**	**209**	**1118**	**1584**
Transfers	-	2102	-	-	-	-	-	-	-	-	-
Statistical Differences	-51	25	136	67	-178	29	-49	-560	-8	-48	530
TRANSFORMATION	**-**	**25**	**-**	**-**	**-**	**-**	**512**	**113**	**-**	**-**	**-**
Electricity Plants	-	-	-	-	-	-	512	89	-	-	-
CHP Plants	-	-	-	-	-	-	-	-	-	-	-
Heat Plants	-	-	-	-	-	-	-	-	-	-	-
Transfer to Gases	-	25	-	-	-	-	-	-	-	-	-
Transfer to Solids	-	-	-	-	-	-	-	24	-	-	-
Petroleum Refineries	-	-	-	-	-	-	-	-	-	-	-
Petrochemical Industry	-	-	-	-	-	-	-	-	-	-	-
Liquefaction	-	-	-	-	-	-	-	-	-	-	-
Other Transformation Sector	-	-	-	-	-	-	-	-	-	-	-
ENERGY SECTOR	**1020**	**37**	**-**	**-**	**-**	**-**	**301**	**157**	**-**	**516**	**-**
Coal Mines	-	-	-	-	-	-	296	1	-	-	-
Oil and Gas Extraction	-	37	-	-	-	-	5	-	-	-	-
Petroleum Refineries	1020	-	-	-	-	-	-	156	-	516	-
Electricity, CHP+Heat plants	-	-	-	-	-	-	-	-	-	-	-
Pumped Storage (Elec.)	-	-	-	-	-	-	-	-	-	-	-
Other Energy Sector	-	-	-	-	-	-	-	-	-	-	-
Distribution Losses	-	-	-	-	-	-	-	-	-	-	-
FINAL CONSUMPTION	**8**	**1913**	**12451**	**70**	**2743**	**158**	**7654**	**1240**	**201**	**554**	**2114**
INDUSTRY SECTOR	**8**	**903**	**-**	**-**	**-**	**8**	**1516**	**857**	**201**	**56**	**19**
Iron and Steel	-	15	-	-	-	-	3	10	-	-	-
Chemical and Petrochemical	8	696	-	-	-	-	5	12	183	15	1
of which: Feedstocks	-	667	-	-	-	-	-	-	183	-	-
Non-Ferrous Metals	-	43	-	-	-	1	61	694	18	-	4
Non-Metallic Minerals	-	29	-	-	-	1	23	19	-	41	13
Transport Equipment	-	4	-	-	-	-	2	-	-	-	-
Machinery	-	26	-	-	-	-	2	-	-	-	-
Mining and Quarrying	-	3	-	-	-	-	530	34	-	-	1
Food and Tobacco	-	61	-	-	-	-	22	48	-	-	-
Paper, Pulp and Print	-	9	-	-	-	-	1	18	-	-	-
Wood and Wood Products	-	4	-	-	-	-	19	16	-	-	-
Construction	-	1	-	-	-	6	845	1	-	-	-
Textile and Leather	-	12	-	-	-	-	3	5	-	-	-
Non-specified	-	-	-	-	-	-	-	-	-	-	-
TRANSPORT SECTOR	**-**	**667**	**12451**	**70**	**2743**	**-**	**4955**	**348**	**-**	**-**	**-**
International Civil Aviation	-	-	-	-	1498	-	-	-	-	-	-
Domestic Air	-	-	-	70	1245	-	1	-	-	-	-
Road	-	667	12451	-	-	-	4330	-	-	-	-
Rail	-	-	-	-	-	-	526	-	-	-	-
Pipeline Transport	-	-	-	-	-	-	-	-	-	-	-
Internal Navigation	-	-	-	-	-	-	98	348	-	-	-
Non-specified	-	-	-	-	-	-	-	-	-	-	-
OTHER SECTORS	**-**	**343**	**-**	**-**	**-**	**150**	**1183**	**35**	**-**	**-**	**-**
Agriculture	-	18	-	-	-	3	1076	-	-	-	-
Commerce and Publ. Serv.	-	153	-	-	-	14	57	35	-	-	-
Residential	-	172	-	-	-	133	50	-	-	-	-
Non-specified	-	-	-	-	-	-	-	-	-	-	-
NON-ENERGY USE	**-**	**-**	**-**	**-**	**-**	**-**	**-**	**-**	**-**	**498**	**2095**
in Industry/Transf./Energy	-	-	-	-	-	-	-	-	-	498	2063
in Transport	-	-	-	-	-	-	-	-	-	-	-
in Other Sectors	-	-	-	-	-	-	-	-	-	-	32

Australia / Australie : 1992

CONSUMPTION APPROVISIONNEMENT ET DEMANDE	Gas / Gaz (TJ)				Combust. Renew. & Waste / En. Re. Comb. & Déchets (TJ)				(GWh)	(TJ)
	Natural Gas Gaz naturel	Gas Works Usines à gaz	Coke Ovens Cokeries	Blast Furnaces Hauts fourneaux	Solid Biomass & Anim. Prod. Biomasse solide & prod. anim.	Gas/Liquids from Biomass Gaz/Liquides tirés de biomasse	Municipal Waste Déchets urbains	Industrial Waste Déchets industriels	Electricity Electricité	Heat Chaleur
Production	902611	-	35703	33671	156852	-	-	7570	159649	-
From Other Sources	-	8403	-	-	-	-	-	-	-	-
Imports	-	-	-	-	-	-	-	-	-	-
Exports	-235400	-	-	-	-	-	-	-	-	-
Intl. Marine Bunkers	-	-	-	-	-	-	-	-	-	-
Stock Changes	-	-	-	-	-	-	-	-	-	-
DOMESTIC SUPPLY	**667211**	**8403**	**35703**	**33671**	**156852**	**-**	**-**	**7570**	**159649**	**-**
Transfers	-	-	-	-	-	-	-	-	-	-
Statistical Differences	-2	-	-	-	-	-	-	-	-	-
TRANSFORMATION	**150140**	**-**	**-**	**524**	**-**	**-**	**-**	**-**	**-**	**-**
Electricity Plants	131947	-	-	524	-	-	-	-	-	-
CHP Plants	-	-	-	-	-	-	-	-	-	-
Heat Plants	-	-	-	-	-	-	-	-	-	-
Transfer to Gases	18193	-	-	-	-	-	-	-	-	-
Transfer to Solids	-	-	-	-	-	-	-	-	-	-
Petroleum Refineries	-	-	-	-	-	-	-	-	-	-
Petrochemical Industry	-	-	-	-	-	-	-	-	-	-
Liquefaction	-	-	-	-	-	-	-	-	-	-
Other Transformation Sector	-	-	-	-	-	-	-	-	-	-
ENERGY SECTOR	**99252**	**241**	**5671**	**9422**	**-**	**-**	**-**	**-**	**16059**	**-**
Coal Mines	-	-	-	-	-	-	-	-	3166	-
Oil and Gas Extraction	88249	-	-	-	-	-	-	-	923	-
Petroleum Refineries	11003	-	-	-	-	-	-	-	1307	-
Electricity, CHP+Heat plants	-	-	-	-	-	-	-	-	9664	-
Pumped Storage (Elec.)	-	-	-	-	-	-	-	-	783	-
Other Energy Sector	-	241	5671	9422	-	-	-	-	216	-
Distribution Losses	-	-	-	-	-	-	-	-	10625	-
FINAL CONSUMPTION	**417817**	**8162**	**30032**	**23725**	**156852**	**-**	**-**	**7570**	**132965**	**-**
INDUSTRY SECTOR	**280964**	**5783**	**30032**	**23725**	**81678**	**-**	**-**	**7570**	**60168**	**-**
Iron and Steel	18831	-	28266	23725	147	-	-	-	4881	-
Chemical and Petrochemical	46974	5682	-	-	-	-	-	7537	3822	-
of which: Feedstocks	11869	-	-	-	-	-	-	-	-	-
Non-Ferrous Metals	99931	-	-	-	1789	-	-	-	26874	-
Non-Metallic Minerals	50620	-	-	-	736	-	-	-	2861	-
Transport Equipment	6298	6	-	-	-	-	-	-	1413	-
Machinery	6902	2	-	-	-	-	-	-	2625	-
Mining and Quarrying	1199	-	1766	-	-	-	-	-	6150	-
Food and Tobacco	25199	93	-	-	63587	-	-	33	4546	-
Paper, Pulp and Print	17219	-	-	-	7763	-	-	-	4114	-
Wood and Wood Products	1258	-	-	-	7656	-	-	-	939	-
Construction	244	-	-	-	-	-	-	-	28	-
Textile and Leather	6289	-	-	-	-	-	-	-	1915	-
Non-specified	-	-	-	-	-	-	-	-	-	-
TRANSPORT SECTOR	**5702**	**-**	**-**	**-**	**-**	**-**	**-**	**-**	**1878**	**-**
International Civil Aviation	-	-	-	-	-	-	-	-	-	-
Domestic Air	-	-	-	-	-	-	-	-	-	-
Road	608	-	-	-	-	-	-	-	-	-
Rail	-	-	-	-	-	-	-	-	1625	-
Pipeline Transport	4584	-	-	-	-	-	-	-	3	-
Internal Navigation	-	-	-	-	-	-	-	-	-	-
Non-specified	510	-	-	-	-	-	-	-	250	-
OTHER SECTORS	**130741**	**2379**	**-**	**-**	**75174**	**-**	**-**	**-**	**70919**	**-**
Agriculture	52	-	-	-	-	-	-	-	2583	-
Commerce and Publ. Serv.	37359	726	-	-	701	-	-	-	29018	-
Residential	93330	1653	-	-	74473	-	-	-	39318	-
Non-specified	-	-	-	-	-	-	-	-	-	-
NON-ENERGY USE	**410**	**-**	**-**	**-**	**-**	**-**	**-**	**-**	**-**	**-**
in Industry/Transf./Energy	410	-	-	-	-	-	-	-	-	-
in Transport	-	-	-	-	-	-	-	-	-	-
in Other Sectors	-	-	-	-	-	-	-	-	-	-

Australia / Australie : 1993

SUPPLY AND CONSUMPTION *APPROVISIONNEMENT ET DEMANDE*	Coal / *Charbon* (1000 tonnes)							Oil / *Pétrole* (1000 tonnes)			
	Coking Coal *Charbon à coke*	Steam Coal *Charbon vapeur*	Sub-Bit. Coal *Charbon sous-bit.*	Lignite *Lignite*	Peat *Tourbe*	Oven and Gas Coke *Coke de four/gaz*	Pat. Fuel and BKB *Agg./briq. de lignite*	Crude Oil *Pétrole brut*	NGL *LGN*	Feedstocks *Produits d'aliment.*	Additives *Additifs*
Production	77970	80500	18057	47648	-	4101	516	24438	2216	-	-
From Other Sources	-	-	-	-	-	-	-	-	-	-	-
Imports	-	-	-	-	-	-	-	10445	-	6160	-
Exports	-72419	-55986	-	-	-	-599	-61	-7812	-	-286	-
Intl. Marine Bunkers	-	-	-	-	-	-	-	-	-	-	-
Stock Changes	130	3673	-	-	-	-36	50	-195	-	112	-
DOMESTIC SUPPLY	**5681**	**28187**	**18057**	**47648**	**-**	**3466**	**505**	**26876**	**2216**	**5986**	**-**
Transfers	-	-	-	-	-	-	-	-	-2216	-	-
Statistical Differences	-	-	-	-	-	-	-	2223	-	-2441	-
TRANSFORMATION	**5681**	**25698**	**15288**	**47597**	**-**	**950**	**65**	**29095**	**-**	**3545**	**-**
Electricity Plants	-	25698	15288	46333	-	-	65	1	-	-	-
CHP Plants	-	-	-	-	-	-	-	-	-	-	-
Heat Plants	-	-	-	-	-	-	-	-	-	-	-
Transfer to Gases	-	-	-	-	-	950	-	-	-	-	-
Transfer to Solids	5681	-	-	1264	-	-	-	-	-	-	-
Petroleum Refineries	-	-	-	-	-	-	-	29094	-	3545	-
Petrochemical Industry	-	-	-	-	-	-	-	-	-	-	-
Liquefaction	-	-	-	-	-	-	-	-	-	-	-
Other Transformation Sector	-	-	-	-	-	-	-	-	-	-	-
ENERGY SECTOR	**-**	**-**	**-**	**-**	**-**	**-**	**-**	**4**	**-**	**-**	**-**
Coal Mines	-	-	-	-	-	-	-	-	-	-	-
Oil and Gas Extraction	-	-	-	-	-	-	-	4	-	-	-
Petroleum Refineries	-	-	-	-	-	-	-	-	-	-	-
Electricity, CHP+Heat plants	-	-	-	-	-	-	-	-	-	-	-
Pumped Storage (Elec.)	-	-	-	-	-	-	-	-	-	-	-
Other Energy Sector	-	-	-	-	-	-	-	-	-	-	-
Distribution Losses	-	-	-	-	-	-	-	-	-	-	-
FINAL CONSUMPTION	**-**	**2489**	**2769**	**51**	**-**	**2516**	**440**	**-**	**-**	**-**	**-**
INDUSTRY SECTOR	**-**	**2395**	**2571**	**51**	**-**	**2358**	**356**	**-**	**-**	**-**	**-**
Iron and Steel	-	368	-	-	-	2157	-	-	-	-	-
Chemical and Petrochemical	-	117	-	-	-	-	134	-	-	-	-
of which: Feedstocks	-	-	-	-	-	-	-	-	-	-	-
Non-Ferrous Metals	-	494	2030	-	-	189	-	-	-	-	-
Non-Metallic Minerals	-	670	233	2	-	4	6	-	-	-	-
Transport Equipment	-	-	-	-	-	-	2	-	-	-	-
Machinery	-	-	-	-	-	-	-	-	-	-	-
Mining and Quarrying	-	16	305	-	-	8	-	-	-	-	-
Food and Tobacco	-	384	3	-	-	-	157	-	-	-	-
Paper, Pulp and Print	-	301	-	-	-	-	32	-	-	-	-
Wood and Wood Products	-	22	-	49	-	-	-	-	-	-	-
Construction	-	-	-	-	-	-	-	-	-	-	-
Textile and Leather	-	23	-	-	-	-	25	-	-	-	-
Non-specified	-	-	-	-	-	-	-	-	-	-	-
TRANSPORT SECTOR	**-**	**1**	**198**	**-**	**-**	**-**	**-**	**-**	**-**	**-**	**-**
International Civil Aviation	-	-	-	-	-	-	-	-	-	-	-
Domestic Air	-	-	-	-	-	-	-	-	-	-	-
Road	-	-	-	-	-	-	-	-	-	-	-
Rail	-	1	-	-	-	-	-	-	-	-	-
Pipeline Transport	-	-	-	-	-	-	-	-	-	-	-
Internal Navigation	-	-	198	-	-	-	-	-	-	-	-
Non-specified	-	-	-	-	-	-	-	-	-	-	-
OTHER SECTORS	**-**	**93**	**-**	**-**	**-**	**-**	**84**	**-**	**-**	**-**	**-**
Agriculture	-	-	-	-	-	-	-	-	-	-	-
Commerce and Publ. Serv.	-	88	-	-	-	-	77	-	-	-	-
Residential	-	5	-	-	-	-	7	-	-	-	-
Non-specified	-	-	-	-	-	-	-	-	-	-	-
NON-ENERGY USE	**-**	**-**	**-**	**-**	**-**	**158**	**-**	**-**	**-**	**-**	**-**
in Industry/Transf./Energy	-	-	-	-	-	158	-	-	-	-	-
in Transport	-	-	-	-	-	-	-	-	-	-	-
in Other Sectors	-	-	-	-	-	-	-	-	-	-	-

Australia / Australie : 1993

SUPPLY AND CONSUMPTION / APPROVISIONNEMENT ET DEMANDE	Refinery Gas / Gaz de raffinerie	LPG + Ethane / GPL + éthane	Motor Gasoline / Essence moteur	Aviation Gasoline / Essence aviation	Jet Fuel / Carbu-réacteur	Kerosene / Kérosène	Gas/Diesel / Gazole	Heavy Fuel Oil / Fioul lourd	Naphtha / Naphta	Pétrol. Coke / Coke de pétrole	Other Prod. / Autres prod.
Production	1048	772	13020	125	3322	243	8948	2567	260	506	2226
From Other Sources	-	-	-	-	-	-	-	-	-	-	-
Imports	-	59	282	-	29	-	567	1125	-	770	129
Exports	-	-813	-496	-49	-309	-59	-557	-998	-	-	-684
Intl. Marine Bunkers	-	-	-	-	-	-	-113	-579	-	-	-
Stock Changes	-	-24	-13	-2	-60	14	-165	66	9	-	-22
DOMESTIC SUPPLY	**1048**	**-6**	**12793**	**74**	**2982**	**198**	**8680**	**2181**	**269**	**1276**	**1649**
Transfers	-	2216	-	-	-	-	-	-	-	-	-
Statistical Differences	-35	-35	-241	-4	-60	-28	68	-752	23	-244	578
TRANSFORMATION	**-**	**26**	**-**	**-**	**-**	**-**	**508**	**116**	**-**	**-**	**-**
Electricity Plants	-	-	-	-	-	-	508	97	-	-	-
CHP Plants	-	-	-	-	-	-	-	-	-	-	-
Heat Plants	-	-	-	-	-	-	-	-	-	-	-
Transfer to Gases	-	26	-	-	-	-	-	-	-	-	-
Transfer to Solids	-	-	-	-	-	-	-	19	-	-	-
Petroleum Refineries	-	-	-	-	-	-	-	-	-	-	-
Petrochemical Industry	-	-	-	-	-	-	-	-	-	-	-
Liquefaction	-	-	-	-	-	-	-	-	-	-	-
Other Transformation Sector	-	-	-	-	-	-	-	-	-	-	-
ENERGY SECTOR	**1005**	**31**	**-**	**-**	**-**	**-**	**314**	**162**	**-**	**506**	**-**
Coal Mines	-	-	-	-	-	-	308	1	-	-	-
Oil and Gas Extraction	-	31	-	-	-	-	6	-	-	-	-
Petroleum Refineries	1005	-	-	-	-	-	-	161	-	506	-
Electricity, CHP+Heat plants	-	-	-	-	-	-	-	-	-	-	-
Pumped Storage (Elec.)	-	-	-	-	-	-	-	-	-	-	-
Other Energy Sector	-	-	-	-	-	-	-	-	-	-	-
Distribution Losses	-	-	-	-	-	-	-	-	-	-	-
FINAL CONSUMPTION	**8**	**2118**	**12552**	**70**	**2922**	**170**	**7926**	**1151**	**292**	**526**	**2227**
INDUSTRY SECTOR	**8**	**998**	**-**	**-**	**-**	**8**	**1599**	**830**	**292**	**18**	**27**
Iron and Steel	-	17	-	-	-	-	3	10	-	-	-
Chemical and Petrochemical	8	769	-	-	-	-	4	10	273	18	-
of which: Feedstocks	-	738	-	-	-	-	-	-	273	-	-
Non-Ferrous Metals	-	45	-	-	-	1	66	665	19	-	6
Non-Metallic Minerals	-	32	-	-	-	1	23	18	-	-	19
Transport Equipment	-	4	-	-	-	-	2	-	-	-	-
Machinery	-	30	-	-	-	-	1	-	-	-	-
Mining and Quarrying	-	3	-	-	-	-	558	36	-	-	2
Food and Tobacco	-	69	-	-	-	-	22	49	-	-	-
Paper, Pulp and Print	-	10	-	-	-	-	1	19	-	-	-
Wood and Wood Products	-	5	-	-	-	-	20	17	-	-	-
Construction	-	1	-	-	-	6	897	1	-	-	-
Textile and Leather	-	13	-	-	-	-	2	5	-	-	-
Non-specified	-	-	-	-	-	-	-	-	-	-	-
TRANSPORT SECTOR	**-**	**756**	**12552**	**70**	**2922**	**-**	**5106**	**286**	**-**	**-**	**-**
International Civil Aviation	-	-	-	-	1619	-	-	-	-	-	-
Domestic Air	-	-	-	70	1303	-	1	-	-	-	-
Road	-	756	12552	-	-	-	4506	-	-	-	-
Rail	-	-	-	-	-	-	514	-	-	-	-
Pipeline Transport	-	-	-	-	-	-	-	-	-	-	-
Internal Navigation	-	-	-	-	-	-	85	286	-	-	-
Non-specified	-	-	-	-	-	-	-	-	-	-	-
OTHER SECTORS	**-**	**364**	**-**	**-**	**-**	**162**	**1221**	**35**	**-**	**-**	**-**
Agriculture	-	19	-	-	-	2	1114	-	-	-	-
Commerce and Publ. Serv.	-	165	-	-	-	14	56	35	-	-	-
Residential	-	180	-	-	-	146	51	-	-	-	-
Non-specified	-	-	-	-	-	-	-	-	-	-	-
NON-ENERGY USE	**-**	**-**	**-**	**-**	**-**	**-**	**-**	**-**	**-**	**508**	**2200**
in Industry/Transf./Energy	-	-	-	-	-	-	-	-	-	508	2191
in Transport	-	-	-	-	-	-	-	-	-	-	-
in Other Sectors	-	-	-	-	-	-	-	-	-	-	9

Australia / Australie : 1993

CONSUMPTION *APPROVISIONNEMENT* *ET DEMANDE*	Natural Gas *Gaz* *naturel*	Gas Works *Usines* *à gaz*	Coke Ovens *Cokeries*	Blast Furnaces *Hauts* *fourneaux*	Solid Biomass & Anim. Prod. *Biomasse solide* *& prod. anim.*	Gas/Liquids from Biomass *Gaz/Liquides* *tirés de biomasse*	Municipal Waste *Déchets* *urbains*	Industrial Waste *Déchets* *industriels*	Electricity *Electricité*	Heat *Chaleur*
	Gas / *Gaz* (TJ)				Combust. Renew. & Waste / *En. Re. Comb. & Déchets* (TJ)				(GWh)	(TJ)
Production	970880	-	34932	33608	173611	-	-	8435	163751	-
From Other Sources	-	9743	-	-	-	-	-	-	-	-
Imports	-	-	-	-	-	-	-	-	-	-
Exports	-276600	-	-	-	-	-	-	-	-	-
Intl. Marine Bunkers	-	-	-	-	-	-	-	-	-	-
Stock Changes	-	-	-	-	-	-	-	-	-	-
DOMESTIC SUPPLY	**694280**	**9743**	**34932**	**33608**	**173611**	**-**	**-**	**8435**	**163751**	**-**
Transfers	-	-	-	-	-	-	-	-	-	-
Statistical Differences	-1	-	-	-	-	-	-	-	-	-
TRANSFORMATION	**153856**	**-**	**-**	**524**	**-**	**-**	**-**	**-**	**-**	**-**
Electricity Plants	136366	-	-	524	-	-	-	-	-	-
CHP Plants	-	-	-	-	-	-	-	-	-	-
Heat Plants	-	-	-	-	-	-	-	-	-	-
Transfer to Gases	17490	-	-	-	-	-	-	-	-	-
Transfer to Solids	-	-	-	-	-	-	-	-	-	-
Petroleum Refineries	-	-	-	-	-	-	-	-	-	-
Petrochemical Industry	-	-	-	-	-	-	-	-	-	-
Liquefaction	-	-	-	-	-	-	-	-	-	-
Other Transformation Sector	-	-	-	-	-	-	-	-	-	-
ENERGY SECTOR	**111861**	**223**	**5482**	**9144**	**-**	**-**	**-**	**-**	**16460**	**-**
Coal Mines	-	-	-	-	-	-	-	-	3354	-
Oil and Gas Extraction	100699	-	-	-	-	-	-	-	910	-
Petroleum Refineries	11162	-	-	-	-	-	-	-	1336	-
Electricity, CHP+Heat plants	-	-	-	-	-	-	-	-	9830	-
Pumped Storage (Elec.)	-	-	-	-	-	-	-	-	814	-
Other Energy Sector	-	223	5482	9144	-	-	-	-	216	-
Distribution Losses	-	-	-	-	-	-	-	-	10533	-
FINAL CONSUMPTION	**428562**	**9520**	**29450**	**23940**	**173611**	**-**	**-**	**8435**	**136758**	**-**
INDUSTRY SECTOR	**284687**	**7065**	**29450**	**23940**	**96292**	**-**	**-**	**8435**	**61786**	**-**
Iron and Steel	19470	-	27506	23940	58	-	-	-	5093	-
Chemical and Petrochemical	44179	7018	-	-	-	-	-	8392	3920	-
of which: Feedstocks	*11448*	-	-	-	-	-	-	-	-	-
Non-Ferrous Metals	104101	-	-	-	1855	-	-	-	27757	-
Non-Metallic Minerals	50976	-	-	-	671	-	-	-	2643	-
Transport Equipment	5931	6	-	-	-	-	-	-	1429	-
Machinery	7125	4	-	-	-	-	-	-	2680	-
Mining and Quarrying	1121	-	1944	-	-	-	-	-	6263	-
Food and Tobacco	25615	37	-	-	77275	-	-	43	4720	-
Paper, Pulp and Print	18031	-	-	-	8583	-	-	-	4322	-
Wood and Wood Products	1121	-	-	-	7850	-	-	-	969	-
Construction	247	-	-	-	-	-	-	-	29	-
Textile and Leather	6770	-	-	-	-	-	-	-	1961	-
Non-specified	-	-	-	-	-	-	-	-	-	-
TRANSPORT SECTOR	**6803**	**-**	**-**	**-**	**-**	**-**	**-**	**-**	**1890**	**-**
International Civil Aviation	-	-	-	-	-	-	-	-	-	-
Domestic Air	-	-	-	-	-	-	-	-	-	-
Road	880	-	-	-	-	-	-	-	-	-
Rail	-	-	-	-	-	-	-	-	1626	-
Pipeline Transport	5395	-	-	-	-	-	-	-	3	-
Internal Navigation	-	-	-	-	-	-	-	-	-	-
Non-specified	528	-	-	-	-	-	-	-	261	-
OTHER SECTORS	**136605**	**2455**	**-**	**-**	**77319**	**-**	**-**	**-**	**73082**	**-**
Agriculture	53	-	-	-	-	-	-	-	2640	-
Commerce and Publ. Serv.	38773	773	-	-	691	-	-	-	29800	-
Residential	97779	1682	-	-	76628	-	-	-	40642	-
Non-specified	-	-	-	-	-	-	-	-	-	-
NON-ENERGY USE	**467**	**-**	**-**	**-**	**-**	**-**	**-**	**-**	**-**	**-**
in Industry/Transf./Energy	467	-	-	-	-	-	-	-	-	-
in Transport	-	-	-	-	-	-	-	-	-	-
in Other Sectors	-	-	-	-	-	-	-	-	-	-

Austria / Autriche : 1992

SUPPLY AND CONSUMPTION / APPROVISIONNEMENT ET DEMANDE	Coal / *Charbon* (1000 tonnes)							Oil / *Pétrole* (1000 tonnes)			
	Coking Coal *Charbon à coke*	Steam Coal *Charbon vapeur*	Sub-Bit. Coal *Charbon sous-bit.*	Lignite *Lignite*	Peat *Tourbe*	Oven and Gas Coke *Coke de four/gaz*	Pat. Fuel and BKB *Agg./briq. de lignite*	Crude Oil *Pétrole brut*	NGL *LGN*	Feedstocks *Produits d'aliment.*	Additives *Additifs*
Production	-	-	-	1771	-	1470	-	1180	40	-	-
From Other Sources	-	-	-	-	-	-	-	-	-	-	-
Imports	2067	1745	-	9	-	685	252	7550	-	790	63
Exports	-	-9	-	-3	-	-2	-	-	-	-	-
Intl. Marine Bunkers	-	-	-	-	-	-	-	-	-	-	-
Stock Changes	-	-250	-	-330	-	-15	-	-19	-	-12	-27
DOMESTIC SUPPLY	**2067**	**1486**	**-**	**1447**	**-**	**2138**	**252**	**8711**	**40**	**778**	**36**
Transfers	-	-	-	-	-	-	-	-	-	-	-
Statistical Differences	-	-	-	-1	-	1	-	21	-	26	-21
TRANSFORMATION	**2067**	**1050**	**-**	**1110**	**-**	**526**	**13**	**8732**	**40**	**804**	**15**
Electricity Plants	-	997	-	1086	-	-	6	-	-	-	-
CHP Plants	-	-	-	-	-	-	-	-	-	-	-
Heat Plants	-	53	-	24	-	-	7	-	-	-	-
Transfer to Gases	-	-	-	-	-	526	-	-	-	-	-
Transfer to Solids	2067	-	-	-	-	-	-	-	-	-	-
Petroleum Refineries	-	-	-	-	-	-	-	8732	40	804	15
Petrochemical Industry	-	-	-	-	-	-	-	-	-	-	-
Liquefaction	-	-	-	-	-	-	-	-	-	-	-
Other Transformation Sector	-	-	-	-	-	-	-	-	-	-	-
ENERGY SECTOR	**-**	**-**	**-**	**2**	**-**	**-**	**-**	**-**	**-**	**-**	**-**
Coal Mines	-	-	-	2	-	-	-	-	-	-	-
Oil and Gas Extraction	-	-	-	-	-	-	-	-	-	-	-
Petroleum Refineries	-	-	-	-	-	-	-	-	-	-	-
Electricity, CHP+Heat plants	-	-	-	-	-	-	-	-	-	-	-
Pumped Storage (Elec.)	-	-	-	-	-	-	-	-	-	-	-
Other Energy Sector	-	-	-	-	-	-	-	-	-	-	-
Distribution Losses	-	-	-	-	-	-	-	-	-	-	-
FINAL CONSUMPTION	**-**	**436**	**-**	**334**	**-**	**1613**	**239**	**-**	**-**	**-**	**-**
INDUSTRY SECTOR	**-**	**315**	**-**	**204**	**-**	**1044**	**23**	**-**	**-**	**-**	**-**
Iron and Steel	-	-	-	-	-	1007	-	-	-	-	-
Chemical and Petrochemical	-	43	-	-	-	12	-	-	-	-	-
of which: Feedstocks	-	-	-	-	-	-	-	-	-	-	-
Non-Ferrous Metals	-	-	-	-	-	-	-	-	-	-	-
Non-Metallic Minerals	-	234	-	8	-	17	-	-	-	-	-
Transport Equipment	-	-	-	-	-	-	-	-	-	-	-
Machinery	-	-	-	-	-	-	-	-	-	-	-
Mining and Quarrying	-	-	-	3	-	3	-	-	-	-	-
Food and Tobacco	-	-	-	-	-	5	-	-	-	-	-
Paper, Pulp and Print	-	38	-	193	-	-	18	-	-	-	-
Wood and Wood Products	-	-	-	-	-	-	5	-	-	-	-
Construction	-	-	-	-	-	-	-	-	-	-	-
Textile and Leather	-	-	-	-	-	-	-	-	-	-	-
Non-specified	-	-	-	-	-	-	-	-	-	-	-
TRANSPORT SECTOR	**-**	**5**	**-**	**2**	**-**	**5**	**-**	**-**	**-**	**-**	**-**
International Civil Aviation	-	-	-	-	-	-	-	-	-	-	-
Domestic Air	-	-	-	-	-	-	-	-	-	-	-
Road	-	-	-	-	-	-	-	-	-	-	-
Rail	-	5	-	2	-	5	-	-	-	-	-
Pipeline Transport	-	-	-	-	-	-	-	-	-	-	-
Internal Navigation	-	-	-	-	-	-	-	-	-	-	-
Non-specified	-	-	-	-	-	-	-	-	-	-	-
OTHER SECTORS	**-**	**114**	**-**	**128**	**-**	**542**	**216**	**-**	**-**	**-**	**-**
Agriculture	-	-	-	-	-	-	-	-	-	-	-
Commerce and Publ. Serv.	-	-	-	-	-	-	-	-	-	-	-
Residential	-	114	-	128	-	542	216	-	-	-	-
Non-specified	-	-	-	-	-	-	-	-	-	-	-
NON-ENERGY USE	**-**	**2**	**-**	**-**	**-**	**22**	**-**	**-**	**-**	**-**	**-**
in Industry/Transf./Energy	-	2	-	-	-	22	-	-	-	-	-
in Transport	-	-	-	-	-	-	-	-	-	-	-
in Other Sectors	-	-	-	-	-	-	-	-	-	-	-

Austria / Autriche : 1992

SUPPLY AND CONSUMPTION	Oil cont. / *Pétrole cont.* (1000 tonnes)										
	Refinery Gas	LPG + Ethane	Motor Gasoline	Aviation Gasoline	Jet Fuel	Kerosene	Gas/ Diesel	Heavy Fuel Oil	Naphtha	Pétrol. Coke	Other Prod.
APPROVISIONNEMENT ET DEMANDE	*Gaz de raffinerie*	*GPL + éthane*	*Essence moteur*	*Essence aviation*	*Carbu- réacteur*	*Kérosène*	*Gazole*	*Fioul lourd*	*Naphta*	*Coke de pétrole*	*Autres prod.*
Production	339	18	2461	-	389	8	3245	1821	-	-	1310
From Other Sources	-	-	-	-	-	-	-	-	-	-	-
Imports	-	145	475	3	9	16	631	469	-	-	453
Exports	-	-1	-209	-	-	-5	-73	-65	-	-	-124
Intl. Marine Bunkers	-	-	-	-	-	-	-	-	-	-	-
Stock Changes	-	-	-47	-	-2	1	76	-244	-	-	9
DOMESTIC SUPPLY	**339**	**162**	**2680**	**3**	**396**	**20**	**3879**	**1981**	**-**	**-**	**1648**
Transfers	-	-	-	-	-	-	-	-	-	-	-
Statistical Differences	-	-2	-5	-	-3	-1	-6	9	-	-	20
TRANSFORMATION	**-**	**9**	**-**	**-**	**-**	**-**	**3**	**696**	**-**	**-**	**-**
Electricity Plants	-	-	-	-	-	-	1	126	-	-	-
CHP Plants	-	-	-	-	-	-	1	348	-	-	-
Heat Plants	-	2	-	-	-	-	1	222	-	-	-
Transfer to Gases	-	7	-	-	-	-	-	-	-	-	-
Transfer to Solids	-	-	-	-	-	-	-	-	-	-	-
Petroleum Refineries	-	-	-	-	-	-	-	-	-	-	-
Petrochemical Industry	-	-	-	-	-	-	-	-	-	-	-
Liquefaction	-	-	-	-	-	-	-	-	-	-	-
Other Transformation Sector	-	-	-	-	-	-	-	-	-	-	-
ENERGY SECTOR	**339**	**-**	**-**	**-**	**-**	**-**	**-**	**-**	**-**	**-**	**231**
Coal Mines	-	-	-	-	-	-	-	-	-	-	-
Oil and Gas Extraction	-	-	-	-	-	-	-	-	-	-	-
Petroleum Refineries	339	-	-	-	-	-	-	-	-	-	231
Electricity, CHP+Heat plants	-	-	-	-	-	-	-	-	-	-	-
Pumped Storage (Elec.)	-	-	-	-	-	-	-	-	-	-	-
Other Energy Sector	-	-	-	-	-	-	-	-	-	-	-
Distribution Losses	-	-	-	-	-	-	-	-	-	-	-
FINAL CONSUMPTION	**-**	**151**	**2675**	**3**	**393**	**19**	**3870**	**1294**	**-**	**-**	**1437**
INDUSTRY SECTOR	**-**	**46**	**-**	**-**	**-**	**-**	**-**	**715**	**-**	**-**	**-**
Iron and Steel	-	4	-	-	-	-	-	65	-	-	-
Chemical and Petrochemical	-	-	-	-	-	-	-	74	-	-	-
of which: Feedstocks	-	-	-	-	-	-	-	-	-	-	-
Non-Ferrous Metals	-	7	-	-	-	-	-	15	-	-	-
Non-Metallic Minerals	-	12	-	-	-	-	-	148	-	-	-
Transport Equipment	-	4	-	-	-	-	-	5	-	-	-
Machinery	-	5	-	-	-	-	-	60	-	-	-
Mining and Quarrying	-	-	-	-	-	-	-	17	-	-	-
Food and Tobacco	-	1	-	-	-	-	-	88	-	-	-
Paper, Pulp and Print	-	1	-	-	-	-	-	103	-	-	-
Wood and Wood Products	-	-	-	-	-	-	-	31	-	-	-
Construction	-	8	-	-	-	-	-	46	-	-	-
Textile and Leather	-	1	-	-	-	-	-	63	-	-	-
Non-specified	-	3	-	-	-	-	-	-	-	-	-
TRANSPORT SECTOR	**-**	**12**	**2675**	**3**	**393**	**-**	**2443**	**14**	**-**	**-**	**-**
International Civil Aviation	-	-	-	2	197	-	-	-	-	-	-
Domestic Air	-	-	-	1	196	-	-	-	-	-	-
Road	-	12	2675	-	-	-	2384	-	-	-	-
Rail	-	-	-	-	-	-	59	14	-	-	-
Pipeline Transport	-	-	-	-	-	-	-	-	-	-	-
Internal Navigation	-	-	-	-	-	-	-	-	-	-	-
Non-specified	-	-	-	-	-	-	-	-	-	-	-
OTHER SECTORS	**-**	**93**	**-**	**-**	**-**	**19**	**1427**	**565**	**-**	**-**	**-**
Agriculture	-	-	-	-	-	-	-	-	-	-	-
Commerce and Publ. Serv.	-	-	-	-	-	-	-	-	-	-	-
Residential	-	93	-	-	-	-	1427	565	-	-	-
Non-specified	-	-	-	-	-	19	-	-	-	-	-
NON-ENERGY USE	**-**	**-**	**-**	**-**	**-**	**-**	**-**	**-**	**-**	**-**	**1437**
in Industry/Transf./Energy	-	-	-	-	-	-	-	-	-	-	1437
in Transport	-	-	-	-	-	-	-	-	-	-	-
in Other Sectors	-	-	-	-	-	-	-	-	-	-	-

Austria / Autriche : 1992

CONSUMPTION *APPROVISIONNEMENT ET DEMANDE*	Gas / Gaz (TJ)				Combust. Renew. & Waste / En. Re. Comb. & Déchets (TJ)				(GWh)	(TJ)
	Natural Gas *Gaz naturel*	Gas Works *Usines à gaz*	Coke Ovens *Cokeries*	Blast Furnaces *Hauts fourneaux*	Solid Biomass & Anim. Prod. *Biomasse solide & prod. anim.*	Gas/Liquids from Biomass *Gaz/Liquides tirés de biomasse*	Municipal Waste *Déchets urbains*	Industrial Waste *Déchets industriels*	Electricity *Electricité*	Heat *Chaleur*
Production	56919	-	11164	14273	19359	-	25730	91125	51180	30835
From Other Sources	-	11	-	-	-	-	-	-	-	-
Imports	202280	-	-	-	-	-	-	2913	9175	-
Exports	-	-	-	-	-	-	-	-68	-8620	-
Intl. Marine Bunkers	-	-	-	-	-	-	-	-	-	-
Stock Changes	-8769	-	-	-	-	-	-	279	-	-
DOMESTIC SUPPLY	**250430**	**11**	**11164**	**14273**	**19359**	**-**	**25730**	**94249**	**51735**	**30835**
Transfers	-	-	-	-	-	-	-	-	-	-
Statistical Differences	4	-	-	-	-	-	-	-	-	-
TRANSFORMATION	**80375**	**-**	**2818**	**4455**	**2673**	**-**	**9957**	**-**	**-**	**-**
Electricity Plants	67000	-	2457	4226	1568	-	6261	-	-	-
CHP Plants	13375	-	-	-	-	-	-	-	-	-
Heat Plants	-	-	361	229	1105	-	3696	-	-	-
Transfer to Gases	-	-	-	-	-	-	-	-	-	-
Transfer to Solids	-	-	-	-	-	-	-	-	-	-
Petroleum Refineries	-	-	-	-	-	-	-	-	-	-
Petrochemical Industry	-	-	-	-	-	-	-	-	-	-
Liquefaction	-	-	-	-	-	-	-	-	-	-
Other Transformation Sector	-	-	-	-	-	-	-	-	-	-
ENERGY SECTOR	**14847**	**-**	**2808**	**1740**	**2**	**-**	**-**	**-**	**4373**	**21**
Coal Mines	-	-	-	-	-	-	-	-	42	-
Oil and Gas Extraction	14847	-	-	-	-	-	-	-	86	-
Petroleum Refineries	-	-	-	-	-	-	-	-	684	-
Electricity, CHP+Heat plants	-	-	-	-	2	-	-	-	1546	-
Pumped Storage (Elec.)	-	-	-	-	-	-	-	-	1571	-
Other Energy Sector	-	-	2808	1740	-	-	-	-	444	21
Distribution Losses	3585	-	56	11	-	-	-	-	2968	3084
FINAL CONSUMPTION	**151627**	**11**	**5482**	**8067**	**16684**	**-**	**15773**	**94249**	**44394**	**27730**
INDUSTRY SECTOR	**77910**	**7**	**5482**	**8067**	**6720**	**-**	**15632**	**161**	**17333**	**3073**
Iron and Steel	15495	-	5230	8067	-	-	-	-	4014	68
Chemical and Petrochemical	23192	-	252	-	2806	-	638	-	3212	1061
of which: Feedstocks	*13726*	-	-	-	-	-	-	-	-	-
Non-Ferrous Metals	-	-	-	-	-	-	-	-	-	-
Non-Metallic Minerals	10318	7	-	-	-	-	185	2	1709	15
Transport Equipment	1511	-	-	-	-	-	-	-	523	466
Machinery	1655	-	-	-	-	-	16	9	972	753
Mining and Quarrying	2291	-	-	-	-	-	-	-	271	22
Food and Tobacco	6389	-	-	-	-	-	27	2	1254	510
Paper, Pulp and Print	12221	-	-	-	1598	-	14766	-	3799	53
Wood and Wood Products	1503	-	-	-	2316	-	-	148	787	80
Construction	-	-	-	-	-	-	-	-	-	-
Textile and Leather	2291	-	-	-	-	-	-	-	792	45
Non-specified	1044	-	-	-	-	-	-	-	-	-
TRANSPORT SECTOR	**990**	**-**	**-**	**-**	**-**	**-**	**6**	**65**	**3042**	**-**
International Civil Aviation	-	-	-	-	-	-	-	-	-	-
Domestic Air	-	-	-	-	-	-	-	-	-	-
Road	-	-	-	-	-	-	-	-	-	-
Rail	-	-	-	-	-	-	6	65	1913	-
Pipeline Transport	-	-	-	-	-	-	-	-	174	-
Internal Navigation	-	-	-	-	-	-	-	-	-	-
Non-specified	990	-	-	-	-	-	-	-	955	-
OTHER SECTORS	**72727**	**4**	**-**	**-**	**9964**	**-**	**135**	**94023**	**24019**	**24657**
Agriculture	-	-	-	-	-	-	-	-	1424	-
Commerce and Publ. Serv.	-	-	-	-	-	-	-	-	4341	-
Residential	72727	4	-	-	9964	-	135	-	11949	24657
Non-specified	-	-	-	-	-	-	-	94023	6305	-
NON-ENERGY USE	**-**	**-**	**-**	**-**	**-**	**-**	**-**	**-**	**-**	**-**
in Industry/Transf./Energy	-	-	-	-	-	-	-	-	-	-
in Transport	-	-	-	-	-	-	-	-	-	-
in Other Sectors	-	-	-	-	-	-	-	-	-	-

Austria / Autriche : 1993

SUPPLY AND CONSUMPTION	Coal / *Charbon* (1000 tonnes)							Oil / *Pétrole* (1000 tonnes)			
	Coking Coal	Steam Coal	Sub-Bit. Coal	Lignite	Peat	Oven and Gas Coke	Pat. Fuel and BKB	Crude Oil	NGL	Feedstocks	Additives
APPROVISIONNEMENT ET DEMANDE	*Charbon à coke*	*Charbon vapeur*	*Charbon sous-bit.*	*Lignite*	*Tourbe*	*Coke de four/gaz*	*Agg./briq. de lignite*	*Pétrole brut*	*LGN*	*Produits d'aliment.*	*Additifs*
Production	-	-	-	1691	-	1402	-	1155	40	-	-
From Other Sources	-	-	-	-	-	-	-	-	-	-	-
Imports	1987	1202	-	1	-	579	237	7453	-	684	34
Exports	-	-	-	-	-	-	-	-	-	-	-
Intl. Marine Bunkers	-	-	-	-	-	-	-	-	-	-	-
Stock Changes	-	-170	-	-337	-	59	-	-38	-	73	11
DOMESTIC SUPPLY	**1987**	**1032**	**-**	**1355**	**-**	**2040**	**237**	**8570**	**40**	**757**	**45**
Transfers	-	-	-	-	-	-	-	-	-	-	-
Statistical Differences	-	-	-	-	-	-	-	-47	-	267	-1
TRANSFORMATION	**1987**	**764**	**-**	**1065**	**-**	**520**	**12**	**8523**	**40**	**1024**	**44**
Electricity Plants	-	728	-	1045	-	-	5	-	-	-	-
CHP Plants	-	-	-	-	-	-	-	-	-	-	-
Heat Plants	-	36	-	20	-	-	7	-	-	-	-
Transfer to Gases	-	-	-	-	-	520	-	-	-	-	-
Transfer to Solids	1987	-	-	-	-	-	-	-	-	-	-
Petroleum Refineries	-	-	-	-	-	-	-	8523	40	1024	44
Petrochemical Industry	-	-	-	-	-	-	-	-	-	-	-
Liquefaction	-	-	-	-	-	-	-	-	-	-	-
Other Transformation Sector	-	-	-	-	-	-	-	-	-	-	-
ENERGY SECTOR	**-**	**-**	**-**	**-**	**-**	**-**	**-**	**-**	**-**	**-**	**-**
Coal Mines	-	-	-	-	-	-	-	-	-	-	-
Oil and Gas Extraction	-	-	-	-	-	-	-	-	-	-	-
Petroleum Refineries	-	-	-	-	-	-	-	-	-	-	-
Electricity, CHP+Heat plants	-	-	-	-	-	-	-	-	-	-	-
Pumped Storage (Elec.)	-	-	-	-	-	-	-	-	-	-	-
Other Energy Sector	-	-	-	-	-	-	-	-	-	-	-
Distribution Losses	-	-	-	-	-	-	-	-	-	-	-
FINAL CONSUMPTION	**-**	**268**	**-**	**290**	**-**	**1520**	**225**	**-**	**-**	**-**	**-**
INDUSTRY SECTOR	**-**	**253**	**-**	**171**	**-**	**960**	**19**	**-**	**-**	**-**	**-**
Iron and Steel	-	-	-	-	-	929	-	-	-	-	-
Chemical and Petrochemical	-	17	-	-	-	11	-	-	-	-	-
of which: Feedstocks	-	-	-	-	-	-	-	-	-	-	-
Non-Ferrous Metals	-	-	-	-	-	-	-	-	-	-	-
Non-Metallic Minerals	-	203	-	-	-	12	-	-	-	-	-
Transport Equipment	-	-	-	-	-	-	-	-	-	-	-
Machinery	-	-	-	-	-	-	-	-	-	-	-
Mining and Quarrying	-	-	-	3	-	3	-	-	-	-	-
Food and Tobacco	-	-	-	-	-	5	-	-	-	-	-
Paper, Pulp and Print	-	33	-	168	-	-	18	-	-	-	-
Wood and Wood Products	-	-	-	-	-	-	1	-	-	-	-
Construction	-	-	-	-	-	-	-	-	-	-	-
Textile and Leather	-	-	-	-	-	-	-	-	-	-	-
Non-specified	-	-	-	-	-	-	-	-	-	-	-
TRANSPORT SECTOR	**-**	**5**	**-**	**1**	**-**	**5**	**2**	**-**	**-**	**-**	**-**
International Civil Aviation	-	-	-	-	-	-	-	-	-	-	-
Domestic Air	-	-	-	-	-	-	-	-	-	-	-
Road	-	-	-	-	-	-	-	-	-	-	-
Rail	-	5	-	1	-	5	2	-	-	-	-
Pipeline Transport	-	-	-	-	-	-	-	-	-	-	-
Internal Navigation	-	-	-	-	-	-	-	-	-	-	-
Non-specified	-	-	-	-	-	-	-	-	-	-	-
OTHER SECTORS	**-**	**8**	**-**	**118**	**-**	**531**	**204**	**-**	**-**	**-**	**-**
Agriculture	-	-	-	-	-	-	-	-	-	-	-
Commerce and Publ. Serv.	-	-	-	-	-	-	-	-	-	-	-
Residential	-	8	-	118	-	531	204	-	-	-	-
Non-specified	-	-	-	-	-	-	-	-	-	-	-
NON-ENERGY USE	**-**	**2**	**-**	**-**	**-**	**24**	**-**	**-**	**-**	**-**	**-**
in Industry/Transf./Energy	-	2	-	-	-	24	-	-	-	-	-
in Transport	-	-	-	-	-	-	-	-	-	-	-
in Other Sectors	-	-	-	-	-	-	-	-	-	-	-

Austria / Autriche : 1993

SUPPLY AND CONSUMPTION / APPROVISIONNEMENT ET DEMANDE	Oil cont. / Pétrole cont. (1000 tonnes)										
	Refinery Gas / Gaz de raffinerie	LPG + Ethane / GPL + éthane	Motor Gasoline / Essence moteur	Aviation Gasoline / Essence aviation	Jet Fuel / Carbu-réacteur	Kerosene / Kérosène	Gas/Diesel / Gazole	Heavy Fuel Oil / Fioul lourd	Naphtha / Naphta	Pétrol. Coke / Coke de pétrole	Other Prod. / Autres prod.
Production	319	1	2329	-	375	2	3605	1678	-	-	1322
From Other Sources	-	-	-	-	-	-	-	-	-	-	-
Imports	-	169	541	3	10	21	780	540	-	-	395
Exports	-	-	-300	-	-3	-	-133	-83	-	-	-143
Intl. Marine Bunkers	-	-	-	-	-	-	-	-	-	-	-
Stock Changes	-	-	70	-	1	1	-35	13	-	-	-12
DOMESTIC SUPPLY	319	170	2640	3	383	24	4217	2148	-	-	1562
Transfers	-	-	-	-	-	-	-	-	-	-	-
Statistical Differences	-	-	-74	-	-	-3	-7	-8	-	-	-146
TRANSFORMATION	-	4	-	-	-	-	5	778	-	-	-
Electricity Plants	-	-	-	-	-	-	1	156	-	-	-
CHP Plants	-	-	-	-	-	-	3	416	-	-	-
Heat Plants	-	3	-	-	-	-	1	206	-	-	-
Transfer to Gases	-	1	-	-	-	-	-	-	-	-	-
Transfer to Solids	-	-	-	-	-	-	-	-	-	-	-
Petroleum Refineries	-	-	-	-	-	-	-	-	-	-	-
Petrochemical Industry	-	-	-	-	-	-	-	-	-	-	-
Liquefaction	-	-	-	-	-	-	-	-	-	-	-
Other Transformation Sector	-	-	-	-	-	-	-	-	-	-	-
ENERGY SECTOR	319	-	-	-	-	-	-	3	-	-	236
Coal Mines	-	-	-	-	-	-	-	-	-	-	-
Oil and Gas Extraction	-	-	-	-	-	-	-	-	-	-	-
Petroleum Refineries	319	-	-	-	-	-	-	3	-	-	236
Electricity, CHP+Heat plants	-	-	-	-	-	-	-	-	-	-	-
Pumped Storage (Elec.)	-	-	-	-	-	-	-	-	-	-	-
Other Energy Sector	-	-	-	-	-	-	-	-	-	-	-
Distribution Losses	-	-	-	-	-	-	-	-	-	-	-
FINAL CONSUMPTION	-	166	2566	3	383	21	4205	1359	-	-	1180
INDUSTRY SECTOR	-	56	-	-	-	-	-	754	-	-	-
Iron and Steel	-	4	-	-	-	-	-	111	-	-	-
Chemical and Petrochemical	-	-	-	-	-	-	-	62	-	-	-
of which: Feedstocks	-	-	-	-	-	-	-	-	-	-	-
Non-Ferrous Metals	-	8	-	-	-	-	-	14	-	-	-
Non-Metallic Minerals	-	17	-	-	-	-	-	165	-	-	-
Transport Equipment	-	2	-	-	-	-	-	4	-	-	-
Machinery	-	7	-	-	-	-	-	58	-	-	-
Mining and Quarrying	-	-	-	-	-	-	-	10	-	-	-
Food and Tobacco	-	2	-	-	-	-	-	91	-	-	-
Paper, Pulp and Print	-	1	-	-	-	-	-	104	-	-	-
Wood and Wood Products	-	-	-	-	-	-	-	29	-	-	-
Construction	-	12	-	-	-	-	-	49	-	-	-
Textile and Leather	-	-	-	-	-	-	-	57	-	-	-
Non-specified	-	3	-	-	-	-	-	-	-	-	-
TRANSPORT SECTOR	-	13	2566	3	383	-	2631	27	-	-	-
International Civil Aviation	-	-	-	2	192	-	-	-	-	-	-
Domestic Air	-	-	-	1	191	-	-	-	-	-	-
Road	-	13	2566	-	-	-	2566	-	-	-	-
Rail	-	-	-	-	-	-	65	15	-	-	-
Pipeline Transport	-	-	-	-	-	-	-	-	-	-	-
Internal Navigation	-	-	-	-	-	-	-	-	-	-	-
Non-specified	-	-	-	-	-	-	-	12	-	-	-
OTHER SECTORS	-	97	-	-	-	21	1574	578	-	-	-
Agriculture	-	-	-	-	-	-	-	-	-	-	-
Commerce and Publ. Serv.	-	-	-	-	-	-	-	-	-	-	-
Residential	-	97	-	-	-	-	1574	578	-	-	-
Non-specified	-	-	-	-	-	21	-	-	-	-	-
NON-ENERGY USE	-	-	-	-	-	-	-	-	-	-	1180
in Industry/Transf./Energy	-	-	-	-	-	-	-	-	-	-	1180
in Transport	-	-	-	-	-	-	-	-	-	-	-
in Other Sectors	-	-	-	-	-	-	-	-	-	-	-

Austria / Autriche : 1993

CONSUMPTION / APPROVISIONNEMENT ET DEMANDE	Gas / Gaz (TJ)				Combust. Renew. & Waste / En. Re. Comb. & Déchets (TJ)				(GWh)	(TJ)
	Natural Gas / Gaz naturel	Gas Works / Usines à gaz	Coke Ovens / Cokeries	Blast Furnaces / Hauts fourneaux	Solid Biomass & Anim. Prod. / Biomasse solide & prod. anim.	Gas/Liquids from Biomass / Gaz/Liquides tirés de biomasse	Municipal Waste / Déchets urbains	Industrial Waste / Déchets industriels	Electricity / Electricité	Heat / Chaleur
Production	58776	-	10636	14281	20006	-	25555	80780	52675	33503
From Other Sources	-	43	-	-	-	-	-	-	-	-
Imports	212511	-	-	-	-	-	-	2657	8072	-
Exports	-	-	-	-	-	-	-	-20	-8805	-
Intl. Marine Bunkers	-	-	-	-	-	-	-	-	-	-
Stock Changes	-7939	-	-	-	-	-	-	150	-	-
DOMESTIC SUPPLY	**263348**	**43**	**10636**	**14281**	**20006**	**-**	**25555**	**83567**	**51942**	**33503**
Transfers	-	-	-	-	-	-	-	-	-	-
Statistical Differences	38	-	-	-	-	-	-	-	-	-
TRANSFORMATION	**84532**	**-**	**3117**	**4477**	**3468**	**-**	**10243**	**-**	**-**	**-**
Electricity Plants	70465	-	2728	4230	1837	-	6229	-	-	-
CHP Plants	14067	-	-	-	-	-	-	-	-	-
Heat Plants	-	-	389	247	1631	-	4014	-	-	-
Transfer to Gases	-	-	-	-	-	-	-	-	-	-
Transfer to Solids	-	-	-	-	-	-	-	-	-	-
Petroleum Refineries	-	-	-	-	-	-	-	-	-	-
Petrochemical Industry	-	-	-	-	-	-	-	-	-	-
Liquefaction	-	-	-	-	-	-	-	-	-	-
Other Transformation Sector	-	-	-	-	-	-	-	-	-	-
ENERGY SECTOR	**15615**	**-**	**2423**	**1741**	**-**	**-**	**-**	**-**	**4244**	**22**
Coal Mines	-	-	-	-	-	-	-	-	43	-
Oil and Gas Extraction	15615	-	-	-	-	-	-	-	87	-
Petroleum Refineries	-	-	-	-	-	-	-	-	695	-
Electricity, CHP+Heat plants	-	-	-	-	-	-	-	-	1450	-
Pumped Storage (Elec.)	-	-	-	-	-	-	-	-	1517	-
Other Energy Sector	-	-	2423	1741	-	-	-	-	452	22
Distribution Losses	3770	-	52	9	-	-	-	-	3169	3350
FINAL CONSUMPTION	**159469**	**43**	**5044**	**8054**	**16538**	**-**	**15312**	**83567**	**44529**	**30131**
INDUSTRY SECTOR	**81940**	**-**	**5044**	**8054**	**5881**	**-**	**15212**	**125**	**16666**	**3316**
Iron and Steel	16296	-	5044	8054	-	-	-	-	3860	73
Chemical and Petrochemical	24391	-	-	-	2613	-	245	-	3088	1160
of which: Feedstocks	*13726*	-	-	-	-	-	-	-	-	-
Non-Ferrous Metals	-	-	-	-	-	-	-	-	-	-
Non-Metallic Minerals	10852	-	-	-	-	-	172	-	1643	16
Transport Equipment	1589	-	-	-	-	-	6	-	503	499
Machinery	1741	-	-	-	-	-	15	-	935	807
Mining and Quarrying	2409	-	-	-	-	-	-	-	260	23
Food and Tobacco	6719	-	-	-	-	-	4	-	1206	547
Paper, Pulp and Print	12853	-	-	-	1391	-	14770	-	3653	57
Wood and Wood Products	1581	-	-	-	1877	-	-	125	757	86
Construction	-	-	-	-	-	-	-	-	-	-
Textile and Leather	2409	-	-	-	-	-	-	-	761	48
Non-specified	1100	-	-	-	-	-	-	-	-	-
TRANSPORT SECTOR	**1041**	**-**	**-**	**-**	**371**	**-**	**7**	**65**	**3060**	**-**
International Civil Aviation	-	-	-	-	-	-	-	-	-	-
Domestic Air	-	-	-	-	-	-	-	-	-	-
Road	-	-	-	-	-	-	-	-	-	-
Rail	-	-	-	-	371	-	7	65	1899	-
Pipeline Transport	-	-	-	-	-	-	-	-	172	-
Internal Navigation	-	-	-	-	-	-	-	-	-	-
Non-specified	1041	-	-	-	-	-	-	-	989	-
OTHER SECTORS	**76488**	**42**	**-**	**-**	**10286**	**-**	**93**	**83377**	**24803**	**26815**
Agriculture	-	-	-	-	-	-	-	-	1462	-
Commerce and Publ. Serv.	-	-	-	-	-	-	-	-	4528	-
Residential	76488	42	-	-	10286	-	93	83377	12322	26815
Non-specified	-	-	-	-	-	-	-	-	6491	-
NON-ENERGY USE	**-**	**1**	**-**	**-**	**-**	**-**	**-**	**-**	**-**	**-**
in Industry/Transf./Energy	-	1	-	-	-	-	-	-	-	-
in Transport	-	-	-	-	-	-	-	-	-	-
in Other Sectors	-	-	-	-	-	-	-	-	-	-

Belgium / Belgique : 1992

SUPPLY AND CONSUMPTION *APPROVISIONNEMENT ET DEMANDE*	Coal / *Charbon* (1000 tonnes)							Oil / *Pétrole* (1000 tonnes)			
	Coking Coal *Charbon à coke*	Steam Coal *Charbon vapeur*	Sub-Bit. Coal *Charbon sous-bit.*	Lignite *Lignite*	Peat *Tourbe*	Oven and Gas Coke *Coke de four/gaz*	Pat. Fuel and BKB *Agg./briq. de lignite*	Crude Oil *Pétrole brut*	NGL *LGN*	Feedstocks *Produits d'aliment.*	Additives *Additifs*
Production	-	218	-	-	-	4575	9	-	-	-	-
From Other Sources	-	-	979	-	-	-	-	-	-	-	-
Imports	5795	8219	-	244	-	616	47	29043	-	3554	-
Exports	-	-655	-14	-	-	-760	-5	-	-	-2825	-
Intl. Marine Bunkers	-	-	-	-	-	-	-	-	-	-	-
Stock Changes	-97	-239	-63	-	-	-142	-	-169	-	7	-
DOMESTIC SUPPLY	**5698**	**7543**	**902**	**244**	**-**	**4289**	**51**	**28874**	**-**	**736**	**-**
Transfers	-	-	-	-	-	-	-	-	-	3069	-
Statistical Differences	-	144	-51	-	-	-1	-	5	-	-59	-
TRANSFORMATION	**5698**	**5457**	**607**	**-**	**-**	**1342**	**-**	**28879**	**-**	**3746**	**-**
Electricity Plants	-	3363	527	-	-	-	-	-	-	-	-
CHP Plants	-	2092	80	-	-	-	-	-	-	-	-
Heat Plants	-	-	-	-	-	-	-	-	-	-	-
Transfer to Gases	-	-	-	-	-	1342	-	-	-	-	-
Transfer to Solids	5698	2	-	-	-	-	-	-	-	-	-
Petroleum Refineries	-	-	-	-	-	-	-	28879	-	3746	-
Petrochemical Industry	-	-	-	-	-	-	-	-	-	-	-
Liquefaction	-	-	-	-	-	-	-	-	-	-	-
Other Transformation Sector	-	-	-	-	-	-	-	-	-	-	-
ENERGY SECTOR	**-**	**3**	**-**	**-**	**-**	**13**	**-**	**-**	**-**	**-**	**-**
Coal Mines	-	3	-	-	-	-	-	-	-	-	-
Oil and Gas Extraction	-	-	-	-	-	-	-	-	-	-	-
Petroleum Refineries	-	-	-	-	-	-	-	-	-	-	-
Electricity, CHP+Heat plants	-	-	-	-	-	-	-	-	-	-	-
Pumped Storage (Elec.)	-	-	-	-	-	-	-	-	-	-	-
Other Energy Sector	-	-	-	-	-	13	-	-	-	-	-
Distribution Losses	-	-	-	-	-	-	-	-	-	-	-
FINAL CONSUMPTION	**-**	**2227**	**244**	**244**	**-**	**2933**	**51**	**-**	**-**	**-**	**-**
INDUSTRY SECTOR	**-**	**1548**	**244**	**244**	**-**	**2916**	**-**	**-**	**-**	**-**	**-**
Iron and Steel	-	954	-	-	-	2817	-	-	-	-	-
Chemical and Petrochemical	-	52	-	-	-	20	-	-	-	-	-
of which: Feedstocks	-	-	-	-	-	-	-	-	-	-	-
Non-Ferrous Metals	-	-	-	-	-	-	-	-	-	-	-
Non-Metallic Minerals	-	383	244	244	-	26	-	-	-	-	-
Transport Equipment	-	-	-	-	-	-	-	-	-	-	-
Machinery	-	-	-	-	-	34	-	-	-	-	-
Mining and Quarrying	-	-	-	-	-	-	-	-	-	-	-
Food and Tobacco	-	103	-	-	-	9	-	-	-	-	-
Paper, Pulp and Print	-	45	-	-	-	-	-	-	-	-	-
Wood and Wood Products	-	-	-	-	-	-	-	-	-	-	-
Construction	-	-	-	-	-	-	-	-	-	-	-
Textile and Leather	-	7	-	-	-	-	-	-	-	-	-
Non-specified	-	4	-	-	-	10	-	-	-	-	-
TRANSPORT SECTOR	**-**	**-**	**-**	**-**	**-**	**-**	**-**	**-**	**-**	**-**	**-**
International Civil Aviation	-	-	-	-	-	-	-	-	-	-	-
Domestic Air	-	-	-	-	-	-	-	-	-	-	-
Road	-	-	-	-	-	-	-	-	-	-	-
Rail	-	-	-	-	-	-	-	-	-	-	-
Pipeline Transport	-	-	-	-	-	-	-	-	-	-	-
Internal Navigation	-	-	-	-	-	-	-	-	-	-	-
Non-specified	-	-	-	-	-	-	-	-	-	-	-
OTHER SECTORS	**-**	**679**	**-**	**-**	**-**	**17**	**51**	**-**	**-**	**-**	**-**
Agriculture	-	2	-	-	-	-	-	-	-	-	-
Commerce and Publ. Serv.	-	-	-	-	-	-	-	-	-	-	-
Residential	-	677	-	-	-	17	51	-	-	-	-
Non-specified	-	-	-	-	-	-	-	-	-	7	-
NON-ENERGY USE	**-**	**-**	**-**	**-**	**-**	**-**	**-**	**-**	**-**	**-**	**-**
in Industry/Transf./Energy	-	-	-	-	-	-	-	-	-	-	-
in Transport	-	-	-	-	-	-	-	-	-	-	-
in Other Sectors	-	-	-	-	-	-	-	-	-	-	-

Belgium / Belgique : 1992

SUPPLY AND CONSUMPTION / APPROVISIONNEMENT ET DEMANDE	Oil cont. / *Pétrole cont.* (1000 tonnes)										
	Refinery Gas *Gaz de raffinerie*	LPG + Ethane *GPL + éthane*	Motor Gasoline *Essence moteur*	Aviation Gasoline *Essence aviation*	Jet Fuel *Carbu-réacteur*	Kerosene *Kérosène*	Gas/ Diesel *Gazole*	Heavy Fuel Oil *Fioul lourd*	Naphtha *Naphta*	Pétrol. Coke *Coke de pétrole*	Other Prod. *Autres prod.*
Production	458	374	6162	-	1715	74	10795	6733	715	441	4783
From Other Sources	-	-	-	-	-	-	-	-	-	-	-
Imports	-	608	1738	4	388	52	4537	3036	993	239	1149
Exports	-	-290	-5113	-1	-1075	-6	-5428	-3215	-373	-11	-1634
Intl. Marine Bunkers	-	-	-	-	-	-	-725	-3544	-	-	-32
Stock Changes	-	-5	125	-	-31	-5	-6	-41	43	-	42
DOMESTIC SUPPLY	**458**	**687**	**2912**	**3**	**997**	**115**	**9173**	**2969**	**1378**	**669**	**4308**
Transfers	-	-27	-3	-	-101	94	3	-3	-	-	-3032
Statistical Differences	-	-5	-6	-	9	-	1	28	-1	-1	26
TRANSFORMATION	**6**	**-**	**-**	**-**	**-**	**-**	**5**	**208**	**-**	**-**	**1**
Electricity Plants	6	-	-	-	-	-	5	115	-	-	1
CHP Plants	-	-	-	-	-	-	-	93	-	-	-
Heat Plants	-	-	-	-	-	-	-	-	-	-	-
Transfer to Gases	-	-	-	-	-	-	-	-	-	-	-
Transfer to Solids	-	-	-	-	-	-	-	-	-	-	-
Petroleum Refineries	-	-	-	-	-	-	-	-	-	-	-
Petrochemical Industry	-	-	-	-	-	-	-	-	-	-	-
Liquefaction	-	-	-	-	-	-	-	-	-	-	-
Other Transformation Sector	-	-	-	-	-	-	-	-	-	-	-
ENERGY SECTOR	**452**	**52**	**-**	**-**	**-**	**1**	**27**	**510**	**-**	**444**	**5**
Coal Mines	-	2	-	-	-	-	5	12	-	-	2
Oil and Gas Extraction	-	-	-	-	-	-	-	-	-	-	-
Petroleum Refineries	452	-	-	-	-	-	21	498	-	441	-
Electricity, CHP+Heat plants	-	-	-	-	-	-	-	-	-	-	-
Pumped Storage (Elec.)	-	-	-	-	-	-	-	-	-	-	-
Other Energy Sector	-	50	-	-	-	1	1	-	-	3	3
Distribution Losses	-	-	-	-	-	-	-	-	-	-	-
FINAL CONSUMPTION	**-**	**603**	**2903**	**3**	**905**	**208**	**9145**	**2276**	**1377**	**224**	**1296**
INDUSTRY SECTOR	**-**	**265**	**-**	**-**	**-**	**7**	**371**	**1652**	**1377**	**166**	**-**
Iron and Steel	-	1	-	-	-	-	7	103	-	-	-
Chemical and Petrochemical	-	233	-	-	-	3	18	497	1377	-	-
of which: Feedstocks	-	*218*	-	-	-	-	-	-	*1375*	-	-
Non-Ferrous Metals	-	1	-	-	-	-	6	72	-	-	-
Non-Metallic Minerals	-	-	-	-	-	-	8	233	-	77	-
Transport Equipment	-	-	-	-	-	-	-	-	-	-	-
Machinery	-	1	-	-	-	1	17	101	-	-	-
Mining and Quarrying	-	-	-	-	-	-	-	-	-	-	-
Food and Tobacco	-	2	-	-	-	-	40	205	-	-	-
Paper, Pulp and Print	-	-	-	-	-	-	3	76	-	-	-
Wood and Wood Products	-	-	-	-	-	-	-	-	-	-	-
Construction	-	2	-	-	-	-	40	104	-	-	-
Textile and Leather	-	-	-	-	-	-	12	68	-	-	-
Non-specified	-	25	-	-	-	3	220	193	-	89	-
TRANSPORT SECTOR	**-**	**45**	**2903**	**3**	**905**	**-**	**3838**	**291**	**-**	**-**	**-**
International Civil Aviation	-	-	-	-	902	-	-	-	-	-	-
Domestic Air	-	-	-	3	3	-	-	-	-	-	-
Road	-	45	2903	-	-	-	3610	-	-	-	-
Rail	-	-	-	-	-	-	80	-	-	-	-
Pipeline Transport	-	-	-	-	-	-	-	-	-	-	-
Internal Navigation	-	-	-	-	-	-	148	291	-	-	-
Non-specified	-	-	-	-	-	-	-	-	-	-	-
OTHER SECTORS	**-**	**293**	**-**	**-**	**-**	**201**	**4936**	**333**	**-**	**58**	**-**
Agriculture	-	5	-	-	-	72	410	225	-	-	-
Commerce and Publ. Serv.	-	124	-	-	-	29	1045	100	-	-	-
Residential	-	164	-	-	-	100	3481	8	-	58	-
Non-specified	-	-	-	-	-	-	-	-	-	-	-
NON-ENERGY USE	**-**	**-**	**-**	**-**	**-**	**-**	**-**	**-**	**-**	**-**	**1296**
in Industry/Transf./Energy	-	-	-	-	-	-	-	-	-	-	1172
in Transport	-	-	-	-	-	-	-	-	-	-	67
in Other Sectors	-	-	-	-	-	-	-	-	-	-	57

Belgium / Belgique : 1992

CONSUMPTION / APPROVISIONNEMENT ET DEMANDE	Gas / Gaz (TJ)				Combust. Renew. & Waste / En. Re. Comb. & Déchets (TJ)				Electricity (GWh)	Heat (TJ)
	Natural Gas / Gaz naturel	Gas Works / Usines à gaz	Coke Ovens / Cokeries	Blast Furnaces / Hauts fourneaux	Solid Biomass & Anim. Prod. / Biomasse solide & prod. anim.	Gas/Liquids from Biomass / Gaz/Liquides tirés de biomasse	Municipal Waste / Déchets urbains	Industrial Waste / Déchets industriels	Electricity / Electricité	Heat / Chaleur
Production	221	-	31700	39336	1474	-	7640	4462	72259	9988
From Other Sources	-	-	-	-	-	-	-	-	-	-
Imports	425078	-	-	-	-	-	-	-	5849	-
Exports	-	-	-	-	-	-	-	-	-5721	-
Intl. Marine Bunkers	-	-	-	-	-	-	-	-	-	-
Stock Changes	-4306	-	-1	-	-	-	-	-	-	-
DOMESTIC SUPPLY	**420993**	**-**	**31699**	**39336**	**1474**	**-**	**7640**	**4462**	**72387**	**9988**
Transfers	-	-	-	-	-	-	-	-	-	-
Statistical Differences	-188	-	-	-167	-	-	-	-	-	-
TRANSFORMATION	**71652**	**-**	**8861**	**18068**	**1474**	**-**	**7640**	**4462**	**-**	**-**
Electricity Plants	66406	-	8861	8361	1474	-	7640	4280	-	-
CHP Plants	5246	-	-	9707	-	-	-	182	-	-
Heat Plants	-	-	-	-	-	-	-	-	-	-
Transfer to Gases	-	-	-	-	-	-	-	-	-	-
Transfer to Solids	-	-	-	-	-	-	-	-	-	-
Petroleum Refineries	-	-	-	-	-	-	-	-	-	-
Petrochemical Industry	-	-	-	-	-	-	-	-	-	-
Liquefaction	-	-	-	-	-	-	-	-	-	-
Other Transformation Sector	-	-	-	-	-	-	-	-	-	-
ENERGY SECTOR	**5039**	**-**	**12400**	**3031**	**-**	**-**	**-**	**-**	**6236**	**-**
Coal Mines	-	-	-	-	-	-	-	-	119	-
Oil and Gas Extraction	4939	-	-	-	-	-	-	-	-	-
Petroleum Refineries	100	-	-	-	-	-	-	-	1045	-
Electricity, CHP+Heat plants	-	-	-	-	-	-	-	-	3880	-
Pumped Storage (Elec.)	-	-	-	-	-	-	-	-	1068	-
Other Energy Sector	-	-	12400	3031	-	-	-	-	124	-
Distribution Losses	-	-	-	-	-	-	-	-	3568	565
FINAL CONSUMPTION	**344114**	**-**	**10438**	**18070**	**-**	**-**	**-**	**-**	**62583**	**9423**
INDUSTRY SECTOR	**154342**	**-**	**10438**	**18070**	**-**	**-**	**-**	**-**	**32212**	**8258**
Iron and Steel	25862	-	9514	18070	-	-	-	-	5566	365
Chemical and Petrochemical	61415	-	924	-	-	-	-	-	10636	3331
of which: Feedstocks	28600	-	-	-	-	-	-	-	-	-
Non-Ferrous Metals	3762	-	-	-	-	-	-	-	1804	-
Non-Metallic Minerals	19750	-	-	-	-	-	-	-	2222	-
Transport Equipment	4383	-	-	-	-	-	-	-	1010	-
Machinery	2444	-	-	-	-	-	-	-	1896	-
Mining and Quarrying	-	-	-	-	-	-	-	-	354	-
Food and Tobacco	5278	-	-	-	-	-	-	-	3168	-
Paper, Pulp and Print	3065	-	-	-	-	-	-	-	2229	-
Wood and Wood Products	-	-	-	-	-	-	-	-	675	-
Construction	-	-	-	-	-	-	-	-	99	-
Textile and Leather	2043	-	-	-	-	-	-	-	1766	-
Non-specified	26340	-	-	-	-	-	-	-	787	4562
TRANSPORT SECTOR	**-**	**-**	**-**	**-**	**-**	**-**	**-**	**-**	**1305**	**-**
International Civil Aviation	-	-	-	-	-	-	-	-	-	-
Domestic Air	-	-	-	-	-	-	-	-	-	-
Road	-	-	-	-	-	-	-	-	-	-
Rail	-	-	-	-	-	-	-	-	1305	-
Pipeline Transport	-	-	-	-	-	-	-	-	-	-
Internal Navigation	-	-	-	-	-	-	-	-	-	-
Non-specified	-	-	-	-	-	-	-	-	-	-
OTHER SECTORS	**189772**	**-**	**-**	**-**	**-**	**-**	**-**	**-**	**29066**	**1165**
Agriculture	-	-	-	-	-	-	-	-	-	-
Commerce and Publ. Serv.	55874	-	-	-	-	-	-	-	8821	572
Residential	133898	-	-	-	-	-	-	-	20245	593
Non-specified	-	-	-	-	-	-	-	-	-	-
NON-ENERGY USE	**-**	**-**	**-**	**-**	**-**	**-**	**-**	**-**	**-**	**-**
in Industry/Transf./Energy	-	-	-	-	-	-	-	-	-	-
in Transport	-	-	-	-	-	-	-	-	-	-
in Other Sectors	-	-	-	-	-	-	-	-	-	-

Belgium / Belgique : 1993

SUPPLY AND CONSUMPTION / APPROVISIONNEMENT ET DEMANDE	Coal / *Charbon* (1000 tonnes)							Oil / *Pétrole* (1000 tonnes)			
	Coking Coal / *Charbon à coke*	Steam Coal / *Charbon vapeur*	Sub-Bit. Coal / *Charbon sous-bit.*	Lignite / *Lignite*	Peat / *Tourbe*	Oven and Gas Coke / *Coke de four/gaz*	Pat. Fuel and BKB / *Agg./briq. de lignite*	Crude Oil / *Pétrole brut*	NGL / *LGN*	Feedstocks / *Produits d'aliment.*	Additives / *Additifs*
Production	-	-	-	-	-	3975	25	-	-	-	-
From Other Sources	-	-	971	-	-	-	-	-	-	-	-
Imports	4748	7146	-	226	-	623	42	27558	-	3376	-
Exports	-	-645	-16	-	-	-797	-10	-	-	-2618	-
Intl. Marine Bunkers	-	-	-	-	-	-	-	-	-	-	-
Stock Changes	282	623	-298	-	-	117	-	212	-	24	-
DOMESTIC SUPPLY	**5030**	**7124**	**657**	**226**	**-**	**3918**	**57**	**27770**	**-**	**782**	**-**
Transfers	-	-	-	-	-	-	-	-	-	3081	-
Statistical Differences	-	418	35	-	-	30	-	4	-	12	-
TRANSFORMATION	**5030**	**5588**	**539**	**-**	**-**	**1253**	**-**	**27774**	**-**	**3875**	**-**
Electricity Plants	-	3662	526	-	-	-	-	-	-	-	-
CHP Plants	-	1921	13	-	-	-	-	-	-	-	-
Heat Plants	-	-	-	-	-	-	-	-	-	-	-
Transfer to Gases	-	-	-	-	-	1253	-	-	-	-	-
Transfer to Solids	5030	5	-	-	-	-	-	-	-	-	-
Petroleum Refineries	-	-	-	-	-	-	-	27774	-	3875	-
Petrochemical Industry	-	-	-	-	-	-	-	-	-	-	-
Liquefaction	-	-	-	-	-	-	-	-	-	-	-
Other Transformation Sector	-	-	-	-	-	-	-	-	-	-	-
ENERGY SECTOR	**-**	**-**	**-**	**-**	**-**	**14**	**-**	**-**	**-**	**-**	**-**
Coal Mines	-	-	-	-	-	-	-	-	-	-	-
Oil and Gas Extraction	-	-	-	-	-	-	-	-	-	-	-
Petroleum Refineries	-	-	-	-	-	-	-	-	-	-	-
Electricity, CHP+Heat plants	-	-	-	-	-	-	-	-	-	-	-
Pumped Storage (Elec.)	-	-	-	-	-	-	-	-	-	-	-
Other Energy Sector	-	-	-	-	-	14	-	-	-	-	-
Distribution Losses	-	-	-	-	-	-	-	-	-	-	-
FINAL CONSUMPTION	**-**	**1954**	**153**	**226**	**-**	**2681**	**57**	**-**	**-**	**-**	**-**
INDUSTRY SECTOR	**-**	**1330**	**153**	**226**	**-**	**2667**	**-**	**-**	**-**	**-**	**-**
Iron and Steel	-	731	-	-	-	2544	-	-	-	-	-
Chemical and Petrochemical	-	50	-	-	-	19	-	-	-	-	-
of which: Feedstocks	-	-	-	-	-	-	-	-	-	-	-
Non-Ferrous Metals	-	-	-	-	-	5	-	-	-	-	-
Non-Metallic Minerals	-	385	153	226	-	29	-	-	-	-	-
Transport Equipment	-	-	-	-	-	-	-	-	-	-	-
Machinery	-	-	-	-	-	29	-	-	-	-	-
Mining and Quarrying	-	-	-	-	-	-	-	-	-	-	-
Food and Tobacco	-	113	-	-	-	14	-	-	-	-	-
Paper, Pulp and Print	-	44	-	-	-	-	-	-	-	-	-
Wood and Wood Products	-	-	-	-	-	-	-	-	-	-	-
Construction	-	-	-	-	-	-	-	-	-	-	-
Textile and Leather	-	5	-	-	-	-	-	-	-	-	-
Non-specified	-	2	-	-	-	27	-	-	-	-	-
TRANSPORT SECTOR	**-**	**-**	**-**	**-**	**-**	**-**	**-**	**-**	**-**	**-**	**-**
International Civil Aviation	-	-	-	-	-	-	-	-	-	-	-
Domestic Air	-	-	-	-	-	-	-	-	-	-	-
Road	-	-	-	-	-	-	-	-	-	-	-
Rail	-	-	-	-	-	-	-	-	-	-	-
Pipeline Transport	-	-	-	-	-	-	-	-	-	-	-
Internal Navigation	-	-	-	-	-	-	-	-	-	-	-
Non-specified	-	-	-	-	-	-	-	-	-	-	-
OTHER SECTORS	**-**	**624**	**-**	**-**	**-**	**14**	**57**	**-**	**-**	**-**	**-**
Agriculture	-	-	-	-	-	-	-	-	-	-	-
Commerce and Publ. Serv.	-	-	-	-	-	-	-	-	-	-	-
Residential	-	624	-	-	-	14	57	-	-	-	-
Non-specified	-	-	-	-	-	-	-	-	-	-	-
NON-ENERGY USE	**-**	**-**	**-**	**-**	**-**	**-**	**-**	**-**	**-**	**-**	**-**
in Industry/Transf./Energy	-	-	-	-	-	-	-	-	-	-	-
in Transport	-	-	-	-	-	-	-	-	-	-	-
in Other Sectors	-	-	-	-	-	-	-	-	-	-	-

Belgium / Belgique : 1993

SUPPLY AND CONSUMPTION / APPROVISIONNEMENT ET DEMANDE	Oil cont. / Pétrole cont. (1000 tonnes)										
	Refinery Gas / Gaz de raffinerie	LPG + Ethane / GPL + éthane	Motor Gasoline / Essence moteur	Aviation Gasoline / Essence aviation	Jet Fuel / Carbu-réacteur	Kerosene / Kérosène	Gas/Diesel / Gazole	Heavy Fuel Oil / Fioul lourd	Naphtha / Naphta	Pétrol. Coke / Coke de pétrole	Other Prod. / Autres prod.
Production	444	409	5614	-	1514	14	10707	6599	820	444	4728
From Other Sources	-	-	-	-	-	-	-	-	-	-	-
Imports	-	557	1589	3	314	67	4609	3100	1093	193	1115
Exports	-	-345	-4312	-	-857	-7	-5534	-3273	-425	-11	-1589
Intl. Marine Bunkers	-	-	-	-	-	-	-649	-3746	-	-	-35
Stock Changes	-	23	-55	-	3	-3	3	10	-31	-	-24
DOMESTIC SUPPLY	444	644	2836	3	974	71	9136	2690	1457	626	4195
Transfers	-	-77	-4	-	-88	88	-5	7	-	-	-3002
Statistical Differences	-	-7	7	-	5	6	21	-3	-4	-	-3
TRANSFORMATION	-	-	-	-	-	-	9	183	-	-	1
Electricity Plants	-	-	-	-	-	-	9	114	-	-	1
CHP Plants	-	-	-	-	-	-	-	69	-	-	-
Heat Plants	-	-	-	-	-	-	-	-	-	-	-
Transfer to Gases	-	-	-	-	-	-	-	-	-	-	-
Transfer to Solids	-	-	-	-	-	-	-	-	-	-	-
Petroleum Refineries	-	-	-	-	-	-	-	-	-	-	-
Petrochemical Industry	-	-	-	-	-	-	-	-	-	-	-
Liquefaction	-	-	-	-	-	-	-	-	-	-	-
Other Transformation Sector	-	-	-	-	-	-	-	-	-	-	-
ENERGY SECTOR	444	39	-	-	-	-	24	473	-	446	2
Coal Mines	-	2	-	-	-	-	5	18	-	-	1
Oil and Gas Extraction	-	-	-	-	-	-	-	-	-	-	-
Petroleum Refineries	444	-	-	-	-	-	18	455	-	444	-
Electricity, CHP+Heat plants	-	-	-	-	-	-	-	-	-	-	-
Pumped Storage (Elec.)	-	-	-	-	-	-	-	-	-	-	-
Other Energy Sector	-	37	-	-	-	-	1	-	-	2	1
Distribution Losses	-	-	-	-	-	-	-	-	-	-	-
FINAL CONSUMPTION	-	521	2839	3	891	165	9119	2038	1453	180	1187
INDUSTRY SECTOR	-	224	-	-	3	6	409	1468	1453	131	-
Iron and Steel	-	-	-	-	-	-	7	67	-	1	-
Chemical and Petrochemical	-	190	-	-	1	3	10	512	1453	-	-
of which: Feedstocks	-	166	-	-	-	-	-	-	1443	-	-
Non-Ferrous Metals	-	1	-	-	-	-	-	-	-	-	-
Non-Metallic Minerals	-	-	-	-	-	-	9	65	-	-	-
Transport Equipment	-	-	-	-	-	-	12	170	-	55	-
Machinery	-	1	-	-	-	-	-	-	-	-	-
Mining and Quarrying	-	-	-	-	2	-	14	90	-	-	-
Food and Tobacco	-	2	-	-	-	-	-	-	-	-	-
Paper, Pulp and Print	-	-	-	-	-	-	38	174	-	-	-
Wood and Wood Products	-	-	-	-	-	-	3	45	-	-	-
Construction	-	2	-	-	-	-	13	47	-	-	-
Textile and Leather	-	-	-	-	-	-	43	56	-	-	-
Non-specified	-	28	-	-	-	3	260	242	-	75	-
TRANSPORT SECTOR	-	40	2839	3	888	-	4032	227	-	-	-
International Civil Aviation	-	-	-	-	795	-	-	-	-	-	-
Domestic Air	-	-	-	3	93	-	-	-	-	-	-
Road	-	40	2839	-	-	-	3838	-	-	-	-
Rail	-	-	-	-	-	-	81	-	-	-	-
Pipeline Transport	-	-	-	-	-	-	-	-	-	-	-
Internal Navigation	-	-	-	-	-	-	113	227	-	-	-
Non-specified	-	-	-	-	-	-	-	-	-	-	-
OTHER SECTORS	-	257	-	-	-	159	4678	343	-	49	-
Agriculture	-	7	-	-	-	55	468	252	-	-	-
Commerce and Publ. Serv.	-	107	-	-	-	24	935	91	-	-	-
Residential	-	143	-	-	-	80	3275	-	-	48	-
Non-specified	-	-	-	-	-	-	-	-	-	1	-
NON-ENERGY USE	-	-	-	-	-	-	-	-	-	-	1187
in Industry/Transf./Energy	-	-	-	-	-	-	-	-	-	-	1064
in Transport	-	-	-	-	-	-	-	-	-	-	62
in Other Sectors	-	-	-	-	-	-	-	-	-	-	61

Belgium / Belgique : 1993

CONSUMPTION *APPROVISIONNEMENT ET DEMANDE*	Gas / *Gaz* (TJ)				Combust. Renew. & Waste / *En. Re. Comb. & Déchets* (TJ)				(GWh)	(TJ)
	Natural Gas *Gaz naturel*	Gas Works *Usines à gaz*	Coke Ovens *Cokeries*	Blast Furnaces *Hauts fourneaux*	Solid Biomass & Anim. Prod. *Biomasse solide & prod. anim.*	Gas/Liquids from Biomass *Gaz/Liquides tirés de biomasse*	Municipal Waste *Déchets urbains*	Industrial Waste *Déchets industriels*	Electricity *Electricité*	Heat *Chaleur*
Production	178	-	29856	36722	673	-	8455	4399	70845	9503
From Other Sources	-	-	-	-	-	-	-	-	-	-
Imports	440441	-	-	-	-	-	-	-	7590	-
Exports	-	-	-	-	-	-	-	-	-5359	-
Intl. Marine Bunkers	-	-	-	-	-	-	-	-	-	-
Stock Changes	-3023	-	2	-	-	-	-	-	-	-
DOMESTIC SUPPLY	**437596**	**-**	**29858**	**36722**	**673**	**-**	**8455**	**4399**	**73076**	**9503**
Transfers	-	-	-	-	-	-	-	-	-	-
Statistical Differences	2776	-	-	-47	-	-	-	-	-	-
TRANSFORMATION	**74852**	**-**	**5778**	**19796**	**673**	**-**	**8455**	**4399**	**-**	**-**
Electricity Plants	66621	-	5778	9118	673	-	8455	4283	-	-
CHP Plants	8231	-	-	10678	-	-	-	116	-	-
Heat Plants	-	-	-	-	-	-	-	-	-	-
Transfer to Gases	-	-	-	-	-	-	-	-	-	-
Transfer to Solids	-	-	-	-	-	-	-	-	-	-
Petroleum Refineries	-	-	-	-	-	-	-	-	-	-
Petrochemical Industry	-	-	-	-	-	-	-	-	-	-
Liquefaction	-	-	-	-	-	-	-	-	-	-
Other Transformation Sector	-	-	-	-	-	-	-	-	-	-
ENERGY SECTOR	**4506**	**-**	**13561**	**1229**	**-**	**-**	**-**	**-**	**5911**	**-**
Coal Mines	-	-	-	-	-	-	-	-	56	-
Oil and Gas Extraction	4446	-	-	-	-	-	-	-	-	-
Petroleum Refineries	60	-	-	-	-	-	-	-	999	-
Electricity, CHP+Heat plants	-	-	-	-	-	-	-	-	3737	-
Pumped Storage (Elec.)	-	-	-	-	-	-	-	-	1011	-
Other Energy Sector	-	-	13561	1229	-	-	-	-	108	-
Distribution Losses	-	-	-	-	-	-	-	-	3684	539
FINAL CONSUMPTION	**361014**	**-**	**10519**	**15650**	**-**	**-**	**-**	**-**	**63481**	**8964**
INDUSTRY SECTOR	**159457**	**-**	**10519**	**15650**	**-**	**-**	**-**	**-**	**31269**	**7722**
Iron and Steel	24585	-	9742	15650	-	-	-	-	5324	355
Chemical and Petrochemical	65881	-	777	-	-	-	-	-	10382	3336
of which: Feedstocks	*28650*	-	-	-	-	-	-	-	-	-
Non-Ferrous Metals	3820	-	-	-	-	-	-	-	1736	-
Non-Metallic Minerals	19535	-	-	-	-	-	-	-	2259	-
Transport Equipment	4537	-	-	-	-	-	-	-	931	-
Machinery	2346	-	-	-	-	-	-	-	1634	-
Mining and Quarrying	-	-	-	-	-	-	-	-	375	-
Food and Tobacco	4890	-	-	-	-	-	-	-	2956	-
Paper, Pulp and Print	3197	-	-	-	-	-	-	-	2045	-
Wood and Wood Products	-	-	-	-	-	-	-	-	523	-
Construction	-	-	-	-	-	-	-	-	204	-
Textile and Leather	2473	-	-	-	-	-	-	-	1599	-
Non-specified	28193	-	-	-	-	-	-	-	1301	4031
TRANSPORT SECTOR	**-**	**-**	**-**	**-**	**-**	**-**	**-**	**-**	**1360**	**-**
International Civil Aviation	-	-	-	-	-	-	-	-	-	-
Domestic Air	-	-	-	-	-	-	-	-	-	-
Road	-	-	-	-	-	-	-	-	-	-
Rail	-	-	-	-	-	-	-	-	1360	-
Pipeline Transport	-	-	-	-	-	-	-	-	-	-
Internal Navigation	-	-	-	-	-	-	-	-	-	-
Non-specified	-	-	-	-	-	-	-	-	-	-
OTHER SECTORS	**201557**	**-**	**-**	**-**	**-**	**-**	**-**	**-**	**30852**	**1242**
Agriculture	-	-	-	-	-	-	-	-	-	-
Commerce and Publ. Serv.	60360	-	-	-	-	-	-	-	9762	606
Residential	141197	-	-	-	-	-	-	-	21090	636
Non-specified	-	-	-	-	-	-	-	-	-	-
NON-ENERGY USE	**-**	**-**	**-**	**-**	**-**	**-**	**-**	**-**	**-**	**-**
in Industry/Transf./Energy	-	-	-	-	-	-	-	-	-	-
in Transport	-	-	-	-	-	-	-	-	-	-
in Other Sectors	-	-	-	-	-	-	-	-	-	-

Canada / Canada : 1992

SUPPLY AND CONSUMPTION	Coal / *Charbon* (1000 tonnes)							Oil / *Pétrole* (1000 tonnes)			
	Coking Coal	Steam Coal	Sub-Bit. Coal	Lignite	Peat	Oven and Gas Coke	Pat. Fuel and BKB	Crude Oil	NGL	Feedstocks	Additives
APPROVISIONNEMENT ET DEMANDE	*Charbon à coke*	*Charbon vapeur*	*Charbon sous-bit.*	*Lignite*	*Tourbe*	*Coke de four/gaz*	*Agg./briq. de lignite*	*Pétrole brut*	*LGN*	*Produits d'aliment.*	*Additifs*
Production	21790	10525	23020	10027	-	3711	-	81257	14647	-	-
From Other Sources	-	-	-	-	-	-	-	-	-	-	-
Imports	4848	7985	-	-	-	309	-	25405	47	-	-
Exports	-22364	-5037	-	-9	-	-99	-	-37649	-8151	-	-
Intl. Marine Bunkers	-	-	-	-	-	-	-	-	-	-	-
Stock Changes	638	974	175	-186	-	209	-	269	143	-	-
DOMESTIC SUPPLY	**4912**	**14447**	**23195**	**9832**	**-**	**4130**	**-**	**69282**	**6686**	**-**	**-**
Transfers	-	-	-	-	-	-	-	-	-4937	6919	-
Statistical Differences	-27	61	-1	-12	-	-26	-	-202	1192	-	-
TRANSFORMATION	**4885**	**13076**	**23156**	**9576**	**-**	**1115**	**-**	**68871**	**2941**	**6919**	**-**
Electricity Plants	-	13076	23156	9576	-	-	-	-	-	-	-
CHP Plants	-	-	-	-	-	-	-	-	-	-	-
Heat Plants	-	-	-	-	-	-	-	-	-	-	-
Transfer to Gases	-	-	-	-	-	1115	-	-	-	-	-
Transfer to Solids	4885	-	-	-	-	-	-	-	-	-	-
Petroleum Refineries	-	-	-	-	-	-	-	70954	2941	6919	-
Petrochemical Industry	-	-	-	-	-	-	-	-	-	-	-
Liquefaction	-	-	-	-	-	-	-	-2083	-	-	-
Other Transformation Sector	-	-	-	-	-	-	-	-	-	-	-
ENERGY SECTOR	**-**	**88**	**-**	**-**	**-**	**-**	**-**	**209**	**-**	**-**	**-**
Coal Mines	-	88	-	-	-	-	-	-	-	-	-
Oil and Gas Extraction	-	-	-	-	-	-	-	209	-	-	-
Petroleum Refineries	-	-	-	-	-	-	-	-	-	-	-
Electricity, CHP+Heat plants	-	-	-	-	-	-	-	-	-	-	-
Pumped Storage (Elec.)	-	-	-	-	-	-	-	-	-	-	-
Other Energy Sector	-	-	-	-	-	-	-	-	-	-	-
Distribution Losses	-	-	-	-	-	-	-	-	-	-	-
FINAL CONSUMPTION	**-**	**1344**	**38**	**244**	**-**	**2989**	**-**	**-**	**-**	**-**	**-**
INDUSTRY SECTOR	**-**	**1148**	**-**	**231**	**-**	**2933**	**-**	**-**	**-**	**-**	**-**
Iron and Steel	-	-	-	-	-	2548	-	-	-	-	-
Chemical and Petrochemical	-	-	-	-	-	-	-	-	-	-	-
of which: Feedstocks	-	-	-	-	-	-	-	-	-	-	-
Non-Ferrous Metals	-	371	-	-	-	94	-	-	-	-	-
Non-Metallic Minerals	-	673	-	-	-	74	-	-	-	-	-
Transport Equipment	-	-	-	-	-	-	-	-	-	-	-
Machinery	-	-	-	-	-	-	-	-	-	-	-
Mining and Quarrying	-	45	-	-	-	114	-	-	-	-	-
Food and Tobacco	-	-	-	-	-	-	-	-	-	-	-
Paper, Pulp and Print	-	19	-	96	-	-	-	-	-	-	-
Wood and Wood Products	-	-	-	-	-	-	-	-	-	-	-
Construction	-	-	-	-	-	-	-	-	-	-	-
Textile and Leather	-	-	-	-	-	-	-	-	-	-	-
Non-specified	-	40	-	135	-	103	-	-	-	-	-
TRANSPORT SECTOR	**-**	**-**	**-**	**-**	**-**	**-**	**-**	**-**	**-**	**-**	**-**
International Civil Aviation	-	-	-	-	-	-	-	-	-	-	-
Domestic Air	-	-	-	-	-	-	-	-	-	-	-
Road	-	-	-	-	-	-	-	-	-	-	-
Rail	-	-	-	-	-	-	-	-	-	-	-
Pipeline Transport	-	-	-	-	-	-	-	-	-	-	-
Internal Navigation	-	-	-	-	-	-	-	-	-	-	-
Non-specified	-	-	-	-	-	-	-	-	-	-	-
OTHER SECTORS	**-**	**37**	**38**	**13**	**-**	**-**	**-**	**-**	**-**	**-**	**-**
Agriculture	-	-	-	-	-	-	-	-	-	-	-
Commerce and Publ. Serv.	-	-	-	-	-	-	-	-	-	-	-
Residential	-	37	38	13	-	-	-	-	-	-	-
Non-specified	-	-	-	-	-	-	-	-	-	-	-
NON-ENERGY USE	**-**	**159**	**-**	**-**	**-**	**56**	**-**	**-**	**-**	**-**	**-**
in Industry/Transf./Energy	-	159	-	-	-	56	-	-	-	-	-
in Transport	-	-	-	-	-	-	-	-	-	-	-
in Other Sectors	-	-	-	-	-	-	-	-	-	-	-

Canada / Canada : 1992

SUPPLY AND CONSUMPTION *APPROVISIONNEMENT ET DEMANDE*	Oil cont. / *Pétrole cont.* (1000 tonnes)										
	Refinery Gas *Gaz de raffinerie*	LPG + Ethane *GPL + éthane*	Motor Gasoline *Essence moteur*	Aviation Gasoline *Essence aviation*	Jet Fuel *Carbu-réacteur*	Kerosene *Kérosène*	Gas/ Diesel *Gazole*	Heavy Fuel Oil *Fioul lourd*	Naphtha *Naphta*	Pétrol. Coke *Coke de pétrole*	Other Prod. *Autres prod.*
Production	3896	2027	25335	80	3613	2070	21261	6967	3917	2091	8165
From Other Sources	-	-	-	-	-	-	-	-	-	-	-
Imports	-	4	503	5	488	95	318	2760	10	1093	2815
Exports	-	-6	-3084	-5	-440	-84	-4296	-1969	-430	-86	-1117
Intl. Marine Bunkers	-	-	-	-	-	-	-105	-486	-	-	-
Stock Changes	-9	-11	417	6	50	207	416	250	24	-25	-20
DOMESTIC SUPPLY	**3887**	**2014**	**23171**	**86**	**3711**	**2288**	**17594**	**7522**	**3521**	**3073**	**9843**
Transfers	-81	4057	1461	2	69	-1807	1136	621	-721	-33	-5462
Statistical Differences	32	-13	-167	-8	-61	54	241	86	65	65	-186
TRANSFORMATION	-	-	-	-	-	-	**479**	**3165**	-	-	-
Electricity Plants	-	-	-	-	-	-	479	3118	-	-	-
CHP Plants	-	-	-	-	-	-	-	47	-	-	-
Heat Plants	-	-	-	-	-	-	-	-	-	-	-
Transfer to Gases	-	-	-	-	-	-	-	-	-	-	-
Transfer to Solids	-	-	-	-	-	-	-	-	-	-	-
Petroleum Refineries	-	-	-	-	-	-	-	-	-	-	-
Petrochemical Industry	-	-	-	-	-	-	-	-	-	-	-
Liquefaction	-	-	-	-	-	-	-	-	-	-	-
Other Transformation Sector	-	-	-	-	-	-	-	-	-	-	-
ENERGY SECTOR	**3838**	**61**	**3**	-	-	-	**18**	**877**	-	**1653**	**5**
Coal Mines	-	-	-	-	-	-	-	-	-	-	-
Oil and Gas Extraction	-	-	-	-	-	-	-	-	-	738	-
Petroleum Refineries	3838	61	3	-	-	-	18	877	-	915	5
Electricity, CHP+Heat plants	-	-	-	-	-	-	-	-	-	-	-
Pumped Storage (Elec.)	-	-	-	-	-	-	-	-	-	-	-
Other Energy Sector	-	-	-	-	-	-	-	-	-	-	-
Distribution Losses	-	-	-	-	-	-	-	-	-	-	-
FINAL CONSUMPTION	-	**5997**	**24462**	**80**	**3719**	**535**	**18474**	**4187**	**2865**	**1452**	**4190**
INDUSTRY SECTOR	-	**4208**	-	-	-	**22**	**2173**	**2922**	**2865**	**297**	-
Iron and Steel	-	-	-	-	-	-	25	215	-	-	-
Chemical and Petrochemical	-	3670	-	-	-	-	6	154	2865	-	-
of which: Feedstocks	-	*3670*	-	-	-	-	-	-	*2865*	-	-
Non-Ferrous Metals	-	-	-	-	-	-	15	197	-	-	-
Non-Metallic Minerals	-	-	-	-	-	-	8	53	-	108	-
Transport Equipment	-	-	-	-	-	-	-	-	-	-	-
Machinery	-	-	-	-	-	-	-	-	-	-	-
Mining and Quarrying	-	142	-	-	-	8	896	347	-	-	-
Food and Tobacco	-	-	-	-	-	-	-	-	-	-	-
Paper, Pulp and Print	-	-	-	-	-	-	135	1597	-	-	-
Wood and Wood Products	-	-	-	-	-	1	160	69	-	-	-
Construction	-	180	-	-	-	5	647	19	-	-	-
Textile and Leather	-	-	-	-	-	-	-	-	-	-	-
Non-specified	-	216	-	-	-	8	281	271	-	189	-
TRANSPORT SECTOR	-	**575**	**24462**	**80**	**3719**	-	**8130**	**990**	-	-	-
International Civil Aviation	-	-	-	-	844	-	-	-	-	-	-
Domestic Air	-	-	-	80	2875	-	-	-	-	-	-
Road	-	575	24462	-	-	-	5322	-	-	-	-
Rail	-	-	-	-	-	-	1927	-	-	-	-
Pipeline Transport	-	-	-	-	-	-	11	-	-	-	-
Internal Navigation	-	-	-	-	-	-	870	990	-	-	-
Non-specified	-	-	-	-	-	-	-	-	-	-	-
OTHER SECTORS	-	**1214**	-	-	-	**513**	**8171**	**275**	-	-	-
Agriculture	-	133	-	-	-	54	2525	16	-	-	-
Commerce and Publ. Serv.	-	800	-	-	-	134	2946	221	-	-	-
Residential	-	281	-	-	-	325	2700	38	-	-	-
Non-specified	-	-	-	-	-	-	-	-	-	-	-
NON-ENERGY USE	-	-	-	-	-	-	-	-	-	**1155**	**4190**
in Industry/Transf./Energy	-	-	-	-	-	-	-	-	-	1155	3105
in Transport	-	-	-	-	-	-	-	-	-	-	266
in Other Sectors	-	-	-	-	-	-	-	-	-	-	819

Canada / Canada : 1992

CONSUMPTION / APPROVISIONNEMENT ET DEMANDE	Gas / Gaz (TJ)				Combust. Renew. & Waste / En. Re. Comb. & Déchets (TJ)				Electricity (GWh)	Heat (TJ)
	Natural Gas / Gaz naturel	Gas Works / Usines à gaz	Coke Ovens / Cokeries	Blast Furnaces / Hauts fourneaux	Solid Biomass & Anim. Prod. / Biomasse solide & prod. anim.	Gas/Liquids from Biomass / Gaz/Liquides tirés de biomasse	Municipal Waste / Déchets urbains	Industrial Waste / Déchets industriels	Electricity / Electricité	Heat / Chaleur
Production	4761464	-	32154	30546	369441	-	-	-	520924	16880
From Other Sources	-	-	-	-	-	-	-	-	-	-
Imports	17109	-	-	-	-	-	-	-	6477	-
Exports	-2195274	-	-	-	-	-	-	-	-31528	-
Intl. Marine Bunkers	-	-	-	-	-	-	-	-	-	-
Stock Changes	113777	-	-	-	-	-	-	-	-	-
DOMESTIC SUPPLY	**2697076**	**-**	**32154**	**30546**	**369441**	**-**	**-**	**-**	**495873**	**16880**
Transfers	-	-	-	-	-	-	-	-	-	-
Statistical Differences	-33441	-	-	-	-	-	-	-	-	-
TRANSFORMATION	**230019**	**-**	**640**	**608**	**15571**	**-**	**-**	**-**	**-**	**-**
Electricity Plants	105639	-	640	608	15571	-	-	-	-	-
CHP Plants	16732	-	-	-	-	-	-	-	-	-
Heat Plants	-	-	-	-	-	-	-	-	-	-
Transfer to Gases	-	-	-	-	-	-	-	-	-	-
Transfer to Solids	-	-	-	-	-	-	-	-	-	-
Petroleum Refineries	-	-	-	-	-	-	-	-	-	-
Petrochemical Industry	-	-	-	-	-	-	-	-	-	-
Liquefaction	94965	-	-	-	-	-	-	-	-	-
Other Transformation Sector	12683	-	-	-	-	-	-	-	-	-
ENERGY SECTOR	**310617**	**-**	**-**	**-**	**-**	**-**	**-**	**-**	**35603**	**-**
Coal Mines	4161	-	-	-	-	-	-	-	1058	-
Oil and Gas Extraction	246955	-	-	-	-	-	-	-	12562	-
Petroleum Refineries	59501	-	-	-	-	-	-	-	5937	-
Electricity, CHP+Heat plants	-	-	-	-	-	-	-	-	15792	-
Pumped Storage (Elec.)	-	-	-	-	-	-	-	-	254	-
Other Energy Sector	-	-	-	-	-	-	-	-	-	-
Distribution Losses	-	-	-	-	-	-	-	-	37163	-
FINAL CONSUMPTION	**2122999**	**-**	**31514**	**29938**	**353870**	**-**	**-**	**-**	**423107**	**16880**
INDUSTRY SECTOR	**933529**	**-**	**31514**	**29938**	**271575**	**-**	**-**	**-**	**167498**	**16776**
Iron and Steel	69323	-	31514	29938	-	-	-	-	8296	-
Chemical and Petrochemical	307923	-	-	-	-	-	-	-	16899	15313
of which: Feedstocks	165664	-	-	-	-	-	-	-	-	-
Non-Ferrous Metals	26744	-	-	-	-	-	-	-	42051	-
Non-Metallic Minerals	13107	-	-	-	-	-	-	-	-	-
Transport Equipment	-	-	-	-	-	-	-	-	-	-
Machinery	-	-	-	-	-	-	-	-	-	-
Mining and Quarrying	45916	-	-	-	-	-	-	-	15345	-
Food and Tobacco	-	-	-	-	-	-	-	-	-	-
Paper, Pulp and Print	117284	-	-	-	271575	-	-	-	49696	1304
Wood and Wood Products	-	-	-	-	-	-	-	-	-	-
Construction	-	-	-	-	-	-	-	-	-	-
Textile and Leather	-	-	-	-	-	-	-	-	-	-
Non-specified	353232	-	-	-	-	-	-	-	35211	159
TRANSPORT SECTOR	**194661**	**-**	**-**	**-**	**-**	**-**	**-**	**-**	**3407**	**-**
International Civil Aviation	-	-	-	-	-	-	-	-	-	-
Domestic Air	-	-	-	-	-	-	-	-	-	-
Road	2871	-	-	-	-	-	-	-	-	-
Rail	-	-	-	-	-	-	-	-	815	-
Pipeline Transport	191790	-	-	-	-	-	-	-	2592	-
Internal Navigation	-	-	-	-	-	-	-	-	-	-
Non-specified	-	-	-	-	-	-	-	-	-	-
OTHER SECTORS	**994809**	**-**	**-**	**-**	**82295**	**-**	**-**	**-**	**252202**	**104**
Agriculture	25134	-	-	-	-	-	-	-	9482	91
Commerce and Publ. Serv.	416355	-	-	-	-	-	-	-	111647	13
Residential	553320	-	-	-	82295	-	-	-	131073	-
Non-specified	-	-	-	-	-	-	-	-	-	-
NON-ENERGY USE	**-**	**-**	**-**	**-**	**-**	**-**	**-**	**-**	**-**	**-**
in Industry/Transf./Energy	-	-	-	-	-	-	-	-	-	-
in Transport	-	-	-	-	-	-	-	-	-	-
in Other Sectors	-	-	-	-	-	-	-	-	-	-

Canada / Canada : 1993

SUPPLY AND CONSUMPTION	Coal / *Charbon* (1000 tonnes)							Oil / *Pétrole* (1000 tonnes)			
	Coking Coal	Steam Coal	Sub-Bit. Coal	Lignite	Peat	Oven and Gas Coke	Pat. Fuel and BKB	Crude Oil	NGL	Feedstocks	Additives
APPROVISIONNEMENT ET DEMANDE	*Charbon à coke*	*Charbon vapeur*	*Charbon sous-bit.*	*Lignite*	*Tourbe*	*Coke de four/gaz*	*Agg./briq. de lignite*	*Pétrole brut*	*LGN*	*Produits d'aliment.*	*Additifs*
Production	25790	9520	23661	10045	-	3657	-	84761	15979	-	-
From Other Sources	-	-	-	-	-	-	-	-	-	-	-
Imports	4684	3718	-	-	-	445	-	29270	71	-	-
Exports	-23950	-4275	-	-29	-	-307	-	-42070	-7908	-	-
Intl. Marine Bunkers	-	-	-	-	-	-	-	-	-	-	-
Stock Changes	-1784	2143	34	118	-	49	-	61	-189	-	-
DOMESTIC SUPPLY	**4740**	**11106**	**23695**	**10134**	**-**	**3844**	**-**	**72022**	**7953**	**-**	**-**
Transfers	-	-	-	-	-	-	-	-	-5070	5461	-
Statistical Differences	-70	-26	-1	-8	-	68	-	26	971	-	-
TRANSFORMATION	**4670**	**9640**	**23651**	**9822**	**-**	**1066**	**-**	**71938**	**3854**	**5461**	**-**
Electricity Plants	-	9640	23651	9822	-	-	-	-	-	-	-
CHP Plants	-	-	-	-	-	-	-	-	-	-	-
Heat Plants	-	-	-	-	-	-	-	-	-	-	-
Transfer to Gases	-	-	-	-	-	1066	-	-	-	-	-
Transfer to Solids	4670	-	-	-	-	-	-	-	-	-	-
Petroleum Refineries	-	-	-	-	-	-	-	74169	3854	5461	-
Petrochemical Industry	-	-	-	-	-	-	-	-	-	-	-
Liquefaction	-	-	-	-	-	-	-	-2231	-	-	-
Other Transformation Sector	-	-	-	-	-	-	-	-	-	-	-
ENERGY SECTOR	**-**	**128**	**-**	**-**	**-**	**-**	**-**	**110**	**-**	**-**	**-**
Coal Mines	-	128	-	-	-	-	-	-	-	-	-
Oil and Gas Extraction	-	-	-	-	-	-	-	110	-	-	-
Petroleum Refineries	-	-	-	-	-	-	-	-	-	-	-
Electricity, CHP+Heat plants	-	-	-	-	-	-	-	-	-	-	-
Pumped Storage (Elec.)	-	-	-	-	-	-	-	-	-	-	-
Other Energy Sector	-	-	-	-	-	-	-	-	-	-	-
Distribution Losses	-	-	-	-	-	-	-	-	-	-	-
FINAL CONSUMPTION	**-**	**1312**	**43**	**304**	**-**	**2846**	**-**	**-**	**-**	**-**	**-**
INDUSTRY SECTOR	**-**	**1105**	**-**	**298**	**-**	**2795**	**-**	**-**	**-**	**-**	**-**
Iron and Steel	-	-	-	-	-	2466	-	-	-	-	-
Chemical and Petrochemical	-	-	-	-	-	-	-	-	-	-	-
of which: Feedstocks	-	-	-	-	-	-	-	-	-	-	-
Non-Ferrous Metals	-	306	-	-	-	85	-	-	-	-	-
Non-Metallic Minerals	-	711	-	-	-	10	-	-	-	-	-
Transport Equipment	-	-	-	-	-	-	-	-	-	-	-
Machinery	-	-	-	-	-	-	-	-	-	-	-
Mining and Quarrying	-	22	-	-	-	131	-	-	-	-	-
Food and Tobacco	-	-	-	-	-	-	-	-	-	-	-
Paper, Pulp and Print	-	24	-	82	-	-	-	-	-	-	-
Wood and Wood Products	-	-	-	-	-	-	-	-	-	-	-
Construction	-	-	-	-	-	-	-	-	-	-	-
Textile and Leather	-	-	-	-	-	-	-	-	-	-	-
Non-specified	-	42	-	216	-	103	-	-	-	-	-
TRANSPORT SECTOR	**-**	**-**	**-**	**-**	**-**	**-**	**-**	**-**	**-**	**-**	**-**
International Civil Aviation	-	-	-	-	-	-	-	-	-	-	-
Domestic Air	-	-	-	-	-	-	-	-	-	-	-
Road	-	-	-	-	-	-	-	-	-	-	-
Rail	-	-	-	-	-	-	-	-	-	-	-
Pipeline Transport	-	-	-	-	-	-	-	-	-	-	-
Internal Navigation	-	-	-	-	-	-	-	-	-	-	-
Non-specified	-	-	-	-	-	-	-	-	-	-	-
OTHER SECTORS	**-**	**34**	**43**	**6**	**-**	**-**	**-**	**-**	**-**	**-**	**-**
Agriculture	-	-	-	-	-	-	-	-	-	-	-
Commerce and Publ. Serv.	-	-	-	-	-	-	-	-	-	-	-
Residential	-	34	43	6	-	-	-	-	-	-	-
Non-specified	-	-	-	-	-	-	-	-	-	-	-
NON-ENERGY USE	**-**	**173**	**-**	**-**	**-**	**51**	**-**	**-**	**-**	**-**	**-**
in Industry/Transf./Energy	-	173	-	-	-	51	-	-	-	-	-
in Transport	-	-	-	-	-	-	-	-	-	-	-
in Other Sectors	-	-	-	-	-	-	-	-	-	-	-

Canada / Canada : 1993

SUPPLY AND CONSUMPTION / APPROVISIONNEMENT ET DEMANDE	Oil cont. / *Pétrole cont.* (1000 tonnes)										
	Refinery Gas / *Gaz de raffinerie*	LPG + Ethane / *GPL + éthane*	Motor Gasoline / *Essence moteur*	Aviation Gasoline / *Essence aviation*	Jet Fuel / *Carbu-réacteur*	Kerosene / *Kérosène*	Gas/ Diesel / *Gazole*	Heavy Fuel Oil / *Fioul lourd*	Naphtha / *Naphta*	Pétrol. Coke / *Coke de pétrole*	Other Prod. / *Autres prod.*
Production	3757	2028	26555	88	3274	2297	22852	6727	3478	2264	8311
From Other Sources	-	-	-	-	-	-	-	-	-	-	-
Imports	-	20	827	7	351	103	359	2168	9	1140	2453
Exports	-	-26	-2779	-10	-155	-91	-5327	-1477	-429	-91	-1905
Intl. Marine Bunkers	-	-	-	-	-	-	-93	-481	-	-	-
Stock Changes	-3	25	-133	-2	26	-15	138	-46	-3	21	197
DOMESTIC SUPPLY	**3754**	**2047**	**24470**	**83**	**3496**	**2294**	**17929**	**6891**	**3055**	**3334**	**9056**
Transfers	-8	4157	750	5	104	-1819	1591	631	-287	9	-4727
Statistical Differences	-6	198	-201	-9	-42	38	14	-5	71	57	2
TRANSFORMATION	-	-	-	-	-	-	**228**	**2332**	-	-	-
Electricity Plants	-	-	-	-	-	-	228	2286	-	-	-
CHP Plants	-	-	-	-	-	-	-	46	-	-	-
Heat Plants	-	-	-	-	-	-	-	-	-	-	-
Transfer to Gases	-	-	-	-	-	-	-	-	-	-	-
Transfer to Solids	-	-	-	-	-	-	-	-	-	-	-
Petroleum Refineries	-	-	-	-	-	-	-	-	-	-	-
Petrochemical Industry	-	-	-	-	-	-	-	-	-	-	-
Liquefaction	-	-	-	-	-	-	-	-	-	-	-
Other Transformation Sector	-	-	-	-	-	-	-	-	-	-	-
ENERGY SECTOR	**3740**	**77**	**13**	-	-	**2**	**27**	**953**	-	**1814**	**10**
Coal Mines	-	-	-	-	-	-	-	-	-	-	-
Oil and Gas Extraction	-	-	-	-	-	-	-	-	-	756	-
Petroleum Refineries	3740	77	13	-	-	2	27	953	-	1058	10
Electricity, CHP+Heat plants	-	-	-	-	-	-	-	-	-	-	-
Pumped Storage (Elec.)	-	-	-	-	-	-	-	-	-	-	-
Other Energy Sector	-	-	-	-	-	-	-	-	-	-	-
Distribution Losses	-	-	-	-	-	-	-	-	-	-	-
FINAL CONSUMPTION	-	**6325**	**25006**	**79**	**3558**	**511**	**19279**	**4232**	**2839**	**1586**	**4321**
INDUSTRY SECTOR	-	**4534**	-	-	-	**31**	**2270**	**3203**	**2839**	**177**	-
Iron and Steel	-	-	-	-	-	-	22	227	-	-	-
Chemical and Petrochemical	-	3961	-	-	-	-	4	238	2839	-	-
of which: Feedstocks	-	3961	-	-	-	-	-	-	2839	-	-
Non-Ferrous Metals	-	-	-	-	-	-	17	227	-	-	-
Non-Metallic Minerals	-	-	-	-	-	-	6	38	-	103	-
Transport Equipment	-	-	-	-	-	-	-	-	-	-	-
Machinery	-	-	-	-	-	-	-	-	-	-	-
Mining and Quarrying	-	-	-	-	-	11	1006	365	-	-	-
Food and Tobacco	-	-	-	-	-	-	-	-	-	-	-
Paper, Pulp and Print	-	-	-	-	-	-	121	1556	-	-	-
Wood and Wood Products	-	-	-	-	-	3	167	111	-	-	-
Construction	-	64	-	-	-	4	645	12	-	-	-
Textile and Leather	-	-	-	-	-	-	-	-	-	-	-
Non-specified	-	509	-	-	-	13	282	429	-	74	-
TRANSPORT SECTOR	-	**638**	**25006**	**79**	**3558**	-	**8486**	**794**	-	-	-
International Civil Aviation	-	-	-	-	778	-	-	-	-	-	-
Domestic Air	-	-	-	79	2780	-	-	-	-	-	-
Road	-	638	25006	-	-	-	5731	-	-	-	-
Rail	-	-	-	-	-	-	1920	-	-	-	-
Pipeline Transport	-	-	-	-	-	-	7	-	-	-	-
Internal Navigation	-	-	-	-	-	-	828	794	-	-	-
Non-specified	-	-	-	-	-	-	-	-	-	-	-
OTHER SECTORS	-	**1153**	-	-	-	**480**	**8523**	**235**	-	-	-
Agriculture	-	121	-	-	-	34	1968	18	-	-	-
Commerce and Publ. Serv.	-	800	-	-	-	136	3069	183	-	-	-
Residential	-	232	-	-	-	310	3486	34	-	-	-
Non-specified	-	-	-	-	-	-	-	-	-	-	-
NON-ENERGY USE	-	-	-	-	-	-	-	-	-	**1409**	**4321**
in Industry/Transf./Energy	-	-	-	-	-	-	-	-	-	1409	3031
in Transport	-	-	-	-	-	-	-	-	-	-	233
in Other Sectors	-	-	-	-	-	-	-	-	-	-	1057

Canada / Canada : 1993

CONSUMPTION / APPROVISIONNEMENT ET DEMANDE	Gas / Gaz (TJ)				Combust. Renew. & Waste / En. Re. Comb. & Déchets (TJ)				(GWh)	(TJ)
	Natural Gas / Gaz naturel	Gas Works / Usines à gaz	Coke Ovens / Cokeries	Blast Furnaces / Hauts fourneaux	Solid Biomass & Anim. Prod. / Biomasse solide & prod. anim.	Gas/Liquids from Biomass / Gaz/Liquides tirés de biomasse	Municipal Waste / Déchets urbains	Industrial Waste / Déchets industriels	Electricity / Electricité	Heat / Chaleur
Production	5234352	-	30733	29196	366881	-	-	-	527386	11022
From Other Sources	-	-	-	-	-	-	-	-	-	-
Imports	30895	-	-	-	-	-	-	-	7551	-
Exports	-2395257	-	-	-	-	-	-	-	-34967	-
Intl. Marine Bunkers	-	-	-	-	-	-	-	-	-	-
Stock Changes	-23201	-	-	-	-	-	-	-	-	-
DOMESTIC SUPPLY	**2846789**	**-**	**30733**	**29196**	**366881**	**-**	**-**	**-**	**499970**	**11022**
Transfers	-	-	-	-	-	-	-	-	-	-
Statistical Differences	-50420	-	-	-	-	-	-	-	-	-
TRANSFORMATION	**253011**	**-**	**739**	**702**	**12141**	**-**	**-**	**-**	**-**	**-**
Electricity Plants	115807	-	739	702	12141	-	-	-	-	-
CHP Plants	27517	-	-	-	-	-	-	-	-	-
Heat Plants	-	-	-	-	-	-	-	-	-	-
Transfer to Gases	-	-	-	-	-	-	-	-	-	-
Transfer to Solids	-	-	-	-	-	-	-	-	-	-
Petroleum Refineries	-	-	-	-	-	-	-	-	-	-
Petrochemical Industry	-	-	-	-	-	-	-	-	-	-
Liquefaction	97371	-	-	-	-	-	-	-	-	-
Other Transformation Sector	12316	-	-	-	-	-	-	-	-	-
ENERGY SECTOR	**314817**	**-**	**-**	**-**	**-**	**-**	**-**	**-**	**31887**	**-**
Coal Mines	4377	-	-	-	-	-	-	-	1005	-
Oil and Gas Extraction	260459	-	-	-	-	-	-	-	13040	-
Petroleum Refineries	49981	-	-	-	-	-	-	-	5988	-
Electricity, CHP+Heat plants	-	-	-	-	-	-	-	-	11629	-
Pumped Storage (Elec.)	-	-	-	-	-	-	-	-	225	-
Other Energy Sector	-	-	-	-	-	-	-	-	-	-
Distribution Losses	-	-	-	-	-	-	-	-	36696	-
FINAL CONSUMPTION	**2228541**	**-**	**29994**	**28494**	**354740**	**-**	**-**	**-**	**431387**	**11022**
INDUSTRY SECTOR	**965210**	**-**	**29994**	**28494**	**273084**	**-**	**-**	**-**	**172497**	**10561**
Iron and Steel	71809	-	29994	28494	-	-	-	-	8445	-
Chemical and Petrochemical	318311	-	-	-	-	-	-	-	16355	9326
of which: Feedstocks	168932	-	-	-	-	-	-	-	-	-
Non-Ferrous Metals	28156	-	-	-	-	-	-	-	46800	-
Non-Metallic Minerals	12677	-	-	-	-	-	-	-	-	-
Transport Equipment	-	-	-	-	-	-	-	-	-	-
Machinery	-	-	-	-	-	-	-	-	-	-
Mining and Quarrying	99718	-	-	-	-	-	-	-	14543	-
Food and Tobacco	-	-	-	-	-	-	-	-	-	-
Paper, Pulp and Print	116180	-	-	-	273084	-	-	-	51327	1087
Wood and Wood Products	-	-	-	-	-	-	-	-	-	-
Construction	-	-	-	-	-	-	-	-	-	-
Textile and Leather	-	-	-	-	-	-	-	-	-	-
Non-specified	318359	-	-	-	-	-	-	-	35027	148
TRANSPORT SECTOR	**205063**	**-**	**-**	**-**	**-**	**-**	**-**	**-**	**3630**	**-**
International Civil Aviation	-	-	-	-	-	-	-	-	-	-
Domestic Air	-	-	-	-	-	-	-	-	-	-
Road	3005	-	-	-	-	-	-	-	-	-
Rail	-	-	-	-	-	-	-	-	810	-
Pipeline Transport	202058	-	-	-	-	-	-	-	2820	-
Internal Navigation	-	-	-	-	-	-	-	-	-	-
Non-specified	-	-	-	-	-	-	-	-	-	-
OTHER SECTORS	**1058268**	**-**	**-**	**-**	**81656**	**-**	**-**	**-**	**255260**	**461**
Agriculture	31207	-	-	-	-	-	-	-	9481	180
Commerce and Publ. Serv.	433577	-	-	-	-	-	-	-	113074	281
Residential	593484	-	-	-	81656	-	-	-	132705	-
Non-specified	-	-	-	-	-	-	-	-	-	-
NON-ENERGY USE	**-**	**-**	**-**	**-**	**-**	**-**	**-**	**-**	**-**	**-**
in Industry/Transf./Energy	-	-	-	-	-	-	-	-	-	-
in Transport	-	-	-	-	-	-	-	-	-	-
in Other Sectors	-	-	-	-	-	-	-	-	-	-

Denmark / Danemark : 1992

SUPPLY AND CONSUMPTION	Coal / *Charbon* (1000 tonnes)							Oil / *Pétrole* (1000 tonnes)			
	Coking Coal	Steam Coal	Sub-Bit. Coal	Lignite	Peat	Oven and Gas Coke	Pat. Fuel and BKB	Crude Oil	NGL	Feedstocks	Additives
APPROVISIONNEMENT ET DEMANDE	*Charbon à coke*	*Charbon vapeur*	*Charbon sous-bit.*	*Lignite*	*Tourbe*	*Coke de four/gaz*	*Agg./briq. de lignite*	*Pétrole brut*	*LGN*	*Produits d'aliment.*	*Additifs*
Production	-	-	-	-	-	-	-	7756	-	-	-
From Other Sources	-	-	-	-	-	-	-	-	-	-	-
Imports	-	11942	-	-	-	39	4	5245	-	325	-
Exports	-	-35	-	-	-	-	-	-4426	-	-113	-
Intl. Marine Bunkers	-	-	-	-	-	-	-	-	-	-	-
Stock Changes	-	-863	-	-	-	1	1	-216	-	-27	-
DOMESTIC SUPPLY	-	**11044**	-	-	-	**40**	**5**	**8359**	-	**185**	-
Transfers	-	-	-	-	-	-	-	-	-	-	-
Statistical Differences	-	28	-	-	-	-	-	-35	-	2	-
TRANSFORMATION	-	**10565**	-	-	-	-	-	**8324**	-	**187**	-
Electricity Plants	-	1634	-	-	-	-	-	-	-	-	-
CHP Plants	-	8736	-	-	-	-	-	-	-	-	-
Heat Plants	-	195	-	-	-	-	-	-	-	-	-
Transfer to Gases	-	-	-	-	-	-	-	-	-	-	-
Transfer to Solids	-	-	-	-	-	-	-	-	-	-	-
Petroleum Refineries	-	-	-	-	-	-	-	8324	-	187	-
Petrochemical Industry	-	-	-	-	-	-	-	-	-	-	-
Liquefaction	-	-	-	-	-	-	-	-	-	-	-
Other Transformation Sector	-	-	-	-	-	-	-	-	-	-	-
ENERGY SECTOR	-	-	-	-	-	-	-	-	-	-	-
Coal Mines	-	-	-	-	-	-	-	-	-	-	-
Oil and Gas Extraction	-	-	-	-	-	-	-	-	-	-	-
Petroleum Refineries	-	-	-	-	-	-	-	-	-	-	-
Electricity, CHP+Heat plants	-	-	-	-	-	-	-	-	-	-	-
Pumped Storage (Elec.)	-	-	-	-	-	-	-	-	-	-	-
Other Energy Sector	-	-	-	-	-	-	-	-	-	-	-
Distribution Losses	-	-	-	-	-	-	-	-	-	-	-
FINAL CONSUMPTION	-	**507**	-	-	-	**40**	**5**	-	-	-	-
INDUSTRY SECTOR	-	**387**	-	-	-	**36**	-	-	-	-	-
Iron and Steel	-	3	-	-	-	3	-	-	-	-	-
Chemical and Petrochemical	-	-	-	-	-	-	-	-	-	-	-
of which: Feedstocks	-	-	-	-	-	-	-	-	-	-	-
Non-Ferrous Metals	-	-	-	-	-	-	-	-	-	-	-
Non-Metallic Minerals	-	218	-	-	-	25	-	-	-	-	-
Transport Equipment	-	-	-	-	-	-	-	-	-	-	-
Machinery	-	1	-	-	-	1	-	-	-	-	-
Mining and Quarrying	-	39	-	-	-	1	-	-	-	-	-
Food and Tobacco	-	95	-	-	-	6	-	-	-	-	-
Paper, Pulp and Print	-	31	-	-	-	-	-	-	-	-	-
Wood and Wood Products	-	-	-	-	-	-	-	-	-	-	-
Construction	-	-	-	-	-	-	-	-	-	-	-
Textile and Leather	-	-	-	-	-	-	-	-	-	-	-
Non-specified	-	-	-	-	-	-	-	-	-	-	-
TRANSPORT SECTOR	-	-	-	-	-	-	-	-	-	-	-
International Civil Aviation	-	-	-	-	-	-	-	-	-	-	-
Domestic Air	-	-	-	-	-	-	-	-	-	-	-
Road	-	-	-	-	-	-	-	-	-	-	-
Rail	-	-	-	-	-	-	-	-	-	-	-
Pipeline Transport	-	-	-	-	-	-	-	-	-	-	-
Internal Navigation	-	-	-	-	-	-	-	-	-	-	-
Non-specified	-	-	-	-	-	-	-	-	-	-	-
OTHER SECTORS	-	**120**	-	-	-	**4**	**5**	-	-	-	-
Agriculture	-	83	-	-	-	1	3	-	-	-	-
Commerce and Publ. Serv.	-	4	-	-	-	-	-	-	-	-	-
Residential	-	33	-	-	-	3	2	-	-	-	-
Non-specified	-	-	-	-	-	-	-	-	-	-	-
NON-ENERGY USE	-	-	-	-	-	-	-	-	-	-	-
in Industry/Transf./Energy	-	-	-	-	-	-	-	-	-	-	-
in Transport	-	-	-	-	-	-	-	-	-	-	-
in Other Sectors	-	-	-	-	-	-	-	-	-	-	-

Denmark / Danemark : 1992

SUPPLY AND CONSUMPTION / APPROVISIONNEMENT ET DEMANDE	Oil cont. / *Pétrole cont.* (1000 tonnes)										
	Refinery Gas / *Gaz de raffinerie*	LPG + Ethane / *GPL + éthane*	Motor Gasoline / *Essence moteur*	Aviation Gasoline / *Essence aviation*	Jet Fuel / *Carbu-réacteur*	Kerosene / *Kérosène*	Gas/ Diesel / *Gazole*	Heavy Fuel Oil / *Fioul lourd*	Naphtha / *Naphta*	Pétrol. Coke / *Coke de pétrole*	Other Prod. / *Autres prod.*
Production	286	129	1537	-	147	22	4000	2189	131	-	-
From Other Sources	-	-	-	-	-	-	-	-	-	-	-
Imports	-	13	824	7	596	1	1690	552	-	153	322
Exports	-	-66	-560	-3	-87	-	-1313	-1536	-126	-10	-11
Intl. Marine Bunkers	-	-	-	-	-	-	-395	-520	-	-	-3
Stock Changes	-	4	-22	-1	45	-1	187	278	-5	-5	3
DOMESTIC SUPPLY	**286**	**80**	**1779**	**3**	**701**	**22**	**4169**	**963**	**-**	**138**	**311**
Transfers	-	-1	14	-	-54	-3	28	12	-	-	4
Statistical Differences	1	3	-8	-	-7	-1	-6	12	-	-1	3
TRANSFORMATION	**35**	**1**	**-**	**-**	**-**	**-**	**35**	**310**	**-**	**-**	**-**
Electricity Plants	-	-	-	-	-	-	-	88	-	-	-
CHP Plants	35	-	-	-	-	-	17	206	-	-	-
Heat Plants	-	-	-	-	-	-	18	16	-	-	-
Transfer to Gases	-	1	-	-	-	-	-	-	-	-	-
Transfer to Solids	-	-	-	-	-	-	-	-	-	-	-
Petroleum Refineries	-	-	-	-	-	-	-	-	-	-	-
Petrochemical Industry	-	-	-	-	-	-	-	-	-	-	-
Liquefaction	-	-	-	-	-	-	-	-	-	-	-
Other Transformation Sector	-	-	-	-	-	-	-	-	-	-	-
ENERGY SECTOR	**250**	**-**	**-**	**-**	**-**	**-**	**1**	**88**	**-**	**-**	**-**
Coal Mines	-	-	-	-	-	-	-	-	-	-	-
Oil and Gas Extraction	-	-	-	-	-	-	-	-	-	-	-
Petroleum Refineries	250	-	-	-	-	-	1	88	-	-	-
Electricity, CHP+Heat plants	-	-	-	-	-	-	-	-	-	-	-
Pumped Storage (Elec.)	-	-	-	-	-	-	-	-	-	-	-
Other Energy Sector	-	-	-	-	-	-	-	-	-	-	-
Distribution Losses	-	-	-	-	-	-	-	-	-	-	-
FINAL CONSUMPTION	**2**	**81**	**1785**	**3**	**640**	**18**	**4155**	**589**	**-**	**137**	**318**
INDUSTRY SECTOR	**2**	**55**	**5**	**-**	**-**	**1**	**378**	**423**	**-**	**-**	**-**
Iron and Steel	-	2	-	-	-	-	4	-	-	-	-
Chemical and Petrochemical	2	6	-	-	-	-	44	84	-	-	-
of which: Feedstocks	-	-	-	-	-	-	-	-	-	-	-
Non-Ferrous Metals	-	2	-	-	-	-	2	1	-	-	-
Non-Metallic Minerals	-	8	2	-	-	-	33	95	-	-	-
Transport Equipment	-	1	-	-	-	-	11	3	-	-	-
Machinery	-	8	-	-	-	-	58	18	-	-	-
Mining and Quarrying	-	-	-	-	-	-	6	-	-	-	-
Food and Tobacco	-	9	1	-	-	1	105	142	-	-	-
Paper, Pulp and Print	-	1	-	-	-	-	7	23	-	-	-
Wood and Wood Products	-	1	1	-	-	-	11	8	-	-	-
Construction	-	15	1	-	-	-	90	39	-	-	-
Textile and Leather	-	2	-	-	-	-	7	10	-	-	-
Non-specified	-	-	-	-	-	-	-	-	-	-	-
TRANSPORT SECTOR	**-**	**5**	**1774**	**3**	**640**	**3**	**1593**	**70**	**-**	**-**	**-**
International Civil Aviation	-	-	-	-	586	-	-	-	-	-	-
Domestic Air	-	-	-	3	54	-	-	-	-	-	-
Road	-	5	1774	-	-	3	1410	-	-	-	-
Rail	-	-	-	-	-	-	101	-	-	-	-
Pipeline Transport	-	-	-	-	-	-	-	-	-	-	-
Internal Navigation	-	-	-	-	-	-	82	70	-	-	-
Non-specified	-	-	-	-	-	-	-	-	-	-	-
OTHER SECTORS	**-**	**21**	**6**	**-**	**-**	**14**	**2184**	**96**	**-**	**32**	**-**
Agriculture	-	10	6	-	-	1	646	55	-	15	-
Commerce and Publ. Serv.	-	1	-	-	-	4	266	15	-	2	-
Residential	-	10	-	-	-	9	1272	4	-	15	-
Non-specified	-	-	-	-	-	-	-	22	-	-	-
NON-ENERGY USE	**-**	**-**	**-**	**-**	**-**	**-**	**-**	**-**	**-**	**105**	**318**
in Industry/Transf./Energy	-	-	-	-	-	-	-	-	-	105	271
in Transport	-	-	-	-	-	-	-	-	-	-	35
in Other Sectors	-	-	-	-	-	-	-	-	-	-	12

Denmark / Danemark : 1992

CONSUMPTION *APPROVISIONNEMENT ET DEMANDE*	Gas / *Gaz* (TJ)				Combust. Renew. & Waste / *En. Re. Comb. & Déchets* (TJ)				(GWh) Electricity *Electricité*	(TJ) Heat *Chaleur*
	Natural Gas *Gaz naturel*	Gas Works *Usines à gaz*	Coke Ovens *Cokeries*	Blast Furnaces *Hauts fourneaux*	Solid Biomass & Anim. Prod. *Biomasse solide & prod. anim.*	Gas/Liquids from Biomass *Gaz/Liquides tirés de biomasse*	Municipal Waste *Déchets urbains*	Industrial Waste *Déchets industriels*		
Production	166955	-	-	-	33170	-	17320	-	30849	103718
From Other Sources	-	1514	-	-	-	-	-	-	-	-
Imports	-	-	-	-	-	-	-	-	8647	-
Exports	-63794	-	-	-	-	-	-	-	-4901	-
Intl. Marine Bunkers	-	-	-	-	-	-	-	-	-	-
Stock Changes	-4133	-	-	-	-	-	-	-	-	-
DOMESTIC SUPPLY	**99028**	**1514**	**-**	**-**	**33170**	**-**	**17320**	**-**	**34595**	**103718**
Transfers	-	-	-	-	-	-	-	-	-	-
Statistical Differences	375	-	-	-	-	-	-	-	-	-
TRANSFORMATION	**27402**	**-**	**-**	**-**	**12010**	**-**	**17320**	**-**	**-**	**-**
Electricity Plants	894	-	-	-	950	-	-	-	-	-
CHP Plants	12198	-	-	-	110	-	5900	-	-	-
Heat Plants	12665	-	-	-	10950	-	11420	-	-	-
Transfer to Gases	1645	-	-	-	-	-	-	-	-	-
Transfer to Solids	-	-	-	-	-	-	-	-	-	-
Petroleum Refineries	-	-	-	-	-	-	-	-	-	-
Petrochemical Industry	-	-	-	-	-	-	-	-	-	-
Liquefaction	-	-	-	-	-	-	-	-	-	-
Other Transformation Sector	-	-	-	-	-	-	-	-	-	-
ENERGY SECTOR	**11969**	**61**	**-**	**-**	**-**	**-**	**-**	**-**	**2236**	**-**
Coal Mines	-	-	-	-	-	-	-	-	-	-
Oil and Gas Extraction	11969	-	-	-	-	-	-	-	-	-
Petroleum Refineries	-	-	-	-	-	-	-	-	261	-
Electricity, CHP+Heat plants	-	-	-	-	-	-	-	-	1975	-
Pumped Storage (Elec.)	-	-	-	-	-	-	-	-	-	-
Other Energy Sector	-	61	-	-	-	-	-	-	-	-
Distribution Losses	129	-	-	-	-	-	-	-	2151	19598
FINAL CONSUMPTION	**59903**	**1453**	**-**	**-**	**21160**	**-**	**-**	**-**	**30208**	**84120**
INDUSTRY SECTOR	**23750**	**116**	**-**	**-**	**4090**	**-**	**-**	**-**	**9194**	**1770**
Iron and Steel	1357	-	-	-	-	-	-	-	674	-
Chemical and Petrochemical	1313	-	-	-	15	-	-	-	1813	-
of which: Feedstocks	-	-	-	-	-	-	-	-	-	-
Non-Ferrous Metals	108	-	-	-	-	-	-	-	-	-
Non-Metallic Minerals	3766	60	-	-	8	-	-	-	767	-
Transport Equipment	291	-	-	-	-	-	-	-	393	-
Machinery	1784	35	-	-	64	-	-	-	1177	-
Mining and Quarrying	398	-	-	-	-	-	-	-	-	-
Food and Tobacco	8693	18	-	-	23	-	-	-	2362	-
Paper, Pulp and Print	1279	3	-	-	46	-	-	-	751	-
Wood and Wood Products	35	-	-	-	3930	-	-	-	323	-
Construction	159	-	-	-	-	-	-	-	333	-
Textile and Leather	1246	-	-	-	4	-	-	-	271	-
Non-specified	3321	-	-	-	-	-	-	-	330	1770
TRANSPORT SECTOR	**-**	**-**	**-**	**-**	**-**	**-**	**-**	**-**	**202**	**-**
International Civil Aviation	-	-	-	-	-	-	-	-	-	-
Domestic Air	-	-	-	-	-	-	-	-	-	-
Road	-	-	-	-	-	-	-	-	-	-
Rail	-	-	-	-	-	-	-	-	202	-
Pipeline Transport	-	-	-	-	-	-	-	-	-	-
Internal Navigation	-	-	-	-	-	-	-	-	-	-
Non-specified	-	-	-	-	-	-	-	-	-	-
OTHER SECTORS	**36153**	**1337**	**-**	**-**	**17070**	**-**	**-**	**-**	**20812**	**82350**
Agriculture	2615	-	-	-	2150	-	-	-	2437	1870
Commerce and Publ. Serv.	10741	87	-	-	-	-	-	-	8400	25030
Residential	22161	1250	-	-	14920	-	-	-	9554	55450
Non-specified	636	-	-	-	-	-	-	-	421	-
NON-ENERGY USE	**-**	**-**	**-**	**-**	**-**	**-**	**-**	**-**	**-**	**-**
in Industry/Transf./Energy	-	-	-	-	-	-	-	-	-	-
in Transport	-	-	-	-	-	-	-	-	-	-
in Other Sectors	-	-	-	-	-	-	-	-	-	-

Denmark / Danemark : 1993

SUPPLY AND CONSUMPTION	Coal / *Charbon* (1000 tonnes)							Oil / *Pétrole* (1000 tonnes)			
	Coking Coal	Steam Coal	Sub-Bit. Coal	Lignite	Peat	Oven and Gas Coke	Pat. Fuel and BKB	Crude Oil	NGL	Feedstocks	Additives
APPROVISIONNEMENT ET DEMANDE	*Charbon à coke*	*Charbon vapeur*	*Charbon sous-bit.*	*Lignite*	*Tourbe*	*Coke de four/gaz*	*Agg./briq. de lignite*	*Pétrole brut*	*LGN*	*Produits d'aliment.*	*Additifs*
Production	-	-	-	-	-	-	-	8265	-	-	-
From Other Sources	-	-	-	-	-	-	-	-	-	-	-
Imports	-	10467	-	-	-	40	5	5087	-	325	-
Exports	-	-24	-	-	-	-	-	-5115	-	-65	-
Intl. Marine Bunkers	-	-	-	-	-	-	-	-	-	-	-
Stock Changes	-	1455	-	-	-	-1	-	132	-	-6	-
DOMESTIC SUPPLY	**-**	**11898**	**-**	**-**	**-**	**39**	**5**	**8369**	**-**	**254**	**-**
Transfers	-	-	-	-	-	-	-	-	-	-	-
Statistical Differences	-	-35	-	-	-	-	2	-13	-	-5	-
TRANSFORMATION	**-**	**11312**	**-**	**-**	**-**	**-**	**-**	**8356**	**-**	**249**	**-**
Electricity Plants	-	1074	-	-	-	-	-	-	-	-	-
CHP Plants	-	10071	-	-	-	-	-	-	-	-	-
Heat Plants	-	167	-	-	-	-	-	-	-	-	-
Transfer to Gases	-	-	-	-	-	-	-	-	-	-	-
Transfer to Solids	-	-	-	-	-	-	-	-	-	-	-
Petroleum Refineries	-	-	-	-	-	-	-	8356	-	249	-
Petrochemical Industry	-	-	-	-	-	-	-	-	-	-	-
Liquefaction	-	-	-	-	-	-	-	-	-	-	-
Other Transformation Sector	-	-	-	-	-	-	-	-	-	-	-
ENERGY SECTOR	**-**	**-**	**-**	**-**	**-**	**-**	**-**	**-**	**-**	**-**	**-**
Coal Mines	-	-	-	-	-	-	-	-	-	-	-
Oil and Gas Extraction	-	-	-	-	-	-	-	-	-	-	-
Petroleum Refineries	-	-	-	-	-	-	-	-	-	-	-
Electricity, CHP+Heat plants	-	-	-	-	-	-	-	-	-	-	-
Pumped Storage (Elec.)	-	-	-	-	-	-	-	-	-	-	-
Other Energy Sector	-	-	-	-	-	-	-	-	-	-	-
Distribution Losses	-	-	-	-	-	-	-	-	-	-	-
FINAL CONSUMPTION	**-**	**551**	**-**	**-**	**-**	**39**	**7**	**-**	**-**	**-**	**-**
INDUSTRY SECTOR	**-**	**439**	**-**	**-**	**-**	**37**	**1**	**-**	**-**	**-**	**-**
Iron and Steel	-	-	-	-	-	-	-	-	-	-	-
Chemical and Petrochemical	-	-	-	-	-	-	-	-	-	-	-
of which: Feedstocks	-	-	-	-	-	-	-	-	-	-	-
Non-Ferrous Metals	-	-	-	-	-	-	-	-	-	-	-
Non-Metallic Minerals	-	255	-	-	-	27	1	-	-	-	-
Transport Equipment	-	-	-	-	-	-	-	-	-	-	-
Machinery	-	-	-	-	-	1	-	-	-	-	-
Mining and Quarrying	-	49	-	-	-	-	-	-	-	-	-
Food and Tobacco	-	132	-	-	-	6	-	-	-	-	-
Paper, Pulp and Print	-	-	-	-	-	-	-	-	-	-	-
Wood and Wood Products	-	-	-	-	-	-	-	-	-	-	-
Construction	-	-	-	-	-	-	-	-	-	-	-
Textile and Leather	-	-	-	-	-	-	-	-	-	-	-
Non-specified	-	3	-	-	-	3	-	-	-	-	-
TRANSPORT SECTOR	**-**	**-**	**-**	**-**	**-**	**-**	**-**	**-**	**-**	**-**	**-**
International Civil Aviation	-	-	-	-	-	-	-	-	-	-	-
Domestic Air	-	-	-	-	-	-	-	-	-	-	-
Road	-	-	-	-	-	-	-	-	-	-	-
Rail	-	-	-	-	-	-	-	-	-	-	-
Pipeline Transport	-	-	-	-	-	-	-	-	-	-	-
Internal Navigation	-	-	-	-	-	-	-	-	-	-	-
Non-specified	-	-	-	-	-	-	-	-	-	-	-
OTHER SECTORS	**-**	**112**	**-**	**-**	**-**	**2**	**6**	**-**	**-**	**-**	**-**
Agriculture	-	79	-	-	-	-	1	-	-	-	-
Commerce and Publ. Serv.	-	3	-	-	-	-	1	-	-	-	-
Residential	-	30	-	-	-	2	4	-	-	-	-
Non-specified	-	-	-	-	-	-	-	-	-	-	-
NON-ENERGY USE	**-**	**-**	**-**	**-**	**-**	**-**	**-**	**-**	**-**	**-**	**-**
in Industry/Transf./Energy	-	-	-	-	-	-	-	-	-	-	-
in Transport	-	-	-	-	-	-	-	-	-	-	-
in Other Sectors	-	-	-	-	-	-	-	-	-	-	-

Denmark / Danemark : 1993

SUPPLY AND CONSUMPTION / APPROVISIONNEMENT ET DEMANDE	Oil cont. / *Pétrole cont.* (1000 tonnes)										
	Refinery Gas / *Gaz de raffinerie*	LPG + Ethane / *GPL + éthane*	Motor Gasoline / *Essence moteur*	Aviation Gasoline / *Essence aviation*	Jet Fuel / *Carbu-réacteur*	Kerosene / *Kérosène*	Gas/ Diesel / *Gazole*	Heavy Fuel Oil / *Fioul lourd*	Naphtha / *Naphta*	Pétrol. Coke / *Coke de pétrole*	Other Prod. / *Autres prod.*
Production	296	134	1477	-	200	11	3929	2360	149	-	-
From Other Sources	-	-	-	-	-	-	-	-	-	-	-
Imports	-	20	908	3	589	2	1876	860	-	272	324
Exports	-	-70	-683	-	-95	-	-1550	-1351	-147	-54	-13
Intl. Marine Bunkers	-	-	-	-	-	-	-448	-916	-	-	-4
Stock Changes	-	-	136	-	18	5	274	-124	-2	-36	11
DOMESTIC SUPPLY	**296**	**84**	**1838**	**3**	**712**	**18**	**4081**	**829**	**-**	**182**	**318**
Transfers	-	-	-1	-	-12	1	-22	32	-	-	2
Statistical Differences	-	-	-7	-	-1	-1	-10	19	-	-1	1
TRANSFORMATION	**43**	**1**	**-**	**-**	**-**	**-**	**31**	**301**	**-**	**39**	**-**
Electricity Plants	-	-	-	-	-	-	2	72	-	-	-
CHP Plants	43	-	-	-	-	-	6	202	-	39	-
Heat Plants	-	-	-	-	-	-	23	27	-	-	-
Transfer to Gases	-	1	-	-	-	-	-	-	-	-	-
Transfer to Solids	-	-	-	-	-	-	-	-	-	-	-
Petroleum Refineries	-	-	-	-	-	-	-	-	-	-	-
Petrochemical Industry	-	-	-	-	-	-	-	-	-	-	-
Liquefaction	-	-	-	-	-	-	-	-	-	-	-
Other Transformation Sector	-	-	-	-	-	-	-	-	-	-	-
ENERGY SECTOR	**251**	**-**	**-**	**-**	**-**	**-**	**1**	**86**	**-**	**-**	**-**
Coal Mines	-	-	-	-	-	-	-	-	-	-	-
Oil and Gas Extraction	-	-	-	-	-	-	-	-	-	-	-
Petroleum Refineries	251	-	-	-	-	-	1	86	-	-	-
Electricity, CHP+Heat plants	-	-	-	-	-	-	-	-	-	-	-
Pumped Storage (Elec.)	-	-	-	-	-	-	-	-	-	-	-
Other Energy Sector	-	-	-	-	-	-	-	-	-	-	-
Distribution Losses	-	-	-	-	-	-	-	-	-	-	-
FINAL CONSUMPTION	**2**	**83**	**1830**	**3**	**699**	**18**	**4017**	**493**	**-**	**142**	**321**
INDUSTRY SECTOR	**2**	**53**	**3**	**-**	**-**	**1**	**377**	**367**	**-**	**-**	**-**
Iron and Steel	-	-	-	-	-	-	9	1	-	-	-
Chemical and Petrochemical	2	2	-	-	-	-	11	28	-	-	-
of which: Feedstocks	-	-	-	-	-	-	-	-	-	-	-
Non-Ferrous Metals	-	-	-	-	-	-	4	2	-	-	-
Non-Metallic Minerals	-	-	-	-	-	-	49	106	-	-	-
Transport Equipment	-	-	-	-	-	-	6	2	-	-	-
Machinery	-	5	2	-	-	-	44	9	-	-	-
Mining and Quarrying	-	-	-	-	-	-	12	3	-	-	-
Food and Tobacco	-	14	1	-	-	1	97	102	-	-	-
Paper, Pulp and Print	-	5	-	-	-	-	7	12	-	-	-
Wood and Wood Products	-	9	-	-	-	-	9	6	-	-	-
Construction	-	13	-	-	-	-	91	12	-	-	-
Textile and Leather	-	1	-	-	-	-	9	3	-	-	-
Non-specified	-	4	-	-	-	-	29	81	-	-	-
TRANSPORT SECTOR	**-**	**7**	**1822**	**3**	**699**	**3**	**1640**	**65**	**-**	**-**	**-**
International Civil Aviation	-	-	-	-	553	-	-	-	-	-	-
Domestic Air	-	-	-	3	146	-	-	-	-	-	-
Road	-	7	1822	-	-	3	1398	-	-	-	-
Rail	-	-	-	-	-	-	105	-	-	-	-
Pipeline Transport	-	-	-	-	-	-	-	-	-	-	-
Internal Navigation	-	-	-	-	-	-	137	65	-	-	-
Non-specified	-	-	-	-	-	-	-	-	-	-	-
OTHER SECTORS	**-**	**23**	**5**	**-**	**-**	**14**	**2000**	**61**	**-**	**35**	**-**
Agriculture	-	6	5	-	-	1	547	45	-	16	-
Commerce and Publ. Serv.	-	3	-	-	-	4	210	13	-	3	-
Residential	-	14	-	-	-	9	1243	3	-	16	-
Non-specified	-	-	-	-	-	-	-	-	-	-	-
NON-ENERGY USE	**-**	**-**	**-**	**-**	**-**	**-**	**-**	**-**	**-**	**107**	**321**
in Industry/Transf./Energy	-	-	-	-	-	-	-	-	-	107	274
in Transport	-	-	-	-	-	-	-	-	-	-	40
in Other Sectors	-	-	-	-	-	-	-	-	-	-	7

Denmark / Danemark : 1993

CONSUMPTION / APPROVISIONNEMENT ET DEMANDE	Gas / *Gaz* (TJ)				Combust. Renew. & Waste / *En. Re. Comb. & Déchets* (TJ)				(GWh)	(TJ)
	Natural Gas / *Gaz naturel*	Gas Works / *Usines à gaz*	Coke Ovens / *Cokeries*	Blast Furnaces / *Hauts fourneaux*	Solid Biomass & Anim. Prod. / *Biomasse solide & prod. anim.*	Gas/Liquids from Biomass / *Gaz/Liquides tirés de biomasse*	Municipal Waste / *Déchets urbains*	Industrial Waste / *Déchets industriels*	Electricity / *Electricité*	Heat / *Chaleur*
Production	183896	-	-	-	32480	1460	18960	-	33738	112162
From Other Sources	-	1500	-	-	-	-	-	-	6280	-
Imports	-	-	-	-	-	-	-	-	6280	-
Exports	-66621	-	-	-	-	-	-	-	-5095	-
Intl. Marine Bunkers	-	-	-	-	-	-	-	-	-	-
Stock Changes	-4969	-	-	-	-	-	-	-	-	-
DOMESTIC SUPPLY	**112306**	**1500**	**-**	**-**	**32480**	**1460**	**18960**	**-**	**34923**	**112162**
Transfers	-	-	-	-	-	-	-	-	-	-
Statistical Differences	331	-	-	-	-	-	-	-	-	-
TRANSFORMATION	**32991**	**-**	**-**	**-**	**12126**	**750**	**18960**	**-**	**-**	**-**
Electricity Plants	976	-	-	-	592	-	-	-	-	-
CHP Plants	18567	-	-	-	2371	702	8136	-	-	-
Heat Plants	11810	-	-	-	9163	48	10824	-	-	-
Transfer to Gases	1638	-	-	-	-	-	-	-	-	-
Transfer to Solids	-	-	-	-	-	-	-	-	-	-
Petroleum Refineries	-	-	-	-	-	-	-	-	-	-
Petrochemical Industry	-	-	-	-	-	-	-	-	-	-
Liquefaction	-	-	-	-	-	-	-	-	-	-
Other Transformation Sector	-	-	-	-	-	-	-	-	-	-
ENERGY SECTOR	**12020**	**-**	**-**	**-**	**-**	**-**	**-**	**-**	**2045**	**-**
Coal Mines	-	-	-	-	-	-	-	-	-	-
Oil and Gas Extraction	12020	-	-	-	-	-	-	-	-	-
Petroleum Refineries	-	-	-	-	-	-	-	-	263	-
Electricity, CHP+Heat plants	-	-	-	-	-	-	-	-	1782	-
Pumped Storage (Elec.)	-	-	-	-	-	-	-	-	-	-
Other Energy Sector	-	-	-	-	-	-	-	-	-	-
Distribution Losses	129	60	-	-	-	-	-	-	2257	22832
FINAL CONSUMPTION	**67497**	**1440**	**-**	**-**	**20354**	**710**	**-**	**-**	**30621**	**89330**
INDUSTRY SECTOR	**25774**	**110**	**-**	**-**	**3034**	**69**	**-**	**-**	**9073**	**3130**
Iron and Steel	1471	-	-	-	-	-	-	-	669	21
Chemical and Petrochemical	1423	14	-	-	-	-	-	-	1703	199
of which: Feedstocks	-	-	-	-	-	-	-	-	-	-
Non-Ferrous Metals	117	-	-	-	-	-	-	-	-	28
Non-Metallic Minerals	4084	79	-	-	-	-	-	-	773	17
Transport Equipment	316	-	-	-	18	-	-	-	368	108
Machinery	1935	8	-	-	-	-	-	-	1102	485
Mining and Quarrying	432	-	-	-	47	-	-	-	20	2
Food and Tobacco	9429	9	-	-	-	69	-	-	2309	528
Paper, Pulp and Print	1387	-	-	-	32	-	-	-	797	1177
Wood and Wood Products	38	-	-	-	2020	-	-	-	388	3
Construction	187	-	-	-	-	-	-	-	316	-
Textile and Leather	1351	-	-	-	-	-	-	-	269	66
Non-specified	3604	-	-	-	917	-	-	-	359	496
TRANSPORT SECTOR	**-**	**-**	**-**	**-**	**-**	**-**	**-**	**-**	**206**	**-**
International Civil Aviation	-	-	-	-	-	-	-	-	-	-
Domestic Air	-	-	-	-	-	-	-	-	-	-
Road	-	-	-	-	-	-	-	-	-	-
Rail	-	-	-	-	-	-	-	-	206	-
Pipeline Transport	-	-	-	-	-	-	-	-	-	-
Internal Navigation	-	-	-	-	-	-	-	-	-	-
Non-specified	-	-	-	-	-	-	-	-	-	-
OTHER SECTORS	**41723**	**1330**	**-**	**-**	**17320**	**641**	**-**	**-**	**21342**	**86200**
Agriculture	2682	-	-	-	2150	5	-	-	1883	1870
Commerce and Publ. Serv.	12480	105	-	-	320	629	-	-	8951	26223
Residential	25836	1225	-	-	14850	7	-	-	10508	58107
Non-specified	725	-	-	-	-	-	-	-	-	-
NON-ENERGY USE	**-**	**-**	**-**	**-**	**-**	**-**	**-**	**-**	**-**	**-**
in Industry/Transf./Energy	-	-	-	-	-	-	-	-	-	-
in Transport	-	-	-	-	-	-	-	-	-	-
in Other Sectors	-	-	-	-	-	-	-	-	-	-

Finland / Finlande : 1992

SUPPLY AND CONSUMPTION *APPROVISIONNEMENT ET DEMANDE*	Coal / *Charbon* (1000 tonnes)							Oil / *Pétrole* (1000 tonnes)			
	Coking Coal *Charbon à coke*	Steam Coal *Charbon vapeur*	Sub-Bit. Coal *Charbon sous-bit.*	Lignite *Lignite*	Peat *Tourbe*	Oven and Gas Coke *Coke de four/gaz*	Pat. Fuel and BKB *Agg./briq. de lignite*	Crude Oil *Pétrole brut*	NGL *LGN*	Feedstocks *Produits d'aliment.*	Additives *Additifs*
Production	-	-	-	-	7028	498	-	-	-	-	-
From Other Sources	-	-	-	-	-	-	-	-	-	55	-
Imports	775	3488	-	-	7	687	-	8869	-	-	-
Exports	-	-	-	-	-153	-	-	-4	-	-	-
Intl. Marine Bunkers	-	-	-	-	-	-	-	-	-	-	-
Stock Changes	-	563	-	-	648	-	-	450	-	-	-
DOMESTIC SUPPLY	**775**	**4051**	**-**	**-**	**7530**	**1185**	**-**	**9315**	**-**	**55**	**-**
Transfers	-	-	-	-	-	-	-	-	-	1224	-
Statistical Differences	-	1	-	-	-	-	-	83	-	-	-
TRANSFORMATION	**775**	**3232**	**-**	**-**	**3971**	**443**	**-**	**9398**	**-**	**1279**	**-**
Electricity Plants	-	857	-	-	953	-	-	-	-	-	-
CHP Plants	-	2178	-	-	2681	-	-	-	-	-	-
Heat Plants	-	197	-	-	337	-	-	-	-	-	-
Transfer to Gases	-	-	-	-	-	443	-	-	-	-	-
Transfer to Solids	775	-	-	-	-	-	-	-	-	-	-
Petroleum Refineries	-	-	-	-	-	-	-	9398	-	1279	-
Petrochemical Industry	-	-	-	-	-	-	-	-	-	-	-
Liquefaction	-	-	-	-	-	-	-	-	-	-	-
Other Transformation Sector	-	-	-	-	-	-	-	-	-	-	-
ENERGY SECTOR	**-**	**-**	**-**	**-**	**-**	**-**	**-**	**-**	**-**	**-**	**-**
Coal Mines	-	-	-	-	-	-	-	-	-	-	-
Oil and Gas Extraction	-	-	-	-	-	-	-	-	-	-	-
Petroleum Refineries	-	-	-	-	-	-	-	-	-	-	-
Electricity, CHP+Heat plants	-	-	-	-	-	-	-	-	-	-	-
Pumped Storage (Elec.)	-	-	-	-	-	-	-	-	-	-	-
Other Energy Sector	-	-	-	-	-	-	-	-	-	-	-
Distribution Losses	-	-	-	-	-	-	-	-	-	-	-
FINAL CONSUMPTION	**-**	**820**	**-**	**-**	**3559**	**742**	**-**	**-**	**-**	**-**	**-**
INDUSTRY SECTOR	**-**	**808**	**-**	**-**	**3398**	**87**	**-**	**-**	**-**	**-**	**-**
Iron and Steel	-	60	-	-	-	84	-	-	-	-	-
Chemical and Petrochemical	-	64	-	-	-	-	-	-	-	-	-
of which: Feedstocks	-	-	-	-	-	-	-	-	-	-	-
Non-Ferrous Metals	-	-	-	-	-	3	-	-	-	-	-
Non-Metallic Minerals	-	590	-	-	-	-	-	-	-	-	-
Transport Equipment	-	-	-	-	-	-	-	-	-	-	-
Machinery	-	4	-	-	-	-	-	-	-	-	-
Mining and Quarrying	-	-	-	-	-	-	-	-	-	-	-
Food and Tobacco	-	14	-	-	-	-	-	-	-	-	-
Paper, Pulp and Print	-	-	-	-	-	-	-	-	-	-	-
Wood and Wood Products	-	72	-	-	-	-	-	-	-	-	-
Construction	-	-	-	-	-	-	-	-	-	-	-
Textile and Leather	-	-	-	-	-	-	-	-	-	-	-
Non-specified	-	4	-	-	3398	-	-	-	-	-	-
TRANSPORT SECTOR	**-**	**-**	**-**	**-**	**-**	**-**	**-**	**-**	**-**	**-**	**-**
International Civil Aviation	-	-	-	-	-	-	-	-	-	-	-
Domestic Air	-	-	-	-	-	-	-	-	-	-	-
Road	-	-	-	-	-	-	-	-	-	-	-
Rail	-	-	-	-	-	-	-	-	-	-	-
Pipeline Transport	-	-	-	-	-	-	-	-	-	-	-
Internal Navigation	-	-	-	-	-	-	-	-	-	-	-
Non-specified	-	-	-	-	-	-	-	-	-	-	-
OTHER SECTORS	**-**	**12**	**-**	**-**	**161**	**-**	**-**	**-**	**-**	**-**	**-**
Agriculture	-	-	-	-	94	-	-	-	-	-	-
Commerce and Publ. Serv.	-	-	-	-	-	-	-	-	-	-	-
Residential	-	12	-	-	67	-	-	-	-	-	-
Non-specified	-	-	-	-	-	-	-	-	-	-	-
NON-ENERGY USE	**-**	**-**	**-**	**-**	**-**	**655**	**-**	**-**	**-**	**-**	**-**
in Industry/Transf./Energy	-	-	-	-	-	655	-	-	-	-	-
in Transport	-	-	-	-	-	-	-	-	-	-	-
in Other Sectors	-	-	-	-	-	-	-	-	-	-	-

Finland / Finlande : 1992

SUPPLY AND CONSUMPTION / APPROVISIONNEMENT ET DEMANDE	Oil cont. / *Pétrole cont.* (1000 tonnes)										
	Refinery Gas / *Gaz de raffinerie*	LPG + Ethane / *GPL + éthane*	Motor Gasoline / *Essence moteur*	Aviation Gasoline / *Essence aviation*	Jet Fuel / *Carbu-réacteur*	Kerosene / *Kérosène*	Gas/Diesel / *Gazole*	Heavy Fuel Oil / *Fioul lourd*	Naphtha / *Naphta*	Pétrol. Coke / *Coke de pétrole*	Other Prod. / *Autres prod.*
Production	546	271	3570	-	421	2	4036	1147	149	-	463
From Other Sources	-	-	-	-	-	-	-	-	-	-	-
Imports	-	15	329	2	29	26	1235	793	202	8	1741
Exports	-	-33	-1877	-	-71	-	-1430	-156	-38	-	-106
Intl. Marine Bunkers	-	-	-	-	-	-	-132	-564	-	-	-
Stock Changes	-	11	-23	-3	29	-	-13	-140	-30	-	-
DOMESTIC SUPPLY	**546**	**264**	**1999**	**-1**	**408**	**28**	**3696**	**1080**	**283**	**8**	**2098**
Transfers	-	-	-89	-	-	-	-844	-319	28	-	-
Statistical Differences	-	-132	82	4	-20	-26	1041	1035	55	-	-914
TRANSFORMATION	**18**	**11**	**-**	**-**	**-**	**-**	**10**	**474**	**34**	**-**	**-**
Electricity Plants	7	-	-	-	-	-	10	40	-	-	-
CHP Plants	-	-	-	-	-	-	-	194	-	-	-
Heat Plants	-	-	-	-	-	-	-	237	-	-	-
Transfer to Gases	-	4	-	-	-	-	-	-	-	-	-
Transfer to Solids	-	-	-	-	-	-	-	-	-	-	-
Petroleum Refineries	-	-	-	-	-	-	-	-	-	-	-
Petrochemical Industry	11	7	-	-	-	-	-	3	34	-	-
Liquefaction	-	-	-	-	-	-	-	-	-	-	-
Other Transformation Sector	-	-	-	-	-	-	-	-	-	-	-
ENERGY SECTOR	**423**	**-**	**-**	**-**	**-**	**-**	**-**	**-**	**-**	**-**	**-**
Coal Mines	-	-	-	-	-	-	-	-	-	-	-
Oil and Gas Extraction	-	-	-	-	-	-	-	-	-	-	-
Petroleum Refineries	423	-	-	-	-	-	-	-	-	-	-
Electricity, CHP+Heat plants	-	-	-	-	-	-	-	-	-	-	-
Pumped Storage (Elec.)	-	-	-	-	-	-	-	-	-	-	-
Other Energy Sector	-	-	-	-	-	-	-	-	-	-	-
Distribution Losses	-	-	-	-	-	-	-	-	-	-	-
FINAL CONSUMPTION	**105**	**121**	**1992**	**3**	**388**	**2**	**3883**	**1322**	**332**	**8**	**1184**
INDUSTRY SECTOR	**105**	**117**	**-**	**-**	**-**	**-**	**182**	**841**	**332**	**8**	**-**
Iron and Steel	-	11	-	-	-	-	23	133	-	-	-
Chemical and Petrochemical	105	73	-	-	-	-	28	161	332	-	-
of which: Feedstocks	*105*	*73*	-	-	-	-	-	*27*	*332*	-	-
Non-Ferrous Metals	-	-	-	-	-	-	3	25	-	-	-
Non-Metallic Minerals	-	9	-	-	-	-	13	80	-	8	-
Transport Equipment	-	-	-	-	-	-	5	34	-	-	-
Machinery	-	-	-	-	-	-	10	83	-	-	-
Mining and Quarrying	-	-	-	-	-	-	6	53	-	-	-
Food and Tobacco	-	2	-	-	-	-	28	129	-	-	-
Paper, Pulp and Print	-	19	-	-	-	-	10	63	-	-	-
Wood and Wood Products	-	-	-	-	-	-	5	38	-	-	-
Construction	-	-	-	-	-	-	51	-	-	-	-
Textile and Leather	-	-	-	-	-	-	-	31	-	-	-
Non-specified	-	3	-	-	-	-	-	11	-	-	-
TRANSPORT SECTOR	**-**	**-**	**1979**	**3**	**388**	**1**	**1520**	**36**	**-**	**-**	**-**
International Civil Aviation	-	-	-	-	265	-	-	-	-	-	-
Domestic Air	-	-	-	3	123	-	-	-	-	-	-
Road	-	-	1979	-	-	1	1430	-	-	-	-
Rail	-	-	-	-	-	-	58	-	-	-	-
Pipeline Transport	-	-	-	-	-	-	-	-	-	-	-
Internal Navigation	-	-	-	-	-	-	32	36	-	-	-
Non-specified	-	-	-	-	-	-	-	-	-	-	-
OTHER SECTORS	**-**	**4**	**13**	**-**	**-**	**1**	**2181**	**445**	**-**	**-**	**-**
Agriculture	-	-	13	-	-	-	490	78	-	-	-
Commerce and Publ. Serv.	-	-	-	-	-	-	-	-	-	-	-
Residential	-	4	-	-	-	1	1691	367	-	-	-
Non-specified	-	-	-	-	-	-	-	-	-	-	-
NON-ENERGY USE	**-**	**-**	**-**	**-**	**-**	**-**	**-**	**-**	**-**	**-**	**1184**
in Industry/Transf./Energy	-	-	-	-	-	-	-	-	-	-	1184
in Transport	-	-	-	-	-	-	-	-	-	-	-
in Other Sectors	-	-	-	-	-	-	-	-	-	-	-

Finland / Finlande : 1992

CONSUMPTION APPROVISIONNEMENT ET DEMANDE	Gas / Gaz (TJ)				Combust. Renew. & Waste / En. Re. Comb. & Déchets (TJ)				(GWh)	(TJ)
	Natural Gas Gaz naturel	Gas Works Usines à gaz	Coke Ovens Cokeries	Blast Furnaces Hauts fourneaux	Solid Biomass & Anim. Prod. Biomasse solide & prod. anim.	Gas/Liquids from Biomass Gaz/Liquides tirés de biomasse	Municipal Waste Déchets urbains	Industrial Waste Déchets industriels	Electricity Electricité	Heat Chaleur
Production	-	-	4322	12983	157364	-	730	-	57722	92042
From Other Sources	-	137	-	-	-	-	-	-	-	-
Imports	115204	-	-	-	-	-	-	-	9067	-
Exports	-	-	-	-	-	-	-	-	-673	-
Intl. Marine Bunkers	-	-	-	-	-	-	-	-	-	-
Stock Changes	-	-	-	-	2690	-	-	-	-	-
DOMESTIC SUPPLY	**115204**	**137**	**4322**	**12983**	**160054**	**-**	**730**	**-**	**66116**	**92042**
Transfers	-	-	-	-	-	-	-	-	-	-
Statistical Differences	-	-	-	-	-	-	-17	-	-	-
TRANSFORMATION	**51132**	**-**	**281**	**3920**	**33838**	**-**	**713**	**-**	**-**	**-**
Electricity Plants	6307	-	-	-	6091	-	-	-	-	-
CHP Plants	38563	-	281	3920	24755	-	-	-	-	-
Heat Plants	6262	-	-	-	2992	-	713	-	-	-
Transfer to Gases	-	-	-	-	-	-	-	-	-	-
Transfer to Solids	-	-	-	-	-	-	-	-	-	-
Petroleum Refineries	-	-	-	-	-	-	-	-	-	-
Petrochemical Industry	-	-	-	-	-	-	-	-	-	-
Liquefaction	-	-	-	-	-	-	-	-	-	-
Other Transformation Sector	-	-	-	-	-	-	-	-	-	-
ENERGY SECTOR	**-**	**-**	**-**	**-**	**-**	**-**	**-**	**-**	**3338**	**-**
Coal Mines	-	-	-	-	-	-	-	-	-	-
Oil and Gas Extraction	-	-	-	-	-	-	-	-	-	-
Petroleum Refineries	-	-	-	-	-	-	-	-	570	-
Electricity, CHP+Heat plants	-	-	-	-	-	-	-	-	2768	-
Pumped Storage (Elec.)	-	-	-	-	-	-	-	-	-	-
Other Energy Sector	-	-	-	-	-	-	-	-	-	-
Distribution Losses	-	31	-	-	-	-	-	-	3021	7190
FINAL CONSUMPTION	**64072**	**106**	**4041**	**9063**	**126216**	**-**	**-**	**-**	**59757**	**84852**
INDUSTRY SECTOR	**61684**	**72**	**4041**	**9063**	**91697**	**-**	**-**	**-**	**31664**	**7596**
Iron and Steel	7803	-	4041	9063	8	-	-	-	1875	-
Chemical and Petrochemical	2904	-	-	-	12845	-	-	-	3690	-
of which: Feedstocks	1136	-	-	-	-	-	-	-	-	-
Non-Ferrous Metals	-	-	-	-	8	-	-	-	1485	-
Non-Metallic Minerals	6275	-	-	-	81	-	-	-	780	-
Transport Equipment	-	-	-	-	-	-	-	-	-	-
Machinery	-	15	-	-	95	-	-	-	1760	-
Mining and Quarrying	-	-	-	-	-	-	-	-	500	-
Food and Tobacco	1861	57	-	-	3449	-	-	-	1320	-
Paper, Pulp and Print	41590	-	-	-	46762	-	-	-	18230	-
Wood and Wood Products	1251	-	-	-	10423	-	-	-	1100	-
Construction	-	-	-	-	-	-	-	-	312	-
Textile and Leather	-	-	-	-	-	-	-	-	240	-
Non-specified	-	-	-	-	18026	-	-	-	372	7596
TRANSPORT SECTOR	**-**	**-**	**-**	**-**	**-**	**-**	**-**	**-**	**435**	**-**
International Civil Aviation	-	-	-	-	-	-	-	-	-	-
Domestic Air	-	-	-	-	-	-	-	-	-	-
Road	-	-	-	-	-	-	-	-	-	-
Rail	-	-	-	-	-	-	-	-	380	-
Pipeline Transport	-	-	-	-	-	-	-	-	-	-
Internal Navigation	-	-	-	-	-	-	-	-	-	-
Non-specified	-	-	-	-	-	-	-	-	55	-
OTHER SECTORS	**2388**	**34**	**-**	**-**	**34519**	**-**	**-**	**-**	**27658**	**77256**
Agriculture	766	-	-	-	6092	-	-	-	850	-
Commerce and Publ. Serv.	-	-	-	-	-	-	-	-	10952	-
Residential	1622	34	-	-	28427	-	-	-	15856	46980
Non-specified	-	-	-	-	-	-	-	-	-	30276
NON-ENERGY USE	**-**	**-**	**-**	**-**	**-**	**-**	**-**	**-**	**-**	**-**
in Industry/Transf./Energy	-	-	-	-	-	-	-	-	-	-
in Transport	-	-	-	-	-	-	-	-	-	-
in Other Sectors	-	-	-	-	-	-	-	-	-	-

Finland / Finlande : 1993

SUPPLY AND CONSUMPTION APPROVISIONNEMENT ET DEMANDE	Coal / *Charbon* (1000 tonnes)							Oil / *Pétrole* (1000 tonnes)			
	Coking Coal *Charbon à coke*	Steam Coal *Charbon vapeur*	Sub-Bit. Coal *Charbon sous-bit.*	Lignite *Lignite*	Peat *Tourbe*	Oven and Gas Coke *Coke de four/gaz*	Pat. Fuel and BKB *Agg./briq. de lignite*	Crude Oil *Pétrole brut*	NGL *LGN*	Feedstocks *Produits d'aliment.*	Additives *Additifs*
Production	-	-	-	-	6987	874	-	-	-	-	-
From Other Sources	-	-	-	-	-	-	-	-	-	85	-
Imports	1093	4840	-	-	36	418	-	8226	-	-	242
Exports	-	-	-	-	-123	-	-	-	-	-	-
Intl. Marine Bunkers	-	-	-	-	-	-	-	-	-	-	-
Stock Changes	-	69	-	-	404	-	-	389	-	-	-
DOMESTIC SUPPLY	**1093**	**4909**	**-**	**-**	**7304**	**1292**	**-**	**8615**	**-**	**85**	**242**
Transfers	-	-	-	-	-	-	-	-	-	1032	-
Statistical Differences	-	-	-	-	-	-	-	482	-	-172	-70
TRANSFORMATION	**1093**	**4145**	**-**	**-**	**4469**	**227**	**-**	**9097**	**-**	**945**	**172**
Electricity Plants	-	1651	-	-	1467	-	-	-	-	-	-
CHP Plants	-	2289	-	-	2638	-	-	-	-	-	-
Heat Plants	-	205	-	-	364	-	-	-	-	-	-
Transfer to Gases	-	-	-	-	-	227	-	-	-	-	-
Transfer to Solids	1093	-	-	-	-	-	-	-	-	-	-
Petroleum Refineries	-	-	-	-	-	-	-	9097	-	945	172
Petrochemical Industry	-	-	-	-	-	-	-	-	-	-	-
Liquefaction	-	-	-	-	-	-	-	-	-	-	-
Other Transformation Sector	-	-	-	-	-	-	-	-	-	-	-
ENERGY SECTOR	**-**	**-**	**-**	**-**	**-**	**-**	**-**	**-**	**-**	**-**	**-**
Coal Mines	-	-	-	-	-	-	-	-	-	-	-
Oil and Gas Extraction	-	-	-	-	-	-	-	-	-	-	-
Petroleum Refineries	-	-	-	-	-	-	-	-	-	-	-
Electricity, CHP+Heat plants	-	-	-	-	-	-	-	-	-	-	-
Pumped Storage (Elec.)	-	-	-	-	-	-	-	-	-	-	-
Other Energy Sector	-	-	-	-	-	-	-	-	-	-	-
Distribution Losses	-	-	-	-	-	-	-	-	-	-	-
FINAL CONSUMPTION	**-**	**764**	**-**	**-**	**2835**	**1065**	**-**	**-**	**-**	**-**	**-**
INDUSTRY SECTOR	**-**	**756**	**-**	**-**	**2756**	**659**	**-**	**-**	**-**	**-**	**-**
Iron and Steel	-	56	-	-	-	655	-	-	-	-	-
Chemical and Petrochemical	-	60	-	-	-	-	-	-	-	-	-
of which: Feedstocks	-	-	-	-	-	-	-	-	-	-	-
Non-Ferrous Metals	-	-	-	-	-	4	-	-	-	-	-
Non-Metallic Minerals	-	551	-	-	-	-	-	-	-	-	-
Transport Equipment	-	-	-	-	-	-	-	-	-	-	-
Machinery	-	4	-	-	-	-	-	-	-	-	-
Mining and Quarrying	-	-	-	-	-	-	-	-	-	-	-
Food and Tobacco	-	14	-	-	-	-	-	-	-	-	-
Paper, Pulp and Print	-	-	-	-	-	-	-	-	-	-	-
Wood and Wood Products	-	67	-	-	-	-	-	-	-	-	-
Construction	-	-	-	-	-	-	-	-	-	-	-
Textile and Leather	-	-	-	-	-	-	-	-	-	-	-
Non-specified	-	4	-	-	2756	-	-	-	-	-	-
TRANSPORT SECTOR	**-**	**-**	**-**	**-**	**-**	**-**	**-**	**-**	**-**	**-**	**-**
International Civil Aviation	-	-	-	-	-	-	-	-	-	-	-
Domestic Air	-	-	-	-	-	-	-	-	-	-	-
Road	-	-	-	-	-	-	-	-	-	-	-
Rail	-	-	-	-	-	-	-	-	-	-	-
Pipeline Transport	-	-	-	-	-	-	-	-	-	-	-
Internal Navigation	-	-	-	-	-	-	-	-	-	-	-
Non-specified	-	-	-	-	-	-	-	-	-	-	-
OTHER SECTORS	**-**	**8**	**-**	**-**	**79**	**-**	**-**	**-**	**-**	**-**	**-**
Agriculture	-	-	-	-	49	-	-	-	-	-	-
Commerce and Publ. Serv.	-	-	-	-	-	-	-	-	-	-	-
Residential	-	8	-	-	30	-	-	-	-	-	-
Non-specified	-	-	-	-	-	-	-	-	-	-	-
NON-ENERGY USE	**-**	**-**	**-**	**-**	**-**	**406**	**-**	**-**	**-**	**-**	**-**
in Industry/Transf./Energy	-	-	-	-	-	406	-	-	-	-	-
in Transport	-	-	-	-	-	-	-	-	-	-	-
in Other Sectors	-	-	-	-	-	-	-	-	-	-	-

Finland / Finlande : 1993

SUPPLY AND CONSUMPTION *APPROVISIONNEMENT ET DEMANDE*	Oil cont. / *Pétrole cont.* (1000 tonnes)										
	Refinery Gas *Gaz de raffinerie*	LPG + Ethane *GPL + éthane*	Motor Gasoline *Essence moteur*	Aviation Gasoline *Essence aviation*	Jet Fuel *Carbu-réacteur*	Kerosene *Kérosène*	Gas/Diesel *Gazole*	Heavy Fuel Oil *Fioul lourd*	Naphtha *Naphta*	Pétrol. Coke *Coke de pétrole*	Other Prod. *Autres prod.*
Production	514	280	3394	-	410	2	3881	1085	149	-	354
From Other Sources	-	-	-	-	-	-	-	-	-	-	-
Imports	-	39	319	2	27	6	1335	954	201	13	1359
Exports	-	-20	-1859	-	-53	-	-1196	-64	-34	-	-102
Intl. Marine Bunkers	-	-	-	-	-	-	-144	-401	-	-	-
Stock Changes	-	-12	12	1	-30	-	160	86	11	-	-
DOMESTIC SUPPLY	**514**	**287**	**1866**	**3**	**354**	**8**	**4036**	**1660**	**327**	**13**	**1611**
Transfers	-	-	-	-	-	-	-489	-474	-69	-	-
Statistical Differences	-	-158	10	-	15	-6	182	478	85	-	-476
TRANSFORMATION	**26**	**15**	**-**	**-**	**-**	**-**	**-**	**471**	**56**	**-**	**-**
Electricity Plants	13	-	-	-	-	-	-	60	-	-	-
CHP Plants	-	-	-	-	-	-	-	172	-	-	-
Heat Plants	-	-	-	-	-	-	-	235	-	-	-
Transfer to Gases	-	3	-	-	-	-	-	-	-	-	-
Transfer to Solids	-	-	-	-	-	-	-	-	-	-	-
Petroleum Refineries	-	-	-	-	-	-	-	-	-	-	-
Petrochemical Industry	13	12	-	-	-	-	-	4	56	-	-
Liquefaction	-	-	-	-	-	-	-	-	-	-	-
Other Transformation Sector	-	-	-	-	-	-	-	-	-	-	-
ENERGY SECTOR	**422**	**-**	**-**	**-**	**-**	**-**	**-**	**-**	**-**	**-**	**-**
Coal Mines	-	-	-	-	-	-	-	-	-	-	-
Oil and Gas Extraction	-	-	-	-	-	-	-	-	-	-	-
Petroleum Refineries	422	-	-	-	-	-	-	-	-	-	-
Electricity, CHP+Heat plants	-	-	-	-	-	-	-	-	-	-	-
Pumped Storage (Elec.)	-	-	-	-	-	-	-	-	-	-	-
Other Energy Sector	-	-	-	-	-	-	-	-	-	-	-
Distribution Losses	-	-	-	-	-	-	-	-	-	-	-
FINAL CONSUMPTION	**66**	**114**	**1876**	**3**	**369**	**2**	**3729**	**1193**	**287**	**13**	**1135**
INDUSTRY SECTOR	**66**	**107**	**-**	**-**	**-**	**-**	**164**	**736**	**287**	**13**	**-**
Iron and Steel	-	11	-	-	-	-	21	117	-	-	-
Chemical and Petrochemical	66	65	-	-	-	-	26	140	287	-	-
of which: Feedstocks	66	65	-	-	-	-	-	21	287	-	-
Non-Ferrous Metals	-	-	-	-	-	-	2	22	-	-	-
Non-Metallic Minerals	-	8	-	-	-	-	12	70	-	13	-
Transport Equipment	-	-	-	-	-	-	4	30	-	-	-
Machinery	-	-	-	-	-	-	9	72	-	-	-
Mining and Quarrying	-	-	-	-	-	-	5	46	-	-	-
Food and Tobacco	-	2	-	-	-	-	26	113	-	-	-
Paper, Pulp and Print	-	18	-	-	-	-	9	55	-	-	-
Wood and Wood Products	-	-	-	-	-	-	4	34	-	-	-
Construction	-	-	-	-	-	-	46	-	-	-	-
Textile and Leather	-	-	-	-	-	-	-	27	-	-	-
Non-specified	-	3	-	-	-	-	-	10	-	-	-
TRANSPORT SECTOR	**-**	**-**	**1862**	**3**	**369**	**1**	**1592**	**42**	**-**	**-**	**-**
International Civil Aviation	-	-	-	-	249	-	-	-	-	-	-
Domestic Air	-	-	-	3	120	-	-	-	-	-	-
Road	-	-	1862	-	-	1	1496	-	-	-	-
Rail	-	-	-	-	-	-	64	-	-	-	-
Pipeline Transport	-	-	-	-	-	-	-	-	-	-	-
Internal Navigation	-	-	-	-	-	-	32	42	-	-	-
Non-specified	-	-	-	-	-	-	-	-	-	-	-
OTHER SECTORS	**-**	**7**	**14**	**-**	**-**	**1**	**1973**	**415**	**-**	**-**	**-**
Agriculture	-	-	14	-	-	-	503	76	-	-	-
Commerce and Publ. Serv.	-	-	-	-	-	-	-	-	-	-	-
Residential	-	7	-	-	-	1	1470	339	-	-	-
Non-specified	-	-	-	-	-	-	-	-	-	-	-
NON-ENERGY USE	**-**	**-**	**-**	**-**	**-**	**-**	**-**	**-**	**-**	**-**	**1135**
in Industry/Transf./Energy	-	-	-	-	-	-	-	-	-	-	1135
in Transport	-	-	-	-	-	-	-	-	-	-	-
in Other Sectors	-	-	-	-	-	-	-	-	-	-	-

Finland / Finlande : 1993

CONSUMPTION / APPROVISIONNEMENT ET DEMANDE	Gas / Gaz (TJ) Natural Gas / Gaz naturel	Gas Works / Usines à gaz	Coke Ovens / Cokeries	Blast Furnaces / Hauts fourneaux	Combust. Renew. & Waste / En. Re. Comb. & Déchets (TJ) Solid Biomass & Anim. Prod. / Biomasse solide & prod. anim.	Gas/Liquids from Biomass / Gaz/Liquides tirés de biomasse	Municipal Waste / Déchets urbains	Industrial Waste / Déchets industriels	(GWh) Electricity / Electricité	(TJ) Heat / Chaleur
Production	-	-	6704	13317	175678	-	691	-	61172	96012
From Other Sources	-	86	-	-	-	-	-	-	-	-
Imports	119625	-	-	-	-	-	-	-	8013	-
Exports	-	-	-	-	-	-	-	-	-429	-
Intl. Marine Bunkers	-	-	-	-	-	-	-	-	-	-
Stock Changes	-	-	-	-	1345	-	-	-	-	-
DOMESTIC SUPPLY	**119625**	**86**	**6704**	**13317**	**177023**	**-**	**691**	**-**	**68756**	**96012**
Transfers	-	-	-	-	-	-	-	-	-	-
Statistical Differences	-392	-	-	-	-	-	4	-	-	-
TRANSFORMATION	**58160**	**-**	**565**	**4946**	**39274**	**-**	**695**	**-**	**-**	**-**
Electricity Plants	8560	-	-	-	6904	-	-	-	-	-
CHP Plants	42599	-	565	4946	29720	-	-	-	-	-
Heat Plants	7001	-	-	-	2650	-	695	-	-	-
Transfer to Gases	-	-	-	-	-	-	-	-	-	-
Transfer to Solids	-	-	-	-	-	-	-	-	-	-
Petroleum Refineries	-	-	-	-	-	-	-	-	-	-
Petrochemical Industry	-	-	-	-	-	-	-	-	-	-
Liquefaction	-	-	-	-	-	-	-	-	-	-
Other Transformation Sector	-	-	-	-	-	-	-	-	-	-
ENERGY SECTOR	**-**	**-**	**-**	**-**	**-**	**-**	**-**	**-**	**3601**	**-**
Coal Mines	-	-	-	-	-	-	-	-	-	-
Oil and Gas Extraction	-	-	-	-	-	-	-	-	-	-
Petroleum Refineries	-	-	-	-	-	-	-	-	530	-
Electricity, CHP+Heat plants	-	-	-	-	-	-	-	-	3071	-
Pumped Storage (Elec.)	-	-	-	-	-	-	-	-	-	-
Other Energy Sector	-	-	-	-	-	-	-	-	-	-
Distribution Losses	-	31	-	-	-	-	-	-	2829	7308
FINAL CONSUMPTION	**61073**	**55**	**6139**	**8371**	**137749**	**-**	**-**	**-**	**62326**	**88704**
INDUSTRY SECTOR	**58505**	**55**	**6139**	**8371**	**103434**	**-**	**-**	**-**	**33677**	**8424**
Iron and Steel	7368	-	6139	8371	9	-	-	-	2003	-
Chemical and Petrochemical	3001	-	-	-	14489	-	-	-	3910	-
of which: Feedstocks	1332	-	-	-	-	-	-	-	-	-
Non-Ferrous Metals	-	-	-	-	9	-	-	-	1587	-
Non-Metallic Minerals	5925	-	-	-	91	-	-	-	740	-
Transport Equipment	-	-	-	-	-	-	-	-	-	-
Machinery	-	11	-	-	108	-	-	-	1820	-
Mining and Quarrying	-	-	-	-	-	-	-	-	500	-
Food and Tobacco	1757	44	-	-	3891	-	-	-	1330	-
Paper, Pulp and Print	39273	-	-	-	52747	-	-	-	19760	-
Wood and Wood Products	1181	-	-	-	11757	-	-	-	1200	-
Construction	-	-	-	-	-	-	-	-	249	-
Textile and Leather	-	-	-	-	-	-	-	-	240	-
Non-specified	-	-	-	-	20333	-	-	-	338	8424
TRANSPORT SECTOR	**-**	**-**	**-**	**-**	**-**	**-**	**-**	**-**	**450**	**-**
International Civil Aviation	-	-	-	-	-	-	-	-	-	-
Domestic Air	-	-	-	-	-	-	-	-	-	-
Road	-	-	-	-	-	-	-	-	-	-
Rail	-	-	-	-	-	-	-	-	397	-
Pipeline Transport	-	-	-	-	-	-	-	-	-	-
Internal Navigation	-	-	-	-	-	-	-	-	-	-
Non-specified	-	-	-	-	-	-	-	-	53	-
OTHER SECTORS	**2568**	**-**	**-**	**-**	**34315**	**-**	**-**	**-**	**28199**	**80280**
Agriculture	811	-	-	-	5888	-	-	-	850	-
Commerce and Publ. Serv.	-	-	-	-	-	-	-	-	11213	-
Residential	1757	-	-	-	28427	-	-	-	16136	49860
Non-specified	-	-	-	-	-	-	-	-	-	30420
NON-ENERGY USE	**-**	**-**	**-**	**-**	**-**	**-**	**-**	**-**	**-**	**-**
in Industry/Transf./Energy	-	-	-	-	-	-	-	-	-	-
in Transport	-	-	-	-	-	-	-	-	-	-
in Other Sectors	-	-	-	-	-	-	-	-	-	-

France / France : 1992

SUPPLY AND CONSUMPTION / APPROVISIONNEMENT ET DEMANDE	Coal / Charbon (1000 tonnes)							Oil / Pétrole (1000 tonnes)			
	Coking Coal / Charbon à coke	Steam Coal / Charbon vapeur	Sub-Bit. Coal / Charbon sous-bit.	Lignite / Lignite	Peat / Tourbe	Oven and Gas Coke / Coke de four/gaz	Pat. Fuel and BKB / Agg./briq. de lignite	Crude Oil / Pétrole brut	NGL / LGN	Feedstocks / Produits d'aliment.	Additives / Additifs
Production	1433	8045	-	1578	-	6795	526	2866	447	-	-
From Other Sources	-	771	-	-	-	-	-	-	-	1896	246
Imports	7457	14532	-	2	-	553	188	71003	-	5322	-
Exports	-	-497	-	-	-	-403	-38	-	-	-429	-
Intl. Marine Bunkers	-	-	-	-	-	-	-	-	-	-	-
Stock Changes	-	-3899	-	-86	-	-98	8	-639	-	-80	5
DOMESTIC SUPPLY	**8890**	**18952**	**-**	**1494**	**-**	**6847**	**684**	**73230**	**447**	**6709**	**251**
Transfers	-	-	-	-	-	-	-	-	-447	48	-
Statistical Differences	-51	178	-	-3	-	1	-7	-338	-	813	-
TRANSFORMATION	**8839**	**11941**	**-**	**1245**	**-**	**2537**	**-**	**72892**	**-**	**7570**	**251**
Electricity Plants	-	11488	-	1245	-	-	-	-	-	-	-
CHP Plants	-	-	-	-	-	-	-	-	-	-	-
Heat Plants	-	-	-	-	-	-	-	-	-	-	-
Transfer to Gases	-	-	-	-	-	2537	-	-	-	-	-
Transfer to Solids	8839	453	-	-	-	-	-	-	-	-	-
Petroleum Refineries	-	-	-	-	-	-	-	72892	-	7570	251
Petrochemical Industry	-	-	-	-	-	-	-	-	-	-	-
Liquefaction	-	-	-	-	-	-	-	-	-	-	-
Other Transformation Sector	-	-	-	-	-	-	-	-	-	-	-
ENERGY SECTOR	**-**	**103**	**-**	**-**	**-**	**164**	**-**	**-**	**-**	**-**	**-**
Coal Mines	-	103	-	-	-	-	-	-	-	-	-
Oil and Gas Extraction	-	-	-	-	-	-	-	-	-	-	-
Petroleum Refineries	-	-	-	-	-	-	-	-	-	-	-
Electricity, CHP+Heat plants	-	-	-	-	-	-	-	-	-	-	-
Pumped Storage (Elec.)	-	-	-	-	-	-	-	-	-	-	-
Other Energy Sector	-	-	-	-	-	164	-	-	-	-	-
Distribution Losses	-	-	-	-	-	-	-	-	-	-	-
FINAL CONSUMPTION	**-**	**7086**	**-**	**246**	**-**	**4147**	**677**	**-**	**-**	**-**	**-**
INDUSTRY SECTOR	**-**	**5776**	**-**	**166**	**-**	**4012**	**-**	**-**	**-**	**-**	**-**
Iron and Steel	-	1788	-	-	-	3215	-	-	-	-	-
Chemical and Petrochemical	-	830	-	65	-	170	-	-	-	-	-
of which: Feedstocks	-	-	-	-	-	-	-	-	-	-	-
Non-Ferrous Metals	-	-	-	35	-	222	-	-	-	-	-
Non-Metallic Minerals	-	1970	-	-	-	95	-	-	-	-	-
Transport Equipment	-	-	-	-	-	-	-	-	-	-	-
Machinery	-	150	-	-	-	255	-	-	-	-	-
Mining and Quarrying	-	90	-	-	-	-	-	-	-	-	-
Food and Tobacco	-	365	-	45	-	55	-	-	-	-	-
Paper, Pulp and Print	-	145	-	-	-	-	-	-	-	-	-
Wood and Wood Products	-	-	-	-	-	-	-	-	-	-	-
Construction	-	-	-	-	-	-	-	-	-	-	-
Textile and Leather	-	100	-	15	-	-	-	-	-	-	-
Non-specified	-	338	-	6	-	-	-	-	-	-	-
TRANSPORT SECTOR	**-**	**-**	**-**	**-**	**-**	**-**	**-**	**-**	**-**	**-**	**-**
International Civil Aviation	-	-	-	-	-	-	-	-	-	-	-
Domestic Air	-	-	-	-	-	-	-	-	-	-	-
Road	-	-	-	-	-	-	-	-	-	-	-
Rail	-	-	-	-	-	-	-	-	-	-	-
Pipeline Transport	-	-	-	-	-	-	-	-	-	-	-
Internal Navigation	-	-	-	-	-	-	-	-	-	-	-
Non-specified	-	-	-	-	-	-	-	-	-	-	-
OTHER SECTORS	**-**	**1310**	**-**	**80**	**-**	**135**	**677**	**-**	**-**	**-**	**-**
Agriculture	-	-	-	-	-	-	-	-	-	-	-
Commerce and Publ. Serv.	-	-	-	-	-	-	-	-	-	-	-
Residential	-	1310	-	80	-	135	677	-	-	-	-
Non-specified	-	-	-	-	-	-	-	-	-	-	-
NON-ENERGY USE	**-**	**-**	**-**	**-**	**-**	**-**	**-**	**-**	**-**	**-**	**-**
in Industry/Transf./Energy	-	-	-	-	-	-	-	-	-	-	-
in Transport	-	-	-	-	-	-	-	-	-	-	-
in Other Sectors	-	-	-	-	-	-	-	-	-	-	-

France / France : 1992

SUPPLY AND CONSUMPTION *APPROVISIONNEMENT ET DEMANDE*	Oil cont. / *Pétrole cont.* (1000 tonnes)										
	Refinery Gas *Gaz de raffinerie*	LPG + Ethane *GPL + éthane*	Motor Gasoline *Essence moteur*	Aviation Gasoline *Essence aviation*	Jet Fuel *Carbu-réacteur*	Kerosene *Kérosène*	Gas/Diesel *Gazole*	Heavy Fuel Oil *Fioul lourd*	Naphtha *Naphta*	Pétrol. Coke *Coke de pétrole*	Other Prod. *Autres prod.*
Production	2311	2530	17874	73	4645	82	29330	12481	3194	907	6797
From Other Sources	-	-	-	-	-	-	-	-	-	-	-
Imports	-	1799	3487	13	1218	13	11893	755	3794	1027	866
Exports	-	-889	-3495	-59	-940	-35	-2956	-3051	-411	-	-2430
Intl. Marine Bunkers	-	-	-	-	-	-	-352	-2227	-	-	-45
Stock Changes	-	32	10	11	22	-3	-228	-591	68	-	32
DOMESTIC SUPPLY	**2311**	**3472**	**17876**	**38**	**4945**	**57**	**37687**	**7367**	**6645**	**1934**	**5220**
Transfers	-	229	141	-	-	-	18	31	-	-	49
Statistical Differences	20	44	-420	-6	-809	-30	1575	-49	1204	395	357
TRANSFORMATION	**-**	**179**	**-**	**-**	**-**	**-**	**182**	**1317**	**1565**	**243**	**-**
Electricity Plants	-	-	-	-	-	-	10	1317	-	20	-
CHP Plants	-	-	-	-	-	-	-	-	-	-	-
Heat Plants	-	-	-	-	-	-	-	-	-	-	-
Transfer to Gases	-	20	-	-	-	-	-	-	-	-	-
Transfer to Solids	-	-	-	-	-	-	-	-	-	223	-
Petroleum Refineries	-	-	-	-	-	-	-	-	-	-	-
Petrochemical Industry	-	159	-	-	-	-	172	-	1565	-	-
Liquefaction	-	-	-	-	-	-	-	-	-	-	-
Other Transformation Sector	-	-	-	-	-	-	-	-	-	-	-
ENERGY SECTOR	**2118**	**29**	**-**	**-**	**-**	**-**	**-**	**1110**	**-**	**907**	**919**
Coal Mines	-	-	-	-	-	-	-	-	-	-	-
Oil and Gas Extraction	-	-	-	-	-	-	-	58	-	-	-
Petroleum Refineries	2118	29	-	-	-	-	-	1052	-	907	919
Electricity, CHP+Heat plants	-	-	-	-	-	-	-	-	-	-	-
Pumped Storage (Elec.)	-	-	-	-	-	-	-	-	-	-	-
Other Energy Sector	-	-	-	-	-	-	-	-	-	-	-
Distribution Losses	-	-	-	-	-	-	-	-	-	-	-
FINAL CONSUMPTION	**213**	**3537**	**17597**	**32**	**4136**	**27**	**39098**	**4922**	**6284**	**1179**	**4707**
INDUSTRY SECTOR	**213**	**1219**	**-**	**-**	**-**	**8**	**3055**	**3293**	**6284**	**1038**	**268**
Iron and Steel	-	-	-	-	-	-	30	101	-	65	-
Chemical and Petrochemical	213	637	-	-	-	-	1444	672	6284	-	268
of which: Feedstocks	-	*637*	-	-	-	-	*738*	-	*6284*	-	-
Non-Ferrous Metals	-	168	-	-	-	-	240	133	-	-	-
Non-Metallic Minerals	-	59	-	-	-	-	25	650	-	514	-
Transport Equipment	-	-	-	-	-	-	74	106	-	-	-
Machinery	-	-	-	-	-	-	158	55	-	-	-
Mining and Quarrying	-	-	-	-	-	-	31	66	-	-	-
Food and Tobacco	-	173	-	-	-	-	101	834	-	-	-
Paper, Pulp and Print	-	-	-	-	-	-	20	408	-	-	-
Wood and Wood Products	-	-	-	-	-	-	-	-	-	-	-
Construction	-	-	-	-	-	-	732	129	-	-	-
Textile and Leather	-	-	-	-	-	-	71	139	-	-	-
Non-specified	-	182	-	-	-	8	129	-	-	459	-
TRANSPORT SECTOR	**-**	**40**	**17559**	**32**	**4136**	**3**	**20243**	**15**	**-**	**-**	**-**
International Civil Aviation	-	-	-	-	3315	-	-	-	-	-	-
Domestic Air	-	-	-	32	821	-	-	-	-	-	-
Road	-	40	17354	-	-	-	19412	-	-	-	-
Rail	-	-	-	-	-	-	424	3	-	-	-
Pipeline Transport	-	-	-	-	-	-	-	-	-	-	-
Internal Navigation	-	-	205	-	-	3	407	12	-	-	-
Non-specified	-	-	-	-	-	-	-	-	-	-	-
OTHER SECTORS	**-**	**2278**	**38**	**-**	**-**	**16**	**15800**	**1614**	**-**	**-**	**-**
Agriculture	-	345	38	-	-	-	2200	122	-	-	-
Commerce and Publ. Serv.	-	270	-	-	-	-	13600	1492	-	-	-
Residential	-	1663	-	-	-	16	-	-	-	-	-
Non-specified	-	-	-	-	-	-	-	-	-	-	-
NON-ENERGY USE	**-**	**-**	**-**	**-**	**-**	**-**	**-**	**-**	**-**	**141**	**4439**
in Industry/Transf./Energy	-	-	-	-	-	-	-	-	-	141	3956
in Transport	-	-	-	-	-	-	-	-	-	-	406
in Other Sectors	-	-	-	-	-	-	-	-	-	-	77

France / France : 1992

CONSUMPTION / APPROVISIONNEMENT ET DEMANDE	Gas / Gaz (TJ)				Combust. Renew. & Waste / En. Re. Comb. & Déchets (TJ)				(GWh)	(TJ)
	Natural Gas / Gaz naturel	Gas Works / Usines à gaz	Coke Ovens / Cokeries	Blast Furnaces / Hauts fourneaux	Solid Biomass & Anim. Prod. / Biomasse solide & prod. anim.	Gas/Liquids from Biomass / Gaz/Liquides tirés de biomasse	Municipal Waste / Déchets urbains	Industrial Waste / Déchets industriels	Electricity / Electricité	Heat / Chaleur
Production	129460	694	48528	70250	175800	-	-	-	462841	-
From Other Sources	-	800	-	-	-	-	-	-	-	-
Imports	1281068	-	-	-	-	-	-	-	4737	-
Exports	-42988	-	-	-	-	-	-	-	-58533	-
Intl. Marine Bunkers	-	-	-	-	-	-	-	-	-	-
Stock Changes	-61920	-	-	-	-	-	-	-	-	-
DOMESTIC SUPPLY	**1305620**	**1494**	**48528**	**70250**	**175800**	**-**	**-**	**-**	**409045**	**-**
Transfers	-	-	-	-	-	-	-	-	-	-
Statistical Differences	-	-	-170	-	-	-	-	-	-	-
TRANSFORMATION	**19078**	**-**	**8636**	**27518**	**8100**	**-**	**-**	**-**	**-**	**-**
Electricity Plants	19078	-	5486	27518	8100	-	-	-	-	-
CHP Plants	-	-	-	-	-	-	-	-	-	-
Heat Plants	-	-	-	-	-	-	-	-	-	-
Transfer to Gases	-	-	3150	-	-	-	-	-	-	-
Transfer to Solids	-	-	-	-	-	-	-	-	-	-
Petroleum Refineries	-	-	-	-	-	-	-	-	-	-
Petrochemical Industry	-	-	-	-	-	-	-	-	-	-
Liquefaction	-	-	-	-	-	-	-	-	-	-
Other Transformation Sector	-	-	-	-	-	-	-	-	-	-
ENERGY SECTOR	**11218**	**-**	**13986**	**-**	**-**	**-**	**-**	**-**	**51554**	**-**
Coal Mines	-	-	-	-	-	-	-	-	1239	-
Oil and Gas Extraction	6894	-	-	-	-	-	-	-	4352	-
Petroleum Refineries	-	-	-	-	-	-	-	-	-	-
Electricity, CHP+Heat plants	-	-	-	-	-	-	-	-	20694	-
Pumped Storage (Elec.)	-	-	-	-	-	-	-	-	5005	-
Other Energy Sector	4324	-	13986	-	-	-	-	-	20264	-
Distribution Losses	2033	-	1343	4561	-	-	-	-	27472	-
FINAL CONSUMPTION	**1273291**	**1494**	**24393**	**38171**	**167700**	**-**	**-**	**-**	**330019**	**-**
INDUSTRY SECTOR	**545792**	**1494**	**24393**	**38171**	**25100**	**-**	**-**	**-**	**121052**	**-**
Iron and Steel	34974	-	21377	38171	-	-	-	-	11870	-
Chemical and Petrochemical	183874	-	2419	-	-	-	-	-	28426	-
of which: Feedstocks	95850	-	-	-	-	-	-	-	-	-
Non-Ferrous Metals	15739	1494	-	-	-	-	-	-	11497	-
Non-Metallic Minerals	65516	-	18	-	-	-	-	-	6322	-
Transport Equipment	-	-	-	-	-	-	-	-	8233	-
Machinery	67032	-	-	-	-	-	-	-	14368	-
Mining and Quarrying	6894	-	-	-	-	-	-	-	3294	-
Food and Tobacco	79096	-	-	-	-	-	-	-	15161	-
Paper, Pulp and Print	45140	-	-	-	-	-	-	-	10708	-
Wood and Wood Products	-	-	-	-	-	-	-	-	4310	-
Construction	1868	-	565	-	-	-	-	-	2008	-
Textile and Leather	19242	-	-	-	-	-	-	-	4194	-
Non-specified	26417	-	14	-	25100	-	-	-	661	-
TRANSPORT SECTOR	**7**	**-**	**-**	**-**	**-**	**-**	**-**	**-**	**9420**	**-**
International Civil Aviation	-	-	-	-	-	-	-	-	-	-
Domestic Air	-	-	-	-	-	-	-	-	-	-
Road	7	-	-	-	-	-	-	-	-	-
Rail	-	-	-	-	-	-	-	-	7123	-
Pipeline Transport	-	-	-	-	-	-	-	-	-	-
Internal Navigation	-	-	-	-	-	-	-	-	-	-
Non-specified	-	-	-	-	-	-	-	-	2297	-
OTHER SECTORS	**727492**	**-**	**-**	**-**	**142600**	**-**	**-**	**-**	**199547**	**-**
Agriculture	10724	-	-	-	-	-	-	-	2294	-
Commerce and Publ. Serv.	337360	-	-	-	-	-	-	-	87660	-
Residential	379408	-	-	-	142600	-	-	-	109593	-
Non-specified	-	-	-	-	-	-	-	-	-	-
NON-ENERGY USE	**-**	**-**	**-**	**-**	**-**	**-**	**-**	**-**	**-**	**-**
in Industry/Transf./Energy	-	-	-	-	-	-	-	-	-	-
in Transport	-	-	-	-	-	-	-	-	-	-
in Other Sectors	-	-	-	-	-	-	-	-	-	-

France / France : 1993

SUPPLY AND CONSUMPTION *APPROVISIONNEMENT ET DEMANDE*	Coal / *Charbon* (1000 tonnes)							Oil / *Pétrole* (1000 tonnes)			
	Coking Coal *Charbon à coke*	Steam Coal *Charbon vapeur*	Sub-Bit. Coal *Charbon sous-bit.*	Lignite *Lignite*	Peat *Tourbe*	Oven and Gas Coke *Coke de four/gaz*	Pat. Fuel and BKB *Agg./briq. de lignite*	Crude Oil *Pétrole brut*	NGL *LGN*	Feedstocks *Produits d'aliment.*	Additives *Additifs*
Production	1350	7226	-	1672	-	6197	427	2752	453	-	-
From Other Sources	-	414	-	-	-	-	-	-	-	1904	270
Imports	6904	7327	-	-	-	638	153	74668	-	3850	-
Exports	-	-622	-	-	-	-487	-27	-	-	-1308	-
Intl. Marine Bunkers	-	-	-	-	-	-	-	-	-	-	-
Stock Changes	-	-1190	-	56	-	-182	5	464	-	95	10
DOMESTIC SUPPLY	**8254**	**13155**	**-**	**1728**	**-**	**6166**	**558**	**77884**	**453**	**4541**	**280**
Transfers	-	-	-	-	-	-	-	-	-453	122	-
Statistical Differences	-	42	-	27	-	-44	-5	-349	-	793	-27
TRANSFORMATION	**8254**	**7169**	**-**	**1556**	**-**	**2366**	**-**	**77535**	**-**	**5456**	**253**
Electricity Plants	-	6810	-	1556	-	-	-	-	-	-	-
CHP Plants	-	-	-	-	-	-	-	-	-	-	-
Heat Plants	-	-	-	-	-	-	-	-	-	-	-
Transfer to Gases	-	-	-	-	-	2366	-	-	-	-	-
Transfer to Solids	8254	359	-	-	-	-	-	-	-	-	-
Petroleum Refineries	-	-	-	-	-	-	-	77535	-	5456	253
Petrochemical Industry	-	-	-	-	-	-	-	-	-	-	-
Liquefaction	-	-	-	-	-	-	-	-	-	-	-
Other Transformation Sector	-	-	-	-	-	-	-	-	-	-	-
ENERGY SECTOR	**-**	**66**	**-**	**-**	**-**	**120**	**-**	**-**	**-**	**-**	**-**
Coal Mines	-	66	-	-	-	-	-	-	-	-	-
Oil and Gas Extraction	-	-	-	-	-	-	-	-	-	-	-
Petroleum Refineries	-	-	-	-	-	-	-	-	-	-	-
Electricity, CHP+Heat plants	-	-	-	-	-	-	-	-	-	-	-
Pumped Storage (Elec.)	-	-	-	-	-	-	-	-	-	-	-
Other Energy Sector	-	-	-	-	-	120	-	-	-	-	-
Distribution Losses	-	-	-	-	-	-	-	-	-	-	-
FINAL CONSUMPTION	**-**	**5962**	**-**	**199**	**-**	**3636**	**553**	**-**	**-**	**-**	**-**
INDUSTRY SECTOR	**-**	**4670**	**-**	**156**	**-**	**3509**	**-**	**-**	**-**	**-**	**-**
Iron and Steel	-	1745	-	-	-	2791	-	-	-	-	-
Chemical and Petrochemical	-	610	-	60	-	153	-	-	-	-	-
of which: Feedstocks	-	-	-	-	-	-	-	-	-	-	-
Non-Ferrous Metals	-	-	-	30	-	200	-	-	-	-	-
Non-Metallic Minerals	-	1445	-	-	-	85	-	-	-	-	-
Transport Equipment	-	-	-	-	-	-	-	-	-	-	-
Machinery	-	110	-	-	-	230	-	-	-	-	-
Mining and Quarrying	-	65	-	-	-	-	-	-	-	-	-
Food and Tobacco	-	270	-	40	-	50	-	-	-	-	-
Paper, Pulp and Print	-	105	-	-	-	-	-	-	-	-	-
Wood and Wood Products	-	-	-	-	-	-	-	-	-	-	-
Construction	-	-	-	-	-	-	-	-	-	-	-
Textile and Leather	-	70	-	15	-	-	-	-	-	-	-
Non-specified	-	250	-	11	-	-	-	-	-	-	-
TRANSPORT SECTOR	**-**	**-**	**-**	**-**	**-**	**-**	**-**	**-**	**-**	**-**	**-**
International Civil Aviation	-	-	-	-	-	-	-	-	-	-	-
Domestic Air	-	-	-	-	-	-	-	-	-	-	-
Road	-	-	-	-	-	-	-	-	-	-	-
Rail	-	-	-	-	-	-	-	-	-	-	-
Pipeline Transport	-	-	-	-	-	-	-	-	-	-	-
Internal Navigation	-	-	-	-	-	-	-	-	-	-	-
Non-specified	-	-	-	-	-	-	-	-	-	-	-
OTHER SECTORS	**-**	**1292**	**-**	**43**	**-**	**127**	**553**	**-**	**-**	**-**	**-**
Agriculture	-	-	-	-	-	-	-	-	-	-	-
Commerce and Publ. Serv.	-	-	-	-	-	-	-	-	-	-	-
Residential	-	1292	-	43	-	127	553	-	-	-	-
Non-specified	-	-	-	-	-	-	-	-	-	-	-
NON-ENERGY USE	**-**	**-**	**-**	**-**	**-**	**-**	**-**	**-**	**-**	**-**	**-**
in Industry/Transf./Energy	-	-	-	-	-	-	-	-	-	-	-
in Transport	-	-	-	-	-	-	-	-	-	-	-
in Other Sectors	-	-	-	-	-	-	-	-	-	-	-

France / France : 1993

SUPPLY AND CONSUMPTION APPROVISIONNEMENT ET DEMANDE	Oil cont. / Pétrole cont. (1000 tonnes)										
	Refinery Gas Gaz de raffinerie	LPG + Ethane GPL + éthane	Motor Gasoline Essence moteur	Aviation Gasoline Essence aviation	Jet Fuel Carbu-réacteur	Kerosene Kérosène	Gas/Diesel Gazole	Heavy Fuel Oil Fioul lourd	Naphtha Naphta	Pétrol. Coke Coke de pétrole	Other Prod. Autres prod.
Production	2277	2694	17815	17	4907	62	31501	12621	3381	875	6527
From Other Sources	-	-	-	-	-	-	-	-	-	-	-
Imports	-	2115	3826	50	786	45	10673	632	3043	979	1251
Exports	-	-1122	-3852	-20	-704	-12	-3317	-3723	-223	-14	-2220
Intl. Marine Bunkers	-	-	-	-	-6	-	-282	-2177	-	-	-20
Stock Changes	-	25	-399	-6	-56	-1	312	213	43	-	-4
DOMESTIC SUPPLY	**2277**	**3712**	**17390**	**41**	**4927**	**94**	**38887**	**7566**	**6244**	**1840**	**5534**
Transfers	-	228	151	-	-	-	-31	-	-	-	44
Statistical Differences	-	-488	-472	-12	-680	-73	1306	-1015	252	14	-71
TRANSFORMATION	**-**	**157**	**-**	**-**	**-**	**-**	**304**	**449**	**1474**	**167**	**-**
Electricity Plants	-	-	-	-	-	-	10	449	-	14	-
CHP Plants	-	-	-	-	-	-	-	-	-	-	-
Heat Plants	-	-	-	-	-	-	-	-	-	-	-
Transfer to Gases	-	21	-	-	-	-	-	-	-	-	-
Transfer to Solids	-	-	-	-	-	-	-	-	-	153	-
Petroleum Refineries	-	-	-	-	-	-	-	-	-	-	-
Petrochemical Industry	-	136	-	-	-	-	294	-	1474	-	-
Liquefaction	-	-	-	-	-	-	-	-	-	-	-
Other Transformation Sector	-	-	-	-	-	-	-	-	-	-	-
ENERGY SECTOR	**2087**	**31**	**-**	**-**	**-**	**-**	**-**	**1347**	**-**	**875**	**783**
Coal Mines	-	-	-	-	-	-	-	-	-	-	-
Oil and Gas Extraction	-	-	-	-	-	-	-	49	-	-	-
Petroleum Refineries	2087	31	-	-	-	-	-	1298	-	875	783
Electricity, CHP+Heat plants	-	-	-	-	-	-	-	-	-	-	-
Pumped Storage (Elec.)	-	-	-	-	-	-	-	-	-	-	-
Other Energy Sector	-	-	-	-	-	-	-	-	-	-	-
Distribution Losses	-	-	-	-	-	-	-	-	-	-	-
FINAL CONSUMPTION	**190**	**3264**	**17069**	**29**	**4247**	**21**	**39858**	**4755**	**5022**	**812**	**4724**
INDUSTRY SECTOR	**190**	**947**	**-**	**-**	**-**	**6**	**3705**	**3199**	**5022**	**691**	**-**
Iron and Steel	-	-	-	-	-	-	25	66	-	85	-
Chemical and Petrochemical	190	465	-	-	-	-	1074	678	5022	-	-
of which: Feedstocks	-	465	-	-	-	-	1074	-	5022	-	-
Non-Ferrous Metals	-	173	-	-	-	-	240	131	-	-	-
Non-Metallic Minerals	-	51	-	-	-	-	14	682	-	354	-
Transport Equipment	-	-	-	-	-	-	39	75	-	-	-
Machinery	-	-	-	-	-	-	158	89	-	-	-
Mining and Quarrying	-	-	-	-	-	-	31	49	-	-	-
Food and Tobacco	-	181	-	-	-	-	63	801	-	-	-
Paper, Pulp and Print	-	-	-	-	-	-	20	358	-	-	-
Wood and Wood Products	-	-	-	-	-	-	-	-	-	-	-
Construction	-	-	-	-	-	-	732	124	-	-	-
Textile and Leather	-	-	-	-	-	-	53	146	-	-	-
Non-specified	-	77	-	-	-	6	1256	-	-	252	-
TRANSPORT SECTOR	**-**	**35**	**17035**	**29**	**4247**	**2**	**21153**	**20**	**-**	**-**	**-**
International Civil Aviation	-	-	-	-	3375	-	-	-	-	-	-
Domestic Air	-	-	-	29	872	-	-	-	-	-	-
Road	-	35	16816	-	-	-	20249	-	-	-	-
Rail	-	-	-	-	-	-	446	4	-	-	-
Pipeline Transport	-	-	-	-	-	-	-	-	-	-	-
Internal Navigation	-	-	219	-	-	2	458	16	-	-	-
Non-specified	-	-	-	-	-	-	-	-	-	-	-
OTHER SECTORS	**-**	**2282**	**34**	**-**	**-**	**13**	**15000**	**1536**	**-**	**-**	**-**
Agriculture	-	367	34	-	-	-	1900	139	-	-	-
Commerce and Publ. Serv.	-	297	-	-	-	-	13100	1397	-	-	-
Residential	-	1618	-	-	-	13	-	-	-	-	-
Non-specified	-	-	-	-	-	-	-	-	-	-	-
NON-ENERGY USE	**-**	**-**	**-**	**-**	**-**	**-**	**-**	**-**	**-**	**121**	**4724**
in Industry/Transf./Energy	-	-	-	-	-	-	-	-	-	121	4232
in Transport	-	-	-	-	-	-	-	-	-	-	421
in Other Sectors	-	-	-	-	-	-	-	-	-	-	71

France / France : 1993

CONSUMPTION / APPROVISIONNEMENT ET DEMANDE	Gas / Gaz (TJ) Natural Gas / Gaz naturel	Gas Works / Usines à gaz	Coke Ovens / Cokeries	Blast Furnaces / Hauts fourneaux	Combust. Renew. & Waste / En. Re. Comb. & Déchets (TJ) Solid Biomass & Anim. Prod. / Biomasse solide & prod. anim.	Gas/Liquids from Biomass / Gaz/Liquides tirés de biomasse	Municipal Waste / Déchets urbains	Industrial Waste / Déchets industriels	(GWh) Electricity / Electricité	(TJ) Heat / Chaleur
Production	134147	640	46516	65509	175600	-	-	-	472004	-
From Other Sources	-	800	-	-	-	-	-	-	-	-
Imports	1200654	-	-	-	-	-	-	-	3663	-
Exports	-23245	-	-	-	-	-	-	-	-65093	-
Intl. Marine Bunkers	-	-	-	-	-	-	-	-	-	-
Stock Changes	35629	-	-	-	-	-	-	-	-	-
DOMESTIC SUPPLY	**1347185**	**1440**	**46516**	**65509**	**175600**	**-**	**-**	**-**	**410574**	**-**
Transfers	-	-	-	-	-	-	-	-	-	-
Statistical Differences	-	-	-	-	-	-	-	-	-	-
TRANSFORMATION	**22924**	**-**	**7666**	**25704**	**7900**	**-**	**-**	**-**	**-**	**-**
Electricity Plants	22924	-	4630	25704	7900	-	-	-	-	-
CHP Plants	-	-	-	-	-	-	-	-	-	-
Heat Plants	-	-	-	-	-	-	-	-	-	-
Transfer to Gases	-	-	3036	-	-	-	-	-	-	-
Transfer to Solids	-	-	-	-	-	-	-	-	-	-
Petroleum Refineries	-	-	-	-	-	-	-	-	-	-
Petrochemical Industry	-	-	-	-	-	-	-	-	-	-
Liquefaction	-	-	-	-	-	-	-	-	-	-
Other Transformation Sector	-	-	-	-	-	-	-	-	-	-
ENERGY SECTOR	**11721**	**-**	**13310**	**-**	**-**	**-**	**-**	**-**	**49498**	**-**
Coal Mines	-	-	-	-	-	-	-	-	1153	-
Oil and Gas Extraction	6577	-	-	-	-	-	-	-	4420	-
Petroleum Refineries	-	-	-	-	-	-	-	-	-	-
Electricity, CHP+Heat plants	-	-	-	-	-	-	-	-	21421	-
Pumped Storage (Elec.)	-	-	-	-	-	-	-	-	4187	-
Other Energy Sector	5144	-	13310	-	-	-	-	-	18317	-
Distribution Losses	2100	-	1245	4231	-	-	-	-	28778	-
FINAL CONSUMPTION	**1310440**	**1440**	**24295**	**35574**	**167700**	**-**	**-**	**-**	**332298**	**-**
INDUSTRY SECTOR	**572271**	**1440**	**24295**	**35574**	**25100**	**-**	**-**	**-**	**120648**	**-**
Iron and Steel	35413	-	21290	35574	-	-	-	-	11620	-
Chemical and Petrochemical	186809	-	2394	-	-	-	-	-	28920	-
of which: Feedstocks	97290	-	-	-	-	-	-	-	-	-
Non-Ferrous Metals	15390	1440	-	-	-	-	-	-	11480	-
Non-Metallic Minerals	66658	-	43	-	-	-	-	-	6340	-
Transport Equipment	-	-	-	-	-	-	-	-	7950	-
Machinery	66251	-	-	-	-	-	-	-	13967	-
Mining and Quarrying	5659	-	-	-	-	-	-	-	2998	-
Food and Tobacco	88081	-	-	-	-	-	-	-	15228	-
Paper, Pulp and Print	48323	-	-	-	-	-	-	-	11230	-
Wood and Wood Products	-	-	-	-	-	-	-	-	4185	-
Construction	2012	-	554	-	-	-	-	-	1918	-
Textile and Leather	19796	-	-	-	-	-	-	-	3980	-
Non-specified	37879	-	14	-	25100	-	-	-	832	-
TRANSPORT SECTOR	**50**	**-**	**-**	**-**	**-**	**-**	**-**	**-**	**9345**	**-**
International Civil Aviation	-	-	-	-	-	-	-	-	-	-
Domestic Air	-	-	-	-	-	-	-	-	-	-
Road	50	-	-	-	-	-	-	-	-	-
Rail	-	-	-	-	-	-	-	-	6925	-
Pipeline Transport	-	-	-	-	-	-	-	-	-	-
Internal Navigation	-	-	-	-	-	-	-	-	-	-
Non-specified	-	-	-	-	-	-	-	-	2420	-
OTHER SECTORS	**738119**	**-**	**-**	**-**	**142600**	**-**	**-**	**-**	**202305**	**-**
Agriculture	9644	-	-	-	-	-	-	-	2235	-
Commerce and Publ. Serv.	353272	-	-	-	-	-	-	-	88600	-
Residential	375203	-	-	-	142600	-	-	-	111470	-
Non-specified	-	-	-	-	-	-	-	-	-	-
NON-ENERGY USE	**-**	**-**	**-**	**-**	**-**	**-**	**-**	**-**	**-**	**-**
in Industry/Transf./Energy	-	-	-	-	-	-	-	-	-	-
in Transport	-	-	-	-	-	-	-	-	-	-
in Other Sectors	-	-	-	-	-	-	-	-	-	-

Germany / Allemagne : 1992

SUPPLY AND CONSUMPTION *APPROVISIONNEMENT ET DEMANDE*	Coal / *Charbon* (1000 tonnes)							Oil / *Pétrole* (1000 tonnes)			
	Coking Coal *Charbon à coke*	Steam Coal *Charbon vapeur*	Sub-Bit. Coal *Charbon sous-bit.*	Lignite *Lignite*	Peat *Tourbe*	Oven and Gas Coke *Coke de four/gaz*	Pat. Fuel and BKB *Agg./briq. de lignite*	Crude Oil *Pétrole brut*	NGL *LGN*	Feedstocks *Produits d'aliment.*	Additives *Additifs*
Production	39182	32971	-	241812	195	15296	17613	3279	-	-	-
From Other Sources	-	-	-	-	-	-	-	98	-	4207	1019
Imports	1357	14095	-	3640	-	1843	283	99065	-	-	-
Exports	-687	-960	-	-2	-185	-1287	-866	-208	-	-	-
Intl. Marine Bunkers	-	-	-	-	-	-	-	-	-	-	-
Stock Changes	-3609	-250	-	1460	-	-909	217	-1598	-	-	-
DOMESTIC SUPPLY	**36243**	**45856**	**-**	**246910**	**10**	**14943**	**17247**	**100636**	**-**	**4207**	**1019**
Transfers	-	-	-	-	-	-	-	-	-	6931	-
Statistical Differences	-	-298	-	-	-	-178	-	426	-	-	-
TRANSFORMATION	**36243**	**37832**	**-**	**234981**	**-**	**3924**	**2669**	**101062**	**-**	**11138**	**1019**
Electricity Plants	16973	35790	-	191128	-	-	1493	-	-	-	-
CHP Plants	-	-	-	-	-	-	-	-	-	-	-
Heat Plants	-	772	-	2579	-	5	547	-	-	-	-
Transfer to Gases	-	581	-	-	-	3836	392	-	-	-	-
Transfer to Solids	19270	689	-	41274	-	83	237	-	-	-	-
Petroleum Refineries	-	-	-	-	-	-	-	101062	-	11138	1019
Petrochemical Industry	-	-	-	-	-	-	-	-	-	-	-
Liquefaction	-	-	-	-	-	-	-	-	-	-	-
Other Transformation Sector	-	-	-	-	-	-	-	-	-	-	-
ENERGY SECTOR	**-**	**74**	**-**	**1747**	**-**	**7**	**277**	**-**	**-**	**-**	**-**
Coal Mines	-	69	-	-	-	-	-	-	-	-	-
Oil and Gas Extraction	-	-	-	-	-	-	-	-	-	-	-
Petroleum Refineries	-	-	-	146	-	-	36	-	-	-	-
Electricity, CHP+Heat plants	-	-	-	-	-	-	-	-	-	-	-
Pumped Storage (Elec.)	-	-	-	-	-	-	-	-	-	-	-
Other Energy Sector	-	5	-	1601	-	7	241	-	-	-	-
Distribution Losses	-	-	-	-	-	-	-	-	-	-	-
FINAL CONSUMPTION	**-**	**7652**	**-**	**10182**	**10**	**10834**	**14301**	**-**	**-**	**-**	**-**
INDUSTRY SECTOR	**-**	**6568**	**-**	**7816**	**-**	**9048**	**4017**	**-**	**-**	**-**	**-**
Iron and Steel	-	1345	-	-	-	8304	-	-	-	-	-
Chemical and Petrochemical	-	1845	-	-	-	27	-	-	-	-	-
of which: Feedstocks	-	-	-	-	-	-	-	-	-	-	-
Non-Ferrous Metals	-	78	-	-	-	246	-	-	-	-	-
Non-Metallic Minerals	-	1786	-	-	-	247	-	-	-	-	-
Transport Equipment	-	90	-	-	-	24	-	-	-	-	-
Machinery	-	200	-	-	-	72	-	-	-	-	-
Mining and Quarrying	-	107	-	-	-	7	-	-	-	-	-
Food and Tobacco	-	393	-	-	-	72	-	-	-	-	-
Paper, Pulp and Print	-	580	-	-	-	43	-	-	-	-	-
Wood and Wood Products	-	23	-	-	-	1	-	-	-	-	-
Construction	-	-	-	-	-	-	-	-	-	-	-
Textile and Leather	-	121	-	-	-	5	-	-	-	-	-
Non-specified	-	-	-	7816	-	-	4017	-	-	-	-
TRANSPORT SECTOR	**-**	**20**	**-**	**-**	**-**	**-**	**-**	**-**	**-**	**-**	**-**
International Civil Aviation	-	-	-	-	-	-	-	-	-	-	-
Domestic Air	-	-	-	-	-	-	-	-	-	-	-
Road	-	-	-	-	-	-	-	-	-	-	-
Rail	-	20	-	-	-	-	-	-	-	-	-
Pipeline Transport	-	-	-	-	-	-	-	-	-	-	-
Internal Navigation	-	-	-	-	-	-	-	-	-	-	-
Non-specified	-	-	-	-	-	-	-	-	-	-	-
OTHER SECTORS	**-**	**967**	**-**	**2309**	**10**	**805**	**10032**	**-**	**-**	**-**	**-**
Agriculture	-	80	-	300	-	50	400	-	-	-	-
Commerce and Publ. Serv.	-	377	-	1863	-	170	2300	-	-	-	-
Residential	-	281	-	-	10	550	6583	-	-	-	-
Non-specified	-	229	-	146	-	35	749	-	-	-	-
NON-ENERGY USE	**-**	**97**	**-**	**57**	**-**	**981**	**252**	**-**	**-**	**-**	**-**
in Industry/Transf./Energy	-	97	-	57	-	981	252	-	-	-	-
in Transport	-	-	-	-	-	-	-	-	-	-	-
in Other Sectors	-	-	-	-	-	-	-	-	-	-	-

Germany / Allemagne : 1992

SUPPLY AND CONSUMPTION / APPROVISIONNEMENT ET DEMANDE	Oil cont. / Pétrole cont. (1000 tonnes)										
	Refinery Gas / Gaz de raffinerie	LPG + Ethane / GPL + éthane	Motor Gasoline / Essence moteur	Aviation Gasoline / Essence aviation	Jet Fuel / Carbu-réacteur	Kerosene / Kérosène	Gas/Diesel / Gazole	Heavy Fuel Oil / Fioul lourd	Naphtha / Naphta	Pétrol. Coke / Coke de pétrole	Other Prod. / Autres prod.
Production	3710	2655	25330	-	2219	29	45527	14162	7588	1561	9064
From Other Sources	-	-	-	-	-	-	-	-	-	-	-
Imports	-	1000	9978	33	3269	36	19465	3961	5927	1178	1182
Exports	-	-553	-2627	-5	-80	-	-3528	-4421	-442	-522	-1156
Intl. Marine Bunkers	-	-	-	-	-	-	-444	-1317	-	-	-56
Stock Changes	1	13	-522	-	-95	3	-700	21	-21	12	-108
DOMESTIC SUPPLY	**3711**	**3115**	**32159**	**28**	**5313**	**68**	**60320**	**12406**	**13052**	**2229**	**8926**
Transfers	32	-201	-1177	-	-109	-37	-814	-1988	-386	-5	-1991
Statistical Differences	9	52	448	2	-58	-8	1411	2	67	2	44
TRANSFORMATION	**167**	**251**	**-**	**-**	**-**	**-**	**1144**	**3274**	**3188**	**877**	**29**
Electricity Plants	56	-	-	-	-	-	845	2055	-	-	-
CHP Plants	-	-	-	-	-	-	-	532	-	-	-
Heat Plants	-	8	-	-	-	-	-	260	-	-	-
Transfer to Gases	-	25	-	-	-	-	1	-	35	-	-
Transfer to Solids	-	-	-	-	-	-	-	-	-	877	-
Petroleum Refineries	-	-	-	-	-	-	-	-	-	-	-
Petrochemical Industry	111	218	-	-	-	-	298	427	3153	-	-
Liquefaction	-	-	-	-	-	-	-	-	-	-	-
Other Transformation Sector	-	-	-	-	-	-	-	-	-	-	29
ENERGY SECTOR	**3182**	**73**	**-**	**-**	**-**	**-**	**101**	**1515**	**27**	**553**	**577**
Coal Mines	-	-	-	-	-	-	52	23	-	-	-
Oil and Gas Extraction	-	-	-	-	-	-	-	-	-	-	-
Petroleum Refineries	3168	73	-	-	-	-	47	1481	27	553	577
Electricity, CHP+Heat plants	-	-	-	-	-	-	-	-	-	-	-
Pumped Storage (Elec.)	-	-	-	-	-	-	-	-	-	-	-
Other Energy Sector	14	-	-	-	-	-	2	11	-	-	-
Distribution Losses	-	-	-	-	-	-	-	-	-	-	-
FINAL CONSUMPTION	**403**	**2642**	**31430**	**30**	**5146**	**23**	**59672**	**5631**	**9518**	**796**	**6373**
INDUSTRY SECTOR	**403**	**1631**	**-**	**-**	**-**	**15**	**4808**	**5463**	**9518**	**791**	**-**
Iron and Steel	-	70	-	-	-	-	142	1186	-	-	-
Chemical and Petrochemical	333	873	-	-	-	8	1414	2061	9518	-	-
of which: Feedstocks	333	873	-	-	-	-	1196	1717	9518	-	-
Non-Ferrous Metals	-	58	-	-	-	-	100	42	-	-	-
Non-Metallic Minerals	-	223	-	-	-	6	310	742	-	310	-
Transport Equipment	-	49	-	-	-	-	247	41	-	-	-
Machinery	-	88	-	-	-	-	899	107	-	-	-
Mining and Quarrying	-	-	-	-	-	-	85	58	-	-	-
Food and Tobacco	-	92	-	-	-	-	801	537	-	-	-
Paper, Pulp and Print	51	30	-	-	-	-	197	387	-	-	-
Wood and Wood Products	-	5	-	-	-	-	295	76	-	-	-
Construction	-	-	-	-	-	-	-	-	-	-	-
Textile and Leather	-	38	-	-	-	-	197	147	-	-	-
Non-specified	19	105	-	-	-	1	121	79	-	481	-
TRANSPORT SECTOR	**-**	**5**	**31205**	**30**	**5146**	**-**	**21042**	**-**	**-**	**-**	**-**
International Civil Aviation	-	-	-	-	4785	-	-	-	-	-	-
Domestic Air	-	-	-	30	361	-	-	-	-	-	-
Road	-	3	31205	-	-	-	19533	-	-	-	-
Rail	-	2	-	-	-	-	810	-	-	-	-
Pipeline Transport	-	-	-	-	-	-	-	-	-	-	-
Internal Navigation	-	-	-	-	-	-	699	-	-	-	-
Non-specified	-	-	-	-	-	-	-	-	-	-	-
OTHER SECTORS	**-**	**1006**	**225**	**-**	**-**	**8**	**33822**	**168**	**-**	**-**	**-**
Agriculture	-	-	-	-	-	-	2130	-	-	-	-
Commerce and Publ. Serv.	-	481	-	-	-	3	11500	168	-	-	-
Residential	-	525	225	-	-	-	20192	-	-	-	-
Non-specified	-	-	-	-	-	5	-	-	-	-	-
NON-ENERGY USE	**-**	**-**	**-**	**-**	**-**	**-**	**-**	**-**	**-**	**5**	**6373**
in Industry/Transf./Energy	-	-	-	-	-	-	-	-	-	5	5960
in Transport	-	-	-	-	-	-	-	-	-	-	408
in Other Sectors	-	-	-	-	-	-	-	-	-	-	5

INTERNATIONAL ENERGY AGENCY

Germany / Allemagne : 1992

CONSUMPTION APPROVISIONNEMENT ET DEMANDE	Gas / Gaz (TJ)				Combust. Renew. & Waste / En. Re. Comb. & Déchets (TJ)				(GWh)	(TJ)
	Natural Gas Gaz naturel	Gas Works Usines à gaz	Coke Ovens Cokeries	Blast Furnaces Hauts fourneaux	Solid Biomass & Anim. Prod. Biomasse solide & prod. anim.	Gas/Liquids from Biomass Gaz/Liquides tirés de biomasse	Municipal Waste Déchets urbains	Industrial Waste Déchets industriels	Electricity Electricité	Heat Chaleur
Production	638317	64001	126021	164771	51563	-	39000	11000	537134	350000
From Other Sources	-	-	-	-	-	-	-	-	-	-
Imports	2115799	-	-	-	-	-	-	-	28418	-
Exports	-52041	-198	-	-	-	-	-	-	-33738	-
Intl. Marine Bunkers	-	-	-	-	-	-	-	-	-	-
Stock Changes	-59731	3564	-	-	-	-	-	-	-	-
DOMESTIC SUPPLY	**2642344**	**67367**	**126021**	**164771**	**51563**	**-**	**39000**	**11000**	**531814**	**350000**
Transfers	-	-	-	-	-	-	-	-	-	-
Statistical Differences	50536	-	-	-	-	-	-	-	-	-
TRANSFORMATION	**628327**	**630**	**22900**	**57127**	**8497**	**-**	**39000**	**11000**		**-**
Electricity Plants	307737	-	22900	57123	7956	-	39000	11000		
CHP Plants	129977	-			-	-	-	-		
Heat Plants	130183	630	-	-	-	-	-	-		
Transfer to Gases	59347	-	-	-	-	-	-	-		
Transfer to Solids	1083	-	-	4	541	-	-	-		
Petroleum Refineries	-	-	-	-	-	-	-	-		
Petrochemical Industry	-	-	-	-	-	-	-	-		
Liquefaction	-	-	-	-	-	-	-	-		
Other Transformation Sector	-	-	-	-	-	-	-	-		
ENERGY SECTOR	**69872**	**1404**	**42739**	**17343**	**-**	**-**	**-**	**-**	**68769**	**6000**
Coal Mines	-	-	2376	-	-	-	-	-	6523	-
Oil and Gas Extraction	24220	-	-	-	-	-	-	-	495	-
Petroleum Refineries	13399	288	5473	-	-	-	-	-	6295	-
Electricity, CHP+Heat plants	-	-	-	-	-	-	-	-	38688	-
Pumped Storage (Elec.)	-	-	-	-	-	-	-	-	5129	-
Other Energy Sector	32253	1116	34890	17343	-	-	-	-	11639	6000
Distribution Losses	26694	720	90	12712	-	-	-	-	12119	25000
FINAL CONSUMPTION	**1967987**	**64613**	**60292**	**77589**	**43066**	**-**	**-**	**-**	**450926**	**319000**
INDUSTRY SECTOR	**858877**	**11144**	**59572**	**77589**	**5129**	**-**	**-**	**-**	**211912**	**64000**
Iron and Steel	106773	1764	44162	77589	-	-	-	-	25359	2600
Chemical and Petrochemical	303596	1026	4987	-	-	-	-	-	53899	15000
of which: Feedstocks	74439	-	-	-	-	-	-	-	-	-
Non-Ferrous Metals	28457	360	936	-	-	-	-	-	17792	-
Non-Metallic Minerals	108647	2701	1674	-	-	-	-	-	14098	-
Transport Equipment	63471	522	306	-	-	-	-	-	13870	-
Machinery	81517	2485	4177	-	-	-	-	-	8224	19000
Mining and Quarrying	13470	-	-	-	-	-	-	-	5114	-
Food and Tobacco	76637	1836	1296	-	-	-	-	-	13137	-
Paper, Pulp and Print	41539	108	1260	-	2199	-	-	-	17364	1600
Wood and Wood Products	2573	108	18	-	2930	-	-	-	3757	-
Construction	-	-	-	-	-	-	-	-	1141	-
Textile and Leather	24228	234	756	-	-	-	-	-	6289	-
Non-specified	7969	-	-	-	-	-	-	-	31868	25800
TRANSPORT SECTOR	**-**	**-**	**-**	**-**	**-**	**-**	**-**	**-**	**14895**	**-**
International Civil Aviation	-	-	-	-	-	-	-	-		-
Domestic Air	-	-	-	-	-	-	-	-		-
Road	-	-	-	-	-	-	-	-		-
Rail	-	-	-	-	-	-	-	-	14895	-
Pipeline Transport	-	-	-	-	-	-	-	-		-
Internal Navigation	-	-	-	-	-	-	-	-		-
Non-specified	-	-	-	-	-	-	-	-	-	-
OTHER SECTORS	**1109110**	**53469**	**720**	**-**	**37937**	**-**	**-**	**-**	**224119**	**255000**
Agriculture	9137	216	-	-	-	-	-	-	8755	-
Commerce and Publ. Serv.	247361	12620	-	-	-	-	-	-	92561	-
Residential	762320	40633	720	-	37937	-	-	-	122803	140000
Non-specified	90292	-	-	-	-	-	-	-	-	115000
NON-ENERGY USE	**-**	**-**	**-**	**-**	**-**	**-**	**-**	**-**	**-**	**-**
in Industry/Transf./Energy	-	-	-	-	-	-	-	-	-	-
in Transport	-	-	-	-	-	-	-	-	-	-
in Other Sectors	-	-	-	-	-	-	-	-	-	-

Germany / Allemagne : 1993

SUPPLY AND CONSUMPTION	Coal / *Charbon* (1000 tonnes)							Oil / *Pétrole* (1000 tonnes)			
	Coking Coal	Steam Coal	Sub-Bit. Coal	Lignite	Peat	Oven and Gas Coke	Pat. Fuel and BKB	Crude Oil	NGL	Feedstocks	Additives
APPROVISIONNEMENT ET DEMANDE	*Charbon à coke*	*Charbon vapeur*	*Charbon sous-bit.*	*Lignite*	*Tourbe*	*Coke de four/gaz*	*Agg./briq. de lignite*	*Pétrole brut*	*LGN*	*Produits d'aliment.*	*Additifs*
Production	34653	29521	-	221802	190	12265	14645	3064	-	-	-
From Other Sources	-	-	-	-	-	-	-	84	-	4276	1026
Imports	987	12103	-	2991	-	2070	444	99584	-	-	-
Exports	-71	-899	-	-1	-180	-640	-971	-108	-	-	-
Intl. Marine Bunkers	-	-	-	-	-	-	-	-	-	-	-
Stock Changes	-1563	3153	-	1294	-	-94	14	395	-	-	-
DOMESTIC SUPPLY	**34006**	**43878**	**-**	**226086**	**10**	**13601**	**14132**	**103019**	**-**	**4276**	**1026**
Transfers	-	-	-	-	-	-	-	-	-	9170	-
Statistical Differences	-	1260	-	-	-	-160	5	-47	-	-	-
TRANSFORMATION	**34006**	**38599**	**-**	**218983**	**-**	**3509**	**1732**	**102972**	**-**	**13446**	**1026**
Electricity Plants	18645	36671	-	181152	-	-	1059	-	-	-	-
CHP Plants	-	-	-	-	-	-	-	-	-	-	-
Heat Plants	-	780	-	2836	-	11	457	-	-	-	-
Transfer to Gases	-	550	-	-	-	3498	-	-	-	-	-
Transfer to Solids	15361	598	-	34995	-	-	216	-	-	-	-
Petroleum Refineries	-	-	-	-	-	-	-	102972	-	13446	1026
Petrochemical Industry	-	-	-	-	-	-	-	-	-	-	-
Liquefaction	-	-	-	-	-	-	-	-	-	-	-
Other Transformation Sector	-	-	-	-	-	-	-	-	-	-	-
ENERGY SECTOR	**-**	**64**	**-**	**1609**	**-**	**11**	**115**	**-**	**-**	**-**	**-**
Coal Mines	-	60	-	-	-	-	-	-	-	-	-
Oil and Gas Extraction	-	-	-	-	-	-	-	-	-	-	-
Petroleum Refineries	-	-	-	-	-	-	-	-	-	-	-
Electricity, CHP+Heat plants	-	-	-	-	-	-	-	-	-	-	-
Pumped Storage (Elec.)	-	-	-	-	-	-	-	-	-	-	-
Other Energy Sector	-	4	-	1609	-	11	115	-	-	-	-
Distribution Losses	-	-	-	-	-	-	-	-	-	-	-
FINAL CONSUMPTION	**-**	**6475**	**-**	**5494**	**10**	**9921**	**12290**	**-**	**-**	**-**	**-**
INDUSTRY SECTOR	**-**	**5572**	**-**	**4001**	**-**	**8280**	**3514**	**-**	**-**	**-**	**-**
Iron and Steel	-	1191	-	-	-	7574	-	-	-	-	-
Chemical and Petrochemical	-	1611	-	-	-	20	-	-	-	-	-
of which: Feedstocks	-	-	-	-	-	-	-	-	-	-	-
Non-Ferrous Metals	-	59	-	-	-	201	-	-	-	-	-
Non-Metallic Minerals	-	1595	-	-	-	280	-	-	-	-	-
Transport Equipment	-	77	-	-	-	18	-	-	-	-	-
Machinery	-	94	-	-	-	50	-	-	-	-	-
Mining and Quarrying	-	67	-	-	-	8	-	-	-	-	-
Food and Tobacco	-	272	-	-	-	76	-	-	-	-	-
Paper, Pulp and Print	-	521	-	-	-	45	-	-	-	-	-
Wood and Wood Products	-	16	-	-	-	-	-	-	-	-	-
Construction	-	-	-	-	-	-	-	-	-	-	-
Textile and Leather	-	69	-	-	-	8	-	-	-	-	-
Non-specified	-	-	-	4001	-	-	3514	-	-	-	-
TRANSPORT SECTOR	**-**	**16**	**-**	**-**	**-**	**-**	**-**	**-**	**-**	**-**	**-**
International Civil Aviation	-	-	-	-	-	-	-	-	-	-	-
Domestic Air	-	-	-	-	-	-	-	-	-	-	-
Road	-	-	-	-	-	-	-	-	-	-	-
Rail	-	16	-	-	-	-	-	-	-	-	-
Pipeline Transport	-	-	-	-	-	-	-	-	-	-	-
Internal Navigation	-	-	-	-	-	-	-	-	-	-	-
Non-specified	-	-	-	-	-	-	-	-	-	-	-
OTHER SECTORS	**-**	**796**	**-**	**1440**	**10**	**781**	**8574**	**-**	**-**	**-**	**-**
Agriculture	-	70	-	200	-	50	350	-	-	-	-
Commerce and Publ. Serv.	-	345	-	1117	-	172	2000	-	-	-	-
Residential	-	221	-	-	10	540	5758	-	-	-	-
Non-specified	-	160	-	123	-	19	466	-	-	-	-
NON-ENERGY USE	**-**	**91**	**-**	**53**	**-**	**860**	**202**	**-**	**-**	**-**	**-**
in Industry/Transf./Energy	-	91	-	53	-	860	202	-	-	-	-
in Transport	-	-	-	-	-	-	-	-	-	-	-
in Other Sectors	-	-	-	-	-	-	-	-	-	-	-

Germany / Allemagne : 1993

SUPPLY AND CONSUMPTION / APPROVISIONNEMENT ET DEMANDE	Oil cont. / Pétrole cont. (1000 tonnes)										
	Refinery Gas / Gaz de raffinerie	LPG + Ethane / GPL + éthane	Motor Gasoline / Essence moteur	Aviation Gasoline / Essence aviation	Jet Fuel / Carbu-réacteur	Kerosene / Kérosène	Gas/Diesel / Gazole	Heavy Fuel Oil / Fioul lourd	Naphtha / Naphta	Pétrol. Coke / Coke de pétrole	Other Prod. / Autres prod.
Production	3974	2873	26848	-	2579	16	47324	14318	8393	1626	8178
From Other Sources	-	-	-	-	-	-	-	-	-	-	-
Imports	-	957	8533	32	3126	5	19737	5382	5556	1214	1199
Exports	-	-633	-3501	-2	-65	-	-3599	-4787	-581	-479	-1162
Intl. Marine Bunkers	-	-	-	-	-	-	-491	-1725	-	-	-55
Stock Changes	-2	2	78	-1	-71	6	-521	-65	19	29	98
DOMESTIC SUPPLY	**3972**	**3199**	**31958**	**29**	**5569**	**27**	**62450**	**13123**	**13387**	**2390**	**8258**
Transfers	-44	-184	-1152	-	-116	6	-1036	-3781	-842	-1	-1798
Statistical Differences	69	157	722	-	-50	-11	1763	-121	457	-32	-24
TRANSFORMATION	**271**	**287**	**-**	**-**	**-**	**-**	**1225**	**2678**	**3276**	**822**	**31**
Electricity Plants	44	1	-	-	-	-	941	1354	-	-	-
CHP Plants	-	-	-	-	-	-	-	308	-	-	-
Heat Plants	113	7	-	-	-	-	-	289	-	-	-
Transfer to Gases	-	19	-	-	-	-	1	346	38	-	-
Transfer to Solids	-	-	-	-	-	-	-	-	-	822	-
Petroleum Refineries	-	-	-	-	-	-	-	-	-	-	-
Petrochemical Industry	114	260	-	-	-	-	283	381	3238		-
Liquefaction	-	-	-	-	-	-	-	-	-		-
Other Transformation Sector	-	-	-	-	-	-	-	-	-	-	31
ENERGY SECTOR	**3356**	**103**	**-**	**-**	**-**	**-**	**113**	**1576**	**16**	**629**	**620**
Coal Mines	-	-	-	-	-	-	51	15	-	-	-
Oil and Gas Extraction	-	-	-	-	-	-	-	-	-	-	-
Petroleum Refineries	3356	103	-	-	-	-	48	1552	16	629	620
Electricity, CHP+Heat plants	-	-	-	-	-	-	-	-	-	-	-
Pumped Storage (Elec.)	-	-	-	-	-	-	-	-	-	-	-
Other Energy Sector	-	-	-	-	-	-	14	9	-	-	-
Distribution Losses	-	-	-	-	-	-	-	-	-	-	-
FINAL CONSUMPTION	**370**	**2782**	**31528**	**29**	**5403**	**22**	**61839**	**4967**	**9710**	**906**	**5785**
INDUSTRY SECTOR	**370**	**1486**	**-**	**-**	**-**	**15**	**5005**	**4884**	**9710**	**906**	**-**
Iron and Steel	-	24	-	-	-	-	148	851	-	-	-
Chemical and Petrochemical	363	782	-	-	-	9	1167	2143	9710	-	-
of which: Feedstocks	*363*	*782*	-	-	-	-	*1133*	*1522*	*9710*	-	-
Non-Ferrous Metals	-	31	-	-	-	-	103	35	-	-	-
Non-Metallic Minerals	-	192	-	-	-	5	403	695	-	318	-
Transport Equipment	-	58	-	-	-	-	247	24	-	-	-
Machinery	-	111	-	-	-	-	800	73	-	-	-
Mining and Quarrying	-	-	-	-	-	-	92	10	-	-	-
Food and Tobacco	-	104	-	-	-	-	773	531	-	-	-
Paper, Pulp and Print	7	37	-	-	-	-	158	324	-	-	-
Wood and Wood Products	-	6	-	-	-	-	148	83	-	-	-
Construction	-	-	-	-	-	-	610	-	-	-	-
Textile and Leather	-	17	-	-	-	-	184	95	-	-	-
Non-specified	-	124	-	-	-	1	172	20	-	588	-
TRANSPORT SECTOR	**-**	**9**	**31308**	**29**	**5403**	**-**	**22406**	**-**	**-**	**-**	**-**
International Civil Aviation	-	-	-	-	5035	-	-	-	-	-	-
Domestic Air	-	-	-	29	368	-	-	-	-	-	-
Road	-	4	31308	-	-	-	20907	-	-	-	-
Rail	-	5	-	-	-	-	790	-	-	-	-
Pipeline Transport	-	-	-	-	-	-	-	-	-	-	-
Internal Navigation	-	-	-	-	-	-	709	-	-	-	-
Non-specified	-	-	-	-	-	-	-	-	-	-	-
OTHER SECTORS	**-**	**1287**	**220**	**-**	**-**	**7**	**34428**	**25**	**-**	**-**	**-**
Agriculture	-	-	-	-	-	-	1670	-	-	-	-
Commerce and Publ. Serv.	-	292	-	-	-	2	10990	25	-	-	-
Residential	-	995	220	-	-	-	21768	-	-	-	-
Non-specified	-	-	-	-	-	5	-	-	-	-	-
NON-ENERGY USE	**-**	**-**	**-**	**-**	**-**	**-**	**-**	**58**	**-**	**-**	**5785**
in Industry/Transf./Energy	-	-	-	-	-	-	-	58	-	-	5361
in Transport	-	-	-	-	-	-	-	-	-	-	420
in Other Sectors	-	-	-	-	-	-	-	-	-	-	4

Germany / Allemagne : 1993

CONSUMPTION APPROVISIONNEMENT ET DEMANDE	Gas / Gaz (TJ)				Combust. Renew. & Waste / En. Re. Comb. & Déchets (TJ)				(GWh)	(TJ)
	Natural Gas Gaz naturel	Gas Works Usines à gaz	Coke Ovens Cokeries	Blast Furnaces Hauts fourneaux	Solid Biomass & Anim. Prod. Biomasse solide & prod. anim.	Gas/Liquids from Biomass Gaz/Liquides tirés de biomasse	Municipal Waste Déchets urbains	Industrial Waste Déchets industriels	Electricity Electricité	Heat Chaleur
Production	639745	36186	104993	154538	53700	-	39000	11000	525721	350000
From Other Sources	-	-	-	-	-	-	-	-	-	-
Imports	2265243	-	-	-	-	-	-	-	33628	-
Exports	-60998	-180	-	-	-	-	-	-	-32758	-
Intl. Marine Bunkers	-	-	-	-	-	-	-	-	-	-
Stock Changes	-67328	2484	-	-	-	-	-	-	-	-
DOMESTIC SUPPLY	**2776662**	**38490**	**104993**	**154538**	**53700**	**-**	**39000**	**11000**	**526591**	**350000**
Transfers	-	-	-	-	-	-	-	-	-	-
Statistical Differences	95284	-	3547	-	-	-	-	-	-	-
TRANSFORMATION	**672403**	**-**	**16725**	**52681**	**8600**	**-**	**39000**	**11000**	**-**	**-**
Electricity Plants	322272	-	16725	52681	8060	-	39000	11000	-	-
CHP Plants	115978	-	-	-	-	-	-	-	-	-
Heat Plants	194916	-	-	-	-	-	-	-	-	-
Transfer to Gases	37554	-	-	-	-	-	-	-	-	-
Transfer to Solids	1683	-	-	-	540	-	-	-	-	-
Petroleum Refineries	-	-	-	-	-	-	-	-	-	-
Petrochemical Industry	-	-	-	-	-	-	-	-	-	-
Liquefaction	-	-	-	-	-	-	-	-	-	-
Other Transformation Sector	-	-	-	-	-	-	-	-	-	-
ENERGY SECTOR	**75643**	**162**	**31217**	**15986**	**-**	**-**	**-**	**-**	**64284**	**6000**
Coal Mines	-	-	1620	-	-	-	-	-	6022	-
Oil and Gas Extraction	27323	-	-	-	-	-	-	-	509	-
Petroleum Refineries	11601	-	2232	-	-	-	-	-	6428	-
Electricity, CHP+Heat plants	-	-	-	-	-	-	-	-	38060	-
Pumped Storage (Elec.)	-	-	-	-	-	-	-	-	5126	-
Other Energy Sector	36719	162	27365	15986	-	-	-	-	8139	6000
Distribution Losses	19414	324	54	10342	-	-	-	-	16241	25000
FINAL CONSUMPTION	**2104486**	**38004**	**60544**	**75529**	**45100**	**-**	**-**	**-**	**446066**	**319000**
INDUSTRY SECTOR	**870132**	**4933**	**59608**	**75529**	**5100**	**-**	**-**	**-**	**202200**	**64000**
Iron and Steel	95242	1891	44575	75529	-	-	-	-	20435	2600
Chemical and Petrochemical	321622	594	3853	-	-	-	-	-	57595	15000
of which: Feedstocks	61673	-	-	-	-	-	-	-	-	-
Non-Ferrous Metals	26530	72	270	-	-	-	-	-	21488	-
Non-Metallic Minerals	116016	504	4915	-	-	-	-	-	10581	-
Transport Equipment	59982	126	180	-	-	-	-	-	12518	-
Machinery	77883	720	3961	-	-	-	-	-	8733	19000
Mining and Quarrying	12518	-	-	-	-	-	-	-	5353	-
Food and Tobacco	75227	738	1152	-	-	-	-	-	12731	-
Paper, Pulp and Print	51096	54	450	-	2200	-	-	-	16504	1600
Wood and Wood Products	2313	36	-	-	2900	-	-	-	5145	-
Construction	-	-	-	-	-	-	-	-	1124	-
Textile and Leather	24157	198	252	-	-	-	-	-	5395	-
Non-specified	7546	-	-	-	-	-	-	-	24598	25800
TRANSPORT SECTOR	**-**	**-**	**-**	**-**	**-**	**-**	**-**	**-**	**14997**	**-**
International Civil Aviation	-	-	-	-	-	-	-	-	-	-
Domestic Air	-	-	-	-	-	-	-	-	-	-
Road	-	-	-	-	-	-	-	-	-	-
Rail	-	-	-	-	-	-	-	-	14997	-
Pipeline Transport	-	-	-	-	-	-	-	-	-	-
Internal Navigation	-	-	-	-	-	-	-	-	-	-
Non-specified	-	-	-	-	-	-	-	-	-	-
OTHER SECTORS	**1234354**	**33071**	**936**	**-**	**40000**	**-**	**-**	**-**	**228869**	**255000**
Agriculture	10333	108	-	-	-	-	-	-	8712	-
Commerce and Publ. Serv.	263598	10081	-	-	-	-	-	-	94064	-
Residential	862265	22882	936	-	40000	-	-	-	126093	140000
Non-specified	98158	-	-	-	-	-	-	-	-	115000
NON-ENERGY USE	**-**	**-**	**-**	**-**	**-**	**-**	**-**	**-**	**-**	**-**
in Industry/Transf./Energy	-	-	-	-	-	-	-	-	-	-
in Transport	-	-	-	-	-	-	-	-	-	-
in Other Sectors	-	-	-	-	-	-	-	-	-	-

Greece / Grèce : 1992

SUPPLY AND CONSUMPTION *APPROVISIONNEMENT ET DEMANDE*	Coal / *Charbon* (1000 tonnes)							Oil / *Pétrole* (1000 tonnes)			
	Coking Coal *Charbon à coke*	Steam Coal *Charbon vapeur*	Sub-Bit. Coal *Charbon sous-bit.*	Lignite *Lignite*	Peat *Tourbe*	Oven and Gas Coke *Coke de four/gaz*	Pat. Fuel and BKB *Agg./briq. de lignite*	Crude Oil *Pétrole brut*	NGL *LGN*	Feedstocks *Produits d'aliment.*	Additives *Additifs*
Production	-	-	-	55051	-	-	62	653	34	-	-
From Other Sources	-	-	-	-	-	-	-	-	-	-	-
Imports	-	2132	-	-	-	22	-	13967	-	2270	41
Exports	-	-	-	-14	-	-	-	-470	-24	-	-
Intl. Marine Bunkers	-	-	-	-	-	-	-	-	-	-	-
Stock Changes	-	-215	-	-544	-	-3	-19	-727	-	-87	-
DOMESTIC SUPPLY	-	**1917**	-	**54493**	-	**19**	**43**	**13423**	**10**	**2183**	**41**
Transfers	-	-	-	-	-	-	-	-	-	416	-
Statistical Differences	-	-	-	-	-	-	-	-	-	-	-
TRANSFORMATION	-	**529**	-	**53993**	-	-	-	**13423**	**10**	**2599**	**41**
Electricity Plants	-	529	-	53790	-	-	-	-	-	-	-
CHP Plants	-	-	-	-	-	-	-	-	-	-	-
Heat Plants	-	-	-	-	-	-	-	-	-	-	-
Transfer to Gases	-	-	-	-	-	-	-	-	-	-	-
Transfer to Solids	-	-	-	203	-	-	-	-	-	-	-
Petroleum Refineries	-	-	-	-	-	-	-	13423	10	2599	41
Petrochemical Industry	-	-	-	-	-	-	-	-	-	-	-
Liquefaction	-	-	-	-	-	-	-	-	-	-	-
Other Transformation Sector	-	-	-	-	-	-	-	-	-	-	-
ENERGY SECTOR	-	-	-	-	-	-	-	-	-	-	-
Coal Mines	-	-	-	-	-	-	-	-	-	-	-
Oil and Gas Extraction	-	-	-	-	-	-	-	-	-	-	-
Petroleum Refineries	-	-	-	-	-	-	-	-	-	-	-
Electricity, CHP+Heat plants	-	-	-	-	-	-	-	-	-	-	-
Pumped Storage (Elec.)	-	-	-	-	-	-	-	-	-	-	-
Other Energy Sector	-	-	-	-	-	-	-	-	-	-	-
Distribution Losses	-	-	-	-	-	-	-	-	-	-	-
FINAL CONSUMPTION	-	**1388**	-	**500**	-	**19**	**43**	-	-	-	-
INDUSTRY SECTOR	-	**1384**	-	**379**	-	**19**	**1**	-	-	-	-
Iron and Steel	-	-	-	-	-	-	-	-	-	-	-
Chemical and Petrochemical	-	-	-	7	-	-	-	-	-	-	-
of which: Feedstocks	-	-	-	-	-	-	-	-	-	-	-
Non-Ferrous Metals	-	84	-	359	-	-	1	-	-	-	-
Non-Metallic Minerals	-	1300	-	13	-	-	-	-	-	-	-
Transport Equipment	-	-	-	-	-	-	-	-	-	-	-
Machinery	-	-	-	-	-	5	-	-	-	-	-
Mining and Quarrying	-	-	-	-	-	-	-	-	-	-	-
Food and Tobacco	-	-	-	-	-	14	-	-	-	-	-
Paper, Pulp and Print	-	-	-	-	-	-	-	-	-	-	-
Wood and Wood Products	-	-	-	-	-	-	-	-	-	-	-
Construction	-	-	-	-	-	-	-	-	-	-	-
Textile and Leather	-	-	-	-	-	-	-	-	-	-	-
Non-specified	-	-	-	-	-	-	-	-	-	-	-
TRANSPORT SECTOR	-	**2**	-	-	-	-	-	-	-	-	-
International Civil Aviation	-	-	-	-	-	-	-	-	-	-	-
Domestic Air	-	-	-	-	-	-	-	-	-	-	-
Road	-	-	-	-	-	-	-	-	-	-	-
Rail	-	2	-	-	-	-	-	-	-	-	-
Pipeline Transport	-	-	-	-	-	-	-	-	-	-	-
Internal Navigation	-	-	-	-	-	-	-	-	-	-	-
Non-specified	-	-	-	-	-	-	-	-	-	-	-
OTHER SECTORS	-	**2**	-	**121**	-	-	**42**	-	-	-	-
Agriculture	-	-	-	33	-	-	-	-	-	-	-
Commerce and Publ. Serv.	-	-	-	-	-	-	2	-	-	-	-
Residential	-	2	-	88	-	-	40	-	-	-	-
Non-specified	-	-	-	-	-	-	-	-	-	-	-
NON-ENERGY USE	-	-	-	-	-	-	-	-	-	-	-
in Industry/Transf./Energy	-	-	-	-	-	-	-	-	-	-	-
in Transport	-	-	-	-	-	-	-	-	-	-	-
in Other Sectors	-	-	-	-	-	-	-	-	-	-	-

Greece / Grèce : 1992

SUPPLY AND CONSUMPTION	Oil cont. / Pétrole cont. (1000 tonnes)										
	Refinery Gas	LPG + Ethane	Motor Gasoline	Aviation Gasoline	Jet Fuel	Kerosene	Gas/ Diesel	Heavy Fuel Oil	Naphtha	Pétrol. Coke	Other Prod.
APPROVISIONNEMENT ET DEMANDE	Gaz de raffinerie	GPL + éthane	Essence moteur	Essence aviation	Carbu- réacteur	Kérosène	Gazole	Fioul lourd	Naphta	Coke de pétrole	Autres prod.
Production	383	423	3581	-	1479	13	3786	5284	404	148	475
From Other Sources	-	-	-	-	-	-	-	-	-	-	-
Imports	-	2	345	2	372	-	2042	2040	280	269	60
Exports	-	-100	-1238	-	-759	-	-509	-1710	-335	-	-165
Intl. Marine Bunkers	-	-	-	-	-	-	-657	-2052	-	-	-41
Stock Changes	-	5	-171	-	88	3	99	121	-130	-82	92
DOMESTIC SUPPLY	**383**	**330**	**2517**	**2**	**1180**	**16**	**4761**	**3683**	**219**	**335**	**421**
Transfers	-	-	-	-	-	-	-	-287	-129	-	-
Statistical Differences	-	5	65	-	-	-	47	-143	-19	-	-66
TRANSFORMATION	**108**	**-**	**-**	**-**	**-**	**-**	**339**	**1564**	**19**	**-**	**-**
Electricity Plants	-	-	-	-	-	-	338	1506	-	-	-
CHP Plants	108	-	-	-	-	-	1	58	-	-	-
Heat Plants	-	-	-	-	-	-	-	-	-	-	-
Transfer to Gases	-	-	-	-	-	-	-	-	19	-	-
Transfer to Solids	-	-	-	-	-	-	-	-	-	-	-
Petroleum Refineries	-	-	-	-	-	-	-	-	-	-	-
Petrochemical Industry	-	-	-	-	-	-	-	-	-	-	-
Liquefaction	-	-	-	-	-	-	-	-	-	-	-
Other Transformation Sector	-	-	-	-	-	-	-	-	-	-	-
ENERGY SECTOR	**250**	**14**	**-**	**-**	**-**	**-**	**-**	**260**	**-**	**148**	**-**
Coal Mines	-	-	-	-	-	-	-	-	-	-	-
Oil and Gas Extraction	-	-	-	-	-	-	-	-	-	-	-
Petroleum Refineries	250	14	-	-	-	-	-	260	-	148	-
Electricity, CHP+Heat plants	-	-	-	-	-	-	-	-	-	-	-
Pumped Storage (Elec.)	-	-	-	-	-	-	-	-	-	-	-
Other Energy Sector	-	-	-	-	-	-	-	-	-	-	-
Distribution Losses	-	-	-	-	-	-	-	-	-	-	-
FINAL CONSUMPTION	**25**	**321**	**2582**	**2**	**1180**	**16**	**4469**	**1429**	**52**	**187**	**355**
INDUSTRY SECTOR	**25**	**148**	**-**	**-**	**-**	**-**	**290**	**1096**	**52**	**117**	**-**
Iron and Steel	-	-	-	-	-	-	20	97	-	-	-
Chemical and Petrochemical	25	27	-	-	-	-	11	43	52	-	-
of which: Feedstocks	-	-	-	-	-	-	-	-	52	-	-
Non-Ferrous Metals	-	-	-	-	-	-	24	161	-	-	-
Non-Metallic Minerals	-	-	-	-	-	-	31	188	-	117	-
Transport Equipment	-	-	-	-	-	-	2	-	-	-	-
Machinery	-	-	-	-	-	-	-	-	-	-	-
Mining and Quarrying	-	-	-	-	-	-	31	23	-	-	-
Food and Tobacco	-	-	-	-	-	-	33	255	-	-	-
Paper, Pulp and Print	-	-	-	-	-	-	10	80	-	-	-
Wood and Wood Products	-	-	-	-	-	-	-	2	-	-	-
Construction	-	-	-	-	-	-	1	26	-	-	-
Textile and Leather	-	-	-	-	-	-	15	108	-	-	-
Non-specified	-	121	-	-	-	-	112	113	-	-	-
TRANSPORT SECTOR	**-**	**42**	**2532**	**2**	**1180**	**-**	**1952**	**255**	**-**	**-**	**-**
International Civil Aviation	-	-	-	-	699	-	-	-	-	-	-
Domestic Air	-	-	-	2	481	-	-	-	-	-	-
Road	-	42	2532	-	-	-	1557	-	-	-	-
Rail	-	-	-	-	-	-	47	-	-	-	-
Pipeline Transport	-	-	-	-	-	-	-	-	-	-	-
Internal Navigation	-	-	-	-	-	-	348	255	-	-	-
Non-specified	-	-	-	-	-	-	-	-	-	-	-
OTHER SECTORS	**-**	**131**	**50**	**-**	**-**	**16**	**2227**	**78**	**-**	**-**	**-**
Agriculture	-	-	50	-	-	-	822	21	-	-	-
Commerce and Publ. Serv.	-	19	-	-	-	-	155	19	-	-	-
Residential	-	112	-	-	-	16	1250	38	-	-	-
Non-specified	-	-	-	-	-	-	-	-	-	-	-
NON-ENERGY USE	**-**	**-**	**-**	**-**	**-**	**-**	**-**	**-**	**-**	**70**	**355**
in Industry/Transf./Energy	-	-	-	-	-	-	-	-	-	70	276
in Transport	-	-	-	-	-	-	-	-	-	-	77
in Other Sectors	-	-	-	-	-	-	-	-	-	-	2

Greece / Grèce : 1992

CONSUMPTION	Gas / Gaz (TJ)				Combust. Renew. & Waste / En. Re. Comb. & Déchets (TJ)				(GWh)	(TJ)
APPROVISIONNEMENT ET DEMANDE	Natural Gas / Gaz naturel	Gas Works / Usines à gaz	Coke Ovens / Cokeries	Blast Furnaces / Hauts fourneaux	Solid Biomass & Anim. Prod. / Biomasse solide & prod. anim.	Gas/Liquids from Biomass / Gaz/Liquides tirés de biomasse	Municipal Waste / Déchets urbains	Industrial Waste / Déchets industriels	Electricity / Electricité	Heat / Chaleur
Production	5866	-	-	-	23023	-	-	1850	37410	-
From Other Sources	-	747	-	-	-	-	-	-	-	-
Imports	-	-	-	-	-	-	-	-	967	-
Exports	-	-	-	-	-	-	-	-	-362	-
Intl. Marine Bunkers	-	-	-	-	-	-	-	-	-	-
Stock Changes	-	-	-	-	-	-	-	-	-	-
DOMESTIC SUPPLY	**5866**	**747**	**-**	**-**	**23023**	**-**	**-**	**1850**	**38015**	**-**
Transfers	-	-	-	-	-	-	-	-	-	-
Statistical Differences	-	-24	-	-	-	-	-	-	-	-
TRANSFORMATION	**725**	**-**	**-**	**-**	**-**	**-**	**-**	**1850**	**-**	**-**
Electricity Plants	-	-	-	-	-	-	-	-	-	-
CHP Plants	725	-	-	-	-	-	-	1850	-	-
Heat Plants	-	-	-	-	-	-	-	-	-	-
Transfer to Gases	-	-	-	-	-	-	-	-	-	-
Transfer to Solids	-	-	-	-	-	-	-	-	-	-
Petroleum Refineries	-	-	-	-	-	-	-	-	-	-
Petrochemical Industry	-	-	-	-	-	-	-	-	-	-
Liquefaction	-	-	-	-	-	-	-	-	-	-
Other Transformation Sector	-	-	-	-	-	-	-	-	-	-
ENERGY SECTOR	**1056**	**-**	**-**	**-**	**-**	**-**	**-**	**-**	**4639**	**-**
Coal Mines	-	-	-	-	-	-	-	-	645	-
Oil and Gas Extraction	1056	-	-	-	-	-	-	-	-	-
Petroleum Refineries	-	-	-	-	-	-	-	-	678	-
Electricity, CHP+Heat plants	-	-	-	-	-	-	-	-	3051	-
Pumped Storage (Elec.)	-	-	-	-	-	-	-	-	265	-
Other Energy Sector	-	-	-	-	-	-	-	-	-	-
Distribution Losses	-	28	-	-	-	-	-	-	2675	-
FINAL CONSUMPTION	**4085**	**695**	**-**	**-**	**23023**	**-**	**-**	**-**	**30701**	**-**
INDUSTRY SECTOR	**4085**	**272**	**-**	**-**	**-**	**-**	**-**	**-**	**11746**	**-**
Iron and Steel	-	-	-	-	-	-	-	-	821	-
Chemical and Petrochemical	4085	15	-	-	-	-	-	-	1050	-
of which: Feedstocks	4085	-	-	-	-	-	-	-	-	-
Non-Ferrous Metals	-	-	-	-	-	-	-	-	3424	-
Non-Metallic Minerals	-	-	-	-	-	-	-	-	1802	-
Transport Equipment	-	-	-	-	-	-	-	-	160	-
Machinery	-	-	-	-	-	-	-	-	374	-
Mining and Quarrying	-	-	-	-	-	-	-	-	231	-
Food and Tobacco	-	131	-	-	-	-	-	-	797	-
Paper, Pulp and Print	-	67	-	-	-	-	-	-	469	-
Wood and Wood Products	-	-	-	-	-	-	-	-	113	-
Construction	-	2	-	-	-	-	-	-	20	-
Textile and Leather	-	57	-	-	-	-	-	-	952	-
Non-specified	-	-	-	-	-	-	-	-	1533	-
TRANSPORT SECTOR	**-**	**-**	**-**	**-**	**-**	**-**	**-**	**-**	**130**	**-**
International Civil Aviation	-	-	-	-	-	-	-	-	-	-
Domestic Air	-	-	-	-	-	-	-	-	-	-
Road	-	-	-	-	-	-	-	-	-	-
Rail	-	-	-	-	-	-	-	-	70	-
Pipeline Transport	-	-	-	-	-	-	-	-	-	-
Internal Navigation	-	-	-	-	-	-	-	-	-	-
Non-specified	-	-	-	-	-	-	-	-	60	-
OTHER SECTORS	**-**	**423**	**-**	**-**	**23023**	**-**	**-**	**-**	**18825**	**-**
Agriculture	-	-	-	-	-	-	-	-	1623	-
Commerce and Publ. Serv.	-	258	-	-	2303	-	-	-	6590	-
Residential	-	165	-	-	20720	-	-	-	10612	-
Non-specified	-	-	-	-	-	-	-	-	-	-
NON-ENERGY USE	**-**	**-**	**-**	**-**	**-**	**-**	**-**	**-**	**-**	**-**
in Industry/Transf./Energy	-	-	-	-	-	-	-	-	-	-
in Transport	-	-	-	-	-	-	-	-	-	-
in Other Sectors	-	-	-	-	-	-	-	-	-	-

Greece / Grèce : 1993

SUPPLY AND CONSUMPTION *APPROVISIONNEMENT ET DEMANDE*	Coal / *Charbon* (1000 tonnes)							Oil / *Pétrole* (1000 tonnes)			
	Coking Coal *Charbon à coke*	Steam Coal *Charbon vapeur*	Sub-Bit. Coal *Charbon sous-bit.*	Lignite *Lignite*	Peat *Tourbe*	Oven and Gas Coke *Coke de four/gaz*	Pat. Fuel and BKB *Agg./briq. de lignite*	Crude Oil *Pétrole brut*	NGL *LGN*	Feedstocks *Produits d'aliment.*	Additives *Additifs*
Production	-	-	-	54800	-	-	57	537	25	-	-
From Other Sources	-	-	-	-	-	-	-	-	-	-	-
Imports	-	1337	-	-	-	21	-	11777	-	2470	24
Exports	-	-	-	-	-	-	-	-723	-17	-	-
Intl. Marine Bunkers	-	-	-	-	-	-	-	-	-	-	-
Stock Changes	-	115	-	366	-	-5	1	-401	-	-86	-1
DOMESTIC SUPPLY	-	1452	-	55166	-	16	58	11190	8	2384	23
Transfers	-	-	-	-	-	-	-	-	-	581	-
Statistical Differences	-	-	-	-	-	-	-	-	-	-	-
TRANSFORMATION	-	97	-	54484	-	-	17	11190	8	2965	23
Electricity Plants	-	97	-	54306	-	-	17	-	-	-	-
CHP Plants	-	-	-	-	-	-	-	-	-	-	-
Heat Plants	-	-	-	-	-	-	-	-	-	-	-
Transfer to Gases	-	-	-	-	-	-	-	-	-	-	-
Transfer to Solids	-	-	-	178	-	-	-	-	-	-	-
Petroleum Refineries	-	-	-	-	-	-	-	11190	8	2965	23
Petrochemical Industry	-	-	-	-	-	-	-	-	-	-	-
Liquefaction	-	-	-	-	-	-	-	-	-	-	-
Other Transformation Sector	-	-	-	-	-	-	-	-	-	-	-
ENERGY SECTOR	-	-	-	-	-	-	-	-	-	-	-
Coal Mines	-	-	-	-	-	-	-	-	-	-	-
Oil and Gas Extraction	-	-	-	-	-	-	-	-	-	-	-
Petroleum Refineries	-	-	-	-	-	-	-	-	-	-	-
Electricity, CHP+Heat plants	-	-	-	-	-	-	-	-	-	-	-
Pumped Storage (Elec.)	-	-	-	-	-	-	-	-	-	-	-
Other Energy Sector	-	-	-	-	-	-	-	-	-	-	-
Distribution Losses	-	-	-	-	-	-	-	-	-	-	-
FINAL CONSUMPTION	-	1355	-	682	-	16	41	-	-	-	-
INDUSTRY SECTOR	-	1353	-	552	-	16	-	-	-	-	-
Iron and Steel	-	-	-	-	-	-	-	-	-	-	-
Chemical and Petrochemical	-	-	-	85	-	-	-	-	-	-	-
of which: Feedstocks	-	-	-	-	-	-	-	-	-	-	-
Non-Ferrous Metals	-	66	-	445	-	-	-	-	-	-	-
Non-Metallic Minerals	-	1287	-	22	-	-	-	-	-	-	-
Transport Equipment	-	-	-	-	-	-	-	-	-	-	-
Machinery	-	-	-	-	-	4	-	-	-	-	-
Mining and Quarrying	-	-	-	-	-	-	-	-	-	-	-
Food and Tobacco	-	-	-	-	-	12	-	-	-	-	-
Paper, Pulp and Print	-	-	-	-	-	-	-	-	-	-	-
Wood and Wood Products	-	-	-	-	-	-	-	-	-	-	-
Construction	-	-	-	-	-	-	-	-	-	-	-
Textile and Leather	-	-	-	-	-	-	-	-	-	-	-
Non-specified	-	-	-	-	-	-	-	-	-	-	-
TRANSPORT SECTOR	-	1	-	-	-	-	-	-	-	-	-
International Civil Aviation	-	-	-	-	-	-	-	-	-	-	-
Domestic Air	-	-	-	-	-	-	-	-	-	-	-
Road	-	-	-	-	-	-	-	-	-	-	-
Rail	-	1	-	-	-	-	-	-	-	-	-
Pipeline Transport	-	-	-	-	-	-	-	-	-	-	-
Internal Navigation	-	-	-	-	-	-	-	-	-	-	-
Non-specified	-	-	-	-	-	-	-	-	-	-	-
OTHER SECTORS	-	1	-	130	-	-	41	-	-	-	-
Agriculture	-	-	-	40	-	-	-	-	-	-	-
Commerce and Publ. Serv.	-	-	-	-	-	-	1	-	-	-	-
Residential	-	1	-	90	-	-	40	-	-	-	-
Non-specified	-	-	-	-	-	-	-	-	-	-	-
NON-ENERGY USE	-	-	-	-	-	-	-	-	-	-	-
in Industry/Transf./Energy	-	-	-	-	-	-	-	-	-	-	-
in Transport	-	-	-	-	-	-	-	-	-	-	-
in Other Sectors	-	-	-	-	-	-	-	-	-	-	-

Greece / Grèce : 1993

SUPPLY AND CONSUMPTION *APPROVISIONNEMENT ET DEMANDE*	Oil cont. / *Pétrole cont.* (1000 tonnes)										
	Refinery Gas *Gaz de raffinerie*	LPG + Ethane *GPL + éthane*	Motor Gasoline *Essence moteur*	Aviation Gasoline *Essence aviation*	Jet Fuel *Carbu-réacteur*	Kerosene *Kérosène*	Gas/Diesel *Gazole*	Heavy Fuel Oil *Fioul lourd*	Naphtha *Naphta*	Pétrol. Coke *Coke de pétrole*	Other Prod. *Autres prod.*
Production	414	401	3445	-	1281	10	3259	4419	145	148	584
From Other Sources	-	-	-	-	-	-	-	-	-	-	-
Imports	-	3	242	1	836	-	2370	1955	121	171	32
Exports	-	-48	-1077	-	-659	-	-201	-654	-142	-	-136
Intl. Marine Bunkers	-	-	-	-	-	-	-718	-2444	-	-	-44
Stock Changes	-	1	11	-	-112	1	-51	196	-38	54	15
DOMESTIC SUPPLY	**414**	**357**	**2621**	**1**	**1346**	**11**	**4659**	**3472**	**86**	**373**	**451**
Transfers	-	-	-	-	-	-	-25	-445	-17	-	-94
Statistical Differences	-	-	23	-	81	-	150	19	3	-	-6
TRANSFORMATION	**95**	**-**	**-**	**-**	**-**	**-**	**287**	**1670**	**20**	**-**	**-**
Electricity Plants	-	-	-	-	-	-	287	1603	-	-	-
CHP Plants	95	-	-	-	-	-	-	67	-	-	-
Heat Plants	-	-	-	-	-	-	-	-	-	-	-
Transfer to Gases	-	-	-	-	-	-	-	-	-	-	-
Transfer to Solids	-	-	-	-	-	-	-	-	20	-	-
Petroleum Refineries	-	-	-	-	-	-	-	-	-	-	-
Petrochemical Industry	-	-	-	-	-	-	-	-	-	-	-
Liquefaction	-	-	-	-	-	-	-	-	-	-	-
Other Transformation Sector	-	-	-	-	-	-	-	-	-	-	-
ENERGY SECTOR	**295**	**29**	**-**	**-**	**-**	**-**	**-**	**210**	**-**	**148**	**-**
Coal Mines	-	-	-	-	-	-	-	-	-	-	-
Oil and Gas Extraction	-	-	-	-	-	-	-	-	-	-	-
Petroleum Refineries	295	29	-	-	-	-	-	210	-	148	-
Electricity, CHP+Heat plants	-	-	-	-	-	-	-	-	-	-	-
Pumped Storage (Elec.)	-	-	-	-	-	-	-	-	-	-	-
Other Energy Sector	-	-	-	-	-	-	-	-	-	-	-
Distribution Losses	-	-	-	-	-	-	-	-	-	-	-
FINAL CONSUMPTION	**24**	**328**	**2644**	**1**	**1427**	**11**	**4497**	**1166**	**52**	**225**	**351**
INDUSTRY SECTOR	**24**	**158**	**-**	**-**	**-**	**-**	**296**	**910**	**52**	**171**	**-**
Iron and Steel	-	-	-	-	-	-	26	86	-	-	-
Chemical and Petrochemical	24	30	-	-	-	-	11	26	52	-	-
of which: Feedstocks	-	-	-	-	-	-	-	-	52	-	-
Non-Ferrous Metals	-	-	-	-	-	-	25	157	-	-	-
Non-Metallic Minerals	-	-	-	-	-	-	31	177	-	171	-
Transport Equipment	-	-	-	-	-	-	2	-	-	-	-
Machinery	-	-	-	-	-	-	-	-	-	-	-
Mining and Quarrying	-	-	-	-	-	-	32	21	-	-	-
Food and Tobacco	-	-	-	-	-	-	39	257	-	-	-
Paper, Pulp and Print	-	-	-	-	-	-	14	71	-	-	-
Wood and Wood Products	-	-	-	-	-	-	-	2	-	-	-
Construction	-	-	-	-	-	-	1	22	-	-	-
Textile and Leather	-	-	-	-	-	-	20	91	-	-	-
Non-specified	-	128	-	-	-	-	95	-	-	-	-
TRANSPORT SECTOR	**-**	**45**	**2594**	**1**	**1427**	**-**	**1986**	**201**	**-**	**-**	**-**
International Civil Aviation	-	-	-	-	921	-	-	-	-	-	-
Domestic Air	-	-	-	1	506	-	-	-	-	-	-
Road	-	45	2594	-	-	-	1588	-	-	-	-
Rail	-	-	-	-	-	-	48	-	-	-	-
Pipeline Transport	-	-	-	-	-	-	-	-	-	-	-
Internal Navigation	-	-	-	-	-	-	350	201	-	-	-
Non-specified	-	-	-	-	-	-	-	-	-	-	-
OTHER SECTORS	**-**	**125**	**50**	**-**	**-**	**11**	**2215**	**55**	**-**	**-**	**-**
Agriculture	-	-	50	-	-	-	802	15	-	-	-
Commerce and Publ. Serv.	-	19	-	-	-	-	150	15	-	-	-
Residential	-	106	-	-	-	11	1263	25	-	-	-
Non-specified	-	-	-	-	-	-	-	-	-	-	-
NON-ENERGY USE	**-**	**-**	**-**	**-**	**-**	**-**	**-**	**-**	**-**	**54**	**351**
in Industry/Transf./Energy	-	-	-	-	-	-	-	-	-	54	274
in Transport	-	-	-	-	-	-	-	-	-	-	75
in Other Sectors	-	-	-	-	-	-	-	-	-	-	2

Greece / Grèce : 1993

CONSUMPTION *APPROVISIONNEMENT ET DEMANDE*	Gas / *Gaz* (TJ)				Combust. Renew. & Waste / *En. Re. Comb. & Déchets* (TJ)				(GWh)	(TJ)
	Natural Gas *Gaz naturel*	Gas Works *Usines à gaz*	Coke Ovens *Cokeries*	Blast Furnaces *Hauts fourneaux*	Solid Biomass & Anim. Prod. *Biomasse solide & prod. anim.*	Gas/Liquids from Biomass *Gaz/Liquides tirés de biomasse*	Municipal Waste *Déchets urbains*	Industrial Waste *Déchets industriels*	Electricity *Electricité*	Heat *Chaleur*
Production	4325	-	-	-	23023	-	-	1241	38396	-
From Other Sources	-	695	-	-	-	-	-	-	-	-
Imports	-	-	-	-	-	-	-	-	1093	-
Exports	-	-	-	-	-	-	-	-	-284	-
Intl. Marine Bunkers	-	-	-	-	-	-	-	-	-	-
Stock Changes	-	-	-	-	-	-	-	-	-	-
DOMESTIC SUPPLY	**4325**	**695**	**-**	**-**	**23023**	**-**	**-**	**1241**	**39205**	**-**
Transfers	-	-	-	-	-	-	-	-	-	-
Statistical Differences	1	-	-	-	-	-	-	-	-	-
TRANSFORMATION	**707**	**-**	**-**	**-**	**-**	**-**	**-**	**1241**	**-**	**-**
Electricity Plants	-	-	-	-	-	-	-	-	-	-
CHP Plants	707	-	-	-	-	-	-	1241	-	-
Heat Plants	-	-	-	-	-	-	-	-	-	-
Transfer to Gases	-	-	-	-	-	-	-	-	-	-
Transfer to Solids	-	-	-	-	-	-	-	-	-	-
Petroleum Refineries	-	-	-	-	-	-	-	-	-	-
Petrochemical Industry	-	-	-	-	-	-	-	-	-	-
Liquefaction	-	-	-	-	-	-	-	-	-	-
Other Transformation Sector	-	-	-	-	-	-	-	-	-	-
ENERGY SECTOR	**986**	**-**	**-**	**-**	**-**	**-**	**-**	**-**	**5009**	**-**
Coal Mines	-	-	-	-	-	-	-	-	771	-
Oil and Gas Extraction	986	-	-	-	-	-	-	-	-	-
Petroleum Refineries	-	-	-	-	-	-	-	-	663	-
Electricity, CHP+Heat plants	-	-	-	-	-	-	-	-	3205	-
Pumped Storage (Elec.)	-	-	-	-	-	-	-	-	370	-
Other Energy Sector	-	-	-	-	-	-	-	-	-	-
Distribution Losses	-	8	-	-	-	-	-	-	3017	-
FINAL CONSUMPTION	**2633**	**687**	**-**	**-**	**23023**	**-**	**-**	**-**	**31179**	**-**
INDUSTRY SECTOR	**2633**	**284**	**-**	**-**	**-**	**-**	**-**	**-**	**11353**	**-**
Iron and Steel	-	-	-	-	-	-	-	-	824	-
Chemical and Petrochemical	2633	15	-	-	-	-	-	-	968	-
of which: Feedstocks	*2633*	-	-	-	-	-	-	-	-	-
Non-Ferrous Metals	-	-	-	-	-	-	-	-	3087	-
Non-Metallic Minerals	-	-	-	-	-	-	-	-	1801	-
Transport Equipment	-	-	-	-	-	-	-	-	163	-
Machinery	-	-	-	-	-	-	-	-	409	-
Mining and Quarrying	-	-	-	-	-	-	-	-	253	-
Food and Tobacco	-	154	-	-	-	-	-	-	820	-
Paper, Pulp and Print	-	57	-	-	-	-	-	-	461	-
Wood and Wood Products	-	-	-	-	-	-	-	-	119	-
Construction	-	2	-	-	-	-	-	-	38	-
Textile and Leather	-	56	-	-	-	-	-	-	978	-
Non-specified	-	-	-	-	-	-	-	-	1432	-
TRANSPORT SECTOR	**-**	**-**	**-**	**-**	**-**	**-**	**-**	**-**	**125**	**-**
International Civil Aviation	-	-	-	-	-	-	-	-	-	-
Domestic Air	-	-	-	-	-	-	-	-	-	-
Road	-	-	-	-	-	-	-	-	-	-
Rail	-	-	-	-	-	-	-	-	64	-
Pipeline Transport	-	-	-	-	-	-	-	-	-	-
Internal Navigation	-	-	-	-	-	-	-	-	-	-
Non-specified	-	-	-	-	-	-	-	-	61	-
OTHER SECTORS	**-**	**403**	**-**	**-**	**23023**	**-**	**-**	**-**	**19701**	**-**
Agriculture	-	-	-	-	-	-	-	-	2040	-
Commerce and Publ. Serv.	-	251	-	-	2303	-	-	-	7180	-
Residential	-	152	-	-	20720	-	-	-	10481	-
Non-specified	-	-	-	-	-	-	-	-	-	-
NON-ENERGY USE	**-**	**-**	**-**	**-**	**-**	**-**	**-**	**-**	**-**	**-**
in Industry/Transf./Energy	-	-	-	-	-	-	-	-	-	-
in Transport	-	-	-	-	-	-	-	-	-	-
in Other Sectors	-	-	-	-	-	-	-	-	-	-

Iceland / Islande : 1992

SUPPLY AND CONSUMPTION / APPROVISIONNEMENT ET DEMANDE	Coking Coal / Charbon à coke	Steam Coal / Charbon vapeur	Sub-Bit. Coal / Charbon sous-bit.	Lignite / Lignite	Peat / Tourbe	Oven and Gas Coke / Coke de four/gaz	Pat. Fuel and BKB / Agg./briq. de lignite	Crude Oil / Pétrole brut	NGL / LGN	Feedstocks / Produits d'aliment.	Additives / Additifs
Production	-	-	-	-	-	-	-	-	-	-	-
From Other Sources	-	-	-	-	-	-	-	-	-	-	-
Imports	12	38	-	-	-	18	-	-	-	-	-
Exports	-	-	-	-	-	-	-	-	-	-	-
Intl. Marine Bunkers	-	-	-	-	-	-	-	-	-	-	-
Stock Changes	-	-	-	-	-	-	-	-	-	-	-
DOMESTIC SUPPLY	**12**	**38**	-	-	-	**18**	-	-	-	-	-
Transfers	-	-	-	-	-	-	-	-	-	-	-
Statistical Differences	-	-	-	-	-	-	-	-	-	-	-
TRANSFORMATION	-	-	-	-	-	-	-	-	-	-	-
Electricity Plants	-	-	-	-	-	-	-	-	-	-	-
CHP Plants	-	-	-	-	-	-	-	-	-	-	-
Heat Plants	-	-	-	-	-	-	-	-	-	-	-
Transfer to Gases	-	-	-	-	-	-	-	-	-	-	-
Transfer to Solids	-	-	-	-	-	-	-	-	-	-	-
Petroleum Refineries	-	-	-	-	-	-	-	-	-	-	-
Petrochemical Industry	-	-	-	-	-	-	-	-	-	-	-
Liquefaction	-	-	-	-	-	-	-	-	-	-	-
Other Transformation Sector	-	-	-	-	-	-	-	-	-	-	-
ENERGY SECTOR	-	-	-	-	-	-	-	-	-	-	-
Coal Mines	-	-	-	-	-	-	-	-	-	-	-
Oil and Gas Extraction	-	-	-	-	-	-	-	-	-	-	-
Petroleum Refineries	-	-	-	-	-	-	-	-	-	-	-
Electricity, CHP+Heat plants	-	-	-	-	-	-	-	-	-	-	-
Pumped Storage (Elec.)	-	-	-	-	-	-	-	-	-	-	-
Other Energy Sector	-	-	-	-	-	-	-	-	-	-	-
Distribution Losses	-	-	-	-	-	-	-	-	-	-	-
FINAL CONSUMPTION	**12**	**38**	-	-	-	**18**	-	-	-	-	-
INDUSTRY SECTOR	**12**	**38**	-	-	-	-	-	-	-	-	-
Iron and Steel	-	38	-	-	-	-	-	-	-	-	-
Chemical and Petrochemical	-	-	-	-	-	-	-	-	-	-	-
of which: Feedstocks	-	-	-	-	-	-	-	-	-	-	-
Non-Ferrous Metals	-	-	-	-	-	-	-	-	-	-	-
Non-Metallic Minerals	12	-	-	-	-	-	-	-	-	-	-
Transport Equipment	-	-	-	-	-	-	-	-	-	-	-
Machinery	-	-	-	-	-	-	-	-	-	-	-
Mining and Quarrying	-	-	-	-	-	-	-	-	-	-	-
Food and Tobacco	-	-	-	-	-	-	-	-	-	-	-
Paper, Pulp and Print	-	-	-	-	-	-	-	-	-	-	-
Wood and Wood Products	-	-	-	-	-	-	-	-	-	-	-
Construction	-	-	-	-	-	-	-	-	-	-	-
Textile and Leather	-	-	-	-	-	-	-	-	-	-	-
Non-specified	-	-	-	-	-	-	-	-	-	-	-
TRANSPORT SECTOR	-	-	-	-	-	-	-	-	-	-	-
International Civil Aviation	-	-	-	-	-	-	-	-	-	-	-
Domestic Air	-	-	-	-	-	-	-	-	-	-	-
Road	-	-	-	-	-	-	-	-	-	-	-
Rail	-	-	-	-	-	-	-	-	-	-	-
Pipeline Transport	-	-	-	-	-	-	-	-	-	-	-
Internal Navigation	-	-	-	-	-	-	-	-	-	-	-
Non-specified	-	-	-	-	-	-	-	-	-	-	-
OTHER SECTORS	-	-	-	-	-	-	-	-	-	-	-
Agriculture	-	-	-	-	-	-	-	-	-	-	-
Commerce and Publ. Serv.	-	-	-	-	-	-	-	-	-	-	-
Residential	-	-	-	-	-	-	-	-	-	-	-
Non-specified	-	-	-	-	-	-	-	-	-	-	-
NON-ENERGY USE	-	-	-	-	-	**18**	-	-	-	-	-
in Industry/Transf./Energy	-	-	-	-	-	18	-	-	-	-	-
in Transport	-	-	-	-	-	-	-	-	-	-	-
in Other Sectors	-	-	-	-	-	-	-	-	-	-	-

Iceland / Islande : 1992

SUPPLY AND CONSUMPTION APPROVISIONNEMENT ET DEMANDE	Oil cont. / *Pétrole cont.* (1000 tonnes)										
	Refinery Gas *Gaz de raffinerie*	LPG + Ethane *GPL + éthane*	Motor Gasoline *Essence moteur*	Aviation Gasoline *Essence aviation*	Jet Fuel *Carbu-réacteur*	Kerosene *Kérosène*	Gas/ Diesel *Gazole*	Heavy Fuel Oil *Fioul lourd*	Naphtha *Naphta*	Pétrol. Coke *Coke de pétrole*	Other Prod. *Autres prod.*
Production	-	-	-	-	-	-	-	-	-	-	-
From Other Sources	-	-	-	-	-	-	-	-	-	-	-
Imports	-	1	141	2	77	-	310	122	-	55	30
Exports	-	-	-	-	-	-	-	-	-	-	-
Intl. Marine Bunkers	-	-	-	-	-	-	-18	-1	-	-	-
Stock Changes	-	-	-6	-	3	-	-14	-34	-	-	-
DOMESTIC SUPPLY	**-**	**1**	**135**	**2**	**80**	**-**	**278**	**87**	**-**	**55**	**30**
Transfers	-	-	-	-	-	-	-	-	-	-	-
Statistical Differences	-	-	-	-	-	-	2	35	-	-	-
TRANSFORMATION	**-**	**-**	**-**	**-**	**-**	**-**	**2**	**-**	**-**	**-**	**-**
Electricity Plants	-	-	-	-	-	-	2	-	-	-	-
CHP Plants	-	-	-	-	-	-	-	-	-	-	-
Heat Plants	-	-	-	-	-	-	-	-	-	-	-
Transfer to Gases	-	-	-	-	-	-	-	-	-	-	-
Transfer to Solids	-	-	-	-	-	-	-	-	-	-	-
Petroleum Refineries	-	-	-	-	-	-	-	-	-	-	-
Petrochemical Industry	-	-	-	-	-	-	-	-	-	-	-
Liquefaction	-	-	-	-	-	-	-	-	-	-	-
Other Transformation Sector	-	-	-	-	-	-	-	-	-	-	-
ENERGY SECTOR	**-**	**-**	**-**	**-**	**-**	**-**	**-**	**-**	**-**	**-**	**-**
Coal Mines	-	-	-	-	-	-	-	-	-	-	-
Oil and Gas Extraction	-	-	-	-	-	-	-	-	-	-	-
Petroleum Refineries	-	-	-	-	-	-	-	-	-	-	-
Electricity, CHP+Heat plants	-	-	-	-	-	-	-	-	-	-	-
Pumped Storage (Elec.)	-	-	-	-	-	-	-	-	-	-	-
Other Energy Sector	-	-	-	-	-	-	-	-	-	-	-
Distribution Losses	-	-	-	-	-	-	-	-	-	-	-
FINAL CONSUMPTION	**-**	**1**	**135**	**2**	**80**	**-**	**278**	**122**	**-**	**55**	**30**
INDUSTRY SECTOR	**-**	**-**	**-**	**-**	**-**	**-**	**6**	**59**	**-**	**-**	**-**
Iron and Steel	-	-	-	-	-	-	-	-	-	-	-
Chemical and Petrochemical	-	-	-	-	-	-	-	-	-	-	-
of which: Feedstocks	-	-	-	-	-	-	-	-	-	-	-
Non-Ferrous Metals	-	-	-	-	-	-	-	-	-	-	-
Non-Metallic Minerals	-	-	-	-	-	-	-	-	-	-	-
Transport Equipment	-	-	-	-	-	-	-	-	-	-	-
Machinery	-	-	-	-	-	-	-	-	-	-	-
Mining and Quarrying	-	-	-	-	-	-	-	-	-	-	-
Food and Tobacco	-	-	-	-	-	-	-	-	-	-	-
Paper, Pulp and Print	-	-	-	-	-	-	-	-	-	-	-
Wood and Wood Products	-	-	-	-	-	-	-	-	-	-	-
Construction	-	-	-	-	-	-	-	-	-	-	-
Textile and Leather	-	-	-	-	-	-	-	-	-	-	-
Non-specified	-	-	-	-	-	-	6	59	-	-	-
TRANSPORT SECTOR	**-**	**-**	**135**	**2**	**80**	**-**	**59**	**8**	**-**	**-**	**-**
International Civil Aviation	-	-	-	-	73	-	-	-	-	-	-
Domestic Air	-	-	-	2	7	-	-	-	-	-	-
Road	-	-	135	-	-	-	48	-	-	-	-
Rail	-	-	-	-	-	-	-	-	-	-	-
Pipeline Transport	-	-	-	-	-	-	-	-	-	-	-
Internal Navigation	-	-	-	-	-	-	11	8	-	-	-
Non-specified	-	-	-	-	-	-	-	-	-	-	-
OTHER SECTORS	**-**	**1**	**-**	**-**	**-**	**-**	**213**	**55**	**-**	**-**	**-**
Agriculture	-	-	-	-	-	-	182	52	-	-	-
Commerce and Publ. Serv.	-	-	-	-	-	-	-	-	-	-	-
Residential	-	1	-	-	-	-	14	3	-	-	-
Non-specified	-	-	-	-	-	-	17	-	-	-	-
NON-ENERGY USE	**-**	**-**	**-**	**-**	**-**	**-**	**-**	**-**	**-**	**55**	**30**
in Industry/Transf./Energy	-	-	-	-	-	-	-	-	-	55	23
in Transport	-	-	-	-	-	-	-	-	-	-	7
in Other Sectors	-	-	-	-	-	-	-	-	-	-	-

Iceland / Islande : 1992

CONSUMPTION / APPROVISIONNEMENT ET DEMANDE	Gas / Gaz (TJ)				Combust. Renew. & Waste / En. Re. Comb. & Déchets (TJ)				Electricity (GWh)	Heat (TJ)
	Natural Gas / Gaz naturel	Gas Works / Usines à gaz	Coke Ovens / Cokeries	Blast Furnaces / Hauts fourneaux	Solid Biomass & Anim. Prod. / Biomasse solide & prod. anim.	Gas/Liquids from Biomass / Gaz/Liquides tirés de biomasse	Municipal Waste / Déchets urbains	Industrial Waste / Déchets industriels	Electricité	Chaleur
Production	-	-	-	-	-	-	-	-	4546	8199
From Other Sources	-	-	-	-	-	-	-	-	-	-
Imports	-	-	-	-	-	-	-	-	-	-
Exports	-	-	-	-	-	-	-	-	-	-
Intl. Marine Bunkers	-	-	-	-	-	-	-	-	-	-
Stock Changes	-	-	-	-	-	-	-	-	-	-
DOMESTIC SUPPLY	-	-	-	-	-	-	-	-	4546	8199
Transfers	-	-	-	-	-	-	-	-	-	-
Statistical Differences	-	-	-	-	-	-	-	-	-	-
TRANSFORMATION	-	-	-	-	-	-	-	-	168	-
Electricity Plants	-	-	-	-	-	-	-	-	-	-
CHP Plants	-	-	-	-	-	-	-	-	-	-
Heat Plants	-	-	-	-	-	-	-	-	168	-
Transfer to Gases	-	-	-	-	-	-	-	-	-	-
Transfer to Solids	-	-	-	-	-	-	-	-	-	-
Petroleum Refineries	-	-	-	-	-	-	-	-	-	-
Petrochemical Industry	-	-	-	-	-	-	-	-	-	-
Liquefaction	-	-	-	-	-	-	-	-	-	-
Other Transformation Sector	-	-	-	-	-	-	-	-	-	-
ENERGY SECTOR	-	-	-	-	-	-	-	-	165	-
Coal Mines	-	-	-	-	-	-	-	-	-	-
Oil and Gas Extraction	-	-	-	-	-	-	-	-	-	-
Petroleum Refineries	-	-	-	-	-	-	-	-	-	-
Electricity, CHP+Heat plants	-	-	-	-	-	-	-	-	56	-
Pumped Storage (Elec.)	-	-	-	-	-	-	-	-	-	-
Other Energy Sector	-	-	-	-	-	-	-	-	109	-
Distribution Losses	-	-	-	-	-	-	-	-	343	746
FINAL CONSUMPTION	-	-	-	-	-	-	-	-	3870	7453
INDUSTRY SECTOR	-	-	-	-	-	-	-	-	2506	-
Iron and Steel	-	-	-	-	-	-	-	-	501	-
Chemical and Petrochemical	-	-	-	-	-	-	-	-	189	-
of which: Feedstocks	-	-	-	-	-	-	-	-	-	-
Non-Ferrous Metals	-	-	-	-	-	-	-	-	1495	-
Non-Metallic Minerals	-	-	-	-	-	-	-	-	40	-
Transport Equipment	-	-	-	-	-	-	-	-	7	-
Machinery	-	-	-	-	-	-	-	-	3	-
Mining and Quarrying	-	-	-	-	-	-	-	-	1	-
Food and Tobacco	-	-	-	-	-	-	-	-	204	-
Paper, Pulp and Print	-	-	-	-	-	-	-	-	16	-
Wood and Wood Products	-	-	-	-	-	-	-	-	8	-
Construction	-	-	-	-	-	-	-	-	17	-
Textile and Leather	-	-	-	-	-	-	-	-	20	-
Non-specified	-	-	-	-	-	-	-	-	5	-
TRANSPORT SECTOR	-	-	-	-	-	-	-	-	30	-
International Civil Aviation	-	-	-	-	-	-	-	-	-	-
Domestic Air	-	-	-	-	-	-	-	-	-	-
Road	-	-	-	-	-	-	-	-	-	-
Rail	-	-	-	-	-	-	-	-	-	-
Pipeline Transport	-	-	-	-	-	-	-	-	30	-
Internal Navigation	-	-	-	-	-	-	-	-	-	-
Non-specified	-	-	-	-	-	-	-	-	-	-
OTHER SECTORS	-	-	-	-	-	-	-	-	1334	7453
Agriculture	-	-	-	-	-	-	-	-	230	-
Commerce and Publ. Serv.	-	-	-	-	-	-	-	-	481	746
Residential	-	-	-	-	-	-	-	-	542	6707
Non-specified	-	-	-	-	-	-	-	-	81	-
NON-ENERGY USE	-	-	-	-	-	-	-	-	-	-
in Industry/Transf./Energy	-	-	-	-	-	-	-	-	-	-
in Transport	-	-	-	-	-	-	-	-	-	-
in Other Sectors	-	-	-	-	-	-	-	-	-	-

Iceland / Islande : 1993

SUPPLY AND CONSUMPTION *APPROVISIONNEMENT ET DEMANDE*	Coal / *Charbon* (1000 tonnes)							Oil / *Pétrole* (1000 tonnes)			
	Coking Coal *Charbon à coke*	Steam Coal *Charbon vapeur*	Sub-Bit. Coal *Charbon sous-bit.*	Lignite *Lignite*	Peat *Tourbe*	Oven and Gas Coke *Coke de four/gaz*	Pat. Fuel and BKB *Agg./briq. de lignite*	Crude Oil *Pétrole brut*	NGL *LGN*	Feedstocks *Produits d'aliment.*	Additives *Additifs*
Production	-	-	-	-	-	-	-	-	-	-	-
From Other Sources	-	-	-	-	-	-	-	-	-	-	-
Imports	6	47	-	-	-	15	-	-	-	-	-
Exports	-	-	-	-	-	-	-	-	-	-	-
Intl. Marine Bunkers	-	-	-	-	-	-	-	-	-	-	-
Stock Changes	-	-	-	-	-	-	-	-	-	-	-
DOMESTIC SUPPLY	**6**	**47**	**-**	**-**	**-**	**15**	**-**	**-**	**-**	**-**	**-**
Transfers	-	-	-	-	-	-	-	-	-	-	-
Statistical Differences	-	-	-	-	-	-	-	-	-	-	-
TRANSFORMATION	**-**	**-**	**-**	**-**	**-**	**-**	**-**	**-**	**-**	**-**	**-**
Electricity Plants	-	-	-	-	-	-	-	-	-	-	-
CHP Plants	-	-	-	-	-	-	-	-	-	-	-
Heat Plants	-	-	-	-	-	-	-	-	-	-	-
Transfer to Gases	-	-	-	-	-	-	-	-	-	-	-
Transfer to Solids	-	-	-	-	-	-	-	-	-	-	-
Petroleum Refineries	-	-	-	-	-	-	-	-	-	-	-
Petrochemical Industry	-	-	-	-	-	-	-	-	-	-	-
Liquefaction	-	-	-	-	-	-	-	-	-	-	-
Other Transformation Sector	-	-	-	-	-	-	-	-	-	-	-
ENERGY SECTOR	**-**	**-**	**-**	**-**	**-**	**-**	**-**	**-**	**-**	**-**	**-**
Coal Mines	-	-	-	-	-	-	-	-	-	-	-
Oil and Gas Extraction	-	-	-	-	-	-	-	-	-	-	-
Petroleum Refineries	-	-	-	-	-	-	-	-	-	-	-
Electricity, CHP+Heat plants	-	-	-	-	-	-	-	-	-	-	-
Pumped Storage (Elec.)	-	-	-	-	-	-	-	-	-	-	-
Other Energy Sector	-	-	-	-	-	-	-	-	-	-	-
Distribution Losses	-	-	-	-	-	-	-	-	-	-	-
FINAL CONSUMPTION	**6**	**47**	**-**	**-**	**-**	**15**	**-**	**-**	**-**	**-**	**-**
INDUSTRY SECTOR	**6**	**47**	**-**	**-**	**-**	**-**	**-**	**-**	**-**	**-**	**-**
Iron and Steel	-	47	-	-	-	-	-	-	-	-	-
Chemical and Petrochemical	-	-	-	-	-	-	-	-	-	-	-
of which: Feedstocks	-	-	-	-	-	-	-	-	-	-	-
Non-Ferrous Metals	-	-	-	-	-	-	-	-	-	-	-
Non-Metallic Minerals	6	-	-	-	-	-	-	-	-	-	-
Transport Equipment	-	-	-	-	-	-	-	-	-	-	-
Machinery	-	-	-	-	-	-	-	-	-	-	-
Mining and Quarrying	-	-	-	-	-	-	-	-	-	-	-
Food and Tobacco	-	-	-	-	-	-	-	-	-	-	-
Paper, Pulp and Print	-	-	-	-	-	-	-	-	-	-	-
Wood and Wood Products	-	-	-	-	-	-	-	-	-	-	-
Construction	-	-	-	-	-	-	-	-	-	-	-
Textile and Leather	-	-	-	-	-	-	-	-	-	-	-
Non-specified	-	-	-	-	-	-	-	-	-	-	-
TRANSPORT SECTOR	**-**	**-**	**-**	**-**	**-**	**-**	**-**	**-**	**-**	**-**	**-**
International Civil Aviation	-	-	-	-	-	-	-	-	-	-	-
Domestic Air	-	-	-	-	-	-	-	-	-	-	-
Road	-	-	-	-	-	-	-	-	-	-	-
Rail	-	-	-	-	-	-	-	-	-	-	-
Pipeline Transport	-	-	-	-	-	-	-	-	-	-	-
Internal Navigation	-	-	-	-	-	-	-	-	-	-	-
Non-specified	-	-	-	-	-	-	-	-	-	-	-
OTHER SECTORS	**-**	**-**	**-**	**-**	**-**	**-**	**-**	**-**	**-**	**-**	**-**
Agriculture	-	-	-	-	-	-	-	-	-	-	-
Commerce and Publ. Serv.	-	-	-	-	-	-	-	-	-	-	-
Residential	-	-	-	-	-	-	-	-	-	-	-
Non-specified	-	-	-	-	-	-	-	-	-	-	-
NON-ENERGY USE	**-**	**-**	**-**	**-**	**-**	**15**	**-**	**-**	**-**	**-**	**-**
in Industry/Transf./Energy	-	-	-	-	-	15	-	-	-	-	-
in Transport	-	-	-	-	-	-	-	-	-	-	-
in Other Sectors	-	-	-	-	-	-	-	-	-	-	-

Iceland / Islande : 1993

SUPPLY AND CONSUMPTION *APPROVISIONNEMENT ET DEMANDE*	Oil cont. / *Pétrole cont.* (1000 tonnes)										
	Refinery Gas *Gaz de raffinerie*	LPG + Ethane *GPL + éthane*	Motor Gasoline *Essence moteur*	Aviation Gasoline *Essence aviation*	Jet Fuel *Carbu-réacteur*	Kerosene *Kérosène*	Gas/ Diesel *Gazole*	Heavy Fuel Oil *Fioul lourd*	Naphtha *Naphta*	Pétrol. Coke *Coke de pétrole*	Other Prod. *Autres prod.*
Production	-	-	-	-	-	-	-	-	-	-	-
From Other Sources	-	-	-	-	-	-	-	-	-	-	-
Imports	-	1	119	1	64	-	332	130	-	46	30
Exports	-	-	-	-	-	-	-	-	-	-	-
Intl. Marine Bunkers	-	-	-	-	-	-	-30	-1	-	-	-
Stock Changes	-	-	7	-	1	-	5	7	-	-	-
DOMESTIC SUPPLY	-	**1**	**126**	**1**	**65**	-	**307**	**136**	-	**46**	**30**
Transfers	-	-	-	-	-	-	-	-	-	-	-
Statistical Differences	-	-	8	-	-	-	-17	-10	-	-	-
TRANSFORMATION	-	-	-	-	-	-	**2**	-	-	-	-
Electricity Plants	-	-	-	-	-	-	2	-	-	-	-
CHP Plants	-	-	-	-	-	-	-	-	-	-	-
Heat Plants	-	-	-	-	-	-	-	-	-	-	-
Transfer to Gases	-	-	-	-	-	-	-	-	-	-	-
Transfer to Solids	-	-	-	-	-	-	-	-	-	-	-
Petroleum Refineries	-	-	-	-	-	-	-	-	-	-	-
Petrochemical Industry	-	-	-	-	-	-	-	-	-	-	-
Liquefaction	-	-	-	-	-	-	-	-	-	-	-
Other Transformation Sector	-	-	-	-	-	-	-	-	-	-	-
ENERGY SECTOR	-	-	-	-	-	-	-	-	-	-	-
Coal Mines	-	-	-	-	-	-	-	-	-	-	-
Oil and Gas Extraction	-	-	-	-	-	-	-	-	-	-	-
Petroleum Refineries	-	-	-	-	-	-	-	-	-	-	-
Electricity, CHP+Heat plants	-	-	-	-	-	-	-	-	-	-	-
Pumped Storage (Elec.)	-	-	-	-	-	-	-	-	-	-	-
Other Energy Sector	-	-	-	-	-	-	-	-	-	-	-
Distribution Losses	-	-	-	-	-	-	-	-	-	-	-
FINAL CONSUMPTION	-	**1**	**134**	**1**	**65**	-	**288**	**126**	-	**46**	**30**
INDUSTRY SECTOR	-	-	-	-	-	-	**8**	**65**	-	-	-
Iron and Steel	-	-	-	-	-	-	-	-	-	-	-
Chemical and Petrochemical	-	-	-	-	-	-	-	-	-	-	-
of which: Feedstocks	-	-	-	-	-	-	-	-	-	-	-
Non-Ferrous Metals	-	-	-	-	-	-	-	-	-	-	-
Non-Metallic Minerals	-	-	-	-	-	-	-	-	-	-	-
Transport Equipment	-	-	-	-	-	-	-	-	-	-	-
Machinery	-	-	-	-	-	-	-	-	-	-	-
Mining and Quarrying	-	-	-	-	-	-	-	-	-	-	-
Food and Tobacco	-	-	-	-	-	-	-	-	-	-	-
Paper, Pulp and Print	-	-	-	-	-	-	-	-	-	-	-
Wood and Wood Products	-	-	-	-	-	-	-	-	-	-	-
Construction	-	-	-	-	-	-	-	-	-	-	-
Textile and Leather	-	-	-	-	-	-	-	-	-	-	-
Non-specified	-	-	-	-	-	-	8	65	-	-	-
TRANSPORT SECTOR	-	-	**134**	**1**	**65**	-	**57**	**7**	-	-	-
International Civil Aviation	-	-	-	-	58	-	-	-	-	-	-
Domestic Air	-	-	-	1	7	-	-	-	-	-	-
Road	-	-	134	-	-	-	49	-	-	-	-
Rail	-	-	-	-	-	-	-	-	-	-	-
Pipeline Transport	-	-	-	-	-	-	-	-	-	-	-
Internal Navigation	-	-	-	-	-	-	8	7	-	-	-
Non-specified	-	-	-	-	-	-	-	-	-	-	-
OTHER SECTORS	-	**1**	-	-	-	-	**223**	**54**	-	-	-
Agriculture	-	-	-	-	-	-	194	51	-	-	-
Commerce and Publ. Serv.	-	-	-	-	-	-	-	-	-	-	-
Residential	-	1	-	-	-	-	13	3	-	-	-
Non-specified	-	-	-	-	-	-	16	-	-	-	-
NON-ENERGY USE	-	-	-	-	-	-	-	-	-	**46**	**30**
in Industry/Transf./Energy	-	-	-	-	-	-	-	-	-	46	23
in Transport	-	-	-	-	-	-	-	-	-	-	7
in Other Sectors	-	-	-	-	-	-	-	-	-	-	-

Iceland / Islande : 1993

CONSUMPTION *APPROVISIONNEMENT ET DEMANDE*	Gas / *Gaz* (TJ)				Combust. Renew. & Waste / *En. Re. Comb. & Déchets* (TJ)				(GWh)	(TJ)
	Natural Gas *Gaz naturel*	Gas Works *Usines à gaz*	Coke Ovens *Cokeries*	Blast Furnaces *Hauts fourneaux*	Solid Biomass & Anim. Prod. *Biomasse solide & prod. anim.*	Gas/Liquids from Biomass *Gaz/Liquides tirés de biomasse*	Municipal Waste *Déchets urbains*	Industrial Waste *Déchets industriels*	Electricity *Electricité*	Heat *Chaleur*
Production	-	-	-	-	-	-	-	-	4727	7746
From Other Sources	-	-	-	-	-	-	-	-	-	-
Imports	-	-	-	-	-	-	-	-	-	-
Exports	-	-	-	-	-	-	-	-	-	-
Intl. Marine Bunkers	-	-	-	-	-	-	-	-	-	-
Stock Changes	-	-	-	-	-	-	-	-	-	-
DOMESTIC SUPPLY	**-**	**-**	**-**	**-**	**-**	**-**	**-**	**-**	**4727**	**7746**
Transfers	-	-	-	-	-	-	-	-	-	-
Statistical Differences	-	-	-	-	-	-	-	-	-	-
TRANSFORMATION	**-**	**-**	**-**	**-**	**-**	**-**	**-**	**-**	**166**	**-**
Electricity Plants	-	-	-	-	-	-	-	-	-	-
CHP Plants	-	-	-	-	-	-	-	-	-	-
Heat Plants	-	-	-	-	-	-	-	-	166	-
Transfer to Gases	-	-	-	-	-	-	-	-	-	-
Transfer to Solids	-	-	-	-	-	-	-	-	-	-
Petroleum Refineries	-	-	-	-	-	-	-	-	-	-
Petrochemical Industry	-	-	-	-	-	-	-	-	-	-
Liquefaction	-	-	-	-	-	-	-	-	-	-
Other Transformation Sector	-	-	-	-	-	-	-	-	-	-
ENERGY SECTOR	**-**	**-**	**-**	**-**	**-**	**-**	**-**	**-**	**166**	**-**
Coal Mines	-	-	-	-	-	-	-	-	-	-
Oil and Gas Extraction	-	-	-	-	-	-	-	-	-	-
Petroleum Refineries	-	-	-	-	-	-	-	-	-	-
Electricity, CHP+Heat plants	-	-	-	-	-	-	-	-	60	-
Pumped Storage (Elec.)	-	-	-	-	-	-	-	-	-	-
Other Energy Sector	-	-	-	-	-	-	-	-	106	-
Distribution Losses	-	-	-	-	-	-	-	-	313	697
FINAL CONSUMPTION	**-**	**-**	**-**	**-**	**-**	**-**	**-**	**-**	**4082**	**7049**
INDUSTRY SECTOR	**-**	**-**	**-**	**-**	**-**	**-**	**-**	**-**	**2677**	**-**
Iron and Steel	-	-	-	-	-	-	-	-	616	-
Chemical and Petrochemical	-	-	-	-	-	-	-	-	204	-
of which: Feedstocks	-	-	-	-	-	-	-	-	-	-
Non-Ferrous Metals	-	-	-	-	-	-	-	-	1536	-
Non-Metallic Minerals	-	-	-	-	-	-	-	-	37	-
Transport Equipment	-	-	-	-	-	-	-	-	7	-
Machinery	-	-	-	-	-	-	-	-	3	-
Mining and Quarrying	-	-	-	-	-	-	-	-	5	-
Food and Tobacco	-	-	-	-	-	-	-	-	206	-
Paper, Pulp and Print	-	-	-	-	-	-	-	-	12	-
Wood and Wood Products	-	-	-	-	-	-	-	-	7	-
Construction	-	-	-	-	-	-	-	-	18	-
Textile and Leather	-	-	-	-	-	-	-	-	19	-
Non-specified	-	-	-	-	-	-	-	-	7	-
TRANSPORT SECTOR	**-**	**-**	**-**	**-**	**-**	**-**	**-**	**-**	**29**	**-**
International Civil Aviation	-	-	-	-	-	-	-	-	-	-
Domestic Air	-	-	-	-	-	-	-	-	-	-
Road	-	-	-	-	-	-	-	-	-	-
Rail	-	-	-	-	-	-	-	-	-	-
Pipeline Transport	-	-	-	-	-	-	-	-	29	-
Internal Navigation	-	-	-	-	-	-	-	-	-	-
Non-specified	-	-	-	-	-	-	-	-	-	-
OTHER SECTORS	**-**	**-**	**-**	**-**	**-**	**-**	**-**	**-**	**1376**	**7049**
Agriculture	-	-	-	-	-	-	-	-	232	-
Commerce and Publ. Serv.	-	-	-	-	-	-	-	-	505	705
Residential	-	-	-	-	-	-	-	-	559	6344
Non-specified	-	-	-	-	-	-	-	-	80	-
NON-ENERGY USE	**-**	**-**	**-**	**-**	**-**	**-**	**-**	**-**	**-**	**-**
in Industry/Transf./Energy	-	-	-	-	-	-	-	-	-	-
in Transport	-	-	-	-	-	-	-	-	-	-
in Other Sectors	-	-	-	-	-	-	-	-	-	-

Ireland / Irlande : 1992

SUPPLY AND CONSUMPTION *APPROVISIONNEMENT ET DEMANDE*	Coal / *Charbon* (1000 tonnes)							Oil / *Pétrole* (1000 tonnes)			
	Coking Coal *Charbon à coke*	Steam Coal *Charbon vapeur*	Sub-Bit. Coal *Charbon sous-bit.*	Lignite *Lignite*	Peat *Tourbe*	Oven and Gas Coke *Coke de four/gaz*	Pat. Fuel and BKB *Agg./briq. de lignite*	Crude Oil *Pétrole brut*	NGL *LGN*	Feedstocks *Produits d'aliment.*	Additives *Additifs*
Production	-	1	-	-	4371	-	432	-	-	-	-
From Other Sources	-	-	-	-	-	-	-	-	-	-	-
Imports	29	2989	-	59	-	20	-	2002	-	2	-
Exports	-	-30	-	-5	-	-	-10	-	-	-	-
Intl. Marine Bunkers	-	-	-	-	-	-	-	-	-	-	-
Stock Changes	-	-113	-	-	1585	-	-54	-24	-	-2	-
DOMESTIC SUPPLY	**29**	**2847**	**-**	**54**	**5956**	**20**	**368**	**1978**	**-**	**-**	**-**
Transfers	-	-	-	-	-	-	-	-	-	-	-
Statistical Differences	-	-	-	-	-	-	-	-1	-	-	-
TRANSFORMATION	**-**	**2193**	**-**	**-**	**4372**	**-**	**-**	**1977**	**-**	**-**	**-**
Electricity Plants	-	2175	-	-	3185	-	-	-	-	-	-
CHP Plants	-	18	-	-	141	-	-	-	-	-	-
Heat Plants	-	-	-	-	-	-	-	-	-	-	-
Transfer to Gases	-	-	-	-	-	-	-	-	-	-	-
Transfer to Solids	-	-	-	-	1046	-	-	-	-	-	-
Petroleum Refineries	-	-	-	-	-	-	-	1977	-	-	-
Petrochemical Industry	-	-	-	-	-	-	-	-	-	-	-
Liquefaction	-	-	-	-	-	-	-	-	-	-	-
Other Transformation Sector	-	-	-	-	-	-	-	-	-	-	-
ENERGY SECTOR	**-**	**-**	**-**	**-**	**-**	**-**	**-**	**-**	**-**	**-**	**-**
Coal Mines	-	-	-	-	-	-	-	-	-	-	-
Oil and Gas Extraction	-	-	-	-	-	-	-	-	-	-	-
Petroleum Refineries	-	-	-	-	-	-	-	-	-	-	-
Electricity, CHP+Heat plants	-	-	-	-	-	-	-	-	-	-	-
Pumped Storage (Elec.)	-	-	-	-	-	-	-	-	-	-	-
Other Energy Sector	-	-	-	-	-	-	-	-	-	-	-
Distribution Losses	-	-	-	-	-	-	-	-	-	-	-
FINAL CONSUMPTION	**29**	**654**	**-**	**54**	**1584**	**20**	**368**	**-**	**-**	**-**	**-**
INDUSTRY SECTOR	**29**	**169**	**-**	**-**	**-**	**20**	**-**	**-**	**-**	**-**	**-**
Iron and Steel	29	1	-	-	-	20	-	-	-	-	-
Chemical and Petrochemical	-	13	-	-	-	-	-	-	-	-	-
of which: Feedstocks	-	-	-	-	-	-	-	-	-	-	-
Non-Ferrous Metals	-	-	-	-	-	-	-	-	-	-	-
Non-Metallic Minerals	-	104	-	-	-	-	-	-	-	-	-
Transport Equipment	-	-	-	-	-	-	-	-	-	-	-
Machinery	-	-	-	-	-	-	-	-	-	-	-
Mining and Quarrying	-	-	-	-	-	-	-	-	-	-	-
Food and Tobacco	-	49	-	-	-	-	-	-	-	-	-
Paper, Pulp and Print	-	-	-	-	-	-	-	-	-	-	-
Wood and Wood Products	-	-	-	-	-	-	-	-	-	-	-
Construction	-	-	-	-	-	-	-	-	-	-	-
Textile and Leather	-	2	-	-	-	-	-	-	-	-	-
Non-specified	-	-	-	-	-	-	-	-	-	-	-
TRANSPORT SECTOR	**-**	**-**	**-**	**-**	**-**	**-**	**-**	**-**	**-**	**-**	**-**
International Civil Aviation	-	-	-	-	-	-	-	-	-	-	-
Domestic Air	-	-	-	-	-	-	-	-	-	-	-
Road	-	-	-	-	-	-	-	-	-	-	-
Rail	-	-	-	-	-	-	-	-	-	-	-
Pipeline Transport	-	-	-	-	-	-	-	-	-	-	-
Internal Navigation	-	-	-	-	-	-	-	-	-	-	-
Non-specified	-	-	-	-	-	-	-	-	-	-	-
OTHER SECTORS	**-**	**485**	**-**	**54**	**1584**	**-**	**368**	**-**	**-**	**-**	**-**
Agriculture	-	-	-	-	-	-	-	-	-	-	-
Commerce and Publ. Serv.	-	1	-	-	6	-	27	-	-	-	-
Residential	-	484	-	54	1578	-	341	-	-	-	-
Non-specified	-	-	-	-	-	-	-	-	-	-	-
NON-ENERGY USE	**-**	**-**	**-**	**-**	**-**	**-**	**-**	**-**	**-**	**-**	**-**
in Industry/Transf./Energy	-	-	-	-	-	-	-	-	-	-	-
in Transport	-	-	-	-	-	-	-	-	-	-	-
in Other Sectors	-	-	-	-	-	-	-	-	-	-	-

Ireland / Irlande : 1992

SUPPLY AND CONSUMPTION *APPROVISIONNEMENT ET DEMANDE*	Oil cont. / *Pétrole cont.* (1000 tonnes)										
	Refinery Gas *Gaz de raffinerie*	LPG + Ethane *GPL + éthane*	Motor Gasoline *Essence moteur*	Aviation Gasoline *Essence aviation*	Jet Fuel *Carbu- réacteur*	Kerosene *Kérosène*	Gas/ Diesel *Gazole*	Heavy Fuel Oil *Fioul lourd*	Naphtha *Naphta*	Pétrol. Coke *Coke de pétrole*	Other Prod. *Autres prod.*
Production	46	35	361	-	-	-	796	694	41	-	-
From Other Sources	-	-	-	-	-	-	-	-	-	-	-
Imports	-	102	594	1	312	122	1224	906	-	94	196
Exports	-	-7	-18	-	-	-	-132	-618	-40	-	-3
Intl. Marine Bunkers	-	-	-	-	-	-	-5	-12	-	-	-
Stock Changes	-	1	-5	-	-8	1	20	64	-1	-	9
DOMESTIC SUPPLY	**46**	**131**	**932**	**1**	**304**	**123**	**1903**	**1034**	**-**	**94**	**202**
Transfers	-	-	-	-	-	-	-	-	-	-	-
Statistical Differences	-	2	39	-	-4	-7	-51	184	-	-	-6
TRANSFORMATION	**-**	**-**	**-**	**-**	**-**	**-**	**14**	**578**	**-**	**-**	**-**
Electricity Plants	-	-	-	-	-	-	11	577	-	-	-
CHP Plants	-	-	-	-	-	-	3	1	-	-	-
Heat Plants	-	-	-	-	-	-	-	-	-	-	-
Transfer to Gases	-	-	-	-	-	-	-	-	-	-	-
Transfer to Solids	-	-	-	-	-	-	-	-	-	-	-
Petroleum Refineries	-	-	-	-	-	-	-	-	-	-	-
Petrochemical Industry	-	-	-	-	-	-	-	-	-	-	-
Liquefaction	-	-	-	-	-	-	-	-	-	-	-
Other Transformation Sector	-	-	-	-	-	-	-	-	-	-	-
ENERGY SECTOR	**46**	**3**	**-**	**-**	**-**	**-**	**-**	**12**	**-**	**-**	**-**
Coal Mines	-	-	-	-	-	-	-	-	-	-	-
Oil and Gas Extraction	-	-	-	-	-	-	-	-	-	-	-
Petroleum Refineries	46	3	-	-	-	-	-	12	-	-	-
Electricity, CHP+Heat plants	-	-	-	-	-	-	-	-	-	-	-
Pumped Storage (Elec.)	-	-	-	-	-	-	-	-	-	-	-
Other Energy Sector	-	-	-	-	-	-	-	-	-	-	-
Distribution Losses	-	-	-	-	-	-	-	-	-	-	-
FINAL CONSUMPTION	**-**	**130**	**971**	**1**	**300**	**116**	**1838**	**628**	**-**	**94**	**196**
INDUSTRY SECTOR	**-**	**53**	**-**	**-**	**-**	**16**	**154**	**449**	**-**	**66**	**-**
Iron and Steel	-	4	-	-	-	-	1	-	-	-	-
Chemical and Petrochemical	-	4	-	-	-	12	12	35	-	-	-
of which: Feedstocks	-	-	-	-	-	-	-	-	-	-	-
Non-Ferrous Metals	-	-	-	-	-	-	-	243	-	66	-
Non-Metallic Minerals	-	7	-	-	-	-	18	18	-	-	-
Transport Equipment	-	4	-	-	-	-	3	3	-	-	-
Machinery	-	4	-	-	-	2	19	26	-	-	-
Mining and Quarrying	-	-	-	-	-	-	20	6	-	-	-
Food and Tobacco	-	2	-	-	-	-	62	84	-	-	-
Paper, Pulp and Print	-	-	-	-	-	-	3	6	-	-	-
Wood and Wood Products	-	-	-	-	-	-	2	2	-	-	-
Construction	-	-	-	-	-	-	-	-	-	-	-
Textile and Leather	-	3	-	-	-	-	9	17	-	-	-
Non-specified	-	25	-	-	-	2	5	9	-	-	-
TRANSPORT SECTOR	**-**	**7**	**971**	**1**	**300**	**-**	**772**	**21**	**-**	**-**	**-**
International Civil Aviation	-	-	-	-	295	-	-	-	-	-	-
Domestic Air	-	-	-	1	5	-	-	-	-	-	-
Road	-	7	971	-	-	-	709	-	-	-	-
Rail	-	-	-	-	-	-	55	-	-	-	-
Pipeline Transport	-	-	-	-	-	-	-	-	-	-	-
Internal Navigation	-	-	-	-	-	-	8	21	-	-	-
Non-specified	-	-	-	-	-	-	-	-	-	-	-
OTHER SECTORS	**-**	**70**	**-**	**-**	**-**	**100**	**912**	**158**	**-**	**28**	**-**
Agriculture	-	-	-	-	-	-	219	-	-	-	-
Commerce and Publ. Serv.	-	9	-	-	-	-	493	158	-	-	-
Residential	-	61	-	-	-	100	200	-	-	28	-
Non-specified	-	-	-	-	-	-	-	-	-	-	-
NON-ENERGY USE	**-**	**-**	**-**	**-**	**-**	**-**	**-**	**-**	**-**	**-**	**196**
in Industry/Transf./Energy	-	-	-	-	-	-	-	-	-	-	170
in Transport	-	-	-	-	-	-	-	-	-	-	26
in Other Sectors	-	-	-	-	-	-	-	-	-	-	-

Ireland / Irlande : 1992

CONSUMPTION / APPROVISIONNEMENT ET DEMANDE	Gas / Gaz (TJ)				Combust. Renew. & Waste / En. Re. Comb. & Déchets (TJ)				(GWh)	(TJ)
	Natural Gas / Gaz naturel	Gas Works / Usines à gaz	Coke Ovens / Cokeries	Blast Furnaces / Hauts fourneaux	Solid Biomass & Anim. Prod. / Biomasse solide & prod. anim.	Gas/Liquids from Biomass / Gaz/Liquides tirés de biomasse	Municipal Waste / Déchets urbains	Industrial Waste / Déchets industriels	Electricity / Electricité	Heat / Chaleur
Production	88319	-	-	-	-	-	-	-	16011	-
From Other Sources	-	-	-	-	-	-	-	-	-	-
Imports	-	-	-	-	-	-	-	-	-	-
Exports	-	-	-	-	-	-	-	-	-	-
Intl. Marine Bunkers	-	-	-	-	-	-	-	-	-	-
Stock Changes	-	-	-	-	-	-	-	-	-	-
DOMESTIC SUPPLY	**88319**	-	-	-	-	-	-	-	**16011**	-
Transfers	-	-	-	-	-	-	-	-	-	-
Statistical Differences	-	-	-	-	-	-	-	-	-	-
TRANSFORMATION	**35495**	-	-	-	-	-	-	-	-	-
Electricity Plants	34245	-	-	-	-	-	-	-	-	-
CHP Plants	1250	-	-	-	-	-	-	-	-	-
Heat Plants	-	-	-	-	-	-	-	-	-	-
Transfer to Gases	-	-	-	-	-	-	-	-	-	-
Transfer to Solids	-	-	-	-	-	-	-	-	-	-
Petroleum Refineries	-	-	-	-	-	-	-	-	-	-
Petrochemical Industry	-	-	-	-	-	-	-	-	-	-
Liquefaction	-	-	-	-	-	-	-	-	-	-
Other Transformation Sector	-	-	-	-	-	-	-	-	-	-
ENERGY SECTOR	-	-	-	-	-	-	-	-	**1399**	-
Coal Mines	-	-	-	-	-	-	-	-	64	-
Oil and Gas Extraction	-	-	-	-	-	-	-	-	-	-
Petroleum Refineries	-	-	-	-	-	-	-	-	27	-
Electricity, CHP+Heat plants	-	-	-	-	-	-	-	-	974	-
Pumped Storage (Elec.)	-	-	-	-	-	-	-	-	328	-
Other Energy Sector	-	-	-	-	-	-	-	-	6	-
Distribution Losses	1554	-	-	-	-	-	-	-	1406	-
FINAL CONSUMPTION	**51270**	-	-	-	-	-	-	-	**13206**	-
INDUSTRY SECTOR	**36749**	-	-	-	-	-	-	-	**4879**	-
Iron and Steel	702	-	-	-	-	-	-	-	206	-
Chemical and Petrochemical	24833	-	-	-	-	-	-	-	561	-
of which: Feedstocks	20255	-	-	-	-	-	-	-	-	-
Non-Ferrous Metals	-	-	-	-	-	-	-	-	450	-
Non-Metallic Minerals	1979	-	-	-	-	-	-	-	376	-
Transport Equipment	-	-	-	-	-	-	-	-	57	-
Machinery	-	-	-	-	-	-	-	-	568	-
Mining and Quarrying	201	-	-	-	-	-	-	-	165	-
Food and Tobacco	6350	-	-	-	-	-	-	-	1322	-
Paper, Pulp and Print	-	-	-	-	-	-	-	-	129	-
Wood and Wood Products	-	-	-	-	-	-	-	-	124	-
Construction	-	-	-	-	-	-	-	-	32	-
Textile and Leather	-	-	-	-	-	-	-	-	230	-
Non-specified	2684	-	-	-	-	-	-	-	659	-
TRANSPORT SECTOR	-	-	-	-	-	-	-	-	**17**	-
International Civil Aviation	-	-	-	-	-	-	-	-	-	-
Domestic Air	-	-	-	-	-	-	-	-	-	-
Road	-	-	-	-	-	-	-	-	-	-
Rail	-	-	-	-	-	-	-	-	-	-
Pipeline Transport	-	-	-	-	-	-	-	-	17	-
Internal Navigation	-	-	-	-	-	-	-	-	-	-
Non-specified	-	-	-	-	-	-	-	-	-	-
OTHER SECTORS	**14521**	-	-	-	-	-	-	-	**8310**	-
Agriculture	-	-	-	-	-	-	-	-	-	-
Commerce and Publ. Serv.	5848	-	-	-	-	-	-	-	3239	-
Residential	8673	-	-	-	-	-	-	-	5071	-
Non-specified	-	-	-	-	-	-	-	-	-	-
NON-ENERGY USE	-	-	-	-	-	-	-	-	-	-
in Industry/Transf./Energy	-	-	-	-	-	-	-	-	-	-
in Transport	-	-	-	-	-	-	-	-	-	-
in Other Sectors	-	-	-	-	-	-	-	-	-	-

Ireland / Irlande : 1993

SUPPLY AND CONSUMPTION	Coal / *Charbon* (1000 tonnes)							Oil / *Pétrole* (1000 tonnes)			
	Coking Coal	Steam Coal	Sub-Bit. Coal	Lignite	Peat	Oven and Gas Coke	Pat. Fuel and BKB	Crude Oil	NGL	Feedstocks	Additives
APPROVISIONNEMENT ET DEMANDE	*Charbon à coke*	*Charbon vapeur*	*Charbon sous-bit.*	*Lignite*	*Tourbe*	*Coke de four/gaz*	*Agg./briq. de lignite*	*Pétrole brut*	*LGN*	*Produits d'aliment.*	*Additifs*
Production	-	1	-	-	5082	-	364	-	-	-	-
From Other Sources	-	-	-	-	-	-	-	-	-	-	-
Imports	20	2887	-	50	-	15	4	1858	-	31	-
Exports	-	-15	-	-6	-	-	-13	-	-	-	-
Intl. Marine Bunkers	-	-	-	-	-	-	-	-	-	-	-
Stock Changes	-	-5	-	-	405	-	30	6	-	5	-
DOMESTIC SUPPLY	**20**	**2868**	**-**	**44**	**5487**	**15**	**385**	**1864**	**-**	**36**	**-**
Transfers	-	-	-	-	-	-	-	-	-	-	-
Statistical Differences	-	-	-	-	-	-	-	-	-	-5	-
TRANSFORMATION	**-**	**2149**	**-**	**-**	**4027**	**-**	**-**	**1864**	**-**	**31**	**-**
Electricity Plants	-	2131	-	-	2945	-	-	-	-	-	-
CHP Plants	-	18	-	-	72	-	-	-	-	-	-
Heat Plants	-	-	-	-	-	-	-	-	-	-	-
Transfer to Gases	-	-	-	-	-	-	-	-	-	-	-
Transfer to Solids	-	-	-	-	1010	-	-	-	-	-	-
Petroleum Refineries	-	-	-	-	-	-	-	1864	-	31	-
Petrochemical Industry	-	-	-	-	-	-	-	-	-	-	-
Liquefaction	-	-	-	-	-	-	-	-	-	-	-
Other Transformation Sector	-	-	-	-	-	-	-	-	-	-	-
ENERGY SECTOR	**-**	**-**	**-**	**-**	**-**	**-**	**-**	**-**	**-**	**-**	**-**
Coal Mines	-	-	-	-	-	-	-	-	-	-	-
Oil and Gas Extraction	-	-	-	-	-	-	-	-	-	-	-
Petroleum Refineries	-	-	-	-	-	-	-	-	-	-	-
Electricity, CHP+Heat plants	-	-	-	-	-	-	-	-	-	-	-
Pumped Storage (Elec.)	-	-	-	-	-	-	-	-	-	-	-
Other Energy Sector	-	-	-	-	-	-	-	-	-	-	-
Distribution Losses	-	-	-	-	-	-	-	-	-	-	-
FINAL CONSUMPTION	**20**	**719**	**-**	**44**	**1460**	**15**	**385**	**-**	**-**	**-**	**-**
INDUSTRY SECTOR	**20**	**208**	**-**	**-**	**-**	**15**	**-**	**-**	**-**	**-**	**-**
Iron and Steel	20	1	-	-	-	15	-	-	-	-	-
Chemical and Petrochemical	-	16	-	-	-	-	-	-	-	-	-
of which: Feedstocks	-	-	-	-	-	-	-	-	-	-	-
Non-Ferrous Metals	-	-	-	-	-	-	-	-	-	-	-
Non-Metallic Minerals	-	128	-	-	-	-	-	-	-	-	-
Transport Equipment	-	-	-	-	-	-	-	-	-	-	-
Machinery	-	-	-	-	-	-	-	-	-	-	-
Mining and Quarrying	-	-	-	-	-	-	-	-	-	-	-
Food and Tobacco	-	60	-	-	-	-	-	-	-	-	-
Paper, Pulp and Print	-	-	-	-	-	-	-	-	-	-	-
Wood and Wood Products	-	-	-	-	-	-	-	-	-	-	-
Construction	-	-	-	-	-	-	-	-	-	-	-
Textile and Leather	-	3	-	-	-	-	-	-	-	-	-
Non-specified	-	-	-	-	-	-	-	-	-	-	-
TRANSPORT SECTOR	**-**	**-**	**-**	**-**	**-**	**-**	**-**	**-**	**-**	**-**	**-**
International Civil Aviation	-	-	-	-	-	-	-	-	-	-	-
Domestic Air	-	-	-	-	-	-	-	-	-	-	-
Road	-	-	-	-	-	-	-	-	-	-	-
Rail	-	-	-	-	-	-	-	-	-	-	-
Pipeline Transport	-	-	-	-	-	-	-	-	-	-	-
Internal Navigation	-	-	-	-	-	-	-	-	-	-	-
Non-specified	-	-	-	-	-	-	-	-	-	-	-
OTHER SECTORS	**-**	**511**	**-**	**44**	**1460**	**-**	**385**	**-**	**-**	**-**	**-**
Agriculture	-	-	-	-	-	-	-	-	-	-	-
Commerce and Publ. Serv.	-	1	-	-	15	-	21	-	-	-	-
Residential	-	510	-	44	1445	-	364	-	-	-	-
Non-specified	-	-	-	-	-	-	-	-	-	-	-
NON-ENERGY USE	**-**	**-**	**-**	**-**	**-**	**-**	**-**	**-**	**-**	**-**	**-**
in Industry/Transf./Energy	-	-	-	-	-	-	-	-	-	-	-
in Transport	-	-	-	-	-	-	-	-	-	-	-
in Other Sectors	-	-	-	-	-	-	-	-	-	-	-

Ireland / Irlande : 1993

SUPPLY AND CONSUMPTION / APPROVISIONNEMENT ET DEMANDE	Oil cont. / Pétrole cont. (1000 tonnes)										
	Refinery Gas / Gaz de raffinerie	LPG + Ethane / GPL + éthane	Motor Gasoline / Essence moteur	Aviation Gasoline / Essence aviation	Jet Fuel / Carbu-réacteur	Kerosene / Kérosène	Gas/ Diesel / Gazole	Heavy Fuel Oil / Fioul lourd	Naphtha / Naphta	Pétrol. Coke / Coke de pétrole	Other Prod. / Autres prod.
Production	44	28	367	-	-	-	737	681	32	-	-
From Other Sources	-	-	-	-	-	-	-	-	-	-	-
Imports	-	111	586	1	433	138	1229	1267	-	85	168
Exports	-	-	-9	-	-	-	-65	-689	-29	-	-
Intl. Marine Bunkers	-	-	-	-	-	-	-34	-20	-	-	-
Stock Changes	-	-	3	-	-2	-6	-19	-52	-	-	-
DOMESTIC SUPPLY	**44**	**139**	**947**	**1**	**431**	**132**	**1848**	**1187**	**3**	**85**	**168**
Transfers	-	-	-	-	-	-	-	-	-	-	-
Statistical Differences	-	-4	6	-	6	2	14	16	-3	-	-
TRANSFORMATION	-	-	-	-	-	-	9	573	-	-	-
Electricity Plants	-	-	-	-	-	-	8	570	-	-	-
CHP Plants	-	-	-	-	-	-	1	3	-	-	-
Heat Plants	-	-	-	-	-	-	-	-	-	-	-
Transfer to Gases	-	-	-	-	-	-	-	-	-	-	-
Transfer to Solids	-	-	-	-	-	-	-	-	-	-	-
Petroleum Refineries	-	-	-	-	-	-	-	-	-	-	-
Petrochemical Industry	-	-	-	-	-	-	-	-	-	-	-
Liquefaction	-	-	-	-	-	-	-	-	-	-	-
Other Transformation Sector	-	-	-	-	-	-	-	-	-	-	-
ENERGY SECTOR	**44**	**4**	-	-	-	-	**3**	**10**	-	-	-
Coal Mines	-	-	-	-	-	-	-	-	-	-	-
Oil and Gas Extraction	-	-	-	-	-	-	-	-	-	-	-
Petroleum Refineries	44	4	-	-	-	-	3	10	-	-	-
Electricity, CHP+Heat plants	-	-	-	-	-	-	-	-	-	-	-
Pumped Storage (Elec.)	-	-	-	-	-	-	-	-	-	-	-
Other Energy Sector	-	-	-	-	-	-	-	-	-	-	-
Distribution Losses	-	-	-	-	-	-	-	-	-	-	-
FINAL CONSUMPTION	-	**131**	**953**	**1**	**437**	**134**	**1850**	**620**	-	**85**	**168**
INDUSTRY SECTOR	-	**54**	-	-	-	**18**	**153**	**443**	-	**60**	-
Iron and Steel	-	4	-	-	-	-	1	-	-	-	-
Chemical and Petrochemical	-	4	-	-	-	14	12	36	-	-	-
of which: Feedstocks	-	-	-	-	-	-	-	-	-	-	-
Non-Ferrous Metals	-	-	-	-	-	-	-	240	-	60	-
Non-Metallic Minerals	-	6	-	-	-	-	18	18	-	-	-
Transport Equipment	-	4	-	-	-	-	3	3	-	-	-
Machinery	-	4	-	-	-	2	19	25	-	-	-
Mining and Quarrying	-	-	-	-	-	-	20	6	-	-	-
Food and Tobacco	-	2	-	-	-	-	62	82	-	-	-
Paper, Pulp and Print	-	-	-	-	-	-	3	6	-	-	-
Wood and Wood Products	-	-	-	-	-	-	2	2	-	-	-
Construction	-	-	-	-	-	-	-	-	-	-	-
Textile and Leather	-	3	-	-	-	-	9	17	-	-	-
Non-specified	-	27	-	-	-	2	4	8	-	-	-
TRANSPORT SECTOR	-	**6**	**953**	**1**	**437**	-	**783**	**21**	-	-	-
International Civil Aviation	-	-	-	1	416	-	-	-	-	-	-
Domestic Air	-	-	-	-	21	-	-	-	-	-	-
Road	-	6	953	-	-	-	720	-	-	-	-
Rail	-	-	-	-	-	-	55	-	-	-	-
Pipeline Transport	-	-	-	-	-	-	-	-	-	-	-
Internal Navigation	-	-	-	-	-	-	-	-	-	-	-
Non-specified	-	-	-	-	-	-	8	21	-	-	-
OTHER SECTORS	-	**71**	-	-	-	**116**	**914**	**156**	-	**25**	-
Agriculture	-	-	-	-	-	-	220	-	-	-	-
Commerce and Publ. Serv.	-	9	-	-	-	-	494	156	-	-	-
Residential	-	62	-	-	-	116	200	-	-	25	-
Non-specified	-	-	-	-	-	-	-	-	-	-	-
NON-ENERGY USE	-	-	-	-	-	-	-	-	-	-	**168**
in Industry/Transf./Energy	-	-	-	-	-	-	-	-	-	-	168
in Transport	-	-	-	-	-	-	-	-	-	-	141
in Other Sectors	-	-	-	-	-	-	-	-	-	-	27

Ireland / Irlande : 1993

CONSUMPTION / APPROVISIONNEMENT ET DEMANDE	Gas / Gaz (TJ)				Combust. Renew. & Waste / En. Re. Comb. & Déchets (TJ)				Electricity (GWh)	Heat (TJ)
	Natural Gas / Gaz naturel	Gas Works / Usines à gaz	Coke Ovens / Cokeries	Blast Furnaces / Hauts fourneaux	Solid Biomass & Anim. Prod. / Biomasse solide & prod. anim.	Gas/Liquids from Biomass / Gaz/Liquides tirés de biomasse	Municipal Waste / Déchets urbains	Industrial Waste / Déchets industriels	Electricity / Electricité	Heat / Chaleur
Production	100312	-	-	-	438	11	4	1	16396	-
From Other Sources	-	-	-	-	-	-	-	-	-	-
Imports	190	-	-	-	-	-	-	-	-	-
Exports	-	-	-	-	-	-	-	-	-	-
Intl. Marine Bunkers	-	-	-	-	-	-	-	-	-	-
Stock Changes	-190	-	-	-	-	-	-	-	-	-
DOMESTIC SUPPLY	**100312**	**-**	**-**	**-**	**438**	**11**	**4**	**1**	**16396**	**-**
Transfers	-	-	-	-	-	-	-	-	-	-
Statistical Differences	-	-	-	-	-	-	-	-	-	-
TRANSFORMATION	**44646**	**-**	**-**	**-**	**-**	**-**	**4**	**1**	**-**	**-**
Electricity Plants	43239	-	-	-	-	-	4	1	-	-
CHP Plants	1407	-	-	-	-	-	-	-	-	-
Heat Plants	-	-	-	-	-	-	-	-	-	-
Transfer to Gases	-	-	-	-	-	-	-	-	-	-
Transfer to Solids	-	-	-	-	-	-	-	-	-	-
Petroleum Refineries	-	-	-	-	-	-	-	-	-	-
Petrochemical Industry	-	-	-	-	-	-	-	-	-	-
Liquefaction	-	-	-	-	-	-	-	-	-	-
Other Transformation Sector	-	-	-	-	-	-	-	-	-	-
ENERGY SECTOR	**-**	**-**	**-**	**-**	**-**	**-**	**-**	**-**	**1424**	**-**
Coal Mines	-	-	-	-	-	-	-	-	53	-
Oil and Gas Extraction	-	-	-	-	-	-	-	-	-	-
Petroleum Refineries	-	-	-	-	-	-	-	-	33	-
Electricity, CHP+Heat plants	-	-	-	-	-	-	-	-	983	-
Pumped Storage (Elec.)	-	-	-	-	-	-	-	-	349	-
Other Energy Sector	-	-	-	-	-	-	-	-	6	-
Distribution Losses	1370	-	-	-	-	-	-	-	1423	-
FINAL CONSUMPTION	**54296**	**-**	**-**	**-**	**438**	**11**	**-**	**-**	**13549**	**-**
INDUSTRY SECTOR	**37177**	**-**	**-**	**-**	**275**	**11**	**-**	**-**	**5054**	**-**
Iron and Steel	805	-	-	-	-	-	-	-	230	-
Chemical and Petrochemical	23241	-	-	-	-	-	-	-	642	-
of which: Feedstocks	19097	-	-	-	-	-	-	-	-	-
Non-Ferrous Metals	-	-	-	-	-	-	-	-	428	-
Non-Metallic Minerals	2532	-	-	-	-	-	-	-	383	-
Transport Equipment	-	-	-	-	-	-	-	-	61	-
Machinery	-	-	-	-	-	-	-	-	652	-
Mining and Quarrying	468	-	-	-	-	-	-	-	96	-
Food and Tobacco	5311	-	-	-	-	-	-	-	1325	-
Paper, Pulp and Print	-	-	-	-	-	-	-	-	140	-
Wood and Wood Products	-	-	-	-	-	-	-	-	128	-
Construction	-	-	-	-	-	-	-	-	25	-
Textile and Leather	-	-	-	-	-	-	-	-	234	-
Non-specified	4820	-	-	-	275	11	-	-	710	-
TRANSPORT SECTOR	**-**	**-**	**-**	**-**	**-**	**-**	**-**	**-**	**18**	**-**
International Civil Aviation	-	-	-	-	-	-	-	-	-	-
Domestic Air	-	-	-	-	-	-	-	-	-	-
Road	-	-	-	-	-	-	-	-	18	-
Rail	-	-	-	-	-	-	-	-	-	-
Pipeline Transport	-	-	-	-	-	-	-	-	-	-
Internal Navigation	-	-	-	-	-	-	-	-	-	-
Non-specified	-	-	-	-	-	-	-	-	-	-
OTHER SECTORS	**17119**	**-**	**-**	**-**	**163**	**-**	**-**	**-**	**8477**	**-**
Agriculture	-	-	-	-	-	-	-	-	-	-
Commerce and Publ. Serv.	7057	-	-	-	-	-	-	-	3314	-
Residential	10062	-	-	-	163	-	-	-	5163	-
Non-specified	-	-	-	-	-	-	-	-	-	-
NON-ENERGY USE	**-**	**-**	**-**	**-**	**-**	**-**	**-**	**-**	**-**	**-**
in Industry/Transf./Energy	-	-	-	-	-	-	-	-	-	-
in Transport	-	-	-	-	-	-	-	-	-	-
in Other Sectors	-	-	-	-	-	-	-	-	-	-

Italy / Italie : 1992

SUPPLY AND CONSUMPTION	Coal / *Charbon* (1000 tonnes)							Oil / *Pétrole* (1000 tonnes)			
APPROVISIONNEMENT ET DEMANDE	Coking Coal *Charbon à coke*	Steam Coal *Charbon vapeur*	Sub-Bit. Coal *Charbon sous-bit.*	Lignite *Lignite*	Peat *Tourbe*	Oven and Gas Coke *Coke de four/gaz*	Pat. Fuel and BKB *Agg./briq. de lignite*	Crude Oil *Pétrole brut*	NGL *LGN*	Feedstocks *Produits d'aliment.*	Additives *Additifs*
Production	-	111	-	714	-	5413	-	4479	22	-	-
From Other Sources	-	-	-	-	-	-	-	-	-	2400	393
Imports	7392	10320	-	84	-	298	-	77985	-	11358	-
Exports	-	-	-	-	-	-186	-	-246	-	-	-
Intl. Marine Bunkers	-	-	-	-	-	-	-	-	-	-	-
Stock Changes	177	-348	-	-61	-	-22	-	-613	-	-99	-
DOMESTIC SUPPLY	**7569**	**10083**	**-**	**737**	**-**	**5503**	**-**	**81605**	**22**	**13659**	**393**
Transfers	-	-	-	-	-	-	-	-	-	-	-
Statistical Differences	-	-	-	-	-	-	-	-	-	-	-
TRANSFORMATION	**7311**	**7242**	**-**	**676**	**-**	**1536**	**-**	**81397**	**22**	**13659**	**393**
Electricity Plants	-	7207	-	676	-	-	-	-	-	-	-
CHP Plants	-	35	-	-	-	-	-	-	-	-	-
Heat Plants	-	-	-	-	-	-	-	-	-	-	-
Transfer to Gases	-	-	-	-	-	1536	-	-	-	-	-
Transfer to Solids	7311	-	-	-	-	-	-	-	-	-	-
Petroleum Refineries	-	-	-	-	-	-	-	81397	22	13659	393
Petrochemical Industry	-	-	-	-	-	-	-	-	-	-	-
Liquefaction	-	-	-	-	-	-	-	-	-	-	-
Other Transformation Sector	-	-	-	-	-	-	-	-	-	-	-
ENERGY SECTOR	**2**	**-**	**-**	**-**	**-**	**52**	**-**	**208**	**-**	**-**	**-**
Coal Mines	-	-	-	-	-	-	-	-	-	-	-
Oil and Gas Extraction	-	-	-	-	-	-	-	208	-	-	-
Petroleum Refineries	-	-	-	-	-	-	-	-	-	-	-
Electricity, CHP+Heat plants	-	-	-	-	-	-	-	-	-	-	-
Pumped Storage (Elec.)	-	-	-	-	-	-	-	-	-	-	-
Other Energy Sector	2	-	-	-	-	52	-	-	-	-	-
Distribution Losses	14	-	-	-	-	7	-	-	-	-	-
FINAL CONSUMPTION	**242**	**2841**	**-**	**61**	**-**	**3908**	**-**	**-**	**-**	**-**	**-**
INDUSTRY SECTOR	**-**	**2772**	**-**	**61**	**-**	**3803**	**-**	**-**	**-**	**-**	**-**
Iron and Steel	-	1206	-	21	-	3515	-	-	-	-	-
Chemical and Petrochemical	-	5	-	4	-	55	-	-	-	-	-
of which: Feedstocks	-	-	-	-	-	-	-	-	-	-	-
Non-Ferrous Metals	-	44	-	-	-	17	-	-	o	-	-
Non-Metallic Minerals	-	1481	-	10	-	62	-	-	-	-	-
Transport Equipment	-	-	-	-	-	-	-	-	-	-	-
Machinery	-	24	-	16	-	121	-	-	-	-	-
Mining and Quarrying	-	-	-	-	-	-	-	-	-	-	-
Food and Tobacco	-	-	-	5	-	33	-	-	-	-	-
Paper, Pulp and Print	-	-	-	-	-	-	-	-	-	-	-
Wood and Wood Products	-	-	-	-	-	-	-	-	-	-	-
Construction	-	-	-	-	-	-	-	-	-	-	-
Textile and Leather	-	8	-	-	-	-	-	-	-	-	-
Non-specified	-	4	-	5	-	-	-	-	-	-	-
TRANSPORT SECTOR	**-**	**-**	**-**	**-**	**-**	**-**	**-**	**-**	**-**	**-**	**-**
International Civil Aviation	-	-	-	-	-	-	-	-	-	-	-
Domestic Air	-	-	-	-	-	-	-	-	-	-	-
Road	-	-	-	-	-	-	-	-	-	-	-
Rail	-	-	-	-	-	-	-	-	-	-	-
Pipeline Transport	-	-	-	-	-	-	-	-	-	-	-
Internal Navigation	-	-	-	-	-	-	-	-	-	-	-
Non-specified	-	-	-	-	-	-	-	-	-	-	-
OTHER SECTORS	**-**	**69**	**-**	**-**	**-**	**105**	**-**	**-**	**-**	**-**	**-**
Agriculture	-	-	-	-	-	-	-	-	-	-	-
Commerce and Publ. Serv.	-	-	-	-	-	-	-	-	-	-	-
Residential	-	69	-	-	-	105	-	-	-	-	-
Non-specified	-	-	-	-	-	-	-	-	-	-	-
NON-ENERGY USE	**242**	**-**	**-**	**-**	**-**	**-**	**-**	**-**	**-**	**-**	**-**
in Industry/Transf./Energy	242	-	-	-	-	-	-	-	-	-	-
in Transport	-	-	-	-	-	-	-	-	-	-	-
in Other Sectors	-	-	-	-	-	-	-	-	-	-	-

Italy / Italie : 1992

SUPPLY AND CONSUMPTION *APPROVISIONNEMENT ET DEMANDE*	Oil cont. / *Pétrole cont.* (1000 tonnes)										
	Refinery Gas *Gaz de raffinerie*	LPG + Ethane *GPL + éthane*	Motor Gasoline *Essence moteur*	Aviation Gasoline *Essence aviation*	Jet Fuel *Carbu-réacteur*	Kerosene *Kérosène*	Gas/Diesel *Gazole*	Heavy Fuel Oil *Fioul lourd*	Naphtha *Naphta*	Pétrol. Coke *Coke de pétrole*	Other Prod. *Autres prod.*
Production	2810	2247	19612	44	2738	2095	30955	24315	3566	1217	4214
From Other Sources	-	-	-	-	-	-	-	-	-	-	-
Imports	-	1337	1137	-	-	7	3473	14414	912	1776	307
Exports	-	-239	-3619	-36	-353	-1190	-7276	-7032	-484	-	-985
Intl. Marine Bunkers	-	-	-	-	-	-	-572	-1880	-	-	-52
Stock Changes	-	72	-37	-	4	89	118	299	164	4	50
DOMESTIC SUPPLY	**2810**	**3417**	**17093**	**8**	**2389**	**1001**	**26698**	**30116**	**4158**	**2997**	**3534**
Transfers	-	-	-243	-	243	-	-	-	-	-	-
Statistical Differences	-	-	-36	-	-279	-	-	-	-	-	37
TRANSFORMATION	**215**	**67**	**398**	**-**	**-**	**262**	**786**	**24488**	**1056**	**276**	**-**
Electricity Plants	-	-	-	-	-	-	213	22936	9	-	-
CHP Plants	215	-	-	-	-	-	4	1453	-	276	-
Heat Plants	-	-	-	-	-	-	-	-	-	-	-
Transfer to Gases	-	29	-	-	-	-	-	-	13	-	-
Transfer to Solids	-	-	-	-	-	-	-	-	-	-	-
Petroleum Refineries	-	-	-	-	-	-	-	-	-	-	-
Petrochemical Industry	-	38	398	-	-	262	569	99	1034	-	-
Liquefaction	-	-	-	-	-	-	-	-	-	-	-
Other Transformation Sector	-	-	-	-	-	-	-	-	-	-	-
ENERGY SECTOR	**2353**	**44**	**-**	**-**	**1**	**6**	**-**	**1119**	**34**	**606**	**-**
Coal Mines	-	-	-	-	-	-	-	-	-	-	-
Oil and Gas Extraction	-	-	-	-	-	-	-	-	-	-	-
Petroleum Refineries	2353	44	-	-	1	6	-	1119	34	606	-
Electricity, CHP+Heat plants	-	-	-	-	-	-	-	-	-	-	-
Pumped Storage (Elec.)	-	-	-	-	-	-	-	-	-	-	-
Other Energy Sector	-	-	-	-	-	-	-	-	-	-	-
Distribution Losses	-	16	74	-	21	4	48	53	-	-	-
FINAL CONSUMPTION	**242**	**3290**	**16342**	**8**	**2331**	**729**	**25864**	**4456**	**3068**	**2115**	**3571**
INDUSTRY SECTOR	**242**	**313**	**864**	**-**	**20**	**553**	**1561**	**3914**	**3068**	**1986**	**-**
Iron and Steel	-	9	-	-	-	-	16	73	-	-	-
Chemical and Petrochemical	242	129	812	-	-	542	1186	1228	3068	247	-
of which: Feedstocks	*242*	*89*	*812*	-	-	*542*	*1176*	*203*	*2139*	-	-
Non-Ferrous Metals	-	5	-	-	-	-	5	-	-	-	-
Non-Metallic Minerals	-	34	-	-	-	-	57	908	-	1687	-
Transport Equipment	-	-	-	-	-	-	-	-	-	-	-
Machinery	-	88	52	-	20	11	133	377	-	9	-
Mining and Quarrying	-	2	-	-	-	-	17	3	-	-	-
Food and Tobacco	-	13	-	-	-	-	29	337	-	-	-
Paper, Pulp and Print	-	6	-	-	-	-	13	289	-	4	-
Wood and Wood Products	-	-	-	-	-	-	-	-	-	-	-
Construction	-	4	-	-	-	-	56	23	-	-	-
Textile and Leather	-	7	-	-	-	-	14	420	-	39	-
Non-specified	-	16	-	-	-	-	35	256	-	-	-
TRANSPORT SECTOR	**-**	**1187**	**15334**	**8**	**2311**	**-**	**15350**	**-**	**-**	**-**	**6**
International Civil Aviation	-	-	-	-	2311	-	-	-	-	-	-
Domestic Air	-	-	-	8	-	-	-	-	-	-	-
Road	-	1187	15151	-	-	-	14955	-	-	-	6
Rail	-	-	-	-	-	-	193	-	-	-	-
Pipeline Transport	-	-	-	-	-	-	-	-	-	-	-
Internal Navigation	-	-	183	-	-	-	202	-	-	-	-
Non-specified	-	-	-	-	-	-	-	-	-	-	-
OTHER SECTORS	**-**	**1790**	**144**	**-**	**-**	**176**	**8953**	**542**	**-**	**-**	**13**
Agriculture	-	78	144	-	-	10	2185	60	-	-	6
Commerce and Publ. Serv.	-	-	-	-	-	-	621	173	-	-	7
Residential	-	1712	-	-	-	166	6147	309	-	-	-
Non-specified	-	-	-	-	-	-	-	-	-	-	-
NON-ENERGY USE	**-**	**-**	**-**	**-**	**-**	**-**	**-**	**-**	**-**	**129**	**3552**
in Industry/Transf./Energy	-	-	-	-	-	-	-	-	-	129	3182
in Transport	-	-	-	-	-	-	-	-	-	-	330
in Other Sectors	-	-	-	-	-	-	-	-	-	-	40

Italy / Italie : 1992

CONSUMPTION / APPROVISIONNEMENT ET DEMANDE	Gas / Gaz (TJ)				Combust. Renew. & Waste / En. Re. Comb. & Déchets (TJ)				(GWh)	(TJ)
	Natural Gas / Gaz naturel	Gas Works / Usines à gaz	Coke Ovens / Cokeries	Blast Furnaces / Hauts fourneaux	Solid Biomass & Anim. Prod. / Biomasse solide & prod. anim.	Gas/Liquids from Biomass / Gaz/Liquides tirés de biomasse	Municipal Waste / Déchets urbains	Industrial Waste / Déchets industriels	Electricity / Electricité	Heat / Chaleur
Production	685403	-	46791	49604	37000	151	1800	3850	226243	-
From Other Sources	-	9146	-	-	-	-	-	-	-	-
Imports	1316877	-	-	-	4900	-	-	-	35947	-
Exports	-1112	-	-	-	-	-	-	-	-647	-
Intl. Marine Bunkers	-	-	-	-	-	-	-	-	-	-
Stock Changes	-88630	-	-	-	-	-	-	-	-	-
DOMESTIC SUPPLY	**1912538**	**9146**	**46791**	**49604**	**41900**	**151**	**1800**	**3850**	**261543**	**-**
Transfers	-	-	-	-	-	-	-	-	-	-
Statistical Differences	-	-	-	-1	-	-	-	-	-	-
TRANSFORMATION	**344520**	**-**	**10549**	**25693**	**3700**	**151**	**1800**	**3850**	**-**	**-**
Electricity Plants	272857	-	10549	19286	-	113	1423	794	-	-
CHP Plants	63106	-	-	6407	-	38	377	3056	-	-
Heat Plants	-	-	-	-	-	-	-	-	-	-
Transfer to Gases	8557	-	-	-	-	-	-	-	-	-
Transfer to Solids	-	-	-	-	3700	-	-	-	-	-
Petroleum Refineries	-	-	-	-	-	-	-	-	-	-
Petrochemical Industry	-	-	-	-	-	-	-	-	-	-
Liquefaction	-	-	-	-	-	-	-	-	-	-
Other Transformation Sector	-	-	-	-	-	-	-	-	-	-
ENERGY SECTOR	**19176**	**17**	**19159**	**12026**	**-**	**-**	**-**	**-**	**21339**	**-**
Coal Mines	-	-	-	-	-	-	-	-	66	-
Oil and Gas Extraction	19176	-	-	-	-	-	-	-	93	-
Petroleum Refineries	-	-	-	-	-	-	-	-	3316	-
Electricity, CHP+Heat plants	-	-	-	-	-	-	-	-	11810	-
Pumped Storage (Elec.)	-	-	-	-	-	-	-	-	4946	-
Other Energy Sector	-	17	19159	12026	-	-	-	-	1108	-
Distribution Losses	37599	142	218	406	-	-	-	-	16779	-
FINAL CONSUMPTION	**1511243**	**8987**	**16865**	**11478**	**38200**	**-**	**-**	**-**	**223425**	**-**
INDUSTRY SECTOR	**690287**	**268**	**16865**	**11478**	**5700**	**-**	**-**	**-**	**111244**	**-**
Iron and Steel	79577	-	14802	11478	-	-	-	-	18802	-
Chemical and Petrochemical	190653	-	996	-	-	-	-	-	18929	-
of which: Feedstocks	*69025*	-	-	-	-	-	-	-	-	-
Non-Ferrous Metals	14464	-	-	-	-	-	-	-	4954	-
Non-Metallic Minerals	138933	142	364	-	5700	-	-	-	11800	-
Transport Equipment	-	-	-	-	-	-	-	-	3707	-
Machinery	71978	126	-	-	-	-	-	-	14611	-
Mining and Quarrying	1651	-	-	-	-	-	-	-	1281	-
Food and Tobacco	73090	-	-	-	-	-	-	-	8334	-
Paper, Pulp and Print	54329	-	-	-	-	-	-	-	7487	-
Wood and Wood Products	-	-	-	-	-	-	-	-	1830	-
Construction	-	-	-	-	-	-	-	-	1128	-
Textile and Leather	45121	-	-	-	-	-	-	-	9939	-
Non-specified	20491	-	703	-	-	-	-	-	8442	-
TRANSPORT SECTOR	**9976**	**-**	**-**	**-**	**-**	**-**	**-**	**-**	**7191**	**-**
International Civil Aviation	-	-	-	-	-	-	-	-	-	-
Domestic Air	-	-	-	-	-	-	-	-	-	-
Road	9976	-	-	-	-	-	-	-	-	-
Rail	-	-	-	-	-	-	-	-	4400	-
Pipeline Transport	-	-	-	-	-	-	-	-	546	-
Internal Navigation	-	-	-	-	-	-	-	-	-	-
Non-specified	-	-	-	-	-	-	-	-	2245	-
OTHER SECTORS	**810980**	**8719**	**-**	**-**	**32500**	**-**	**-**	**-**	**104990**	**-**
Agriculture	4181	-	-	-	-	-	-	-	4331	-
Commerce and Publ. Serv.	-	-	-	-	-	-	-	-	44920	-
Residential	806799	8719	-	-	32500	-	-	-	55739	-
Non-specified	-	-	-	-	-	-	-	-	-	-
NON-ENERGY USE	**-**	**-**	**-**	**-**	**-**	**-**	**-**	**-**	**-**	**-**
in Industry/Transf./Energy	-	-	-	-	-	-	-	-	-	-
in Transport	-	-	-	-	-	-	-	-	-	-
in Other Sectors	-	-	-	-	-	-	-	-	-	-

Italy / Italie : 1993

SUPPLY AND CONSUMPTION / APPROVISIONNEMENT ET DEMANDE	Coal / Charbon (1000 tonnes)							Oil / Pétrole (1000 tonnes)			
	Coking Coal / Charbon à coke	Steam Coal / Charbon vapeur	Sub-Bit. Coal / Charbon sous-bit.	Lignite / Lignite	Peat / Tourbe	Oven and Gas Coke / Coke de four/gaz	Pat. Fuel and BKB / Agg./briq. de lignite	Crude Oil / Pétrole brut	NGL / LGN	Feedstocks / Produits d'aliment.	Additives / Additifs
Production	-	10	-	620	-	4929	-	4620	20	-	-
From Other Sources	-	-	-	-	-	-	-	-	-	3443	449
Imports	6796	7503	-	20	-	301	-	77208	-	9569	-
Exports	-	-	-	-	-	-167	-	-420	-	-	-
Intl. Marine Bunkers	-	-	-	-	-	-	-	-	-	-	-
Stock Changes	65	645	-	-	-	287	-	28	-	39	-
DOMESTIC SUPPLY	**6861**	**8158**	**-**	**640**	**-**	**5350**	**-**	**81436**	**20**	**13051**	**449**
Transfers	-	-	-	-	-	-	-	-	-	-	-
Statistical Differences	-	-	-	-	-	-	-	200	-	-	-
TRANSFORMATION	**6639**	**5569**	**-**	**620**	**-**	**1496**	**-**	**81436**	**20**	**13051**	**449**
Electricity Plants	-	5523	-	620	-	-	-	-	-	-	-
CHP Plants	-	46	-	-	-	-	-	-	-	-	-
Heat Plants	-	-	-	-	-	-	-	-	-	-	-
Transfer to Gases	-	-	-	-	-	1496	-	-	-	-	-
Transfer to Solids	6639	-	-	-	-	-	-	-	-	-	-
Petroleum Refineries	-	-	-	-	-	-	-	81436	20	13051	449
Petrochemical Industry	-	-	-	-	-	-	-	-	-	-	-
Liquefaction	-	-	-	-	-	-	-	-	-	-	-
Other Transformation Sector	-	-	-	-	-	-	-	-	-	-	-
ENERGY SECTOR	**2**	**-**	**-**	**-**	**-**	**50**	**-**	**200**	**-**	**-**	**-**
Coal Mines	-	-	-	-	-	-	-	-	-	-	-
Oil and Gas Extraction	-	-	-	-	-	-	-	200	-	-	-
Petroleum Refineries	-	-	-	-	-	-	-	-	-	-	-
Electricity, CHP+Heat plants	-	-	-	-	-	-	-	-	-	-	-
Pumped Storage (Elec.)	-	-	-	-	-	-	-	-	-	-	-
Other Energy Sector	2	-	-	-	-	50	-	-	-	-	-
Distribution Losses	10	-	-	-	-	6	-	-	-	-	-
FINAL CONSUMPTION	**210**	**2589**	**-**	**20**	**-**	**3798**	**-**	**-**	**-**	**-**	**-**
INDUSTRY SECTOR	**-**	**2519**	**-**	**20**	**-**	**3698**	**-**	**-**	**-**	**-**	**-**
Iron and Steel	-	1322	-	-	-	3493	-	-	-	-	-
Chemical and Petrochemical	-	9	-	-	-	12	-	-	-	-	-
of which: Feedstocks	-	-	-	-	-	-	-	-	-	-	-
Non-Ferrous Metals	-	40	-	-	-	13	-	-	-	-	-
Non-Metallic Minerals	-	1093	-	7	-	44	-	-	-	-	-
Transport Equipment	-	-	-	-	-	-	-	-	-	-	-
Machinery	-	26	-	13	-	87	-	-	-	-	-
Mining and Quarrying	-	-	-	-	-	-	-	-	-	-	-
Food and Tobacco	-	-	-	-	-	49	-	-	-	-	-
Paper, Pulp and Print	-	5	-	-	-	-	-	-	-	-	-
Wood and Wood Products	-	-	-	-	-	-	-	-	-	-	-
Construction	-	-	-	-	-	-	-	-	-	-	-
Textile and Leather	-	18	-	-	-	-	-	-	-	-	-
Non-specified	-	6	-	-	-	-	-	-	-	-	-
TRANSPORT SECTOR	**-**	**-**	**-**	**-**	**-**	**-**	**-**	**-**	**-**	**-**	**-**
International Civil Aviation	-	-	-	-	-	-	-	-	-	-	-
Domestic Air	-	-	-	-	-	-	-	-	-	-	-
Road	-	-	-	-	-	-	-	-	-	-	-
Rail	-	-	-	-	-	-	-	-	-	-	-
Pipeline Transport	-	-	-	-	-	-	-	-	-	-	-
Internal Navigation	-	-	-	-	-	-	-	-	-	-	-
Non-specified	-	-	-	-	-	-	-	-	-	-	-
OTHER SECTORS	**-**	**70**	**-**	**-**	**-**	**100**	**-**	**-**	**-**	**-**	**-**
Agriculture	-	-	-	-	-	-	-	-	-	-	-
Commerce and Publ. Serv.	-	-	-	-	-	-	-	-	-	-	-
Residential	-	70	-	-	-	100	-	-	-	-	-
Non-specified	-	-	-	-	-	-	-	-	-	-	-
NON-ENERGY USE	**210**	**-**	**-**	**-**	**-**	**-**	**-**	**-**	**-**	**-**	**-**
in Industry/Transf./Energy	210	-	-	-	-	-	-	-	-	-	-
in Transport	-	-	-	-	-	-	-	-	-	-	-
in Other Sectors	-	-	-	-	-	-	-	-	-	-	-

Italy / Italie : 1993

SUPPLY AND CONSUMPTION / APPROVISIONNEMENT ET DEMANDE	Oil cont. / *Pétrole cont.* (1000 tonnes)										
	Refinery Gas / *Gaz de raffinerie*	LPG + Ethane / *GPL + éthane*	Motor Gasoline / *Essence moteur*	Aviation Gasoline / *Essence aviation*	Jet Fuel / *Carbu-réacteur*	Kerosene / *Kérosène*	Gas/ Diesel / *Gazole*	Heavy Fuel Oil / *Fioul lourd*	Naphtha / *Naphta*	Pétrol. Coke / *Coke de pétrole*	Other Prod. / *Autres prod.*
Production	2809	2392	19485	64	3105	1831	32215	23139	3475	1227	3853
From Other Sources	-	-	-	-	-	-	-	-	-	-	-
Imports	-	1545	2069	-	-	-	2806	14284	1333	1593	324
Exports	-	-232	-3731	-56	-611	-826	-9148	-6581	-515	-14	-883
Intl. Marine Bunkers	-	-	-	-	-	-	-555	-1889	-	-	-52
Stock Changes	-	1	-258	-	-1	-44	764	452	64	-4	127
DOMESTIC SUPPLY	**2809**	**3706**	**17565**	**8**	**2493**	**961**	**26082**	**29405**	**4357**	**2802**	**3369**
Transfers	-	-	-245	-	245	-	-	-	-	-	-
Statistical Differences	-	-	203	-	-301	-	-	-51	-	-	-80
TRANSFORMATION	**248**	**133**	**510**	**-**	**-**	**379**	**995**	**24062**	**1546**	**170**	**-**
Electricity Plants	1	-	-	-	-	-	147	22507	5	-	-
CHP Plants	247	-	-	-	-	-	8	1473	-	170	-
Heat Plants	-	-	-	-	-	-	-	-	-	-	-
Transfer to Gases	-	30	-	-	-	-	-	-	12	-	-
Transfer to Solids	-	-	-	-	-	-	-	-	-	-	-
Petroleum Refineries	-	-	-	-	-	-	-	-	-	-	-
Petrochemical Industry	-	103	510	-	-	379	840	82	1529	-	-
Liquefaction	-	-	-	-	-	-	-	-	-	-	-
Other Transformation Sector	-	-	-	-	-	-	-	-	-	-	-
ENERGY SECTOR	**2288**	**34**	**-**	**-**	**-**	**5**	**-**	**1503**	**14**	**609**	**9**
Coal Mines	-	-	-	-	-	-	-	-	-	-	-
Oil and Gas Extraction	-	-	-	-	-	-	-	-	-	-	-
Petroleum Refineries	2288	34	-	-	-	5	-	1503	14	609	9
Electricity, CHP+Heat plants	-	-	-	-	-	-	-	-	-	-	-
Pumped Storage (Elec.)	-	-	-	-	-	-	-	-	-	-	-
Other Energy Sector	-	-	-	-	-	-	-	-	-	-	-
Distribution Losses	-	17	81	-	12	1	46	53	-	-	-
FINAL CONSUMPTION	**273**	**3522**	**16932**	**8**	**2425**	**576**	**25041**	**3736**	**2797**	**2023**	**3280**
INDUSTRY SECTOR	**273**	**333**	**830**	**-**	**14**	**440**	**1264**	**3356**	**2797**	**1933**	**-**
Iron and Steel	-	10	-	-	-	-	19	85	-	-	-
Chemical and Petrochemical	273	157	793	-	-	431	977	1114	2797	215	-
of which: Feedstocks	*273*	*108*	*582*	*-*	*-*	*431*	*962*	*98*	*1746*	*-*	*-*
Non-Ferrous Metals	-	7	-	-	-	-	4	-	-	-	-
Non-Metallic Minerals	-	35	-	-	-	-	29	610	-	1702	-
Transport Equipment	-	-	-	-	-	-	-	-	-	-	-
Machinery	-	72	37	-	14	9	97	263	-	14	-
Mining and Quarrying	-	1	-	-	-	-	4	5	-	-	-
Food and Tobacco	-	14	-	-	-	-	16	249	-	2	-
Paper, Pulp and Print	-	5	-	-	-	-	16	242	-	-	-
Wood and Wood Products	-	-	-	-	-	-	-	-	-	-	-
Construction	-	3	-	-	-	-	52	28	-	-	-
Textile and Leather	-	7	-	-	-	-	14	453	-	-	-
Non-specified	-	22	-	-	-	-	36	307	-	-	-
TRANSPORT SECTOR	**-**	**1294**	**15982**	**8**	**2411**	**-**	**15257**	**-**	**-**	**-**	**5**
International Civil Aviation	-	-	-	-	2411	-	-	-	-	-	-
Domestic Air	-	-	-	8	-	-	-	-	-	-	-
Road	-	1294	15797	-	-	-	14861	-	-	-	5
Rail	-	-	-	-	-	-	188	-	-	-	-
Pipeline Transport	-	-	-	-	-	-	-	-	-	-	-
Internal Navigation	-	-	185	-	-	-	208	-	-	-	-
Non-specified	-	-	-	-	-	-	-	-	-	-	-
OTHER SECTORS	**-**	**1895**	**120**	**-**	**-**	**136**	**8520**	**380**	**-**	**-**	**12**
Agriculture	-	71	120	-	-	6	2445	48	-	-	5
Commerce and Publ. Serv.	-	-	-	-	-	-	642	122	-	-	7
Residential	-	1824	-	-	-	130	5433	210	-	-	-
Non-specified	-	-	-	-	-	-	-	-	-	-	-
NON-ENERGY USE	**-**	**-**	**-**	**-**	**-**	**-**	**-**	**-**	**-**	**90**	**3263**
in Industry/Transf./Energy	-	-	-	-	-	-	-	-	-	90	2812
in Transport	-	-	-	-	-	-	-	-	-	-	412
in Other Sectors	-	-	-	-	-	-	-	-	-	-	39

Italy / Italie : 1993

CONSUMPTION APPROVISIONNEMENT ET DEMANDE	Gas / Gaz (TJ)				Combust. Renew. & Waste / En. Re. Comb. & Déchets (TJ)				Electricity (GWh)	Heat (TJ)
	Natural Gas Gaz naturel	Gas Works Usines à gaz	Coke Ovens Cokeries	Blast Furnaces Hauts fourneaux	Solid Biomass & Anim. Prod. Biomasse solide & prod. anim.	Gas/Liquids from Biomass Gaz/Liquides tirés de biomasse	Municipal Waste Déchets urbains	Industrial Waste Déchets industriels	Electricité	Chaleur
Production	729510	-	44853	48219	34639	151	1884	3558	222788	-
From Other Sources	-	10287	-	-	-	-	-	-	-	-
Imports	1245746	-	-	-	4960	-	-	-	40109	-
Exports	-1265	-	-	-	-	-	-	-	-677	-
Intl. Marine Bunkers	-	-	-	-	-	-	-	-	-	-
Stock Changes	-22483	-	-	-	-	-	-	-	-	-
DOMESTIC SUPPLY	**1951508**	**10287**	**44853**	**48219**	**39599**	**151**	**1884**	**3558**	**262220**	**-**
Transfers	-	-	-	-	-	-	-	-	-	-
Statistical Differences	-7	-	-	-	-	-	-	-	-	-
TRANSFORMATION	**386338**	**-**	**11373**	**22378**	**4165**	**151**	**1884**	**3558**	**-**	**-**
Electricity Plants	281034	-	8887	16899	-	113	1465	753	-	-
CHP Plants	96512	-	2486	5479	-	38	419	2805	-	-
Heat Plants	-	-	-	-	-	-	-	-	-	-
Transfer to Gases	8792	-	-	-	-	-	-	-	-	-
Transfer to Solids	-	-	-	-	4165	-	-	-	-	-
Petroleum Refineries	-	-	-	-	-	-	-	-	-	-
Petrochemical Industry	-	-	-	-	-	-	-	-	-	-
Liquefaction	-	-	-	-	-	-	-	-	-	-
Other Transformation Sector	-	-	-	-	-	-	-	-	-	-
ENERGY SECTOR	**14580**	**18**	**17203**	**13109**	**-**	**-**	**-**	**-**	**20221**	**-**
Coal Mines	-	-	-	-	-	-	-	-	59	-
Oil and Gas Extraction	14580	-	-	-	-	-	-	-	93	-
Petroleum Refineries	-	-	-	-	-	-	-	-	3435	-
Electricity, CHP+Heat plants	-	-	-	-	-	-	-	-	11431	-
Pumped Storage (Elec.)	-	-	-	-	-	-	-	-	4189	-
Other Energy Sector	-	18	17203	13109	-	-	-	-	1014	-
Distribution Losses	19003	152	230	433	-	-	-	-	17694	-
FINAL CONSUMPTION	**1531580**	**10117**	**16047**	**12299**	**35434**	**-**	**-**	**-**	**224305**	**-**
INDUSTRY SECTOR	**672671**	**314**	**16047**	**12299**	**5316**	**-**	**-**	**-**	**109788**	**-**
Iron and Steel	75898	-	14306	12299	-	-	-	-	18589	-
Chemical and Petrochemical	175048	-	723	-	-	-	-	-	18746	-
of which: Feedstocks	44469	-	-	-	-	-	-	-	-	-
Non-Ferrous Metals	13575	-	-	-	-	-	-	-	4776	-
Non-Metallic Minerals	140294	157	1018	-	5316	-	-	-	11200	-
Transport Equipment	-	-	-	-	-	-	-	-	3517	-
Machinery	69554	157	-	-	-	-	-	-	14541	-
Mining and Quarrying	3787	-	-	-	-	-	-	-	1184	-
Food and Tobacco	66763	-	-	-	-	-	-	-	8339	-
Paper, Pulp and Print	56669	-	-	-	-	-	-	-	7622	-
Wood and Wood Products	-	-	-	-	-	-	-	-	1872	-
Construction	-	-	-	-	-	-	-	-	1079	-
Textile and Leather	44544	-	-	-	-	-	-	-	9718	-
Non-specified	26539	-	-	-	-	-	-	-	8605	-
TRANSPORT SECTOR	**10020**	**-**	**-**	**-**	**-**	**-**	**-**	**-**	**7158**	**-**
International Civil Aviation	-	-	-	-	-	-	-	-	-	-
Domestic Air	-	-	-	-	-	-	-	-	-	-
Road	10020	-	-	-	-	-	-	-	4318	-
Rail	-	-	-	-	-	-	-	-	521	-
Pipeline Transport	-	-	-	-	-	-	-	-	-	-
Internal Navigation	-	-	-	-	-	-	-	-	-	-
Non-specified	-	-	-	-	-	-	-	-	2319	-
OTHER SECTORS	**848889**	**9803**	**-**	**-**	**30118**	**-**	**-**	**-**	**107359**	**-**
Agriculture	4625	-	-	-	-	-	-	-	4605	-
Commerce and Publ. Serv.	-	-	-	-	-	-	-	-	46342	-
Residential	844264	9803	-	-	30118	-	-	-	56412	-
Non-specified	-	-	-	-	-	-	-	-	-	-
NON-ENERGY USE	**-**	**-**	**-**	**-**	**-**	**-**	**-**	**-**	**-**	**-**
in Industry/Transf./Energy	-	-	-	-	-	-	-	-	-	-
in Transport	-	-	-	-	-	-	-	-	-	-
in Other Sectors	-	-	-	-	-	-	-	-	-	-

Japan / Japon : 1992

SUPPLY AND CONSUMPTION *APPROVISIONNEMENT ET DEMANDE*	Coal / *Charbon* (1000 tonnes)							Oil / *Pétrole* (1000 tonnes)			
	Coking Coal *Charbon à coke*	Steam Coal *Charbon vapeur*	Sub-Bit. Coal *Charbon sous-bit.*	Lignite *Lignite*	Peat *Tourbe*	Oven and Gas Coke *Coke de four/gaz*	Pat. Fuel and BKB *Agg./briq. de lignite*	Crude Oil *Pétrole brut*	NGL *LGN*	Feedstocks *Produits d'aliment.*	Additives *Additifs*
Production	-	7598	-	-	-	44499	112	858	-	-	-
From Other Sources	-	-	-	-	-	-	-	-	-	4879	132
Imports	64468	44653	-	-	-	-	-	208290	5448	-	-
Exports	-	-	-	-	-	-2899	-	-	-	-	-
Intl. Marine Bunkers	-	-	-	-	-	-	-	-	-	-	-
Stock Changes	-	60	-	-	-	154	-	1085	-	-756	-
DOMESTIC SUPPLY	**64468**	**52311**	-	-	-	**41754**	**112**	**210233**	**5448**	**4123**	**132**
Transfers	-	-	-	-	-	-	-	-	-12	-	-
Statistical Differences	-	-1685	-	-	-	142	-	-368	-	-	-
TRANSFORMATION	**64407**	**33976**	-	-	-	**12920**	-	**209854**	**1879**	**4123**	**132**
Electricity Plants	-	33835	-	-	-	-	-	17575	217	-	-
CHP Plants	-	-	-	-	-	-	-	-	-	-	-
Heat Plants	-	29	-	-	-	-	-	-	-	-	-
Transfer to Gases	1042	-	-	-	-	12920	-	-	-	-	-
Transfer to Solids	63365	112	-	-	-	-	-	-	-	-	-
Petroleum Refineries	-	-	-	-	-	-	-	192279	1662	4123	132
Petrochemical Industry	-	-	-	-	-	-	-	-	-	-	-
Liquefaction	-	-	-	-	-	-	-	-	-	-	-
Other Transformation Sector	-	-	-	-	-	-	-	-	-	-	-
ENERGY SECTOR	-	**219**	-	-	-	**110**	-	-	-	-	-
Coal Mines	-	219	-	-	-	-	-	-	-	-	-
Oil and Gas Extraction	-	-	-	-	-	-	-	-	-	-	-
Petroleum Refineries	-	-	-	-	-	-	-	-	-	-	-
Electricity, CHP+Heat plants	-	-	-	-	-	-	-	-	-	-	-
Pumped Storage (Elec.)	-	-	-	-	-	-	-	-	-	-	-
Other Energy Sector	-	-	-	-	-	110	-	-	-	-	-
Distribution Losses	-	-	-	-	-	-	-	-	-	-	-
FINAL CONSUMPTION	**61**	**16431**	-	-	-	**28866**	**112**	**11**	**3557**	-	-
INDUSTRY SECTOR	**61**	**16342**	-	-	-	**28866**	-	**11**	**3557**	-	-
Iron and Steel	-	1878	-	-	-	25333	-	-	-	-	-
Chemical and Petrochemical	61	2530	-	-	-	125	-	11	3557	-	-
of which: Feedstocks	-	-	-	-	-	-	-	-	3557	-	-
Non-Ferrous Metals	-	-	-	-	-	276	-	-	-	-	-
Non-Metallic Minerals	-	9135	-	-	-	302	-	-	-	-	-
Transport Equipment	-	-	-	-	-	-	-	-	-	-	-
Machinery	-	-	-	-	-	-	-	-	-	-	-
Mining and Quarrying	-	-	-	-	-	-	-	-	-	-	-
Food and Tobacco	-	-	-	-	-	-	-	-	-	-	-
Paper, Pulp and Print	-	1906	-	-	-	-	-	-	-	-	-
Wood and Wood Products	-	-	-	-	-	-	-	-	-	-	-
Construction	-	-	-	-	-	-	-	-	-	-	-
Textile and Leather	-	-	-	-	-	-	-	-	-	-	-
Non-specified	-	893	-	-	-	2830	-	-	-	-	-
TRANSPORT SECTOR	-	-	-	-	-	-	-	-	-	-	-
International Civil Aviation	-	-	-	-	-	-	-	-	-	-	-
Domestic Air	-	-	-	-	-	-	-	-	-	-	-
Road	-	-	-	-	-	-	-	-	-	-	-
Rail	-	-	-	-	-	-	-	-	-	-	-
Pipeline Transport	-	-	-	-	-	-	-	-	-	-	-
Internal Navigation	-	-	-	-	-	-	-	-	-	-	-
Non-specified	-	-	-	-	-	-	-	-	-	-	-
OTHER SECTORS	-	**89**	-	-	-	-	**112**	-	-	-	-
Agriculture	-	-	-	-	-	-	-	-	-	-	-
Commerce and Publ. Serv.	-	-	-	-	-	-	-	-	-	-	-
Residential	-	89	-	-	-	-	112	-	-	-	-
Non-specified	-	-	-	-	-	-	-	-	-	-	-
NON-ENERGY USE	-	-	-	-	-	-	-	-	-	-	-
in Industry/Transf./Energy	-	-	-	-	-	-	-	-	-	-	-
in Transport	-	-	-	-	-	-	-	-	-	-	-
in Other Sectors	-	-	-	-	-	-	-	-	-	-	-

Japan / Japon : 1992

SUPPLY AND CONSUMPTION / APPROVISIONNEMENT ET DEMANDE	Oil cont. / Pétrole cont. (1000 tonnes)										
	Refinery Gas / Gaz de raffinerie	LPG + Ethane / GPL + éthane	Motor Gasoline / Essence moteur	Aviation Gasoline / Essence aviation	Jet Fuel / Carbu-réacteur	Kerosene / Kérosène	Gas/Diesel / Gazole	Heavy Fuel Oil / Fioul lourd	Naphtha / Naphta	Pétrol. Coke / Coke de pétrole	Other Prod. / Autres prod.
Production	7764	4724	34013	9	4707	21168	56785	43488	11793	300	10271
From Other Sources	-	-	-	-	-	-	-	-	-	-	-
Imports	-	15286	822	-	3129	1906	2586	6863	15238	4208	123
Exports	-	-7	-	-	-136	-422	-1870	-2398	-461	-96	-314
Intl. Marine Bunkers	-	-	-	-	-	-	-348	-5470	-	-	-49
Stock Changes	-	-313	-178	-	-38	278	285	234	227	-1	-78
DOMESTIC SUPPLY	**7764**	**19690**	**34657**	**9**	**7662**	**22930**	**57438**	**42717**	**26797**	**4411**	**9953**
Transfers	-	12	-	-	-	-	-	-	-	-	-
Statistical Differences	-	58	-49	-	-58	-518	225	-120	-191	-	5
TRANSFORMATION	**214**	**3886**	**-**	**-**	**-**	**12**	**539**	**26701**	**5651**	**1737**	**812**
Electricity Plants	-	993	-	-	-	-	539	26683	909	908	812
CHP Plants	-	-	-	-	-	-	-	-	-	-	-
Heat Plants	-	6	-	-	-	12	-	18	-	-	-
Transfer to Gases	214	2487	-	-	-	-	-	-	263	-	-
Transfer to Solids	-	-	-	-	-	-	-	-	-	829	-
Petroleum Refineries	-	-	-	-	-	-	-	-	-	-	-
Petrochemical Industry	-	400	-	-	-	-	-	-	4479	-	-
Liquefaction	-	-	-	-	-	-	-	-	-	-	-
Other Transformation Sector	-	-	-	-	-	-	-	-	-	-	-
ENERGY SECTOR	**7550**	**7**	**-**	**-**	**-**	**7**	**64**	**2383**	**105**	**34**	**41**
Coal Mines	-	-	-	-	-	-	-	-	-	-	-
Oil and Gas Extraction	-	-	-	-	-	-	-	-	-	-	-
Petroleum Refineries	7550	6	-	-	-	7	26	2227	105	34	41
Electricity, CHP+Heat plants	-	1	-	-	-	-	38	156	-	-	-
Pumped Storage (Elec.)	-	-	-	-	-	-	-	-	-	-	-
Other Energy Sector	-	-	-	-	-	-	-	-	-	-	-
Distribution Losses	-	-	-	-	-	-	-	-	-	-	-
FINAL CONSUMPTION	**-**	**15867**	**34608**	**9**	**7604**	**22393**	**57060**	**13513**	**20850**	**2640**	**9105**
INDUSTRY SECTOR	**-**	**6309**	**-**	**-**	**-**	**4792**	**14030**	**7395**	**20850**	**2546**	**-**
Iron and Steel	-	617	-	-	-	288	625	920	-	108	-
Chemical and Petrochemical	-	1903	-	-	-	260	1295	705	20720	586	-
of which: Feedstocks	-	1903	-	-	-	-	-	-	20720	-	-
Non-Ferrous Metals	-	195	-	-	-	163	730	407	-	62	-
Non-Metallic Minerals	-	195	-	-	-	96	868	1599	-	405	-
Transport Equipment	-	-	-	-	-	-	-	-	-	-	-
Machinery	-	423	-	-	-	362	883	7	-	-	-
Mining and Quarrying	-	-	-	-	-	29	314	59	-	-	-
Food and Tobacco	-	-	-	-	-	-	1675	470	-	-	-
Paper, Pulp and Print	-	59	-	-	-	33	280	1864	-	159	-
Wood and Wood Products	-	-	-	-	-	-	-	-	-	-	-
Construction	-	-	-	-	-	1001	3644	10	-	-	-
Textile and Leather	-	117	-	-	-	15	682	966	-	30	-
Non-specified	-	2800	-	-	-	2545	3034	388	130	1196	-
TRANSPORT SECTOR	**-**	**2175**	**34608**	**9**	**7604**	**-**	**31821**	**1739**	**-**	**-**	**-**
International Civil Aviation	-	-	-	-	4515	-	-	-	-	-	-
Domestic Air	-	-	-	9	3089	-	-	-	-	-	-
Road	-	2175	34608	-	-	-	25774	49	-	-	-
Rail	-	-	-	-	-	-	555	-	-	-	-
Pipeline Transport	-	-	-	-	-	-	-	-	-	-	-
Internal Navigation	-	-	-	-	-	-	5492	1658	-	-	-
Non-specified	-	-	-	-	-	-	-	32	-	-	-
OTHER SECTORS	**-**	**7383**	**-**	**-**	**-**	**17601**	**11209**	**4379**	**-**	**-**	**-**
Agriculture	-	-	-	-	-	2764	3769	72	-	-	-
Commerce and Publ. Serv.	-	1681	-	-	-	4166	7440	4307	-	-	-
Residential	-	5702	-	-	-	10671	-	-	-	-	-
Non-specified	-	-	-	-	-	-	-	-	-	-	-
NON-ENERGY USE	**-**	**-**	**-**	**-**	**-**	**-**	**-**	**-**	**-**	**94**	**9105**
in Industry/Transf./Energy	-	-	-	-	-	-	-	-	-	94	8191
in Transport	-	-	-	-	-	-	-	-	-	-	223
in Other Sectors	-	-	-	-	-	-	-	-	-	-	691

Japan / Japon : 1992

CONSUMPTION / APPROVISIONNEMENT ET DEMANDE	Gas / Gaz (TJ)				Combust. Renew. & Waste / En. Re. Comb. & Déchets (TJ)				(GWh)	(TJ)
	Natural Gas / Gaz naturel	Gas Works / Usines à gaz	Coke Ovens / Cokeries	Blast Furnaces / Hauts fourneaux	Solid Biomass & Anim. Prod. / Biomasse solide & prod. anim.	Gas/Liquids from Biomass / Gaz/Liquides tirés de biomasse	Municipal Waste / Déchets urbains	Industrial Waste / Déchets industriels	Electricity / Electricité	Heat / Chaleur
Production	88569	587135	280029	338886	78567	-	13389	-	895266	13680
From Other Sources	-	165579	-	-	-	-	-	-	-	-
Imports	2124285	-	-	-	-	-	-	-	-	-
Exports	-	-	-	-	-	-	-	-	-	-
Intl. Marine Bunkers	-	-	-	-	-	-	-	-	-	-
Stock Changes	-13514	-	-	-	-	-	-	-	-	-
DOMESTIC SUPPLY	**2199340**	**752714**	**280029**	**338886**	**78567**	**-**	**13389**	**-**	**895266**	**13680**
Transfers	-	-	-	-	-	-	-	-	-	-
Statistical Differences	33503	1657	-21678	37661	-	-	-	-	-	-
TRANSFORMATION	**2161650**	**-**	**82070**	**189123**	**78567**	**-**	**13389**	**-**	**1019**	
Electricity Plants	1585332	-	75156	189123	78567	-	13389	-	-	
CHP Plants	-	-	-	-	-	-	-	-	-	
Heat Plants	8402	-	-	-	-	-	-	-	1019	
Transfer to Gases	567916	-	6914	-	-	-	-	-	-	
Transfer to Solids	-	-	-	-	-	-	-	-	-	
Petroleum Refineries	-	-	-	-	-	-	-	-	-	
Petrochemical Industry	-	-	-	-	-	-	-	-	-	
Liquefaction	-	-	-	-	-	-	-	-	-	
Other Transformation Sector	-	-	-	-	-	-	-	-	-	
ENERGY SECTOR	**14407**	**16691**	**35146**	**49691**	**-**	**-**	**-**	**-**	**70116**	**262**
Coal Mines	-	-	-	-	-	-	-	-	653	-
Oil and Gas Extraction	14407	-	-	-	-	-	-	-	-	-
Petroleum Refineries	-	-	-	-	-	-	-	-	6937	-
Electricity, CHP+Heat plants	-	-	-	-	-	-	-	-	51544	262
Pumped Storage (Elec.)	-	-	-	-	-	-	-	-	10982	-
Other Energy Sector	-	16691	35146	49691	-	-	-	-	-	-
Distribution Losses	-	8642	-	-	-	-	-	-	33969	2675
FINAL CONSUMPTION	**56786**	**729038**	**141135**	**137733**	**-**	**-**	**-**	**-**	**790162**	**10743**
INDUSTRY SECTOR	**53245**	**214986**	**141135**	**137733**	**-**	**-**	**-**	**-**	**439737**	**-**
Iron and Steel	33276	-	141135	137733	-	-	-	-	75204	-
Chemical and Petrochemical	18093	-	-	-	-	-	-	-	56183	-
of which: Feedstocks	-	-	-	-	-	-	-	-	-	-
Non-Ferrous Metals	-	-	-	-	-	-	-	-	14944	-
Non-Metallic Minerals	-	-	-	-	-	-	-	-	19711	-
Transport Equipment	-	-	-	-	-	-	-	-	25314	-
Machinery	-	-	-	-	-	-	-	-	35698	-
Mining and Quarrying	-	-	-	-	-	-	-	-	1723	-
Food and Tobacco	-	-	-	-	-	-	-	-	13316	-
Paper, Pulp and Print	-	-	-	-	-	-	-	-	31543	-
Wood and Wood Products	-	-	-	-	-	-	-	-	-	-
Construction	-	-	-	-	-	-	-	-	-	-
Textile and Leather	-	-	-	-	-	-	-	-	7348	-
Non-specified	1876	214986	-	-	-	-	-	-	158753	-
TRANSPORT SECTOR	**-**	**-**	**-**	**-**	**-**	**-**	**-**	**-**	**20713**	**-**
International Civil Aviation	-	-	-	-	-	-	-	-	-	-
Domestic Air	-	-	-	-	-	-	-	-	-	-
Road	-	-	-	-	-	-	-	-	-	-
Rail	-	-	-	-	-	-	-	-	20713	-
Pipeline Transport	-	-	-	-	-	-	-	-	-	-
Internal Navigation	-	-	-	-	-	-	-	-	-	-
Non-specified	-	-	-	-	-	-	-	-	-	-
OTHER SECTORS	**3541**	**514052**	**-**	**-**	**-**	**-**	**-**	**-**	**329712**	**10743**
Agriculture	-	-	-	-	-	-	-	-	1624	-
Commerce and Publ. Serv.	-	114951	-	-	-	-	-	-	129005	9380
Residential	-	399101	-	-	-	-	-	-	199083	1363
Non-specified	3541	-	-	-	-	-	-	-	-	-
NON-ENERGY USE	**-**	**-**	**-**	**-**	**-**	**-**	**-**	**-**	**-**	**-**
in Industry/Transf./Energy	-	-	-	-	-	-	-	-	-	-
in Transport	-	-	-	-	-	-	-	-	-	-
in Other Sectors	-	-	-	-	-	-	-	-	-	-

Japan / Japon : 1993

SUPPLY AND CONSUMPTION *APPROVISIONNEMENT ET DEMANDE*	Coal / *Charbon* (1000 tonnes)							Oil / *Pétrole* (1000 tonnes)			
	Coking Coal *Charbon à coke*	Steam Coal *Charbon vapeur*	Sub-Bit. Coal *Charbon sous-bit.*	Lignite *Lignite*	Peat *Tourbe*	Oven and Gas Coke *Coke de four/gaz*	Pat. Fuel and BKB *Agg./briq. de lignite*	Crude Oil *Pétrole brut*	NGL *LGN*	Feedstocks *Produits d'aliment.*	Additives *Additifs*
Production	-	7217	-	-	-	43815	113	778	-	-	-
From Other Sources	-	-	-	-	-	-	-	-	-	4863	131
Imports	64972	46432	-	-	-	-	-	212102	5021	-	-
Exports	-	-	-	-	-	-2877	-	-	-	-	-
Intl. Marine Bunkers	-	-	-	-	-	-	-	-	-	-	-
Stock Changes	-	241	-	-	-	618	-	-2160	-	116	-
DOMESTIC SUPPLY	**64972**	**53890**	**-**	**-**	**-**	**41556**	**113**	**210720**	**5021**	**4979**	**131**
Transfers	-	-	-	-	-	-	-	-	-12	-	-
Statistical Differences	-	-1277	-	-	-	-1	-	-939	-	-	-
TRANSFORMATION	**64969**	**38619**	**-**	**-**	**-**	**13067**	**-**	**209771**	**2176**	**4979**	**131**
Electricity Plants	-	38444	-	-	-	-	-	13563	214	-	-
CHP Plants	-	-	-	-	-	-	-	-	-	-	-
Heat Plants	-	47	-	-	-	-	-	-	-	-	-
Transfer to Gases	1005	15	-	-	-	13067	-	-	-	-	-
Transfer to Solids	63964	113	-	-	-	-	-	-	-	-	-
Petroleum Refineries	-	-	-	-	-	-	-	196208	1962	4979	131
Petrochemical Industry	-	-	-	-	-	-	-	-	-	-	-
Liquefaction	-	-	-	-	-	-	-	-	-	-	-
Other Transformation Sector	-	-	-	-	-	-	-	-	-	-	-
ENERGY SECTOR	**-**	**199**	**-**	**-**	**-**	**104**	**-**	**-**	**-**	**-**	**-**
Coal Mines	-	199	-	-	-	-	-	-	-	-	-
Oil and Gas Extraction	-	-	-	-	-	-	-	-	-	-	-
Petroleum Refineries	-	-	-	-	-	-	-	-	-	-	-
Electricity, CHP+Heat plants	-	-	-	-	-	-	-	-	-	-	-
Pumped Storage (Elec.)	-	-	-	-	-	-	-	-	-	-	-
Other Energy Sector	-	-	-	-	-	104	-	-	-	-	-
Distribution Losses	-	-	-	-	-	-	-	-	-	-	-
FINAL CONSUMPTION	**3**	**13795**	**-**	**-**	**-**	**28384**	**113**	**10**	**2833**	**-**	**-**
INDUSTRY SECTOR	**3**	**13722**	**-**	**-**	**-**	**28384**	**-**	**10**	**2833**	**-**	**-**
Iron and Steel	-	1760	-	-	-	25089	-	-	-	-	-
Chemical and Petrochemical	3	1613	-	-	-	118	-	10	2833	-	-
of which: Feedstocks	-	-	-	-	-	-	-	-	*2833*	-	-
Non-Ferrous Metals	-	-	-	-	-	230	-	-	-	-	-
Non-Metallic Minerals	-	8555	-	-	-	290	-	-	-	-	-
Transport Equipment	-	-	-	-	-	-	-	-	-	-	-
Machinery	-	-	-	-	-	-	-	-	-	-	-
Mining and Quarrying	-	-	-	-	-	-	-	-	-	-	-
Food and Tobacco	-	-	-	-	-	-	-	-	-	-	-
Paper, Pulp and Print	-	1716	-	-	-	-	-	-	-	-	-
Wood and Wood Products	-	-	-	-	-	-	-	-	-	-	-
Construction	-	-	-	-	-	-	-	-	-	-	-
Textile and Leather	-	-	-	-	-	-	-	-	-	-	-
Non-specified	-	78	-	-	-	2657	-	-	-	-	-
TRANSPORT SECTOR	**-**	**-**	**-**	**-**	**-**	**-**	**-**	**-**	**-**	**-**	**-**
International Civil Aviation	-	-	-	-	-	-	-	-	-	-	-
Domestic Air	-	-	-	-	-	-	-	-	-	-	-
Road	-	-	-	-	-	-	-	-	-	-	-
Rail	-	-	-	-	-	-	-	-	-	-	-
Pipeline Transport	-	-	-	-	-	-	-	-	-	-	-
Internal Navigation	-	-	-	-	-	-	-	-	-	-	-
Non-specified	-	-	-	-	-	-	-	-	-	-	-
OTHER SECTORS	**-**	**73**	**-**	**-**	**-**	**-**	**113**	**-**	**-**	**-**	**-**
Agriculture	-	-	-	-	-	-	-	-	-	-	-
Commerce and Publ. Serv.	-	-	-	-	-	-	-	-	-	-	-
Residential	-	73	-	-	-	-	113	-	-	-	-
Non-specified	-	-	-	-	-	-	-	-	-	-	-
NON-ENERGY USE	**-**	**-**	**-**	**-**	**-**	**-**	**-**	**-**	**-**	**-**	**-**
in Industry/Transf./Energy	-	-	-	-	-	-	-	-	-	-	-
in Transport	-	-	-	-	-	-	-	-	-	-	-
in Other Sectors	-	-	-	-	-	-	-	-	-	-	-

Japan / Japon : 1993

SUPPLY AND CONSUMPTION / APPROVISIONNEMENT ET DEMANDE	Oil cont. / *Pétrole cont.* (1000 tonnes)										
	Refinery Gas / *Gaz de raffinerie*	LPG + Ethane / *GPL + éthane*	Motor Gasoline / *Essence moteur*	Aviation Gasoline / *Essence aviation*	Jet Fuel / *Carbu-réacteur*	Kerosene / *Kérosène*	Gas/Diesel / *Gazole*	Heavy Fuel Oil / *Fioul lourd*	Naphtha / *Naphta*	Pétrol. Coke / *Coke de pétrole*	Other Prod. / *Autres prod.*
Production	8020	4601	35295	8	5053	21945	58276	43556	12794	603	10360
From Other Sources	-	-	-	-	-	-	-	-	-	-	-
Imports	-	15235	437	-	2734	1683	2194	4369	14212	4598	68
Exports	-	-10	-473	-	-108	-246	-1969	-2838	-163	-112	-397
Intl. Marine Bunkers	-	-	-	-	-	-	-379	-6383	-	-	-31
Stock Changes	-	130	-73	-	-34	105	-35	-217	60	-16	-16
DOMESTIC SUPPLY	**8020**	**19956**	**35186**	**8**	**7645**	**23487**	**58087**	**38487**	**26903**	**5073**	**9984**
Transfers	-	12	-	-	-	-	-	-	-	-	-
Statistical Differences	-	1	-38	-	176	-653	221	140	-219	-	21
TRANSFORMATION	**248**	**3782**	**-**	**-**	**-**	**11**	**547**	**24910**	**5616**	**1714**	**838**
Electricity Plants	-	813	-	-	-	-	547	24892	886	853	838
CHP Plants	-	-	-	-	-	-	-	-	-	-	-
Heat Plants	-	6	-	-	-	11	-	18	-	-	-
Transfer to Gases	248	2555	-	-	-	-	-	-	275	-	-
Transfer to Solids	-	-	-	-	-	-	-	-	-	861	-
Petroleum Refineries	-	-	-	-	-	-	-	-	-	-	-
Petrochemical Industry	-	408	-	-	-	-	-	-	4455	-	-
Liquefaction	-	-	-	-	-	-	-	-	-	-	-
Other Transformation Sector	-	-	-	-	-	-	-	-	-	-	-
ENERGY SECTOR	**7772**	**12**	**-**	**-**	**-**	**10**	**86**	**2537**	**83**	**30**	**23**
Coal Mines	-	-	-	-	-	-	-	-	-	-	-
Oil and Gas Extraction	-	-	-	-	-	-	-	-	-	-	-
Petroleum Refineries	7772	11	-	-	-	10	53	2385	83	30	23
Electricity, CHP+Heat plants	-	1	-	-	-	-	33	152	-	-	-
Pumped Storage (Elec.)	-	-	-	-	-	-	-	-	-	-	-
Other Energy Sector	-	-	-	-	-	-	-	-	-	-	-
Distribution Losses	-	-	-	-	-	-	-	-	-	-	-
FINAL CONSUMPTION	**-**	**16175**	**35148**	**8**	**7821**	**22813**	**57675**	**11180**	**20985**	**3329**	**9144**
INDUSTRY SECTOR	**-**	**7171**	**-**	**-**	**-**	**4375**	**14277**	**7465**	**20985**	**3240**	**-**
Iron and Steel	-	588	-	-	-	302	532	930	-	163	-
Chemical and Petrochemical	-	1919	-	-	-	252	980	943	20886	671	-
of which: Feedstocks	-	*1919*	-	-	-	-	-	-	*20886*	-	-
Non-Ferrous Metals	-	195	-	-	-	158	821	376	-	60	-
Non-Metallic Minerals	-	191	-	-	-	92	863	1508	-	761	-
Transport Equipment	-	-	-	-	-	-	-	-	-	-	-
Machinery	-	410	-	-	-	346	808	7	-	-	-
Mining and Quarrying	-	-	-	-	-	44	340	74	-	-	-
Food and Tobacco	-	-	-	-	-	-	1748	432	-	-	-
Paper, Pulp and Print	-	58	-	-	-	58	394	1995	-	147	-
Wood and Wood Products	-	-	-	-	-	-	-	-	-	-	-
Construction	-	-	-	-	-	984	3967	9	-	-	-
Textile and Leather	-	115	-	-	-	13	808	1080	-	30	-
Non-specified	-	3695	-	-	-	2126	3016	111	99	1408	-
TRANSPORT SECTOR	**-**	**1520**	**35148**	**8**	**7821**	**-**	**31578**	**2126**	**-**	**-**	**-**
International Civil Aviation	-	-	-	-	4546	-	-	-	-	-	-
Domestic Air	-	-	-	8	3275	-	-	-	-	-	-
Road	-	1520	35148	-	-	-	26020	41	-	-	-
Rail	-	-	-	-	-	-	514	-	-	-	-
Pipeline Transport	-	-	-	-	-	-	-	-	-	-	-
Internal Navigation	-	-	-	-	-	-	5044	2004	-	-	-
Non-specified	-	-	-	-	-	-	-	81	-	-	-
OTHER SECTORS	**-**	**7484**	**-**	**-**	**-**	**18438**	**11820**	**1589**	**-**	**-**	**-**
Agriculture	-	-	-	-	-	2706	4098	43	-	-	-
Commerce and Publ. Serv.	-	1693	-	-	-	4468	7722	1546	-	-	-
Residential	-	5791	-	-	-	11264	-	-	-	-	-
Non-specified	-	-	-	-	-	-	-	-	-	-	-
NON-ENERGY USE	**-**	**-**	**-**	**-**	**-**	**-**	**-**	**-**	**-**	**89**	**9144**
in Industry/Transf./Energy	-	-	-	-	-	-	-	-	-	89	8345
in Transport	-	-	-	-	-	-	-	-	-	-	214
in Other Sectors	-	-	-	-	-	-	-	-	-	-	585

Japan / Japon : 1993

CONSUMPTION / APPROVISIONNEMENT ET DEMANDE	Gas / Gaz (TJ)				Combust. Renew. & Waste / En. Re. Comb. & Déchets (TJ)				(GWh)	(TJ)
	Natural Gas / Gaz naturel	Gas Works / Usines à gaz	Coke Ovens / Cokeries	Blast Furnaces / Hauts fourneaux	Solid Biomass & Anim. Prod. / Biomasse solide & prod. anim.	Gas/Liquids from Biomass / Gaz/Liquides tirés de biomasse	Municipal Waste / Déchets urbains	Industrial Waste / Déchets industriels	Electricity / Electricité	Heat / Chaleur
Production	90394	575299	278026	393289	77042	-	14184	-	906705	14498
From Other Sources	-	225944	-	-	-	-	-	-	-	-
Imports	2134762	-	-	-	-	-	-	-	-	-
Exports	-	-	-	-	-	-	-	-	-	-
Intl. Marine Bunkers	-	-	-	-	-	-	-	-	-	-
Stock Changes	-7393	-	-	-	-	-	-	-	-	-
DOMESTIC SUPPLY	**2217763**	**801243**	**278026**	**393289**	**77042**	**-**	**14184**	**-**	**906705**	**14498**
Transfers	-	-	-	-	-	-	-	-	-	-
Statistical Differences	26681	-245	-20247	-2910	-	-	-	-	-	-
TRANSFORMATION	**2172775**	**-**	**89406**	**206042**	**77042**	**-**	**14184**	**-**	**990**	**-**
Electricity Plants	1557894	-	82001	206042	77042	-	14184	-	-	-
CHP Plants	-	-	-	-	-	-	-	-	-	-
Heat Plants	9252	-	-	-	-	-	-	-	990	-
Transfer to Gases	605629	-	7405	-	-	-	-	-	-	-
Transfer to Solids	-	-	-	-	-	-	-	-	-	-
Petroleum Refineries	-	-	-	-	-	-	-	-	-	-
Petrochemical Industry	-	-	-	-	-	-	-	-	-	-
Liquefaction	-	-	-	-	-	-	-	-	-	-
Other Transformation Sector	-	-	-	-	-	-	-	-	-	-
ENERGY SECTOR	**15016**	**15603**	**32296**	**51677**	**-**	**-**	**-**	**-**	**74493**	**106**
Coal Mines	-	-	-	-	-	-	-	-	640	-
Oil and Gas Extraction	15016	-	-	-	-	-	-	-	-	-
Petroleum Refineries	-	-	-	-	-	-	-	-	7455	-
Electricity, CHP+Heat plants	-	-	-	-	-	-	-	-	51248	106
Pumped Storage (Elec.)	-	-	-	-	-	-	-	-	15150	-
Other Energy Sector	-	15603	32296	51677	-	-	-	-	-	-
Distribution Losses	-	8968	-	-	-	-	-	-	34623	2490
FINAL CONSUMPTION	**56653**	**776427**	**136077**	**132660**	**-**	**-**	**-**	**-**	**796599**	**11902**
INDUSTRY SECTOR	**53865**	**240561**	**136077**	**132660**	**-**	**-**	**-**	**-**	**435501**	**-**
Iron and Steel	33257	-	136077	132660	-	-	-	-	73710	-
Chemical and Petrochemical	18782	-	-	-	-	-	-	-	55351	-
of which: Feedstocks	-	-	-	-	-	-	-	-	-	-
Non-Ferrous Metals	-	-	-	-	-	-	-	-	14943	-
Non-Metallic Minerals	-	-	-	-	-	-	-	-	19467	-
Transport Equipment	-	-	-	-	-	-	-	-	24076	-
Machinery	-	-	-	-	-	-	-	-	35951	-
Mining and Quarrying	-	-	-	-	-	-	-	-	1683	-
Food and Tobacco	-	-	-	-	-	-	-	-	13622	-
Paper, Pulp and Print	-	-	-	-	-	-	-	-	31101	-
Wood and Wood Products	-	-	-	-	-	-	-	-	-	-
Construction	-	-	-	-	-	-	-	-	-	-
Textile and Leather	-	-	-	-	-	-	-	-	6541	-
Non-specified	1826	240561	-	-	-	-	-	-	159056	-
TRANSPORT SECTOR	**-**	**-**	**-**	**-**	**-**	**-**	**-**	**-**	**20943**	**-**
International Civil Aviation	-	-	-	-	-	-	-	-	-	-
Domestic Air	-	-	-	-	-	-	-	-	-	-
Road	-	-	-	-	-	-	-	-	-	-
Rail	-	-	-	-	-	-	-	-	20943	-
Pipeline Transport	-	-	-	-	-	-	-	-	-	-
Internal Navigation	-	-	-	-	-	-	-	-	-	-
Non-specified	-	-	-	-	-	-	-	-	-	-
OTHER SECTORS	**2788**	**535866**	**-**	**-**	**-**	**-**	**-**	**-**	**340155**	**11902**
Agriculture	-	-	-	-	-	-	-	-	1447	-
Commerce and Publ. Serv.	-	120177	-	-	-	-	-	-	134106	10519
Residential	-	415689	-	-	-	-	-	-	204602	1383
Non-specified	2788	-	-	-	-	-	-	-	-	-
NON-ENERGY USE	**-**	**-**	**-**	**-**	**-**	**-**	**-**	**-**	**-**	**-**
in Industry/Transf./Energy	-	-	-	-	-	-	-	-	-	-
in Transport	-	-	-	-	-	-	-	-	-	-
in Other Sectors	-	-	-	-	-	-	-	-	-	-

Luxembourg / Luxembourg : 1992

SUPPLY AND CONSUMPTION	Coal / *Charbon* (1000 tonnes)							Oil / *Pétrole* (1000 tonnes)			
	Coking Coal	Steam Coal	Sub-Bit. Coal	Lignite	Peat	Oven and Gas Coke	Pat. Fuel and BKB	Crude Oil	NGL	Feedstocks	Additives
APPROVISIONNEMENT ET DEMANDE	*Charbon à coke*	*Charbon vapeur*	*Charbon sous-bit.*	*Lignite*	*Tourbe*	*Coke de four/gaz*	*Agg./briq. de lignite*	*Pétrole brut*	*LGN*	*Produits d'aliment.*	*Additifs*
Production	-	-	-	-	-	-	-	-	-	-	-
From Other Sources	-	-	-	-	-	-	-	-	-	-	-
Imports	-	278	-	9	-	1181	12	-	-	-	-
Exports	-	-	-	-	-	-	-	-	-	-	-
Intl. Marine Bunkers	-	-	-	-	-	-	-	-	-	-	-
Stock Changes	-	-	-	-	-	-	-	-	-	-	-
DOMESTIC SUPPLY	-	278	-	9	-	1181	12	-	-	-	-
Transfers	-	-	-	-	-	-	-	-	-	-	-
Statistical Differences	-	-	-	-	-	-	-	-	-	-	-
TRANSFORMATION	-	-	-	-	-	437	-	-	-	-	-
Electricity Plants	-	-	-	-	-	-	-	-	-	-	-
CHP Plants	-	-	-	-	-	-	-	-	-	-	-
Heat Plants	-	-	-	-	-	-	-	-	-	-	-
Transfer to Gases	-	-	-	-	-	437	-	-	-	-	-
Transfer to Solids	-	-	-	-	-	-	-	-	-	-	-
Petroleum Refineries	-	-	-	-	-	-	-	-	-	-	-
Petrochemical Industry	-	-	-	-	-	-	-	-	-	-	-
Liquefaction	-	-	-	-	-	-	-	-	-	-	-
Other Transformation Sector	-	-	-	-	-	-	-	-	-	-	-
ENERGY SECTOR	-	-	-	-	-	-	-	-	-	-	-
Coal Mines	-	-	-	-	-	-	-	-	-	-	-
Oil and Gas Extraction	-	-	-	-	-	-	-	-	-	-	-
Petroleum Refineries	-	-	-	-	-	-	-	-	-	-	-
Electricity, CHP+Heat plants	-	-	-	-	-	-	-	-	-	-	-
Pumped Storage (Elec.)	-	-	-	-	-	-	-	-	-	-	-
Other Energy Sector	-	-	-	-	-	-	-	-	-	-	-
Distribution Losses	-	-	-	-	-	-	-	-	-	-	-
FINAL CONSUMPTION	-	278	-	9	-	744	12	-	-	-	-
INDUSTRY SECTOR	-	278	-	9	-	744	-	-	-	-	-
Iron and Steel	-	138	-	-	-	744	-	-	-	-	-
Chemical and Petrochemical	-	-	-	-	-	-	-	-	-	-	-
of which: Feedstocks	-	-	-	-	-	-	-	-	-	-	-
Non-Ferrous Metals	-	-	-	-	-	-	-	-	-	-	-
Non-Metallic Minerals	-	140	-	9	-	-	-	-	-	-	-
Transport Equipment	-	-	-	-	-	-	-	-	-	-	-
Machinery	-	-	-	-	-	-	-	-	-	-	-
Mining and Quarrying	-	-	-	-	-	-	-	-	-	-	-
Food and Tobacco	-	-	-	-	-	-	-	-	-	-	-
Paper, Pulp and Print	-	-	-	-	-	-	-	-	-	-	-
Wood and Wood Products	-	-	-	-	-	-	-	-	-	-	-
Construction	-	-	-	-	-	-	-	-	-	-	-
Textile and Leather	-	-	-	-	-	-	-	-	-	-	-
Non-specified	-	-	-	-	-	-	-	-	-	-	-
TRANSPORT SECTOR	-	-	-	-	-	-	-	-	-	-	-
International Civil Aviation	-	-	-	-	-	-	-	-	-	-	-
Domestic Air	-	-	-	-	-	-	-	-	-	-	-
Road	-	-	-	-	-	-	-	-	-	-	-
Rail	-	-	-	-	-	-	-	-	-	-	-
Pipeline Transport	-	-	-	-	-	-	-	-	-	-	-
Internal Navigation	-	-	-	-	-	-	-	-	-	-	-
Non-specified	-	-	-	-	-	-	-	-	-	-	-
OTHER SECTORS	-	-	-	-	-	-	12	-	-	-	-
Agriculture	-	-	-	-	-	-	-	-	-	-	-
Commerce and Publ. Serv.	-	-	-	-	-	-	-	-	-	-	-
Residential	-	-	-	-	-	-	12	-	-	-	-
Non-specified	-	-	-	-	-	-	-	-	-	-	-
NON-ENERGY USE	-	-	-	-	-	-	-	-	-	-	-
in Industry/Transf./Energy	-	-	-	-	-	-	-	-	-	-	-
in Transport	-	-	-	-	-	-	-	-	-	-	-
in Other Sectors	-	-	-	-	-	-	-	-	-	-	-

Luxembourg / Luxembourg : 1992

SUPPLY AND CONSUMPTION	Oil cont. / *Pétrole cont.* (1000 tonnes)										
	Refinery Gas	LPG + Ethane	Motor Gasoline	Aviation Gasoline	Jet Fuel	Kerosene	Gas/ Diesel	Heavy Fuel Oil	Naphtha	Pétrol. Coke	Other Prod.
APPROVISIONNEMENT ET DEMANDE	*Gaz de raffinerie*	*GPL + éthane*	*Essence moteur*	*Essence aviation*	*Carbu- réacteur*	*Kérosène*	*Gazole*	*Fioul lourd*	*Naphta*	*Coke de pétrole*	*Autres prod.*
Production	-	-	-	-	-	-	-	-	-	-	-
From Other Sources	-	-	-	-	-	-	-	-	-	-	-
Imports	-	18	532	1	127	1	987	241	-	-	16
Exports	-	-	-	-	-	-	-1	-	-	-	-
Intl. Marine Bunkers	-	-	-	-	-	-	-	-	-	-	-
Stock Changes	-	-	-9	-	1	-	-16	-2	-	-	-
DOMESTIC SUPPLY	-	18	523	1	128	1	970	239	-	-	16
Transfers	-	-	-	-	-	-	-	-	-	-	-
Statistical Differences	-	-	-	-	1	-	-3	1	-	-	-
TRANSFORMATION	-	-	-	-	-	-	-	18	-	-	-
Electricity Plants	-	-	-	-	-	-	-	18	-	-	-
CHP Plants	-	-	-	-	-	-	-	-	-	-	-
Heat Plants	-	-	-	-	-	-	-	-	-	-	-
Transfer to Gases	-	-	-	-	-	-	-	-	-	-	-
Transfer to Solids	-	-	-	-	-	-	-	-	-	-	-
Petroleum Refineries	-	-	-	-	-	-	-	-	-	-	-
Petrochemical Industry	-	-	-	-	-	-	-	-	-	-	-
Liquefaction	-	-	-	-	-	-	-	-	-	-	-
Other Transformation Sector	-	-	-	-	-	-	-	-	-	-	-
ENERGY SECTOR	-	-	-	-	-	-	-	-	-	-	-
Coal Mines	-	-	-	-	-	-	-	-	-	-	-
Oil and Gas Extraction	-	-	-	-	-	-	-	-	-	-	-
Petroleum Refineries	-	-	-	-	-	-	-	-	-	-	-
Electricity, CHP+Heat plants	-	-	-	-	-	-	-	-	-	-	-
Pumped Storage (Elec.)	-	-	-	-	-	-	-	-	-	-	-
Other Energy Sector	-	-	-	-	-	-	-	-	-	-	-
Distribution Losses	-	-	-	-	-	-	-	-	-	-	-
FINAL CONSUMPTION	-	18	523	1	129	1	967	222	-	-	16
INDUSTRY SECTOR	-	4	-	-	-	1	49	222	-	-	-
Iron and Steel	-	2	-	-	-	-	7	187	-	-	-
Chemical and Petrochemical	-	1	-	-	-	-	7	31	-	-	-
of which: Feedstocks	-	*1*	-	-	-	-	-	-	-	-	-
Non-Ferrous Metals	-	-	-	-	-	-	-	-	-	-	-
Non-Metallic Minerals	-	-	-	-	-	-	7	-	-	-	-
Transport Equipment	-	-	-	-	-	-	-	-	-	-	-
Machinery	-	-	-	-	-	-	-	-	-	-	-
Mining and Quarrying	-	-	-	-	-	-	2	-	-	-	-
Food and Tobacco	-	-	-	-	-	-	4	1	-	-	-
Paper, Pulp and Print	-	-	-	-	-	-	-	-	-	-	-
Wood and Wood Products	-	-	-	-	-	-	-	-	-	-	-
Construction	-	-	-	-	-	-	6	-	-	-	-
Textile and Leather	-	-	-	-	-	-	-	-	-	-	-
Non-specified	-	1	-	-	-	1	16	3	-	-	-
TRANSPORT SECTOR	-	3	523	1	129	-	580	-	-	-	-
International Civil Aviation	-	-	-	-	129	-	-	-	-	-	-
Domestic Air	-	-	-	1	-	-	-	-	-	-	-
Road	-	3	523	-	-	-	573	-	-	-	-
Rail	-	-	-	-	-	-	7	-	-	-	-
Pipeline Transport	-	-	-	-	-	-	-	-	-	-	-
Internal Navigation	-	-	-	-	-	-	-	-	-	-	-
Non-specified	-	-	-	-	-	-	-	-	-	-	-
OTHER SECTORS	-	11	-	-	-	-	338	-	-	-	-
Agriculture	-	-	-	-	-	-	6	-	-	-	-
Commerce and Publ. Serv.	-	-	-	-	-	-	-	-	-	-	-
Residential	-	11	-	-	-	-	317	-	-	-	-
Non-specified	-	-	-	-	-	-	15	-	-	-	-
NON-ENERGY USE	-	-	-	-	-	-	-	-	-	-	16
in Industry/Transf./Energy	-	-	-	-	-	-	-	-	-	-	14
in Transport	-	-	-	-	-	-	-	-	-	-	2
in Other Sectors	-	-	-	-	-	-	-	-	-	-	-

Luxembourg / Luxembourg : 1992

CONSUMPTION *APPROVISIONNEMENT ET DEMANDE*	Gas / *Gaz* (TJ)				Combust. Renew. & Waste / *En. Re. Comb. & Déchets* (TJ)				(GWh)	(TJ)
	Natural Gas *Gaz naturel*	Gas Works *Usines à gaz*	Coke Ovens *Cokeries*	Blast Furnaces *Hauts fourneaux*	Solid Biomass & Anim. Prod. *Biomasse solide & prod. anim.*	Gas/Liquids from Biomass *Gaz/Liquides tirés de biomasse*	Municipal Waste *Déchets urbains*	Industrial Waste *Déchets industriels*	Electricity *Electricité*	Heat *Chaleur*
Production	-	-	-	13844	-	-	1087	-	1198	-
From Other Sources	-	-	-	-	-	-	-	-	-	-
Imports	21669	-	-	-	-	-	-	-	4511	-
Exports	-	-	-	-	-	-	-	-	-533	-
Intl. Marine Bunkers	-	-	-	-	-	-	-	-	-	-
Stock Changes	-	-	-	-	-	-	-	-	-	-
DOMESTIC SUPPLY	**21669**	**-**	**-**	**13844**	**-**	**-**	**1087**	**-**	**5176**	**-**
Transfers	-	-	-	-	-	-	-	-	-	-
Statistical Differences	-	-	-	-	-	-	-	-	-	-
TRANSFORMATION	**393**	**-**	**-**	**6282**	**-**	**-**	**1087**	**-**	**-**	**-**
Electricity Plants	393	-	-	6282	-	-	1087	-	-	-
CHP Plants	-	-	-	-	-	-	-	-	-	-
Heat Plants	-	-	-	-	-	-	-	-	-	-
Transfer to Gases	-	-	-	-	-	-	-	-	-	-
Transfer to Solids	-	-	-	-	-	-	-	-	-	-
Petroleum Refineries	-	-	-	-	-	-	-	-	-	-
Petrochemical Industry	-	-	-	-	-	-	-	-	-	-
Liquefaction	-	-	-	-	-	-	-	-	-	-
Other Transformation Sector	-	-	-	-	-	-	-	-	-	-
ENERGY SECTOR	**-**	**-**	**-**	**-**	**-**	**-**	**-**	**-**	**820**	**-**
Coal Mines	-	-	-	-	-	-	-	-	-	-
Oil and Gas Extraction	-	-	-	-	-	-	-	-	-	-
Petroleum Refineries	-	-	-	-	-	-	-	-	-	-
Electricity, CHP+Heat plants	-	-	-	-	-	-	-	-	45	-
Pumped Storage (Elec.)	-	-	-	-	-	-	-	-	775	-
Other Energy Sector	-	-	-	-	-	-	-	-	-	-
Distribution Losses	53	-	-	1355	-	-	-	-	106	-
FINAL CONSUMPTION	**21223**	**-**	**-**	**6207**	**-**	**-**	**-**	**-**	**4250**	**-**
INDUSTRY SECTOR	**13778**	**-**	**-**	**6207**	**-**	**-**	**-**	**-**	**2588**	**-**
Iron and Steel	5886	-	-	6207	-	-	-	-	1103	-
Chemical and Petrochemical	-	-	-	-	-	-	-	-	542	-
of which: Feedstocks	-	-	-	-	-	-	-	-	-	-
Non-Ferrous Metals	-	-	-	-	-	-	-	-	-	-
Non-Metallic Minerals	-	-	-	-	-	-	-	-	-	-
Transport Equipment	-	-	-	-	-	-	-	-	-	-
Machinery	-	-	-	-	-	-	-	-	431	-
Mining and Quarrying	-	-	-	-	-	-	-	-	17	-
Food and Tobacco	-	-	-	-	-	-	-	-	61	-
Paper, Pulp and Print	-	-	-	-	-	-	-	-	-	-
Wood and Wood Products	-	-	-	-	-	-	-	-	-	-
Construction	-	-	-	-	-	-	-	-	-	-
Textile and Leather	-	-	-	-	-	-	-	-	229	-
Non-specified	7892	-	-	-	-	-	-	-	205	-
TRANSPORT SECTOR	**-**	**-**	**-**	**-**	**-**	**-**	**-**	**-**	**63**	**-**
International Civil Aviation	-	-	-	-	-	-	-	-	-	-
Domestic Air	-	-	-	-	-	-	-	-	-	-
Road	-	-	-	-	-	-	-	-	-	-
Rail	-	-	-	-	-	-	-	-	63	-
Pipeline Transport	-	-	-	-	-	-	-	-	-	-
Internal Navigation	-	-	-	-	-	-	-	-	-	-
Non-specified	-	-	-	-	-	-	-	-	-	-
OTHER SECTORS	**7445**	**-**	**-**	**-**	**-**	**-**	**-**	**-**	**1599**	**-**
Agriculture	-	-	-	-	-	-	-	-	84	-
Commerce and Publ. Serv.	-	-	-	-	-	-	-	-	810	-
Residential	7445	-	-	-	-	-	-	-	705	-
Non-specified	-	-	-	-	-	-	-	-	-	-
NON-ENERGY USE	**-**	**-**	**-**	**-**	**-**	**-**	**-**	**-**	**-**	**-**
in Industry/Transf./Energy	-	-	-	-	-	-	-	-	-	-
in Transport	-	-	-	-	-	-	-	-	-	-
in Other Sectors	-	-	-	-	-	-	-	-	-	-

Luxembourg / Luxembourg : 1993

SUPPLY AND CONSUMPTION *APPROVISIONNEMENT ET DEMANDE*	Coal / *Charbon* (1000 tonnes)							Oil / *Pétrole* (1000 tonnes)			
	Coking Coal *Charbon à coke*	Steam Coal *Charbon vapeur*	Sub-Bit. Coal *Charbon sous-bit.*	Lignite *Lignite*	Peat *Tourbe*	Oven and Gas Coke *Coke de four/gaz*	Pat. Fuel and BKB *Agg./briq. de lignite*	Crude Oil *Pétrole brut*	NGL *LGN*	Feedstocks *Produits d'aliment.*	Additives *Additifs*
Production	-	-	-	-	-	-	-	-	-	-	-
From Other Sources	-	-	-	-	-	-	-	-	-	-	-
Imports	-	277	-	8	-	1230	10	-	-	-	-
Exports	-	-	-	-	-	-	-	-	-	-	-
Intl. Marine Bunkers	-	-	-	-	-	-	-	-	-	-	-
Stock Changes	-	-	-	-	-	-	-	-	-	-	-
DOMESTIC SUPPLY	-	277	-	8	-	1230	10	-	-	-	-
Transfers	-	-	-	-	-	-	-	-	-	-	-
Statistical Differences	-	-	-	-	-	-	-	-	-	-	-
TRANSFORMATION	-	-	-	-	-	455	-	-	-	-	-
Electricity Plants	-	-	-	-	-	-	-	-	-	-	-
CHP Plants	-	-	-	-	-	-	-	-	-	-	-
Heat Plants	-	-	-	-	-	-	-	-	-	-	-
Transfer to Gases	-	-	-	-	-	455	-	-	-	-	-
Transfer to Solids	-	-	-	-	-	-	-	-	-	-	-
Petroleum Refineries	-	-	-	-	-	-	-	-	-	-	-
Petrochemical Industry	-	-	-	-	-	-	-	-	-	-	-
Liquefaction	-	-	-	-	-	-	-	-	-	-	-
Other Transformation Sector	-	-	-	-	-	-	-	-	-	-	-
ENERGY SECTOR	-	-	-	-	-	-	-	-	-	-	-
Coal Mines	-	-	-	-	-	-	-	-	-	-	-
Oil and Gas Extraction	-	-	-	-	-	-	-	-	-	-	-
Petroleum Refineries	-	-	-	-	-	-	-	-	-	-	-
Electricity, CHP+Heat plants	-	-	-	-	-	-	-	-	-	-	-
Pumped Storage (Elec.)	-	-	-	-	-	-	-	-	-	-	-
Other Energy Sector	-	-	-	-	-	-	-	-	-	-	-
Distribution Losses	-	-	-	-	-	-	-	-	-	-	-
FINAL CONSUMPTION	-	277	-	8	-	775	10	-	-	-	-
INDUSTRY SECTOR	-	277	-	8	-	775	-	-	-	-	-
Iron and Steel	-	160	-	-	-	775	-	-	-	-	-
Chemical and Petrochemical	-	-	-	-	-	-	-	-	-	-	-
of which: Feedstocks	-	-	-	-	-	-	-	-	-	-	-
Non-Ferrous Metals	-	-	-	-	-	-	-	-	-	-	-
Non-Metallic Minerals	-	117	-	8	-	-	-	-	-	-	-
Transport Equipment	-	-	-	-	-	-	-	-	-	-	-
Machinery	-	-	-	-	-	-	-	-	-	-	-
Mining and Quarrying	-	-	-	-	-	-	-	-	-	-	-
Food and Tobacco	-	-	-	-	-	-	-	-	-	-	-
Paper, Pulp and Print	-	-	-	-	-	-	-	-	-	-	-
Wood and Wood Products	-	-	-	-	-	-	-	-	-	-	-
Construction	-	-	-	-	-	-	-	-	-	-	-
Textile and Leather	-	-	-	-	-	-	-	-	-	-	-
Non-specified	-	-	-	-	-	-	-	-	-	-	-
TRANSPORT SECTOR	-	-	-	-	-	-	-	-	-	-	-
International Civil Aviation	-	-	-	-	-	-	-	-	-	-	-
Domestic Air	-	-	-	-	-	-	-	-	-	-	-
Road	-	-	-	-	-	-	-	-	-	-	-
Rail	-	-	-	-	-	-	-	-	-	-	-
Pipeline Transport	-	-	-	-	-	-	-	-	-	-	-
Internal Navigation	-	-	-	-	-	-	-	-	-	-	-
Non-specified	-	-	-	-	-	-	-	-	-	-	-
OTHER SECTORS	-	-	-	-	-	-	10	-	-	-	-
Agriculture	-	-	-	-	-	-	-	-	-	-	-
Commerce and Publ. Serv.	-	-	-	-	-	-	-	-	-	-	-
Residential	-	-	-	-	-	-	10	-	-	-	-
Non-specified	-	-	-	-	-	-	-	-	-	-	-
NON-ENERGY USE	-	-	-	-	-	-	-	-	-	-	-
in Industry/Transf./Energy	-	-	-	-	-	-	-	-	-	-	-
in Transport	-	-	-	-	-	-	-	-	-	-	-
in Other Sectors	-	-	-	-	-	-	-	-	-	-	-

Luxembourg / Luxembourg : 1993

SUPPLY AND CONSUMPTION / *APPROVISIONNEMENT ET DEMANDE*	Oil cont. / *Pétrole cont.* (1000 tonnes)										
	Refinery Gas / *Gaz de raffinerie*	LPG + Ethane / *GPL + éthane*	Motor Gasoline / *Essence moteur*	Aviation Gasoline / *Essence aviation*	Jet Fuel / *Carbu-réacteur*	Kerosene / *Kérosène*	Gas/ Diesel / *Gazole*	Heavy Fuel Oil / *Fioul lourd*	Naphtha / *Naphta*	Pétrol. Coke / *Coke de pétrole*	Other Prod. / *Autres prod.*
Production	-	-	-	-	-	-	-	-	-	-	-
From Other Sources	-	-	-	-	-	-	-	-	-	-	-
Imports	-	15	517	-	128	1	953	250	-	-	13
Exports	-	-	-1	-	-	-	-1	-	-	-	-
Intl. Marine Bunkers	-	-	-	-	-	-	-	-	-	-	-
Stock Changes	-	-	12	-	-3	-	9	-	-	-	1
DOMESTIC SUPPLY	-	15	528	-	125	1	961	250	-	-	14
Transfers	-	-	-	-	-	-	-	-	-	-	-
Statistical Differences	-	-	-2	-	3	-	-4	-	-	-	-1
TRANSFORMATION	-	-	-	-	-	-	-	18	-	-	-
Electricity Plants	-	-	-	-	-	-	-	18	-	-	-
CHP Plants	-	-	-	-	-	-	-	-	-	-	-
Heat Plants	-	-	-	-	-	-	-	-	-	-	-
Transfer to Gases	-	-	-	-	-	-	-	-	-	-	-
Transfer to Solids	-	-	-	-	-	-	-	-	-	-	-
Petroleum Refineries	-	-	-	-	-	-	-	-	-	-	-
Petrochemical Industry	-	-	-	-	-	-	-	-	-	-	-
Liquefaction	-	-	-	-	-	-	-	-	-	-	-
Other Transformation Sector	-	-	-	-	-	-	-	-	-	-	-
ENERGY SECTOR	-	-	-	-	-	-	-	-	-	-	-
Coal Mines	-	-	-	-	-	-	-	-	-	-	-
Oil and Gas Extraction	-	-	-	-	-	-	-	-	-	-	-
Petroleum Refineries	-	-	-	-	-	-	-	-	-	-	-
Electricity, CHP+Heat plants	-	-	-	-	-	-	-	-	-	-	-
Pumped Storage (Elec.)	-	-	-	-	-	-	-	-	-	-	-
Other Energy Sector	-	-	-	-	-	-	-	-	-	-	-
Distribution Losses	-	-	-	-	-	-	-	-	-	-	-
FINAL CONSUMPTION	-	15	526	-	128	1	957	232	-	-	13
INDUSTRY SECTOR	-	1	-	-	-	1	46	232	-	-	-
Iron and Steel	-	-	-	-	-	-	9	193	-	-	-
Chemical and Petrochemical	-	1	-	-	-	-	7	35	-	-	-
of which: Feedstocks	-	*1*	-	-	-	-	-	-	-	-	-
Non-Ferrous Metals	-	-	-	-	-	-	-	-	-	-	-
Non-Metallic Minerals	-	-	-	-	-	-	8	-	-	-	-
Transport Equipment	-	-	-	-	-	-	-	-	-	-	-
Machinery	-	-	-	-	-	-	-	-	-	-	-
Mining and Quarrying	-	-	-	-	-	-	2	-	-	-	-
Food and Tobacco	-	-	-	-	-	-	2	1	-	-	-
Paper, Pulp and Print	-	-	-	-	-	-	-	-	-	-	-
Wood and Wood Products	-	-	-	-	-	-	-	-	-	-	-
Construction	-	-	-	-	-	-	8	-	-	-	-
Textile and Leather	-	-	-	-	-	-	-	-	-	-	-
Non-specified	-	-	-	-	-	1	10	3	-	-	-
TRANSPORT SECTOR	-	3	526	-	128	-	588	-	-	-	-
International Civil Aviation	-	-	-	-	128	-	-	-	-	-	-
Domestic Air	-	-	-	-	-	-	-	-	-	-	-
Road	-	3	526	-	-	-	584	-	-	-	-
Rail	-	-	-	-	-	-	4	-	-	-	-
Pipeline Transport	-	-	-	-	-	-	-	-	-	-	-
Internal Navigation	-	-	-	-	-	-	-	-	-	-	-
Non-specified	-	-	-	-	-	-	-	-	-	-	-
OTHER SECTORS	-	11	-	-	-	-	323	-	-	-	-
Agriculture	-	-	-	-	-	-	5	-	-	-	-
Commerce and Publ. Serv.	-	-	-	-	-	-	-	-	-	-	-
Residential	-	10	-	-	-	-	305	-	-	-	-
Non-specified	-	1	-	-	-	-	13	-	-	-	-
NON-ENERGY USE	-	-	-	-	-	-	-	-	-	-	13
in Industry/Transf./Energy	-	-	-	-	-	-	-	-	-	-	11
in Transport	-	-	-	-	-	-	-	-	-	-	2
in Other Sectors	-	-	-	-	-	-	-	-	-	-	-

Luxembourg / Luxembourg : 1993

CONSUMPTION *APPROVISIONNEMENT ET DEMANDE*	Gas / *Gaz* (TJ)				Combust. Renew. & Waste / *En. Re. Comb. & Déchets* (TJ)				(GWh)	(TJ)
	Natural Gas *Gaz naturel*	Gas Works *Usines à gaz*	Coke Ovens *Cokeries*	Blast Furnaces *Hauts fourneaux*	Solid Biomass & Anim. Prod. *Biomasse solide & prod. anim.*	Gas/Liquids from Biomass *Gaz/Liquides tirés de biomasse*	Municipal Waste *Déchets urbains*	Industrial Waste *Déchets industriels*	Electricity *Electricité*	Heat *Chaleur*
Production	-	-	-	14256	-	-	1040	-	1067	-
From Other Sources	-	-	-	-	-	-	-	-	-	-
Imports	22509	-	-	-	-	-	-	-	4445	-
Exports	-	-	-	-	-	-	-	-	-394	-
Intl. Marine Bunkers	-	-	-	-	-	-	-	-	-	-
Stock Changes	-	-	-	-	-	-	-	-	-	-
DOMESTIC SUPPLY	**22509**	-	-	**14256**	-	-	**1040**	-	**5118**	-
Transfers	-	-	-	-	-	-	-	-	-	-
Statistical Differences	-	-	-	-	-	-	-	-	-	-
TRANSFORMATION	**284**	-	-	**6457**	-	-	**1040**	-	-	-
Electricity Plants	284	-	-	6457	-	-	1040	-	-	-
CHP Plants	-	-	-	-	-	-	-	-	-	-
Heat Plants	-	-	-	-	-	-	-	-	-	-
Transfer to Gases	-	-	-	-	-	-	-	-	-	-
Transfer to Solids	-	-	-	-	-	-	-	-	-	-
Petroleum Refineries	-	-	-	-	-	-	-	-	-	-
Petrochemical Industry	-	-	-	-	-	-	-	-	-	-
Liquefaction	-	-	-	-	-	-	-	-	-	-
Other Transformation Sector	-	-	-	-	-	-	-	-	-	-
ENERGY SECTOR	-	-	-	-	-	-	-	-	**645**	-
Coal Mines	-	-	-	-	-	-	-	-	-	-
Oil and Gas Extraction	-	-	-	-	-	-	-	-	-	-
Petroleum Refineries	-	-	-	-	-	-	-	-	-	-
Electricity, CHP+Heat plants	-	-	-	-	-	-	-	-	46	-
Pumped Storage (Elec.)	-	-	-	-	-	-	-	-	599	-
Other Energy Sector	-	-	-	-	-	-	-	-	-	-
Distribution Losses	155	-	-	1297	-	-	-	-	97	-
FINAL CONSUMPTION	**22070**	-	-	**6502**	-	-	-	-	**4376**	-
INDUSTRY SECTOR	**14151**	-	-	**6502**	-	-	-	-	**2638**	-
Iron and Steel	5923	-	-	6502	-	-	-	-	1118	-
Chemical and Petrochemical	-	-	-	-	-	-	-	-	538	-
of which: Feedstocks	-	-	-	-	-	-	-	-	-	-
Non-Ferrous Metals	-	-	-	-	-	-	-	-	-	-
Non-Metallic Minerals	-	-	-	-	-	-	-	-	-	-
Transport Equipment	-	-	-	-	-	-	-	-	-	-
Machinery	-	-	-	-	-	-	-	-	448	-
Mining and Quarrying	-	-	-	-	-	-	-	-	16	-
Food and Tobacco	-	-	-	-	-	-	-	-	61	-
Paper, Pulp and Print	-	-	-	-	-	-	-	-	-	-
Wood and Wood Products	-	-	-	-	-	-	-	-	-	-
Construction	-	-	-	-	-	-	-	-	-	-
Textile and Leather	-	-	-	-	-	-	-	-	231	-
Non-specified	8228	-	-	-	-	-	-	-	226	-
TRANSPORT SECTOR	-	-	-	-	-	-	-	-	**60**	-
International Civil Aviation	-	-	-	-	-	-	-	-	-	-
Domestic Air	-	-	-	-	-	-	-	-	-	-
Road	-	-	-	-	-	-	-	-	-	-
Rail	-	-	-	-	-	-	-	-	60	-
Pipeline Transport	-	-	-	-	-	-	-	-	-	-
Internal Navigation	-	-	-	-	-	-	-	-	-	-
Non-specified	-	-	-	-	-	-	-	-	-	-
OTHER SECTORS	**7919**	-	-	-	-	-	-	-	**1678**	-
Agriculture	-	-	-	-	-	-	-	-	83	-
Commerce and Publ. Serv.	-	-	-	-	-	-	-	-	877	-
Residential	7919	-	-	-	-	-	-	-	718	-
Non-specified	-	-	-	-	-	-	-	-	-	-
NON-ENERGY USE	-	-	-	-	-	-	-	-	-	-
in Industry/Transf./Energy	-	-	-	-	-	-	-	-	-	-
in Transport	-	-	-	-	-	-	-	-	-	-
in Other Sectors	-	-	-	-	-	-	-	-	-	-

Mexico / Mexique : 1992

SUPPLY AND CONSUMPTION	Coal / Charbon (1000 tonnes)							Oil / Pétrole (1000 tonnes)			
	Coking Coal	Steam Coal	Sub-Bit. Coal	Lignite	Peat	Oven and Gas Coke	Pat. Fuel and BKB	Crude Oil	NGL	Feedstocks	Additives
APPROVISIONNEMENT ET DEMANDE	Charbon à coke	Charbon vapeur	Charbon sous-bit.	Lignite	Tourbe	Coke de four/gaz	Agg./briq. de lignite	Pétrole brut	LGN	Produits d'aliment.	Additifs
Production	1605	-	4499	-	-	2033	-	140185	15322	-	-
From Other Sources	-	-	-	-	-	-	-	-	-	-	-
Imports	634	-	-	-	-	167	-	-	-	-	-
Exports	-	-	-	-	-	-	-	-72165	-	-	-
Intl. Marine Bunkers	-	-	-	-	-	-	-	-	-	-	-
Stock Changes	475	-	-507	-	-	182	-	138	-	-	-
DOMESTIC SUPPLY	**2714**	**-**	**3992**	**-**	**-**	**2382**	**-**	**68158**	**15322**	**-**	**-**
Transfers	-	-	-	-	-	-	-	-	-12395	-	-
Statistical Differences	-160	-	257	-	-	-	-	-1292	-	-	-
TRANSFORMATION	**2554**	**-**	**4249**	**-**	**-**	**-**	**-**	**66866**	**2927**	**-**	**-**
Electricity Plants	-	-	4249	-	-	-	-	-	-	-	-
CHP Plants	-	-	-	-	-	-	-	-	-	-	-
Heat Plants	-	-	-	-	-	-	-	-	-	-	-
Transfer to Gases	-	-	-	-	-	-	-	-	-	-	-
Transfer to Solids	2554	-	-	-	-	-	-	-	-	-	-
Petroleum Refineries	-	-	-	-	-	-	-	66866	2927	-	-
Petrochemical Industry	-	-	-	-	-	-	-	-	-	-	-
Liquefaction	-	-	-	-	-	-	-	-	-	-	-
Other Transformation Sector	-	-	-	-	-	-	-	-	-	-	-
ENERGY SECTOR	**-**	**-**	**-**	**-**	**-**	**-**	**-**	**-**	**-**	**-**	**-**
Coal Mines	-	-	-	-	-	-	-	-	-	-	-
Oil and Gas Extraction	-	-	-	-	-	-	-	-	-	-	-
Petroleum Refineries	-	-	-	-	-	-	-	-	-	-	-
Electricity, CHP+Heat plants	-	-	-	-	-	-	-	-	-	-	-
Pumped Storage (Elec.)	-	-	-	-	-	-	-	-	-	-	-
Other Energy Sector	-	-	-	-	-	-	-	-	-	-	-
Distribution Losses	-	-	-	-	-	-	-	-	-	-	-
FINAL CONSUMPTION	**-**	**-**	**-**	**-**	**-**	**2382**	**-**	**-**	**-**	**-**	**-**
INDUSTRY SECTOR	**-**	**-**	**-**	**-**	**-**	**2382**	**-**	**-**	**-**	**-**	**-**
Iron and Steel	-	-	-	-	-	2203	-	-	-	-	-
Chemical and Petrochemical	-	-	-	-	-	-	-	-	-	-	-
of which: Feedstocks	-	-	-	-	-	-	-	-	-	-	-
Non-Ferrous Metals	-	-	-	-	-	-	-	-	-	-	-
Non-Metallic Minerals	-	-	-	-	-	-	-	-	-	-	-
Transport Equipment	-	-	-	-	-	-	-	-	-	-	-
Machinery	-	-	-	-	-	-	-	-	-	-	-
Mining and Quarrying	-	-	-	-	-	145	-	-	-	-	-
Food and Tobacco	-	-	-	-	-	-	-	-	-	-	-
Paper, Pulp and Print	-	-	-	-	-	-	-	-	-	-	-
Wood and Wood Products	-	-	-	-	-	-	-	-	-	-	-
Construction	-	-	-	-	-	-	-	-	-	-	-
Textile and Leather	-	-	-	-	-	-	-	-	-	-	-
Non-specified	-	-	-	-	-	34	-	-	-	-	-
TRANSPORT SECTOR	**-**	**-**	**-**	**-**	**-**	**-**	**-**	**-**	**-**	**-**	**-**
International Civil Aviation	-	-	-	-	-	-	-	-	-	-	-
Domestic Air	-	-	-	-	-	-	-	-	-	-	-
Road	-	-	-	-	-	-	-	-	-	-	-
Rail	-	-	-	-	-	-	-	-	-	-	-
Pipeline Transport	-	-	-	-	-	-	-	-	-	-	-
Internal Navigation	-	-	-	-	-	-	-	-	-	-	-
Non-specified	-	-	-	-	-	-	-	-	-	-	-
OTHER SECTORS	**-**	**-**	**-**	**-**	**-**	**-**	**-**	**-**	**-**	**-**	**-**
Agriculture	-	-	-	-	-	-	-	-	-	-	-
Commerce and Publ. Serv.	-	-	-	-	-	-	-	-	-	-	-
Residential	-	-	-	-	-	-	-	-	-	-	-
Non-specified	-	-	-	-	-	-	-	-	-	-	-
NON-ENERGY USE	**-**	**-**	**-**	**-**	**-**	**-**	**-**	**-**	**-**	**-**	**-**
in Industry/Transf./Energy	-	-	-	-	-	-	-	-	-	-	-
in Transport	-	-	-	-	-	-	-	-	-	-	-
in Other Sectors	-	-	-	-	-	-	-	-	-	-	-

Mexico / Mexique : 1992

SUPPLY AND CONSUMPTION *APPROVISIONNEMENT ET DEMANDE*	Oil cont. / *Pétrole cont.* (1000 tonnes)										
	Refinery Gas *Gaz de raffinerie*	LPG + Ethane *GPL + éthane*	Motor Gasoline *Essence moteur*	Aviation Gasoline *Essence aviation*	Jet Fuel *Carbu-réacteur*	Kerosene *Kérosène*	Gas/ Diesel *Gazole*	Heavy Fuel Oil *Fioul lourd*	Naphtha *Naphta*	Pétrol. Coke *Coke de pétrole*	Other Prod. *Autres prod.*
Production	1128	1306	16343	-	2623	971	15174	25542	1342	79	2577
From Other Sources	-	-	-	-	-	-	-	-	-	-	-
Imports	-	934	3820	-	-	-	-	2920	-	-	-
Exports	-	-601	-965	-	-712	-	-1908	-873	-	-	-
Intl. Marine Bunkers	-	-	-	-	-	-	-	-400	-	-	-
Stock Changes	-	20	114	-	29	-	141	-96	-	-	-
DOMESTIC SUPPLY	**1128**	**1659**	**19312**	**-**	**1940**	**971**	**13407**	**27093**	**1342**	**79**	**2577**
Transfers	-	9398	2997	-	-	-	-	-	-	-	-
Statistical Differences	-	-	40	-	-	-4	-1	-	-	-	-
TRANSFORMATION	**-**	**-**	**-**	**-**	**-**	**-**	**281**	**14824**	**-**	**-**	**-**
Electricity Plants	-	-	-	-	-	-	281	14824	-	-	-
CHP Plants	-	-	-	-	-	-	-	-	-	-	-
Heat Plants	-	-	-	-	-	-	-	-	-	-	-
Transfer to Gases	-	-	-	-	-	-	-	-	-	-	-
Transfer to Solids	-	-	-	-	-	-	-	-	-	-	-
Petroleum Refineries	-	-	-	-	-	-	-	-	-	-	-
Petrochemical Industry	-	-	-	-	-	-	-	-	-	-	-
Liquefaction	-	-	-	-	-	-	-	-	-	-	-
Other Transformation Sector	-	-	-	-	-	-	-	-	-	-	-
ENERGY SECTOR	**1128**	**-**	**-**	**-**	**-**	**-**	**-**	**3000**	**-**	**-**	**-**
Coal Mines	-	-	-	-	-	-	-	-	-	-	-
Oil and Gas Extraction	-	-	-	-	-	-	-	-	-	-	-
Petroleum Refineries	1128	-	-	-	-	-	-	3000	-	-	-
Electricity, CHP+Heat plants	-	-	-	-	-	-	-	-	-	-	-
Pumped Storage (Elec.)	-	-	-	-	-	-	-	-	-	-	-
Other Energy Sector	-	-	-	-	-	-	-	-	-	-	-
Distribution Losses	-	-	-	-	-	-	-	-	-	-	-
FINAL CONSUMPTION	**-**	**11057**	**22349**	**-**	**1940**	**967**	**13125**	**9269**	**1342**	**79**	**2577**
INDUSTRY SECTOR	**-**	**3403**	**-**	**-**	**-**	**48**	**1687**	**6097**	**1342**	**-**	**-**
Iron and Steel	-	7	-	-	-	-	21	332	-	-	-
Chemical and Petrochemical	-	3045	-	-	-	-	116	1215	1244	-	-
of which: Feedstocks	-	-	-	-	-	-	-	-	*1244*	-	-
Non-Ferrous Metals	-	2	-	-	-	-	-	-	-	-	-
Non-Metallic Minerals	-	2	-	-	-	-	31	1973	-	-	-
Transport Equipment	-	-	-	-	-	-	-	-	-	-	-
Machinery	-	27	-	-	-	-	10	-	-	-	-
Mining and Quarrying	-	23	-	-	-	-	92	130	-	-	-
Food and Tobacco	-	32	-	-	-	-	115	1095	-	-	-
Paper, Pulp and Print	-	3	-	-	-	-	134	291	-	-	-
Wood and Wood Products	-	-	-	-	-	-	-	-	-	-	-
Construction	-	-	-	-	-	-	124	-	-	-	-
Textile and Leather	-	-	-	-	-	-	-	-	-	-	-
Non-specified	-	262	-	-	-	48	1044	1061	98	-	-
TRANSPORT SECTOR	**-**	**368**	**22349**	**-**	**1940**	**-**	**8450**	**-**	**-**	**-**	**-**
International Civil Aviation	-	-	-	-	1940	-	-	-	-	-	-
Domestic Air	-	-	-	-	-	-	-	-	-	-	-
Road	-	368	22349	-	-	-	8450	-	-	-	-
Rail	-	-	-	-	-	-	-	-	-	-	-
Pipeline Transport	-	-	-	-	-	-	-	-	-	-	-
Internal Navigation	-	-	-	-	-	-	-	-	-	-	-
Non-specified	-	-	-	-	-	-	-	-	-	-	-
OTHER SECTORS	**-**	**7286**	**-**	**-**	**-**	**919**	**2988**	**3172**	**-**	**-**	**-**
Agriculture	-	22	-	-	-	97	1574	-	-	-	-
Commerce and Publ. Serv.	-	-	-	-	-	-	40	772	-	-	-
Residential	-	6610	-	-	-	180	-	-	-	-	-
Non-specified	-	654	-	-	-	642	1374	2400	-	-	-
NON-ENERGY USE	**-**	**-**	**-**	**-**	**-**	**-**	**-**	**-**	**-**	**79**	**2577**
in Industry/Transf./Energy	-	-	-	-	-	-	-	-	-	79	2577
in Transport	-	-	-	-	-	-	-	-	-	-	-
in Other Sectors	-	-	-	-	-	-	-	-	-	-	-

Mexico / Mexique : 1992

CONSUMPTION *APPROVISIONNEMENT ET DEMANDE*	Gas / *Gaz* (TJ)				Combust. Renew. & Waste / *En. Re. Comb. & Déchets* (TJ)				(GWh)	(TJ)
	Natural Gas *Gaz naturel*	Gas Works *Usines à gaz*	Coke Ovens *Cokeries*	Blast Furnaces *Hauts fourneaux*	Solid Biomass & Anim. Prod. *Biomasse solide & prod. anim.*	Gas/Liquids from Biomass *Gaz/Liquides tirés de biomasse*	Municipal Waste *Déchets urbains*	Industrial Waste *Déchets industriels*	Electricity *Electricité*	Heat *Chaleur*
Production	1148262	-	-	-	370398	-	-	-	121653	-
From Other Sources	-	-	-	-	-	-	-	-	-	-
Imports	112462	-	-	-	-	-	-	-	990	-
Exports	-	-	-	-	-	-	-	-	-2041	-
Intl. Marine Bunkers	-	-	-	-	-	-	-	-	-	-
Stock Changes	-8076	-	-	-	-	-	-	-	-	-
DOMESTIC SUPPLY	**1252648**	**-**	**-**	**-**	**370398**	**-**	**-**	**-**	**120602**	**-**
Transfers	-	-	-	-	-	-	-	-	-	-
Statistical Differences	-4652	-	-	-	-465	-	-	-	-	-
TRANSFORMATION	**174017**	**-**	**-**	**-**	**-**	**-**	**-**	**-**	**-**	**-**
Electricity Plants	174017	-	-	-	-	-	-	-	-	-
CHP Plants	-	-	-	-	-	-	-	-	-	-
Heat Plants	-	-	-	-	-	-	-	-	-	-
Transfer to Gases	-	-	-	-	-	-	-	-	-	-
Transfer to Solids	-	-	-	-	-	-	-	-	-	-
Petroleum Refineries	-	-	-	-	-	-	-	-	-	-
Petrochemical Industry	-	-	-	-	-	-	-	-	-	-
Liquefaction	-	-	-	-	-	-	-	-	-	-
Other Transformation Sector	-	-	-	-	-	-	-	-	-	-
ENERGY SECTOR	**303915**	**-**	**-**	**-**	**-**	**-**	**-**	**-**	**5994**	**-**
Coal Mines	-	-	-	-	-	-	-	-	-	-
Oil and Gas Extraction	-	-	-	-	-	-	-	-	-	-
Petroleum Refineries	-	-	-	-	-	-	-	-	-	-
Electricity, CHP+Heat plants	-	-	-	-	-	-	-	-	5994	-
Pumped Storage (Elec.)	-	-	-	-	-	-	-	-	-	-
Other Energy Sector	303915	-	-	-	-	-	-	-	-	-
Distribution Losses	-	-	-	-	-	-	-	-	17039	-
FINAL CONSUMPTION	**770064**	**-**	**-**	**-**	**369933**	**-**	**-**	**-**	**97569**	**-**
INDUSTRY SECTOR	**723809**	**-**	**-**	**-**	**69890**	**-**	**-**	**-**	**52831**	**-**
Iron and Steel	94571	-	-	-	-	-	-	-	6662	-
Chemical and Petrochemical	395350	-	-	-	-	-	-	-	5227	-
of which: Feedstocks	*120222*	-	-	-	-	-	-	-	-	-
Non-Ferrous Metals	2726	-	-	-	-	-	-	-	107	-
Non-Metallic Minerals	48483	-	-	-	-	-	-	-	4200	-
Transport Equipment	-	-	-	-	-	-	-	-	-	-
Machinery	1996	-	-	-	-	-	-	-	715	-
Mining and Quarrying	27112	-	-	-	-	-	-	-	4262	-
Food and Tobacco	7680	-	-	-	69890	-	-	-	748	-
Paper, Pulp and Print	30112	-	-	-	-	-	-	-	2367	-
Wood and Wood Products	-	-	-	-	-	-	-	-	-	-
Construction	-	-	-	-	-	-	-	-	330	-
Textile and Leather	-	-	-	-	-	-	-	-	-	-
Non-specified	115779	-	-	-	-	-	-	-	28213	-
TRANSPORT SECTOR	**-**	**-**	**-**	**-**	**-**	**-**	**-**	**-**	**873**	**-**
International Civil Aviation	-	-	-	-	-	-	-	-	-	-
Domestic Air	-	-	-	-	-	-	-	-	-	-
Road	-	-	-	-	-	-	-	-	-	-
Rail	-	-	-	-	-	-	-	-	873	-
Pipeline Transport	-	-	-	-	-	-	-	-	-	-
Internal Navigation	-	-	-	-	-	-	-	-	-	-
Non-specified	-	-	-	-	-	-	-	-	-	-
OTHER SECTORS	**46255**	**-**	**-**	**-**	**300043**	**-**	**-**	**-**	**43865**	**-**
Agriculture	-	-	-	-	-	-	-	-	5671	-
Commerce and Publ. Serv.	-	-	-	-	-	-	-	-	14143	-
Residential	46255	-	-	-	300043	-	-	-	24051	-
Non-specified	-	-	-	-	-	-	-	-	-	-
NON-ENERGY USE	**-**	**-**	**-**	**-**	**-**	**-**	**-**	**-**	**-**	**-**
in Industry/Transf./Energy	-	-	-	-	-	-	-	-	-	-
in Transport	-	-	-	-	-	-	-	-	-	-
in Other Sectors	-	-	-	-	-	-	-	-	-	-

Mexico / Mexique : 1993

SUPPLY AND CONSUMPTION	Coal / *Charbon* (1000 tonnes)							Oil / *Pétrole* (1000 tonnes)			
	Coking Coal	Steam Coal	Sub-Bit. Coal	Lignite	Peat	Oven and Gas Coke	Pat. Fuel and BKB	Crude Oil	NGL	Feedstocks	Additives
APPROVISIONNEMENT ET DEMANDE	*Charbon à coke*	*Charbon vapeur*	*Charbon sous-bit.*	*Lignite*	*Tourbe*	*Coke de four/gaz*	*Agg./briq. de lignite*	*Pétrole brut*	*LGN*	*Produits d'aliment.*	*Additifs*
Production	1710	-	4905	-	-	1942	-	140099	15152	-	-
From Other Sources	-	-	-	-	-	-	-	-	-	-	-
Imports	18	-	-	-	-	608	-	-	-	-	-
Exports	-5	-	-	-	-	-	-	-71086	-	-	-
Intl. Marine Bunkers	-	-	-	-	-	-	-	-	-	-	-
Stock Changes	873	-	488	-	-	-146	-	-132	-	-	-
DOMESTIC SUPPLY	**2596**	**-**	**5393**	**-**	**-**	**2404**	**-**	**68881**	**15152**	**-**	**-**
Transfers	-	-	-	-	-	-	-	-	-12253	-	-
Statistical Differences	-157	-	-	-	-	-	-	-660	-	-	-
TRANSFORMATION	**2439**	**-**	**5393**	**-**	**-**	**-**	**-**	**68221**	**2899**	**-**	**-**
Electricity Plants	-	-	5393	-	-	-	-	-	-	-	-
CHP Plants	-	-	-	-	-	-	-	-	-	-	-
Heat Plants	-	-	-	-	-	-	-	-	-	-	-
Transfer to Gases	-	-	-	-	-	-	-	-	-	-	-
Transfer to Solids	2439	-	-	-	-	-	-	-	-	-	-
Petroleum Refineries	-	-	-	-	-	-	-	68221	2899	-	-
Petrochemical Industry	-	-	-	-	-	-	-	-	-	-	-
Liquefaction	-	-	-	-	-	-	-	-	-	-	-
Other Transformation Sector	-	-	-	-	-	-	-	-	-	-	-
ENERGY SECTOR	**-**	**-**	**-**	**-**	**-**	**-**	**-**	**-**	**-**	**-**	**-**
Coal Mines	-	-	-	-	-	-	-	-	-	-	-
Oil and Gas Extraction	-	-	-	-	-	-	-	-	-	-	-
Petroleum Refineries	-	-	-	-	-	-	-	-	-	-	-
Electricity, CHP+Heat plants	-	-	-	-	-	-	-	-	-	-	-
Pumped Storage (Elec.)	-	-	-	-	-	-	-	-	-	-	-
Other Energy Sector	-	-	-	-	-	-	-	-	-	-	-
Distribution Losses	-	-	-	-	-	-	-	-	-	-	-
FINAL CONSUMPTION	**-**	**-**	**-**	**-**	**-**	**2404**	**-**	**-**	**-**	**-**	**-**
INDUSTRY SECTOR	**-**	**-**	**-**	**-**	**-**	**2404**	**-**	**-**	**-**	**-**	**-**
Iron and Steel	-	-	-	-	-	2218	-	-	-	-	-
Chemical and Petrochemical	-	-	-	-	-	-	-	-	-	-	-
of which: Feedstocks	-	-	-	-	-	-	-	-	-	-	-
Non-Ferrous Metals	-	-	-	-	-	-	-	-	-	-	-
Non-Metallic Minerals	-	-	-	-	-	-	-	-	-	-	-
Transport Equipment	-	-	-	-	-	-	-	-	-	-	-
Machinery	-	-	-	-	-	-	-	-	-	-	-
Mining and Quarrying	-	-	-	-	-	152	-	-	-	-	-
Food and Tobacco	-	-	-	-	-	-	-	-	-	-	-
Paper, Pulp and Print	-	-	-	-	-	-	-	-	-	-	-
Wood and Wood Products	-	-	-	-	-	-	-	-	-	-	-
Construction	-	-	-	-	-	-	-	-	-	-	-
Textile and Leather	-	-	-	-	-	-	-	-	-	-	-
Non-specified	-	-	-	-	-	34	-	-	-	-	-
TRANSPORT SECTOR	**-**	**-**	**-**	**-**	**-**	**-**	**-**	**-**	**-**	**-**	**-**
International Civil Aviation	-	-	-	-	-	-	-	-	-	-	-
Domestic Air	-	-	-	-	-	-	-	-	-	-	-
Road	-	-	-	-	-	-	-	-	-	-	-
Rail	-	-	-	-	-	-	-	-	-	-	-
Pipeline Transport	-	-	-	-	-	-	-	-	-	-	-
Internal Navigation	-	-	-	-	-	-	-	-	-	-	-
Non-specified	-	-	-	-	-	-	-	-	-	-	-
OTHER SECTORS	**-**	**-**	**-**	**-**	**-**	**-**	**-**	**-**	**-**	**-**	**-**
Agriculture	-	-	-	-	-	-	-	-	-	-	-
Commerce and Publ. Serv.	-	-	-	-	-	-	-	-	-	-	-
Residential	-	-	-	-	-	-	-	-	-	-	-
Non-specified	-	-	-	-	-	-	-	-	-	-	-
NON-ENERGY USE	**-**	**-**	**-**	**-**	**-**	**-**	**-**	**-**	**-**	**-**	**-**
in Industry/Transf./Energy	-	-	-	-	-	-	-	-	-	-	-
in Transport	-	-	-	-	-	-	-	-	-	-	-
in Other Sectors	-	-	-	-	-	-	-	-	-	-	-

Mexico / Mexique : 1993

SUPPLY AND CONSUMPTION APPROVISIONNEMENT ET DEMANDE	Oil cont. / Pétrole cont. (1000 tonnes)										
	Refinery Gas Gaz de raffinerie	LPG + Ethane GPL + éthane	Motor Gasoline Essence moteur	Aviation Gasoline Essence aviation	Jet Fuel Carbu-réacteur	Kerosene Kérosène	Gas/Diesel Gazole	Heavy Fuel Oil Fioul lourd	Naphtha Naphta	Pétrol. Coke Coke de pétrole	Other Prod. Autres prod.
Production	1148	1849	16680	-	2839	1088	14625	26234	1302	79	2832
From Other Sources	-	-	-	-	-	-	-	-	-	-	-
Imports	-	946	3872	-	-	-	-	3071	-	-	-
Exports	-	-558	-1549	-	-789	-	-2216	-1947	-	-	-
Intl. Marine Bunkers	-	-	-	-	-	-	-	-400	-	-	-
Stock Changes	-	50	253	-	5	-	61	86	-	-	-
DOMESTIC SUPPLY	**1148**	**2287**	**19256**	**-**	**2055**	**1088**	**12470**	**27044**	**1302**	**79**	**2832**
Transfers	-	9189	3064	-	-	-	-	-	-	-	-
Statistical Differences	-	-	39	-	-	-5	-3	-2	-	-	-
TRANSFORMATION	**-**	**-**	**-**	**-**	**-**	**-**	**267**	**15031**	**-**	**-**	**-**
Electricity Plants	-	-	-	-	-	-	267	15031	-	-	-
CHP Plants	-	-	-	-	-	-	-	-	-	-	-
Heat Plants	-	-	-	-	-	-	-	-	-	-	-
Transfer to Gases	-	-	-	-	-	-	-	-	-	-	-
Transfer to Solids	-	-	-	-	-	-	-	-	-	-	-
Petroleum Refineries	-	-	-	-	-	-	-	-	-	-	-
Petrochemical Industry	-	-	-	-	-	-	-	-	-	-	-
Liquefaction	-	-	-	-	-	-	-	-	-	-	-
Other Transformation Sector	-	-	-	-	-	-	-	-	-	-	-
ENERGY SECTOR	**1148**	**-**	**-**	**-**	**-**	**-**	**-**	**3000**	**-**	**-**	**-**
Coal Mines	-	-	-	-	-	-	-	-	-	-	-
Oil and Gas Extraction	-	-	-	-	-	-	-	-	-	-	-
Petroleum Refineries	1148	-	-	-	-	-	-	3000	-	-	-
Electricity, CHP+Heat plants	-	-	-	-	-	-	-	-	-	-	-
Pumped Storage (Elec.)	-	-	-	-	-	-	-	-	-	-	-
Other Energy Sector	-	-	-	-	-	-	-	-	-	-	-
Distribution Losses	-	-	-	-	-	-	-	-	-	-	-
FINAL CONSUMPTION	**-**	**11476**	**22359**	**-**	**2055**	**1083**	**12200**	**9011**	**1302**	**79**	**2832**
INDUSTRY SECTOR	**-**	**3444**	**-**	**-**	**-**	**24**	**1591**	**6004**	**1302**	**-**	**-**
Iron and Steel	-	6	-	-	-	-	21	409	-	-	-
Chemical and Petrochemical	-	3077	-	-	-	-	104	1162	1200	-	-
of which: Feedstocks	-	-	-	-	-	-	-	-	1200	-	-
Non-Ferrous Metals	-	2	-	-	-	-	-	-	-	-	-
Non-Metallic Minerals	-	2	-	-	-	-	29	1949	-	-	-
Transport Equipment	-	-	-	-	-	-	-	-	-	-	-
Machinery	-	27	-	-	-	-	7	-	-	-	-
Mining and Quarrying	-	24	-	-	-	-	95	135	-	-	-
Food and Tobacco	-	14	-	-	-	-	74	974	-	-	-
Paper, Pulp and Print	-	6	-	-	-	-	67	410	-	-	-
Wood and Wood Products	-	-	-	-	-	-	-	-	-	-	-
Construction	-	-	-	-	-	-	126	-	-	-	-
Textile and Leather	-	-	-	-	-	-	-	-	-	-	-
Non-specified	-	286	-	-	-	24	1068	965	102	-	-
TRANSPORT SECTOR	**-**	**372**	**22359**	**-**	**2055**	**-**	**8664**	**-**	**-**	**-**	**-**
International Civil Aviation	-	-	-	-	2055	-	-	-	-	-	-
Domestic Air	-	-	-	-	-	-	-	-	-	-	-
Road	-	372	22359	-	-	-	8664	-	-	-	-
Rail	-	-	-	-	-	-	-	-	-	-	-
Pipeline Transport	-	-	-	-	-	-	-	-	-	-	-
Internal Navigation	-	-	-	-	-	-	-	-	-	-	-
Non-specified	-	-	-	-	-	-	-	-	-	-	-
OTHER SECTORS	**-**	**7660**	**-**	**-**	**-**	**1059**	**1945**	**3007**	**-**	**-**	**-**
Agriculture	-	23	-	-	-	79	1603	-	-	-	-
Commerce and Publ. Serv.	-	-	-	-	-	-	39	762	-	-	-
Residential	-	6998	-	-	-	97	-	-	-	-	-
Non-specified	-	639	-	-	-	883	303	2245	-	-	-
NON-ENERGY USE	**-**	**-**	**-**	**-**	**-**	**-**	**-**	**-**	**-**	**79**	**2832**
in Industry/Transf./Energy	-	-	-	-	-	-	-	-	-	79	2832
in Transport	-	-	-	-	-	-	-	-	-	-	-
in Other Sectors	-	-	-	-	-	-	-	-	-	-	-

Mexico / Mexique : 1993

CONSUMPTION *APPROVISIONNEMENT ET DEMANDE*	Gas / *Gaz* (TJ)				Combust. Renew. & Waste / *En. Re. Comb. & Déchets* (TJ)				(GWh)	(TJ)
	Natural Gas *Gaz naturel*	Gas Works *Usines à gaz*	Coke Ovens *Cokeries*	Blast Furnaces *Hauts fourneaux*	Solid Biomass & Anim. Prod. *Biomasse solide & prod. anim.*	Gas/Liquids from Biomass *Gaz/Liquides tirés de biomasse*	Municipal Waste *Déchets urbains*	Industrial Waste *Déchets industriels*	Electricity *Electricité*	Heat *Chaleur*
Production	1123746	-	-	-	383130	-	-	-	126566	-
From Other Sources	-	-	-	-	-	-	-	-	-	-
Imports	43464	-	-	-	-	-	-	-	909	-
Exports	-2219	-	-	-	-	-	-	-	-2015	-
Intl. Marine Bunkers	-	-	-	-	-	-	-	-	-	-
Stock Changes	8941	-	-	-	-	-	-	-	-	-
DOMESTIC SUPPLY	**1173932**	**-**	**-**	**-**	**383130**	**-**	**-**	**-**	**125460**	**-**
Transfers	-	-	-	-	-	-	-	-	-	-
Statistical Differences	-	-	-	-	-616	-	-	-	-	-
TRANSFORMATION	**170407**	**-**	**-**	**-**	**-**	**-**	**-**	**-**	**-**	**-**
Electricity Plants	170407	-	-	-	-	-	-	-	-	-
CHP Plants	-	-	-	-	-	-	-	-	-	-
Heat Plants	-	-	-	-	-	-	-	-	-	-
Transfer to Gases	-	-	-	-	-	-	-	-	-	-
Transfer to Solids	-	-	-	-	-	-	-	-	-	-
Petroleum Refineries	-	-	-	-	-	-	-	-	-	-
Petrochemical Industry	-	-	-	-	-	-	-	-	-	-
Liquefaction	-	-	-	-	-	-	-	-	-	-
Other Transformation Sector	-	-	-	-	-	-	-	-	-	-
ENERGY SECTOR	**245477**	**-**	**-**	**-**	**-**	**-**	**-**	**-**	**6030**	**-**
Coal Mines	-	-	-	-	-	-	-	-	-	-
Oil and Gas Extraction	-	-	-	-	-	-	-	-	-	-
Petroleum Refineries	-	-	-	-	-	-	-	-	-	-
Electricity, CHP+Heat plants	-	-	-	-	-	-	-	-	6030	-
Pumped Storage (Elec.)	-	-	-	-	-	-	-	-	-	-
Other Energy Sector	245477	-	-	-	-	-	-	-	-	-
Distribution Losses	-	-	-	-	-	-	-	-	17220	-
FINAL CONSUMPTION	**758048**	**-**	**-**	**-**	**382514**	**-**	**-**	**-**	**102210**	**-**
INDUSTRY SECTOR	**708476**	**-**	**-**	**-**	**80633**	**-**	**-**	**-**	**55145**	**-**
Iron and Steel	98641	-	-	-	-	-	-	-	6820	-
Chemical and Petrochemical	345095	-	-	-	-	-	-	-	6497	-
of which: Feedstocks	98176	-	-	-	-	-	-	-	-	-
Non-Ferrous Metals	3405	-	-	-	-	-	-	-	245	-
Non-Metallic Minerals	47181	-	-	-	-	-	-	-	4355	-
Transport Equipment	-	-	-	-	-	-	-	-	-	-
Machinery	2521	-	-	-	-	-	-	-	718	-
Mining and Quarrying	28521	-	-	-	-	-	-	-	4312	-
Food and Tobacco	9383	-	-	-	80633	-	-	-	763	-
Paper, Pulp and Print	21134	-	-	-	-	-	-	-	2436	-
Wood and Wood Products	-	-	-	-	-	-	-	-	-	-
Construction	-	-	-	-	-	-	-	-	365	-
Textile and Leather	-	-	-	-	-	-	-	-	-	-
Non-specified	152595	-	-	-	-	-	-	-	28634	-
TRANSPORT SECTOR	**-**	**-**	**-**	**-**	**-**	**-**	**-**	**-**	**894**	**-**
International Civil Aviation	-	-	-	-	-	-	-	-	-	-
Domestic Air	-	-	-	-	-	-	-	-	-	-
Road	-	-	-	-	-	-	-	-	-	-
Rail	-	-	-	-	-	-	-	-	894	-
Pipeline Transport	-	-	-	-	-	-	-	-	-	-
Internal Navigation	-	-	-	-	-	-	-	-	-	-
Non-specified	-	-	-	-	-	-	-	-	-	-
OTHER SECTORS	**49572**	**-**	**-**	**-**	**301881**	**-**	**-**	**-**	**46171**	**-**
Agriculture	-	-	-	-	-	-	-	-	5919	-
Commerce and Publ. Serv.	-	-	-	-	-	-	-	-	14741	-
Residential	49572	-	-	-	301881	-	-	-	25511	-
Non-specified	-	-	-	-	-	-	-	-	-	-
NON-ENERGY USE	**-**	**-**	**-**	**-**	**-**	**-**	**-**	**-**	**-**	**-**
in Industry/Transf./Energy	-	-	-	-	-	-	-	-	-	-
in Transport	-	-	-	-	-	-	-	-	-	-
in Other Sectors	-	-	-	-	-	-	-	-	-	-

Netherlands / Pays-Bas : 1992

SUPPLY AND CONSUMPTION / APPROVISIONNEMENT ET DEMANDE	Coal / *Charbon* (1000 tonnes)							Oil / *Pétrole* (1000 tonnes)			
	Coking Coal / *Charbon à coke*	Steam Coal / *Charbon vapeur*	Sub-Bit. Coal / *Charbon sous-bit.*	Lignite / *Lignite*	Peat / *Tourbe*	Oven and Gas Coke / *Coke de four/gaz*	Pat. Fuel and BKB / *Agg./briq. de lignite*	Crude Oil / *Pétrole brut*	NGL / *LGN*	Feedstocks / *Produits d'aliment.*	Additives / *Additifs*
Production	-	-	-	-	-	2922	-	2845	479	-	-
From Other Sources	-	-	-	-	-	-	-	-	-	-	-
Imports	4816	10151	-	35	-	328	12	52905	3255	-	-
Exports	-6	-2190	-	-	-	-1176	-9	-977	-3	-	-
Intl. Marine Bunkers	-	-	-	-	-	-	-	-	-	-	-
Stock Changes	-91	250	-	-	-	2	-	-1122	-32	-	-
DOMESTIC SUPPLY	**4719**	**8211**	**-**	**35**	**-**	**2076**	**3**	**53651**	**3699**	**-**	**-**
Transfers	-	-	-	-	-	-	-	-	-	14400	-
Statistical Differences	162	3	-	2	-	3	-	128	-5	-	-
TRANSFORMATION	**4105**	**7842**	**-**	**-**	**-**	**1003**	**-**	**53779**	**3694**	**14400**	**-**
Electricity Plants	-	-	-	-	-	-	-	-	-	-	-
CHP Plants	-	7842	-	-	-	-	-	-	-	-	-
Heat Plants	-	-	-	-	-	-	-	-	-	-	-
Transfer to Gases	-	-	-	-	-	1003	-	-	-	-	-
Transfer to Solids	4105	-	-	-	-	-	-	-	-	-	-
Petroleum Refineries	-	-	-	-	-	-	-	53779	3694	14400	-
Petrochemical Industry	-	-	-	-	-	-	-	-	-	-	-
Liquefaction	-	-	-	-	-	-	-	-	-	-	-
Other Transformation Sector	-	-	-	-	-	-	-	-	-	-	-
ENERGY SECTOR	**-**	**-**	**-**	**-**	**-**	**-**	**-**	**-**	**-**	**-**	**-**
Coal Mines	-	-	-	-	-	-	-	-	-	-	-
Oil and Gas Extraction	-	-	-	-	-	-	-	-	-	-	-
Petroleum Refineries	-	-	-	-	-	-	-	-	-	-	-
Electricity, CHP+Heat plants	-	-	-	-	-	-	-	-	-	-	-
Pumped Storage (Elec.)	-	-	-	-	-	-	-	-	-	-	-
Other Energy Sector	-	-	-	-	-	-	-	-	-	-	-
Distribution Losses	-	-	-	-	-	-	-	-	-	-	-
FINAL CONSUMPTION	**776**	**372**	**-**	**37**	**-**	**1076**	**3**	**-**	**-**	**-**	**-**
INDUSTRY SECTOR	**776**	**314**	**-**	**30**	**-**	**941**	**-**	**-**	**-**	**-**	**-**
Iron and Steel	776	-	-	-	-	881	-	-	-	-	-
Chemical and Petrochemical	-	222	-	-	-	9	-	-	-	-	-
of which: Feedstocks	-	-	-	-	-	-	-	-	-	-	-
Non-Ferrous Metals	-	-	-	-	-	-	-	-	-	-	-
Non-Metallic Minerals	-	21	-	29	-	41	-	-	-	-	-
Transport Equipment	-	-	-	-	-	-	-	-	-	-	-
Machinery	-	-	-	-	-	10	-	-	-	-	-
Mining and Quarrying	-	-	-	-	-	-	-	-	-	-	-
Food and Tobacco	-	67	-	-	-	-	-	-	-	-	-
Paper, Pulp and Print	-	-	-	-	-	-	-	-	-	-	-
Wood and Wood Products	-	-	-	-	-	-	-	-	-	-	-
Construction	-	-	-	-	-	-	-	-	-	-	-
Textile and Leather	-	2	-	-	-	-	-	-	-	-	-
Non-specified	-	2	-	1	-	-	-	-	-	-	-
TRANSPORT SECTOR	**-**	**-**	**-**	**-**	**-**	**-**	**-**	**-**	**-**	**-**	**-**
International Civil Aviation	-	-	-	-	-	-	-	-	-	-	-
Domestic Air	-	-	-	-	-	-	-	-	-	-	-
Road	-	-	-	-	-	-	-	-	-	-	-
Rail	-	-	-	-	-	-	-	-	-	-	-
Pipeline Transport	-	-	-	-	-	-	-	-	-	-	-
Internal Navigation	-	-	-	-	-	-	-	-	-	-	-
Non-specified	-	-	-	-	-	-	-	-	-	-	-
OTHER SECTORS	**-**	**50**	**-**	**7**	**-**	**-**	**3**	**-**	**-**	**-**	**-**
Agriculture	-	-	-	-	-	-	-	-	-	-	-
Commerce and Publ. Serv.	-	-	-	-	-	-	-	-	-	-	-
Residential	-	18	-	7	-	-	1	-	-	-	-
Non-specified	-	32	-	-	-	-	2	-	-	-	-
NON-ENERGY USE	**-**	**8**	**-**	**-**	**-**	**135**	**-**	**-**	**-**	**-**	**-**
in Industry/Transf./Energy	-	8	-	-	-	135	-	-	-	-	-
in Transport	-	-	-	-	-	-	-	-	-	-	-
in Other Sectors	-	-	-	-	-	-	-	-	-	-	-

Netherlands / Pays-Bas : 1992

SUPPLY AND CONSUMPTION / APPROVISIONNEMENT ET DEMANDE	Oil cont. / Pétrole cont. (1000 tonnes)										
	Refinery Gas / Gaz de raffinerie	LPG + Ethane / GPL + éthane	Motor Gasoline / Essence moteur	Aviation Gasoline / Essence aviation	Jet Fuel / Carbu-réacteur	Kerosene / Kérosène	Gas/Diesel / Gazole	Heavy Fuel Oil / Fioul lourd	Naphtha / Naphta	Pétrol. Coke / Coke de pétrole	Other Prod. / Autres prod.
Production	3562	2698	12794	46	4979	229	18316	14711	9773	-	4436
From Other Sources	-	-	-	-	-	-	-	-	-	-	-
Imports	-	2565	3552	7	409	598	7684	6657	8016	-	1823
Exports	-	-1137	-9088	-49	-3287	-314	-17752	-9864	-8841	-	-2495
Intl. Marine Bunkers	-	-	-	-	-	-	-2138	-9352	-	-	-87
Stock Changes	-	83	187	1	-17	-68	185	43	156	-	-16
DOMESTIC SUPPLY	**3562**	**4209**	**7445**	**5**	**2084**	**445**	**6295**	**2195**	**9104**	**-**	**3661**
Transfers	-99	-1648	-3813	-1	-168	-360	-338	-949	-6294	-	-694
Statistical Differences	-	-6	-41	-	5	-	87	3	-5	-	6
TRANSFORMATION	**305**	**-**	**-**	**-**	**-**	**-**	**33**	**239**	**-**	**-**	**142**
Electricity Plants	-	-	-	-	-	-	-	-	-	-	-
CHP Plants	305	-	-	-	-	-	32	239	-	-	142
Heat Plants	-	-	-	-	-	-	-	-	-	-	-
Transfer to Gases	-	-	-	-	-	-	-	-	-	-	-
Transfer to Solids	-	-	-	-	-	-	1	-	-	-	-
Petroleum Refineries	-	-	-	-	-	-	-	-	-	-	-
Petrochemical Industry	-	-	-	-	-	-	-	-	-	-	-
Liquefaction	-	-	-	-	-	-	-	-	-	-	-
Other Transformation Sector	-	-	-	-	-	-	-	-	-	-	-
ENERGY SECTOR	**2372**	**6**	**-**	**-**	**-**	**-**	**20**	**835**	**-**	**-**	**363**
Coal Mines	-	-	-	-	-	-	-	-	-	-	-
Oil and Gas Extraction	-	-	-	-	-	-	-	-	-	-	-
Petroleum Refineries	2372	6	-	-	-	-	20	835	-	-	363
Electricity, CHP+Heat plants	-	-	-	-	-	-	-	-	-	-	-
Pumped Storage (Elec.)	-	-	-	-	-	-	-	-	-	-	-
Other Energy Sector	-	-	-	-	-	-	-	-	-	-	-
Distribution Losses	-	-	-	-	-	-	-	-	-	-	-
FINAL CONSUMPTION	**786**	**2549**	**3591**	**4**	**1921**	**85**	**5991**	**175**	**2805**	**-**	**2468**
INDUSTRY SECTOR	**786**	**1601**	**1**	**-**	**-**	**8**	**290**	**150**	**2805**	**-**	**-**
Iron and Steel	-	1	-	-	-	-	4	1	-	-	-
Chemical and Petrochemical	782	1585	-	-	-	6	86	23	2805	-	-
of which: Feedstocks	*71*	*1579*	-	-	-	*6*	*55*	*6*	*2805*	-	-
Non-Ferrous Metals	-	-	-	-	-	-	-	-	-	-	-
Non-Metallic Minerals	-	3	-	-	-	1	22	88	-	-	-
Transport Equipment	-	1	-	-	-	-	6	-	-	-	-
Machinery	-	4	1	-	-	-	13	3	-	-	-
Mining and Quarrying	-	-	-	-	-	-	16	-	-	-	-
Food and Tobacco	4	4	-	-	-	1	11	25	-	-	-
Paper, Pulp and Print	-	2	-	-	-	-	2	-	-	-	-
Wood and Wood Products	-	-	-	-	-	-	6	2	-	-	-
Construction	-	-	-	-	-	-	119	-	-	-	-
Textile and Leather	-	-	-	-	-	-	2	2	-	-	-
Non-specified	-	1	-	-	-	-	3	6	-	-	-
TRANSPORT SECTOR	**-**	**862**	**3590**	**4**	**1921**	**-**	**4306**	**-**	**-**	**-**	**-**
International Civil Aviation	-	-	-	1	1863	-	-	-	-	-	-
Domestic Air	-	-	-	3	58	-	-	-	-	-	-
Road	-	862	3590	-	-	-	3646	-	-	-	-
Rail	-	-	-	-	-	-	-	-	-	-	-
Pipeline Transport	-	-	-	-	-	-	-	-	-	-	-
Internal Navigation	-	-	-	-	-	-	660	-	-	-	-
Non-specified	-	-	-	-	-	-	-	-	-	-	-
OTHER SECTORS	**-**	**86**	**-**	**-**	**-**	**77**	**1395**	**25**	**-**	**-**	**-**
Agriculture	-	24	-	-	-	-	81	-	-	-	-
Commerce and Publ. Serv.	-	-	-	-	-	-	-	-	-	-	-
Residential	-	41	-	-	-	20	149	-	-	-	-
Non-specified	-	21	-	-	-	57	1165	25	-	-	-
NON-ENERGY USE	**-**	**-**	**-**	**-**	**-**	**-**	**-**	**-**	**-**	**-**	**2468**
in Industry/Transf./Energy	-	-	-	-	-	-	-	-	-	-	2281
in Transport	-	-	-	-	-	-	-	-	-	-	58
in Other Sectors	-	-	-	-	-	-	-	-	-	-	129

Netherlands / Pays-Bas : 1992

CONSUMPTION / APPROVISIONNEMENT ET DEMANDE	Gas / Gaz (TJ)				Combust. Renew. & Waste / En. Re. Comb. & Déchets (TJ)				(GWh)	(TJ)
	Natural Gas / Gaz naturel	Gas Works / Usines à gaz	Coke Ovens / Cokeries	Blast Furnaces / Hauts fourneaux	Solid Biomass & Anim. Prod. / Biomasse solide & prod. anim.	Gas/Liquids from Biomass / Gaz/Liquides tirés de biomasse	Municipal Waste / Déchets urbains	Industrial Waste / Déchets industriels	Electricity / Electricité	Heat / Chaleur
Production	2884654	-	27849	30750	-	3435	11601	-	77202	18804
From Other Sources	-	-	-	-	-	-	-	-	-	-
Imports	98413	-	-	-	-	-	-	-	8905	-
Exports	-1430130	-	-	-	-	-	-	-	-227	-
Intl. Marine Bunkers	-	-	-	-	-	-	-	-	-	-
Stock Changes	-66	-	-	-	-	-	-	-	-	-
DOMESTIC SUPPLY	**1552871**	**-**	**27849**	**30750**	**-**	**3435**	**11601**	**-**	**85880**	**18804**
Transfers	-	-	-	-	-	-	-	-	-	-
Statistical Differences	21761	-	-	-3	-	-	-	-	-	-
TRANSFORMATION	**400122**	**-**	**4625**	**19273**	**-**	**985**	**11601**	**-**	**-**	**-**
Electricity Plants	-	-	-	-	-	-	-	-	-	-
CHP Plants	400122	-	4625	19273	-	985	11601	-	-	-
Heat Plants	-	-	-	-	-	-	-	-	-	-
Transfer to Gases	-	-	-	-	-	-	-	-	-	-
Transfer to Solids	-	-	-	-	-	-	-	-	-	-
Petroleum Refineries	-	-	-	-	-	-	-	-	-	-
Petrochemical Industry	-	-	-	-	-	-	-	-	-	-
Liquefaction	-	-	-	-	-	-	-	-	-	-
Other Transformation Sector	-	-	-	-	-	-	-	-	-	-
ENERGY SECTOR	**55269**	**-**	**10197**	**1559**	**-**	**-**	**-**	**-**	**4777**	**-**
Coal Mines	-	-	-	-	-	-	-	-	-	-
Oil and Gas Extraction	33406	-	-	-	-	-	-	-	141	-
Petroleum Refineries	21863	-	-	-	-	-	-	-	1805	-
Electricity, CHP+Heat plants	-	-	-	-	-	-	-	-	2706	-
Pumped Storage (Elec.)	-	-	-	-	-	-	-	-	-	-
Other Energy Sector	-	-	10197	1559	-	-	-	-	125	-
Distribution Losses	-	-	-	-	-	-	-	-	3244	2820
FINAL CONSUMPTION	**1119241**	**-**	**13027**	**9915**	**-**	**2450**	**-**	**-**	**77859**	**15984**
INDUSTRY SECTOR	**414151**	**-**	**13027**	**9915**	**-**	**455**	**-**	**-**	**33666**	**-**
Iron and Steel	16565	-	10747	9915	-	-	-	-	1950	-
Chemical and Petrochemical	253151	-	2280	-	-	91	-	-	12206	-
of which: Feedstocks	112486	-	-	-	-	-	-	-	-	-
Non-Ferrous Metals	3999	-	-	-	-	131	-	-	4872	-
Non-Metallic Minerals	31564	-	-	-	-	-	-	-	1649	-
Transport Equipment	4074	-	-	-	-	-	-	-	525	-
Machinery	16598	-	-	-	-	-	-	-	2789	-
Mining and Quarrying	169	-	-	-	-	-	-	-	109	-
Food and Tobacco	56684	-	-	-	-	172	-	-	5060	-
Paper, Pulp and Print	18152	-	-	-	-	61	-	-	3012	-
Wood and Wood Products	1158	-	-	-	-	-	-	-	281	-
Construction	4291	-	-	-	-	-	-	-	500	-
Textile and Leather	5990	-	-	-	-	-	-	-	530	-
Non-specified	1756	-	-	-	-	-	-	-	183	-
TRANSPORT SECTOR	**-**	**-**	**-**	**-**	**-**	**-**	**-**	**-**	**1385**	**-**
International Civil Aviation	-	-	-	-	-	-	-	-	-	-
Domestic Air	-	-	-	-	-	-	-	-	-	-
Road	-	-	-	-	-	-	-	-	-	-
Rail	-	-	-	-	-	-	-	-	1385	-
Pipeline Transport	-	-	-	-	-	-	-	-	-	-
Internal Navigation	-	-	-	-	-	-	-	-	-	-
Non-specified	-	-	-	-	-	-	-	-	-	-
OTHER SECTORS	**705090**	**-**	**-**	**-**	**-**	**1995**	**-**	**-**	**42808**	**15984**
Agriculture	156471	-	-	-	-	-	-	-	1823	2686
Commerce and Publ. Serv.	-	-	-	-	-	-	-	-	23485	6268
Residential	372802	-	-	-	-	-	-	-	17500	7030
Non-specified	175817	-	-	-	-	1995	-	-	-	-
NON-ENERGY USE	**-**	**-**	**-**	**-**	**-**	**-**	**-**	**-**	**-**	**-**
in Industry/Transf./Energy	-	-	-	-	-	-	-	-	-	-
in Transport	-	-	-	-	-	-	-	-	-	-
in Other Sectors	-	-	-	-	-	-	-	-	-	-

Netherlands / Pays-Bas : 1993

SUPPLY AND CONSUMPTION / APPROVISIONNEMENT ET DEMANDE	Coal / Charbon (1000 tonnes)							Oil / Pétrole (1000 tonnes)			
	Coking Coal / Charbon à coke	Steam Coal / Charbon vapeur	Sub-Bit. Coal / Charbon sous-bit.	Lignite / Lignite	Peat / Tourbe	Oven and Gas Coke / Coke de four/gaz	Pat. Fuel and BKB / Agg./briq. de lignite	Crude Oil / Pétrole brut	NGL / LGN	Feedstocks / Produits d'aliment.	Additives / Additifs
Production	-	-	-	-	-	2879	-	2672	576	-	-
From Other Sources	-	-	-	-	-	-	-	-	-	-	-
Imports	4831	10290	-	78	-	207	8	51459	3817	-	-
Exports	-2	-2240	-	-39	-	-920	-2	-825	-35	-	-
Intl. Marine Bunkers	-	-	-	-	-	-	-	-	-	-	-
Stock Changes	39	170	-	-3	-	100	-	828	37	-	-
DOMESTIC SUPPLY	**4868**	**8220**	**-**	**36**	**-**	**2266**	**6**	**54134**	**4395**	**-**	**-**
Transfers	-	-	-	-	-	-	-	-	-	15111	-
Statistical Differences	31	-156	-	-	-	25	-	120	-2	-	-
TRANSFORMATION	**4062**	**7669**	**-**	**-**	**-**	**1131**	**-**	**54254**	**4393**	**15111**	**-**
Electricity Plants	-	-	-	-	-	-	-	-	-	-	-
CHP Plants	-	7669	-	-	-	-	-	-	-	-	-
Heat Plants	-	-	-	-	-	-	-	-	-	-	-
Transfer to Gases	-	-	-	-	-	1131	-	-	-	-	-
Transfer to Solids	4062	-	-	-	-	-	-	-	-	-	-
Petroleum Refineries	-	-	-	-	-	-	-	54254	4393	15111	-
Petrochemical Industry	-	-	-	-	-	-	-	-	-	-	-
Liquefaction	-	-	-	-	-	-	-	-	-	-	-
Other Transformation Sector	-	-	-	-	-	-	-	-	-	-	-
ENERGY SECTOR	**-**	**-**	**-**	**-**	**-**	**-**	**-**	**-**	**-**	**-**	**-**
Coal Mines	-	-	-	-	-	-	-	-	-	-	-
Oil and Gas Extraction	-	-	-	-	-	-	-	-	-	-	-
Petroleum Refineries	-	-	-	-	-	-	-	-	-	-	-
Electricity, CHP+Heat plants	-	-	-	-	-	-	-	-	-	-	-
Pumped Storage (Elec.)	-	-	-	-	-	-	-	-	-	-	-
Other Energy Sector	-	-	-	-	-	-	-	-	-	-	-
Distribution Losses	-	-	-	-	-	-	-	-	-	-	-
FINAL CONSUMPTION	**837**	**395**	**-**	**36**	**-**	**1160**	**6**	**-**	**-**	**-**	**-**
INDUSTRY SECTOR	**836**	**336**	**-**	**27**	**-**	**1037**	**3**	**-**	**-**	**-**	**-**
Iron and Steel	836	-	-	-	-	993	-	-	-	-	-
Chemical and Petrochemical	-	235	-	-	-	8	-	-	-	-	-
of which: Feedstocks	-	-	-	-	-	-	-	-	-	-	-
Non-Ferrous Metals	-	-	-	-	-	-	-	-	-	-	-
Non-Metallic Minerals	-	20	-	27	-	36	3	-	-	-	-
Transport Equipment	-	-	-	-	-	-	-	-	-	-	-
Machinery	-	-	-	-	-	-	-	-	-	-	-
Mining and Quarrying	-	-	-	-	-	-	-	-	-	-	-
Food and Tobacco	-	80	-	-	-	-	-	-	-	-	-
Paper, Pulp and Print	-	-	-	-	-	-	-	-	-	-	-
Wood and Wood Products	-	-	-	-	-	-	-	-	-	-	-
Construction	-	-	-	-	-	-	-	-	-	-	-
Textile and Leather	-	1	-	-	-	-	-	-	-	-	-
Non-specified	-	-	-	-	-	-	-	-	-	-	-
TRANSPORT SECTOR	**-**	**-**	**-**	**-**	**-**	**-**	**-**	**-**	**-**	**-**	**-**
International Civil Aviation	-	-	-	-	-	-	-	-	-	-	-
Domestic Air	-	-	-	-	-	-	-	-	-	-	-
Road	-	-	-	-	-	-	-	-	-	-	-
Rail	-	-	-	-	-	-	-	-	-	-	-
Pipeline Transport	-	-	-	-	-	-	-	-	-	-	-
Internal Navigation	-	-	-	-	-	-	-	-	-	-	-
Non-specified	-	-	-	-	-	-	-	-	-	-	-
OTHER SECTORS	**-**	**56**	**-**	**9**	**-**	**-**	**3**	**-**	**-**	**-**	**-**
Agriculture	-	-	-	-	-	-	-	-	-	-	-
Commerce and Publ. Serv.	-	-	-	-	-	-	-	-	-	-	-
Residential	-	14	-	9	-	-	1	-	-	-	-
Non-specified	-	42	-	-	-	-	2	-	-	-	-
NON-ENERGY USE	**1**	**3**	**-**	**-**	**-**	**123**	**-**	**-**	**-**	**-**	**-**
in Industry/Transf./Energy	1	3	-	-	-	123	-	-	-	-	-
in Transport	-	-	-	-	-	-	-	-	-	-	-
in Other Sectors	-	-	-	-	-	-	-	-	-	-	-

Netherlands / Pays-Bas : 1993

SUPPLY AND CONSUMPTION / APPROVISIONNEMENT ET DEMANDE	Refinery Gas / Gaz de raffinerie	LPG + Ethane / GPL + éthane	Motor Gasoline / Essence moteur	Aviation Gasoline / Essence aviation	Jet Fuel / Carbu-réacteur	Kerosene / Kérosène	Gas/ Diesel / Gazole	Heavy Fuel Oil / Fioul lourd	Naphtha / Naphta	Pétrol. Coke / Coke de pétrole	Other Prod. / Autres prod.
Production	3678	2729	14794	80	4938	262	18749	14850	8579	-	4804
From Other Sources	-	-	-	-	-	-	-	-	-	-	-
Imports	-	2560	3353	3	467	554	7128	8144	7735	-	1999
Exports	-	-1305	-9317	-77	-3238	-275	-18608	-10267	-8066	-	-2795
Intl. Marine Bunkers	-	-	-	-	-	-	-1874	-10035	-	-	-97
Stock Changes	-	18	-560	-	36	50	367	-56	-124	-	-32
DOMESTIC SUPPLY	**3678**	**4002**	**8270**	**6**	**2203**	**591**	**5762**	**2636**	**8124**	**-**	**3879**
Transfers	-86	-1680	-4491	-1	-102	-496	179	-1423	-6072	-	-903
Statistical Differences	-	1	10	-	-6	2	12	19	4	-	5
TRANSFORMATION	**273**	**-**	**-**	**-**	**-**	**-**	**24**	**278**	**-**	**-**	**112**
Electricity Plants	-	-	-	-	-	-	-	-	-	-	-
CHP Plants	273	-	-	-	-	-	23	278	-	-	112
Heat Plants	-	-	-	-	-	-	-	-	-	-	-
Transfer to Gases	-	-	-	-	-	-	-	-	-	-	-
Transfer to Solids	-	-	-	-	-	-	1	-	-	-	-
Petroleum Refineries	-	-	-	-	-	-	-	-	-	-	-
Petrochemical Industry	-	-	-	-	-	-	-	-	-	-	-
Liquefaction	-	-	-	-	-	-	-	-	-	-	-
Other Transformation Sector	-	-	-	-	-	-	-	-	-	-	-
ENERGY SECTOR	**2545**	**1**	**-**	**-**	**-**	**-**	**11**	**788**	**-**	**-**	**384**
Coal Mines	-	-	-	-	-	-	-	-	-	-	-
Oil and Gas Extraction	-	-	-	-	-	-	-	-	-	-	-
Petroleum Refineries	2545	1	-	-	-	-	11	788	-	-	384
Electricity, CHP+Heat plants	-	-	-	-	-	-	-	-	-	-	-
Pumped Storage (Elec.)	-	-	-	-	-	-	-	-	-	-	-
Other Energy Sector	-	-	-	-	-	-	-	-	-	-	-
Distribution Losses	-	-	-	-	-	-	-	-	-	-	-
FINAL CONSUMPTION	**774**	**2322**	**3789**	**5**	**2095**	**97**	**5918**	**166**	**2056**	**-**	**2485**
INDUSTRY SECTOR	**774**	**1401**	**-**	**-**	**-**	**5**	**221**	**141**	**2056**	**-**	**5**
Iron and Steel	-	1	-	-	-	-	4	-	-	-	-
Chemical and Petrochemical	770	1388	-	-	-	5	22	19	2056	-	5
of which: Feedstocks	32	1293	-	-	-	5	-	2	2056	-	-
Non-Ferrous Metals	-	-	-	-	-	-	1	-	-	-	-
Non-Metallic Minerals	-	1	-	-	-	-	13	97	-	-	-
Transport Equipment	-	2	-	-	-	-	4	-	-	-	-
Machinery	-	3	-	-	-	-	11	1	-	-	-
Mining and Quarrying	-	-	-	-	-	-	17	-	-	-	-
Food and Tobacco	4	5	-	-	-	-	16	21	-	-	-
Paper, Pulp and Print	-	1	-	-	-	-	2	1	-	-	-
Wood and Wood Products	-	-	-	-	-	-	1	-	-	-	-
Construction	-	-	-	-	-	-	126	-	-	-	-
Textile and Leather	-	-	-	-	-	-	-	-	-	-	-
Non-specified	-	-	-	-	-	-	4	2	-	-	-
TRANSPORT SECTOR	**-**	**822**	**3789**	**5**	**2095**	**-**	**4330**	**-**	**-**	**-**	**-**
International Civil Aviation	-	-	-	1	2035	-	-	-	-	-	-
Domestic Air	-	-	-	4	60	-	-	-	-	-	-
Road	-	822	3789	-	-	-	3665	-	-	-	-
Rail	-	-	-	-	-	-	-	-	-	-	-
Pipeline Transport	-	-	-	-	-	-	-	-	-	-	-
Internal Navigation	-	-	-	-	-	-	665	-	-	-	-
Non-specified	-	-	-	-	-	-	-	-	-	-	-
OTHER SECTORS	**-**	**99**	**-**	**-**	**-**	**92**	**1367**	**25**	**-**	**-**	**-**
Agriculture	-	24	-	-	-	-	56	7	-	-	-
Commerce and Publ. Serv.	-	-	-	-	-	-	-	-	-	-	-
Residential	-	44	-	-	-	21	158	-	-	-	-
Non-specified	-	31	-	-	-	71	1153	18	-	-	-
NON-ENERGY USE	**-**	**-**	**-**	**-**	**-**	**-**	**-**	**-**	**-**	**-**	**2480**
in Industry/Transf./Energy	-	-	-	-	-	-	-	-	-	-	2384
in Transport	-	-	-	-	-	-	-	-	-	-	26
in Other Sectors	-	-	-	-	-	-	-	-	-	-	70

Netherlands / Pays-Bas : 1993

CONSUMPTION *APPROVISIONNEMENT ET DEMANDE*	Gas / *Gaz* (TJ)				Combust. Renew. & Waste / *En. Re. Comb. & Déchets* (TJ)				(GWh)	(TJ)
	Natural Gas *Gaz naturel*	Gas Works *Usines à gaz*	Coke Ovens *Cokeries*	Blast Furnaces *Hauts fourneaux*	Solid Biomass & Anim. Prod. *Biomasse solide & prod. anim.*	Gas/Liquids from Biomass *Gaz/Liquides tirés de biomasse*	Municipal Waste *Déchets urbains*	Industrial Waste *Déchets industriels*	Electricity *Electricité*	Heat *Chaleur*
Production	2936245	-	27274	35449	-	4196	11884	-	76992	20945
From Other Sources	-	-	-	-	-	-	-	-	-	-
Imports	122787	-	-	-	-	-	-	-	10572	-
Exports	-1464228	-	-	-	-	-	-	-	-269	-
Intl. Marine Bunkers	-	-	-	-	-	-	-	-	-	-
Stock Changes	-512	-	-	-	-	-	-	-	-	-
DOMESTIC SUPPLY	**1594292**	**-**	**27274**	**35449**	**-**	**4196**	**11884**	**-**	**87295**	**20945**
Transfers	-	-	-	-	-	-	-	-	-	-
Statistical Differences	22702	-	-1197	-	-	-	-	-	-	-
TRANSFORMATION	**404995**	**-**	**3976**	**22298**	**-**	**1466**	**11884**	**-**	**-**	**-**
Electricity Plants	-	-	-	-	-	-	-	-	-	-
CHP Plants	404995	-	3976	22298	-	1466	11884	-	-	-
Heat Plants	-	-	-	-	-	-	-	-	-	-
Transfer to Gases	-	-	-	-	-	-	-	-	-	-
Transfer to Solids	-	-	-	-	-	-	-	-	-	-
Petroleum Refineries	-	-	-	-	-	-	-	-	-	-
Petrochemical Industry	-	-	-	-	-	-	-	-	-	-
Liquefaction	-	-	-	-	-	-	-	-	-	-
Other Transformation Sector	-	-	-	-	-	-	-	-	-	-
ENERGY SECTOR	**54418**	**-**	**10004**	**1441**	**-**	**-**	**-**	**-**	**5285**	**-**
Coal Mines	-	-	-	-	-	-	-	-	-	-
Oil and Gas Extraction	26148	-	-	-	-	-	-	-	144	-
Petroleum Refineries	28270	-	-	-	-	-	-	-	2035	-
Electricity, CHP+Heat plants	-	-	-	-	-	-	-	-	2976	-
Pumped Storage (Elec.)	-	-	-	-	-	-	-	-	-	-
Other Energy Sector	-	-	10004	1441	-	-	-	-	130	-
Distribution Losses	-	-	-	-	-	-	-	-	3286	3142
FINAL CONSUMPTION	**1157581**	**-**	**12097**	**11710**	**-**	**2730**	**-**	**-**	**78724**	**17803**
INDUSTRY SECTOR	**424981**	**-**	**12097**	**11710**	**-**	**423**	**-**	**-**	**34823**	**-**
Iron and Steel	15566	-	10838	11710	-	-	-	-	2088	-
Chemical and Petrochemical	252586	-	1259	-	-	55	-	-	10830	-
of which: Feedstocks	*107296*	-	-	-	-	-	-	-	-	-
Non-Ferrous Metals	3895	-	-	-	-	149	-	-	4728	-
Non-Metallic Minerals	29624	-	-	-	-	-	-	-	1480	-
Transport Equipment	3913	-	-	-	-	-	-	-	537	-
Machinery	17237	-	-	-	-	-	-	-	3005	-
Mining and Quarrying	317	-	-	-	-	-	-	-	49	-
Food and Tobacco	60584	-	-	-	-	154	-	-	6241	-
Paper, Pulp and Print	20520	-	-	-	-	65	-	-	3129	-
Wood and Wood Products	1026	-	-	-	-	-	-	-	280	-
Construction	4537	-	-	-	-	-	-	-	490	-
Textile and Leather	6549	-	-	-	-	-	-	-	529	-
Non-specified	8627	-	-	-	-	-	-	-	1437	-
TRANSPORT SECTOR	**-**	**-**	**-**	**-**	**-**	**-**	**-**	**-**	**1382**	**-**
International Civil Aviation	-	-	-	-	-	-	-	-	-	-
Domestic Air	-	-	-	-	-	-	-	-	-	-
Road	-	-	-	-	-	-	-	-	-	-
Rail	-	-	-	-	-	-	-	-	1382	-
Pipeline Transport	-	-	-	-	-	-	-	-	-	-
Internal Navigation	-	-	-	-	-	-	-	-	-	-
Non-specified	-	-	-	-	-	-	-	-	-	-
OTHER SECTORS	**732600**	**-**	**-**	**-**	**-**	**2307**	**-**	**-**	**42519**	**17803**
Agriculture	166917	-	-	-	-	-	-	-	1975	2990
Commerce and Publ. Serv.	-	-	-	-	-	-	-	-	22644	6980
Residential	395663	-	-	-	-	-	-	-	17900	7833
Non-specified	170020	-	-	-	-	2307	-	-	-	-
NON-ENERGY USE	**-**	**-**	**-**	**-**	**-**	**-**	**-**	**-**	**-**	**-**
in Industry/Transf./Energy	-	-	-	-	-	-	-	-	-	-
in Transport	-	-	-	-	-	-	-	-	-	-
in Other Sectors	-	-	-	-	-	-	-	-	-	-

New Zealand / Nouvelle-Zélande : 1992

SUPPLY AND CONSUMPTION	Coal / *Charbon* (1000 tonnes)							Oil / *Pétrole* (1000 tonnes)			
	Coking Coal	Steam Coal	Sub-Bit. Coal	Lignite	Peat	Oven and Gas Coke	Pat. Fuel and BKB	Crude Oil	NGL	Feedstocks	Additives
APPROVISIONNEMENT ET DEMANDE	*Charbon à coke*	*Charbon vapeur*	*Charbon sous-bit.*	*Lignite*	*Tourbe*	*Coke de four/gaz*	*Agg./briq. de lignite*	*Pétrole brut*	*LGN*	*Produits d'aliment.*	*Additifs*
Production	773	168	1828	179	-	-	-	1739	157	-	-
From Other Sources	-	-	-	-	-	-	-	-	-	-	-
Imports	-	1	-	-	-	-	-	3111	-	77	-
Exports	-758	-	-	-	-	-	-	-886	-	-	-
Intl. Marine Bunkers	-	-	-	-	-	-	-	-	-	-	-
Stock Changes	-15	-51	300	43	-	-	-	-22	-	21	-
DOMESTIC SUPPLY	-	118	2128	222	-	-	-	3942	157	98	-
Transfers	-	-	-	-	-	-	-	-588	-142	48	-
Statistical Differences	-	-	-	1	-	-	-	93	-15	-24	-
TRANSFORMATION	-	-	431	-	-	-	-	3447	-	122	-
Electricity Plants	-	-	431	-	-	-	-	-	-	-	-
CHP Plants	-	-	-	-	-	-	-	-	-	-	-
Heat Plants	-	-	-	-	-	-	-	-	-	-	-
Transfer to Gases	-	-	-	-	-	-	-	-	-	-	-
Transfer to Solids	-	-	-	-	-	-	-	-	-	-	-
Petroleum Refineries	-	-	-	-	-	-	-	4606	-	122	-
Petrochemical Industry	-	-	-	-	-	-	-	-	-	-	-
Liquefaction	-	-	-	-	-	-	-	-1159	-	-	-
Other Transformation Sector	-	-	-	-	-	-	-	-	-	-	-
ENERGY SECTOR	-	-	-	-	-	-	-	-	-	-	-
Coal Mines	-	-	-	-	-	-	-	-	-	-	-
Oil and Gas Extraction	-	-	-	-	-	-	-	-	-	-	-
Petroleum Refineries	-	-	-	-	-	-	-	-	-	-	-
Electricity, CHP+Heat plants	-	-	-	-	-	-	-	-	-	-	-
Pumped Storage (Elec.)	-	-	-	-	-	-	-	-	-	-	-
Other Energy Sector	-	-	-	-	-	-	-	-	-	-	-
Distribution Losses	-	-	-	-	-	-	-	-	-	-	-
FINAL CONSUMPTION	-	118	1697	223	-	-	-	-	-	-	-
INDUSTRY SECTOR	-	107	1591	116	-	-	-	-	-	-	-
Iron and Steel	-	-	698	-	-	-	-	-	-	-	-
Chemical and Petrochemical	-	-	-	-	-	-	-	-	-	-	-
of which: Feedstocks	-	-	-	-	-	-	-	-	-	-	-
Non-Ferrous Metals	-	-	-	-	-	-	-	-	-	-	-
Non-Metallic Minerals	-	-	-	-	-	-	-	-	-	-	-
Transport Equipment	-	-	-	-	-	-	-	-	-	-	-
Machinery	-	-	-	-	-	-	-	-	-	-	-
Mining and Quarrying	-	-	-	-	-	-	-	-	-	-	-
Food and Tobacco	-	-	-	-	-	-	-	-	-	-	-
Paper, Pulp and Print	-	-	-	-	-	-	-	-	-	-	-
Wood and Wood Products	-	-	-	-	-	-	-	-	-	-	-
Construction	-	-	-	-	-	-	-	-	-	-	-
Textile and Leather	-	-	-	-	-	-	-	-	-	-	-
Non-specified	-	107	893	116	-	-	-	-	-	-	-
TRANSPORT SECTOR	-	-	-	-	-	-	-	-	-	-	-
International Civil Aviation	-	-	-	-	-	-	-	-	-	-	-
Domestic Air	-	-	-	-	-	-	-	-	-	-	-
Road	-	-	-	-	-	-	-	-	-	-	-
Rail	-	-	-	-	-	-	-	-	-	-	-
Pipeline Transport	-	-	-	-	-	-	-	-	-	-	-
Internal Navigation	-	-	-	-	-	-	-	-	-	-	-
Non-specified	-	-	-	-	-	-	-	-	-	-	-
OTHER SECTORS	-	11	106	107	-	-	-	-	-	-	-
Agriculture	-	2	13	-	-	-	-	-	-	-	-
Commerce and Publ. Serv.	-	8	69	-	-	-	-	-	-	-	-
Residential	-	1	24	45	-	-	-	-	-	-	-
Non-specified	-	-	-	62	-	-	-	-	-	-	-
NON-ENERGY USE	-	-	-	-	-	-	-	-	-	-	-
in Industry/Transf./Energy	-	-	-	-	-	-	-	-	-	-	-
in Transport	-	-	-	-	-	-	-	-	-	-	-
in Other Sectors	-	-	-	-	-	-	-	-	-	-	-

New Zealand / Nouvelle-Zélande : 1992

SUPPLY AND CONSUMPTION *APPROVISIONNEMENT ET DEMANDE*	Oil cont. / *Pétrole cont.* (1000 tonnes)										
	Refinery Gas *Gaz de raffinerie*	LPG + Ethane *GPL + éthane*	Motor Gasoline *Essence moteur*	Aviation Gasoline *Essence aviation*	Jet Fuel *Carbu-réacteur*	Kerosene *Kérosène*	Gas/ Diesel *Gazole*	Heavy Fuel Oil *Fioul lourd*	Naphtha *Naphta*	Pétrol. Coke *Coke de pétrole*	Other Prod. *Autres prod.*
Production	195	-	1791	-	701	-	1405	415	-	-	234
From Other Sources	-	-	-	-	-	-	-	-	-	-	-
Imports	-	-	225	15	31	-	33	52	-	76	89
Exports	-	-24	-74	-	-33	-	-96	-37	-	-	-
Intl. Marine Bunkers	-	-	-	-	-	-	-104	-168	-	-	-
Stock Changes	-	-	25	2	7	-	-31	42	-	-	-19
DOMESTIC SUPPLY	**195**	**-24**	**1967**	**17**	**706**	**-**	**1207**	**304**	**-**	**76**	**304**
Transfers	-	142	59	-	-5	4	1	20	-	-	461
Statistical Differences	-	-1	-53	3	-90	4	-34	-80	-	-	53
TRANSFORMATION	**-**	**-**	**-**	**-**	**-**	**-**	**13**	**45**	**-**	**-**	**-**
Electricity Plants	-	-	-	-	-	-	13	45	-	-	-
CHP Plants	-	-	-	-	-	-	-	-	-	-	-
Heat Plants	-	-	-	-	-	-	-	-	-	-	-
Transfer to Gases	-	-	-	-	-	-	-	-	-	-	-
Transfer to Solids	-	-	-	-	-	-	-	-	-	-	-
Petroleum Refineries	-	-	-	-	-	-	-	-	-	-	-
Petrochemical Industry	-	-	-	-	-	-	-	-	-	-	-
Liquefaction	-	-	-	-	-	-	-	-	-	-	-
Other Transformation Sector	-	-	-	-	-	-	-	-	-	-	-
ENERGY SECTOR	**195**	**-**	**-**	**-**	**-**	**-**	**-**	**-**	**-**	**-**	**69**
Coal Mines	-	-	-	-	-	-	-	-	-	-	-
Oil and Gas Extraction	-	-	-	-	-	-	-	-	-	-	-
Petroleum Refineries	195	-	-	-	-	-	-	-	-	-	69
Electricity, CHP+Heat plants	-	-	-	-	-	-	-	-	-	-	-
Pumped Storage (Elec.)	-	-	-	-	-	-	-	-	-	-	-
Other Energy Sector	-	-	-	-	-	-	-	-	-	-	-
Distribution Losses	-	-	-	-	-	-	-	-	-	-	-
FINAL CONSUMPTION	**-**	**117**	**1973**	**20**	**611**	**8**	**1161**	**199**	**-**	**76**	**749**
INDUSTRY SECTOR	**-**	**20**	**29**	**-**	**-**	**4**	**188**	**52**	**-**	**-**	**-**
Iron and Steel	-	-	2	-	-	-	1	-	-	-	-
Chemical and Petrochemical	-	-	-	-	-	-	-	-	-	-	-
of which: Feedstocks	-	-	-	-	-	-	-	-	-	-	-
Non-Ferrous Metals	-	-	-	-	-	-	-	-	-	-	-
Non-Metallic Minerals	-	-	-	-	-	-	-	-	-	-	-
Transport Equipment	-	-	-	-	-	-	-	-	-	-	-
Machinery	-	-	-	-	-	-	-	-	-	-	-
Mining and Quarrying	-	-	-	-	-	-	54	-	-	-	-
Food and Tobacco	-	-	2	-	-	-	16	7	-	-	-
Paper, Pulp and Print	-	-	-	-	-	-	-	-	-	-	-
Wood and Wood Products	-	-	-	-	-	-	-	-	-	-	-
Construction	-	-	3	-	-	3	63	-	-	-	-
Textile and Leather	-	-	-	-	-	-	-	-	-	-	-
Non-specified	-	20	22	-	-	1	54	45	-	-	-
TRANSPORT SECTOR	**-**	**81**	**1857**	**11**	**608**	**3**	**750**	**73**	**-**	**-**	**-**
International Civil Aviation	-	-	-	-	419	-	-	-	-	-	-
Domestic Air	-	-	-	11	189	-	-	-	-	-	-
Road	-	81	1857	-	-	3	-	-	-	-	-
Rail	-	-	-	-	-	-	-	-	-	-	-
Pipeline Transport	-	-	-	-	-	-	-	-	-	-	-
Internal Navigation	-	-	-	-	-	-	99	-	-	-	-
Non-specified	-	-	-	-	-	-	651	73	-	-	-
OTHER SECTORS	**-**	**16**	**87**	**9**	**3**	**1**	**223**	**74**	**-**	**-**	**-**
Agriculture	-	-	55	3	-	-	103	30	-	-	-
Commerce and Publ. Serv.	-	2	31	6	3	1	117	44	-	-	-
Residential	-	14	1	-	-	-	3	-	-	-	-
Non-specified	-	-	-	-	-	-	-	-	-	-	-
NON-ENERGY USE	**-**	**-**	**-**	**-**	**-**	**-**	**-**	**-**	**-**	**76**	**749**
in Industry/Transf./Energy	-	-	-	-	-	-	-	-	-	76	749
in Transport	-	-	-	-	-	-	-	-	-	-	-
in Other Sectors	-	-	-	-	-	-	-	-	-	-	-

New Zealand / Nouvelle-Zélande : 1992

CONSUMPTION *APPROVISIONNEMENT ET DEMANDE*	Gas / *Gaz* (TJ)				Combust. Renew. & Waste / *En. Re. Comb. & Déchets* (TJ)				(GWh)	(TJ)
	Natural Gas *Gaz naturel*	Gas Works *Usines à gaz*	Coke Ovens *Cokeries*	Blast Furnaces *Hauts fourneaux*	Solid Biomass & Anim. Prod. *Biomasse solide & prod. anim.*	Gas/Liquids from Biomass *Gaz/Liquides tirés de biomasse*	Municipal Waste *Déchets urbains*	Industrial Waste *Déchets industriels*	Electricity *Electricité*	Heat *Chaleur*
Production	210097	-	-	-	40700	59	277	350	31294	-
From Other Sources	-	-	-	-	-	-	-	-	-	-
Imports	-	-	-	-	-	-	-	-	-	-
Exports	-	-	-	-	-	-	-	-	-	-
Intl. Marine Bunkers	-	-	-	-	-	-	-	-	-	-
Stock Changes	-	-	-	-	-	-	-	-	-	-
DOMESTIC SUPPLY	**210097**	**-**	**-**	**-**	**40700**	**59**	**277**	**350**	**31294**	**-**
Transfers	-	-	-	-	-	-	-	-	-	-
Statistical Differences	-33	-	-	-	-	-	-	-	-	-
TRANSFORMATION	**159654**	**-**	**-**	**-**	**-**	**59**	**-**	**350**	**-**	**-**
Electricity Plants	74695	-	-	-	-	59	-	350	-	-
CHP Plants	-	-	-	-	-	-	-	-	-	-
Heat Plants	-	-	-	-	-	-	-	-	-	-
Transfer to Gases	-	-	-	-	-	-	-	-	-	-
Transfer to Solids	-	-	-	-	-	-	-	-	-	-
Petroleum Refineries	-	-	-	-	-	-	-	-	-	-
Petrochemical Industry	-	-	-	-	-	-	-	-	-	-
Liquefaction	84959	-	-	-	-	-	-	-	-	-
Other Transformation Sector	-	-	-	-	-	-	-	-	-	-
ENERGY SECTOR	**4289**	**-**	**-**	**-**	**-**	**-**	**-**	**-**	**919**	**-**
Coal Mines	-	-	-	-	-	-	-	-	16	-
Oil and Gas Extraction	4135	-	-	-	-	-	-	-	21	-
Petroleum Refineries	154	-	-	-	-	-	-	-	-	-
Electricity, CHP+Heat plants	-	-	-	-	-	-	-	-	882	-
Pumped Storage (Elec.)	-	-	-	-	-	-	-	-	-	-
Other Energy Sector	-	-	-	-	-	-	-	-	-	-
Distribution Losses	-	-	-	-	-	-	-	-	2627	-
FINAL CONSUMPTION	**46121**	**-**	**-**	**-**	**40700**	**-**	**277**	**-**	**27748**	**-**
INDUSTRY SECTOR	**34660**	**-**	**-**	**-**	**35700**	**-**	**-**	**-**	**11514**	**-**
Iron and Steel	-	-	-	-	-	-	-	-	4944	-
Chemical and Petrochemical	5160	-	-	-	-	-	-	-	935	-
of which: Feedstocks	*5160*	-	-	-	-	-	-	-	-	-
Non-Ferrous Metals	-	-	-	-	-	-	-	-	-	-
Non-Metallic Minerals	-	-	-	-	-	-	-	-	166	-
Transport Equipment	-	-	-	-	-	-	-	-	-	-
Machinery	-	-	-	-	-	-	-	-	337	-
Mining and Quarrying	-	-	-	-	-	-	-	-	199	-
Food and Tobacco	-	-	-	-	-	-	-	-	1463	-
Paper, Pulp and Print	-	-	-	-	-	-	-	-	2420	-
Wood and Wood Products	-	-	-	-	14600	-	-	-	468	-
Construction	-	-	-	-	-	-	-	-	80	-
Textile and Leather	-	-	-	-	21100	-	-	-	201	-
Non-specified	29500	-	-	-	-	-	-	-	301	-
TRANSPORT SECTOR	**2461**	**-**	**-**	**-**	**-**	**-**	**-**	**-**	**122**	**-**
International Civil Aviation	-	-	-	-	-	-	-	-	-	-
Domestic Air	-	-	-	-	-	-	-	-	-	-
Road	2461	-	-	-	-	-	-	-	-	-
Rail	-	-	-	-	-	-	-	-	122	-
Pipeline Transport	-	-	-	-	-	-	-	-	-	-
Internal Navigation	-	-	-	-	-	-	-	-	-	-
Non-specified	-	-	-	-	-	-	-	-	-	-
OTHER SECTORS	**9000**	**-**	**-**	**-**	**5000**	**-**	**277**	**-**	**16112**	**-**
Agriculture	-	-	-	-	-	-	-	-	713	-
Commerce and Publ. Serv.	4900	-	-	-	-	-	-	-	5275	-
Residential	4100	-	-	-	-	-	277	-	10124	-
Non-specified	-	-	-	-	5000	-	-	-	-	-
NON-ENERGY USE	**-**	**-**	**-**	**-**	**-**	**-**	**-**	**-**	**-**	**-**
in Industry/Transf./Energy	-	-	-	-	-	-	-	-	-	-
in Transport	-	-	-	-	-	-	-	-	-	-
in Other Sectors	-	-	-	-	-	-	-	-	-	-

New Zealand / Nouvelle-Zélande : 1993

SUPPLY AND CONSUMPTION *APPROVISIONNEMENT ET DEMANDE*	Coal / *Charbon* (1000 tonnes)							Oil / *Pétrole* (1000 tonnes)			
	Coking Coal *Charbon à coke*	Steam Coal *Charbon vapeur*	Sub-Bit. Coal *Charbon sous-bit.*	Lignite *Lignite*	Peat *Tourbe*	Oven and Gas Coke *Coke de four/gaz*	Pat. Fuel and BKB *Agg./briq. de lignite*	Crude Oil *Pétrole brut*	NGL *LGN*	Feedstocks *Produits d'aliment.*	Additives *Additifs*
Production	1148	89	1688	176	-	-	-	1842	184	-	-
From Other Sources	-	-	-	-	-	-	-	-	-	-	-
Imports	-	1	-	-	-	-	-	3486	-	82	-
Exports	-780	-	-7	-	-	-	-	-1045	-	-	-
Intl. Marine Bunkers	-	-	-	-	-	-	-	-	-	-	-
Stock Changes	-368	79	212	53	-	-	-	1	-	-64	-
DOMESTIC SUPPLY	-	169	1893	229	-	-	-	4284	184	18	-
Transfers	-	-	-	-	-	-	-	-636	-147	-	-
Statistical Differences	-	-	-	1	-	-	-	-20	-37	68	-
TRANSFORMATION	-	-	210	-	-	-	-	3628	-	86	-
Electricity Plants	-	-	210	-	-	-	-	-	-	-	-
CHP Plants	-	-	-	-	-	-	-	-	-	-	-
Heat Plants	-	-	-	-	-	-	-	-	-	-	-
Transfer to Gases	-	-	-	-	-	-	-	-	-	-	-
Transfer to Solids	-	-	-	-	-	-	-	-	-	-	-
Petroleum Refineries	-	-	-	-	-	-	-	4738	-	86	-
Petrochemical Industry	-	-	-	-	-	-	-	-	-	-	-
Liquefaction	-	-	-	-	-	-	-	-1110	-	-	-
Other Transformation Sector	-	-	-	-	-	-	-	-	-	-	-
ENERGY SECTOR	-	-	-	-	-	-	-	-	-	-	-
Coal Mines	-	-	-	-	-	-	-	-	-	-	-
Oil and Gas Extraction	-	-	-	-	-	-	-	-	-	-	-
Petroleum Refineries	-	-	-	-	-	-	-	-	-	-	-
Electricity, CHP+Heat plants	-	-	-	-	-	-	-	-	-	-	-
Pumped Storage (Elec.)	-	-	-	-	-	-	-	-	-	-	-
Other Energy Sector	-	-	-	-	-	-	-	-	-	-	-
Distribution Losses	-	-	-	-	-	-	-	-	-	-	-
FINAL CONSUMPTION	-	169	1683	230	-	-	-	-	-	-	-
INDUSTRY SECTOR	-	155	1412	119	-	-	-	-	-	-	-
Iron and Steel	-	-	725	-	-	-	-	-	-	-	-
Chemical and Petrochemical	-	-	-	-	-	-	-	-	-	-	-
of which: Feedstocks	-	-	-	-	-	-	-	-	-	-	-
Non-Ferrous Metals	-	-	-	-	-	-	-	-	-	-	-
Non-Metallic Minerals	-	-	-	-	-	-	-	-	-	-	-
Transport Equipment	-	-	-	-	-	-	-	-	-	-	-
Machinery	-	-	-	-	-	-	-	-	-	-	-
Mining and Quarrying	-	-	-	-	-	-	-	-	-	-	-
Food and Tobacco	-	-	-	-	-	-	-	-	-	-	-
Paper, Pulp and Print	-	-	-	-	-	-	-	-	-	-	-
Wood and Wood Products	-	-	-	-	-	-	-	-	-	-	-
Construction	-	-	-	-	-	-	-	-	-	-	-
Textile and Leather	-	-	-	-	-	-	-	-	-	-	-
Non-specified	-	155	687	119	-	-	-	-	-	-	-
TRANSPORT SECTOR	-	-	-	-	-	-	-	-	-	-	-
International Civil Aviation	-	-	-	-	-	-	-	-	-	-	-
Domestic Air	-	-	-	-	-	-	-	-	-	-	-
Road	-	-	-	-	-	-	-	-	-	-	-
Rail	-	-	-	-	-	-	-	-	-	-	-
Pipeline Transport	-	-	-	-	-	-	-	-	-	-	-
Internal Navigation	-	-	-	-	-	-	-	-	-	-	-
Non-specified	-	-	-	-	-	-	-	-	-	-	-
OTHER SECTORS	-	14	271	111	-	-	-	-	-	-	-
Agriculture	-	3	12	-	-	-	-	-	-	-	-
Commerce and Publ. Serv.	-	-	-	-	-	-	-	-	-	-	-
Residential	-	-	7	70	-	-	-	-	-	-	-
Non-specified	-	11	252	41	-	-	-	-	-	-	-
NON-ENERGY USE	-	-	-	-	-	-	-	-	-	-	-
in Industry/Transf./Energy	-	-	-	-	-	-	-	-	-	-	-
in Transport	-	-	-	-	-	-	-	-	-	-	-
in Other Sectors	-	-	-	-	-	-	-	-	-	-	-

New Zealand / Nouvelle-Zélande : 1993

SUPPLY AND CONSUMPTION *APPROVISIONNEMENT ET DEMANDE*	Oil cont. / *Pétrole cont.* (1000 tonnes)										
	Refinery Gas *Gaz de raffinerie*	LPG + Ethane *GPL + éthane*	Motor Gasoline *Essence moteur*	Aviation Gasoline *Essence aviation*	Jet Fuel *Carbu-réacteur*	Kerosene *Kérosène*	Gas/Diesel *Gazole*	Heavy Fuel Oil *Fioul lourd*	Naphtha *Naphta*	Pétrol. Coke *Coke de pétrole*	Other Prod. *Autres prod.*
Production	200	-	1809	-	748	-	1488	384	-	-	250
From Other Sources	-	-	-	-	-	-	-	-	-	-	-
Imports	-	-	317	19	1	1	-	2	-	100	65
Exports	-	-27	-122	-	-66	-	-186	-27	-	-	-2
Intl. Marine Bunkers	-	-	-	-	-	-	-102	-185	-	-	-1
Stock Changes	-	-	40	-1	43	1	-17	-10	-	-	6
DOMESTIC SUPPLY	**200**	**-27**	**2044**	**18**	**726**	**2**	**1183**	**164**	**-**	**100**	**318**
Transfers	-	147	94	-	-5	4	2	1	-	-	540
Statistical Differences	-	-	-179	-4	-85	2	16	-20	-	-	-19
TRANSFORMATION	**-**	**-**	**-**	**-**	**-**	**-**	**1**	**-**	**-**	**-**	**-**
Electricity Plants	-	-	-	-	-	-	1	-	-	-	-
CHP Plants	-	-	-	-	-	-	-	-	-	-	-
Heat Plants	-	-	-	-	-	-	-	-	-	-	-
Transfer to Gases	-	-	-	-	-	-	-	-	-	-	-
Transfer to Solids	-	-	-	-	-	-	-	-	-	-	-
Petroleum Refineries	-	-	-	-	-	-	-	-	-	-	-
Petrochemical Industry	-	-	-	-	-	-	-	-	-	-	-
Liquefaction	-	-	-	-	-	-	-	-	-	-	-
Other Transformation Sector	-	-	-	-	-	-	-	-	-	-	-
ENERGY SECTOR	**200**	**-**	**-**	**-**	**-**	**-**	**-**	**-**	**-**	**-**	**85**
Coal Mines	-	-	-	-	-	-	-	-	-	-	-
Oil and Gas Extraction	-	-	-	-	-	-	-	-	-	-	-
Petroleum Refineries	200	-	-	-	-	-	-	-	-	-	85
Electricity, CHP+Heat plants	-	-	-	-	-	-	-	-	-	-	-
Pumped Storage (Elec.)	-	-	-	-	-	-	-	-	-	-	-
Other Energy Sector	-	-	-	-	-	-	-	-	-	-	-
Distribution Losses	-	-	-	-	-	-	-	-	-	-	-
FINAL CONSUMPTION	**-**	**120**	**1959**	**14**	**636**	**8**	**1200**	**145**	**-**	**100**	**754**
INDUSTRY SECTOR	**-**	**21**	**11**	**-**	**-**	**5**	**185**	**41**	**-**	**-**	**-**
Iron and Steel	-	-	1	-	-	-	1	-	-	-	-
Chemical and Petrochemical	-	-	-	-	-	-	-	-	-	-	-
of which: Feedstocks	-	-	-	-	-	-	-	-	-	-	-
Non-Ferrous Metals	-	-	-	-	-	-	-	-	-	-	-
Non-Metallic Minerals	-	-	-	-	-	-	-	-	-	-	-
Transport Equipment	-	-	-	-	-	-	-	-	-	-	-
Machinery	-	-	-	-	-	-	-	-	-	-	-
Mining and Quarrying	-	-	-	-	-	-	60	-	-	-	-
Food and Tobacco	-	-	1	-	-	-	16	5	-	-	-
Paper, Pulp and Print	-	-	-	-	-	-	-	-	-	-	-
Wood and Wood Products	-	-	-	-	-	-	-	-	-	-	-
Construction	-	-	6	-	-	1	40	-	-	-	-
Textile and Leather	-	-	-	-	-	-	-	-	-	-	-
Non-specified	-	21	3	-	-	4	68	36	-	-	-
TRANSPORT SECTOR	**-**	**84**	**1879**	**12**	**628**	**2**	**839**	**66**	**-**	**-**	**-**
International Civil Aviation	-	-	-	-	426	-	-	-	-	-	-
Domestic Air	-	-	-	12	202	-	-	-	-	-	-
Road	-	84	1879	-	-	2	-	-	-	-	-
Rail	-	-	-	-	-	-	-	-	-	-	-
Pipeline Transport	-	-	-	-	-	-	-	-	-	-	-
Internal Navigation	-	-	-	-	-	-	91	-	-	-	-
Non-specified	-	-	-	-	-	-	748	66	-	-	-
OTHER SECTORS	**-**	**15**	**69**	**2**	**8**	**1**	**176**	**38**	**-**	**-**	**-**
Agriculture	-	-	51	2	1	-	111	34	-	-	-
Commerce and Publ. Serv.	-	3	17	-	7	1	62	4	-	-	-
Residential	-	12	1	-	-	-	3	-	-	-	-
Non-specified	-	-	-	-	-	-	-	-	-	-	-
NON-ENERGY USE	**-**	**-**	**-**	**-**	**-**	**-**	**-**	**-**	**-**	**100**	**754**
in Industry/Transf./Energy	-	-	-	-	-	-	-	-	-	100	754
in Transport	-	-	-	-	-	-	-	-	-	-	-
in Other Sectors	-	-	-	-	-	-	-	-	-	-	-

New Zealand / Nouvelle-Zélande : 1993

CONSUMPTION APPROVISIONNEMENT ET DEMANDE	Gas / Gaz (TJ)				Combust. Renew. & Waste / En. Re. Comb. & Déchets (TJ)				(GWh)	(TJ)
	Natural Gas Gaz naturel	Gas Works Usines à gaz	Coke Ovens Cokeries	Blast Furnaces Hauts fourneaux	Solid Biomass & Anim. Prod. Biomasse solide & prod. anim.	Gas/Liquids from Biomass Gaz/Liquides tirés de biomasse	Municipal Waste Déchets urbains	Industrial Waste Déchets industriels	Electricity Electricité	Heat Chaleur
Production	204265	-	-	-	42100	54	240	350	33624	-
From Other Sources	-	-	-	-	-	-	-	-	-	-
Imports	-	-	-	-	-	-	-	-	-	-
Exports	-	-	-	-	-	-	-	-	-	-
Intl. Marine Bunkers	-	-	-	-	-	-	-	-	-	-
Stock Changes	-	-	-	-	-	-	-	-	-	-
DOMESTIC SUPPLY	**204265**	-	-	-	**42100**	**54**	**240**	**350**	**33624**	-
Transfers	-	-	-	-	-	-	-	-	-	-
Statistical Differences	-377	-	-	-	-	-	-	-	-	-
TRANSFORMATION	**153922**	-	-	-	-	**54**	-	**350**	-	-
Electricity Plants	68985	-	-	-	-	54	-	350	-	-
CHP Plants	-	-	-	-	-	-	-	-	-	-
Heat Plants	-	-	-	-	-	-	-	-	-	-
Transfer to Gases	-	-	-	-	-	-	-	-	-	-
Transfer to Solids	-	-	-	-	-	-	-	-	-	-
Petroleum Refineries	-	-	-	-	-	-	-	-	-	-
Petrochemical Industry	-	-	-	-	-	-	-	-	-	-
Liquefaction	84937	-	-	-	-	-	-	-	-	-
Other Transformation Sector	-	-	-	-	-	-	-	-	-	-
ENERGY SECTOR	**4541**	-	-	-	-	-	-	-	**923**	-
Coal Mines	-	-	-	-	-	-	-	-	15	-
Oil and Gas Extraction	4405	-	-	-	-	-	-	-	25	-
Petroleum Refineries	136	-	-	-	-	-	-	-	-	-
Electricity, CHP+Heat plants	-	-	-	-	-	-	-	-	883	-
Pumped Storage (Elec.)	-	-	-	-	-	-	-	-	-	-
Other Energy Sector	-	-	-	-	-	-	-	-	-	-
Distribution Losses	-	-	-	-	-	-	-	-	2772	-
FINAL CONSUMPTION	**45425**	-	-	-	**42100**	-	**240**	-	**29929**	-
INDUSTRY SECTOR	**33650**	-	-	-	**36000**	-	-	-	**12465**	-
Iron and Steel	-	-	-	-	-	-	-	-	6037	-
Chemical and Petrochemical	4950	-	-	-	-	-	-	-	787	-
of which: Feedstocks	4950	-	-	-	-	-	-	-	-	-
Non-Ferrous Metals	-	-	-	-	-	-	-	-	-	-
Non-Metallic Minerals	-	-	-	-	-	-	-	-	208	-
Transport Equipment	-	-	-	-	-	-	-	-	-	-
Machinery	-	-	-	-	-	-	-	-	298	-
Mining and Quarrying	-	-	-	-	-	-	-	-	179	-
Food and Tobacco	-	-	-	-	-	-	-	-	1603	-
Paper, Pulp and Print	-	-	-	-	-	-	-	-	2530	-
Wood and Wood Products	-	-	-	-	14600	-	-	-	482	-
Construction	-	-	-	-	-	-	-	-	23	-
Textile and Leather	-	-	-	-	21400	-	-	-	211	-
Non-specified	28700	-	-	-	-	-	-	-	107	-
TRANSPORT SECTOR	**2275**	-	-	-	-	-	-	-	**64**	-
International Civil Aviation	-	-	-	-	-	-	-	-	-	-
Domestic Air	-	-	-	-	-	-	-	-	-	-
Road	2275	-	-	-	-	-	-	-	-	-
Rail	-	-	-	-	-	-	-	-	64	-
Pipeline Transport	-	-	-	-	-	-	-	-	-	-
Internal Navigation	-	-	-	-	-	-	-	-	-	-
Non-specified	-	-	-	-	-	-	-	-	-	-
OTHER SECTORS	**9500**	-	-	-	**6100**	-	**240**	-	**17400**	-
Agriculture	-	-	-	-	-	-	-	-	755	-
Commerce and Publ. Serv.	5200	-	-	-	-	-	240	-	6022	-
Residential	4300	-	-	-	6100	-	-	-	10623	-
Non-specified	-	-	-	-	-	-	-	-	-	-
NON-ENERGY USE	-	-	-	-	-	-	-	-	-	-
in Industry/Transf./Energy	-	-	-	-	-	-	-	-	-	-
in Transport	-	-	-	-	-	-	-	-	-	-
in Other Sectors	-	-	-	-	-	-	-	-	-	-

Norway / Norvège : 1992

SUPPLY AND CONSUMPTION APPROVISIONNEMENT ET DEMANDE	Coal / Charbon (1000 tonnes)							Oil / Pétrole (1000 tonnes)			
	Coking Coal Charbon à coke	Steam Coal Charbon vapeur	Sub-Bit. Coal Charbon sous-bit.	Lignite Lignite	Peat Tourbe	Oven and Gas Coke Coke de four/gaz	Pat. Fuel and BKB Agg./briq. de lignite	Crude Oil Pétrole brut	NGL LGN	Feedstocks Produits d'aliment.	Additives Additifs
Production	-	359	-	-	-	-	-	104488	2374	-	-
From Other Sources	-	-	-	-	-	-	-	-	-	73	-
Imports	-	619	-	-	-	469	-	986	-	-	-
Exports	-	-168	-	-	-	-	-	-91462	-1535	-	-
Intl. Marine Bunkers	-	-	-	-	-	-	-	-	-	-	-
Stock Changes	-	-155	-	-	-	14	-	-474	-4	-	-
DOMESTIC SUPPLY	-	**655**	-	-	-	**483**	-	**13538**	**835**	**73**	-
Transfers	-	-	-	-	-	-	-	-	-832	586	-
Statistical Differences	-	32	-	-	-	-11	-	-18	-3	-	-
TRANSFORMATION	-	**28**	-	-	-	**16**	-	**13520**	-	**659**	-
Electricity Plants	-	1	-	-	-	-	-	-	-	-	-
CHP Plants	-	27	-	-	-	-	-	-	-	-	-
Heat Plants	-	-	-	-	-	-	-	-	-	-	-
Transfer to Gases	-	-	-	-	-	16	-	-	-	-	-
Transfer to Solids	-	-	-	-	-	-	-	-	-	-	-
Petroleum Refineries	-	-	-	-	-	-	-	13520	-	659	-
Petrochemical Industry	-	-	-	-	-	-	-	-	-	-	-
Liquefaction	-	-	-	-	-	-	-	-	-	-	-
Other Transformation Sector	-	-	-	-	-	-	-	-	-	-	-
ENERGY SECTOR	-	-	-	-	-	-	-	-	-	-	-
Coal Mines	-	-	-	-	-	-	-	-	-	-	-
Oil and Gas Extraction	-	-	-	-	-	-	-	-	-	-	-
Petroleum Refineries	-	-	-	-	-	-	-	-	-	-	-
Electricity, CHP+Heat plants	-	-	-	-	-	-	-	-	-	-	-
Pumped Storage (Elec.)	-	-	-	-	-	-	-	-	-	-	-
Other Energy Sector	-	-	-	-	-	-	-	-	-	-	-
Distribution Losses	-	-	-	-	-	-	-	-	-	-	-
FINAL CONSUMPTION	-	**659**	-	-	-	**456**	-	-	-	-	-
INDUSTRY SECTOR	-	**648**	-	-	-	**454**	-	-	-	-	-
Iron and Steel	-	416	-	-	-	394	-	-	-	-	-
Chemical and Petrochemical	-	88	-	-	-	37	-	-	-	-	-
of which: Feedstocks	-	-	-	-	-	-	-	-	-	-	-
Non-Ferrous Metals	-	-	-	-	-	14	-	-	-	-	-
Non-Metallic Minerals	-	134	-	-	-	9	-	-	-	-	-
Transport Equipment	-	-	-	-	-	-	-	-	-	-	-
Machinery	-	-	-	-	-	-	-	-	-	-	-
Mining and Quarrying	-	-	-	-	-	-	-	-	-	-	-
Food and Tobacco	-	1	-	-	-	-	-	-	-	-	-
Paper, Pulp and Print	-	9	-	-	-	-	-	-	-	-	-
Wood and Wood Products	-	-	-	-	-	-	-	-	-	-	-
Construction	-	-	-	-	-	-	-	-	-	-	-
Textile and Leather	-	-	-	-	-	-	-	-	-	-	-
Non-specified	-	-	-	-	-	-	-	-	-	-	-
TRANSPORT SECTOR	-	-	-	-	-	-	-	-	-	-	-
International Civil Aviation	-	-	-	-	-	-	-	-	-	-	-
Domestic Air	-	-	-	-	-	-	-	-	-	-	-
Road	-	-	-	-	-	-	-	-	-	-	-
Rail	-	-	-	-	-	-	-	-	-	-	-
Pipeline Transport	-	-	-	-	-	-	-	-	-	-	-
Internal Navigation	-	-	-	-	-	-	-	-	-	-	-
Non-specified	-	-	-	-	-	-	-	-	-	-	-
OTHER SECTORS	-	**11**	-	-	-	**2**	-	-	-	-	-
Agriculture	-	6	-	-	-	-	-	-	-	-	-
Commerce and Publ. Serv.	-	-	-	-	-	-	-	-	-	-	-
Residential	-	5	-	-	-	2	-	-	-	-	-
Non-specified	-	-	-	-	-	-	-	-	-	-	-
NON-ENERGY USE	-	-	-	-	-	-	-	-	-	-	-
in Industry/Transf./Energy	-	-	-	-	-	-	-	-	-	-	-
in Transport	-	-	-	-	-	-	-	-	-	-	-
in Other Sectors	-	-	-	-	-	-	-	-	-	-	-

Norway / Norvège : 1992

SUPPLY AND CONSUMPTION / APPROVISIONNEMENT ET DEMANDE	Oil cont. / Pétrole cont. (1000 tonnes)										
	Refinery Gas / Gaz de raffinerie	LPG + Ethane / GPL + éthane	Motor Gasoline / Essence moteur	Aviation Gasoline / Essence aviation	Jet Fuel / Carbu-réacteur	Kerosene / Kérosène	Gas/ Diesel / Gazole	Heavy Fuel Oil / Fioul lourd	Naphtha / Naphta	Pétrol. Coke / Coke de pétrole	Other Prod. / Autres prod.
Production	692	217	3242	-	862	161	6278	1541	740	165	260
From Other Sources	-	-	-	-	-	-	-	-	-	-	-
Imports	-	175	375	5	134	16	610	639	6	320	438
Exports	-	-199	-1842	-	-345	-	-3838	-1444	-801	-111	-8
Intl. Marine Bunkers	-	-	-	-	-	-	-211	-280	-	-	-
Stock Changes	-	-2	29	-	7	-20	-3	-	2	4	1
DOMESTIC SUPPLY	692	191	1804	5	658	157	2836	456	-53	378	691
Transfers	-	832	-	-	-	-	-12	-570	-4	-	-
Statistical Differences	-	-103	-107	-2	-161	-5	56	383	57	9	-107
TRANSFORMATION	-	72	-	-	-	-	1	-	-	-	1
Electricity Plants	-	-	-	-	-	-	-	-	-	-	-
CHP Plants	-	-	-	-	-	-	-	-	-	-	-
Heat Plants	-	-	-	-	-	-	1	-	-	-	-
Transfer to Gases	-	-	-	-	-	-	-	-	-	-	-
Transfer to Solids	-	-	-	-	-	-	-	-	-	-	-
Petroleum Refineries	-	-	-	-	-	-	-	-	-	-	-
Petrochemical Industry	-	72	-	-	-	-	-	-	-	-	1
Liquefaction	-	-	-	-	-	-	-	-	-	-	-
Other Transformation Sector	-	-	-	-	-	-	-	-	-	-	-
ENERGY SECTOR	692	-	4	-	-	-	90	3	-	-	-
Coal Mines	-	-	-	-	-	-	4	-	-	-	-
Oil and Gas Extraction	-	-	-	-	-	-	79	-	-	-	-
Petroleum Refineries	692	-	-	-	-	-	-	3	-	-	-
Electricity, CHP+Heat plants	-	-	4	-	-	-	7	-	-	-	-
Pumped Storage (Elec.)	-	-	-	-	-	-	-	-	-	-	-
Other Energy Sector	-	-	-	-	-	-	-	-	-	-	-
Distribution Losses	-	-	-	-	-	-	-	-	-	-	-
FINAL CONSUMPTION	-	848	1693	3	497	152	2789	266	-	387	583
INDUSTRY SECTOR	-	845	-	-	-	2	240	208	-	6	-
Iron and Steel	-	-	-	-	-	-	6	5	-	-	-
Chemical and Petrochemical	-	801	-	-	-	-	21	38	-	-	-
of which: Feedstocks	-	801	-	-	-	-	-	-	-	-	-
Non-Ferrous Metals	-	6	-	-	-	-	38	17	-	-	-
Non-Metallic Minerals	-	20	-	-	-	-	19	22	-	6	-
Transport Equipment	-	4	-	-	-	-	14	1	-	-	-
Machinery	-	7	-	-	-	-	19	1	-	-	-
Mining and Quarrying	-	-	-	-	-	1	10	7	-	-	-
Food and Tobacco	-	5	-	-	-	-	69	60	-	-	-
Paper, Pulp and Print	-	2	-	-	-	-	4	51	-	-	-
Wood and Wood Products	-	-	-	-	-	-	10	4	-	-	-
Construction	-	-	-	-	-	1	26	-	-	-	-
Textile and Leather	-	-	-	-	-	-	4	2	-	-	-
Non-specified	-	-	-	-	-	-	-	-	-	-	-
TRANSPORT SECTOR	-	-	1684	3	497	-	1944	56	-	-	-
International Civil Aviation	-	-	-	-	80	-	-	-	-	-	-
Domestic Air	-	-	-	3	417	-	-	-	-	-	-
Road	-	-	1681	-	-	-	972	-	-	-	-
Rail	-	-	-	-	-	-	33	-	-	-	-
Pipeline Transport	-	-	-	-	-	-	-	-	-	-	-
Internal Navigation	-	-	3	-	-	-	939	56	-	-	-
Non-specified	-	-	-	-	-	-	-	-	-	-	-
OTHER SECTORS	-	3	9	-	-	150	605	2	-	-	-
Agriculture	-	-	9	-	-	-	176	1	-	-	-
Commerce and Publ. Serv.	-	-	-	-	-	10	262	1	-	-	-
Residential	-	3	-	-	-	140	167	-	-	-	-
Non-specified	-	-	-	-	-	-	-	-	-	-	-
NON-ENERGY USE	-	-	-	-	-	-	-	-	-	381	583
in Industry/Transf./Energy	-	-	-	-	-	-	-	-	-	381	583
in Transport	-	-	-	-	-	-	-	-	-	-	-
in Other Sectors	-	-	-	-	-	-	-	-	-	-	-

Norway / Norvège : 1992

CONSUMPTION APPROVISIONNEMENT ET DEMANDE	Gas / Gaz (TJ)				Combust. Renew. & Waste / En. Re. Comb. & Déchets (TJ)				(GWh)	(TJ)
	Natural Gas Gaz naturel	Gas Works Usines à gaz	Coke Ovens Cokeries	Blast Furnaces Hauts fourneaux	Solid Biomass & Anim. Prod. Biomasse solide & prod. anim.	Gas/Liquids from Biomass Gaz/Liquides tirés de biomasse	Municipal Waste Déchets urbains	Industrial Waste Déchets industriels	Electricity Electricité	Heat Chaleur
Production	1171974	-	-	1123	37649	311	4128	398	117506	6197
From Other Sources	-	-	-	-	-	-	-	-	-	-
Imports	-	-	-	-	-	-	-	-	1379	-
Exports	-1049926	-	-	-	-	-	-	-	-10109	-
Intl. Marine Bunkers	-	-	-	-	-	-	-	-	-	-
Stock Changes	-	-	-	-	-	-	-	-	-	-
DOMESTIC SUPPLY	**122048**	**-**	**-**	**1123**	**37649**	**311**	**4128**	**398**	**108776**	**6197**
Transfers	-	-	-	-	-	-	-	-	-	-
Statistical Differences	2	-	-	-	1115	-	-	-	-	-
TRANSFORMATION	**-**	**-**	**-**	**761**	**1248**	**-**	**4128**	**398**	**383**	**-**
Electricity Plants	-	-	-	710	1059	-	-	-	-	-
CHP Plants	-	-	-	-	-	-	1921	-	-	-
Heat Plants	-	-	-	51	189	-	2207	398	383	-
Transfer to Gases	-	-	-	-	-	-	-	-	-	-
Transfer to Solids	-	-	-	-	-	-	-	-	-	-
Petroleum Refineries	-	-	-	-	-	-	-	-	-	-
Petrochemical Industry	-	-	-	-	-	-	-	-	-	-
Liquefaction	-	-	-	-	-	-	-	-	-	-
Other Transformation Sector	-	-	-	-	-	-	-	-	-	-
ENERGY SECTOR	**122050**	**-**	**-**	**-**	**-**	**-**	**-**	**-**	**2196**	**143**
Coal Mines	-	-	-	-	-	-	-	-	23	-
Oil and Gas Extraction	122050	-	-	-	-	-	-	-	140	-
Petroleum Refineries	-	-	-	-	-	-	-	-	472	-
Electricity, CHP+Heat plants	-	-	-	-	-	-	-	-	963	143
Pumped Storage (Elec.)	-	-	-	-	-	-	-	-	558	-
Other Energy Sector	-	-	-	-	-	-	-	-	40	-
Distribution Losses	-	-	-	-	-	-	-	-	6814	2209
FINAL CONSUMPTION	**-**	**-**	**-**	**362**	**37516**	**311**	**-**	**-**	**99383**	**3845**
INDUSTRY SECTOR	**-**	**-**	**-**	**362**	**19843**	**-**	**-**	**-**	**44808**	**794**
Iron and Steel	-	-	-	362	-	-	-	-	7391	9
Chemical and Petrochemical	-	-	-	-	1	-	-	-	5772	320
of which: Feedstocks	-	-	-	-	-	-	-	-	-	-
Non-Ferrous Metals	-	-	-	-	-	-	-	-	16421	-
Non-Metallic Minerals	-	-	-	-	-	-	-	-	970	-
Transport Equipment	-	-	-	-	-	-	-	-	786	47
Machinery	-	-	-	-	-	-	-	-	1520	-
Mining and Quarrying	-	-	-	-	-	-	-	-	672	-
Food and Tobacco	-	-	-	-	4	-	-	-	2903	407
Paper, Pulp and Print	-	-	-	-	15472	-	-	-	6678	-
Wood and Wood Products	-	-	-	-	4358	-	-	-	916	11
Construction	-	-	-	-	-	-	-	-	430	-
Textile and Leather	-	-	-	-	-	-	-	-	210	-
Non-specified	-	-	-	-	8	-	-	-	139	-
TRANSPORT SECTOR	**-**	**-**	**-**	**-**	**-**	**-**	**-**	**-**	**1523**	**-**
International Civil Aviation	-	-	-	-	-	-	-	-	-	-
Domestic Air	-	-	-	-	-	-	-	-	-	-
Road	-	-	-	-	-	-	-	-	-	-
Rail	-	-	-	-	-	-	-	-	494	-
Pipeline Transport	-	-	-	-	-	-	-	-	-	-
Internal Navigation	-	-	-	-	-	-	-	-	-	-
Non-specified	-	-	-	-	-	-	-	-	1029	-
OTHER SECTORS	**-**	**-**	**-**	**-**	**17673**	**311**	**-**	**-**	**53052**	**3051**
Agriculture	-	-	-	-	-	-	-	-	678	23
Commerce and Publ. Serv.	-	-	-	-	-	311	-	-	19724	1926
Residential	-	-	-	-	17673	-	-	-	32650	984
Non-specified	-	-	-	-	-	-	-	-	-	118
NON-ENERGY USE	**-**	**-**	**-**	**-**	**-**	**-**	**-**	**-**	**-**	**-**
in Industry/Transf./Energy	-	-	-	-	-	-	-	-	-	-
in Transport	-	-	-	-	-	-	-	-	-	-
in Other Sectors	-	-	-	-	-	-	-	-	-	-

Norway / Norvège : 1993

SUPPLY AND CONSUMPTION *APPROVISIONNEMENT ET DEMANDE*	Coal / *Charbon* (1000 tonnes)							Oil / *Pétrole* (1000 tonnes)			
	Coking Coal *Charbon à coke*	Steam Coal *Charbon vapeur*	Sub-Bit. Coal *Charbon sous-bit.*	Lignite *Lignite*	Peat *Tourbe*	Oven and Gas Coke *Coke de four/gaz*	Pat. Fuel and BKB *Agg./briq. de lignite*	Crude Oil *Pétrole brut*	NGL *LGN*	Feedstocks *Produits d'aliment.*	Additives *Additifs*
Production	-	267	-	-	-	-	-	111854	2617	-	-
From Other Sources	-	-	-	-	-	-	-	-	-	73	-
Imports	-	715	-	-	-	464	-	1332	-	-	-
Exports	-	-227	-	-	-	-2	-	-98641	-1684	-	-
Intl. Marine Bunkers	-	-	-	-	-	-	-	-	-	-	-
Stock Changes	-	66	-	-	-	-23	-	-1080	-19	-	-
DOMESTIC SUPPLY	-	**821**	-	-	-	**439**	-	**13465**	**914**	**73**	-
Transfers	-	-	-	-	-	-	-	-	-927	557	-
Statistical Differences	-	-44	-	-	-	31	-	4	13	-	-
TRANSFORMATION	-	**28**	-	-	-	**16**	-	**13469**	-	**630**	-
Electricity Plants	-	1	-	-	-	-	-	-	-	-	-
CHP Plants	-	27	-	-	-	-	-	-	-	-	-
Heat Plants	-	-	-	-	-	-	-	-	-	-	-
Transfer to Gases	-	-	-	-	-	16	-	-	-	-	-
Transfer to Solids	-	-	-	-	-	-	-	-	-	-	-
Petroleum Refineries	-	-	-	-	-	-	-	13469	-	630	-
Petrochemical Industry	-	-	-	-	-	-	-	-	-	-	-
Liquefaction	-	-	-	-	-	-	-	-	-	-	-
Other Transformation Sector	-	-	-	-	-	-	-	-	-	-	-
ENERGY SECTOR	-	-	-	-	-	-	-	-	-	-	-
Coal Mines	-	-	-	-	-	-	-	-	-	-	-
Oil and Gas Extraction	-	-	-	-	-	-	-	-	-	-	-
Petroleum Refineries	-	-	-	-	-	-	-	-	-	-	-
Electricity, CHP+Heat plants	-	-	-	-	-	-	-	-	-	-	-
Pumped Storage (Elec.)	-	-	-	-	-	-	-	-	-	-	-
Other Energy Sector	-	-	-	-	-	-	-	-	-	-	-
Distribution Losses	-	-	-	-	-	-	-	-	-	-	-
FINAL CONSUMPTION	-	**749**	-	-	-	**454**	-	-	-	-	-
INDUSTRY SECTOR	-	**744**	-	-	-	**453**	-	-	-	-	-
Iron and Steel	-	468	-	-	-	402	-	-	-	-	-
Chemical and Petrochemical	-	89	-	-	-	31	-	-	-	-	-
of which: Feedstocks	-	-	-	-	-	-	-	-	-	-	-
Non-Ferrous Metals	-	-	-	-	-	11	-	-	-	-	-
Non-Metallic Minerals	-	179	-	-	-	9	-	-	-	-	-
Transport Equipment	-	-	-	-	-	-	-	-	-	-	-
Machinery	-	-	-	-	-	-	-	-	-	-	-
Mining and Quarrying	-	-	-	-	-	-	-	-	-	-	-
Food and Tobacco	-	-	-	-	-	-	-	-	-	-	-
Paper, Pulp and Print	-	8	-	-	-	-	-	-	-	-	-
Wood and Wood Products	-	-	-	-	-	-	-	-	-	-	-
Construction	-	-	-	-	-	-	-	-	-	-	-
Textile and Leather	-	-	-	-	-	-	-	-	-	-	-
Non-specified	-	-	-	-	-	-	-	-	-	-	-
TRANSPORT SECTOR	-	-	-	-	-	-	-	-	-	-	-
International Civil Aviation	-	-	-	-	-	-	-	-	-	-	-
Domestic Air	-	-	-	-	-	-	-	-	-	-	-
Road	-	-	-	-	-	-	-	-	-	-	-
Rail	-	-	-	-	-	-	-	-	-	-	-
Pipeline Transport	-	-	-	-	-	-	-	-	-	-	-
Internal Navigation	-	-	-	-	-	-	-	-	-	-	-
Non-specified	-	-	-	-	-	-	-	-	-	-	-
OTHER SECTORS	-	**5**	-	-	-	**1**	-	-	-	-	-
Agriculture	-	1	-	-	-	-	-	-	-	-	-
Commerce and Publ. Serv.	-	-	-	-	-	-	-	-	-	-	-
Residential	-	4	-	-	-	1	-	-	-	-	-
Non-specified	-	-	-	-	-	-	-	-	-	-	-
NON-ENERGY USE	-	-	-	-	-	-	-	-	-	-	-
in Industry/Transf./Energy	-	-	-	-	-	-	-	-	-	-	-
in Transport	-	-	-	-	-	-	-	-	-	-	-
in Other Sectors	-	-	-	-	-	-	-	-	-	-	-

Norway / Norvège : 1993

SUPPLY AND CONSUMPTION / APPROVISIONNEMENT ET DEMANDE	Oil cont. / Pétrole cont. (1000 tonnes)										
	Refinery Gas / Gaz de raffinerie	LPG + Ethane / GPL + éthane	Motor Gasoline / Essence moteur	Aviation Gasoline / Essence aviation	Jet Fuel / Carbu-réacteur	Kerosene / Kérosène	Gas/ Diesel / Gazole	Heavy Fuel Oil / Fioul lourd	Naphtha / Naphta	Pétrol. Coke / Coke de pétrole	Other Prod. / Autres prod.
Production	683	230	3233	-	934	136	6445	1463	651	198	157
From Other Sources	-	-	-	-	-	-	-	-	-	-	-
Imports	-	342	419	2	27	34	518	872	5	344	371
Exports	-	-259	-1800	-	-397	-4	-3731	-1417	-839	-136	-21
Intl. Marine Bunkers	-	-	-	-	-	-	-230	-296	-	-	-
Stock Changes	-	-3	-65	-	-54	-11	70	26	-2	4	13
DOMESTIC SUPPLY	683	310	1787	2	510	155	3072	648	-185	410	520
Transfers	-	927	-	-	-	-	-81	-476	-	-	-
Statistical Differences	-	-247	-104	-	-29	-	97	120	185	-4	-59
TRANSFORMATION	-	72	-	-	-	-	1	-	-	-	1
Electricity Plants	-	-	-	-	-	-	-	-	-	-	-
CHP Plants	-	-	-	-	-	-	-	-	-	-	-
Heat Plants	-	-	-	-	-	-	1	-	-	-	-
Transfer to Gases	-	-	-	-	-	-	-	-	-	-	-
Transfer to Solids	-	-	-	-	-	-	-	-	-	-	-
Petroleum Refineries	-	-	-	-	-	-	-	-	-	-	-
Petrochemical Industry	-	72	-	-	-	-	-	-	-	-	1
Liquefaction	-	-	-	-	-	-	-	-	-	-	-
Other Transformation Sector	-	-	-	-	-	-	-	-	-	-	-
ENERGY SECTOR	683	-	4	-	-	-	91	1	-	-	-
Coal Mines	-	-	-	-	-	-	2	-	-	-	-
Oil and Gas Extraction	-	-	-	-	-	-	82	-	-	-	-
Petroleum Refineries	683	-	-	-	-	-	-	1	-	-	-
Electricity, CHP+Heat plants	-	-	4	-	-	-	7	-	-	-	-
Pumped Storage (Elec.)	-	-	-	-	-	-	-	-	-	-	-
Other Energy Sector	-	-	-	-	-	-	-	-	-	-	-
Distribution Losses	-	-	-	-	-	-	-	-	-	-	-
FINAL CONSUMPTION	-	918	1679	2	481	155	2996	291	-	406	460
INDUSTRY SECTOR	-	915	-	-	-	1	244	214	-	7	-
Iron and Steel	-	-	-	-	-	-	6	11	-	-	-
Chemical and Petrochemical	-	861	-	-	-	-	21	41	-	-	-
of which: Feedstocks	-	861	-	-	-	-	-	-	-	-	-
Non-Ferrous Metals	-	7	-	-	-	-	40	15	-	-	-
Non-Metallic Minerals	-	25	-	-	-	-	19	18	-	7	-
Transport Equipment	-	5	-	-	-	-	14	2	-	-	-
Machinery	-	8	-	-	-	-	19	-	-	-	-
Mining and Quarrying	-	-	-	-	-	1	10	14	-	-	-
Food and Tobacco	-	6	-	-	-	-	69	57	-	-	-
Paper, Pulp and Print	-	3	-	-	-	-	4	50	-	-	-
Wood and Wood Products	-	-	-	-	-	-	10	3	-	-	-
Construction	-	-	-	-	-	-	27	-	-	-	-
Textile and Leather	-	-	-	-	-	-	5	2	-	-	-
Non-specified	-	-	-	-	-	-	-	1	-	-	-
TRANSPORT SECTOR	-	-	1671	2	481	-	2154	73	-	-	-
International Civil Aviation	-	-	-	-	84	-	-	-	-	-	-
Domestic Air	-	-	-	2	397	-	-	-	-	-	-
Road	-	-	1668	-	-	-	1113	-	-	-	-
Rail	-	-	-	-	-	-	34	-	-	-	-
Pipeline Transport	-	-	-	-	-	-	-	-	-	-	-
Internal Navigation	-	-	3	-	-	-	1007	73	-	-	-
Non-specified	-	-	-	-	-	-	-	-	-	-	-
OTHER SECTORS	-	3	8	-	-	154	598	4	-	-	-
Agriculture	-	-	8	-	-	1	176	2	-	-	-
Commerce and Publ. Serv.	-	-	-	-	-	6	256	1	-	-	-
Residential	-	3	-	-	-	147	166	1	-	-	-
Non-specified	-	-	-	-	-	-	-	-	-	-	-
NON-ENERGY USE	-	-	-	-	-	-	-	-	-	399	460
in Industry/Transf./Energy	-	-	-	-	-	-	-	-	-	399	460
in Transport	-	-	-	-	-	-	-	-	-	-	-
in Other Sectors	-	-	-	-	-	-	-	-	-	-	-

Norway / Norvège : 1993

CONSUMPTION *APPROVISIONNEMENT ET DEMANDE*	Gas / *Gaz* (TJ)				Combust. Renew. & Waste / *En. Re. Comb. & Déchets* (TJ)				(GWh)	(TJ)
	Natural Gas *Gaz naturel*	Gas Works *Usines à gaz*	Coke Ovens *Cokeries*	Blast Furnaces *Hauts fourneaux*	Solid Biomass & Anim. Prod. *Biomasse solide & prod. anim.*	Gas/Liquids from Biomass *Gaz/Liquides tirés de biomasse*	Municipal Waste *Déchets urbains*	Industrial Waste *Déchets industriels*	Electricity *Electricité*	Heat *Chaleur*
Production	1126696	-	-	1163	37789	311	4293	406	120004	6319
From Other Sources	-	-	-	-	-	-	-	-	-	-
Imports	-	-	-	-	-	-	-	-	595	-
Exports	-1009981	-	-	-	-	-	-	-	-8376	-
Intl. Marine Bunkers	-	-	-	-	-	-	-	-	-	-
Stock Changes	-	-	-	-	-	-	-	-	-	-
DOMESTIC SUPPLY	**116715**	**-**	**-**	**1163**	**37789**	**311**	**4293**	**406**	**112223**	**6319**
Transfers	-	-	-	-	-	-	-	-	-	-
Statistical Differences	-1	-	-	-	1154	-	-82	-	-	-
TRANSFORMATION	**-**	**-**	**-**	**819**	**1339**	**-**	**4211**	**406**	**399**	**-**
Electricity Plants	-	-	-	767	1147	-	-	-	-	-
CHP Plants	-	-	-	-	-	-	1960	-	-	-
Heat Plants	-	-	-	52	192	-	2251	406	399	-
Transfer to Gases	-	-	-	-	-	-	-	-	-	-
Transfer to Solids	-	-	-	-	-	-	-	-	-	-
Petroleum Refineries	-	-	-	-	-	-	-	-	-	-
Petrochemical Industry	-	-	-	-	-	-	-	-	-	-
Liquefaction	-	-	-	-	-	-	-	-	-	-
Other Transformation Sector	-	-	-	-	-	-	-	-	-	-
ENERGY SECTOR	**116714**	**-**	**-**	**-**	**-**	**-**	**-**	**-**	**2458**	**145**
Coal Mines	-	-	-	-	-	-	-	-	20	-
Oil and Gas Extraction	116714	-	-	-	-	-	-	-	196	-
Petroleum Refineries	-	-	-	-	-	-	-	-	467	-
Electricity, CHP+Heat plants	-	-	-	-	-	-	-	-	1111	145
Pumped Storage (Elec.)	-	-	-	-	-	-	-	-	620	-
Other Energy Sector	-	-	-	-	-	-	-	-	44	-
Distribution Losses	-	-	-	-	-	-	-	-	7616	2049
FINAL CONSUMPTION	**-**	**-**	**-**	**344**	**37604**	**311**	**-**	**-**	**101750**	**4125**
INDUSTRY SECTOR	**-**	**-**	**-**	**344**	**19931**	**-**	**-**	**-**	**46260**	**852**
Iron and Steel	-	-	-	344	-	-	-	-	7329	9
Chemical and Petrochemical	-	-	-	-	-	-	-	-	5780	344
of which: Feedstocks	-	-	-	-	-	-	-	-	-	-
Non-Ferrous Metals	-	-	-	-	-	-	-	-	16290	-
Non-Metallic Minerals	-	-	-	-	-	-	-	-	953	-
Transport Equipment	-	-	-	-	-	-	-	-	780	51
Machinery	-	-	-	-	-	-	-	-	1528	-
Mining and Quarrying	-	-	-	-	-	-	-	-	825	-
Food and Tobacco	-	-	-	-	4	-	-	-	3066	436
Paper, Pulp and Print	-	-	-	-	15570	-	-	-	7960	-
Wood and Wood Products	-	-	-	-	4347	-	-	-	948	12
Construction	-	-	-	-	-	-	-	-	406	-
Textile and Leather	-	-	-	-	-	-	-	-	250	-
Non-specified	-	-	-	-	10	-	-	-	145	-
TRANSPORT SECTOR	**-**	**-**	**-**	**-**	**-**	**-**	**-**	**-**	**1587**	**-**
International Civil Aviation	-	-	-	-	-	-	-	-	-	-
Domestic Air	-	-	-	-	-	-	-	-	-	-
Road	-	-	-	-	-	-	-	-	-	-
Rail	-	-	-	-	-	-	-	-	510	-
Pipeline Transport	-	-	-	-	-	-	-	-	-	-
Internal Navigation	-	-	-	-	-	-	-	-	-	-
Non-specified	-	-	-	-	-	-	-	-	1077	-
OTHER SECTORS	**-**	**-**	**-**	**-**	**17673**	**311**	**-**	**-**	**53903**	**3273**
Agriculture	-	-	-	-	-	-	-	-	656	24
Commerce and Publ. Serv.	-	-	-	-	-	311	-	-	20409	2057
Residential	-	-	-	-	17673	-	-	-	32838	1056
Non-specified	-	-	-	-	-	-	-	-	-	136
NON-ENERGY USE	**-**	**-**	**-**	**-**	**-**	**-**	**-**	**-**	**-**	**-**
in Industry/Transf./Energy	-	-	-	-	-	-	-	-	-	-
in Transport	-	-	-	-	-	-	-	-	-	-
in Other Sectors	-	-	-	-	-	-	-	-	-	-

Portugal / Portugal : 1992

SUPPLY AND CONSUMPTION	Coal / Charbon (1000 tonnes)							Oil / Pétrole (1000 tonnes)			
	Coking Coal	Steam Coal	Sub-Bit. Coal	Lignite	Peat	Oven and Gas Coke	Pat. Fuel and BKB	Crude Oil	NGL	Feedstocks	Additives
APPROVISIONNEMENT ET DEMANDE	Charbon à coke	Charbon vapeur	Charbon sous-bit.	Lignite	Tourbe	Coke de four/gaz	Agg./briq. de lignite	Pétrole brut	LGN	Produits d'aliment.	Additifs
Production	-	-	221	-	-	268	-	-	-	-	-
From Other Sources	-	-	-	-	-	-	-	-	-	-	-
Imports	350	4132	-	-	-	22	-	11237	-	490	-
Exports	-	-	-	-	-	-41	-	-	-	-	-
Intl. Marine Bunkers	-	-	-	-	-	-	-	-	-	-	-
Stock Changes	23	-21	-3	-	-	31	-	30	-	8	-
DOMESTIC SUPPLY	**373**	**4111**	**218**	**-**	**-**	**280**	**-**	**11267**	**-**	**498**	**-**
Transfers	-	-	-	-	-	-	-	-	-	33	-
Statistical Differences	-	-	-	-	-	-1	-	-	-	-3	-
TRANSFORMATION	**373**	**3333**	**207**	**-**	**-**	**74**	**-**	**11267**	**-**	**528**	**-**
Electricity Plants	-	3333	207	-	-	-	-	-	-	-	-
CHP Plants	-	-	-	-	-	-	-	-	-	-	-
Heat Plants	-	-	-	-	-	-	-	-	-	-	-
Transfer to Gases	-	-	-	-	-	74	-	-	-	-	-
Transfer to Solids	373	-	-	-	-	-	-	-	-	-	-
Petroleum Refineries	-	-	-	-	-	-	-	11267	-	528	-
Petrochemical Industry	-	-	-	-	-	-	-	-	-	-	-
Liquefaction	-	-	-	-	-	-	-	-	-	-	-
Other Transformation Sector	-	-	-	-	-	-	-	-	-	-	-
ENERGY SECTOR	**-**	**-**	**-**	**-**	**-**	**-**	**-**	**-**	**-**	**-**	**-**
Coal Mines	-	-	-	-	-	-	-	-	-	-	-
Oil and Gas Extraction	-	-	-	-	-	-	-	-	-	-	-
Petroleum Refineries	-	-	-	-	-	-	-	-	-	-	-
Electricity, CHP+Heat plants	-	-	-	-	-	-	-	-	-	-	-
Pumped Storage (Elec.)	-	-	-	-	-	-	-	-	-	-	-
Other Energy Sector	-	-	-	-	-	-	-	-	-	-	-
Distribution Losses	-	-	-	-	-	-	-	-	-	-	-
FINAL CONSUMPTION	**-**	**778**	**11**	**-**	**-**	**205**	**-**	**-**	**-**	**-**	**-**
INDUSTRY SECTOR	**-**	**777**	**11**	**-**	**-**	**205**	**-**	**-**	**-**	**-**	**-**
Iron and Steel	-	-	-	-	-	174	-	-	-	-	-
Chemical and Petrochemical	-	-	-	-	-	17	-	-	-	-	-
of which: Feedstocks	-	-	-	-	-	-	-	-	-	-	-
Non-Ferrous Metals	-	1	-	-	-	8	-	-	-	-	-
Non-Metallic Minerals	-	776	11	-	-	6	-	-	-	-	-
Transport Equipment	-	-	-	-	-	-	-	-	-	-	-
Machinery	-	-	-	-	-	-	-	-	-	-	-
Mining and Quarrying	-	-	-	-	-	-	-	-	-	-	-
Food and Tobacco	-	-	-	-	-	-	-	-	-	-	-
Paper, Pulp and Print	-	-	-	-	-	-	-	-	-	-	-
Wood and Wood Products	-	-	-	-	-	-	-	-	-	-	-
Construction	-	-	-	-	-	-	-	-	-	-	-
Textile and Leather	-	-	-	-	-	-	-	-	-	-	-
Non-specified	-	-	-	-	-	-	-	-	-	-	-
TRANSPORT SECTOR	**-**	**-**	**-**	**-**	**-**	**-**	**-**	**-**	**-**	**-**	**-**
International Civil Aviation	-	-	-	-	-	-	-	-	-	-	-
Domestic Air	-	-	-	-	-	-	-	-	-	-	-
Road	-	-	-	-	-	-	-	-	-	-	-
Rail	-	-	-	-	-	-	-	-	-	-	-
Pipeline Transport	-	-	-	-	-	-	-	-	-	-	-
Internal Navigation	-	-	-	-	-	-	-	-	-	-	-
Non-specified	-	-	-	-	-	-	-	-	-	-	-
OTHER SECTORS	**-**	**1**	**-**	**-**	**-**	**-**	**-**	**-**	**-**	**-**	**-**
Agriculture	-	-	-	-	-	-	-	-	-	-	-
Commerce and Publ. Serv.	-	1	-	-	-	-	-	-	-	-	-
Residential	-	-	-	-	-	-	-	-	-	-	-
Non-specified	-	-	-	-	-	-	-	-	-	-	-
NON-ENERGY USE	**-**	**-**	**-**	**-**	**-**	**-**	**-**	**-**	**-**	**-**	**-**
in Industry/Transf./Energy	-	-	-	-	-	-	-	-	-	-	-
in Transport	-	-	-	-	-	-	-	-	-	-	-
in Other Sectors	-	-	-	-	-	-	-	-	-	-	-

Portugal / Portugal : 1992

SUPPLY AND CONSUMPTION / APPROVISIONNEMENT ET DEMANDE	Oil cont. / *Pétrole cont.* (1000 tonnes)										
	Refinery Gas / *Gaz de raffinerie*	LPG + Ethane / *GPL + éthane*	Motor Gasoline / *Essence moteur*	Aviation Gasoline / *Essence aviation*	Jet Fuel / *Carbu-réacteur*	Kerosene / *Kérosène*	Gas/Diesel / *Gazole*	Heavy Fuel Oil / *Fioul lourd*	Naphtha / *Naphta*	Pétrol. Coke / *Coke de pétrole*	Other Prod. / *Autres prod.*
Production	246	369	1860	-	883	23	2987	4220	729	-	336
From Other Sources	-	-	-	-	-	-	-	-	-	-	-
Imports	-	552	101	2	46	-	259	3175	665	-	330
Exports	-	-29	-244	-	-292	-	-315	-2093	-210	-	-99
Intl. Marine Bunkers	-	-	-	-	-	-	-213	-402	-	-	-
Stock Changes	-	6	-28	-	-20	-2	38	-125	21	-	162
DOMESTIC SUPPLY	246	898	1689	2	617	21	2756	4775	1205	-	729
Transfers	4	-4	-1	-	-4	2	-25	18	-	-	-23
Statistical Differences	-3	-2	4	-	-12	-	-24	-19	-1	-	2
TRANSFORMATION	45	-	-	-	-	-	20	3153	28	-	-
Electricity Plants	-	-	-	-	-	-	20	2858	-	-	-
CHP Plants	15	-	-	-	-	-	-	275	-	-	-
Heat Plants	-	-	-	-	-	-	-	-	-	-	-
Transfer to Gases	30	-	-	-	-	-	-	20	28	-	-
Transfer to Solids	-	-	-	-	-	-	-	-	-	-	-
Petroleum Refineries	-	-	-	-	-	-	-	-	-	-	-
Petrochemical Industry	-	-	-	-	-	-	-	-	-	-	-
Liquefaction	-	-	-	-	-	-	-	-	-	-	-
Other Transformation Sector	-	-	-	-	-	-	-	-	-	-	-
ENERGY SECTOR	202	1	-	-	-	-	2	78	-	-	168
Coal Mines	-	-	-	-	-	-	2	-	-	-	-
Oil and Gas Extraction	-	-	-	-	-	-	-	-	-	-	-
Petroleum Refineries	202	1	-	-	-	-	-	78	-	-	167
Electricity, CHP+Heat plants	-	-	-	-	-	-	-	-	-	-	1
Pumped Storage (Elec.)	-	-	-	-	-	-	-	-	-	-	-
Other Energy Sector	-	-	-	-	-	-	-	-	-	-	-
Distribution Losses	-	1	-	-	-	-	4	4	-	-	1
FINAL CONSUMPTION	-	890	1692	2	601	23	2681	1539	1176	-	539
INDUSTRY SECTOR	-	289	-	-	-	-	273	1476	1176	-	-
Iron and Steel	-	13	-	-	-	-	2	20	-	-	-
Chemical and Petrochemical	-	2	-	-	-	-	6	370	1176	-	-
of which: Feedstocks	-	-	-	-	-	-	-	*157*	*1176*	-	-
Non-Ferrous Metals	-	6	-	-	-	-	-	12	-	-	-
Non-Metallic Minerals	-	180	-	-	-	-	30	199	-	-	-
Transport Equipment	-	10	-	-	-	-	2	8	-	-	-
Machinery	-	5	-	-	-	-	1	10	-	-	-
Mining and Quarrying	-	2	-	-	-	-	25	4	-	-	-
Food and Tobacco	-	24	-	-	-	-	37	202	-	-	-
Paper, Pulp and Print	-	6	-	-	-	-	4	260	-	-	-
Wood and Wood Products	-	2	-	-	-	-	14	15	-	-	-
Construction	-	6	-	-	-	-	149	22	-	-	-
Textile and Leather	-	10	-	-	-	-	3	193	-	-	-
Non-specified	-	23	-	-	-	-	-	161	-	-	-
TRANSPORT SECTOR	-	-	1692	2	601	-	1870	-	-	-	-
International Civil Aviation	-	-	-	-	528	-	-	-	-	-	-
Domestic Air	-	-	-	2	73	-	-	-	-	-	-
Road	-	-	1692	-	-	-	1772	-	-	-	-
Rail	-	-	-	-	-	-	58	-	-	-	-
Pipeline Transport	-	-	-	-	-	-	-	-	-	-	-
Internal Navigation	-	-	-	-	-	-	40	-	-	-	-
Non-specified	-	-	-	-	-	-	-	-	-	-	-
OTHER SECTORS	-	601	-	-	-	23	538	63	-	-	-
Agriculture	-	10	-	-	-	-	413	7	-	-	-
Commerce and Publ. Serv.	-	41	-	-	-	3	115	56	-	-	-
Residential	-	550	-	-	-	20	10	-	-	-	-
Non-specified	-	-	-	-	-	-	-	-	-	-	-
NON-ENERGY USE	-	-	-	-	-	-	-	-	-	-	539
in Industry/Transf./Energy	-	-	-	-	-	-	-	-	-	-	435
in Transport	-	-	-	-	-	-	-	-	-	-	71
in Other Sectors	-	-	-	-	-	-	-	-	-	-	33

Portugal / Portugal : 1992

CONSUMPTION / APPROVISIONNEMENT ET DEMANDE	Gas / Gaz (TJ)				Combust. Renew. & Waste / En. Re. Comb. & Déchets (TJ)				Electricity (GWh)	Heat (TJ)
	Natural Gas / Gaz naturel	Gas Works / Usines à gaz	Coke Ovens / Cokeries	Blast Furnaces / Hauts fourneaux	Solid Biomass & Anim. Prod. / Biomasse solide & prod. anim.	Gas/Liquids from Biomass / Gaz/Liquides tirés de biomasse	Municipal Waste / Déchets urbains	Industrial Waste / Déchets industriels	Electricité	Chaleur
Production	-	-	2549	2072	44611	-	-	-	30087	1318
From Other Sources	-	2972	-	-	-	-	-	-	-	-
Imports	-	-	-	-	-	-	-	-	2538	-
Exports	-	-	-	-	-	-	-	-	-1197	-
Intl. Marine Bunkers	-	-	-	-	-	-	-	-	-	-
Stock Changes	-	-	-	-	-	-	-	-	-	-
DOMESTIC SUPPLY	-	**2972**	**2549**	**2072**	**44611**	-	-	-	**31428**	**1318**
Transfers	-	-	-	-	-	-	-	-	-	-
Statistical Differences	-	-	-	-	-	-	-	-	-	-
TRANSFORMATION	-	-	**247**	**1281**	**6100**	-	-	-	-	-
Electricity Plants	-	-	-	-	-	-	-	-	-	-
CHP Plants	-	-	247	1281	6100	-	-	-	-	-
Heat Plants	-	-	-	-	-	-	-	-	-	-
Transfer to Gases	-	-	-	-	-	-	-	-	-	-
Transfer to Solids	-	-	-	-	-	-	-	-	-	-
Petroleum Refineries	-	-	-	-	-	-	-	-	-	-
Petrochemical Industry	-	-	-	-	-	-	-	-	-	-
Liquefaction	-	-	-	-	-	-	-	-	-	-
Other Transformation Sector	-	-	-	-	-	-	-	-	-	-
ENERGY SECTOR	-	-	**1201**	-	-	-	-	-	**2372**	-
Coal Mines	-	-	-	-	-	-	-	-	6	-
Oil and Gas Extraction	-	-	-	-	-	-	-	-	-	-
Petroleum Refineries	-	-	-	-	-	-	-	-	346	-
Electricity, CHP+Heat plants	-	-	-	-	-	-	-	-	1379	-
Pumped Storage (Elec.)	-	-	-	-	-	-	-	-	611	-
Other Energy Sector	-	-	1201	-	-	-	-	-	30	-
Distribution Losses	-	149	46	96	-	-	-	-	3403	-
FINAL CONSUMPTION	-	**2823**	**1055**	**695**	**38511**	-	-	-	**25653**	**1318**
INDUSTRY SECTOR	-	**7**	**1055**	**695**	**20930**	-	-	-	**12800**	**1318**
Iron and Steel	-	-	1055	695	-	-	-	-	691	-
Chemical and Petrochemical	-	-	-	-	1241	-	-	-	2652	1318
of which: Feedstocks	-	-	-	-	-	-	-	-	-	-
Non-Ferrous Metals	-	-	-	-	197	-	-	-	86	-
Non-Metallic Minerals	-	-	-	-	12349	-	-	-	1801	-
Transport Equipment	-	-	-	-	-	-	-	-	224	-
Machinery	-	-	-	-	12	-	-	-	904	-
Mining and Quarrying	-	-	-	-	-	-	-	-	164	-
Food and Tobacco	-	-	-	-	3140	-	-	-	1156	-
Paper, Pulp and Print	-	-	-	-	1256	-	-	-	1643	-
Wood and Wood Products	-	-	-	-	837	-	-	-	645	-
Construction	-	-	-	-	-	-	-	-	137	-
Textile and Leather	-	-	-	-	1884	-	-	-	2252	-
Non-specified	-	7	-	-	14	-	-	-	445	-
TRANSPORT SECTOR	-	-	-	-	-	-	-	-	**332**	-
International Civil Aviation	-	-	-	-	-	-	-	-	-	-
Domestic Air	-	-	-	-	-	-	-	-	-	-
Road	-	-	-	-	-	-	-	-	-	-
Rail	-	-	-	-	-	-	-	-	332	-
Pipeline Transport	-	-	-	-	-	-	-	-	-	-
Internal Navigation	-	-	-	-	-	-	-	-	-	-
Non-specified	-	-	-	-	-	-	-	-	-	-
OTHER SECTORS	-	**2816**	-	-	**17581**	-	-	-	**12521**	-
Agriculture	-	-	-	-	-	-	-	-	285	-
Commerce and Publ. Serv.	-	592	-	-	-	-	-	-	5439	-
Residential	-	2224	-	-	17581	-	-	-	6797	-
Non-specified	-	-	-	-	-	-	-	-	-	-
NON-ENERGY USE	-	-	-	-	-	-	-	-	-	-
in Industry/Transf./Energy	-	-	-	-	-	-	-	-	-	-
in Transport	-	-	-	-	-	-	-	-	-	-
in Other Sectors	-	-	-	-	-	-	-	-	-	-

Portugal / Portugal : 1993

SUPPLY AND CONSUMPTION	Coal / *Charbon* (1000 tonnes)							Oil / *Pétrole* (1000 tonnes)			
	Coking Coal	Steam Coal	Sub-Bit. Coal	Lignite	Peat	Oven and Gas Coke	Pat. Fuel and BKB	Crude Oil	NGL	Feedstocks	Additives
APPROVISIONNEMENT ET DEMANDE	*Charbon à coke*	*Charbon vapeur*	*Charbon sous-bit.*	*Lignite*	*Tourbe*	*Coke de four/gaz*	*Agg./briq. de lignite*	*Pétrole brut*	*LGN*	*Produits d'aliment.*	*Additifs*
Production	-	-	197	-	-	268	-	-	-	-	-
From Other Sources	-	-	-	-	-	-	-	-	-	-	-
Imports	352	4414	-	-	-	35	-	10952	-	556	-
Exports	-	-	-	-	-	-19	-	-	-	-	-
Intl. Marine Bunkers	-	-	-	-	-	-	-	-	-	-	-
Stock Changes	11	96	-119	-	-	14	-	-147	-	-10	-
DOMESTIC SUPPLY	**363**	**4510**	**78**	-	-	**298**	-	**10805**	-	**546**	-
Transfers	-	-	-	-	-	-	-	-	-	24	-
Statistical Differences	-	-1	-	-	-	2	-	-4	-	-5	-
TRANSFORMATION	**363**	**3779**	**73**	-	-	**79**	-	**10801**	-	**565**	-
Electricity Plants	-	3779	73	-	-	-	-	-	-	-	-
CHP Plants	-	-	-	-	-	-	-	-	-	-	-
Heat Plants	-	-	-	-	-	-	-	-	-	-	-
Transfer to Gases	-	-	-	-	-	79	-	-	-	-	-
Transfer to Solids	363	-	-	-	-	-	-	-	-	-	-
Petroleum Refineries	-	-	-	-	-	-	-	10801	-	565	-
Petrochemical Industry	-	-	-	-	-	-	-	-	-	-	-
Liquefaction	-	-	-	-	-	-	-	-	-	-	-
Other Transformation Sector	-	-	-	-	-	-	-	-	-	-	-
ENERGY SECTOR	-	-	-	-	-	-	-	-	-	-	-
Coal Mines	-	-	-	-	-	-	-	-	-	-	-
Oil and Gas Extraction	-	-	-	-	-	-	-	-	-	-	-
Petroleum Refineries	-	-	-	-	-	-	-	-	-	-	-
Electricity, CHP+Heat plants	-	-	-	-	-	-	-	-	-	-	-
Pumped Storage (Elec.)	-	-	-	-	-	-	-	-	-	-	-
Other Energy Sector	-	-	-	-	-	-	-	-	-	-	-
Distribution Losses	-	-	-	-	-	-	-	-	-	-	-
FINAL CONSUMPTION	-	**730**	**5**	-	-	**221**	-	-	-	-	-
INDUSTRY SECTOR	-	**729**	**5**	-	-	**221**	-	-	-	-	-
Iron and Steel	-	1	-	-	-	178	-	-	-	-	-
Chemical and Petrochemical	-	-	-	-	-	15	-	-	-	-	-
of which: Feedstocks	-	-	-	-	-	-	-	-	-	-	-
Non-Ferrous Metals	-	-	-	-	-	-	-	-	-	-	-
Non-Metallic Minerals	-	728	5	-	-	28	-	-	-	-	-
Transport Equipment	-	-	-	-	-	-	-	-	-	-	-
Machinery	-	-	-	-	-	-	-	-	-	-	-
Mining and Quarrying	-	-	-	-	-	-	-	-	-	-	-
Food and Tobacco	-	-	-	-	-	-	-	-	-	-	-
Paper, Pulp and Print	-	-	-	-	-	-	-	-	-	-	-
Wood and Wood Products	-	-	-	-	-	-	-	-	-	-	-
Construction	-	-	-	-	-	-	-	-	-	-	-
Textile and Leather	-	-	-	-	-	-	-	-	-	-	-
Non-specified	-	-	-	-	-	-	-	-	-	-	-
TRANSPORT SECTOR	-	-	-	-	-	-	-	-	-	-	-
International Civil Aviation	-	-	-	-	-	-	-	-	-	-	-
Domestic Air	-	-	-	-	-	-	-	-	-	-	-
Road	-	-	-	-	-	-	-	-	-	-	-
Rail	-	-	-	-	-	-	-	-	-	-	-
Pipeline Transport	-	-	-	-	-	-	-	-	-	-	-
Internal Navigation	-	-	-	-	-	-	-	-	-	-	-
Non-specified	-	-	-	-	-	-	-	-	-	-	-
OTHER SECTORS	-	**1**	-	-	-	-	-	-	-	-	-
Agriculture	-	-	-	-	-	-	-	-	-	-	-
Commerce and Publ. Serv.	-	1	-	-	-	-	-	-	-	-	-
Residential	-	-	-	-	-	-	-	-	-	-	-
Non-specified	-	-	-	-	-	-	-	-	-	-	-
NON-ENERGY USE	-	-	-	-	-	-	-	-	-	-	-
in Industry/Transf./Energy	-	-	-	-	-	-	-	-	-	-	-
in Transport	-	-	-	-	-	-	-	-	-	-	-
in Other Sectors	-	-	-	-	-	-	-	-	-	-	-

Portugal / Portugal : 1993

SUPPLY AND CONSUMPTION *APPROVISIONNEMENT ET DEMANDE*	Oil cont. / *Pétrole cont.* (1000 tonnes)										
	Refinery Gas *Gaz de raffinerie*	LPG + Ethane *GPL + éthane*	Motor Gasoline *Essence moteur*	Aviation Gasoline *Essence aviation*	Jet Fuel *Carbu-réacteur*	Kerosene *Kérosène*	Gas/Diesel *Gazole*	Heavy Fuel Oil *Fioul lourd*	Naphtha *Naphta*	Pétrol. Coke *Coke de pétrole*	Other Prod. *Autres prod.*
Production	245	346	1687	-	710	13	3281	3807	749	-	428
From Other Sources	-	-	-	-	-	-	-	-	-	-	-
Imports	-	620	204	2	13	-	387	2287	549	-	504
Exports	-	-13	-103	-	-156	-	-646	-1961	-229	-	-139
Intl. Marine Bunkers	-	-	-	-	-	-	-187	-334	-	-	-
Stock Changes	-	-1	15	-	7	9	-30	28	10	-	69
DOMESTIC SUPPLY	245	952	1803	2	574	22	2805	3827	1079	-	862
Transfers	1	-2	1	-	-3	-3	-27	48	-29	-	-10
Statistical Differences	-	6	-9	-	-	-	2	9	-	-	-23
TRANSFORMATION	47	-	-	-	-	-	27	2360	28	-	-
Electricity Plants	-	-	-	-	-	-	26	1933	-	-	-
CHP Plants	18	-	-	-	-	-	1	406	-	-	-
Heat Plants	-	-	-	-	-	-	-	-	-	-	-
Transfer to Gases	29	-	-	-	-	-	-	21	28	-	-
Transfer to Solids	-	-	-	-	-	-	-	-	-	-	-
Petroleum Refineries	-	-	-	-	-	-	-	-	-	-	-
Petrochemical Industry	-	-	-	-	-	-	-	-	-	-	-
Liquefaction	-	-	-	-	-	-	-	-	-	-	-
Other Transformation Sector	-	-	-	-	-	-	-	-	-	-	-
ENERGY SECTOR	199	2	-	-	-	-	2	102	-	-	228
Coal Mines	-	-	-	-	-	-	2	-	-	-	-
Oil and Gas Extraction	-	-	-	-	-	-	-	-	-	-	-
Petroleum Refineries	199	2	-	-	-	-	-	102	-	-	226
Electricity, CHP+Heat plants	-	-	-	-	-	-	-	-	-	-	2
Pumped Storage (Elec.)	-	-	-	-	-	-	-	-	-	-	-
Other Energy Sector	-	-	-	-	-	-	-	-	-	-	-
Distribution Losses	-	-	-	-	-	-	2	5	-	-	1
FINAL CONSUMPTION	-	954	1795	2	571	19	2749	1417	1022	-	600
INDUSTRY SECTOR	-	306	-	-	-	-	278	1342	1022	-	-
Iron and Steel	-	15	-	-	-	-	2	20	-	-	-
Chemical and Petrochemical	-	5	-	-	-	-	6	294	1022	-	-
of which: Feedstocks	-	-	-	-	-	-	-	*130*	*1022*	-	-
Non-Ferrous Metals	-	4	-	-	-	-	-	12	-	-	-
Non-Metallic Minerals	-	187	-	-	-	-	30	200	-	-	-
Transport Equipment	-	9	-	-	-	-	3	8	-	-	-
Machinery	-	5	-	-	-	-	1	10	-	-	-
Mining and Quarrying	-	2	-	-	-	-	25	2	-	-	-
Food and Tobacco	-	26	-	-	-	-	37	182	-	-	-
Paper, Pulp and Print	-	6	-	-	-	-	4	267	-	-	-
Wood and Wood Products	-	2	-	-	-	-	14	24	-	-	-
Construction	-	10	-	-	-	-	152	44	-	-	-
Textile and Leather	-	11	-	-	-	-	4	183	-	-	-
Non-specified	-	24	-	-	-	-	-	96	-	-	-
TRANSPORT SECTOR	-	-	1795	2	571	-	1952	-	-	-	-
International Civil Aviation	-	-	-	-	518	-	-	-	-	-	-
Domestic Air	-	-	-	2	53	-	-	-	-	-	-
Road	-	-	1795	-	-	-	1852	-	-	-	-
Rail	-	-	-	-	-	-	53	-	-	-	-
Pipeline Transport	-	-	-	-	-	-	-	-	-	-	-
Internal Navigation	-	-	-	-	-	-	47	-	-	-	-
Non-specified	-	-	-	-	-	-	-	-	-	-	-
OTHER SECTORS	-	648	-	-	-	19	519	75	-	-	-
Agriculture	-	12	-	-	-	-	406	9	-	-	-
Commerce and Publ. Serv.	-	48	-	-	-	-	100	66	-	-	-
Residential	-	588	-	-	-	2	100	66	-	-	-
Non-specified	-	-	-	-	-	17	13	-	-	-	-
NON-ENERGY USE	-	-	-	-	-	-	-	-	-	-	600
in Industry/Transf./Energy	-	-	-	-	-	-	-	-	-	-	493
in Transport	-	-	-	-	-	-	-	-	-	-	58
in Other Sectors	-	-	-	-	-	-	-	-	-	-	49

Portugal / Portugal : 1993

CONSUMPTION APPROVISIONNEMENT ET DEMANDE	Gas / Gaz (TJ)				Combust. Renew. & Waste / En. Re. Comb. & Déchets (TJ)				(GWh)	(TJ)
	Natural Gas Gaz naturel	Gas Works Usines à gaz	Coke Ovens Cokeries	Blast Furnaces Hauts fourneaux	Solid Biomass & Anim. Prod. Biomasse solide & prod. anim.	Gas/Liquids from Biomass Gaz/Liquides tirés de biomasse	Municipal Waste Déchets urbains	Industrial Waste Déchets industriels	Electricity Electricité	Heat Chaleur
Production	-	-	2265	2227	45694	-	-	-	31205	1437
From Other Sources	-	3045	-	-	-	-	-	-	-	-
Imports	-	-	-	-	-	-	-	-	2077	-
Exports	-	-	-	-	-	-	-	-	-1902	-
Intl. Marine Bunkers	-	-	-	-	-	-	-	-	-	-
Stock Changes	-	-	-	-	-	-	-	-	-	-
DOMESTIC SUPPLY	-	3045	2265	2227	45694	-	-	-	31380	1437
Transfers	-	-	-	-	-	-	-	-	-	-
Statistical Differences	-	-	-	-	-	-	-	-	-	-
TRANSFORMATION	-	-	460	1247	6394	-	-	-	-	-
Electricity Plants	-	-	-	-	-	-	-	-	-	-
CHP Plants	-	-	460	1247	6394	-	-	-	-	-
Heat Plants	-	-	-	-	-	-	-	-	-	-
Transfer to Gases	-	-	-	-	-	-	-	-	-	-
Transfer to Solids	-	-	-	-	-	-	-	-	-	-
Petroleum Refineries	-	-	-	-	-	-	-	-	-	-
Petrochemical Industry	-	-	-	-	-	-	-	-	-	-
Liquefaction	-	-	-	-	-	-	-	-	-	-
Other Transformation Sector	-	-	-	-	-	-	-	-	-	-
ENERGY SECTOR	-	-	925	-	-	-	-	-	1951	-
Coal Mines	-	-	-	-	-	-	-	-	5	-
Oil and Gas Extraction	-	-	-	-	-	-	-	-	-	-
Petroleum Refineries	-	-	-	-	-	-	-	-	362	-
Electricity, CHP+Heat plants	-	-	-	-	-	-	-	-	1273	-
Pumped Storage (Elec.)	-	-	-	-	-	-	-	-	284	-
Other Energy Sector	-	-	925	-	-	-	-	-	27	-
Distribution Losses	-	262	46	226	-	-	-	-	3447	-
FINAL CONSUMPTION	-	2783	834	754	39300	-	-	-	25982	1437
INDUSTRY SECTOR	-	65	834	754	20510	-	-	-	12515	1437
Iron and Steel	-	-	834	754	135	-	-	-	688	-
Chemical and Petrochemical	-	-	-	-	1042	-	-	-	2500	1396
of which: Feedstocks	-	-	-	-	-	-	-	-	-	-
Non-Ferrous Metals	-	-	-	-	-	-	-	-	84	-
Non-Metallic Minerals	-	-	-	-	12082	-	-	-	1785	-
Transport Equipment	-	-	-	-	-	-	-	-	225	-
Machinery	-	-	-	-	27	-	-	-	910	-
Mining and Quarrying	-	-	-	-	-	-	-	-	156	-
Food and Tobacco	-	-	-	-	3778	-	-	-	1225	-
Paper, Pulp and Print	-	-	-	-	856	-	-	-	1648	-
Wood and Wood Products	-	-	-	-	1242	-	-	-	620	-
Construction	-	-	-	-	-	-	-	-	164	-
Textile and Leather	-	-	-	-	1344	-	-	-	2145	31
Non-specified	-	65	-	-	4	-	-	-	365	10
TRANSPORT SECTOR	-	-	-	-	-	-	-	-	325	-
International Civil Aviation	-	-	-	-	-	-	-	-	-	-
Domestic Air	-	-	-	-	-	-	-	-	-	-
Road	-	-	-	-	-	-	-	-	-	-
Rail	-	-	-	-	-	-	-	-	325	-
Pipeline Transport	-	-	-	-	-	-	-	-	-	-
Internal Navigation	-	-	-	-	-	-	-	-	-	-
Non-specified	-	-	-	-	-	-	-	-	-	-
OTHER SECTORS	-	2718	-	-	18790	-	-	-	13142	-
Agriculture	-	-	-	-	-	-	-	-	288	-
Commerce and Publ. Serv.	-	644	-	-	-	-	-	-	5738	-
Residential	-	2074	-	-	18790	-	-	-	7116	-
Non-specified	-	-	-	-	-	-	-	-	-	-
NON-ENERGY USE	-	-	-	-	-	-	-	-	-	-
in Industry/Transf./Energy	-	-	-	-	-	-	-	-	-	-
in Transport	-	-	-	-	-	-	-	-	-	-
in Other Sectors	-	-	-	-	-	-	-	-	-	-

Spain / Espagne : 1992

SUPPLY AND CONSUMPTION *APPROVISIONNEMENT ET DEMANDE*	Coal / *Charbon* (1000 tonnes)							Oil / *Pétrole* (1000 tonnes)			
	Coking Coal *Charbon à coke*	Steam Coal *Charbon vapeur*	Sub-Bit. Coal *Charbon sous-bit.*	Lignite *Lignite*	Peat *Tourbe*	Oven and Gas Coke *Coke de four/gaz*	Pat. Fuel and BKB *Agg./briq. de lignite*	Crude Oil *Pétrole brut*	NGL *LGN*	Feedstocks *Produits d'aliment.*	Additives *Additifs*
Production	28	14690	3902	14779	-	2952	5	1073	329	-	-
From Other Sources	-	72	-	-	-	-	-	-	-	781	-
Imports	4343	9936		-	-	108	-	54037	-	855	-
Exports	-	-	-	-	-	-56	-	-	-	-	-
Intl. Marine Bunkers	-	-	-	-	-	-	-	-	-	-	-
Stock Changes	-75	-789	626	-44	-	-70	-	-150	-	94	-
DOMESTIC SUPPLY	**4296**	**23909**	**4528**	**14735**	**-**	**2934**	**5**	**54960**	**329**	**1730**	**-**
Transfers	-	-	-	-	-	-	-	-	-329	351	-
Statistical Differences	-247	-	19	-	-	-	-	-	-	243	-
TRANSFORMATION	**3948**	**20699**	**4501**	**14735**	**-**	**803**	**-**	**54940**	**-**	**2324**	**-**
Electricity Plants	-	20612	4501	14735	-	-	-	-	-	-	-
CHP Plants	-	82	-	-	-	-	-	-	-	-	-
Heat Plants	-	-	-	-	-	-	-	-	-	-	-
Transfer to Gases	-	-	-	-	-	803	-	-	-	-	-
Transfer to Solids	3948	5	-	-	-	-	-	-	-	-	-
Petroleum Refineries	-	-	-	-	-	-	-	54940	-	2324	-
Petrochemical Industry	-	-	-	-	-	-	-	-	-	-	-
Liquefaction	-	-	-	-	-	-	-	-	-	-	-
Other Transformation Sector	-	-	-	-	-	-	-	-	-	-	-
ENERGY SECTOR	**58**	**26**	**33**	**-**	**-**	**-**	**-**	**-**	**-**	**-**	**-**
Coal Mines	-	26	33	-	-	-	-	-	-	-	-
Oil and Gas Extraction	-	-	-	-	-	-	-	-	-	-	-
Petroleum Refineries	-	-	-	-	-	-	-	-	-	-	-
Electricity, CHP+Heat plants	-	-	-	-	-	-	-	-	-	-	-
Pumped Storage (Elec.)	-	-	-	-	-	-	-	-	-	-	-
Other Energy Sector	58	-	-	-	-	-	-	-	-	-	-
Distribution Losses	-	-	-	-	-	-	-	-	-	-	-
FINAL CONSUMPTION	**43**	**3184**	**13**	**-**	**-**	**2131**	**5**	**20**	**-**	**-**	**-**
INDUSTRY SECTOR	**43**	**2384**	**6**	**-**	**-**	**2131**	**-**	**20**	**-**	**-**	**-**
Iron and Steel	-	-	-	-	-	1933	-	-	-	-	-
Chemical and Petrochemical	-	150	4	-	-	48	-	20	-	-	-
of which: Feedstocks	-	-	-	-	-	-	-	-	-	-	-
Non-Ferrous Metals	-	30	-	-	-	40	-	-	-	-	-
Non-Metallic Minerals	-	2114	2	-	-	-	-	-	-	-	-
Transport Equipment	-	-	-	-	-	-	-	-	-	-	-
Machinery	-	30	-	-	-	80	-	-	-	-	-
Mining and Quarrying	-	20	-	-	-	-	-	-	-	-	-
Food and Tobacco	-	-	-	-	-	30	-	-	-	-	-
Paper, Pulp and Print	-	40	-	-	-	-	-	-	-	-	-
Wood and Wood Products	-	-	-	-	-	-	-	-	-	-	-
Construction	-	-	-	-	-	-	-	-	-	-	-
Textile and Leather	-	-	-	-	-	-	-	-	-	-	-
Non-specified	43	-	-	-	-	-	-	-	-	-	-
TRANSPORT SECTOR	**-**	**-**	**-**	**-**	**-**	**-**	**-**	**-**	**-**	**-**	**-**
International Civil Aviation	-	-	-	-	-	-	-	-	-	-	-
Domestic Air	-	-	-	-	-	-	-	-	-	-	-
Road	-	-	-	-	-	-	-	-	-	-	-
Rail	-	-	-	-	-	-	-	-	-	-	-
Pipeline Transport	-	-	-	-	-	-	-	-	-	-	-
Internal Navigation	-	-	-	-	-	-	-	-	-	-	-
Non-specified	-	-	-	-	-	-	-	-	-	-	-
OTHER SECTORS	**-**	**800**	**7**	**-**	**-**	**-**	**5**	**-**	**-**	**-**	**-**
Agriculture	-	-	-	-	-	-	-	-	-	-	-
Commerce and Publ. Serv.	-	100	-	-	-	-	-	-	-	-	-
Residential	-	700	7	-	-	-	5	-	-	-	-
Non-specified	-	-	-	-	-	-	-	-	-	-	-
NON-ENERGY USE	**-**	**-**	**-**	**-**	**-**	**-**	**-**	**-**	**-**	**-**	**-**
in Industry/Transf./Energy	-	-	-	-	-	-	-	-	-	-	-
in Transport	-	-	-	-	-	-	-	-	-	-	-
in Other Sectors	-	-	-	-	-	-	-	-	-	-	-

Spain / Espagne : 1992

SUPPLY AND CONSUMPTION *APPROVISIONNEMENT ET DEMANDE*	Oil cont. / *Pétrole cont.* (1000 tonnes)										
	Refinery Gas *Gaz de raffinerie*	LPG + Ethane *GPL + éthane*	Motor Gasoline *Essence moteur*	Aviation Gasoline *Essence aviation*	Jet Fuel *Carbu-réacteur*	Kerosene *Kérosène*	Gas/Diesel *Gazole*	Heavy Fuel Oil *Fioul lourd*	Naphtha *Naphta*	Pétrol. Coke *Coke de pétrole*	Other Prod. *Autres prod.*
Production	1615	1854	9441	-	3560	170	16119	16953	2551	441	4036
From Other Sources	-	-	-	-	-	-	-	-	-	-	-
Imports	-	759	651	9	-	-	2583	1608	2327	1460	405
Exports	-	-103	-1013	-	-826	-	-1337	-6220	-1442	-33	-1552
Intl. Marine Bunkers	-	-	-	-	-	-	-1300	-2692	-	-	-
Stock Changes	-	-68	-43	-	-2	23	-81	61	45	20	31
DOMESTIC SUPPLY	**1615**	**2442**	**9036**	**9**	**2732**	**193**	**15984**	**9710**	**3481**	**1888**	**2920**
Transfers	15	239	169	-	-38	-45	-419	187	-490	-	360
Statistical Differences	-6	7	-6	-	-4	-9	8	-3	-2	-	27
TRANSFORMATION	**17**	**24**	**-**	**-**	**-**	**-**	**99**	**3583**	**748**	**-**	**-**
Electricity Plants	-	-	-	-	-	-	86	3208	-	-	-
CHP Plants	10	-	-	-	-	-	-	345	-	-	-
Heat Plants	-	-	-	-	-	-	-	-	-	-	-
Transfer to Gases	-	16	-	-	-	-	-	-	25	-	-
Transfer to Solids	-	-	-	-	-	-	-	-	-	-	-
Petroleum Refineries	-	-	-	-	-	-	-	-	-	-	-
Petrochemical Industry	7	8	-	-	-	-	13	30	723	-	-
Liquefaction	-	-	-	-	-	-	-	-	-	-	-
Other Transformation Sector	-	-	-	-	-	-	-	-	-	-	-
ENERGY SECTOR	**1508**	**22**	**5**	**-**	**-**	**-**	**56**	**2005**	**-**	**-**	**187**
Coal Mines	-	-	-	-	-	-	46	-	-	-	-
Oil and Gas Extraction	-	-	-	-	-	-	2	-	-	-	-
Petroleum Refineries	1508	22	5	-	-	-	8	1985	-	-	57
Electricity, CHP+Heat plants	-	-	-	-	-	-	-	-	-	-	-
Pumped Storage (Elec.)	-	-	-	-	-	-	-	-	-	-	-
Other Energy Sector	-	-	-	-	-	-	-	20	-	-	130
Distribution Losses	-	-	-	-	-	-	-	-	-	-	-
FINAL CONSUMPTION	**99**	**2642**	**9194**	**9**	**2690**	**139**	**15418**	**4306**	**2241**	**1888**	**3120**
INDUSTRY SECTOR	**99**	**393**	**-**	**-**	**-**	**-**	**438**	**3455**	**2241**	**1579**	**113**
Iron and Steel	-	25	-	-	-	-	28	320	-	6	-
Chemical and Petrochemical	99	220	-	-	-	-	74	1002	2241	10	13
of which: Feedstocks	-	-	-	-	-	-	-	-	2241	-	-
Non-Ferrous Metals	-	10	-	-	-	-	10	160	-	-	-
Non-Metallic Minerals	-	48	-	-	-	-	21	475	-	1488	-
Transport Equipment	-	10	-	-	-	-	20	73	-	-	-
Machinery	-	35	-	-	-	-	20	75	-	75	-
Mining and Quarrying	-	2	-	-	-	-	45	55	-	-	-
Food and Tobacco	-	22	-	-	-	-	150	735	-	-	-
Paper, Pulp and Print	-	12	-	-	-	-	8	320	-	-	-
Wood and Wood Products	-	3	-	-	-	-	4	20	-	-	-
Construction	-	-	-	-	-	-	14	30	-	-	-
Textile and Leather	-	6	-	-	-	-	32	190	-	-	-
Non-specified	-	-	-	-	-	-	12	-	-	-	100
TRANSPORT SECTOR	**-**	**50**	**9194**	**9**	**2690**	**-**	**11530**	**400**	**-**	**-**	**-**
International Civil Aviation	-	-	-	-	1130	-	-	-	-	-	-
Domestic Air	-	-	-	9	1560	-	-	-	-	-	-
Road	-	50	9194	-	-	-	9900	-	-	-	-
Rail	-	-	-	-	-	-	230	-	-	-	-
Pipeline Transport	-	-	-	-	-	-	-	-	-	-	-
Internal Navigation	-	-	-	-	-	-	1400	400	-	-	-
Non-specified	-	-	-	-	-	-	-	-	-	-	-
OTHER SECTORS	**-**	**2199**	**-**	**-**	**-**	**139**	**3450**	**451**	**-**	**14**	**-**
Agriculture	-	35	-	-	-	139	1370	25	-	-	-
Commerce and Publ. Serv.	-	170	-	-	-	-	680	396	-	5	-
Residential	-	1994	-	-	-	-	1400	30	-	9	-
Non-specified	-	-	-	-	-	-	-	-	-	-	-
NON-ENERGY USE	**-**	**-**	**-**	**-**	**-**	**-**	**-**	**-**	**-**	**295**	**3007**
in Industry/Transf./Energy	-	-	-	-	-	-	-	-	-	295	2806
in Transport	-	-	-	-	-	-	-	-	-	-	186
in Other Sectors	-	-	-	-	-	-	-	-	-	-	15

Spain / Espagne : 1992

CONSUMPTION APPROVISIONNEMENT ET DEMANDE	Natural Gas Gaz naturel	Gas Works Usines à gaz	Coke Ovens Cokeries	Blast Furnaces Hauts fourneaux	Solid Biomass & Anim. Prod. Biomasse solide & prod. anim.	Gas/Liquids from Biomass Gaz/Liquides tirés de biomasse	Municipal Waste Déchets urbains	Industrial Waste Déchets industriels	Electricity Electricité	Heat Chaleur
	Gas / Gaz (TJ)				Combust. Renew. & Waste / En. Re. Comb. & Déchets (TJ)				(GWh)	(TJ)
Production	50664	67	23607	24321	29147	-	-	853	158505	-
From Other Sources	-	8988	-	-	-	-	-	-	-	-
Imports	225149	-	-	-	-	-	-	-	4351	-
Exports	-	-	-	-	-	-	-	-	-3710	-
Intl. Marine Bunkers	-	-	-	-	-	-	-	-	-	-
Stock Changes	-3443	-	-	-	-	-	-	-	-	-\
DOMESTIC SUPPLY	272370	9055	23607	24321	29147	-	-	853	159146	-
Transfers	-	-	-	-	-	-	-	-	-	-
Statistical Differences	1647	-	-	-	-	-	-	-	-	-
TRANSFORMATION	22387	-	1732	6826	3826	-	-	353	-	-
Electricity Plants	9825	-	888	4230	1100	-	-	353	-	-
CHP Plants	4700	-	777	2596	2726	-	-	-	-	-
Heat Plants	-	-	-	-	-	-	-	-	-	-
Transfer to Gases	7862	-	67	-	-	-	-	-	-	-
Transfer to Solids	-	-	-	-	-	-	-	-	-	-
Petroleum Refineries	-	-	-	-	-	-	-	-	-	-
Petrochemical Industry	-	-	-	-	-	-	-	-	-	-
Liquefaction	-	-	-	-	-	-	-	-	-	-
Other Transformation Sector	-	-	-	-	-	-	-	-	-	-
ENERGY SECTOR	2257	12	6233	4243	-	-	-	-	13875	-
Coal Mines	-	-	-	-	-	-	-	-	1250	-
Oil and Gas Extraction	2257	-	-	-	-	-	-	-	18	-
Petroleum Refineries	-	-	-	-	-	-	-	-	2025	-
Electricity, CHP+Heat plants	-	-	-	-	-	-	-	-	7695	-
Pumped Storage (Elec.)	-	-	-	-	-	-	-	-	2697	-
Other Energy Sector	-	12	6233	4243	-	-	-	-	190	-
Distribution Losses	5929	50	-	-	-	-	-	-	14502	-
FINAL CONSUMPTION	243444	8993	15642	13252	25321	-	-	500	130769	-
INDUSTRY SECTOR	196716	197	15642	13252	25321	-	-	500	64876	-
Iron and Steel	14466	-	14042	13100	-	-	-	-	9250	-
Chemical and Petrochemical	62398	-	1600	152	-	-	-	-	10203	-
of which: Feedstocks	24578	-	-	-	-	-	-	-	-	-
Non-Ferrous Metals	3588	-	-	-	-	-	-	-	8472	-
Non-Metallic Minerals	46533	-	-	-	-	-	-	500	7100	-
Transport Equipment	9863	-	-	-	-	-	-	-	2828	-
Machinery	6882	182	-	-	-	-	-	-	4800	-
Mining and Quarrying	632	-	-	-	-	-	-	-	1672	-
Food and Tobacco	15142	14	-	-	7000	-	-	-	6023	-
Paper, Pulp and Print	21595	-	-	-	18321	-	-	-	4083	-
Wood and Wood Products	508	1	-	-	-	-	-	-	1460	-
Construction	215	-	-	-	-	-	-	-	825	-
Textile and Leather	13802	-	-	-	-	-	-	-	3800	-
Non-specified	1092	-	-	-	-	-	-	-	4360	-
TRANSPORT SECTOR	-	-	-	-	-	-	-	-	4107	-
International Civil Aviation	-	-	-	-	-	-	-	-	-	-
Domestic Air	-	-	-	-	-	-	-	-	-	-
Road	-	-	-	-	-	-	-	-	-	-
Rail	-	-	-	-	-	-	-	-	2000	-
Pipeline Transport	-	-	-	-	-	-	-	-	-	-
Internal Navigation	-	-	-	-	-	-	-	-	-	-
Non-specified	-	-	-	-	-	-	-	-	2107	-
OTHER SECTORS	46728	8796	-	-	-	-	-	-	61786	-
Agriculture	189	-	-	-	-	-	-	-	3652	-
Commerce and Publ. Serv.	12811	1911	-	-	-	-	-	-	26727	-
Residential	33728	6885	-	-	-	-	-	-	31407	-
Non-specified	-	-	-	-	-	-	-	-	-	-
NON-ENERGY USE	-	-	-	-	-	-	-	-	-	-
in Industry/Transf./Energy	-	-	-	-	-	-	-	-	-	-
in Transport	-	-	-	-	-	-	-	-	-	-
in Other Sectors	-	-	-	-	-	-	-	-	-	-

Spain / Espagne : 1993

SUPPLY AND CONSUMPTION *APPROVISIONNEMENT ET DEMANDE*	Coal / *Charbon* (1000 tonnes)							Oil / *Pétrole* (1000 tonnes)			
	Coking Coal *Charbon à coke*	Steam Coal *Charbon vapeur*	Sub-Bit. Coal *Charbon sous-bit.*	Lignite *Lignite*	Peat *Tourbe*	Oven and Gas Coke *Coke de four/gaz*	Pat. Fuel and BKB *Agg./briq. de lignite*	Crude Oil *Pétrole brut*	NGL *LGN*	Feedstocks *Produits d'aliment.*	Additives *Additifs*
Production	-	14046	4111	13347	-	3055	-	874	228	-	-
From Other Sources	-	79	-	-	-	-	-	-	-	901	-
Imports	4572	8154	-	-	-	145	-	51395	-	1111	-
Exports	-	-	-	-	-	-85	-	-	-	-	-
Intl. Marine Bunkers	-	-	-	-	-	-	-	-	-	-	-
Stock Changes	-167	-54	319	88	-	-28	-	-253	-	92	-
DOMESTIC SUPPLY	**4405**	**22225**	**4430**	**13435**	**-**	**3087**	**-**	**52016**	**228**	**2104**	**-**
Transfers	-	-	-	-	-	-	-	-	-228	14	-
Statistical Differences	-	-	-	-	-	-	-	-	-	-183	-
TRANSFORMATION	**4306**	**20217**	**4412**	**13435**	**-**	**895**	**-**	**52001**	**-**	**1935**	**-**
Electricity Plants	-	20133	4412	13435	-	-	-	-	-	-	-
CHP Plants	-	84	-	-	-	-	-	-	-	-	-
Heat Plants	-	-	-	-	-	-	-	-	-	-	-
Transfer to Gases	-	-	-	-	-	895	-	-	-	-	-
Transfer to Solids	4306	-	-	-	-	-	-	-	-	-	-
Petroleum Refineries	-	-	-	-	-	-	-	52001	-	1935	-
Petrochemical Industry	-	-	-	-	-	-	-	-	-	-	-
Liquefaction	-	-	-	-	-	-	-	-	-	-	-
Other Transformation Sector	-	-	-	-	-	-	-	-	-	-	-
ENERGY SECTOR	**55**	**32**	**3**	**-**	**-**	**-**	**-**	**-**	**-**	**-**	**-**
Coal Mines	-	32	3	-	-	-	-	-	-	-	-
Oil and Gas Extraction	-	-	-	-	-	-	-	-	-	-	-
Petroleum Refineries	-	-	-	-	-	-	-	-	-	-	-
Electricity, CHP+Heat plants	-	-	-	-	-	-	-	-	-	-	-
Pumped Storage (Elec.)	-	-	-	-	-	-	-	-	-	-	-
Other Energy Sector	55	-	-	-	-	-	-	-	-	-	-
Distribution Losses	-	-	-	-	-	-	-	-	-	-	-
FINAL CONSUMPTION	**44**	**1976**	**15**	**-**	**-**	**2192**	**-**	**15**	**-**	**-**	**-**
INDUSTRY SECTOR	**44**	**1339**	**10**	**-**	**-**	**2192**	**-**	**15**	**-**	**-**	**-**
Iron and Steel	-	-	-	-	-	2014	-	-	-	-	-
Chemical and Petrochemical	-	115	4	-	-	35	-	15	-	-	-
of which: Feedstocks	-	-	-	-	-	-	-	-	-	-	-
Non-Ferrous Metals	-	20	-	-	-	53	-	-	-	-	-
Non-Metallic Minerals	-	1144	2	-	-	-	-	-	-	-	-
Transport Equipment	-	-	-	-	-	-	-	-	-	-	-
Machinery	-	20	-	-	-	60	-	-	-	-	-
Mining and Quarrying	-	10	-	-	-	-	-	-	-	-	-
Food and Tobacco	-	-	-	-	-	30	-	-	-	-	-
Paper, Pulp and Print	-	30	-	-	-	-	-	-	-	-	-
Wood and Wood Products	-	-	-	-	-	-	-	-	-	-	-
Construction	-	-	-	-	-	-	-	-	-	-	-
Textile and Leather	-	-	-	-	-	-	-	-	-	-	-
Non-specified	44	-	4	-	-	-	-	-	-	-	-
TRANSPORT SECTOR	**-**	**-**	**-**	**-**	**-**	**-**	**-**	**-**	**-**	**-**	**-**
International Civil Aviation	-	-	-	-	-	-	-	-	-	-	-
Domestic Air	-	-	-	-	-	-	-	-	-	-	-
Road	-	-	-	-	-	-	-	-	-	-	-
Rail	-	-	-	-	-	-	-	-	-	-	-
Pipeline Transport	-	-	-	-	-	-	-	-	-	-	-
Internal Navigation	-	-	-	-	-	-	-	-	-	-	-
Non-specified	-	-	-	-	-	-	-	-	-	-	-
OTHER SECTORS	**-**	**637**	**5**	**-**	**-**	**-**	**-**	**-**	**-**	**-**	**-**
Agriculture	-	-	5	-	-	-	-	-	-	-	-
Commerce and Publ. Serv.	-	37	-	-	-	-	-	-	-	-	-
Residential	-	600	-	-	-	-	-	-	-	-	-
Non-specified	-	-	-	-	-	-	-	-	-	-	-
NON-ENERGY USE	**-**	**-**	**-**	**-**	**-**	**-**	**-**	**-**	**-**	**-**	**-**
in Industry/Transf./Energy	-	-	-	-	-	-	-	-	-	-	-
in Transport	-	-	-	-	-	-	-	-	-	-	-
in Other Sectors	-	-	-	-	-	-	-	-	-	-	-

Spain / Espagne : 1993

SUPPLY AND CONSUMPTION / APPROVISIONNEMENT ET DEMANDE	Oil cont. / Pétrole cont. (1000 tonnes)										
	Refinery Gas / Gaz de raffinerie	LPG + Ethane / GPL + éthane	Motor Gasoline / Essence moteur	Aviation Gasoline / Essence aviation	Jet Fuel / Carbu-réacteur	Kerosene / Kérosène	Gas/Diesel / Gazole	Heavy Fuel Oil / Fioul lourd	Naphtha / Naphta	Pétrol. Coke / Coke de pétrole	Other Prod. / Autres prod.
Production	1495	1606	8950	19	3427	176	15239	14828	2308	428	5005
From Other Sources	-	-	-	-	-	-	-	-	-	-	-
Imports	-	1137	886	-	-	-	2517	1241	2185	1161	732
Exports	-	-67	-1579	-	-749	-	-1434	-5557	-1237	-26	-1792
Intl. Marine Bunkers	-	-	-	-	-	-	-740	-2755	-	-	-
Stock Changes	-	-64	-133	-	8	-33	119	25	-62	-38	21
DOMESTIC SUPPLY	1495	2612	8124	19	2686	143	15701	7782	3194	1525	3966
Transfers	24	-101	732	-11	-74	-17	202	990	-97	26	-1460
Statistical Differences	-2	9	-5	1	-2	-	-5	-3	6	2	28
TRANSFORMATION	75	16	-	-	-	-	163	2166	921	-	-
Electricity Plants	-	-	-	-	-	-	151	1860	-	-	-
CHP Plants	75	-	-	-	-	-	12	306	-	-	-
Heat Plants	-	-	-	-	-	-	-	-	-	-	-
Transfer to Gases	-	16	-	-	-	-	-	-	-	-	-
Transfer to Solids	-	-	-	-	-	-	-	-	20	-	-
Petroleum Refineries	-	-	-	-	-	-	-	-	-	-	-
Petrochemical Industry	-	-	-	-	-	-	-	-	-	-	-
Liquefaction	-	-	-	-	-	-	-	-	901	-	-
Other Transformation Sector	-	-	-	-	-	-	-	-	-	-	-
ENERGY SECTOR	1394	20	-	-	-	-	69	1929	3	-	157
Coal Mines	-	-	-	-	-	-	-	-	-	-	-
Oil and Gas Extraction	-	-	-	-	-	-	48	-	-	-	-
Petroleum Refineries	1394	20	-	-	-	-	2	-	-	-	-
Electricity, CHP+Heat plants	-	-	-	-	-	-	19	1909	3	-	77
Pumped Storage (Elec.)	-	-	-	-	-	-	-	-	-	-	-
Other Energy Sector	-	-	-	-	-	-	-	20	-	-	80
Distribution Losses	-	-	-	-	-	-	-	-	-	-	-
FINAL CONSUMPTION	48	2484	8851	9	2610	126	15666	4674	2179	1553	2377
INDUSTRY SECTOR	48	324	-	-	-	-	410	3984	2179	1388	-
Iron and Steel	-	22	-	-	-	-	30	300	-	6	-
Chemical and Petrochemical	48	173	-	-	-	-	36	1000	2179	10	-
of which: Feedstocks	48	-	-	-	-	-	-	-	2179	-	-
Non-Ferrous Metals	-	9	-	-	-	-	14	469	-	-	-
Non-Metallic Minerals	-	42	-	-	-	-	10	160	-	1302	-
Transport Equipment	-	9	-	-	-	-	25	500	-	-	-
Machinery	-	30	-	-	-	-	20	75	-	-	-
Mining and Quarrying	-	2	-	-	-	-	20	80	-	70	-
Food and Tobacco	-	20	-	-	-	-	40	60	-	-	-
Paper, Pulp and Print	-	12	-	-	-	-	155	730	-	-	-
Wood and Wood Products	-	2	-	-	-	-	10	350	-	-	-
Construction	-	-	-	-	-	-	5	25	-	-	-
Textile and Leather	-	3	-	-	-	-	15	35	-	-	-
Non-specified	-	-	-	-	-	-	30	200	-	-	-
TRANSPORT SECTOR	-	60	8851	9	2610	-	11600	450	-	-	-
International Civil Aviation	-	-	-	-	2060	-	-	-	-	-	-
Domestic Air	-	-	-	9	550	-	-	-	-	-	-
Road	-	60	8851	-	-	-	9980	-	-	-	-
Rail	-	-	-	-	-	-	220	-	-	-	-
Pipeline Transport	-	-	-	-	-	-	-	-	-	-	-
Internal Navigation	-	-	-	-	-	-	1400	450	-	-	-
Non-specified	-	-	-	-	-	-	-	-	-	-	-
OTHER SECTORS	-	2100	-	-	-	126	3656	240	-	15	-
Agriculture	-	40	-	-	-	-	1436	20	-	-	-
Commerce and Publ. Serv.	-	160	-	-	-	126	720	20	-	5	-
Residential	-	1900	-	-	-	-	1500	200	-	10	-
Non-specified	-	-	-	-	-	-	-	-	-	-	-
NON-ENERGY USE	-	-	-	-	-	-	-	-	-	150	2377
in Industry/Transf./Energy	-	-	-	-	-	-	-	-	-	150	2227
in Transport	-	-	-	-	-	-	-	-	-	-	-
in Other Sectors	-	-	-	-	-	-	-	-	-	-	150

Spain / Espagne : 1993

CONSUMPTION / APPROVISIONNEMENT ET DEMANDE	Gas / Gaz (TJ)				Combust. Renew. & Waste / En. Re. Comb. & Déchets (TJ)				(GWh)	(TJ)
	Natural Gas / Gaz naturel	Gas Works / Usines à gaz	Coke Ovens / Cokeries	Blast Furnaces / Hauts fourneaux	Solid Biomass & Anim. Prod. / Biomasse solide & prod. anim.	Gas/Liquids from Biomass / Gaz/Liquides tirés de biomasse	Municipal Waste / Déchets urbains	Industrial Waste / Déchets industriels	Electricity / Electricité	Heat / Chaleur
Production	27726	93	25765	27024	30510	-	-	1221	156529	-
From Other Sources	-	7513	-	-	-	-	-	-	-	-
Imports	236828	-	-	-	-	-	-	-	4606	-
Exports	-	-	-	-	-	-	-	-	-3339	-
Intl. Marine Bunkers	-	-	-	-	-	-	-	-	-	-
Stock Changes	2616	-	-	-	-	-	-	-	-	-
DOMESTIC SUPPLY	**267170**	**7606**	**25765**	**27024**	**30510**	**-**	**-**	**1221**	**157796**	**-**
Transfers	-	-	-	-	-	-	-	-	-	-
Statistical Differences	3282	54	-	-	-	-	-	-	-	-
TRANSFORMATION	**14127**	**-**	**2096**	**6928**	**3910**	**-**	**-**	**423**	**-**	**-**
Electricity Plants	2041	-	918	4796	1359	-	-	423	-	-
CHP Plants	6138	-	1074	2132	2551	-	-	-	-	-
Heat Plants	-	-	-	-	-	-	-	-	-	-
Transfer to Gases	5948	-	104	-	-	-	-	-	-	-
Transfer to Solids	-	-	-	-	-	-	-	-	-	-
Petroleum Refineries	-	-	-	-	-	-	-	-	-	-
Petrochemical Industry	-	-	-	-	-	-	-	-	-	-
Liquefaction	-	-	-	-	-	-	-	-	-	-
Other Transformation Sector	-	-	-	-	-	-	-	-	-	-
ENERGY SECTOR	**1878**	**12**	**7429**	**4635**	**-**	**-**	**-**	**-**	**12626**	**-**
Coal Mines	-	-	-	-	-	-	-	-	1200	-
Oil and Gas Extraction	1878	-	-	-	-	-	-	-	18	-
Petroleum Refineries	-	-	-	-	-	-	-	-	2000	-
Electricity, CHP+Heat plants	-	-	-	-	-	-	-	-	7330	-
Pumped Storage (Elec.)	-	-	-	-	-	-	-	-	1878	-
Other Energy Sector	-	12	7429	4635	-	-	-	-	200	-
Distribution Losses	3351	-	-	-	-	-	-	-	14487	-
FINAL CONSUMPTION	**251096**	**7648**	**16240**	**15461**	**26600**	**-**	**-**	**798**	**130683**	**-**
INDUSTRY SECTOR	**198436**	**312**	**16191**	**15340**	**26600**	**-**	**-**	**798**	**63253**	**-**
Iron and Steel	14830	-	14677	15180	-	-	-	-	9019	-
Chemical and Petrochemical	52852	-	1514	160	-	-	-	-	9949	-
of which: Feedstocks	17991	-	-	-	-	-	-	-	-	-
Non-Ferrous Metals	3805	-	-	-	-	-	-	-	8260	-
Non-Metallic Minerals	50793	-	-	-	-	-	-	798	6922	-
Transport Equipment	9289	-	-	-	-	-	-	-	2757	-
Machinery	7305	296	-	-	-	-	-	-	4680	-
Mining and Quarrying	707	-	-	-	-	-	-	-	1630	-
Food and Tobacco	15677	14	-	-	7646	-	-	-	5872	-
Paper, Pulp and Print	24300	-	-	-	18954	-	-	-	3981	-
Wood and Wood Products	527	-	-	-	-	-	-	-	1423	-
Construction	71	-	-	-	-	-	-	-	804	-
Textile and Leather	16903	-	-	-	-	-	-	-	3705	-
Non-specified	1377	2	-	-	-	-	-	-	4251	-
TRANSPORT SECTOR	**-**	**-**	**-**	**-**	**-**	**-**	**-**	**-**	**4197**	**-**
International Civil Aviation	-	-	-	-	-	-	-	-	-	-
Domestic Air	-	-	-	-	-	-	-	-	-	-
Road	-	-	-	-	-	-	-	-	-	-
Rail	-	-	-	-	-	-	-	-	1997	-
Pipeline Transport	-	-	-	-	-	-	-	-	-	-
Internal Navigation	-	-	-	-	-	-	-	-	-	-
Non-specified	-	-	-	-	-	-	-	-	2200	-
OTHER SECTORS	**52660**	**7336**	**-**	**-**	**-**	**-**	**-**	**-**	**63233**	**-**
Agriculture	184	-	-	-	-	-	-	-	3446	-
Commerce and Publ. Serv.	14258	1827	-	-	-	-	-	-	27425	-
Residential	38218	5509	-	-	-	-	-	-	32362	-
Non-specified	-	-	-	-	-	-	-	-	-	-
NON-ENERGY USE	**-**	**-**	**49**	**121**	**-**	**-**	**-**	**-**	**-**	**-**
in Industry/Transf./Energy	-	-	49	121	-	-	-	-	-	-
in Transport	-	-	-	-	-	-	-	-	-	-
in Other Sectors	-	-	-	-	-	-	-	-	-	-

Sweden / Suède : 1992

SUPPLY AND CONSUMPTION	Coal / Charbon (1000 tonnes)							Oil / Pétrole (1000 tonnes)			
	Coking Coal	Steam Coal	Sub-Bit. Coal	Lignite	Peat	Oven and Gas Coke	Pat. Fuel and BKB	Crude Oil	NGL	Feedstocks	Additives
APPROVISIONNEMENT ET DEMANDE	Charbon à coke	Charbon vapeur	Charbon sous-bit.	Lignite	Tourbe	Coke de four/gaz	Agg./briq. de lignite	Pétrole brut	LGN	Produits d'aliment.	Additifs
Production	-	37	-	-	1013	1146	-	1	-	-	-
From Other Sources	-	-	-	-	-	-	-	-	-	-	-
Imports	1535	1475	-	-	-	295	3	16786	-	628	-
Exports	-	-15	-	-	-	-23	-3	-1	-	-389	-
Intl. Marine Bunkers	-	-	-	-	-	-	-	-	-	-	-
Stock Changes	6	296	-	-	-	-95	-	9	-	38	-
DOMESTIC SUPPLY	**1541**	**1793**	**-**	**-**	**1013**	**1323**	**-**	**16795**	**-**	**277**	**-**
Transfers	-	-	-	-	-	-	-	-	-	1352	-
Statistical Differences	-	-	-	-	-	-	-	574	-	-585	-
TRANSFORMATION	**1541**	**1086**	**-**	**-**	**976**	**463**	**-**	**17369**	**-**	**1044**	**-**
Electricity Plants	-	-	-	-	-	-	-	-	-	-	-
CHP Plants	-	916	-	-	529	-	-	-	-	-	-
Heat Plants	-	170	-	-	447	-	-	-	-	-	-
Transfer to Gases	-	-	-	-	-	463	-	-	-	-	-
Transfer to Solids	1541	-	-	-	-	-	-	-	-	-	-
Petroleum Refineries	-	-	-	-	-	-	-	17369	-	1044	-
Petrochemical Industry	-	-	-	-	-	-	-	-	-	-	-
Liquefaction	-	-	-	-	-	-	-	-	-	-	-
Other Transformation Sector	-	-	-	-	-	-	-	-	-	-	-
ENERGY SECTOR	**-**	**-**	**-**	**-**	**-**	**-**	**-**	**-**	**-**	**-**	**-**
Coal Mines	-	-	-	-	-	-	-	-	-	-	-
Oil and Gas Extraction	-	-	-	-	-	-	-	-	-	-	-
Petroleum Refineries	-	-	-	-	-	-	-	-	-	-	-
Electricity, CHP+Heat plants	-	-	-	-	-	-	-	-	-	-	-
Pumped Storage (Elec.)	-	-	-	-	-	-	-	-	-	-	-
Other Energy Sector	-	-	-	-	-	-	-	-	-	-	-
Distribution Losses	-	-	-	-	-	-	-	-	-	-	-
FINAL CONSUMPTION	**-**	**707**	**-**	**-**	**37**	**860**	**-**	**-**	**-**	**-**	**-**
INDUSTRY SECTOR	**-**	**686**	**-**	**-**	**37**	**832**	**-**	**-**	**-**	**-**	**-**
Iron and Steel	-	162	-	-	-	754	-	-	-	-	-
Chemical and Petrochemical	-	17	-	-	7	5	-	-	-	-	-
of which: Feedstocks	-	-	-	-	-	-	-	-	-	-	-
Non-Ferrous Metals	-	62	-	-	-	18	-	-	-	-	-
Non-Metallic Minerals	-	270	-	-	-	36	-	-	-	-	-
Transport Equipment	-	-	-	-	-	11	-	-	-	-	-
Machinery	-	-	-	-	-	2	-	-	-	-	-
Mining and Quarrying	-	76	-	-	-	1	-	-	-	-	-
Food and Tobacco	-	16	-	-	-	5	-	-	-	-	-
Paper, Pulp and Print	-	82	-	-	30	-	-	-	-	-	-
Wood and Wood Products	-	1	-	-	-	-	-	-	-	-	-
Construction	-	-	-	-	-	-	-	-	-	-	-
Textile and Leather	-	-	-	-	-	-	-	-	-	-	-
Non-specified	-	-	-	-	-	-	-	-	-	-	-
TRANSPORT SECTOR	**-**	**-**	**-**	**-**	**-**	**-**	**-**	**-**	**-**	**-**	**-**
International Civil Aviation	-	-	-	-	-	-	-	-	-	-	-
Domestic Air	-	-	-	-	-	-	-	-	-	-	-
Road	-	-	-	-	-	-	-	-	-	-	-
Rail	-	-	-	-	-	-	-	-	-	-	-
Pipeline Transport	-	-	-	-	-	-	-	-	-	-	-
Internal Navigation	-	-	-	-	-	-	-	-	-	-	-
Non-specified	-	-	-	-	-	-	-	-	-	-	-
OTHER SECTORS	**-**	**21**	**-**	**-**	**-**	**2**	**-**	**-**	**-**	**-**	**-**
Agriculture	-	20	-	-	-	2	-	-	-	-	-
Commerce and Publ. Serv.	-	1	-	-	-	-	-	-	-	-	-
Residential	-	-	-	-	-	-	-	-	-	-	-
Non-specified	-	-	-	-	-	-	-	-	-	-	-
NON-ENERGY USE	**-**	**-**	**-**	**-**	**-**	**26**	**-**	**-**	**-**	**-**	**-**
in Industry/Transf./Energy	-	-	-	-	-	26	-	-	-	-	-
in Transport	-	-	-	-	-	-	-	-	-	-	-
in Other Sectors	-	-	-	-	-	-	-	-	-	-	-

Sweden / Suède : 1992

SUPPLY AND CONSUMPTION *APPROVISIONNEMENT ET DEMANDE*	Oil cont. / *Pétrole cont.* (1000 tonnes)										
	Refinery Gas *Gaz de raffinerie*	LPG + Ethane *GPL + éthane*	Motor Gasoline *Essence moteur*	Aviation Gasoline *Essence aviation*	Jet Fuel *Carbu-réacteur*	Kerosene *Kérosène*	Gas/Diesel *Gazole*	Heavy Fuel Oil *Fioul lourd*	Naphtha *Naphta*	Pétrol. Coke *Coke de pétrole*	Other Prod. *Autres prod.*
Production	-	291	4363	-	181	5	6503	5689	6	-	964
From Other Sources	-	-	-	-	-	-	-	-	-	-	-
Imports	-	795	1755	6	689	66	1637	1040	383	174	396
Exports	-	-83	-1706	-3	-35	-4	-3526	-3208	-27	-2	-763
Intl. Marine Bunkers	-	-	-	-	-	-	-176	-743	-	-	-
Stock Changes	-	-50	79	1	-27	12	330	175	-16	-57	2
DOMESTIC SUPPLY	-	**953**	**4491**	**4**	**808**	**79**	**4768**	**2953**	**346**	**115**	**599**
Transfers	-	-3	146	-	-27	-16	66	-259	85	-	8
Statistical Differences	-	40	-287	2	16	-61	286	-460	230	-51	30
TRANSFORMATION	-	**86**	**-**	**-**	**-**	**-**	**80**	**621**	**37**	**60**	**-**
Electricity Plants	-	10	-	-	-	-	25	197	-	-	-
CHP Plants	-	20	-	-	-	-	18	243	-	-	-
Heat Plants	-	45	-	-	-	-	37	181	-	-	-
Transfer to Gases	-	11	-	-	-	-	-	-	37	-	-
Transfer to Solids	-	-	-	-	-	-	-	-	-	60	-
Petroleum Refineries	-	-	-	-	-	-	-	-	-	-	-
Petrochemical Industry	-	-	-	-	-	-	-	-	-	-	-
Liquefaction	-	-	-	-	-	-	-	-	-	-	-
Other Transformation Sector	-	-	-	-	-	-	-	-	-	-	-
ENERGY SECTOR	-	**-**	**-**	**-**	**-**	**-**	**-**	**571**	**-**	**-**	**-**
Coal Mines	-	-	-	-	-	-	-	-	-	-	-
Oil and Gas Extraction	-	-	-	-	-	-	-	-	-	-	-
Petroleum Refineries	-	-	-	-	-	-	-	567	-	-	-
Electricity, CHP+Heat plants	-	-	-	-	-	-	-	4	-	-	-
Pumped Storage (Elec.)	-	-	-	-	-	-	-	-	-	-	-
Other Energy Sector	-	-	-	-	-	-	-	-	-	-	-
Distribution Losses	-	-	-	-	-	-	-	-	-	-	-
FINAL CONSUMPTION	-	**904**	**4350**	**6**	**797**	**2**	**5040**	**1042**	**624**	**4**	**637**
INDUSTRY SECTOR	-	**868**	**-**	**-**	**-**	**-**	**368**	**731**	**624**	**4**	**-**
Iron and Steel	-	127	-	-	-	-	25	110	-	-	-
Chemical and Petrochemical	-	510	-	-	-	-	34	88	621	-	-
of which: Feedstocks	-	*510*	-	-	-	-	-	*18*	*621*	-	-
Non-Ferrous Metals	-	15	-	-	-	-	8	5	-	-	-
Non-Metallic Minerals	-	85	-	-	-	-	23	48	-	-	-
Transport Equipment	-	-	-	-	-	-	-	17	-	-	-
Machinery	-	49	-	-	-	-	110	52	-	-	-
Mining and Quarrying	-	-	-	-	-	-	6	30	-	-	-
Food and Tobacco	-	35	-	-	-	-	34	84	-	-	-
Paper, Pulp and Print	-	35	-	-	-	-	22	252	-	4	-
Wood and Wood Products	-	-	-	-	-	-	10	28	-	-	-
Construction	-	-	-	-	-	-	-	-	-	-	-
Textile and Leather	-	12	-	-	-	-	4	17	-	-	-
Non-specified	-	-	-	-	-	-	92	-	3	-	-
TRANSPORT SECTOR	-	**1**	**4350**	**6**	**797**	**-**	**1789**	**42**	**-**	**-**	**-**
International Civil Aviation	-	-	-	-	328	-	-	-	-	-	-
Domestic Air	-	-	-	6	469	-	-	-	-	-	-
Road	-	1	4350	-	-	-	1667	-	-	-	-
Rail	-	-	-	-	-	-	36	-	-	-	-
Pipeline Transport	-	-	-	-	-	-	-	-	-	-	-
Internal Navigation	-	-	-	-	-	-	56	42	-	-	-
Non-specified	-	-	-	-	-	-	30	-	-	-	-
OTHER SECTORS	-	**35**	**-**	**-**	**-**	**2**	**2883**	**269**	**-**	**-**	**-**
Agriculture	-	-	-	-	-	-	376	24	-	-	-
Commerce and Publ. Serv.	-	35	-	-	-	-	830	111	-	-	-
Residential	-	-	-	-	-	2	1677	134	-	-	-
Non-specified	-	-	-	-	-	-	-	-	-	-	-
NON-ENERGY USE	-	**-**	**-**	**-**	**-**	**-**	**-**	**-**	**-**	**-**	**637**
in Industry/Transf./Energy	-	-	-	-	-	-	-	-	-	-	589
in Transport	-	-	-	-	-	-	-	-	-	-	48
in Other Sectors	-	-	-	-	-	-	-	-	-	-	-

Sweden / Suède : 1992

CONSUMPTION *APPROVISIONNEMENT ET DEMANDE*	Gas / *Gaz* (TJ)				Combust. Renew. & Waste / *En. Re. Comb. & Déchets* (TJ)				(GWh)	(TJ)
	Natural Gas *Gaz naturel*	Gas Works *Usines à gaz*	Coke Ovens *Cokeries*	Blast Furnaces *Hauts fourneaux*	Solid Biomass & Anim. Prod. *Biomasse solide & prod. anim.*	Gas/Liquids from Biomass *Gaz/Liquides tirés de biomasse*	Municipal Waste *Déchets urbains*	Industrial Waste *Déchets industriels*	Electricity *Electricité*	Heat *Chaleur*
Production	-	-	9819	12992	230400	517	15132	167	146444	148111
From Other Sources	-	2111	-	-	-	-	-	-	-	-
Imports	29199	-	-	-	-	-	-	-	8847	-
Exports	-	-	-	-	-	-	-	-	-11003	-
Intl. Marine Bunkers	-	-	-	-	-	-	-	-	-	-
Stock Changes	-	-	-	-	-	-	-	-	-	-
DOMESTIC SUPPLY	**29199**	**2111**	**9819**	**12992**	**230400**	**517**	**15132**	**167**	**144288**	**148111**
Transfers	-	-	-	-	-	-	-	-	-	-
Statistical Differences	-623	-	-	-	-	-	-	-	-	-
TRANSFORMATION	**13412**	**25**	**945**	**5881**	**30984**	**517**	**15132**	**-**	**8053**	**-**
Electricity Plants	-	-	125	377	-	-	-	-	-	-
CHP Plants	11312	-	670	5192	17902	69	6288	-	-	-
Heat Plants	2022	25	150	312	13082	448	8844	-	8053	-
Transfer to Gases	39	-	-	-	-	-	-	-	-	-
Transfer to Solids	-	-	-	-	-	-	-	-	-	-
Petroleum Refineries	-	-	-	-	-	-	-	-	-	-
Petrochemical Industry	-	-	-	-	-	-	-	-	-	-
Liquefaction	-	-	-	-	-	-	-	-	-	-
Other Transformation Sector	39	-	-	-	-	-	-	-	-	-
ENERGY SECTOR	**-**	**52**	**3758**	**633**	**-**	**-**	**-**	**-**	**6620**	**-**
Coal Mines	-	-	-	-	-	-	-	-	-	-
Oil and Gas Extraction	-	-	-	-	-	-	-	-	-	-
Petroleum Refineries	-	-	-	-	-	-	-	-	628	-
Electricity, CHP+Heat plants	-	-	-	-	-	-	-	-	3911	-
Pumped Storage (Elec.)	-	-	-	-	-	-	-	-	755	-
Other Energy Sector	-	52	3758	633	-	-	-	-	1326	-
Distribution Losses	-	131	548	1140	-	-	-	-	9569	13100
FINAL CONSUMPTION	**15164**	**1903**	**4568**	**5338**	**199416**	**-**	**-**	**167**	**120046**	**135011**
INDUSTRY SECTOR	**10809**	**694**	**4568**	**5338**	**159432**	**-**	**-**	**167**	**50626**	**12190**
Iron and Steel	622	-	4402	5338	-	-	-	-	4642	-
Chemical and Petrochemical	2449	-	-	-	1842	-	-	-	5631	-
of which: Feedstocks	-	-	-	-	-	-	-	-	-	-
Non-Ferrous Metals	-	-	-	-	-	-	-	-	2368	-
Non-Metallic Minerals	700	-	-	-	-	-	-	-	1253	-
Transport Equipment	-	-	-	-	-	-	-	-	2176	-
Machinery	1128	21	-	-	167	-	-	-	4207	-
Mining and Quarrying	-	-	166	-	-	-	-	-	2311	-
Food and Tobacco	4238	536	-	-	-	-	-	-	2494	-
Paper, Pulp and Print	1477	7	-	-	131214	-	-	167	18945	-
Wood and Wood Products	-	-	-	-	26209	-	-	-	1908	-
Construction	-	-	-	-	-	-	-	-	945	-
Textile and Leather	78	-	-	-	-	-	-	-	451	-
Non-specified	117	130	-	-	-	-	-	-	3295	12190
TRANSPORT SECTOR	**-**	**-**	**-**	**-**	**-**	**-**	**-**	**-**	**2472**	**-**
International Civil Aviation	-	-	-	-	-	-	-	-	-	-
Domestic Air	-	-	-	-	-	-	-	-	-	-
Road	-	-	-	-	-	-	-	-	-	-
Rail	-	-	-	-	-	-	-	-	2472	-
Pipeline Transport	-	-	-	-	-	-	-	-	-	-
Internal Navigation	-	-	-	-	-	-	-	-	-	-
Non-specified	-	-	-	-	-	-	-	-	-	-
OTHER SECTORS	**4355**	**1209**	**-**	**-**	**39984**	**-**	**-**	**-**	**66948**	**122821**
Agriculture	-	-	-	-	293	-	-	-	1163	173
Commerce and Publ. Serv.	-	299	-	-	628	-	-	-	25575	46200
Residential	2022	910	-	-	39063	-	-	-	40210	76448
Non-specified	2333	-	-	-	-	-	-	-	-	-
NON-ENERGY USE	**-**	**-**	**-**	**-**	**-**	**-**	**-**	**-**	**-**	**-**
in Industry/Transf./Energy	-	-	-	-	-	-	-	-	-	-
in Transport	-	-	-	-	-	-	-	-	-	-
in Other Sectors	-	-	-	-	-	-	-	-	-	-

Sweden / Suède : 1993

SUPPLY AND CONSUMPTION *APPROVISIONNEMENT ET DEMANDE*	Coal / *Charbon* (1000 tonnes)							Oil / *Pétrole* (1000 tonnes)			
	Coking Coal *Charbon à coke*	Steam Coal *Charbon vapeur*	Sub-Bit. Coal *Charbon sous-bit.*	Lignite *Lignite*	Peat *Tourbe*	Oven and Gas Coke *Coke de four/gaz*	Pat. Fuel and BKB *Agg./briq. de lignite*	Crude Oil *Pétrole brut*	NGL *LGN*	Feedstocks *Produits d'aliment.*	Additives *Additifs*
Production	-	4	-	-	1023	1137	-	-	-	-	-
From Other Sources	-	-	-	-	-	-	-	-	-	-	-
Imports	1526	1679	-	-	-	220	6	17752	-	529	-
Exports	-	-106	-	-	-	-37	-	-5	-	-444	-
Intl. Marine Bunkers	-	-	-	-	-	-	-	-	-	-	-
Stock Changes	-22	270	-	-	-	66	-	129	-	-2	-
DOMESTIC SUPPLY	**1504**	**1847**	**-**	**-**	**1023**	**1386**	**6**	**17876**	**-**	**83**	**-**
Transfers	-	-	-	-	-	-	-	-	-	1345	-
Statistical Differences	-	-	-	-	-	-	-	393	-	119	-
TRANSFORMATION	**1504**	**1100**	**-**	**-**	**962**	**475**	**-**	**18269**	**-**	**1547**	**-**
Electricity Plants	-	-	-	-	-	-	-	-	-	-	-
CHP Plants	-	928	-	-	562	-	-	-	-	-	-
Heat Plants	-	172	-	-	400	-	-	-	-	-	-
Transfer to Gases	-	-	-	-	-	475	-	-	-	-	-
Transfer to Solids	1504	-	-	-	-	-	-	-	-	-	-
Petroleum Refineries	-	-	-	-	-	-	-	18269	-	1547	-
Petrochemical Industry	-	-	-	-	-	-	-	-	-	-	-
Liquefaction	-	-	-	-	-	-	-	-	-	-	-
Other Transformation Sector	-	-	-	-	-	-	-	-	-	-	-
ENERGY SECTOR	**-**	**-**	**-**	**-**	**-**	**-**	**-**	**-**	**-**	**-**	**-**
Coal Mines	-	-	-	-	-	-	-	-	-	-	-
Oil and Gas Extraction	-	-	-	-	-	-	-	-	-	-	-
Petroleum Refineries	-	-	-	-	-	-	-	-	-	-	-
Electricity, CHP+Heat plants	-	-	-	-	-	-	-	-	-	-	-
Pumped Storage (Elec.)	-	-	-	-	-	-	-	-	-	-	-
Other Energy Sector	-	-	-	-	-	-	-	-	-	-	-
Distribution Losses	-	-	-	-	-	-	-	-	-	-	-
FINAL CONSUMPTION	**-**	**747**	**-**	**-**	**61**	**911**	**6**	**-**	**-**	**-**	**-**
INDUSTRY SECTOR	**-**	**731**	**-**	**-**	**61**	**881**	**6**	**-**	**-**	**-**	**-**
Iron and Steel	-	165	-	-	-	815	-	-	-	-	-
Chemical and Petrochemical	-	8	-	-	28	7	-	-	-	-	-
of which: Feedstocks	-	-	-	-	-	-	-	-	-	-	-
Non-Ferrous Metals	-	77	-	-	-	17	-	-	-	-	-
Non-Metallic Minerals	-	298	-	-	-	27	-	-	-	-	-
Transport Equipment	-	-	-	-	-	11	-	-	-	-	-
Machinery	-	2	-	-	-	1	-	-	-	-	-
Mining and Quarrying	-	77	-	-	-	-	-	-	-	-	-
Food and Tobacco	-	17	-	-	-	3	-	-	-	-	-
Paper, Pulp and Print	-	84	-	-	33	-	-	-	-	-	-
Wood and Wood Products	-	3	-	-	-	-	-	-	-	-	-
Construction	-	-	-	-	-	-	-	-	-	-	-
Textile and Leather	-	-	-	-	-	-	-	-	-	-	-
Non-specified	-	-	-	-	-	-	6	-	-	-	-
TRANSPORT SECTOR	**-**	**-**	**-**	**-**	**-**	**-**	**-**	**-**	**-**	**-**	**-**
International Civil Aviation	-	-	-	-	-	-	-	-	-	-	-
Domestic Air	-	-	-	-	-	-	-	-	-	-	-
Road	-	-	-	-	-	-	-	-	-	-	-
Rail	-	-	-	-	-	-	-	-	-	-	-
Pipeline Transport	-	-	-	-	-	-	-	-	-	-	-
Internal Navigation	-	-	-	-	-	-	-	-	-	-	-
Non-specified	-	-	-	-	-	-	-	-	-	-	-
OTHER SECTORS	**-**	**16**	**-**	**-**	**-**	**2**	**-**	**-**	**-**	**-**	**-**
Agriculture	-	15	-	-	-	2	-	-	-	-	-
Commerce and Publ. Serv.	-	1	-	-	-	-	-	-	-	-	-
Residential	-	-	-	-	-	-	-	-	-	-	-
Non-specified	-	-	-	-	-	-	-	-	-	-	-
NON-ENERGY USE	**-**	**-**	**-**	**-**	**-**	**28**	**-**	**-**	**-**	**-**	**-**
in Industry/Transf./Energy	-	-	-	-	-	28	-	-	-	-	-
in Transport	-	-	-	-	-	-	-	-	-	-	-
in Other Sectors	-	-	-	-	-	-	-	-	-	-	-

Sweden / Suède : 1993

SUPPLY AND CONSUMPTION / APPROVISIONNEMENT ET DEMANDE	Oil cont. / *Pétrole cont.* (1000 tonnes)										
	Refinery Gas / *Gaz de raffinerie*	LPG + Ethane / *GPL + éthane*	Motor Gasoline / *Essence moteur*	Aviation Gasoline / *Essence aviation*	Jet Fuel / *Carbu-réacteur*	Kerosene / *Kérosène*	Gas/Diesel / *Gazole*	Heavy Fuel Oil / *Fioul lourd*	Naphtha / *Naphta*	Pétrol. Coke / *Coke de pétrole*	Other Prod. / *Autres prod.*
Production	-	298	4361	-	77	2	6875	5975	10	-	1130
From Other Sources	-	-	-	-	-	-	-	-	-	-	-
Imports	-	714	1520	7	731	1146	1088	952	310	55	361
Exports	-	-105	-1529	-	-3	-4	-3903	-3239	-8	-1	-831
Intl. Marine Bunkers	-	-	-	-	-	-	-172	-753	-	-	-
Stock Changes	-	32	-140	1	-21	-	-45	4	28	26	-
DOMESTIC SUPPLY	-	**939**	**4212**	**8**	**784**	**1144**	**3843**	**2939**	**340**	**80**	**660**
Transfers	-	13	32	-	9	-1140	1255	-154	-15	-	-
Statistical Differences	-	-68	-125	-2	15	-2	-83	-256	207	28	58
TRANSFORMATION	-	**67**	-	-	-	-	**88**	**745**	**40**	**104**	-
Electricity Plants	-	-	-	-	-	-	23	198	-	-	-
CHP Plants	-	18	-	-	-	-	26	373	-	-	-
Heat Plants	-	45	-	-	-	-	39	174	-	-	-
Transfer to Gases	-	4	-	-	-	-	-	-	40	-	-
Transfer to Solids	-	-	-	-	-	-	-	-	-	104	-
Petroleum Refineries	-	-	-	-	-	-	-	-	-	-	-
Petrochemical Industry	-	-	-	-	-	-	-	-	-	-	-
Liquefaction	-	-	-	-	-	-	-	-	-	-	-
Other Transformation Sector	-	-	-	-	-	-	-	-	-	-	-
ENERGY SECTOR	-	-	-	-	-	-	**2**	**552**	-	-	-
Coal Mines	-	-	-	-	-	-	-	-	-	-	-
Oil and Gas Extraction	-	-	-	-	-	-	-	-	-	-	-
Petroleum Refineries	-	-	-	-	-	-	2	550	-	-	-
Electricity, CHP+Heat plants	-	-	-	-	-	-	-	2	-	-	-
Pumped Storage (Elec.)	-	-	-	-	-	-	-	-	-	-	-
Other Energy Sector	-	-	-	-	-	-	-	-	-	-	-
Distribution Losses	-	-	-	-	-	-	-	-	-	-	-
FINAL CONSUMPTION	-	**817**	**4119**	**6**	**808**	**2**	**4925**	**1232**	**492**	**4**	**718**
INDUSTRY SECTOR	-	**794**	-	-	-	-	**383**	**906**	**492**	**4**	-
Iron and Steel	-	114	-	-	-	-	25	126	-	-	-
Chemical and Petrochemical	-	474	-	-	-	-	36	118	492	-	-
of which: Feedstocks	-	*474*	-	-	-	-	-	*26*	*492*	-	-
Non-Ferrous Metals	-	15	-	-	-	-	8	9	-	-	-
Non-Metallic Minerals	-	68	-	-	-	-	26	62	-	-	-
Transport Equipment	-	-	-	-	-	-	-	21	-	-	-
Machinery	-	40	-	-	-	-	107	65	-	-	-
Mining and Quarrying	-	-	-	-	-	-	8	31	-	-	-
Food and Tobacco	-	35	-	-	-	-	36	96	-	-	-
Paper, Pulp and Print	-	32	-	-	-	-	20	332	-	-	-
Wood and Wood Products	-	-	-	-	-	-	12	27	-	4	-
Construction	-	-	-	-	-	-	-	-	-	-	-
Textile and Leather	-	16	-	-	-	-	5	19	-	-	-
Non-specified	-	-	-	-	-	-	100	-	-	-	-
TRANSPORT SECTOR	-	-	**4119**	**6**	**808**	-	**1891**	**26**	-	-	-
International Civil Aviation	-	-	-	-	412	-	-	-	-	-	-
Domestic Air	-	-	-	6	396	-	-	-	-	-	-
Road	-	-	4119	-	-	-	1811	-	-	-	-
Rail	-	-	-	-	-	-	35	1	-	-	-
Pipeline Transport	-	-	-	-	-	-	-	-	-	-	-
Internal Navigation	-	-	-	-	-	-	45	25	-	-	-
Non-specified	-	-	-	-	-	-	-	-	-	-	-
OTHER SECTORS	-	**23**	-	-	-	**2**	**2651**	**300**	-	-	-
Agriculture	-	-	-	-	-	-	333	24	-	-	-
Commerce and Publ. Serv.	-	21	-	-	-	-	773	141	-	-	-
Residential	-	2	-	-	-	2	1545	130	-	-	-
Non-specified	-	-	-	-	-	-	-	5	-	-	-
NON-ENERGY USE	-	-	-	-	-	-	-	-	-	-	**718**
in Industry/Transf./Energy	-	-	-	-	-	-	-	-	-	-	661
in Transport	-	-	-	-	-	-	-	-	-	-	57

Sweden / Suède : 1993

CONSUMPTION / APPROVISIONNEMENT ET DEMANDE	Gas / Gaz (TJ)				Combust. Renew. & Waste / En. Re. Comb. & Déchets (TJ)				(GWh)	(TJ)
	Natural Gas / Gaz naturel	Gas Works / Usines à gaz	Coke Ovens / Cokeries	Blast Furnaces / Hauts fourneaux	Solid Biomass & Anim. Prod. / Biomasse solide & prod. anim.	Gas/Liquids from Biomass / Gaz/Liquides tirés de biomasse	Municipal Waste / Déchets urbains	Industrial Waste / Déchets industriels	Electricity / Electricité	Heat / Chaleur
Production	-	-	9782	13345	243673	914	15545	42	145975	157944
From Other Sources	-	2083	-	-	-	-	-	-	-	-
Imports	32620	-	-	-	-	-	-	-	7977	-
Exports	-	-	-	-	-	-	-	-	-8566	-
Intl. Marine Bunkers	-	-	-	-	-	-	-	-	-	-
Stock Changes	-	-	-	-	-	-	-	-	-	-
DOMESTIC SUPPLY	**32620**	**2083**	**9782**	**13345**	**243673**	**914**	**15545**	**42**	**145386**	**157944**
Transfers	-	-	-	-	-	-	-	-	-	-
Statistical Differences	-1228	-	-	-	-	-	-	-	-	-
TRANSFORMATION	**15009**	**25**	**1098**	**5074**	**38540**	**853**	**15545**	**-**	**7573**	**-**
Electricity Plants	-	-	74	270	-	-	-	-	-	-
CHP Plants	13220	-	847	4539	20954	133	6485	-	-	-
Heat Plants	1594	25	177	265	17586	720	9060	-	7573	-
Transfer to Gases	117	-	-	-	-	-	-	-	-	-
Transfer to Solids	-	-	-	-	-	-	-	-	-	-
Petroleum Refineries	-	-	-	-	-	-	-	-	-	-
Petrochemical Industry	-	-	-	-	-	-	-	-	-	-
Liquefaction	-	-	-	-	-	-	-	-	-	-
Other Transformation Sector	78	-	-	-	-	-	-	-	-	-
ENERGY SECTOR	**-**	**51**	**3814**	**636**	**-**	**-**	**-**	**-**	**6676**	**-**
Coal Mines	-	-	-	-	-	-	-	-	-	-
Oil and Gas Extraction	-	-	-	-	-	-	-	-	-	-
Petroleum Refineries	-	-	-	-	-	-	-	-	641	-
Electricity, CHP+Heat plants	-	-	-	-	-	-	-	-	3487	-
Pumped Storage (Elec.)	-	-	-	-	-	-	-	-	1114	-
Other Energy Sector	-	51	3814	636	-	-	-	-	1434	-
Distribution Losses	-	182	338	2078	-	-	-	-	10219	10683
FINAL CONSUMPTION	**16383**	**1825**	**4532**	**5557**	**205133**	**61**	**-**	**42**	**120918**	**147261**
INDUSTRY SECTOR	**11212**	**598**	**4532**	**5557**	**163977**	**61**	**-**	**42**	**49621**	**13694**
Iron and Steel	675	-	4385	5557	-	-	-	-	4662	-
Chemical and Petrochemical	2333	-	-	-	1382	-	-	-	5732	-
of which: Feedstocks	-	-	-	-	-	-	-	-	-	-
Non-Ferrous Metals	-	-	-	-	-	-	-	-	2518	-
Non-Metallic Minerals	583	-	-	-	-	-	-	-	1096	-
Transport Equipment	-	-	-	-	-	-	-	-	2004	-
Machinery	1011	25	-	-	167	-	-	-	3979	-
Mining and Quarrying	-	-	147	-	-	-	-	-	2243	-
Food and Tobacco	4743	452	-	-	22	61	-	-	2444	-
Paper, Pulp and Print	1672	-	-	-	136197	-	-	42	19199	-
Wood and Wood Products	-	-	-	-	26209	-	-	-	2064	-
Construction	-	-	-	-	-	-	-	-	817	-
Textile and Leather	117	-	-	-	-	-	-	-	391	-
Non-specified	78	121	-	-	-	-	-	-	2472	13694
TRANSPORT SECTOR	**-**	**-**	**-**	**-**	**-**	**-**	**-**	**-**	**2337**	**-**
International Civil Aviation	-	-	-	-	-	-	-	-	-	-
Domestic Air	-	-	-	-	-	-	-	-	-	-
Road	-	-	-	-	-	-	-	-	-	-
Rail	-	-	-	-	-	-	-	-	2337	-
Pipeline Transport	-	-	-	-	-	-	-	-	-	-
Internal Navigation	-	-	-	-	-	-	-	-	-	-
Non-specified	-	-	-	-	-	-	-	-	-	-
OTHER SECTORS	**5171**	**1227**	**-**	**-**	**41156**	**-**	**-**	**-**	**68960**	**133567**
Agriculture	-	-	-	-	293	-	-	-	1280	180
Commerce and Publ. Serv.	-	283	-	-	586	-	-	-	26147	50619
Residential	2372	944	-	-	40277	-	-	-	41533	82768
Non-specified	2799	-	-	-	-	-	-	-	-	-
NON-ENERGY USE	**-**	**-**	**-**	**-**	**-**	**-**	**-**	**-**	**-**	**-**
in Industry/Transf./Energy	-	-	-	-	-	-	-	-	-	-
in Transport	-	-	-	-	-	-	-	-	-	-
in Other Sectors	-	-	-	-	-	-	-	-	-	-

Switzerland / Suisse : 1992

SUPPLY AND CONSUMPTION	Coal / Charbon (1000 tonnes)							Oil / Pétrole (1000 tonnes)			
	Coking Coal	Steam Coal	Sub-Bit. Coal	Lignite	Peat	Oven and Gas Coke	Pat. Fuel and BKB	Crude Oil	NGL	Feedstocks	Additives
APPROVISIONNEMENT ET DEMANDE	Charbon à coke	Charbon vapeur	Charbon sous-bit.	Lignite	Tourbe	Coke de four/gaz	Agg./briq. de lignite	Pétrole brut	LGN	Produits d'aliment.	Additifs
Production	-	-	-	-	-	-	-	-	-	-	-
From Other Sources	-	-	-	-	-	-	-	-	-	-	-
Imports	-	148	-	-	-	33	18	4124	-	105	88
Exports	-	-3	-	-	-	-	-	-	-	-	-
Intl. Marine Bunkers	-	-	-	-	-	-	-	-	-	-	-
Stock Changes	-	121	-	-	-	4	-1	-14	-	-12	2
DOMESTIC SUPPLY	-	**266**	-	-	-	**37**	**17**	**4110**	-	**93**	**90**
Transfers	-	-	-	-	-	-	-	-	-	-	-
Statistical Differences	-	-	-	-	-	-	-	-	-	-	-
TRANSFORMATION	-	**4**	-	-	-	-	-	**4110**	-	**93**	**90**
Electricity Plants	-	-	-	-	-	-	-	-	-	-	-
CHP Plants	-	4	-	-	-	-	-	-	-	-	-
Heat Plants	-	-	-	-	-	-	-	-	-	-	-
Transfer to Gases	-	-	-	-	-	-	-	-	-	-	-
Transfer to Solids	-	-	-	-	-	-	-	-	-	-	-
Petroleum Refineries	-	-	-	-	-	-	-	4110	-	93	90
Petrochemical Industry	-	-	-	-	-	-	-	-	-	-	-
Liquefaction	-	-	-	-	-	-	-	-	-	-	-
Other Transformation Sector	-	-	-	-	-	-	-	-	-	-	-
ENERGY SECTOR	-	-	-	-	-	-	-	-	-	-	-
Coal Mines	-	-	-	-	-	-	-	-	-	-	-
Oil and Gas Extraction	-	-	-	-	-	-	-	-	-	-	-
Petroleum Refineries	-	-	-	-	-	-	-	-	-	-	-
Electricity, CHP+Heat plants	-	-	-	-	-	-	-	-	-	-	-
Pumped Storage (Elec.)	-	-	-	-	-	-	-	-	-	-	-
Other Energy Sector	-	-	-	-	-	-	-	-	-	-	-
Distribution Losses	-	-	-	-	-	-	-	-	-	-	-
FINAL CONSUMPTION	-	**262**	-	-	-	**37**	**17**	-	-	-	-
INDUSTRY SECTOR	-	**256**	-	-	-	**30**	-	-	-	-	-
Iron and Steel	-	-	-	-	-	-	-	-	-	-	-
Chemical and Petrochemical	-	-	-	-	-	-	-	-	-	-	-
of which: Feedstocks	-	-	-	-	-	-	-	-	-	-	-
Non-Ferrous Metals	-	-	-	-	-	-	-	-	-	-	-
Non-Metallic Minerals	-	247	-	-	-	7	-	-	-	-	-
Transport Equipment	-	-	-	-	-	-	-	-	-	-	-
Machinery	-	1	-	-	-	13	-	-	-	-	-
Mining and Quarrying	-	-	-	-	-	-	-	-	-	-	-
Food and Tobacco	-	3	-	-	-	3	-	-	-	-	-
Paper, Pulp and Print	-	4	-	-	-	-	-	-	-	-	-
Wood and Wood Products	-	-	-	-	-	-	-	-	-	-	-
Construction	-	-	-	-	-	7	-	-	-	-	-
Textile and Leather	-	-	-	-	-	-	-	-	-	-	-
Non-specified	-	1	-	-	-	-	-	-	-	-	-
TRANSPORT SECTOR	-	-	-	-	-	-	-	-	-	-	-
International Civil Aviation	-	-	-	-	-	-	-	-	-	-	-
Domestic Air	-	-	-	-	-	-	-	-	-	-	-
Road	-	-	-	-	-	-	-	-	-	-	-
Rail	-	-	-	-	-	-	-	-	-	-	-
Pipeline Transport	-	-	-	-	-	-	-	-	-	-	-
Internal Navigation	-	-	-	-	-	-	-	-	-	-	-
Non-specified	-	-	-	-	-	-	-	-	-	-	-
OTHER SECTORS	-	**3**	-	-	-	**6**	**17**	-	-	-	-
Agriculture	-	-	-	-	-	-	-	-	-	-	-
Commerce and Publ. Serv.	-	1	-	-	-	-	-	-	-	-	-
Residential	-	2	-	-	-	6	17	-	-	-	-
Non-specified	-	-	-	-	-	-	-	-	-	-	-
NON-ENERGY USE	-	**3**	-	-	-	**1**	-	-	-	-	-
in Industry/Transf./Energy	-	3	-	-	-	1	-	-	-	-	-
in Transport	-	-	-	-	-	-	-	-	-	-	-
in Other Sectors	-	-	-	-	-	-	-	-	-	-	-

Switzerland / Suisse : 1992

SUPPLY AND CONSUMPTION *APPROVISIONNEMENT ET DEMANDE*	Oil cont. / *Pétrole cont.* (1000 tonnes)										
	Refinery Gas *Gaz de raffinerie*	LPG + Ethane *GPL + éthane*	Motor Gasoline *Essence moteur*	Aviation Gasoline *Essence aviation*	Jet Fuel *Carbu-réacteur*	Kerosene *Kérosène*	Gas/ Diesel *Gazole*	Heavy Fuel Oil *Fioul lourd*	Naphtha *Naphta*	Pétrol. Coke *Coke de pétrole*	Other Prod. *Autres prod.*
Production	147	169	988	-	243	2	1706	860	6	-	142
From Other Sources	-	-	-	-	-	-	-	-	-	-	-
Imports	-	34	2925	5	950	18	4808	29	44	49	250
Exports	-	-31	-12	-	-	-	-12	-402	-	-1	-12
Intl. Marine Bunkers	-	-	-	-	-	-	-17	-	-	-	-
Stock Changes	-	1	83	-	-58	-	183	-17	-6	-	-1
DOMESTIC SUPPLY	**147**	**173**	**3984**	**5**	**1135**	**20**	**6668**	**470**	**44**	**48**	**379**
Transfers	-	-	10	-	-	-11	11	-	-10	-	-
Statistical Differences	-	-12	4	-	2	-	350	117	2	7	2
TRANSFORMATION	**-**	**5**	**-**	**-**	**-**	**-**	**58**	**140**	**-**	**-**	**-**
Electricity Plants	-	-	-	-	-	-	-	-	-	-	-
CHP Plants	-	-	-	-	-	-	58	140	-	-	-
Heat Plants	-	-	-	-	-	-	-	-	-	-	-
Transfer to Gases	-	5	-	-	-	-	-	-	-	-	-
Transfer to Solids	-	-	-	-	-	-	-	-	-	-	-
Petroleum Refineries	-	-	-	-	-	-	-	-	-	-	-
Petrochemical Industry	-	-	-	-	-	-	-	-	-	-	-
Liquefaction	-	-	-	-	-	-	-	-	-	-	-
Other Transformation Sector	-	-	-	-	-	-	-	-	-	-	-
ENERGY SECTOR	**147**	**-**	**-**	**-**	**-**	**-**	**-**	**24**	**-**	**-**	**-**
Coal Mines	-	-	-	-	-	-	-	-	-	-	-
Oil and Gas Extraction	-	-	-	-	-	-	-	-	-	-	-
Petroleum Refineries	147	-	-	-	-	-	-	24	-	-	-
Electricity, CHP+Heat plants	-	-	-	-	-	-	-	-	-	-	-
Pumped Storage (Elec.)	-	-	-	-	-	-	-	-	-	-	-
Other Energy Sector	-	-	-	-	-	-	-	-	-	-	-
Distribution Losses	-	-	-	-	-	-	-	-	-	-	-
FINAL CONSUMPTION	**-**	**156**	**3998**	**5**	**1137**	**9**	**6971**	**423**	**36**	**55**	**381**
INDUSTRY SECTOR	**-**	**77**	**4**	**-**	**-**	**4**	**397**	**423**	**36**	**18**	**-**
Iron and Steel	-	-	-	-	-	-	-	-	-	-	-
Chemical and Petrochemical	-	77	-	-	-	-	81	22	36	-	-
of which: Feedstocks	-	69	-	-	-	-	-	-	36	-	-
Non-Ferrous Metals	-	-	-	-	-	-	11	-	-	-	-
Non-Metallic Minerals	-	-	-	-	-	-	7	38	-	-	-
Transport Equipment	-	-	-	-	-	-	-	-	-	-	-
Machinery	-	-	-	-	-	-	129	27	-	-	-
Mining and Quarrying	-	-	-	-	-	-	63	84	-	18	-
Food and Tobacco	-	-	-	-	-	-	34	20	-	-	-
Paper, Pulp and Print	-	-	-	-	-	-	25	93	-	-	-
Wood and Wood Products	-	-	-	-	-	-	-	-	-	-	-
Construction	-	-	4	-	-	-	30	11	-	-	-
Textile and Leather	-	-	-	-	-	-	9	3	-	-	-
Non-specified	-	-	-	-	-	4	8	125	-	-	-
TRANSPORT SECTOR	**-**	**3**	**3975**	**5**	**1137**	**3**	**867**	**-**	**-**	**-**	**-**
International Civil Aviation	-	-	-	-	1012	-	-	-	-	-	-
Domestic Air	-	-	-	5	125	-	-	-	-	-	-
Road	-	3	3974	-	-	3	852	-	-	-	-
Rail	-	-	-	-	-	-	9	-	-	-	-
Pipeline Transport	-	-	-	-	-	-	-	-	-	-	-
Internal Navigation	-	-	1	-	-	-	6	-	-	-	-
Non-specified	-	-	-	-	-	-	-	-	-	-	-
OTHER SECTORS	**-**	**76**	**19**	**-**	**-**	**2**	**5707**	**-**	**-**	**-**	**-**
Agriculture	-	-	19	-	-	-	86	-	-	-	-
Commerce and Publ. Serv.	-	-	-	-	-	-	1941	-	-	-	-
Residential	-	-	-	-	-	2	3680	-	-	-	-
Non-specified	-	76	-	-	-	-	-	-	-	-	-
NON-ENERGY USE	**-**	**-**	**-**	**-**	**-**	**-**	**-**	**-**	**-**	**37**	**381**
in Industry/Transf./Energy	-	-	-	-	-	-	-	-	-	37	346
in Transport	-	-	-	-	-	-	-	-	-	-	35
in Other Sectors	-	-	-	-	-	-	-	-	-	-	-

Switzerland / Suisse : 1992

CONSUMPTION APPROVISIONNEMENT ET DEMANDE	Gas / Gaz (TJ)				Combust. Renew. & Waste / En. Re. Comb. & Déchets (TJ)				(GWh)	(TJ)
	Natural Gas Gaz naturel	Gas Works Usines à gaz	Coke Ovens Cokeries	Blast Furnaces Hauts fourneaux	Solid Biomass & Anim. Prod. Biomasse solide & prod. anim.	Gas/Liquids from Biomass Gaz/Liquides tirés de biomasse	Municipal Waste Déchets urbains	Industrial Waste Déchets industriels	Electricity Electricité	Heat Chaleur
Production	110	-	-	-	12130	-	16270	8370	59117	13070
From Other Sources	-	230	-	-	-	-	-	-	-	-
Imports	89460	-	-	-	590	-	-	-	19571	-
Exports	-	-	-	-	-	-	-	-	-23860	-
Intl. Marine Bunkers	-	-	-	-	-	-	-	-	-	-
Stock Changes	-	-	-	-	-	-	-	-	-	-
DOMESTIC SUPPLY	**89570**	**230**	**-**	**-**	**12720**	**-**	**16270**	**8370**	**54828**	**13070**
Transfers	-	-	-	-	-	-	-	-	-	-
Statistical Differences	-	-	-	-	-	-	-	-	-	-
TRANSFORMATION	**5190**	**-**	**-**	**-**	**-**	**-**	**16270**	**-**	**-**	**-**
Electricity Plants	-	-	-	-	-	-	-	-	-	-
CHP Plants	5190	-	-	-	-	-	16270	-	-	-
Heat Plants	-	-	-	-	-	-	-	-	-	-
Transfer to Gases	-	-	-	-	-	-	-	-	-	-
Transfer to Solids	-	-	-	-	-	-	-	-	-	-
Petroleum Refineries	-	-	-	-	-	-	-	-	-	-
Petrochemical Industry	-	-	-	-	-	-	-	-	-	-
Liquefaction	-	-	-	-	-	-	-	-	-	-
Other Transformation Sector	-	-	-	-	-	-	-	-	-	-
ENERGY SECTOR	**-**	**-**	**-**	**-**	**-**	**-**	**-**	**-**	**3207**	**-**
Coal Mines	-	-	-	-	-	-	-	-	-	-
Oil and Gas Extraction	-	-	-	-	-	-	-	-	-	-
Petroleum Refineries	-	-	-	-	-	-	-	-	-	-
Electricity, CHP+Heat plants	-	-	-	-	-	-	-	-	1769	-
Pumped Storage (Elec.)	-	-	-	-	-	-	-	-	1438	-
Other Energy Sector	-	-	-	-	-	-	-	-	-	-
Distribution Losses	630	10	-	-	-	-	-	-	3755	1100
FINAL CONSUMPTION	**83750**	**220**	**-**	**-**	**12720**	**-**	**-**	**8370**	**47866**	**11970**
INDUSTRY SECTOR	**33230**	**110**	**-**	**-**	**2890**	**-**	**-**	**8370**	**14845**	**2280**
Iron and Steel	-	-	-	-	-	-	-	-	-	-
Chemical and Petrochemical	8794	-	-	-	-	-	-	2780	2173	244
of which: Feedstocks	-	-	-	-	-	-	-	-	-	-
Non-Ferrous Metals	1405	-	-	-	-	-	-	20	1143	-
Non-Metallic Minerals	2050	-	-	-	-	-	-	330	519	-
Transport Equipment	-	-	-	-	-	-	-	-	-	-
Machinery	6170	-	-	-	-	-	-	110	3179	520
Mining and Quarrying	-	-	-	-	-	-	-	-	-	-
Food and Tobacco	1711	-	-	-	-	-	-	170	430	18
Paper, Pulp and Print	5334	-	-	-	-	-	-	2140	1557	1270
Wood and Wood Products	-	-	-	-	2890	-	-	-	-	-
Construction	114	-	-	-	-	-	-	10	78	15
Textile and Leather	1734	-	-	-	-	-	-	120	719	59
Non-specified	5918	110	-	-	-	-	-	2690	5047	154
TRANSPORT SECTOR	**-**	**-**	**-**	**-**	**-**	**-**	**-**	**-**	**2532**	**-**
International Civil Aviation	-	-	-	-	-	-	-	-	-	-
Domestic Air	-	-	-	-	-	-	-	-	-	-
Road	-	-	-	-	-	-	-	-	-	-
Rail	-	-	-	-	-	-	-	-	2532	-
Pipeline Transport	-	-	-	-	-	-	-	-	-	-
Internal Navigation	-	-	-	-	-	-	-	-	-	-
Non-specified	-	-	-	-	-	-	-	-	-	-
OTHER SECTORS	**50520**	**110**	**-**	**-**	**9830**	**-**	**-**	**-**	**30489**	**9690**
Agriculture	611	-	-	-	880	-	-	-	933	-
Commerce and Publ. Serv.	15879	-	-	-	350	-	-	-	15388	4590
Residential	34030	60	-	-	8600	-	-	-	14168	5100
Non-specified	-	50	-	-	-	-	-	-	-	-
NON-ENERGY USE	**-**	**-**	**-**	**-**	**-**	**-**	**-**	**-**	**-**	**-**
in Industry/Transf./Energy	-	-	-	-	-	-	-	-	-	-
in Transport	-	-	-	-	-	-	-	-	-	-
in Other Sectors	-	-	-	-	-	-	-	-	-	-

Switzerland / Suisse : 1993

SUPPLY AND CONSUMPTION / APPROVISIONNEMENT ET DEMANDE	Coal / Charbon (1000 tonnes)							Oil / Pétrole (1000 tonnes)			
	Coking Coal / Charbon à coke	Steam Coal / Charbon vapeur	Sub-Bit. Coal / Charbon sous-bit.	Lignite / Lignite	Peat / Tourbe	Oven and Gas Coke / Coke de four/gaz	Pat. Fuel and BKB / Agg./briq. de lignite	Crude Oil / Pétrole brut	NGL / LGN	Feedstocks / Produits d'aliment.	Additives / Additifs
Production	-	-	-	-	-	-	-	-	-	-	-
From Other Sources	-	-	-	-	-	-	-	-	-	-	-
Imports	-	125	-	-	-	23	15	4499	-	213	52
Exports	-	-	-	-	-	-	-	-	-	-	-
Intl. Marine Bunkers	-	-	-	-	-	-	-	-	-	-	-
Stock Changes	-	95	-	-	-	11	-	25	-	-7	2
DOMESTIC SUPPLY	-	220	-	-	-	34	15	4524	-	206	54
Transfers	-	-	-	-	-	-	-	-	-	-	-
Statistical Differences	-	-	-	-	-	-	-	-	-	-	-
TRANSFORMATION	-	2	-	-	-	-	-	4524	-	206	54
Electricity Plants	-	-	-	-	-	-	-	-	-	-	-
CHP Plants	-	2	-	-	-	-	-	-	-	-	-
Heat Plants	-	-	-	-	-	-	-	-	-	-	-
Transfer to Gases	-	-	-	-	-	-	-	-	-	-	-
Transfer to Solids	-	-	-	-	-	-	-	-	-	-	-
Petroleum Refineries	-	-	-	-	-	-	-	4524	-	206	54
Petrochemical Industry	-	-	-	-	-	-	-	-	-	-	-
Liquefaction	-	-	-	-	-	-	-	-	-	-	-
Other Transformation Sector	-	-	-	-	-	-	-	-	-	-	-
ENERGY SECTOR	-	-	-	-	-	-	-	-	-	-	-
Coal Mines	-	-	-	-	-	-	-	-	-	-	-
Oil and Gas Extraction	-	-	-	-	-	-	-	-	-	-	-
Petroleum Refineries	-	-	-	-	-	-	-	-	-	-	-
Electricity, CHP+Heat plants	-	-	-	-	-	-	-	-	-	-	-
Pumped Storage (Elec.)	-	-	-	-	-	-	-	-	-	-	-
Other Energy Sector	-	-	-	-	-	-	-	-	-	-	-
Distribution Losses	-	-	-	-	-	-	-	-	-	-	-
FINAL CONSUMPTION	-	218	-	-	-	34	15	-	-	-	-
INDUSTRY SECTOR	-	210	-	-	-	30	-	-	-	-	-
Iron and Steel	-	-	-	-	-	-	-	-	-	-	-
Chemical and Petrochemical	-	-	-	-	-	-	-	-	-	-	-
of which: Feedstocks	-	-	-	-	-	-	-	-	-	-	-
Non-Ferrous Metals	-	-	-	-	-	-	-	-	-	-	-
Non-Metallic Minerals	-	209	-	-	-	9	-	-	-	-	-
Transport Equipment	-	-	-	-	-	-	-	-	-	-	-
Machinery	-	-	-	-	-	12	-	-	-	-	-
Mining and Quarrying	-	-	-	-	-	-	-	-	-	-	-
Food and Tobacco	-	-	-	-	-	3	-	-	-	-	-
Paper, Pulp and Print	-	-	-	-	-	-	-	-	-	-	-
Wood and Wood Products	-	-	-	-	-	-	-	-	-	-	-
Construction	-	-	-	-	-	6	-	-	-	-	-
Textile and Leather	-	-	-	-	-	-	-	-	-	-	-
Non-specified	-	1	-	-	-	-	-	-	-	-	-
TRANSPORT SECTOR	-	-	-	-	-	-	-	-	-	-	-
International Civil Aviation	-	-	-	-	-	-	-	-	-	-	-
Domestic Air	-	-	-	-	-	-	-	-	-	-	-
Road	-	-	-	-	-	-	-	-	-	-	-
Rail	-	-	-	-	-	-	-	-	-	-	-
Pipeline Transport	-	-	-	-	-	-	-	-	-	-	-
Internal Navigation	-	-	-	-	-	-	-	-	-	-	-
Non-specified	-	-	-	-	-	-	-	-	-	-	-
OTHER SECTORS	-	4	-	-	-	4	15	-	-	-	-
Agriculture	-	-	-	-	-	-	-	-	-	-	-
Commerce and Publ. Serv.	-	1	-	-	-	-	-	-	-	-	-
Residential	-	3	-	-	-	4	15	-	-	-	-
Non-specified	-	-	-	-	-	-	-	-	-	-	-
NON-ENERGY USE	-	4	-	-	-	-	-	-	-	-	-
in Industry/Transf./Energy	-	4	-	-	-	-	-	-	-	-	-
in Transport	-	-	-	-	-	-	-	-	-	-	-
in Other Sectors	-	-	-	-	-	-	-	-	-	-	-

Switzerland / Suisse : 1993

SUPPLY AND CONSUMPTION *APPROVISIONNEMENT ET DEMANDE*	Oil cont. / *Pétrole cont.* (1000 tonnes)										
	Refinery Gas *Gaz de raffinerie*	LPG + Ethane *GPL + éthane*	Motor Gasoline *Essence moteur*	Aviation Gasoline *Essence aviation*	Jet Fuel *Carbu-réacteur*	Kerosene *Kérosène*	Gas/ Diesel *Gazole*	Heavy Fuel Oil *Fioul lourd*	Naphtha *Naphta*	Pétrol. Coke *Coke de pétrole*	Other Prod. *Autres prod.*
Production	170	190	1084	-	281	2	2001	892	-	-	126
From Other Sources	-	-	-	-	-	-	-	-	-	-	-
Imports	-	27	2627	4	890	16	3689	15	28	61	236
Exports	-	-38	-1	-	-	-	-12	-562	-	-	-7
Intl. Marine Bunkers	-	-	-	-	-	-	-17	-	-	-	-
Stock Changes	-	-	8	-	3	-	677	17	-	-	5
DOMESTIC SUPPLY	170	179	3718	4	1174	18	6338	362	28	61	360
Transfers	-	-	-	-	-	-12	-	12	-	-	-
Statistical Differences	-	-	-13	-	3	-	541	43	-	-	-
TRANSFORMATION	-	5	-	-	-	-	38	42	-	-	-
Electricity Plants	-	-	-	-	-	-	-	-	-	-	-
CHP Plants	-	-	-	-	-	-	38	42	-	-	-
Heat Plants	-	-	-	-	-	-	-	-	-	-	-
Transfer to Gases	-	5	-	-	-	-	-	-	-	-	-
Transfer to Solids	-	-	-	-	-	-	-	-	-	-	-
Petroleum Refineries	-	-	-	-	-	-	-	-	-	-	-
Petrochemical Industry	-	-	-	-	-	-	-	-	-	-	-
Liquefaction	-	-	-	-	-	-	-	-	-	-	-
Other Transformation Sector	-	-	-	-	-	-	-	-	-	-	-
ENERGY SECTOR	170	-	-	-	-	-	-	26	-	-	-
Coal Mines	-	-	-	-	-	-	-	-	-	-	-
Oil and Gas Extraction	-	-	-	-	-	-	-	-	-	-	-
Petroleum Refineries	170	-	-	-	-	-	-	26	-	-	-
Electricity, CHP+Heat plants	-	-	-	-	-	-	-	-	-	-	-
Pumped Storage (Elec.)	-	-	-	-	-	-	-	-	-	-	-
Other Energy Sector	-	-	-	-	-	-	-	-	-	-	-
Distribution Losses	-	-	-	-	-	-	-	-	-	-	-
FINAL CONSUMPTION	-	174	3705	4	1177	6	6841	349	28	61	360
INDUSTRY SECTOR	-	83	8	-	-	3	275	349	28	20	-
Iron and Steel	-	-	-	-	-	-	-	-	-	-	-
Chemical and Petrochemical	-	83	-	-	-	-	57	25	28	-	-
of which: Feedstocks	-	74	-	-	-	-	-	-	28	-	-
Non-Ferrous Metals	-	-	-	-	-	-	7	-	-	-	-
Non-Metallic Minerals	-	-	-	-	-	-	4	37	-	-	-
Transport Equipment	-	-	-	-	-	-	-	-	-	-	-
Machinery	-	-	-	-	-	-	104	19	-	-	-
Mining and Quarrying	-	-	-	-	-	-	7	108	-	20	-
Food and Tobacco	-	-	-	-	-	-	41	8	-	-	-
Paper, Pulp and Print	-	-	-	-	-	-	17	86	-	-	-
Wood and Wood Products	-	-	-	-	-	-	-	-	-	-	-
Construction	-	-	8	-	-	-	19	-	-	-	-
Textile and Leather	-	-	-	-	-	-	18	7	-	-	-
Non-specified	-	-	-	-	-	3	1	59	-	-	-
TRANSPORT SECTOR	-	4	3669	4	1177	2	855	-	-	-	-
International Civil Aviation	-	-	-	-	1069	-	-	-	-	-	-
Domestic Air	-	-	-	4	108	-	-	-	-	-	-
Road	-	4	3668	-	-	2	839	-	-	-	-
Rail	-	-	-	-	-	-	10	-	-	-	-
Pipeline Transport	-	-	-	-	-	-	-	-	-	-	-
Internal Navigation	-	-	1	-	-	-	6	-	-	-	-
Non-specified	-	-	-	-	-	-	-	-	-	-	-
OTHER SECTORS	-	87	28	-	-	1	5711	-	-	-	-
Agriculture	-	-	28	-	-	-	85	-	-	-	-
Commerce and Publ. Serv.	-	-	-	-	-	-	1953	-	-	-	-
Residential	-	-	-	-	-	1	3673	-	-	-	-
Non-specified	-	87	-	-	-	-	-	-	-	-	-
NON-ENERGY USE	-	-	-	-	-	-	-	-	-	41	360
in Industry/Transf./Energy	-	-	-	-	-	-	-	-	-	41	323
in Transport	-	-	-	-	-	-	-	-	-	-	37
in Other Sectors	-	-	-	-	-	-	-	-	-	-	-

Switzerland / Suisse : 1993

CONSUMPTION / APPROVISIONNEMENT ET DEMANDE	Gas / Gaz (TJ)				Combust. Renew. & Waste / En. Re. Comb. & Déchets (TJ)				(GWh)	(TJ)
	Natural Gas / Gaz naturel	Gas Works / Usines à gaz	Coke Ovens / Cokeries	Blast Furnaces / Hauts fourneaux	Solid Biomass & Anim. Prod. / Biomasse solide & prod. anim.	Gas/Liquids from Biomass / Gaz/Liquides tirés de biomasse	Municipal Waste / Déchets urbains	Industrial Waste / Déchets industriels	Electricity / Electricité	Heat / Chaleur
Production	90	-	-	-	12130	-	19610	9720	61070	13310
From Other Sources	-	230	-	-	-	-	-	-	-	-
Imports	93870	-	-	-	590	-	-	-	19520	-
Exports	-	-	-	-	-	-	-	-	-26719	-
Intl. Marine Bunkers	-	-	-	-	-	-	-	-	-	-
Stock Changes	-	-	-	-	-	-	-	-	-	-
DOMESTIC SUPPLY	**93960**	**230**	**-**	**-**	**12720**	**-**	**19610**	**9720**	**53871**	**13310**
Transfers	-	-	-	-	-	-	-	-	-	-
Statistical Differences	-	-	-	-	-	-	-	-	-	-
TRANSFORMATION	**5150**	**-**	**-**	**-**	**-**	**-**	**19610**	**-**	**-**	**-**
Electricity Plants	-	-	-	-	-	-	-	-	-	-
CHP Plants	5150	-	-	-	-	-	19610	-	-	-
Heat Plants	-	-	-	-	-	-	-	-	-	-
Transfer to Gases	-	-	-	-	-	-	-	-	-	-
Transfer to Solids	-	-	-	-	-	-	-	-	-	-
Petroleum Refineries	-	-	-	-	-	-	-	-	-	-
Petrochemical Industry	-	-	-	-	-	-	-	-	-	-
Liquefaction	-	-	-	-	-	-	-	-	-	-
Other Transformation Sector	-	-	-	-	-	-	-	-	-	-
ENERGY SECTOR	**-**	**-**	**-**	**-**	**-**	**-**	**-**	**-**	**2943**	**-**
Coal Mines	-	-	-	-	-	-	-	-	-	-
Oil and Gas Extraction	-	-	-	-	-	-	-	-	-	-
Petroleum Refineries	-	-	-	-	-	-	-	-	-	-
Electricity, CHP+Heat plants	-	-	-	-	-	-	-	-	1757	-
Pumped Storage (Elec.)	-	-	-	-	-	-	-	-	1186	-
Other Energy Sector	-	-	-	-	-	-	-	-	-	-
Distribution Losses	660	20	-	-	-	-	-	-	3689	1070
FINAL CONSUMPTION	**88150**	**210**	**-**	**-**	**12720**	**-**	**-**	**9720**	**47239**	**12240**
INDUSTRY SECTOR	**36910**	**110**	**-**	**-**	**2890**	**-**	**-**	**9720**	**14506**	**2610**
Iron and Steel	-	-	-	-	-	-	-	-	-	-
Chemical and Petrochemical	7746	-	-	-	-	-	-	3330	2023	331
of which: Feedstocks	-	-	-	-	-	-	-	-	-	-
Non-Ferrous Metals	1111	-	-	-	-	-	-	30	864	-
Non-Metallic Minerals	2111	-	-	-	-	-	-	330	489	-
Transport Equipment	-	-	-	-	-	-	-	-	-	-
Machinery	5802	-	-	-	-	-	-	110	2843	456
Mining and Quarrying	-	-	-	-	-	-	-	-	-	-
Food and Tobacco	2355	-	-	-	-	-	-	200	328	16
Paper, Pulp and Print	6094	-	-	-	-	-	-	1930	1518	1550
Wood and Wood Products	-	-	-	-	2890	-	-	-	-	-
Construction	108	-	-	-	-	-	-	10	75	15
Textile and Leather	2677	-	-	-	-	-	-	120	730	62
Non-specified	8906	110	-	-	-	-	-	3660	5636	180
TRANSPORT SECTOR	**-**	**-**	**-**	**-**	**-**	**-**	**-**	**-**	**2458**	**-**
International Civil Aviation	-	-	-	-	-	-	-	-	-	-
Domestic Air	-	-	-	-	-	-	-	-	-	-
Road	-	-	-	-	-	-	-	-	-	-
Rail	-	-	-	-	-	-	-	-	2458	-
Pipeline Transport	-	-	-	-	-	-	-	-	-	-
Internal Navigation	-	-	-	-	-	-	-	-	-	-
Non-specified	-	-	-	-	-	-	-	-	-	-
OTHER SECTORS	**51240**	**100**	**-**	**-**	**9830**	**-**	**-**	**-**	**30275**	**9630**
Agriculture	615	-	-	-	880	-	-	-	929	-
Commerce and Publ. Serv.	16125	-	-	-	350	-	-	-	15174	4560
Residential	34500	50	-	-	8600	-	-	-	14172	5070
Non-specified	-	50	-	-	-	-	-	-	-	-
NON-ENERGY USE	**-**	**-**	**-**	**-**	**-**	**-**	**-**	**-**	**-**	**-**
in Industry/Transf./Energy	-	-	-	-	-	-	-	-	-	-
in Transport	-	-	-	-	-	-	-	-	-	-
in Other Sectors	-	-	-	-	-	-	-	-	-	-

Turkey / Turquie : 1992

SUPPLY AND CONSUMPTION / *APPROVISIONNEMENT ET DEMANDE*	Coal / *Charbon* (1000 tonnes)							Oil / *Pétrole* (1000 tonnes)			
	Coking Coal *Charbon à coke*	Steam Coal *Charbon vapeur*	Sub-Bit. Coal *Charbon sous-bit.*	Lignite *Lignite*	Peat *Tourbe*	Oven and Gas Coke *Coke de four/gaz*	Pat. Fuel and BKB *Agg./briq. de lignite*	Crude Oil *Pétrole brut*	NGL *LGN*	Feedstocks *Produits d'aliment.*	Additives *Additifs*
Production	1378	1452	213	48388	-	3249	25	4276	-	-	-
From Other Sources	-	-	-	-	-	-	-	-	-	-	-
Imports	3562	1852	-	14	-	93	-	19316	-	46	-
Exports	-	-	-	-	-	-	-	-	-	-	-
Intl. Marine Bunkers	-	-	-	-	-	-	-	-	-	-	-
Stock Changes	283	314	-16	2257	-	49	-1	-401	-	53	-
DOMESTIC SUPPLY	**5223**	**3618**	**197**	**50659**	**-**	**3391**	**24**	**23191**	**-**	**99**	**-**
Transfers	-	-	-	-	-	-	-	-	-	-	-
Statistical Differences	-	-	-	-	-	-	-	-65	-	-	-
TRANSFORMATION	**4281**	**1316**	**-**	**35348**	**-**	**1045**	**-**	**23126**	**-**	**99**	**-**
Electricity Plants	23	1316	-	35318	-	-	-	-	-	-	-
CHP Plants	-	-	-	-	-	-	-	-	-	-	-
Heat Plants	-	-	-	-	-	-	-	-	-	-	-
Transfer to Gases	81	-	-	-	-	1039	-	-	-	-	-
Transfer to Solids	4177	-	-	30	-	6	-	-	-	-	-
Petroleum Refineries	-	-	-	-	-	-	-	23126	-	99	-
Petrochemical Industry	-	-	-	-	-	-	-	-	-	-	-
Liquefaction	-	-	-	-	-	-	-	-	-	-	-
Other Transformation Sector	-	-	-	-	-	-	-	-	-	-	-
ENERGY SECTOR	**-**	**-**	**-**	**-**	**-**	**17**	**-**	**-**	**-**	**-**	**-**
Coal Mines	-	-	-	-	-	-	-	-	-	-	-
Oil and Gas Extraction	-	-	-	-	-	-	-	-	-	-	-
Petroleum Refineries	-	-	-	-	-	-	-	-	-	-	-
Electricity, CHP+Heat plants	-	-	-	-	-	-	-	-	-	-	-
Pumped Storage (Elec.)	-	-	-	-	-	-	-	-	-	-	-
Other Energy Sector	-	-	-	-	-	17	-	-	-	-	-
Distribution Losses	-	-	-	-	-	-	-	-	-	-	-
FINAL CONSUMPTION	**942**	**2302**	**197**	**15311**	**-**	**2329**	**24**	**-**	**-**	**-**	**-**
INDUSTRY SECTOR	**439**	**1191**	**23**	**7382**	**-**	**2012**	**-**	**-**	**-**	**-**	**-**
Iron and Steel	-	-	-	-	-	1699	-	-	-	-	-
Chemical and Petrochemical	-	-	-	318	-	-	-	-	-	-	-
of which: Feedstocks	-	-	-	-	-	-	-	-	-	-	-
Non-Ferrous Metals	1	2	-	-	-	-	-	-	-	-	-
Non-Metallic Minerals	-	6	-	-	-	-	-	-	-	-	-
Transport Equipment	-	-	-	-	-	-	-	-	-	-	-
Machinery	4	-	-	43	-	-	-	-	-	-	-
Mining and Quarrying	-	-	-	-	-	-	-	-	-	-	-
Food and Tobacco	121	20	-	1520	-	-	-	-	-	-	-
Paper, Pulp and Print	-	1	-	-	-	59	-	-	-	-	-
Wood and Wood Products	-	-	-	-	-	-	-	-	-	-	-
Construction	272	1057	16	1192	-	-	-	-	-	-	-
Textile and Leather	-	5	-	223	-	-	-	-	-	-	-
Non-specified	41	100	7	4086	-	254	-	-	-	-	-
TRANSPORT SECTOR	**15**	**-**	**-**	**2**	**-**	**-**	**-**	**-**	**-**	**-**	**-**
International Civil Aviation	-	-	-	-	-	-	-	-	-	-	-
Domestic Air	-	-	-	-	-	-	-	-	-	-	-
Road	-	-	-	-	-	-	-	-	-	-	-
Rail	15	-	-	2	-	-	-	-	-	-	-
Pipeline Transport	-	-	-	-	-	-	-	-	-	-	-
Internal Navigation	-	-	-	-	-	-	-	-	-	-	-
Non-specified	-	-	-	-	-	-	-	-	-	-	-
OTHER SECTORS	**488**	**1111**	**174**	**7927**	**-**	**317**	**24**	**-**	**-**	**-**	**-**
Agriculture	-	-	-	-	-	-	-	-	-	-	-
Commerce and Publ. Serv.	-	-	-	-	-	-	-	-	-	-	-
Residential	488	1111	174	7927	-	317	24	-	-	-	-
Non-specified	-	-	-	-	-	-	-	-	-	-	-
NON-ENERGY USE	**-**	**-**	**-**	**-**	**-**	**-**	**-**	**-**	**-**	**-**	**-**
in Industry/Transf./Energy	-	-	-	-	-	-	-	-	-	-	-
in Transport	-	-	-	-	-	-	-	-	-	-	-
in Other Sectors	-	-	-	-	-	-	-	-	-	-	-

Turkey / Turquie : 1992

SUPPLY AND CONSUMPTION / APPROVISIONNEMENT ET DEMANDE	Oil cont. / *Pétrole cont.* (1000 tonnes)										
	Refinery Gas / *Gaz de raffinerie*	LPG + Ethane / *GPL + éthane*	Motor Gasoline / *Essence moteur*	Aviation Gasoline / *Essence aviation*	Jet Fuel / *Carbu-réacteur*	Kerosene / *Kérosène*	Gas/ Diesel / *Gazole*	Heavy Fuel Oil / *Fioul lourd*	Naphtha / *Naphta*	Pétrol. Coke / *Coke de pétrole*	Other Prod. / *Autres prod.*
Production	489	677	3172	-	687	150	6590	8902	1241	-	1210
From Other Sources	-	-	-	-	-	-	-	-	-	-	-
Imports	-	1184	208	-	-	-	339	50	214	-	39
Exports	-	-2	-12	-	-144	-	-22	-1630	-	-	-104
Intl. Marine Bunkers	-	-	-	-	-	-	-70	-40	-	-	-
Stock Changes	-	-	38	-	-8	-9	78	13	-10	-	41
DOMESTIC SUPPLY	**489**	**1859**	**3406**	**-**	**535**	**141**	**6915**	**7295**	**1445**	**-**	**1186**
Transfers	-	-	-	-	-	-	-	-	-	-	-
Statistical Differences	-	-	-	-	-	-	-	-	-	-	-
TRANSFORMATION	**-**	**-**	**-**	**-**	**-**	**-**	**14**	**1210**	**44**	**-**	**2**
Electricity Plants	-	-	-	-	-	-	13	1210	-	-	-
CHP Plants	-	-	-	-	-	-	-	-	-	-	-
Heat Plants	-	-	-	-	-	-	-	-	-	-	-
Transfer to Gases	-	-	-	-	-	-	-	-	-	-	-
Transfer to Solids	-	-	-	-	-	-	-	-	-	-	-
Petroleum Refineries	-	-	-	-	-	-	-	-	-	-	-
Petrochemical Industry	-	-	-	-	-	-	1	-	44	-	1
Liquefaction	-	-	-	-	-	-	-	-	-	-	-
Other Transformation Sector	-	-	-	-	-	-	-	-	-	-	1
ENERGY SECTOR	**489**	**-**	**-**	**-**	**-**	**-**	**-**	**721**	**-**	**-**	**-**
Coal Mines	-	-	-	-	-	-	-	-	-	-	-
Oil and Gas Extraction	-	-	-	-	-	-	-	-	-	-	-
Petroleum Refineries	489	-	-	-	-	-	-	721	-	-	-
Electricity, CHP+Heat plants	-	-	-	-	-	-	-	-	-	-	-
Pumped Storage (Elec.)	-	-	-	-	-	-	-	-	-	-	-
Other Energy Sector	-	-	-	-	-	-	-	-	-	-	-
Distribution Losses	-	-	-	-	-	-	-	-	-	-	-
FINAL CONSUMPTION	**-**	**1859**	**3406**	**-**	**535**	**141**	**6901**	**5364**	**1401**	**-**	**1184**
INDUSTRY SECTOR	**-**	**56**	**40**	**-**	**-**	**-**	**161**	**3954**	**1401**	**-**	**-**
Iron and Steel	-	-	-	-	-	-	20	572	-	-	-
Chemical and Petrochemical	-	23	-	-	-	-	24	670	1401	-	-
of which: Feedstocks	-	-	-	-	-	-	*24*	-	*1401*	-	-
Non-Ferrous Metals	-	-	-	-	-	-	-	360	-	-	-
Non-Metallic Minerals	-	20	-	-	-	-	-	-	-	-	-
Transport Equipment	-	-	-	-	-	-	-	-	-	-	-
Machinery	-	-	-	-	-	-	-	6	-	-	-
Mining and Quarrying	-	-	-	-	-	-	-	-	-	-	-
Food and Tobacco	-	-	-	-	-	-	-	210	-	-	-
Paper, Pulp and Print	-	-	-	-	-	-	-	250	-	-	-
Wood and Wood Products	-	-	-	-	-	-	-	-	-	-	-
Construction	-	-	-	-	-	-	40	-	-	-	-
Textile and Leather	-	-	-	-	-	-	30	360	-	-	-
Non-specified	-	13	40	-	-	-	47	1526	-	-	-
TRANSPORT SECTOR	**-**	**-**	**3366**	**-**	**535**	**-**	**4850**	**150**	**-**	**-**	**-**
International Civil Aviation	-	-	-	-	255	-	-	-	-	-	-
Domestic Air	-	-	-	-	280	-	-	-	-	-	-
Road	-	-	3363	-	-	-	4600	-	-	-	-
Rail	-	-	-	-	-	-	165	30	-	-	-
Pipeline Transport	-	-	-	-	-	-	-	-	-	-	-
Internal Navigation	-	-	3	-	-	-	85	120	-	-	-
Non-specified	-	-	-	-	-	-	-	-	-	-	-
OTHER SECTORS	**-**	**1803**	**-**	**-**	**-**	**141**	**1890**	**1260**	**-**	**-**	**-**
Agriculture	-	-	-	-	-	-	1890	-	-	-	-
Commerce and Publ. Serv.	-	-	-	-	-	-	-	-	-	-	-
Residential	-	1803	-	-	-	141	-	1260	-	-	-
Non-specified	-	-	-	-	-	-	-	-	-	-	-
NON-ENERGY USE	**-**	**-**	**-**	**-**	**-**	**-**	**-**	**-**	**-**	**-**	**1184**
in Industry/Transf./Energy	-	-	-	-	-	-	-	-	-	-	1054
in Transport	-	-	-	-	-	-	-	-	-	-	130
in Other Sectors	-	-	-	-	-	-	-	-	-	-	-

Turkey / Turquie : 1992

CONSUMPTION / APPROVISIONNEMENT ET DEMANDE	Gas / Gaz (TJ)				Combust. Renew. & Waste / En. Re. Comb. & Déchets (TJ)				(GWh)	(TJ)
	Natural Gas / Gaz naturel	Gas Works / Usines à gaz	Coke Ovens / Cokeries	Blast Furnaces / Hauts fourneaux	Solid Biomass & Anim. Prod. / Biomasse solide & prod. anim.	Gas/Liquids from Biomass / Gaz/Liquides tirés de biomasse	Municipal Waste / Déchets urbains	Industrial Waste / Déchets industriels	Electricity / Electricité	Heat / Chaleur
Production	7583	670	22991	30439	332075	-	-	-	67342	-
From Other Sources	-	-	-	-	-	-	-	-	-	-
Imports	169937	-	-	-	-	-	-	-	189	-
Exports	-	-	-	-	-	-	-	-	-314	-
Intl. Marine Bunkers	-	-	-	-	-	-	-	-	-	-
Stock Changes	-39	-	-	-	-	-	-	-	-	-
DOMESTIC SUPPLY	**177481**	**670**	**22991**	**30439**	**332075**	**-**	**-**	**-**	**67217**	**-**
Transfers	-	-	-	-	-	-	-	-	-	-
Statistical Differences	1	-	-	-	-	-	-	-	-	-
TRANSFORMATION	**100171**	**-**	**3666**	**8967**	**-**	**-**	**-**	**-**	**-**	**-**
Electricity Plants	100171	-	3666	8967	-	-	-	-	-	-
CHP Plants	-	-	-	-	-	-	-	-	-	-
Heat Plants	-	-	-	-	-	-	-	-	-	-
Transfer to Gases	-	-	-	-	-	-	-	-	-	-
Transfer to Solids	-	-	-	-	-	-	-	-	-	-
Petroleum Refineries	-	-	-	-	-	-	-	-	-	-
Petrochemical Industry	-	-	-	-	-	-	-	-	-	-
Liquefaction	-	-	-	-	-	-	-	-	-	-
Other Transformation Sector	-	-	-	-	-	-	-	-	-	-
ENERGY SECTOR	**1508**	**3**	**4109**	**8718**	**-**	**-**	**-**	**-**	**6488**	**-**
Coal Mines	-	-	-	-	-	-	-	-	731	-
Oil and Gas Extraction	958	-	-	-	-	-	-	-	-	-
Petroleum Refineries	-	-	-	-	-	-	-	-	1520	-
Electricity, CHP+Heat plants	550	-	-	-	-	-	-	-	4237	-
Pumped Storage (Elec.)	-	-	-	-	-	-	-	-	-	-
Other Energy Sector	-	3	4109	8718	-	-	-	-	-	-
Distribution Losses	114	155	-	462	-	-	-	-	8995	-
FINAL CONSUMPTION	**75689**	**512**	**15216**	**12292**	**332075**	**-**	**-**	**-**	**51734**	**-**
INDUSTRY SECTOR	**60504**	**-**	**15216**	**12292**	**-**	**-**	**-**	**-**	**29285**	**-**
Iron and Steel	2070	-	15216	12292	-	-	-	-	5982	-
Chemical and Petrochemical	32309	-	-	-	-	-	-	-	1937	-
of which: Feedstocks	24091	-	-	-	-	-	-	-	-	-
Non-Ferrous Metals	-	-	-	-	-	-	-	-	2631	-
Non-Metallic Minerals	14565	-	-	-	-	-	-	-	4733	-
Transport Equipment	666	-	-	-	-	-	-	-	-	-
Machinery	1015	-	-	-	-	-	-	-	1440	-
Mining and Quarrying	-	-	-	-	-	-	-	-	500	-
Food and Tobacco	968	-	-	-	-	-	-	-	2577	-
Paper, Pulp and Print	1109	-	-	-	-	-	-	-	-	-
Wood and Wood Products	-	-	-	-	-	-	-	-	1904	-
Construction	-	-	-	-	-	-	-	-	507	-
Textile and Leather	1772	-	-	-	-	-	-	-	4292	-
Non-specified	6030	-	-	-	-	-	-	-	2782	-
TRANSPORT SECTOR	**919**	**-**	**-**	**-**	**-**	**-**	**-**	**-**	**438**	**-**
International Civil Aviation	-	-	-	-	-	-	-	-	-	-
Domestic Air	-	-	-	-	-	-	-	-	-	-
Road	-	-	-	-	-	-	-	-	-	-
Rail	-	-	-	-	-	-	-	-	438	-
Pipeline Transport	919	-	-	-	-	-	-	-	-	-
Internal Navigation	-	-	-	-	-	-	-	-	-	-
Non-specified	-	-	-	-	-	-	-	-	-	-
OTHER SECTORS	**14266**	**512**	**-**	**-**	**332075**	**-**	**-**	**-**	**22011**	**-**
Agriculture	-	-	-	-	-	-	-	-	859	-
Commerce and Publ. Serv.	3	30	-	-	-	-	-	-	9444	-
Residential	14263	482	-	-	332075	-	-	-	11482	-
Non-specified	-	-	-	-	-	-	-	-	226	-
NON-ENERGY USE	**-**	**-**	**-**	**-**	**-**	**-**	**-**	**-**	**-**	**-**
in Industry/Transf./Energy	-	-	-	-	-	-	-	-	-	-
in Transport	-	-	-	-	-	-	-	-	-	-
in Other Sectors	-	-	-	-	-	-	-	-	-	-

Turkey / Turquie : 1993

SUPPLY AND CONSUMPTION	Coal / Charbon (1000 tonnes)							Oil / Pétrole (1000 tonnes)			
	Coking Coal	Steam Coal	Sub-Bit. Coal	Lignite	Peat	Oven and Gas Coke	Pat. Fuel and BKB	Crude Oil	NGL	Feedstocks	Additives
APPROVISIONNEMENT ET DEMANDE	*Charbon à coke*	*Charbon vapeur*	*Charbon sous-bit.*	*Lignite*	*Tourbe*	*Coke de four/gaz*	*Agg./briq. de lignite*	*Pétrole brut*	*LGN*	*Produits d'aliment.*	*Additifs*
Production	1283	1506	86	45286	-	3098	11	3892	-	-	-
From Other Sources	-	-	-	-	-	-	-	-	-	40	-
Imports	3687	1953	-	-	-	90	-	21976	-	-	-
Intl. Marine Bunkers	-	-	-	-	-	-	-	-	-	-	-
Stock Changes	-26	142	16	2054	-	40	-1	-352	-	56	-
DOMESTIC SUPPLY	**4944**	**3601**	**102**	**47340**	**-**	**3228**	**10**	**25516**	**-**	**96**	**-**
Transfers	-	-	-	-	-	-	-	-	-	-	-
Statistical Differences	-	-	-	-	-	-	-	108	-	-	-
TRANSFORMATION	**4182**	**1275**	**-**	**31931**	**-**	**1023**	**-**	**25624**	**-**	**96**	****
Electricity Plants	23	1275	-	31917	-	-	-	-	-	-	-
CHP Plants	-	-	-	-	-	-	-	-	-	-	-
Heat Plants	-	-	-	-	-	-	-	-	-	-	-
Transfer to Gases	37	-	-	-	-	1023	-	-	-	-	-
Transfer to Solids	4122	-	-	14	-	-	-	-	-	-	-
Petroleum Refineries	-	-	-	-	-	-	-	25624	-	96	-
Petrochemical Industry	-	-	-	-	-	-	-	-	-	-	-
Liquefaction	-	-	-	-	-	-	-	-	-	-	-
Other Transformation Sector	-	-	-	-	-	-	-	-	-	-	-
ENERGY SECTOR	**-**	**-**	**-**	**-**	**-**	**10**	**-**	**-**	**-**	**-**	**-**
Coal Mines	-	-	-	-	-	-	-	-	-	-	-
Oil and Gas Extraction	-	-	-	-	-	-	-	-	-	-	-
Petroleum Refineries	-	-	-	-	-	-	-	-	-	-	-
Electricity, CHP+Heat plants	-	-	-	-	-	-	-	-	-	-	-
Pumped Storage (Elec.)	-	-	-	-	-	-	-	-	-	-	-
Other Energy Sector	-	-	-	-	-	10	-	-	-	-	-
Distribution Losses	-	-	-	-	-	-	-	-	-	-	-
FINAL CONSUMPTION	**762**	**2326**	**102**	**15409**	**-**	**2195**	**10**	**-**	**-**	**-**	**-**
INDUSTRY SECTOR	**452**	**1055**	**13**	**7415**	**-**	**2007**	**-**	**-**	**-**	**-**	**-**
Iron and Steel	-	-	-	-	-	1674	-	-	-	-	-
Chemical and Petrochemical	-	-	-	170	-	-	-	-	-	-	-
of which: Feedstocks	-	-	-	-	-	-	-	-	-	-	-
Non-Ferrous Metals	2	1	-	-	-	-	-	-	-	-	-
Non-Metallic Minerals	-	5	-	-	-	-	-	-	-	-	-
Transport Equipment	-	-	-	-	-	-	-	-	-	-	-
Machinery	5	-	-	45	-	-	-	-	-	-	-
Mining and Quarrying	-	-	-	-	-	-	-	-	-	-	-
Food and Tobacco	136	23	-	1570	-	67	-	-	-	-	-
Paper, Pulp and Print	-	2	-	-	-	-	-	-	-	-	-
Wood and Wood Products	-	-	-	-	-	-	-	-	-	-	-
Construction	188	920	12	1287	-	48	-	-	-	-	-
Textile and Leather	-	7	-	265	-	-	-	-	-	-	-
Non-specified	121	97	1	4078	-	218	-	-	-	-	-
TRANSPORT SECTOR	**14**	**-**	**-**	**-**	**-**	**-**	**-**	**-**	**-**	**-**	**-**
International Civil Aviation	-	-	-	-	-	-	-	-	-	-	-
Domestic Air	-	-	-	-	-	-	-	-	-	-	-
Road	-	-	-	-	-	-	-	-	-	-	-
Rail	14	-	-	-	-	-	-	-	-	-	-
Pipeline Transport	-	-	-	-	-	-	-	-	-	-	-
Internal Navigation	-	-	-	-	-	-	-	-	-	-	-
Non-specified	-	-	-	-	-	-	-	-	-	-	-
OTHER SECTORS	**296**	**1271**	**89**	**7994**	**-**	**188**	**10**	**-**	**-**	**-**	**-**
Agriculture	-	-	-	-	-	-	-	-	-	-	-
Commerce and Publ. Serv.	-	-	-	-	-	-	-	-	-	-	-
Residential	296	1271	89	7994	-	188	10	-	-	-	-
Non-specified	-	-	-	-	-	-	-	-	-	-	-
NON-ENERGY USE	**-**	**-**	**-**	**-**	**-**	**-**	**-**	**-**	**-**	**-**	**-**
in Industry/Transf./Energy	-	-	-	-	-	-	-	-	-	-	-
in Transport	-	-	-	-	-	-	-	-	-	-	-
in Other Sectors	-	-	-	-	-	-	-	-	-	-	-

Turkey / Turquie : 1993

SUPPLY AND CONSUMPTION *APPROVISIONNEMENT ET DEMANDE*	Oil cont. / *Pétrole cont.* (1000 tonnes)										
	Refinery Gas *Gaz de raffinerie*	LPG + Ethane *GPL + éthane*	Motor Gasoline *Essence moteur*	Aviation Gasoline *Essence aviation*	Jet Fuel *Carbu-réacteur*	Kerosene *Kérosène*	Gas/ Diesel *Gazole*	Heavy Fuel Oil *Fioul lourd*	Naphtha *Naphta*	Pétrol. Coke *Coke de pétrole*	Other Prod. *Autres prod.*
Production	582	710	3535	-	812	166	7272	9283	1207	-	2001
From Other Sources	-	-	-	-	-	-	-	-	-	-	-
Imports	-	1394	407	-	6	-	1155	350	167	-	252
Exports	-	-	-	-	-136	-20	-	-1707	-	-	-253
Intl. Marine Bunkers	-	-	-	-	-	-	-57	-42	-	-	-
Stock Changes	-	-3	13	-	-9	7	-26	-122	-17	-	-87
DOMESTIC SUPPLY	**582**	**2101**	**3955**	**-**	**673**	**153**	**8344**	**7762**	**1357**	**-**	**1913**
Transfers	-	-	-	-	-	-	-	-	-	-	-
Statistical Differences	-	-	-	-	-	-	-	-	-	-	-
TRANSFORMATION	**-**	**-**	**-**	**-**	**-**	**-**	**14**	**1720**	**38**	**-**	**6**
Electricity Plants	-	-	-	-	-	-	13	1720	-	-	-
CHP Plants	-	-	-	-	-	-	-	-	-	-	-
Heat Plants	-	-	-	-	-	-	-	-	-	-	-
Transfer to Gases	-	-	-	-	-	-	-	-	-	-	-
Transfer to Solids	-	-	-	-	-	-	-	-	-	-	-
Petroleum Refineries	-	-	-	-	-	-	-	-	-	-	-
Petrochemical Industry	-	-	-	-	-	-	1	-	38	-	1
Liquefaction	-	-	-	-	-	-	-	-	-	-	-
Other Transformation Sector	-	-	-	-	-	-	-	-	-	-	5
ENERGY SECTOR	**582**	**-**	**-**	**-**	**-**	**-**	**-**	**824**	**-**	**-**	**-**
Coal Mines	-	-	-	-	-	-	-	-	-	-	-
Oil and Gas Extraction	-	-	-	-	-	-	-	-	-	-	-
Petroleum Refineries	582	-	-	-	-	-	-	824	-	-	-
Electricity, CHP+Heat plants	-	-	-	-	-	-	-	-	-	-	-
Pumped Storage (Elec.)	-	-	-	-	-	-	-	-	-	-	-
Other Energy Sector	-	-	-	-	-	-	-	-	-	-	-
Distribution Losses	-	-	-	-	-	-	-	-	-	-	-
FINAL CONSUMPTION	**-**	**2101**	**3955**	**-**	**673**	**153**	**8330**	**5218**	**1319**	**-**	**1907**
INDUSTRY SECTOR	**-**	**81**	**20**	**-**	**-**	**-**	**179**	**3858**	**1319**	**-**	**-**
Iron and Steel	-	-	-	-	-	-	10	623	-	-	-
Chemical and Petrochemical	-	25	-	-	-	-	19	670	1319	-	-
of which: Feedstocks	-	-	-	-	-	-	*19*	-	*1319*	-	-
Non-Ferrous Metals	-	-	-	-	-	-	16	235	-	-	-
Non-Metallic Minerals	-	30	-	-	-	-	24	110	-	-	-
Transport Equipment	-	-	-	-	-	-	-	-	-	-	-
Machinery	-	-	-	-	-	-	-	-	-	-	-
Mining and Quarrying	-	-	-	-	-	-	-	-	-	-	-
Food and Tobacco	-	-	-	-	-	-	-	200	-	-	-
Paper, Pulp and Print	-	-	-	-	-	-	-	210	-	-	-
Wood and Wood Products	-	-	-	-	-	-	-	-	-	-	-
Construction	-	-	-	-	-	-	45	-	-	-	-
Textile and Leather	-	-	-	-	-	-	30	310	-	-	-
Non-specified	-	26	20	-	-	-	35	1500	-	-	-
TRANSPORT SECTOR	**-**	**-**	**3935**	**-**	**673**	**-**	**5866**	**150**	**-**	**-**	**-**
International Civil Aviation	-	-	-	-	310	-	-	-	-	-	-
Domestic Air	-	-	-	-	363	-	-	-	-	-	-
Road	-	-	3935	-	-	-	5596	-	-	-	-
Rail	-	-	-	-	-	-	183	25	-	-	-
Pipeline Transport	-	-	-	-	-	-	-	-	-	-	-
Internal Navigation	-	-	-	-	-	-	87	125	-	-	-
Non-specified	-	-	-	-	-	-	-	-	-	-	-
OTHER SECTORS	**-**	**2020**	**-**	**-**	**-**	**153**	**2285**	**1210**	**-**	**-**	**-**
Agriculture	-	-	-	-	-	-	2285	-	-	-	-
Commerce and Publ. Serv.	-	-	-	-	-	-	-	-	-	-	-
Residential	-	2020	-	-	-	153	-	1210	-	-	-
Non-specified	-	-	-	-	-	-	-	-	-	-	-
NON-ENERGY USE	**-**	**-**	**-**	**-**	**-**	**-**	**-**	**-**	**-**	**-**	**1907**
in Industry/Transf./Energy	-	-	-	-	-	-	-	-	-	-	1747
in Transport	-	-	-	-	-	-	-	-	-	-	160
in Other Sectors	-	-	-	-	-	-	-	-	-	-	-

Turkey / Turquie : 1993

CONSUMPTION / *APPROVISIONNEMENT ET DEMANDE*	Gas / *Gaz* (TJ)				Combust. Renew. & Waste / *En. Re. Comb. & Déchets* (TJ)				(GWh)	(TJ)
	Natural Gas *Gaz naturel*	Gas Works *Usines à gaz*	Coke Ovens *Cokeries*	Blast Furnaces *Hauts fourneaux*	Solid Biomass & Anim. Prod. *Biomasse solide & prod. anim.*	Gas/Liquids from Biomass *Gaz/Liquides tirés de biomasse*	Municipal Waste *Déchets urbains*	Industrial Waste *Déchets industriels*	Electricity *Electricité*	Heat *Chaleur*
Production	7660	335	23304	28942	332578	-	-	-	73808	-
From Other Sources	-	-	-	-	-	-	-	-	-	-
Imports	189738	-	-	-	-	-	-	-	213	-
Exports	-	-	-	-	-	-	-	-	-589	-
Intl. Marine Bunkers	-	-	-	-	-	-	-	-	-	-
Stock Changes	-153	-	-	-	-	-	-	-	-	-
DOMESTIC SUPPLY	**197245**	**335**	**23304**	**28942**	**332578**	-	-	-	**73432**	-
Transfers	-	-	-	-	-	-	-	-	-	-
Statistical Differences	-	-	-	-	-	-	-	-	-	-
TRANSFORMATION	**99060**	-	**5135**	**9950**	-	-	-	-	-	-
Electricity Plants	99060	-	5135	9950	-	-	-	-	-	-
CHP Plants	-	-	-	-	-	-	-	-	-	-
Heat Plants	-	-	-	-	-	-	-	-	-	-
Transfer to Gases	-	-	-	-	-	-	-	-	-	-
Transfer to Solids	-	-	-	-	-	-	-	-	-	-
Petroleum Refineries	-	-	-	-	-	-	-	-	-	-
Petrochemical Industry	-	-	-	-	-	-	-	-	-	-
Liquefaction	-	-	-	-	-	-	-	-	-	-
Other Transformation Sector	-	-	-	-	-	-	-	-	-	-
ENERGY SECTOR	**850**	**3**	**4135**	**8880**	-	-	-	-	**6434**	-
Coal Mines	-	-	-	-	-	-	-	-	714	-
Oil and Gas Extraction	350	-	-	-	-	-	-	-	-	-
Petroleum Refineries	-	-	-	-	-	-	-	-	1777	-
Electricity, CHP+Heat plants	500	-	-	-	-	-	-	-	3943	-
Pumped Storage (Elec.)	-	-	-	-	-	-	-	-	-	-
Other Energy Sector	-	3	4135	8880	-	-	-	-	-	-
Distribution Losses	689	78	-	366	-	-	-	-	10252	-
FINAL CONSUMPTION	**96646**	**254**	**14034**	**9746**	**332578**	-	-	-	**56746**	-
INDUSTRY SECTOR	**74509**	-	**14034**	**9746**	-	-	-	-	**31756**	-
Iron and Steel	1090	-	14034	9746	-	-	-	-	6734	-
Chemical and Petrochemical	39679	-	-	-	-	-	-	-	2136	-
of which: Feedstocks	29889	-	-	-	-	-	-	-	-	-
Non-Ferrous Metals	5500	-	-	-	-	-	-	-	2673	-
Non-Metallic Minerals	11758	-	-	-	-	-	-	-	4969	-
Transport Equipment	766	-	-	-	-	-	-	-	-	-
Machinery	900	-	-	-	-	-	-	-	1671	-
Mining and Quarrying	-	-	-	-	-	-	-	-	574	-
Food and Tobacco	1762	-	-	-	-	-	-	-	2753	-
Paper, Pulp and Print	1609	-	-	-	-	-	-	-	-	-
Wood and Wood Products	-	-	-	-	-	-	-	-	1813	-
Construction	-	-	-	-	-	-	-	-	631	-
Textile and Leather	5604	-	-	-	-	-	-	-	4720	-
Non-specified	5841	-	-	-	-	-	-	-	3082	-
TRANSPORT SECTOR	**1455**	-	-	-	-	-	-	-	**452**	-
International Civil Aviation	-	-	-	-	-	-	-	-	-	-
Domestic Air	-	-	-	-	-	-	-	-	-	-
Road	-	-	-	-	-	-	-	-	-	-
Rail	-	-	-	-	-	-	-	-	452	-
Pipeline Transport	1455	-	-	-	-	-	-	-	-	-
Internal Navigation	-	-	-	-	-	-	-	-	-	-
Non-specified	-	-	-	-	-	-	-	-	-	-
OTHER SECTORS	**20682**	**254**	-	-	**332578**	-	-	-	**24538**	-
Agriculture	-	-	-	-	-	-	-	-	989	-
Commerce and Publ. Serv.	2	-	-	-	-	-	-	-	10739	-
Residential	20680	254	-	-	332578	-	-	-	12559	-
Non-specified	-	-	-	-	-	-	-	-	251	-
NON-ENERGY USE	-	-	-	-	-	-	-	-	-	-
in Industry/Transf./Energy	-	-	-	-	-	-	-	-	-	-
in Transport	-	-	-	-	-	-	-	-	-	-
in Other Sectors	-	-	-	-	-	-	-	-	-	-

United Kingdom / Royaume-Uni : 1992

SUPPLY AND CONSUMPTION / APPROVISIONNEMENT ET DEMANDE	Coal / Charbon (1000 tonnes)							Oil / Pétrole (1000 tonnes)			
	Coking Coal / Charbon à coke	Steam Coal / Charbon vapeur	Sub-Bit. Coal / Charbon sous-bit.	Lignite / Lignite	Peat / Tourbe	Oven and Gas Coke / Coke de four/gaz	Pat. Fuel and BKB / Agg./briq. de lignite	Crude Oil / Pétrole brut	NGL / LGN	Feedstocks / Produits d'aliment.	Additives / Additifs
Production	450	83537	-	-	-	7029	555	89179	5067	-	144
From Other Sources	-	507	-	-	-	-	-	5	-	832	-
Imports	8385	11954	-	-	-	460	135	47639	-	11330	-
Exports	-21	-952	-	-	-	-267	-	-54441	-1987	-1198	-
Intl. Marine Bunkers	-	-	-	-	-	-	-	-	-	-	-
Stock Changes	360	-4246	-	-	-	-106	-1	-292	-15	192	-
DOMESTIC SUPPLY	**9174**	**90800**	**-**	**-**	**-**	**7116**	**689**	**82090**	**3065**	**11156**	**144**
Transfers	-	-	-	-	-	-	-	-1291	-1636	-	-
Statistical Differences	-143	789	-	-	-	309	-	-145	30	-935	-
TRANSFORMATION	**9031**	**79821**	**-**	**-**	**-**	**2295**	**-**	**80654**	**1459**	**10221**	**144**
Electricity Plants	-	78509	-	-	-	-	-	-	-	-	-
CHP Plants	-	-	-	-	-	-	-	-	-	-	-
Heat Plants	-	-	-	-	-	-	-	-	-	-	-
Transfer to Gases	-	-	-	-	-	2157	-	-	-	-	-
Transfer to Solids	9031	1312	-	-	-	138	-	-	-	-	-
Petroleum Refineries	-	-	-	-	-	-	-	80654	1459	10221	144
Petrochemical Industry	-	-	-	-	-	-	-	-	-	-	-
Liquefaction	-	-	-	-	-	-	-	-	-	-	-
Other Transformation Sector	-	-	-	-	-	-	-	-	-	-	-
ENERGY SECTOR	**-**	**86**	**-**	**-**	**-**	**-**	**-**	**-**	**-**	**-**	**-**
Coal Mines	-	79	-	-	-	-	-	-	-	-	-
Oil and Gas Extraction	-	-	-	-	-	-	-	-	-	-	-
Petroleum Refineries	-	-	-	-	-	-	-	-	-	-	-
Electricity, CHP+Heat plants	-	-	-	-	-	-	-	-	-	-	-
Pumped Storage (Elec.)	-	-	-	-	-	-	-	-	-	-	-
Other Energy Sector	-	7	-	-	-	-	-	-	-	-	-
Distribution Losses	-	-	-	-	-	-	-	-	-	-	-
FINAL CONSUMPTION	**-**	**11682**	**-**	**-**	**-**	**5130**	**689**	**-**	**-**	**-**	**-**
INDUSTRY SECTOR	**-**	**6581**	**-**	**-**	**-**	**4353**	**-**	**-**	**-**	**-**	**-**
Iron and Steel	-	6	-	-	-	3752	-	-	-	-	-
Chemical and Petrochemical	-	1210	-	-	-	76	-	-	-	-	-
of which: Feedstocks	-	-	-	-	-	-	-	-	-	-	-
Non-Ferrous Metals	-	275	-	-	-	210	-	-	-	-	-
Non-Metallic Minerals	-	1155	-	-	-	16	-	-	-	-	-
Transport Equipment	-	291	-	-	-	7	-	-	-	-	-
Machinery	-	45	-	-	-	218	-	-	-	-	-
Mining and Quarrying	-	-	-	-	-	-	-	-	-	-	-
Food and Tobacco	-	640	-	-	-	-	-	-	-	-	-
Paper, Pulp and Print	-	930	-	-	-	-	-	-	-	-	-
Wood and Wood Products	-	-	-	-	-	-	-	-	-	-	-
Construction	-	-	-	-	-	-	-	-	-	-	-
Textile and Leather	-	307	-	-	-	-	-	-	-	-	-
Non-specified	-	1722	-	-	-	74	-	-	-	-	-
TRANSPORT SECTOR	**-**	**-**	**-**	**-**	**-**	**-**	**-**	**-**	**-**	**-**	**-**
International Civil Aviation	-	-	-	-	-	-	-	-	-	-	-
Domestic Air	-	-	-	-	-	-	-	-	-	-	-
Road	-	-	-	-	-	-	-	-	-	-	-
Rail	-	-	-	-	-	-	-	-	-	-	-
Pipeline Transport	-	-	-	-	-	-	-	-	-	-	-
Internal Navigation	-	-	-	-	-	-	-	-	-	-	-
Non-specified	-	-	-	-	-	-	-	-	-	-	-
OTHER SECTORS	**-**	**5101**	**-**	**-**	**-**	**777**	**689**	**-**	**-**	**-**	**-**
Agriculture	-	12	-	-	-	3	-	-	-	-	-
Commerce and Publ. Serv.	-	744	-	-	-	132	-	-	-	-	-
Residential	-	4156	-	-	-	642	689	-	-	-	-
Non-specified	-	189	-	-	-	-	-	-	-	-	-
NON-ENERGY USE	**-**	**-**	**-**	**-**	**-**	**-**	**-**	**-**	**-**	**-**	**-**
in Industry/Transf./Energy	-	-	-	-	-	-	-	-	-	-	-
in Transport	-	-	-	-	-	-	-	-	-	-	-
in Other Sectors	-	-	-	-	-	-	-	-	-	-	-

United Kingdom / Royaume-Uni : 1992

SUPPLY AND CONSUMPTION / APPROVISIONNEMENT ET DEMANDE	Oil cont. / *Pétrole cont.* (1000 tonnes)										
	Refinery Gas / *Gaz de raffinerie*	LPG + Ethane / *GPL + éthane*	Motor Gasoline / *Essence moteur*	Aviation Gasoline / *Essence aviation*	Jet Fuel / *Carbu-réacteur*	Kerosene / *Kérosène*	Gas/Diesel / *Gazole*	Heavy Fuel Oil / *Fioul lourd*	Naphtha / *Naphta*	Pétrol. Coke / *Coke de pétrole*	Other Prod. / *Autres prod.*
Production	2797	1650	28126	-	7681	2450	25651	14651	3069	1582	4350
From Other Sources	-	-	-	-	-	-	-	-	-	-	-
Imports	-	910	929	18	490	37	746	4079	997	-	1075
Exports	-	-720	-5681	-5	-1029	-273	-5665	-5100	-380	-	-1396
Intl. Marine Bunkers	-	-	-	-	-	-	-1239	-1307	-	-	-
Stock Changes	1	4	271	-1	76	95	247	199	7	-54	19
DOMESTIC SUPPLY	**2798**	**1844**	**23645**	**12**	**7218**	**2309**	**19740**	**12522**	**3693**	**1528**	**4048**
Transfers	-	1636	-	-	-	-	-	-	-	-	1291
Statistical Differences	-14	-121	399	15	-552	163	-51	559	-174	201	34
TRANSFORMATION	**20**	**260**	**-**	**-**	**-**	**-**	**159**	**6118**	**431**	**-**	**1286**
Electricity Plants	-	-	-	-	-	-	34	4643	-	-	1286
CHP Plants	-	-	-	-	-	-	39	1398	-	-	-
Heat Plants	-	-	-	-	-	-	-	-	-	-	-
Transfer to Gases	-	40	-	-	-	-	2	-	-	-	-
Transfer to Solids	-	-	-	-	-	-	-	-	-	-	-
Petroleum Refineries	-	-	-	-	-	-	-	-	-	-	-
Petrochemical Industry	20	220	-	-	-	-	84	77	431	-	-
Liquefaction	-	-	-	-	-	-	-	-	-	-	-
Other Transformation Sector	-	-	-	-	-	-	-	-	-	-	-
ENERGY SECTOR	**2625**	**428**	**-**	**-**	**-**	**-**	**2**	**2263**	**29**	**1047**	**46**
Coal Mines	-	-	-	-	-	-	-	-	-	-	-
Oil and Gas Extraction	-	361	-	-	-	-	-	-	-	-	-
Petroleum Refineries	2625	67	-	-	-	-	2	2263	29	1047	46
Electricity, CHP+Heat plants	-	-	-	-	-	-	-	-	-	-	-
Pumped Storage (Elec.)	-	-	-	-	-	-	-	-	-	-	-
Other Energy Sector	-	-	-	-	-	-	-	-	-	-	-
Distribution Losses	-	-	-	-	-	-	-	-	-	-	-
FINAL CONSUMPTION	**139**	**2671**	**24044**	**27**	**6666**	**2472**	**19528**	**4700**	**3059**	**682**	**4041**
INDUSTRY SECTOR	**139**	**2265**	**-**	**-**	**-**	**522**	**2811**	**3205**	**3059**	**-**	**-**
Iron and Steel	-	24	-	-	-	-	129	492	-	-	-
Chemical and Petrochemical	139	1565	-	-	-	-	753	716	3059	-	-
of which: Feedstocks	*139*	*1565*	-	-	-	-	*753*	*393*	*3059*	-	-
Non-Ferrous Metals	-	-	-	-	-	-	23	37	-	-	-
Non-Metallic Minerals	-	-	-	-	-	-	153	292	-	-	-
Transport Equipment	-	-	-	-	-	-	94	112	-	-	-
Machinery	-	-	-	-	-	-	238	293	-	-	-
Mining and Quarrying	-	-	-	-	-	-	318	21	-	-	-
Food and Tobacco	-	-	-	-	-	-	120	687	-	-	-
Paper, Pulp and Print	-	-	-	-	-	-	34	208	-	-	-
Wood and Wood Products	-	-	-	-	-	-	16	5	-	-	-
Construction	-	-	-	-	-	-	648	30	-	-	-
Textile and Leather	-	-	-	-	-	-	38	183	-	-	-
Non-specified	-	676	-	-	-	522	247	129	-	-	-
TRANSPORT SECTOR	**-**	**-**	**24044**	**27**	**6666**	**12**	**12918**	**124**	**-**	**-**	**-**
International Civil Aviation	-	-	-	-	3821	-	-	-	-	-	-
Domestic Air	-	-	-	27	2845	-	-	-	-	-	-
Road	-	-	24044	-	-	-	11132	-	-	-	-
Rail	-	-	-	-	-	12	641	1	-	-	-
Pipeline Transport	-	-	-	-	-	-	-	-	-	-	-
Internal Navigation	-	-	-	-	-	-	1145	123	-	-	-
Non-specified	-	-	-	-	-	-	-	-	-	-	-
OTHER SECTORS	**-**	**406**	**-**	**-**	**-**	**1938**	**3799**	**1371**	**-**	**-**	**-**
Agriculture	-	-	-	-	-	12	664	115	-	-	-
Commerce and Publ. Serv.	-	-	-	-	-	12	2173	963	-	-	-
Residential	-	406	-	-	-	1914	249	11	-	-	-
Non-specified	-	-	-	-	-	-	713	282	-	-	-
NON-ENERGY USE	**-**	**-**	**-**	**-**	**-**	**-**	**-**	**-**	**-**	**682**	**4041**
in Industry/Transf./Energy	-	-	-	-	-	-	-	-	-	682	3694
in Transport	-	-	-	-	-	-	-	-	-	-	330
in Other Sectors	-	-	-	-	-	-	-	-	-	-	17

United Kingdom / Royaume-Uni : 1992

CONSUMPTION / APPROVISIONNEMENT ET DEMANDE	Gas / Gaz (TJ)				Combust. Renew. & Waste / En. Re. Comb. & Déchets (TJ)				Electricity (GWh)	Heat (TJ)
	Natural Gas / Gaz naturel	Gas Works / Usines à gaz	Coke Ovens / Cokeries	Blast Furnaces / Hauts fourneaux	Solid Biomass & Anim. Prod. / Biomasse solide & prod. anim.	Gas/Liquids from Biomass / Gaz/Liquides tirés de biomasse	Municipal Waste / Déchets urbains	Industrial Waste / Déchets industriels	Electricity / Electricité	Heat / Chaleur
Production	2155548	-	51149	64274	13580	11552	8127	520	320963	-
From Other Sources	-	95	-	-	-	-	-	-	16725	-
Imports	220519	-	-	-	-	-	-	-	-32	-
Exports	-2232	-	-	-	-	-	-	-	-	-
Intl. Marine Bunkers	-	-	-	-	-	-	-	-	-	-
Stock Changes	5537	-	-	-	-	-	-	-	-	-
DOMESTIC SUPPLY	**2379372**	**95**	**51149**	**64274**	**13580**	**11552**	**8127**	**520**	**337656**	**-**
Transfers	-	-	-	-	-	-	-	-	-	-
Statistical Differences	-67952	-	-983	-3754	-	-	-	-	-	-
TRANSFORMATION	**120824**	**-**	**5807**	**20873**	**13580**	**11552**	**8127**	**520**	**-**	**-**
Electricity Plants	65204	-	5807	20873	-	8719	4933	-	-	-
CHP Plants	55620	-	-	-	-	-	2732	-	-	-
Heat Plants	-	-	-	-	13580	2833	462	520	-	-
Transfer to Gases	-	-	-	-	-	-	-	-	-	-
Transfer to Solids	-	-	-	-	-	-	-	-	-	-
Petroleum Refineries	-	-	-	-	-	-	-	-	-	-
Petrochemical Industry	-	-	-	-	-	-	-	-	-	-
Liquefaction	-	-	-	-	-	-	-	-	-	-
Other Transformation Sector	-	-	-	-	-	-	-	-	-	-
ENERGY SECTOR	**163167**	**-**	**22003**	**3539**	**-**	**-**	**-**	**-**	**34113**	**-**
Coal Mines	5094	-	-	-	-	-	-	-	3672	-
Oil and Gas Extraction	138619	-	-	-	-	-	-	-	806	-
Petroleum Refineries	6404	-	-	-	-	-	-	-	4051	-
Electricity, CHP+Heat plants	-	-	-	-	-	-	-	-	21872	-
Pumped Storage (Elec.)	-	-	-	-	-	-	-	-	2257	-
Other Energy Sector	13050	-	22003	3539	-	-	-	-	1455	-
Distribution Losses	-	95	-	-	-	-	-	-	22074	-
FINAL CONSUMPTION	**2027429**	**-**	**22356**	**36108**	**-**	**-**	**-**	**-**	**281469**	**-**
INDUSTRY SECTOR	**483574**	**-**	**22356**	**36108**	**-**	**-**	**-**	**-**	**95276**	**-**
Iron and Steel	46818	-	20916	36108	-	-	-	-	8505	-
Chemical and Petrochemical	154120	-	-	-	-	-	-	-	17571	-
of which: Feedstocks	*91134*	-	-	-	-	-	-	-	-	-
Non-Ferrous Metals	12560	-	-	-	-	-	-	-	6585	-
Non-Metallic Minerals	48730	-	-	-	-	-	-	-	7162	-
Transport Equipment	32886	-	-	-	-	-	-	-	19659	-
Machinery	35593	-	-	-	-	-	-	-	-	-
Mining and Quarrying	-	-	-	-	-	-	-	-	-	-
Food and Tobacco	66629	-	-	-	-	-	-	-	10710	-
Paper, Pulp and Print	23494	-	-	-	-	-	-	-	7494	-
Wood and Wood Products	-	-	-	-	-	-	-	-	-	-
Construction	4003	-	-	-	-	-	-	-	1739	-
Textile and Leather	5760	-	-	-	-	-	-	-	2642	-
Non-specified	52981	-	1440	-	-	-	-	-	13209	-
TRANSPORT SECTOR	**-**	**-**	**-**	**-**	**-**	**-**	**-**	**-**	**5361**	**-**
International Civil Aviation	-	-	-	-	-	-	-	-	-	-
Domestic Air	-	-	-	-	-	-	-	-	-	-
Road	-	-	-	-	-	-	-	-	-	-
Rail	-	-	-	-	-	-	-	-	5361	-
Pipeline Transport	-	-	-	-	-	-	-	-	-	-
Internal Navigation	-	-	-	-	-	-	-	-	-	-
Non-specified	-	-	-	-	-	-	-	-	-	-
OTHER SECTORS	**1543855**	**-**	**-**	**-**	**-**	**-**	**-**	**-**	**180832**	**-**
Agriculture	4244	-	-	-	-	-	-	-	3846	-
Commerce and Publ. Serv.	156302	-	-	-	-	-	-	-	77504	-
Residential	1188365	-	-	-	-	-	-	-	99482	-
Non-specified	194944	-	-	-	-	-	-	-	-	-
NON-ENERGY USE	**-**	**-**	**-**	**-**	**-**	**-**	**-**	**-**	**-**	**-**
in Industry/Transf./Energy	-	-	-	-	-	-	-	-	-	-
in Transport	-	-	-	-	-	-	-	-	-	-
in Other Sectors	-	-	-	-	-	-	-	-	-	-

United Kingdom / Royaume-Uni : 1993

SUPPLY AND CONSUMPTION / APPROVISIONNEMENT ET DEMANDE	Coal / *Charbon* (1000 tonnes)							Oil / *Pétrole* (1000 tonnes)			
	Coking Coal *Charbon à coke*	Steam Coal *Charbon vapeur*	Sub-Bit. Coal *Charbon sous-bit.*	Lignite *Lignite*	Peat *Tourbe*	Oven and Gas Coke *Coke de four/gaz*	Pat. Fuel and BKB *Agg./briq. de lignite*	Crude Oil *Pétrole brut*	NGL *LGN*	Feedstocks *Produits d'aliment.*	Additives *Additifs*
Production	219	67244	-	-	-	6539	665	93949	6136	-	143
From Other Sources	-	736	-	-	-	-	-	1	-	852	-
Imports	8602	9798	-	-	-	700	102	51914	-	11203	-
Exports	-23	-1072	-	-	-	-274	-	-60166	-2222	-1834	-
Intl. Marine Bunkers	-	-	-	-	-	-	-	-	-	-	-
Stock Changes	53	1813	-	-	-	-144	3	-419	13	69	-
DOMESTIC SUPPLY	**8851**	**78519**	-	-	-	**6821**	**770**	**85279**	**3927**	**10290**	**143**
Transfers	-	-	-	-	-	-	-	-1417	-1703	-	-
Statistical Differences	-372	-215	-	-	-	331	-2	1388	-732	-759	-
TRANSFORMATION	**8479**	**67394**	-	-	-	**2253**	-	**85250**	**1492**	**9531**	**143**
Electricity Plants	-	66163	-	-	-	-	-	-	-	-	-
CHP Plants	-	-	-	-	-	-	-	-	-	-	-
Heat Plants	-	-	-	-	-	-	-	-	-	-	-
Transfer to Gases	-	-	-	-	-	2169	-	-	-	-	-
Transfer to Solids	8479	1231	-	-	-	84	-	-	-	-	-
Petroleum Refineries	-	-	-	-	-	-	-	85250	1492	9531	143
Petrochemical Industry	-	-	-	-	-	-	-	-	-	-	-
Liquefaction	-	-	-	-	-	-	-	-	-	-	-
Other Transformation Sector	-	-	-	-	-	-	-	-	-	-	-
ENERGY SECTOR	-	**146**	-	-	-	-	-	-	-	-	-
Coal Mines	-	48	-	-	-	-	-	-	-	-	-
Oil and Gas Extraction	-	-	-	-	-	-	-	-	-	-	-
Petroleum Refineries	-	-	-	-	-	-	-	-	-	-	-
Electricity, CHP+Heat plants	-	-	-	-	-	-	-	-	-	-	-
Pumped Storage (Elec.)	-	-	-	-	-	-	-	-	-	-	-
Other Energy Sector	-	98	-	-	-	-	-	-	-	-	-
Distribution Losses	-	-	-	-	-	-	-	-	-	-	-
FINAL CONSUMPTION	-	**10764**	-	-	-	**4899**	**768**	-	-	-	-
INDUSTRY SECTOR	-	**5300**	-	-	-	**4243**	-	-	-	-	-
Iron and Steel	-	3	-	-	-	3579	-	-	-	-	-
Chemical and Petrochemical	-	1020	-	-	-	109	-	-	-	-	-
of which: Feedstocks	-	-	-	-	-	-	-	-	-	-	-
Non-Ferrous Metals	-	198	-	-	-	302	-	-	-	-	-
Non-Metallic Minerals	-	940	-	-	-	23	-	-	-	-	-
Transport Equipment	-	242	-	-	-	10	-	-	-	-	-
Machinery	-	52	-	-	-	198	-	-	-	-	-
Mining and Quarrying	-	-	-	-	-	-	-	-	-	-	-
Food and Tobacco	-	632	-	-	-	-	-	-	-	-	-
Paper, Pulp and Print	-	950	-	-	-	-	-	-	-	-	-
Wood and Wood Products	-	-	-	-	-	-	-	-	-	-	-
Construction	-	-	-	-	-	-	-	-	-	-	-
Textile and Leather	-	343	-	-	-	-	-	-	-	-	-
Non-specified	-	920	-	-	-	22	-	-	-	-	-
TRANSPORT SECTOR	-	-	-	-	-	-	-	-	-	-	-
International Civil Aviation	-	-	-	-	-	-	-	-	-	-	-
Domestic Air	-	-	-	-	-	-	-	-	-	-	-
Road	-	-	-	-	-	-	-	-	-	-	-
Rail	-	-	-	-	-	-	-	-	-	-	-
Pipeline Transport	-	-	-	-	-	-	-	-	-	-	-
Internal Navigation	-	-	-	-	-	-	-	-	-	-	-
Non-specified	-	-	-	-	-	-	-	-	-	-	-
OTHER SECTORS	-	**5464**	-	-	-	**656**	**768**	-	-	-	-
Agriculture	-	13	-	-	-	-	-	-	-	-	-
Commerce and Publ. Serv.	-	609	-	-	-	95	-	-	-	-	-
Residential	-	4638	-	-	-	561	768	-	-	-	-
Non-specified	-	204	-	-	-	-	-	-	-	-	-
NON-ENERGY USE	-	-	-	-	-	-	-	-	-	-	-
in Industry/Transf./Energy	-	-	-	-	-	-	-	-	-	-	-
in Transport	-	-	-	-	-	-	-	-	-	-	-
in Other Sectors	-	-	-	-	-	-	-	-	-	-	-

United Kingdom / Royaume-Uni : 1993

SUPPLY AND CONSUMPTION *APPROVISIONNEMENT ET DEMANDE*	Oil cont. / *Pétrole cont.* (1000 tonnes)										
	Refinery Gas *Gaz de raffinerie*	LPG + Ethane *GPL + éthane*	Motor Gasoline *Essence moteur*	Aviation Gasoline *Essence aviation*	Jet Fuel *Carbu-réacteur*	Kerosene *Kérosène*	Gas/ Diesel *Gazole*	Heavy Fuel Oil *Fioul lourd*	Naphtha *Naphta*	Pétrol. Coke *Coke de pétrole*	Other Prod. *Autres prod.*
Production	3002	1603	28535	-	8341	2707	27366	15539	2721	1691	4603
From Other Sources	-	-	-	-	-	-	-	-	-	-	-
Imports	-	621	1457	26	356	79	718	3068	1282	-	1042
Exports	-	-608	-6562	-	-1065	-416	-6528	-5878	-456	-	-1549
Intl. Marine Bunkers	-	-	-	-	-	-	-1155	-1323	-	-	-
Stock Changes	2	-11	-196	-2	14	-92	-109	182	-25	32	-39
DOMESTIC SUPPLY	**3004**	**1605**	**23234**	**24**	**7646**	**2278**	**20292**	**11588**	**3522**	**1723**	**4057**
Transfers	-	1703	-	-	-	-	-	-	-	-	1417
Statistical Differences	-10	209	532	3	-540	347	-39	753	-159	125	99
TRANSFORMATION	**20**	**285**	**-**	**-**	**-**	**-**	**214**	**4875**	**424**	**-**	**1416**
Electricity Plants	-	-	-	-	-	-	62	3524	-	-	1416
CHP Plants	-	-	-	-	-	-	66	1271	-	-	-
Heat Plants	-	-	-	-	-	-	-	-	-	-	-
Transfer to Gases	-	41	-	-	-	-	2	-	-	-	-
Transfer to Solids	-	-	-	-	-	-	-	-	-	-	-
Petroleum Refineries	-	-	-	-	-	-	-	-	-	-	-
Petrochemical Industry	20	244	-	-	-	-	84	80	424	-	-
Liquefaction	-	-	-	-	-	-	-	-	-	-	-
Other Transformation Sector	-	-	-	-	-	-	-	-	-	-	-
ENERGY SECTOR	**2840**	**419**	**-**	**-**	**-**	**-**	**5**	**2356**	**25**	**1070**	**58**
Coal Mines	-	-	-	-	-	-	-	-	-	-	-
Oil and Gas Extraction	-	390	-	-	-	-	-	-	-	-	-
Petroleum Refineries	2840	29	-	-	-	-	5	2356	25	1070	58
Electricity, CHP+Heat plants	-	-	-	-	-	-	-	-	-	-	-
Pumped Storage (Elec.)	-	-	-	-	-	-	-	-	-	-	-
Other Energy Sector	-	-	-	-	-	-	-	-	-	-	-
Distribution Losses	-	-	-	-	-	-	-	-	-	-	-
FINAL CONSUMPTION	**134**	**2813**	**23766**	**27**	**7106**	**2625**	**20034**	**5110**	**2914**	**778**	**4099**
INDUSTRY SECTOR	**134**	**2407**	**-**	**-**	**-**	**551**	**2746**	**3564**	**2914**	**-**	**-**
Iron and Steel	-	-	-	-	-	-	139	657	-	-	-
Chemical and Petrochemical	134	1672	-	-	-	-	736	1007	2914	-	-
of which: Feedstocks	*134*	*1672*	-	-	-	-	*736*	*391*	*2914*	-	-
Non-Ferrous Metals	-	-	-	-	-	-	23	16	-	-	-
Non-Metallic Minerals	-	-	-	-	-	-	158	335	-	-	-
Transport Equipment	-	-	-	-	-	-	94	111	-	-	-
Machinery	-	-	-	-	-	-	223	309	-	-	-
Mining and Quarrying	-	-	-	-	-	-	303	23	-	-	-
Food and Tobacco	-	-	-	-	-	-	105	612	-	-	-
Paper, Pulp and Print	-	-	-	-	-	-	39	145	-	-	-
Wood and Wood Products	-	-	-	-	-	-	14	4	-	-	-
Construction	-	-	-	-	-	-	602	37	-	-	-
Textile and Leather	-	-	-	-	-	-	37	197	-	-	-
Non-specified	-	735	-	-	-	551	273	111	-	-	-
TRANSPORT SECTOR	**-**	**-**	**23766**	**27**	**7106**	**12**	**13505**	**153**	**-**	**-**	**-**
International Civil Aviation	-	-	-	-	4153	-	-	-	-	-	-
Domestic Air	-	-	-	27	2953	-	-	-	-	-	-
Road	-	-	23766	-	-	-	11806	-	-	-	-
Rail	-	-	-	-	-	12	600	1	-	-	-
Pipeline Transport	-	-	-	-	-	-	-	-	-	-	-
Internal Navigation	-	-	-	-	-	-	1099	152	-	-	-
Non-specified	-	-	-	-	-	-	-	-	-	-	-
OTHER SECTORS	**-**	**406**	**-**	**-**	**-**	**2062**	**3783**	**1393**	**-**	**-**	**-**
Agriculture	-	-	-	-	-	12	655	121	-	-	-
Commerce and Publ. Serv.	-	-	-	-	-	12	2085	1006	-	-	-
Residential	-	406	-	-	-	2038	259	11	-	-	-
Non-specified	-	-	-	-	-	-	784	255	-	-	-
NON-ENERGY USE	**-**	**-**	**-**	**-**	**-**	**-**	**-**	**-**	**-**	**778**	**4099**
in Industry/Transf./Energy	-	-	-	-	-	-	-	-	-	778	3725
in Transport	-	-	-	-	-	-	-	-	-	-	353
in Other Sectors	-	-	-	-	-	-	-	-	-	-	21

United Kingdom / Royaume-Uni : 1993

CONSUMPTION *APPROVISIONNEMENT ET DEMANDE*	Gas / *Gaz* (TJ)				Combust. Renew. & Waste / *En. Re. Comb. & Déchets* (TJ)				(GWh)	(TJ)
	Natural Gas *Gaz naturel*	Gas Works *Usines à gaz*	Coke Ovens *Cokeries*	Blast Furnaces *Hauts fourneaux*	Solid Biomass & Anim. Prod. *Biomasse solide & prod. anim.*	Gas/Liquids from Biomass *Gaz/Liquides tirés de biomasse*	Municipal Waste *Déchets urbains*	Industrial Waste *Déchets industriels*	Electricity *Electricité*	Heat *Chaleur*
Production	2536581	-	47531	64393	14874	12050	10607	786	323029	6034
From Other Sources	-	116	-	-	-	-	-	-	-	-
Imports	174698								16721	-
Exports	-24567	-	-	-	-	-	-	-	-5	-
Intl. Marine Bunkers	-	-	-	-	-	-	-	-	-	-
Stock Changes	5468	-	-	-	-	-	-	-	-	-
DOMESTIC SUPPLY	**2692180**	**116**	**47531**	**64393**	**14874**	**12050**	**10607**	**786**	**339745**	**6034**
Transfers	-	-	-	-	-	-	-	-	-	-
Statistical Differences	-103571	-	-767	-3483	-	-	-	-	-	-
TRANSFORMATION	**378378**	**-**	**6134**	**22156**	**14874**	**12050**	**10607**	**786**	**-**	**-**
Electricity Plants	304261	-	6134	22156	-	10196	7276	-	-	-
CHP Plants	74117	-	-	-	-	-	2785	-	-	-
Heat Plants		-	-	-	14874	1854	546	786	-	-
Transfer to Gases	-	-	-	-	-	-	-	-	-	-
Transfer to Solids	-	-	-	-	-	-	-	-	-	-
Petroleum Refineries	-	-	-	-	-	-	-	-	-	-
Petrochemical Industry	-	-	-	-	-	-	-	-	-	-
Liquefaction	-	-	-	-	-	-	-	-	-	-
Other Transformation Sector	-	-	-	-	-	-	-	-	-	-
ENERGY SECTOR	**170922**	**-**	**19760**	**3528**	**-**	**-**	**-**	**-**	**30624**	**-**
Coal Mines	3384	-	-	-	-	-	-	-	2906	-
Oil and Gas Extraction	146409	-	-	-	-	-	-	-	854	-
Petroleum Refineries	7661	-	-	-	-	-	-	-	4450	-
Electricity, CHP+Heat plants	-	-	-	-	-	-	-	-	19288	-
Pumped Storage (Elec.)	-	-	-	-	-	-	-	-	1948	-
Other Energy Sector	13468	-	19760	3528	-	-	-	-	1178	-
Distribution Losses	-	116	-	-	-	-	-	-	23374	-
FINAL CONSUMPTION	**2039309**	**-**	**20870**	**35226**	**-**	**-**	**-**	**-**	**285747**	**6034**
INDUSTRY SECTOR	**478736**	**-**	**20870**	**35226**	**-**	**-**	**-**	**-**	**96246**	**-**
Iron and Steel	50875	-	19912	35226	-	-	-	-	8771	-
Chemical and Petrochemical	141556	-	-	-	-	-	-	-	18169	-
of which: Feedstocks	*84186*	-	-	-	-	-	-	-	-	-
Non-Ferrous Metals	6790	-	-	-	-	-	-	-	5146	-
Non-Metallic Minerals	39283	-	-	-	-	-	-	-	6638	-
Transport Equipment	29070	-	-	-	-	-	-	-	19576	-
Machinery	23969	-	-	-	-	-	-	-	-	-
Mining and Quarrying	-	-	-	-	-	-	-	-	-	-
Food and Tobacco	57337	-	-	-	-	-	-	-	11534	-
Paper, Pulp and Print	14051	-	-	-	-	-	-	-	8676	-
Wood and Wood Products	-	-	-	-	-	-	-	-	-	-
Construction	4601	-	-	-	-	-	-	-	1639	-
Textile and Leather	8471	-	-	-	-	-	-	-	2722	-
Non-specified	102733	-	958	-	-	-	-	-	13375	-
TRANSPORT SECTOR	**-**	**-**	**-**	**-**	**-**	**-**	**-**	**-**	**6246**	**-**
International Civil Aviation	-	-	-	-	-	-	-	-	-	-
Domestic Air	-	-	-	-	-	-	-	-	-	-
Road	-	-	-	-	-	-	-	-	-	-
Rail	-	-	-	-	-	-	-	-	6246	-
Pipeline Transport	-	-	-	-	-	-	-	-	-	-
Internal Navigation	-	-	-	-	-	-	-	-	-	-
Non-specified	-	-	-	-	-	-	-	-	-	-
OTHER SECTORS	**1560573**	**-**	**-**	**-**	**-**	**-**	**-**	**-**	**183255**	**6034**
Agriculture	4009	-	-	-	-	-	-	-	3942	-
Commerce and Publ. Serv.	121144	-	-	-	-	-	-	-	78908	-
Residential	1224596	-	-	-	-	-	-	-	100405	6034
Non-specified	210824	-	-	-	-	-	-	-	-	-
NON-ENERGY USE	**-**	**-**	**-**	**-**	**-**	**-**	**-**	**-**	**-**	**-**
in Industry/Transf./Energy	-	-	-	-	-	-	-	-	-	-
in Transport	-	-	-	-	-	-	-	-	-	-
in Other Sectors	-	-	-	-	-	-	-	-	-	-

United States / Etats-Unis : 1992

SUPPLY AND CONSUMPTION *APPROVISIONNEMENT ET DEMANDE*	Coal / *Charbon* (1000 tonnes)							Oil / *Pétrole* (1000 tonnes)			
	Coking Coal *Charbon à coke*	Steam Coal *Charbon vapeur*	Sub-Bit. Coal *Charbon sous-bit.*	Lignite *Lignite*	Peat *Tourbe*	Oven and Gas Coke *Coke de four/gaz*	Pat. Fuel and BKB *Agg./briq. de lignite*	Crude Oil *Pétrole brut*	NGL *LGN*	Feedstocks *Produits d'aliment.*	Additives *Additifs*
Production	83113	511388	228754	81703	11	21237	-	357075	50401	-	-
From Other Sources	-	-	-	-	-	-	-	-	-	-	-
Imports	-	3450	-	-	-	1578	-	326165	4725	22646	-
Exports	-53910	-39045	-	-46	-	-583	-	-188	-1562	-	-
Intl. Marine Bunkers	-	-	-	-	-	-	-	-	-	-	-
Stock Changes	159	-6402	-17	444	-	204	-	-533	-277	82	-
DOMESTIC SUPPLY	**29362**	**469391**	**228737**	**82101**	**11**	**22436**	**-**	**682519**	**53287**	**22728**	**-**
Transfers	-	-	-	-	-	-	-	-	-36521	5623	-
Statistical Differences	-	1881	-952	-929	-	-	-	3359	-1	-	-
TRANSFORMATION	**29362**	**443181**	**223835**	**74938**	**11**	**7500**	**-**	**685240**	**16765**	**28351**	**-**
Electricity Plants	-	404275	213473	74938	11	-	-	-	-	-	-
CHP Plants	-	38906	10362	-	-	-	-	-	-	-	-
Heat Plants	-	-	-	-	-	-	-	-	-	-	-
Transfer to Gases	-	-	-	-	-	7500	-	-	-	-	-
Transfer to Solids	29362	-	-	-	-	-	-	-	-	-	-
Petroleum Refineries	-	-	-	-	-	-	-	685240	16765	28351	-
Petrochemical Industry	-	-	-	-	-	-	-	-	-	-	-
Liquefaction	-	-	-	-	-	-	-	-	-	-	-
Other Transformation Sector	-	-	-	-	-	-	-	-	-	-	-
ENERGY SECTOR	**-**	**527**	**-**	**-**	**-**	**-**	**-**	**638**	**-**	**-**	**-**
Coal Mines	-	406	-	-	-	-	-	-	-	-	-
Oil and Gas Extraction	-	-	-	-	-	-	-	638	-	-	-
Petroleum Refineries	-	121	-	-	-	-	-	-	-	-	-
Electricity, CHP+Heat plants	-	-	-	-	-	-	-	-	-	-	-
Pumped Storage (Elec.)	-	-	-	-	-	-	-	-	-	-	-
Other Energy Sector	-	-	-	-	-	-	-	-	-	-	-
Distribution Losses	-	-	-	-	-	-	-	-	-	-	-
FINAL CONSUMPTION	**-**	**27564**	**3950**	**6234**	**-**	**14936**	**-**	**-**	**-**	**-**	**-**
INDUSTRY SECTOR	**-**	**24059**	**3950**	**6234**	**-**	**14936**	**-**	**-**	**-**	**-**	**-**
Iron and Steel	-	596	-	-	-	13365	-	-	-	-	-
Chemical and Petrochemical	-	2547	2976	6178	-	-	-	-	-	-	-
of which: Feedstocks	-	-	-	-	-	-	-	-	-	-	-
Non-Ferrous Metals	-	-	-	-	-	-	-	-	-	-	-
Non-Metallic Minerals	-	9656	509	2	-	-	-	-	-	-	-
Transport Equipment	-	-	-	-	-	-	-	-	-	-	-
Machinery	-	691	48	-	-	-	-	-	-	-	-
Mining and Quarrying	-	-	-	-	-	-	-	-	-	-	-
Food and Tobacco	-	484	417	54	-	-	-	-	-	-	-
Paper, Pulp and Print	-	149	-	-	-	-	-	-	-	-	-
Wood and Wood Products	-	-	-	-	-	-	-	-	-	-	-
Construction	-	-	-	-	-	-	-	-	-	-	-
Textile and Leather	-	-	-	-	-	-	-	-	-	-	-
Non-specified	-	9936	-	-	-	1571	-	-	-	-	-
TRANSPORT SECTOR	**-**	**-**	**-**	**-**	**-**	**-**	**-**	**-**	**-**	**-**	**-**
International Civil Aviation	-	-	-	-	-	-	-	-	-	-	-
Domestic Air	-	-	-	-	-	-	-	-	-	-	-
Road	-	-	-	-	-	-	-	-	-	-	-
Rail	-	-	-	-	-	-	-	-	-	-	-
Pipeline Transport	-	-	-	-	-	-	-	-	-	-	-
Internal Navigation	-	-	-	-	-	-	-	-	-	-	-
Non-specified	-	-	-	-	-	-	-	-	-	-	-
OTHER SECTORS	**-**	**3505**	**-**	**-**	**-**	**-**	**-**	**-**	**-**	**-**	**-**
Agriculture	-	-	-	-	-	-	-	-	-	-	-
Commerce and Publ. Serv.	-	1297	-	-	-	-	-	-	-	-	-
Residential	-	2208	-	-	-	-	-	-	-	-	-
Non-specified	-	-	-	-	-	-	-	-	-	-	-
NON-ENERGY USE	**-**	**-**	**-**	**-**	**-**	**-**	**-**	**-**	**-**	**-**	**-**
in Industry/Transf./Energy	-	-	-	-	-	-	-	-	-	-	-
in Transport	-	-	-	-	-	-	-	-	-	-	-
in Other Sectors	-	-	-	-	-	-	-	-	-	-	-

United States / Etats-Unis : 1992

SUPPLY AND CONSUMPTION	Oil cont. / *Pétrole cont.* (1000 tonnes)										
	Refinery Gas	LPG + Ethane	Motor Gasoline	Aviation Gasoline	Jet Fuel	Kerosene	Gas/ Diesel	Heavy Fuel Oil	Naphtha	Pétrol. Coke	Other Prod.
APPROVISIONNEMENT ET DEMANDE	*Gaz de raffinerie*	*GPL + éthane*	*Essence moteur*	*Essence aviation*	*Carbu- réacteur*	*Kérosène*	*Gazole*	*Fioul lourd*	*Naphta*	*Coke de pétrole*	*Autres prod.*
Production	33059	18513	306562	897	66412	1973	149495	54262	7994	39598	53580
From Other Sources	-	-	-	-	-	-	-	-	-	-	-
Imports	-	221	12817	14	2797	98	8696	19166	856	145	7150
Exports	-	-	-4051	-	-1944	-374	-10780	-10601	-	-14341	-1910
Intl. Marine Bunkers	-	-	-	-	-	-	-7150	-25737	-	-	-
Stock Changes	-	342	281	3	482	25	539	1612	-31	27	699
DOMESTIC SUPPLY	**33059**	**19076**	**315609**	**914**	**67747**	**1722**	**140800**	**38702**	**8819**	**25429**	**59519**
Transfers	-	36521	490	2	-	-	-	-	-	-	-6115
Statistical Differences	-	-	-	1	-	-1	-91	-375	-	-3	-
TRANSFORMATION	**-**	**246**	**-**	**-**	**-**	**-**	**1549**	**20387**	**-**	**905**	**-**
Electricity Plants	-	-	-	-	-	-	1549	20387	-	905	-
CHP Plants	-	-	-	-	-	-	-	-	-	-	-
Heat Plants	-	-	-	-	-	-	-	-	-	-	-
Transfer to Gases	-	246	-	-	-	-	-	-	-	-	-
Transfer to Solids	-	-	-	-	-	-	-	-	-	-	-
Petroleum Refineries	-	-	-	-	-	-	-	-	-	-	-
Petrochemical Industry	-	-	-	-	-	-	-	-	-	-	-
Liquefaction	-	-	-	-	-	-	-	-	-	-	-
Other Transformation Sector	-	-	-	-	-	-	-	-	-	-	-
ENERGY SECTOR	**32415**	**1074**	**100**	**-**	**57**	**-**	**104**	**1888**	**6**	**15315**	**197**
Coal Mines	-	-	-	-	-	-	-	-	-	-	-
Oil and Gas Extraction	-	-	-	-	-	-	-	-	-	-	-
Petroleum Refineries	32415	1074	100	-	57	-	104	1888	6	15315	197
Electricity, CHP+Heat plants	-	-	-	-	-	-	-	-	-	-	-
Pumped Storage (Elec.)	-	-	-	-	-	-	-	-	-	-	-
Other Energy Sector	-	-	-	-	-	-	-	-	-	-	-
Distribution Losses	-	-	-	-	-	-	-	-	-	-	-
FINAL CONSUMPTION	**644**	**54277**	**315999**	**917**	**67690**	**1721**	**139056**	**16052**	**8813**	**9206**	**53207**
INDUSTRY SECTOR	**644**	**46521**	**2171**	**-**	**-**	**142**	**15332**	**10513**	**8813**	**-**	**1234**
Iron and Steel	-	-	-	-	-	-	-	-	-	-	-
Chemical and Petrochemical	644	33981	-	-	-	-	-	-	8813	-	-
of which: Feedstocks	*644*	*33981*	-	-	-	-	-	-	*8813*	-	-
Non-Ferrous Metals	-	-	-	-	-	-	-	-	-	-	-
Non-Metallic Minerals	-	-	-	-	-	-	-	-	-	-	-
Transport Equipment	-	-	-	-	-	-	-	-	-	-	-
Machinery	-	-	-	-	-	-	-	-	-	-	-
Mining and Quarrying	-	-	-	-	-	-	-	-	-	-	-
Food and Tobacco	-	-	-	-	-	-	-	-	-	-	-
Paper, Pulp and Print	-	-	-	-	-	-	-	-	-	-	-
Wood and Wood Products	-	-	-	-	-	-	-	-	-	-	-
Construction	-	-	753	-	-	-	-	-	-	-	-
Textile and Leather	-	-	-	-	-	-	-	-	-	-	-
Non-specified	-	12540	1418	-	-	142	15332	10513	-	-	1234
TRANSPORT SECTOR	**-**	**339**	**309808**	**917**	**67690**	**-**	**81474**	**401**	**-**	**-**	**-**
International Civil Aviation	-	-	-	-	-	-	-	-	-	-	-
Domestic Air	-	-	-	917	67690	-	-	-	-	-	-
Road	-	339	306176	-	-	-	68991	-	-	-	-
Rail	-	-	-	-	-	-	10384	-	-	-	-
Pipeline Transport	-	-	-	-	-	-	-	-	-	-	-
Internal Navigation	-	-	3632	-	-	-	-	401	-	-	-
Non-specified	-	-	-	-	-	-	2099	-	-	-	-
OTHER SECTORS	**-**	**7417**	**4020**	**-**	**-**	**1579**	**42250**	**5138**	**-**	**-**	**-**
Agriculture	-	1537	2223	-	-	54	11312	-	-	-	-
Commerce and Publ. Serv.	-	882	1797	-	-	223	10803	5138	-	-	-
Residential	-	4998	-	-	-	1302	20135	-	-	-	-
Non-specified	-	-	-	-	-	-	-	-	-	-	-
NON-ENERGY USE	**-**	**-**	**-**	**-**	**-**	**-**	**-**	**-**	**-**	**9206**	**51973**
in Industry/Transf./Energy	-	-	-	-	-	-	-	-	-	9206	47383
in Transport	-	-	-	-	-	-	-	-	-	-	4590
in Other Sectors	-	-	-	-	-	-	-	-	-	-	-

United States / Etats-Unis : 1992

CONSUMPTION / APPROVISIONNEMENT ET DEMANDE	Gas / Gaz (TJ) Natural Gas / Gaz naturel	Gas Works / Usines à gaz	Coke Ovens / Cokeries	Blast Furnaces / Hauts fourneaux	Combust. Renew. & Waste (TJ) Solid Biomass & Anim. Prod. / Biomasse solide & prod. anim.	Gas/Liquids from Biomass / Gaz/Liquides tirés de biomasse	Municipal Waste / Déchets urbains	Industrial Waste / Déchets industriels	(GWh) Electricity / Electricité	(TJ) Heat / Chaleur
Production	19515717	-	163573	210365	3092678	36571	236331	165816	3291866	377128
From Other Sources	-	-	-	-	-	-	-	-	-	-
Imports	2280089	-	-	-	-	-	-	-	37204	-
Exports	-232307	-	-	-	-	-	-	-	-8855	-
Intl. Marine Bunkers	-	-	-	-	-	-	-	-	-	-
Stock Changes	246626	-	-	-	-	-	-	-	-	-
DOMESTIC SUPPLY	**21810125**	**-**	**163573**	**210365**	**3092678**	**36571**	**236331**	**165816**	**3320215**	**377128**
Transfers	-	-	-	-	-	-	-	-	-	-
Statistical Differences	-575868	-	1838	2364	-	-	-	-	-	-
TRANSFORMATION	**2982189**	**-**	**165411**	**212729**	**1322644**	**36571**	**236331**	**165816**	**-**	**-**
Electricity Plants	2871082	-	13402	17236	210482	27967	191636	18790	-	-
CHP Plants	111107	-	152009	195493	1112162	8604	44695	147026	-	-
Heat Plants	-	-	-	-	-	-	-	-	-	-
Transfer to Gases	-	-	-	-	-	-	-	-	-	-
Transfer to Solids	-	-	-	-	-	-	-	-	-	-
Petroleum Refineries	-	-	-	-	-	-	-	-	-	-
Petrochemical Industry	-	-	-	-	-	-	-	-	-	-
Liquefaction	-	-	-	-	-	-	-	-	-	-
Other Transformation Sector	-	-	-	-	-	-	-	-	-	-
ENERGY SECTOR	**2042000**	**-**	**-**	**-**	**-**	**-**	**-**	**-**	**307311**	**36912**
Coal Mines	-	-	-	-	-	-	-	-	13507	-
Oil and Gas Extraction	1273629	-	-	-	-	-	-	-	33904	-
Petroleum Refineries	768371	-	-	-	-	-	-	-	42696	36912
Electricity, CHP+Heat plants	-	-	-	-	-	-	-	-	193955	-
Pumped Storage (Elec.)	-	-	-	-	-	-	-	-	23249	-
Other Energy Sector	-	-	-	-	-	-	-	-	-	-
Distribution Losses	-	-	-	-	-	-	-	-	237452	41368
FINAL CONSUMPTION	**16210068**	**-**	**-**	**-**	**1770034**	**-**	**-**	**-**	**2775452**	**298848**
INDUSTRY SECTOR	**7419450**	**-**	**-**	**-**	**1123521**	**-**	**-**	**-**	**984800**	**235200**
Iron and Steel	-	-	-	-	-	-	-	-	56976	337
Chemical and Petrochemical	-	-	-	-	-	-	-	-	216640	123231
of which: Feedstocks	-	-	-	-	-	-	-	-	-	-
Non-Ferrous Metals	-	-	-	-	-	-	-	-	96806	1536
Non-Metallic Minerals	-	-	-	-	-	-	-	-	32410	351
Transport Equipment	-	-	-	-	-	-	-	-	35609	5126
Machinery	-	-	-	-	-	-	-	-	102815	6920
Mining and Quarrying	-	-	-	-	-	-	-	-	33389	-
Food and Tobacco	-	-	-	-	-	-	-	-	58267	19635
Paper, Pulp and Print	-	-	-	-	907641	-	-	-	128607	21919
Wood and Wood Products	-	-	-	-	215880	-	-	-	26437	-
Construction	-	-	-	-	-	-	-	-	-	-
Textile and Leather	-	-	-	-	-	-	-	-	37464	7809
Non-specified	7419450	-	-	-	-	-	-	-	159380	48336
TRANSPORT SECTOR	**639872**	**-**	**-**	**-**	**-**	**-**	**-**	**-**	**4005**	**-**
International Civil Aviation	-	-	-	-	-	-	-	-	-	-
Domestic Air	-	-	-	-	-	-	-	-	-	-
Road	556	-	-	-	-	-	-	-	-	-
Rail	-	-	-	-	-	-	-	-	4005	-
Pipeline Transport	639316	-	-	-	-	-	-	-	-	-
Internal Navigation	-	-	-	-	-	-	-	-	-	-
Non-specified	-	-	-	-	-	-	-	-	-	-
OTHER SECTORS	**8150746**	**-**	**-**	**-**	**646513**	**-**	**-**	**-**	**1786647**	**63648**
Agriculture	-	-	-	-	-	-	-	-	-	-
Commerce and Publ. Serv.	3048855	-	-	-	-	-	-	-	850708	63648
Residential	5101891	-	-	-	646513	-	-	-	935939	-
Non-specified	-	-	-	-	-	-	-	-	-	-
NON-ENERGY USE	**-**	**-**	**-**	**-**	**-**	**-**	**-**	**-**	**-**	**-**
in Industry/Transf./Energy	-	-	-	-	-	-	-	-	-	-
in Transport	-	-	-	-	-	-	-	-	-	-
in Other Sectors	-	-	-	-	-	-	-	-	-	-

United States / Etats-Unis : 1993

SUPPLY AND CONSUMPTION	Coal / *Charbon* (1000 tonnes)							Oil / *Pétrole* (1000 tonnes)			
	Coking Coal	Steam Coal	Sub-Bit. Coal	Lignite	Peat	Oven and Gas Coke	Pat. Fuel and BKB	Crude Oil	NGL	Feedstocks	Additives
APPROVISIONNEMENT ET DEMANDE	*Charbon à coke*	*Charbon vapeur*	*Charbon sous-bit.*	*Lignite*	*Tourbe*	*Coke de four/gaz*	*Agg./briq. de lignite*	*Pétrole brut*	*LGN*	*Produits d'aliment.*	*Additifs*
Production	73282	453769	249386	81238	24	21030	-	338152	51332	-	6544
From Other Sources	-	-	-	-	-	-	-	-	-	-	-
Imports	-	6631	-	-	-	1392	-	360102	5604	26635	870
Exports	-45044	-20627	-1932	-	-	-758	-	-158	-1407	-	-
Intl. Marine Bunkers	-	-	-	-	-	-	-	-	-	-	-
Stock Changes	178	43963	1751	-2592	-	383	-	-2563	-182	828	-1456
DOMESTIC SUPPLY	**28416**	**483736**	**249205**	**78646**	**24**	**22047**	**-**	**695533**	**55347**	**27463**	**5958**
Transfers	-	-	-	-	-	-	-	-	-37853	6922	473
Statistical Differences	-	-17697	14949	2748	-	-	-	-2942	-	-1	-352
TRANSFORMATION	**28416**	**438833**	**260864**	**75620**	**24**	**7792**	**-**	**692098**	**17494**	**34384**	**6079**
Electricity Plants	-	395060	247084	74412	24	-	-	-	-	-	-
CHP Plants	-	43773	13780	1208	-	-	-	-	-	-	-
Heat Plants	-	-	-	-	-	-	-	-	-	-	-
Transfer to Gases	-	-	-	-	-	7792	-	-	-	-	-
Transfer to Solids	28416	-	-	-	-	-	-	-	-	-	-
Petroleum Refineries	-	-	-	-	-	-	-	692098	17494	34384	6079
Petrochemical Industry	-	-	-	-	-	-	-	-	-	-	-
Liquefaction	-	-	-	-	-	-	-	-	-	-	-
Other Transformation Sector	-	-	-	-	-	-	-	-	-	-	-
ENERGY SECTOR	**-**	**149**	**-**	**-**	**-**	**-**	**-**	**493**	**-**	**-**	**-**
Coal Mines	-	20	-	-	-	-	-	-	-	-	-
Oil and Gas Extraction	-	-	-	-	-	-	-	493	-	-	-
Petroleum Refineries	-	129	-	-	-	-	-	-	-	-	-
Electricity, CHP+Heat plants	-	-	-	-	-	-	-	-	-	-	-
Pumped Storage (Elec.)	-	-	-	-	-	-	-	-	-	-	-
Other Energy Sector	-	-	-	-	-	-	-	-	-	-	-
Distribution Losses	-	-	-	-	-	-	-	-	-	-	-
FINAL CONSUMPTION	**-**	**27057**	**3290**	**5774**	**-**	**14255**					
INDUSTRY SECTOR	**-**	**24700**	**3290**	**5774**	**-**	**14255**	**-**	**-**	**-**	**-**	**-**
Iron and Steel	-	451	-	-	-	12712	-	-	-	-	-
Chemical and Petrochemical	-	2686	2828	5546	-	-	-	-	-	-	-
of which: Feedstocks	-	-	-	-	-	-	-	-	-	-	-
Non-Ferrous Metals	-	-	-	-	-	-	-	-	-	-	-
Non-Metallic Minerals	-	10475	379	2	-	-	-	-	-	-	-
Transport Equipment	-	-	-	-	-	-	-	-	-	-	-
Machinery	-	631	83	-	-	-	-	-	-	-	-
Mining and Quarrying	-	-	-	-	-	-	-	-	-	-	-
Food and Tobacco	-	464	-	46	-	-	-	-	-	-	-
Paper, Pulp and Print	-	114	-	-	-	-	-	-	-	-	-
Wood and Wood Products	-	-	-	-	-	-	-	-	-	-	-
Construction	-	-	-	-	-	-	-	-	-	-	-
Textile and Leather	-	-	-	-	-	-	-	-	-	-	-
Non-specified	-	9879	-	180	-	1543	-	-	-	-	-
TRANSPORT SECTOR	**-**	**-**	**-**	**-**	**-**	**-**	**-**	**-**	**-**	**-**	**-**
International Civil Aviation	-	-	-	-	-	-	-	-	-	-	-
Domestic Air	-	-	-	-	-	-	-	-	-	-	-
Road	-	-	-	-	-	-	-	-	-	-	-
Rail	-	-	-	-	-	-	-	-	-	-	-
Pipeline Transport	-	-	-	-	-	-	-	-	-	-	-
Internal Navigation	-	-	-	-	-	-	-	-	-	-	-
Non-specified	-	-	-	-	-	-	-	-	-	-	-
OTHER SECTORS	**-**	**2357**	**-**	**-**	**-**	**-**	**-**	**-**	**-**	**-**	**-**
Agriculture	-	-	-	-	-	-	-	-	-	-	-
Commerce and Publ. Serv.	-	125	-	-	-	-	-	-	-	-	-
Residential	-	2232	-	-	-	-	-	-	-	-	-
Non-specified	-	-	-	-	-	-	-	-	-	-	-
NON-ENERGY USE	**-**	**-**	**-**	**-**	**-**	**-**	**-**	**-**	**-**	**-**	**-**
in Industry/Transf./Energy	-	-	-	-	-	-	-	-	-	-	-
in Transport	-	-	-	-	-	-	-	-	-	-	-
in Other Sectors	-	-	-	-	-	-	-	-	-	-	-

United States / Etats-Unis : 1993

SUPPLY AND CONSUMPTION / APPROVISIONNEMENT ET DEMANDE	Oil cont. / *Pétrole cont.* (1000 tonnes)										
	Refinery Gas / *Gaz de raffinerie*	LPG + Ethane / *GPL + éthane*	Motor Gasoline / *Essence moteur*	Aviation Gasoline / *Essence aviation*	Jet Fuel / *Carbu-réacteur*	Kerosene / *Kérosène*	Gas/ Diesel / *Gazole*	Heavy Fuel Oil / *Fioul lourd*	Naphtha / *Naphta*	Pétrol. Coke / *Coke de pétrole*	Other Prod. / *Autres prod.*
Production	32764	17921	316957	874	67530	2334	157330	50958	7122	41048	55148
From Other Sources	-	-	-	-	-	-	-	-	-	-	-
Imports	-	445	9697	11	3364	40	7308	19057	896	125	7868
Exports	-	-	-4789	-	-2632	-164	-13563	-6857	-	-17121	-1566
Intl. Marine Bunkers	-	-	-	-	-	-	-7150	-25737	-	-	-
Stock Changes	-	-1395	-1478	-27	381	193	35	1199	-22	185	-59
DOMESTIC SUPPLY	**32764**	**16971**	**320387**	**858**	**68643**	**2403**	**143960**	**38620**	**7996**	**24237**	**61391**
Transfers	-	37853	1799	5	-	-	-	-	-	-	-6169
Statistical Differences	-	1	1	-	-1	1	-5	-1406	-1	18	1
TRANSFORMATION	**-**	**240**	**-**	**-**	**-**	**-**	**1765**	**22415**	**-**	**1105**	**-**
Electricity Plants	-	-	-	-	-	-	1765	22415	-	1105	-
CHP Plants	-	-	-	-	-	-	-	-	-	-	-
Heat Plants	-	-	-	-	-	-	-	-	-	-	-
Transfer to Gases	-	240	-	-	-	-	-	-	-	-	-
Transfer to Solids	-	-	-	-	-	-	-	-	-	-	-
Petroleum Refineries	-	-	-	-	-	-	-	-	-	-	-
Petrochemical Industry	-	-	-	-	-	-	-	-	-	-	-
Liquefaction	-	-	-	-	-	-	-	-	-	-	-
Other Transformation Sector	-	-	-	-	-	-	-	-	-	-	-
ENERGY SECTOR	**31704**	**870**	**84**	**-**	**69**	**-**	**102**	**1963**	**3**	**15581**	**255**
Coal Mines	-	-	-	-	-	-	-	-	-	-	-
Oil and Gas Extraction	-	-	-	-	-	-	-	-	-	-	-
Petroleum Refineries	31704	870	84	-	69	-	102	1963	3	15581	255
Electricity, CHP+Heat plants	-	-	-	-	-	-	-	-	-	-	-
Pumped Storage (Elec.)	-	-	-	-	-	-	-	-	-	-	-
Other Energy Sector	-	-	-	-	-	-	-	-	-	-	-
Distribution Losses	-	-	-	-	-	-	-	-	-	-	-
FINAL CONSUMPTION	**1060**	**53715**	**322103**	**863**	**68573**	**2404**	**142088**	**12836**	**7992**	**7569**	**54968**
INDUSTRY SECTOR	**1060**	**46153**	**2209**	**-**	**-**	**198**	**15666**	**8407**	**7992**	**-**	**1016**
Iron and Steel	-	-	-	-	-	-	-	-	-	-	-
Chemical and Petrochemical	1060	33926	-	-	-	-	-	-	7992	-	-
of which: Feedstocks	*1060*	*33926*	-	-	-	-	-	-	*7992*	-	-
Non-Ferrous Metals	-	-	-	-	-	-	-	-	-	-	-
Non-Metallic Minerals	-	-	-	-	-	-	-	-	-	-	-
Transport Equipment	-	-	-	-	-	-	-	-	-	-	-
Machinery	-	-	-	-	-	-	-	-	-	-	-
Mining and Quarrying	-	-	-	-	-	-	-	-	-	-	-
Food and Tobacco	-	-	-	-	-	-	-	-	-	-	-
Paper, Pulp and Print	-	-	-	-	-	-	-	-	-	-	-
Wood and Wood Products	-	-	-	-	-	-	-	-	-	-	-
Construction	-	-	766	-	-	-	-	-	-	-	-
Textile and Leather	-	-	-	-	-	-	-	-	-	-	-
Non-specified	-	12227	1443	-	-	198	15666	8407	-	-	1016
TRANSPORT SECTOR	**-**	**330**	**315804**	**863**	**68573**	**-**	**83250**	**321**	**-**	**-**	**-**
International Civil Aviation	-	-	-	-	-	-	-	-	-	-	-
Domestic Air	-	-	-	863	68573	-	-	-	-	-	-
Road	-	330	312109	-	-	-	70495	-	-	-	-
Rail	-	-	-	-	-	-	10611	-	-	-	-
Pipeline Transport	-	-	-	-	-	-	-	-	-	-	-
Internal Navigation	-	-	3695	-	-	-	-	321	-	-	-
Non-specified	-	-	-	-	-	-	2144	-	-	-	-
OTHER SECTORS	**-**	**7232**	**4090**	**-**	**-**	**2206**	**43172**	**4108**	**-**	**-**	**-**
Agriculture	-	1498	2261	-	-	76	11559	-	-	-	-
Commerce and Publ. Serv.	-	860	1829	-	-	311	11039	4108	-	-	-
Residential	-	4874	-	-	-	1819	20574	-	-	-	-
Non-specified	-	-	-	-	-	-	-	-	-	-	-
NON-ENERGY USE	**-**	**-**	**-**	**-**	**-**	**-**	**-**	**-**	**-**	**7569**	**53952**
in Industry/Transf./Energy	-	-	-	-	-	-	-	-	-	7569	49252
in Transport	-	-	-	-	-	-	-	-	-	-	4700
in Other Sectors	-	-	-	-	-	-	-	-	-	-	-

United States / Etats-Unis : 1993

CONSUMPTION / APPROVISIONNEMENT ET DEMANDE	Gas / Gaz (TJ)				Combust. Renew. & Waste / En. Re. Comb. & Déchets (TJ)				(GWh)	(TJ)
	Natural Gas / Gaz naturel	Gas Works / Usines à gaz	Coke Ovens / Cokeries	Blast Furnaces / Hauts fourneaux	Solid Biomass & Anim. Prod. / Biomasse solide & prod. anim.	Gas/Liquids from Biomass / Gaz/Liquides tirés de biomasse	Municipal Waste / Déchets urbains	Industrial Waste / Déchets industriels	Electricity / Electricité	Heat / Chaleur
Production	20087149	-	150145	218569	3195038	134505	240650	173307	3411281	404634
From Other Sources	-	-	-	-	-	-	-	-	-	-
Imports	2529197	-	-	-	-	844	-	-	36892	-
Exports	-150274	-	-	-	-	-	-	-	-8146	-
Intl. Marine Bunkers	-	-	-	-	-	-	-	-	-	-
Stock Changes	306015	-	-	-	-	1089	-	-	-	-
DOMESTIC SUPPLY	**22772087**	**-**	**150145**	**218569**	**3195038**	**136438**	**240650**	**173307**	**3440027**	**404634**
Transfers	-	-	-	-	-	-82475	-	-	-	-
Statistical Differences	-772860	-	-	-	-	-2150	-	-	-	-
TRANSFORMATION	**2892508**	**-**	**148451**	**216103**	**1346365**	**51813**	**240650**	**173307**	**-**	**-**
Electricity Plants	2793676	-	5792	8432	177489	31498	197532	47124	-	-
CHP Plants	98832	-	142659	207671	1168876	8828	43118	126183	-	-
Heat Plants	-	-	-	-	-	-	-	-	-	-
Transfer to Gases	-	-	-	-	-	-	-	-	-	-
Transfer to Solids	-	-	-	-	-	-	-	-	-	-
Petroleum Refineries	-	-	-	-	-	11487	-	-	-	-
Petrochemical Industry	-	-	-	-	-	-	-	-	-	-
Liquefaction	-	-	-	-	-	-	-	-	-	-
Other Transformation Sector	-	-	-	-	-	-	-	-	-	-
ENERGY SECTOR	**2078073**	**-**	**1694**	**-**	**-**	**-**	**-**	**-**	**313974**	**37514**
Coal Mines	-	-	-	-	-	-	-	-	13080	-
Oil and Gas Extraction	1279842	-	-	-	-	-	-	-	33574	-
Petroleum Refineries	798231	-	-	-	-	-	-	-	43459	37514
Electricity, CHP+Heat plants	-	-	-	-	-	-	-	-	200262	-
Pumped Storage (Elec.)	-	-	-	-	-	-	-	-	23599	-
Other Energy Sector	-	-	1694	-	-	-	-	-	-	-
Distribution Losses	-	-	-	-	-	-	-	-	252186	65181
FINAL CONSUMPTION	**17028646**	**-**	**-**	**2466**	**1848673**	**-**	**-**	**-**	**2873867**	**301939**
INDUSTRY SECTOR	**7815911**	**-**	**-**	**2466**	**1181197**	**-**	**-**	**-**	**994707**	**235840**
Iron and Steel	-	-	-	2466	-	-	-	-	58628	346
Chemical and Petrochemical	-	-	-	-	-	-	-	-	213637	120039
of which: Feedstocks	-	-	-	-	-	-	-	-	-	-
Non-Ferrous Metals	-	-	-	-	-	-	-	-	92322	1493
Non-Metallic Minerals	-	-	-	-	-	-	-	-	33054	359
Transport Equipment	-	-	-	-	-	-	-	-	36152	5204
Machinery	-	-	-	-	-	-	-	-	104956	7096
Mining and Quarrying	-	-	-	-	-	-	-	-	32257	-
Food and Tobacco	-	-	-	-	-	-	-	-	59307	20030
Paper, Pulp and Print	-	-	-	-	940214	-	-	-	130287	22174
Wood and Wood Products	-	-	-	-	240983	-	-	-	27917	-
Construction	-	-	-	-	-	-	-	-	-	-
Textile and Leather	-	-	-	-	-	-	-	-	38678	8084
Non-specified	7815911	-	-	-	-	-	-	-	167512	51015
TRANSPORT SECTOR	**678192**	**-**	**-**	**-**	**-**	**-**	**-**	**-**	**4110**	**-**
International Civil Aviation	-	-	-	-	-	-	-	-	-	-
Domestic Air	-	-	-	-	-	-	-	-	-	-
Road	1041	-	-	-	-	-	-	-	-	-
Rail	-	-	-	-	-	-	-	-	4110	-
Pipeline Transport	677151	-	-	-	-	-	-	-	-	-
Internal Navigation	-	-	-	-	-	-	-	-	-	-
Non-specified	-	-	-	-	-	-	-	-	-	-
OTHER SECTORS	**8534543**	**-**	**-**	**-**	**667476**	**-**	**-**	**-**	**1875050**	**66099**
Agriculture	-	-	-	-	-	-	-	-	-	-
Commerce and Publ. Serv.	3157743	-	-	-	-	-	-	-	881498	66099
Residential	5376800	-	-	-	667476	-	-	-	993552	-
Non-specified	-	-	-	-	-	-	-	-	-	-
NON-ENERGY USE	**-**	**-**	**-**	**-**	**-**	**-**	**-**	**-**	**-**	**-**
in Industry/Transf./Energy	-	-	-	-	-	-	-	-	-	-
in Transport	-	-	-	-	-	-	-	-	-	-
in Other Sectors	-	-	-	-	-	-	-	-	-	-

VII. SUMMARY TABLES

1970, 1973, 1978-1993

VII. TABLEAUX RECAPITULATIFS

1970, 1973, 1978-1993

Production of Hard Coal (1000 tonnes)
Production de houille (1000 tonnes)

	1970	1973	1978	1979	1980	1981	1982	1983	1984
Australia	45407	55483	69906	72007	72389	85830	89453	98267	104583
Austria	-	-	-	-	-	-	-	-	-
Belgium	11362	8842	6590	6125	6324	6186	6576	6119	6342
Canada	8042	12337	17141	18610	20173	21739	22379	22583	32063
Denmark	-	-	-	-	-	-	-	-	-
Finland	-	-	-	-	-	-	-	-	-
France	37354	25682	19690	18694	18146	17889	16895	17021	16594
Germany	118018	104407	90188	93311	94492	95545	96318	89620	84868
Greece	-	-	-	-	-	-	-	-	-
Iceland	-	-	-	-	-	-	-	-	-
Ireland	130	64	21	63	60	69	62	75	70
Italy	295	-	6	-	-	-	-	-	-
Japan	40900	25090	18549	17760	18027	17687	17606	17062	16644
Luxembourg	-	-	-	-	-	-	-	-	-
Mexico	-	2494	3085	3125	3089	3030	3189	3689	3819
Netherlands	4545	1829	-	-	-	-	-	-	-
New Zealand	2196	2325	2019	1719	1930	1992	2107	2255	2307
Norway	461	415	402	282	288	410	440	502	451
Portugal	271	221	180	179	177	184	178	185	194
Spain	10751	9991	11217	11677	12558	13867	15423	15419	15289
Sweden	-	12	16	14	18	16	13	13	13
Switzerland	-	-	-	-	-	-	-	-	-
Turkey	4574	4642	4295	4051	3598	3970	4008	3539	3632
United Kingdom	144563	130154	121695	120637	128209	125301	121427	116448	49549
United States	550387	530064	576801	670037	710178	701346	712381	656568	755550
OECD TOTAL	**979256**	**914052**	**941801**	**1038291**	**1089656**	**1095061**	**1108455**	**1049365**	**1091968**
OECD EUROPE	332324	286259	254300	255033	263870	263437	261340	248941	177002
NORTH AMERICA	558429	544895	597027	691772	733440	726115	737949	682840	791432
PACIFIC	88503	82898	90474	91486	92346	105509	109166	117584	123534
EU	327289	281202	249603	250700	259984	259057	256892	244900	172919
IEA	979256	911558	938716	1035166	1086567	1092031	1105266	1045676	1088149

	1985	1986	1987	1988	1989	1990	1991	1992	1993
Australia	117504	133383	147718	134807	147804	158834	164644	175130	176527
Austria	-	-	-	-	-	-	-	-	-
Belgium	6237	5625	4370	2487	1893	1036	634	218	-
Canada	34310	30542	32651	38585	38794	37672	39911	32315	35310
Denmark	-	-	-	-	-	-	-	-	-
Finland	-	-	-	-	-	-	-	-	-
France	15124	14394	13743	12142	11471	10487	10127	9478	8576
Germany	88849	87125	82380	79319	77451	76553	72744	72153	64174
Greece	-	-	-	-	-	-	-	-	-
Iceland	-	-	-	-	-	-	-	-	-
Ireland	57	54	45	45	43	25	1	1	1
Italy	-	29	14	40	74	58	21	111	10
Japan	16382	16012	13049	11223	10187	8262	8053	7598	7217
Luxembourg	-	-	-	-	-	-	-	-	-
Mexico	3713	3150	3368	2459	2802	2963	2321	1605	1710
Netherlands	-	-	-	-	-	-	-	-	-
New Zealand	2279	2176	2327	2227	2554	2427	2504	2769	2925
Norway	507	437	399	264	339	303	330	359	267
Portugal	237	236	261	230	258	281	270	221	197
Spain	16091	15895	14101	14205	14525	14743	13799	14718	14046
Sweden	13	12	24	16	-	11	28	37	4
Switzerland	-	-	-	-	-	-	-	-	-
Turkey	3605	3526	3461	3256	3038	2745	2762	2830	2789
United Kingdom	90793	104635	101645	101661	98285	91033	92712	83987	67463
United States	738844	738413	762341	784864	811296	853647	825058	823255	776437
OECD TOTAL	**1134545**	**1155644**	**1181897**	**1187830**	**1220814**	**1261080**	**1235919**	**1226785**	**1157653**
OECD EUROPE	221513	231968	220443	213665	207377	197275	193428	184113	157527
NORTH AMERICA	776867	772105	798360	825908	852892	894282	867290	857175	813457
PACIFIC	136165	151571	163094	148257	160545	169523	175201	185497	186669
EU	217401	228005	216583	210145	204000	194227	190336	180924	154471
IEA	1130832	1152494	1178529	1185371	1218012	1258117	1233598	1225180	1155943

Production of Brown Coal (1000 tonnes)
Production de lignite (1000 tonnes)

	1970	1973	1978	1979	1980	1981	1982	1983	1984
Australia	24312	24121	30473	32101	32894	32102	37567	34708	33199
Austria	3670	3634	3076	2741	2865	3061	3297	3041	2928
Belgium	-	-	-	-	-	-	-	-	-
Canada	7021	8135	13343	14588	16515	18349	20528	22224	25339
Denmark	135	-	-	-	-	-	-	-	-
Finland	-	-	-	-	-	-	-	-	-
France	2785	2764	2730	2450	2560	2940	3061	2590	2426
Germany	371490	366409	377891	387679	389726	398596	404552	403501	424250
Greece	7946	13301	21815	23621	23198	27315	27399	30594	32502
Iceland	-	-	-	-	-	-	-	-	-
Ireland	-	-	-	-	-	-	-	-	-
Italy	1393	1190	1202	1412	1286	1214	1905	1750	1779
Japan	200	100	37	29	27	-	-	-	-
Luxembourg	-	-	-	-	-	-	-	-	-
Mexico	-	84	-	-	-	12	469	957	1243
Netherlands	-	-	-	-	-	-	-	-	-
New Zealand	187	143	151	209	208	212	152	229	226
Norway	-	-	-	-	-	-	-	-	-
Portugal	-	-	-	-	-	-	-	-	-
Spain	2831	3003	8261	10696	15454	20886	23882	24534	24303
Sweden	-	-	-	-	-	-	-	-	-
Switzerland	-	-	-	-	-	-	-	-	-
Turkey	3992	7754	15122	13127	15027	17036	18664	21706	26340
United Kingdom	-	-	-	-	-	-	-	-	-
United States	5410	12948	31162	38596	42783	45970	47942	52933	57216
OECD TOTAL	**431372**	**443586**	**505263**	**527249**	**542543**	**567693**	**589418**	**598767**	**631751**
OECD EUROPE	394242	398055	430097	441726	450116	471048	482760	487716	514528
NORTH AMERICA	12431	21167	44505	53184	59298	64331	68939	76114	83798
PACIFIC	24699	24364	30661	32339	33129	32314	37719	34937	33425
EU	390250	390301	414975	428599	435089	454012	464096	466010	488188
IEA	431372	443502	505263	527249	542543	567681	588949	597810	630508

	1985	1986	1987	1988	1989	1990	1991	1992	1993
Australia	38380	36075	41804	43398	48289	45990	49386	50723	47648
Austria	3081	2969	2786	2129	2066	2448	2081	1771	1691
Belgium	-	-	-	-	-	-	-	-	-
Canada	26543	26506	28556	32058	31733	30659	31224	33047	33706
Denmark	-	-	-	-	-	-	-	-	-
Finland	-	-	-	-	-	-	-	-	-
France	1839	2142	2060	1653	2168	2333	1966	1578	1672
Germany	434037	426769	418652	420032	411986	357468	279578	241812	221802
Greece	35888	38096	44612	48323	51866	51896	52695	55051	54800
Iceland	-	-	-	-	-	-	-	-	-
Ireland	-	-	-	-	-	-	-	-	-
Italy	1892	1008	959	1000	1000	956	940	714	620
Japan	-	-	-	-	-	-	-	-	-
Luxembourg	-	-	-	-	-	-	-	-	-
Mexico	1480	2475	2848	3091	3160	3078	3174	4499	4905
Netherlands	-	-	-	-	-	-	-	-	-
New Zealand	247	195	86	174	159	161	173	179	176
Norway	-	-	-	-	-	-	-	-	-
Portugal	-	-	-	-	-	-	-	-	-
Spain	23572	22425	20490	17635	21926	21070	19646	18681	17458
Sweden	-	-	-	-	-	-	-	-	-
Switzerland	-	-	-	-	-	-	-	-	-
Turkey	36392	42891	43527	35962	49171	44683	43346	48601	45372
United Kingdom	-	-	-	-	-	-	-	-	-
United States	62779	69267	71146	77202	78407	79914	78484	81703	81238
OECD TOTAL	**666130**	**670818**	**677526**	**682657**	**701931**	**640656**	**562693**	**538359**	**511088**
OECD EUROPE	536701	536300	533086	526734	540183	480854	400252	368208	343415
NORTH AMERICA	90802	98248	102550	112351	113300	113651	112882	119249	119849
PACIFIC	38627	36270	41890	43572	48448	46151	49559	50902	47824
EU	500309	493409	489559	490772	491012	436171	356906	319607	298043
IEA	664650	668343	674678	679566	698771	637578	559519	533860	506183

Production of Natural Gas (TJ)
Production de gaz naturel (TJ)

	1970	1973	1978	1979	1980	1981	1982	1983	1984
Australia	55990	157311	284560	323187	347366	406233	448025	468474	490073
Austria	77223	91923	98683	95287	78442	58099	53551	48806	51177
Belgium	1880	1913	1369	1323	1532	1277	1218	720	1478
Canada	2190659	2855419	2848933	3116453	2960659	2849802	2937399	2757513	2996246
Denmark	-	-	-	-	-	-	-	1709	12127
Finland	-	-	-	-	-	-	-	-	-
France	270610	292687	307236	302777	294328	276953	257074	259824	246820
Germany	443978	764857	847948	856218	756799	779202	689925	753616	792131
Greece	-	-	-	-	-	-	3375	3215	3538
Iceland	-	-	-	-	-	-	-	-	-
Ireland	-	-	-	21512	34315	52297	76966	82296	87282
Italy	503262	587010	525820	513034	477425	535035	549363	492598	521357
Japan	96799	106475	108363	99047	90146	86248	83991	85549	87517
Luxembourg	-	-	-	-	-	-	-	-	-
Mexico	-	545226	756985	923662	1114486	1196826	1290275	1267157	1248534
Netherlands	1116276	2501073	3120564	3293111	3205762	2975902	2533357	2691648	2716794
New Zealand	4011	13147	59473	39402	42542	45053	79915	86358	109656
Norway	-	-	549894	893467	1059382	1072043	1028772	1041391	1097348
Portugal	-	-	-	-	-	-	-	-	-
Spain	155	59	33	-	-	-	-	2931	9295
Sweden	-	-	-	-	-	-	-	-	-
Switzerland	-	-	-	-	-	-	-	-	-
Turkey	-	-	-	-	-	-	1532	2719	1532
United Kingdom	438170	1137344	1517916	1532792	1457161	1453891	1477735	1523736	1491242
United States	22838337	23388315	20541651	21163047	21152333	20956919	19400350	17567532	19020959
OECD TOTAL	**28037350**	**32442759**	**31569428**	**33174319**	**33072678**	**32745780**	**30912823**	**29137792**	**30985106**
OECD EUROPE	**2851554**	**5376866**	**6969463**	**7509521**	**7365146**	**7204699**	**6672868**	**6905209**	**7032121**
NORTH AMERICA	**25028996**	**26788960**	**24147569**	**25203162**	**25227478**	**25003547**	**23628024**	**21592202**	**23265739**
PACIFIC	**156800**	**276933**	**452396**	**461636**	**480054**	**537534**	**611931**	**640381**	**687246**
EU	**2851554**	**5376866**	**6419569**	**6616054**	**6305764**	**6132656**	**5642564**	**5861099**	**5933241**
IEA	**28037350**	**31897533**	**30812443**	**32250657**	**31958192**	**31548954**	**29622548**	**27870635**	**29736572**

	1985	1986	1987	1988	1989	1990	1991	1992	1993
Australia	522852	571092	588928	610477	627770	797340	829256	902611	970880
Austria	46943	44834	46693	50582	52938	51529	52515	56919	58776
Belgium	1591	1043	1105	664	523	450	383	221	178
Canada	3267512	3061255	3323309	3833834	3987065	4101164	4335607	4761464	5234352
Denmark	49283	83544	107141	107744	125032	127281	160726	166955	183896
Finland	-	-	-	-	-	-	-	-	-
France	209382	164608	152642	125478	121284	117032	132868	129460	134147
Germany	728382	681193	758607	702686	672632	629513	629515	638317	639745
Greece	3324	4555	5200	6237	6290	6426	6348	5866	4325
Iceland	-	-	-	-	-	-	-	-	-
Ireland	92491	62924	62815	75679	85734	87127	89290	88319	100312
Italy	536769	601505	616473	626563	640451	652664	656443	685403	729510
Japan	91293	86369	88953	86025	82415	83851	87584	88569	90394
Luxembourg	-	-	-	-	-	-	-	-	-
Mexico	1231354	1092075	1107241	1118562	1156017	1176617	1175942	1148262	1123746
Netherlands	2838839	2603758	2611144	2307408	2522206	2540607	2872184	2884654	2936245
New Zealand	140083	168521	162678	178157	182770	181925	198150	210097	204265
Norway	1088677	1129393	1193171	1203835	1242770	1123348	1112303	1171974	1126696
Portugal	-	-	-	-	-	-	-	-	-
Spain	10681	15491	29630	37724	66069	59228	55393	50664	27726
Sweden	-	-	-	-	-	-	-	-	-
Switzerland	700	600	340	280	170	140	120	110	90
Turkey	2566	17518	11384	3792	6665	8120	7775	7583	7660
United Kingdom	1661741	1738971	1829288	1761317	1724139	1903851	2119723	2155548	2536581
United States	17959454	17486128	18062977	18594050	18946778	19507097	19355514	19515717	20087149
OECD TOTAL	**30483917**	**29615377**	**30759719**	**31431094**	**32249718**	**33155310**	**33877639**	**34668713**	**36196673**
OECD EUROPE	**7271369**	**7149937**	**7425633**	**7009989**	**7266903**	**7307316**	**7895586**	**8041993**	**8485887**
NORTH AMERICA	**22458320**	**21639458**	**22493527**	**23546446**	**24089860**	**24784878**	**24867063**	**25425443**	**26445247**
PACIFIC	**754228**	**825982**	**840559**	**874659**	**892955**	**1063116**	**1114990**	**1201277**	**1265539**
EU	**6179426**	**6002426**	**6220738**	**5802082**	**6017298**	**6175708**	**6775388**	**6862326**	**7351441**
IEA	**29252563**	**28523302**	**29652478**	**30312532**	**31093701**	**31978693**	**32701697**	**33520451**	**35072927**

Production of Nuclear Electricity (GWh)
Production d'électricité d'origine nucléaire (GWh)

	1970	1973	1978	1979	1980	1981	1982	1983	1984
Australia	-	-	-	-	-	-	-	-	-
Austria		-	-	-	-	-	-	-	-
Belgium	57	76	12513	11407	12549	12859	15664	24106	27743
Canada	1037	15254	31202	35271	38032	40067	38337	48610	52210
Denmark									
Finland	-	-	3264	6742	7022	14665	16776	17720	18867
France	5711	14741	30483	39960	61251	105326	108919	144261	191234
Germany	6494	12106	43873	52064	55589	65533	74426	78063	104317
Greece	-	-	-	-	-	-	-	-	-
Iceland	-	-	-	-	-	-	-	-	-
Ireland	-	-	-	-	-	-	-	-	-
Italy	3176	3142	4428	2628	2208	2707	6804	5783	6887
Japan	4600	9707	59313	70393	82591	87820	102430	114291	134264
Luxembourg	-	-	-	-	-	-	-	-	-
Mexico	-								
Netherlands	368	1108	4060	3489	4200	3658	3897	3589	3711
New Zealand	-	-	-	-	-	-	-	-	-
Norway	-	-	-	-	-	-	-	-	-
Portugal	-	-	-		-	-	-	-	-
Spain	923	6545	7649	6700	5186	9568	8771	10661	23086
Sweden	56	2111	23781	21039	26488	37679	39045	41004	50926
Switzerland	1766	6310	8395	11805	14346	15330	15133	15710	18440
Turkey	-	-	-	-	-	-	-	-	-
United Kingdom	26012	27997	37224	38308	37023	37969	43972	49928	53979
United States	23324	89167	292987	270464	266183	289034	299739	311298	347292
OECD TOTAL	**73524**	**188264**	**559172**	**570270**	**612668**	**722215**	**773913**	**865024**	**1032956**
OECD EUROPE	44563	74136	175670	194142	225862	305294	333407	390825	499190
NORTH AMERICA	24361	104421	324189	305735	304215	329101	338076	359908	399502
PACIFIC	4600	9707	59313	70393	82591	87820	102430	114291	134264
EU	42797	67826	167275	182337	211516	289964	318274	375115	480750
IEA	73524	188264	559172	570270	612668	722215	773913	865024	1032956

	1985	1986	1987	1988	1989	1990	1991	1992	1993
Australia	-	-	-	-	-	-	-	-	-
Austria	-	-	-	-	-	-	-	-	-
Belgium	34601	39394	41967	43102	41217	42722	42861	43456	41927
Canada	60521	71267	77261	82867	79872	72886	84929	80580	94823
Denmark	-	-	-	-	-	-	-	-	-
Finland	19059	19059	19646	19554	19090	19216	19511	19260	19891
France	224100	254155	265520	275521	303931	314081	331340	338445	368188
Germany	138641	130489	141725	156820	161671	152468	147429	158804	153476
Greece	-	-	-	-	-	-	-	-	-
Iceland	-	-	-	-	-	-	-	-	-
Ireland	-	-	-	-	-	-	-	-	-
Italy	7024	8758	174	-	-	-	-	-	-
Japan	159578	168305	187758	178659	182869	202272	213460	223259	249256
Luxembourg	-	-	-	-	-	-	-	-	-
Mexico	-	-	-	-	372	2937	4242	3919	4931
Netherlands	3899	4216	3556	3675	4019	3502	3329	3800	3948
New Zealand	-	-	-	-	-	-	-	-	-
Norway	-	-	-	-	-	-	-	-	-
Portugal	-	-	-	-	-	-	-	-	-
Spain	28044	37458	41271	50466	56126	54268	55578	55782	56060
Sweden	58561	69951	67385	69424	65603	68185	76761	63544	61395
Switzerland	22558	22581	23003	22792	22836	23636	22953	23448	23351
Turkey	-	-	-	-	-	-	-	-	-
United Kingdom	61095	59079	55238	63456	71734	65747	70543	76807	89353
United States	406712	438880	482586	558591	561165	611589	649399	655970	646987
OECD TOTAL	**1224393**	**1323592**	**1407090**	**1524927**	**1570505**	**1633509**	**1722335**	**1747074**	**1813586**
OECD EUROPE	597582	645140	659485	704810	746227	743825	770305	783346	817589
NORTH AMERICA	467233	510147	559847	641458	641409	687412	738570	740469	746741
PACIFIC	159578	168305	187758	178659	182869	202272	213460	223259	249256
EU	575024	622559	636482	682018	723391	720189	747352	759898	794238
IEA	1224393	1323592	1407090	1524927	1570133	1630572	1718093	1743155	1808655

Production of Hydro Electricity (GWh)
Production d'électricité d'origine hydraulique (GWh)

	1970	1973	1978	1979	1980	1981	1982	1983	1984
Australia	9125	11800	14458	16034	13781	14913	14570	12913	12890
Austria	21240	19159	24891	28047	29090	30830	30880	30589	29469
Belgium	246	623	503	575	829	1083	1051	1174	1318
Canada	158276	194771	235374	244233	251249	266106	257865	266024	286196
Denmark	24	24	23	25	30	33	31	39	34
Finland	9258	10515	9742	10870	10216	13653	13088	13579	13246
France	56689	47708	68838	67309	70187	73017	71298	70888	67537
Germany	19010	16784	19777	19832	20307	21694	21411	20634	20218
Greece	2636	2223	2988	3566	3405	3407	3561	2340	2862
Iceland	1431	2207	2634	2850	3087	3120	3445	3628	3779
Ireland	802	644	1030	1203	1155	1242	1203	1178	1045
Italy	41300	39125	47413	48212	47511	45736	44081	44216	45434
Japan	80100	71678	74647	85043	92092	90563	84039	87995	76723
Luxembourg	887	839	320	332	290	573	494	452	450
Mexico	-	16081	16056	17839	16740	24446	22729	20583	23448
Netherlands	-	-	-	-	-	-	-	-	-
New Zealand	11383	14316	16210	18692	18928	19539	17987	20198	20107
Norway	57833	72893	80864	88977	83962	93270	92888	106049	106339
Portugal	5854	7354	10865	11251	8072	5095	6982	8134	9817
Spain	27959	29524	41497	47473	30807	23178	27394	28865	33420
Sweden	41539	59892	57772	61218	59247	60207	55604	64066	68481
Switzerland	31586	29110	32835	32669	33877	36458	37405	36362	31180
Turkey	3029	2621	9335	10289	11348	12617	14167	11343	13426
United Kingdom	5666	4554	5222	5464	5123	5385	5637	6459	6060
United States	250480	265384	283223	282581	278781	263291	312305	335451	324361
OECD TOTAL	**836353**	**919829**	**1056517**	**1104584**	**1090114**	**1109456**	**1140115**	**1193159**	**1197840**
OECD EUROPE	326989	345799	416549	440162	418543	430598	430620	449995	454115
NORTH AMERICA	408756	476236	534653	544653	546770	553843	592899	622058	634005
PACIFIC	100608	97794	105315	119769	124801	125015	116596	121106	109720
EU	233110	238968	290881	305377	286269	285133	282715	292613	299391
IEA	834922	901541	1037827	1083895	1070287	1081890	1113941	1168948	1170613

	1985	1986	1987	1988	1989	1990	1991	1992	1993
Australia	14964	15511	14744	14963	15161	14880	16103	15767	16539
Austria	31603	31680	36725	36541	36146	32492	32728	36082	38020
Belgium	1350	1398	1469	1167	975	897	979	1156	1020
Canada	303720	310697	316288	307553	291448	296919	308479	316484	323690
Denmark	33	29	29	32	27	27	26	28	27
Finland	12333	12389	13795	13361	13029	10859	13197	15107	13599
France	63663	64694	72365	78216	50602	57350	61478	72522	67894
Germany	19345	20311	22313	22451	20713	19722	18460	21115	21465
Greece	2805	3348	2964	2593	2147	1997	3171	2389	2541
Iceland	3704	3884	3957	4211	4259	4204	4204	4310	4466
Ireland	1180	1264	1116	1205	991	983	964	1050	1012
Italy	44595	44531	42585	43547	37484	35079	45606	45786	44482
Japan	87946	86074	80846	95884	97825	95835	105594	89616	105470
Luxembourg	510	534	552	825	825	823	798	608	463
Mexico	26087	19876	18200	20652	24199	23338	21737	26095	26235
Netherlands	3	3	1	2	37	120	80	120	92
New Zealand	19707	21788	22078	23162	22163	23340	23124	20631	23368
Norway	102946	96819	103763	109544	118698	121382	110580	117062	119511
Portugal	10783	8542	9185	12302	6079	9303	9176	5074	8737
Spain	33033	27416	28167	36233	20047	26184	28293	20934	25779
Sweden	71589	61494	72442	70467	71921	73033	63662	74861	75380
Switzerland	33004	33925	35766	36803	30790	30982	33413	34062	36616
Turkey	12045	11872	18618	28949	17939	23148	22683	26568	33951
United Kingdom	6926	7001	6243	7054	6659	7153	6103	7080	5686
United States	283960	293752	252192	225169	273636	288960	309155	274883	303063
OECD TOTAL	**1187834**	**1178832**	**1176393**	**1192886**	**1163800**	**1199010**	**1239793**	**1229390**	**1299106**
OECD EUROPE	451450	431134	472045	505503	439368	455738	455601	485914	500741
NORTH AMERICA	613767	624325	586680	553374	589283	609217	639371	617462	652988
PACIFIC	122617	123373	117668	134009	135149	134055	144821	126014	145377
EU	299751	284634	309951	325996	267682	276022	284721	303912	306197
IEA	1158043	1155072	1154236	1168023	1135342	1171468	1213852	1198985	1268405

Production of Crude Oil + NGL (1000 tonnes)
Production de pétrole brut + LGN (1000 tonnes)

	1970	1973	1978	1979	1980	1981	1982	1983	1984
Australia	8147	19182	21891	21941	20564	20064	19766	19226	23138
Austria	2798	2596	1815	1751	1496	1352	1306	1281	1216
Belgium	-	-	-	-	-	-	-	-	-
Canada	66409	94128	75080	84386	81389	73723	73446	77272	83315
Denmark	-	68	432	432	298	758	1686	2152	2314
Finland	-	-	-	-	-	-	-	-	-
France	2904	2066	1943	2005	2254	2436	2338	2317	2699
Germany	7790	6714	5130	4799	4667	4495	4292	4145	4071
Greece	-	-	-	-	-	196	1032	1241	1320
Iceland	-	-	-	-	-	-	-	-	-
Ireland	-	-	-	-	-	-	-	-	-
Italy	1520	1105	1489	1717	1825	1487	1789	2265	2295
Japan	779	717	565	507	451	408	420	441	426
Luxembourg	-	-	-	-	-	-	-	-	-
Mexico	-	25801	66301	80342	106622	127275	149928	146079	149933
Netherlands	1919	1556	1520	1581	1568	1606	1894	2900	3433
New Zealand	-	161	575	386	338	435	681	672	864
Norway	-	1595	17000	18776	24277	23376	24411	30611	35050
Portugal	-	-	-	-	-	-	-	-	-
Spain	155	654	1211	1368	1755	1445	1757	3185	2512
Sweden	-	-	1	1	25	6	14	23	13
Switzerland	-	-	-	-	-	-	-	-	-
Turkey	3542	3511	2736	2823	2330	2363	2333	2203	2087
United Kingdom	165	515	54100	77944	80467	89481	103218	114921	125924
United States	532428	513296	483076	475465	478626	477059	478452	480024	491474
OECD TOTAL	**628556**	**673665**	**734865**	**776224**	**808952**	**827965**	**868763**	**890958**	**932084**
OECD EUROPE	20793	20380	87377	113197	120962	129001	146070	167244	182934
NORTH AMERICA	598837	633225	624457	640193	666637	678057	701826	703375	724722
PACIFIC	8926	20060	23031	22834	21353	20907	20867	20339	24428
EU	17251	15274	67641	91598	94355	103262	119326	134430	145797
IEA	628556	647864	668564	695882	702330	700690	718835	744879	782151

	1985	1986	1987	1988	1989	1990	1991	1992	1993
Australia	26764	27436	27236	27171	24581	27493	27513	26927	26654
Austria	1161	1133	1082	1217	1198	1190	1321	1220	1195
Belgium	-	-	-	-	-	-	-	-	-
Canada	84049	85448	90266	93932	91821	92147	92000	95904	100740
Denmark	2892	3621	4602	4734	5531	5994	6993	7756	8265
Finland	-	-	-	-	-	-	-	-	-
France	3243	3446	3645	3831	3740	3470	3400	3313	3205
Germany	4136	4068	3767	3986	3837	3648	3405	3279	3064
Greece	1322	1333	1221	1118	916	830	836	687	562
Iceland	-	-	-	-	-	-	-	-	-
Ireland	-	-	-	-	-	-	-	-	-
Italy	2408	2558	3943	4841	4604	4668	4332	4501	4640
Japan	553	647	621	607	560	552	751	858	778
Luxembourg	-	-	-	-	-	-	-	-	-
Mexico	147477	138029	144425	143940	144489	147882	155557	155507	155251
Netherlands	4069	4995	4663	4271	3814	3976	3719	3324	3248
New Zealand	1282	1427	1370	1634	1829	1891	1992	1896	2026
Norway	38431	42375	49541	56351	74872	82088	93716	106862	114471
Portugal	-	-	-	-	-	-	-	-	-
Spain	2383	2094	1852	1718	1333	1144	1422	1402	1102
Sweden	8	4	4	3	3	3	2	1	-
Switzerland	-	-	-	-	-	-	-	-	-
Turkey	2110	2394	2627	2569	2876	3712	4364	4276	3892
United Kingdom	127642	127053	123306	114459	91811	91596	91259	94390	100228
United States	494350	478081	463262	454909	425265	413344	412898	407476	396028
OECD TOTAL	**944280**	**926142**	**927433**	**921291**	**883080**	**885628**	**905480**	**919579**	**925349**
OECD EUROPE	189805	195074	200253	199098	194535	202319	214769	231011	243872
NORTH AMERICA	725876	701558	697953	692781	661575	653373	660455	658887	652019
PACIFIC	28599	29510	29227	29412	26970	29936	30256	29681	29458
EU	149264	150305	148085	140178	116787	116519	116689	119873	125509
IEA	796803	788113	783008	777351	738591	737746	749923	764072	770098

INTERNATIONAL ENERGY AGENCY

Production of Combustible Renewables and Waste (TJ)
Production de renouvelables combustibles et déchets (TJ)

	1970	1973	1978	1979	1980	1981	1982	1983	1984
Australia	148225	147710	154070	148456	151286	160283	166388	164386	160359
Austria	27708	29195	34792	42831	47202	50380	56476	57363	65624
Belgium	-	202	2366	2717	1984	1905	2258	4649	4820
Canada	314782	327225	288800	297500	317800	301974	303761	330500	329711
Denmark	9630	10048	12351	14235	14235	15491	17166	18694	21198
Finland	174909	164266	133415	140320	144668	151985	136832	149658	159589
France	78712	78712	110113	118068	125604	133559	141514	145282	149469
Germany	105669	103471	109447	111727	124986	134890	144542	140843	153753
Greece	18840	18840	18840	18840	18840	18840	18840	18840	18840
Iceland	-	-	-	-	-	-	-	-	-
Ireland	-	-	-	-	-	-	-	-	-
Italy	65209	64791	29957	31987	34198	38476	36082	35576	36907
Japan	-	-	-	-	-	-	-	-	-
Luxembourg	-	-	729	766	879	879	858	858	963
Mexico	-	343308	356792	358511	357105	360062	342361	354109	365094
Netherlands	-	-	11434	10253	9504	8529	2441	2131	155
New Zealand	-	-	21700	21100	22600	23900	23300	21900	22200
Norway	-	-	19824	23542	25573	28948	27872	29345	30489
Portugal	31238	26749	30622	32310	30075	30987	32741	34725	34341
Spain	456	544	3069	2056	11149	13172	14390	14386	16869
Sweden	121836	148421	155487	165084	172970	179336	173811	195740	214155
Switzerland	10110	9890	16310	19070	19550	24370	26970	26980	28680
Turkey	-	270174	313047	325348	321610	323369	331866	337301	332023
United Kingdom	15659	7574	3270	2005	1394	394	1189	992	695
United States	1508311	1612588	2149587	2270158	2343385	2361757	2395762	2545503	2849942
OECD TOTAL	-	-	3976022	4156884	4296597	4363486	4397420	4629761	4995876
OECD EUROPE	-	-	1005073	1061159	1104421	1155510	1165848	1213363	1268570
NORTH AMERICA	-	-	2795179	2926169	3018290	3023793	3041884	3230112	3544747
PACIFIC	-	-	175770	169556	173886	184183	189688	186286	182559
EU	-	-	655892	693199	737688	778823	779140	819737	877378
IEA	-	-	3619230	3798373	3939492	4003424	4055059	4275652	4630782

	1985	1986	1987	1988	1989	1990	1991	1992	1993
Australia	164985	166283	160650	163905	173830	178191	177112	164422	182046
Austria	70522	78339	119221	130711	128318	132064	131403	136214	126341
Belgium	6579	8487	8259	9003	8767	10137	12697	13576	13527
Canada	348260	368062	373323	373735	360386	353911	359968	369441	366881
Denmark	22680	27863	36978	40020	42520	42710	47410	50490	52900
Finland	149863	152178	159162	166340	171777	166259	155740	158094	176369
France	153237	157005	157424	161192	165379	165379	165000	175800	175600
Germany	154569	146897	140475	152330	145216	141341	111599	101563	103700
Greece	18840	18840	20934	20934	20934	23023	23023	24873	24264
Iceland	-	-	-	-	-	-	-	-	-
Ireland	-	-	-	-	-	-	-	-	-
Italy	31694	39683	37513	39389	39194	37205	41077	42801	454
Japan	-	-	-	-	-	-	-	-	40232
Luxembourg	-	-	-	-	-	-	-	91956	91226
Mexico	971	733	1013	1135	1166	1036	1078	1087	1040
Netherlands	369998	342082	343566	344969	346311	347625	349614	370398	383130
New Zealand	3588	4501	5715	7708	8308	8455	9360	15036	16080
Norway	24000	22900	22900	24500	25700	41050	42650	41386	42744
Portugal	34071	37161	38554	37843	40008	41866	41941	42486	42799
Spain	38650	42608	44156	44696	47175	48087	47570	44611	45694
Sweden	18602	18828	20025	21119	21500	20000	30000	30000	31731
Switzerland	225532	226931	230236	234388	230894	230579	241307	246216	260174
Turkey	31420	33540	33950	34180	34450	34760	36910	36770	41460
United Kingdom	324389	330456	330489	331835	331717	331087	331573	332075	332578
United States	188	100	-	-	29152	28481	30141	33779	38317
	2799717	2860468	3146514	3113952	3266684	2971087	4093741	3531396	3743500
OECD TOTAL	4992355	5083945	5431057	5453884	5639386	5354333	6480914	6054470	6332787
OECD EUROPE	1285395	1324150	1384104	1432823	1466475	1462469	1457829	1485471	1523260
NORTH AMERICA	3517975	3570612	3863403	3832656	3973381	3672623	4803323	4271235	4493511
PACIFIC	188985	189183	183550	188405	199530	219241	219762	297764	316016
EU	895515	922993	981111	1028965	1060300	1054756	1047405	1074140	1106423
IEA	4622357	4741863	5087491	5108915	5293075	5006708	6131300	5684072	5949657

As data become available in different years for different countries, no regional totals are shown prior to 1978.
Comme les données pour tous les pays sont disponibles pour des années différentes, les totaux régionaux ne sont pas calculés avant 1978.

INTERNATIONAL ENERGY AGENCY

Total Production of Electricity (GWh)
Production totale d'électricité (GWh)

	1970	1973	1978	1979	1980	1981	1982	1983	1984
Australia	49618	64800	86370	91308	96073	103045	105387	106298	112308
Austria	30036	31325	38068	40645	41965	42892	42891	42625	42382
Belgium	30523	41067	50839	52246	53642	50753	50696	52707	54657
Canada	209651	270198	343081	359216	373375	390636	387482	407981	437098
Denmark	20024	19120	20415	22105	26754	19752	23707	22186	22620
Finland	21991	26102	35732	39243	40747	40909	41175	42197	45287
France	146837	182528	226635	241375	257979	276461	279209	296812	324509
Germany	310254	375903	449393	469028	467578	469526	469783	478741	504977
Greece	9820	14817	21050	22102	22653	23393	23272	23983	24804
Iceland	1488	2320	2707	2955	3184	3315	3633	3828	3977
Ireland	5791	7348	9978	11017	10883	10909	10931	11178	11593
Italy	117423	145518	175041	181264	185741	181656	184445	182880	182669
Japan	359500	470287	562372	589640	576331	583245	581358	618377	648671
Luxembourg	2148	2186	1380	1339	1110	1193	941	830	896
Mexico	-	34244	52967	58070	61868	67879	73225	74831	79507
Netherlands	40858	52627	61596	64464	64806	64053	60312	59650	62778
New Zealand	13983	18531	21912	21749	22273	23132	24598	26138	27064
Norway	58202	73055	80997	89123	84099	93397	93156	106370	106666
Portugal	7488	9821	14653	16153	15263	13900	15418	18161	19247
Spain	56490	76272	99534	105779	110483	111232	114569	117196	120042
Sweden	60646	78080	92903	95204	96695	103300	100050	109391	123843
Switzerland	35452	38024	43203	46575	49247	52811	53580	53137	50566
Turkey	8453	12246	21589	22378	23140	24563	26553	27348	30613
United Kingdom	249193	282048	287689	299864	285303	277735	272783	277474	282469
United States	1623891	1965509	2316442	2359663	2427320	2437024	2376635	2449040	2562773
OECD TOTAL	**3469760**	**4293976**	**5116546**	**5302505**	**5398512**	**5466711**	**5415789**	**5609359**	**5882016**
OECD EUROPE	1213117	1470407	1733402	1822859	1841272	1861750	1867104	1926694	2014595
NORTH AMERICA	1833542	2269951	2712490	2776949	2862563	2895539	2837342	2931852	3079378
PACIFIC	423101	553618	670654	702697	694677	709422	711343	750813	788043
EU	1109522	1344762	1584906	1661828	1681602	1687664	1690182	1736011	1822773
IEA	3468272	4257412	5060872	5241480	5333460	5395517	5338931	5530700	5798532

	1985	1986	1987	1988	1989	1990	1991	1992	1993
Australia	120962	126383	132670	138959	147788	155077	156851	159649	163751
Austria	44534	44653	50517	49025	50174	50414	51484	51180	52675
Belgium	57322	58676	63367	65349	67482	70846	71945	72259	70845
Canada	459045	468593	496335	505966	499538	482025	507913	520924	527386
Denmark	29064	30739	29449	27965	22312	25758	36330	30849	33738
Finland	49716	49266	53402	53878	53817	54377	57985	57722	61172
France	344301	362784	378309	391926	406891	420155	454735	462841	472004
Germany	522534	523557	532442	549489	559867	549877	539391	537134	525721
Greece	27740	28237	30272	33394	34456	35002	35813	37410	38396
Iceland	3900	4114	4210	4478	4537	4510	4494	4546	4727
Ireland	12088	12652	13064	13228	13833	14515	15147	16011	16396
Italy	185740	192330	201372	203561	210750	216891	222041	226243	222788
Japan	671952	676360	719067	753728	798757	857272	888088	895266	906705
Luxembourg	942	1022	1019	1331	1372	1377	1415	1198	1067
Mexico	85352	89383	96310	101905	110063	114249	118357	121653	126566
Netherlands	62947	67158	68419	69611	73050	71866	74252	77202	76992
New Zealand	27334	28169	28686	29471	30955	31632	32725	31294	33624
Norway	103292	97284	104283	110019	119197	121848	111009	117506	120004
Portugal	18900	20355	20135	22489	25808	28500	29871	30087	31205
Spain	127363	129150	133390	139571	147842	151741	155704	158505	156529
Sweden	137140	138651	146571	146230	143091	146508	147384	146444	145975
Switzerland	56492	57564	59890	60690	54767	55796	57803	59117	61070
Turkey	34219	39696	44353	48048	52044	57543	60246	67342	73808
United Kingdom	297555	301590	303750	308825	314585	319695	322805	320963	323029
United States	2621929	2639724	2732532	2874797	3144994	3197267	3273121	3291866	3411281
OECD TOTAL	**6102363**	**6188090**	**6443814**	**6703933**	**7087970**	**7234741**	**7426909**	**7495211**	**7657454**
OECD EUROPE	2115789	2159478	2238214	2299107	2355875	2397219	2449854	2474559	2488141
NORTH AMERICA	3166326	3197700	3325177	3482668	3754595	3793541	3899391	3934443	4065233
PACIFIC	820248	830912	880423	922158	977500	1043981	1077664	1086209	1104080
EU	1917886	1960820	2025478	2075872	2125330	2157522	2216302	2226048	2228532
IEA	6013111	6094593	6343294	6597550	6973370	7115982	7304058	7369012	7526161

Production of Heat (TJ)
Production de chaleur (TJ)

	1970	1973	1978	1979	1980	1981	1982	1983	1984
Australia	-	-	4626	4857	5443	4689	4312	3140	2759
Austria	-	-	6845	6812	7817	7880	18677	18904	19626
Belgium	-	14013	14960	16592	17128	15622	13937	12079	10913
Canada	-	4003	17011	43816	43140	45742	63159	50643	46443
Denmark	-		26921	29496	30806	31523	33662	37322	38878
Finland	17226	26471	46826	47855	52704	56664	60800	65494	70560
France	-		-	-	-	-	-	-	-
Germany	66100	99274	285419	290190	293490	301863	307277	320745	325266
Greece	-	-	-	-	-	-	-	-	-
Iceland	-							3066	2895
Ireland	-	-	-	-	-	-	-	-	-
Italy	-	-	-	-	-	-	-	-	-
Japan	-	1160	3638	3936	4270	4466	4519	5052	5458
Luxembourg	-	-	-	-	-	-	-	-	-
Mexico	-	-	-	-	-	-	-	-	-
Netherlands	-	-	-	-	-	-	6530	7480	8789
New Zealand	-	-	-	-	-	-	-	-	-
Norway	-	-	-	-	-	-	-	1180	1453
Portugal	-	-	-	-	892	1725	1499	1227	1461
Spain	-	-	-	-	-	-	-	-	-
Sweden	-	-	53055	56225	107326	104965	101246	90604	85691
Switzerland	-	-	6636	6984	8930	9328	9416	9617	10216
Turkey	-	-	-	-	-	-	-	-	-
United Kingdom	-	-	4480	4413	5037	3035	1985	528	548
United States	-	-	-	-	-	-	-	83313	85896
OECD TOTAL	-	-	-	-	-	-	-	-	-
OECD EUROPE	-	-	-	-	-	-	-	-	-
NORTH AMERICA	-	-	-	-	-	-	-	-	-
PACIFIC	-	-	-	-	-	-	-	-	-
EU	-	-	-	-	-	-	-	-	-
IEA	-	-	-	-	-	-	-	-	-

	1985	1986	1987	1988	1989	1990	1991	1992	1993
Australia	3446	3383	3262	3169	3567	2269	1972	-	-
Austria	22379	23278	24536	24598	25452	28059	32189	30835	33503
Belgium	9686	9633	9793	9205	9306	9399	9970	9988	9503
Canada	33966	32235	31794	16392	24432	21007	24816	16880	11022
Denmark	45548	47734	51980	52912	50422	96178	102650	103718	112162
Finland	85774	82811	92430	87242	82116	86832	91800	92042	96012
France	-	-	-	-	-	-	-	-	-
Germany	335082	344871	360067	339071	359168	341541	353495	350000	350000
Greece	-	-	-	-	-	-	-	-	-
Iceland	2889	3078	3326	3503	3660	5282	6808	8199	7746
Ireland	-	-	-	-	-	-	-	-	-
Italy	-	-	-	-	-	-	-	-	-
Japan	5776	5892	6379	6460	7192	8458	9835	13680	14498
Luxembourg	-	-	-	-	-	-	-	-	-
Mexico	-	-	-	-	-	-	-	-	-
Netherlands	11742	15684	12633	11574	11852	11914	14550	18804	20945
New Zealand	-	-	-	-	-	-	-	-	-
Norway	2195	3232	3959	4529	4922	5087	5563	6197	6319
Portugal	1373	1348	1398	1264	1411	1188	1182	1318	1437
Spain	-	-	775	679	665	181	160		-
Sweden	114106	109451	108090	91872	78358	78134	91022	148111	157944
Switzerland	10438	10927	12351	11790	11870	11470	13260	13070	13310
Turkey	-	-	-	-	-	-	-	-	-
United Kingdom	615	574	565	484	519	530	289	-	6034
United States	83878	81768	85143	79474	94392	81308	296191	377128	404634
OECD TOTAL	-	-	-	-	-	-	-	-	-
OECD EUROPE	-	-	-	-	-	-	-	-	-
NORTH AMERICA	-	-	-	-	-	-	-	-	-
PACIFIC	-	-	-	-	-	-	-	-	-
EU	-	-	-	-	-	-	-	-	-
IEA	-	-	-	-	-	-	-	-	-

Since data are not available for all countries, regional totals are not shown.
Les données n'étant pas disponibles pour tous les pays, les totaux régionaux ne sont pas montrés.

Refinery Output of Petroleum Products (1000 tonnes)
Production de produits pétroliers en raffineries (1000 tonnes)

	1970	1973	1978	1979	1980	1981	1982	1983	1984
Australia	23317	25251	30065	30204	28933	28202	28770	27654	27824
Austria	5905	8817	9874	10613	10091	8808	7731	6966	7486
Belgium	28241	35510	33545	33862	33439	28991	24708	23009	23397
Canada	62414	82322	88487	95569	92595	86003	74753	71263	73395
Denmark	9709	9760	8020	8715	6616	6208	5968	6883	7284
Finland	8141	9045	11104	12193	12484	11115	9499	10507	10454
France	100350	133792	118583	128510	115717	98478	84483	80124	78736
Germany	121136	139508	126584	139461	136512	120402	117460	111659	110456
Greece	4973	12423	11445	15275	14134	15795	14993	13946	12591
Iceland	-	-	-	-	-	-	-	-	-
Ireland	2648	2675	2236	2302	2014	730	493	1187	1235
Italy	116729	130307	113861	117101	97992	94836	87935	82653	81218
Japan	160883	222333	213895	217169	200694	183263	169743	163453	168265
Luxembourg	-	-	-	-	-	-	-	-	-
Mexico	-	25315	39549	41971	49433	54704	55057	53044	56178
Netherlands	61758	73081	60530	65457	57238	51244	53335	59325	62060
New Zealand	2990	3265	2954	3037	2904	2749	2294	2451	2498
Norway	5664	6112	8237	8442	7770	7209	6937	7220	7594
Portugal	3514	4222	6471	8250	7609	7945	7967	8239	7515
Spain	32369	42423	48265	48256	48517	46294	44990	45587	44994
Sweden	11396	10542	15288	16100	17592	13744	12884	14223	13944
Switzerland	5359	6126	4236	4573	4550	3981	4021	4288	4189
Turkey	7039	12533	13049	11053	12657	13395	16403	16164	17775
United Kingdom	100722	113004	95579	97121	85544	77500	76296	76224	78503
United States	581566	665486	788157	783070	723765	684431	652244	634639	658022
OECD TOTAL	**1456823**	**1773852**	**1850014**	**1898304**	**1768800**	**1646027**	**1558964**	**1520708**	**1555613**
OECD EUROPE	625653	749880	686907	727284	670476	606675	576103	568204	569431
NORTH AMERICA	643980	773123	916193	920610	865793	825138	782054	758946	787595
PACIFIC	187190	250849	246914	250410	232531	214214	200807	193558	198587
EU	607591	725109	661385	703216	645499	582090	548742	540532	539873
IEA	1456823	1748537	1810465	1856333	1719367	1591323	1503907	1467664	1499435

	1985	1986	1987	1988	1989	1990	1991	1992	1993
Australia	27826	26960	27160	29034	29845	30758	31574	31990	33037
Austria	8106	8171	8175	8090	8144	8783	9071	9591	9631
Belgium	20384	27524	28245	29392	30031	29372	32494	32250	31293
Canada	72153	70829	76091	80466	82025	83323	81025	79422	81631
Denmark	6937	7687	7556	7892	8295	7848	8159	8441	8556
Finland	10339	9320	10429	10310	9069	10344	10696	10605	10069
France	79376	76322	72987	77898	77786	78333	81635	80224	82677
Germany	108912	107088	103943	110415	106603	106189	104458	111845	116129
Greece	12054	16035	16352	15786	16349	16442	15114	15976	14106
Iceland	-	-	-	-	-	-	-	-	-
Ireland	1296	1518	1495	1337	1495	1725	1801	1973	1889
Italy	78126	88350	85152	86211	87688	90564	90906	93813	93595
Japan	156125	151180	146318	152166	159160	173817	184840	195022	200511
Luxembourg	-	-	-	-	-	-	-	-	-
Mexico	58046	57964	59694	59158	61632	65462	67337	67085	68676
Netherlands	55592	67272	67432	69064	69540	67905	70332	71544	73463
New Zealand	1500	2538	3613	4088	4551	4682	4645	4741	4879
Norway	7723	7317	9319	8554	9806	13024	12550	14158	14130
Portugal	7166	8484	7631	8534	10586	10879	10191	11653	11266
Spain	45320	49786	48015	51303	51664	52796	54809	56740	53481
Sweden	13395	14596	15479	14657	16549	17082	16564	18002	18728
Switzerland	4166	4267	4147	3981	3050	3047	4691	4263	4746
Turkey	17834	19274	22731	23919	21715	22884	22490	23118	25568
United Kingdom	78076	79493	79874	85321	87207	88120	91532	92007	96108
United States	653493	687249	695157	713140	723405	731487	725391	732345	749986
OECD TOTAL	**1523945**	**1589224**	**1596995**	**1650716**	**1676195**	**1714866**	**1732305**	**1766808**	**1804155**
OECD EUROPE	554802	592504	588962	612664	615577	625337	637493	656203	665435
NORTH AMERICA	783692	816042	830942	852764	867062	880272	873753	878852	900293
PACIFIC	185451	180678	177091	185288	193556	209257	221059	231753	238427
EU	525079	561646	552765	576210	581006	586382	597762	614664	620991
IEA	1465899	1531260	1537301	1591558	1614563	1649404	1664968	1699723	1735479

Net Imports of Hard Coal (1000 tonnes)
Importations nettes de houille (1000 tonnes)

	1970	1973	1978	1979	1980	1981	1982	1983	1984
Australia	-17965	-28149	-37898	-38262	-43159	-47439	-47151	-55544	-66522
Austria	3615	2865	2307	2841	2879	2744	2876	2981	3792
Belgium	7038	6503	6781	9303	9659	9264	9789	6890	8141
Canada	13584	4192	262	3676	365	-738	-331	-1893	-6762
Denmark	3371	3014	6110	7552	9967	10885	9663	8535	9731
Finland	3221	2973	4789	4771	4669	5650	4685	4390	3570
France	12578	11627	22992	26641	28980	26815	22221	17991	20918
Germany	1810	1242	-6226	847	3489	4365	5821	3238	2429
Greece	140	651	349	628	533	287	505	1420	1836
Iceland	1	1	-	10	12	24	25	37	55
Ireland	1137	736	511	1140	1149	1280	1235	1421	1369
Italy	12692	11479	12458	14128	17197	18924	19747	17239	20388
Japan	50900	58000	52802	59341	68509	77912	78518	75112	87223
Luxembourg	127	305	495	349	364	297	283	167	189
Mexico	-	238	570	744	823	681	641	279	234
Netherlands	3486	2740	4550	5215	5609	7526	7956	6713	9677
New Zealand	-	-	-10	-9	-70	-232	-204	-222	-371
Norway	368	322	373	609	648	609	709	421	579
Portugal	480	431	412	380	398	313	345	489	513
Spain	2878	3108	3366	4176	5661	7031	7163	5905	6988
Sweden	1530	1014	1513	2095	2178	2037	2881	3085	3927
Switzerland	364	130	141	312	574	863	471	344	539
Turkey	-274	16	475	824	943	648	1103	1670	1982
United Kingdom	-3112	-1033	86	2035	3292	-5222	-3326	-1884	6454
United States	-65656	-48498	-34591	-58018	-82144	-101105	-95961	-69286	-72744
OECD TOTAL	**32313**	**33907**	**42617**	**51328**	**42525**	**23419**	**29934**	**29498**	**44135**
OECD EUROPE	51450	48124	61482	83856	98201	94340	94152	81052	103077
NORTH AMERICA	-52072	-44068	-33759	-53598	-80956	-101162	-95381	-70900	-79272
PACIFIC	32935	29851	14894	21070	25280	30241	31163	19346	20330
EU	50991	47655	60493	82101	96024	92196	91844	78580	99922
IEA	32312	33668	42047	50574	41690	22714	29268	29182	43846

	1985	1986	1987	1988	1989	1990	1991	1992	1993
Australia	-83799	-89884	-95714	-102200	-99302	-104014	-113182	-123200	-128405
Austria	3599	3752	4155	3871	3732	3608	3788	3803	3189
Belgium	8050	7339	8143	10114	11773	14037	13369	13345	11233
Canada	-12799	-12593	-12395	-14255	-18295	-16889	-21705	-14568	-19823
Denmark	12641	12084	12003	10219	10696	9903	12728	11907	10443
Finland	5070	5454	5067	4797	5565	6101	5173	4263	5933
France	17859	16169	12468	10588	15231	18804	21179	21492	13609
Germany	6307	9667	8372	7989	4702	8068	11891	13805	12120
Greece	1815	1730	1670	1288	1160	1380	1407	2132	1337
Iceland	69	74	60	67	71	65	60	50	53
Ireland	1901	2615	2889	3434	3308	3107	3101	2988	2892
Italy	22213	20570	21285	19824	20733	20445	19829	17712	14299
Japan	93447	90392	90915	101243	101509	103580	109382	109121	111404
Luxembourg	199	183	197	161	195	197	203	278	277
Mexico	590	243	-41	-6	-14	222	24	634	13
Netherlands	10168	9937	11194	12786	13044	14928	13367	12771	12879
New Zealand	-395	-282	-299	-364	-485	-329	-608	-757	-786
Norway	682	648	542	519	396	459	330	451	488
Portugal	1395	1884	2762	2990	3554	4669	4254	4482	4766
Spain	8411	8715	8886	8762	10561	10452	12988	14279	12726
Sweden	4756	4391	3862	3804	3690	3541	3115	2995	3099
Switzerland	468	614	511	411	315	473	359	145	125
Turkey	2661	2996	3917	4503	3613	5557	6083	5414	5640
United Kingdom	10174	7805	7440	9948	10065	12476	17787	19366	17305
United States	-82277	-75536	-70601	-84267	-88870	-93463	-95734	-89505	-60972
OECD TOTAL	**33205**	**28967**	**27288**	**16226**	**16947**	**27377**	**29188**	**33403**	**33844**
OECD EUROPE	118438	116627	115423	116075	122404	138270	151011	151678	132413
NORTH AMERICA	-94486	-87886	-83037	-98528	-107179	-110130	-117415	-103439	-80782
PACIFIC	9253	226	-5098	-1321	1722	-763	-4408	-14836	-17787
EU	114558	112295	110393	110575	118009	131716	144179	145618	126107
IEA	32546	28650	27269	16165	16890	27090	29104	32719	33778

A negative number shows net exports. / *Un chiffre négatif correspond à des exportations nettes.*

Net Imports of Brown Coal (1000 tonnes)
Importations nettes de lignite (1000 tonnes)

	1970	1973	1978	1979	1980	1981	1982	1983	1984
Australia	-	-	-	-	-	-	-	-	-
Austria	129	463	240	199	259	504	586	354	183
Belgium	-	-	-	8	95	112	92	98	196
Canada	-11	-5	-8	-29	-	-	-	-	-
Denmark	-	-	-	-	-	-	-	-	-
Finland	-	-	-	-	-	-	-	-	-
France	-24	-29	-	30	-	-	2	3	7
Germany	4922	6186	4780	4553	2114	3845	3593	2785	2496
Greece	-	-	-	-	-	-	-	-	-
Iceland	-	-	-	-	-	-	-	-	-
Ireland	-	-	-	-	-	-	-	-	-
Italy	239	112	68	40	99	62	41	76	94
Japan	-	-	-	-	-	-	-	-	-
Luxembourg	-	-	17	26	28	6	-	-	-
Mexico	-	-	-	-	-	-	-	-	-
Netherlands	-	20	68	182	156	149	132	94	93
New Zealand	-	-	-	-	-	-	-	-	-
Norway	-	-	-	-	-	-	-	-	-
Portugal	-	-	-	-	-	-	-	-	-
Spain	18	21	6	7	7	7	5	3	3
Sweden	-	-	-	-	-1	-	-	-	1
Switzerland	-	-	-	-	-	-	-	-	-
Turkey	-	-	-245	-131	-197	-	-	-	-
United Kingdom	-	-	-	-	-	-	-	-	-
United States	-	-	-75	-26	-59	-44	-48	-114	-8
OECD TOTAL	**5273**	**6768**	**4851**	**4859**	**2501**	**4641**	**4403**	**3299**	**3065**
OECD EUROPE	5284	6773	4934	4914	2560	4685	4451	3413	3073
NORTH AMERICA	-11	-5	-83	-55	-59	-44	-48	-114	-8
PACIFIC	-	-	-	-	-	-	-	-	-
EU	5284	6773	5179	5045	2757	4685	4451	3413	3073
IEA	5273	6768	4851	4859	2501	4641	4403	3299	3065

	1985	1986	1987	1988	1989	1990	1991	1992	1993
Australia	-	-	-	-	-	-	-	-	-
Austria	333	202	46	35	21	20	20	6	1
Belgium	275	257	258	226	267	276	276	244	226
Canada	-	-	-	-7	-10	-9	-10	-9	-29
Denmark	-	-	-	-	-	-	-	-	-
Finland	-	-	-	-	-	-	-	-	-
France	36	58	49	49	57	69	2	2	-
Germany	2565	2391	2094	1815	1918	1904	3425	3638	2990
Greece	-	-	-	-	-	-	-	-14	-
Iceland	-	-	-	-	-	-	-	-	-
Ireland	-	2	13	18	22	39	70	54	44
Italy	149	80	131	24	28	133	32	84	20
Japan	-	-	-	-	-	-	-	-	-
Luxembourg	-	-	12	4	2	9	9	9	8
Mexico	-	-	-	-	-	-	-	-	-
Netherlands	103	115	91	59	54	69	51	35	39
New Zealand	-	-	-	-	-	-	-	-	-
Norway	-	-	-	-	-	-	-	-	-
Portugal	-	-	-	-	-	-	-	-	-
Spain	2	2	2	-	-	1	-	-	-
Sweden	-	-	4	-	6	2	-	-	-
Switzerland	-	-	-	-	-	-	-	-	-
Turkey	-	-	-	-	-	15	185	14	-
United Kingdom	-	-	-	-	-	-	-	-	-
United States	-30	-37	-32	-	-	-70	-45	-46	-
OECD TOTAL	**3433**	**3070**	**2668**	**2223**	**2365**	**2458**	**4015**	**4017**	**3299**
OECD EUROPE	3463	3107	2700	2230	2375	2537	4070	4072	3328
NORTH AMERICA	-30	-37	-32	-7	-10	-79	-55	-55	-29
PACIFIC	-	-	-	-	-	-	-	-	-
EU	3463	3107	2700	2230	2375	2522	3885	4058	3328
IEA	3433	3070	2668	2223	2365	2458	4015	4017	3299

A negative number shows net exports. / *Un chiffre négatif correspond à des exportations nettes.*

Net Imports of Natural Gas (TJ)
Importations nettes de gaz naturel (TJ)

	1970	1973	1978	1979	1980	1981	1982	1983	1984
Australia	-	-	-	-	-	-	-	-	-
Austria	39658	62974	113518	119598	124841	160317	122394	100371	163976
Belgium	157495	330774	395875	435716	413681	378914	320072	333006	340002
Canada	-804531	-1059771	-929887	-1056081	-855011	-813596	-845519	-766692	-812484
Denmark								687	-4228
Finland	-	-	37828	37761	36949	29316	27608	26800	29236
France	131972	351767	637503	683871	752461	809694	756061	876402	846382
Germany	135049	572272	1347559	1573735	1643313	1518151	1430704	1458047	1498647
Greece	-	-	-	-	-	-	-	-	-
Iceland	-	-	-	-	-	-	-	-	-
Ireland	-	-	-	-	-	-	-	-	-
Italy	-	76543	539260	559951	547403	529316	513833	563376	731166
Japan	44924	129581	625219	775446	909009	937316	973364	1044004	1433158
Luxembourg	515	10170	21131	21918	19741	15119	12669	12079	13000
Mexico	-	-2490		-	-125081	-127980	-118962	-94532	-63559
Netherlands	-398546	-1175009	-1604512	-1767022	-1790091	-1628992	-1258443	-1334639	-1283564
New Zealand									
Norway	-	-	-520850	-860563	-1018958	-1032477	-984719	-988859	-1050765
Portugal	-	-	-	-	-	-	-	-	-
Spain	4266	43283	56141	65921	65674	82673	85306	90728	76752
Sweden	-	-	-	-	-	-	-	-	-
Switzerland	486	6907	31500	35330	40310	43490	45930	50500	56320
Turkey	-	-	-	-	-	-	-	-	-
United Kingdom	35136	30949	199300	348593	418651	447351	414012	448197	530702
United States	816154	1028898	980783	1288237	1008776	903118	945946	932329	834064
OECD TOTAL	**162578**	**406848**	**1930368**	**2262411**	**2191668**	**2251730**	**2440256**	**2751804**	**3338805**
OECD EUROPE	106031	310630	1254253	1254809	1253975	1352872	1485427	1636695	1947626
NORTH AMERICA	11623	-33363	50896	232156	28684	-38458	-18535	71105	-41979
PACIFIC	44924	129581	625219	775446	909009	937316	973364	1044004	1433158
EU	105545	303723	1743603	2080042	2232623	2341859	2424216	2575054	2942071
IEA	162578	409338	1930368	2262411	2316749	2379710	2559218	2846336	3402364

	1985	1986	1987	1988	1989	1990	1991	1992	1993
Australia	-	-	-	-	-	-109300	-185000	-235400	-276600
Austria	169412	163556	157531	150519	160540	208797	202603	202280	212511
Belgium	342451	309384	346487	332510	379494	382255	402887	425078	440441
Canada	-992048	-786947	-1055765	-1345814	-1403143	-1513001	-1791965	-2178165	-2364362
Denmark	-18338	-25158	-30840	-34288	-38151	-43102	-58197	-63794	-66621
Finland	37175	45992	60901	65179	86591	105162	111164	115204	119625
France	959196	1001324	1050628	994828	1033635	1133737	1196665	1238080	1177409
Germany	1594524	1647722	1790140	1752330	1923691	1942285	2019889	2063758	2204245
Greece	-	-	-	-	-	-	-	-	-
Iceland	-	-	-	-	-	-	-	-	-
Ireland	-	-	-	-	-	-	-	-	190
Italy	746184	761851	888694	932675	1087461	1177468	1280369	1315765	1244481
Japan	1534416	1573667	1587572	1674252	1806880	1938808	2072679	2124285	2134762
Luxembourg	14110	14051	15960	16502	18860	19981	20789	21669	22509
Mexico	2490	2141	2531	2759	19907	18711	74584	112462	41245
Netherlands	-1333843	-1091030	-1046968	-889569	-1070641	-1107135	-1269312	-1331717	-1341441
New Zealand	-	-	-	-	-	-	-	-	-
Norway	-1033809	-1030434	-1124152	-1123636	-1159097	-1031422	-1022434	-1049926	-1009981
Portugal	-	-	-	-	-	-	-	-	-
Spain	89531	89840	90749	120243	142508	171653	204584	225149	236828
Sweden	3483	8524	11487	14920	19912	24584	25816	29199	32620
Switzerland	58270	59780	64410	64910	70740	75760	85090	89460	93870
Turkey	-	-	16559	43704	116441	124750	154541	169937	189738
United Kingdom	529647	493565	464023	415572	409558	287407	259228	218287	150131
United States	944009	723171	987424	1287900	1348570	1544182	1757852	2047782	2378923
OECD TOTAL	**3646860**	**3960999**	**4277371**	**4475496**	**4953756**	**5351580**	**5541832**	**5539393**	**5620523**
OECD EUROPE	2157993	2448967	2755609	2856399	3181542	3472180	3613682	3668429	3706555
NORTH AMERICA	-45549	-61635	-65810	-55155	-34666	49892	40471	-17921	55806
PACIFIC	1534416	1573667	1587572	1674252	1806880	1829508	1887679	1888885	1858162
EU	3133532	3419621	3798792	3871421	4153458	4303092	4396485	4458958	4432928
IEA	3644370	3958858	4274840	4472737	4933849	5332869	5467248	5426931	5579278

A negative number shows net exports. / *Un chiffre négatif correspond à des exportations nettes.*

Net Imports of Oil (1000 tonnes)
Importations nettes de pétrole (1000 tonnes)

	1970	1973	1978	1979	1980	1981	1982	1983	1984
Australia	17236	9052	10129	10758	11136	10465	10394	9078	4782
Austria	6716	9635	10321	11234	11178	9783	8622	8297	8732
Belgium	26862	30837	27145	28990	25856	21192	21904	19984	18647
Canada	4588	-13907	10779	8098	8767	9249	-682	-9606	-11028
Denmark	19126	18453	16281	15514	13158	10502	9687	8656	8294
Finland	12339	13695	11786	14668	13743	11657	10524	10917	9239
France	96966	128811	111782	121178	112582	93700	87925	82800	83773
Germany	132541	157949	155818	162785	145824	123455	115493	113224	114719
Greece	6581	11291	11990	12991	13191	12108	10318	9872	9929
Iceland	525	678	614	649	576	557	522	488	493
Ireland	4242	5409	6052	6351	5805	5028	4470	4093	4227
Italy	89282	105030	96147	101112	98051	93434	90498	83783	84958
Japan	198817	268675	258345	271470	246681	222093	208160	209434	219245
Luxembourg	1340	1666	1408	1318	1083	1031	1021	976	964
Mexico	-	5731	-16919	-26324	-44062	-60435	-83175	-84370	-83196
Netherlands	35955	40199	37274	40723	37525	31251	27747	25604	25155
New Zealand	3849	4246	3700	3890	3980	3389	3103	3160	3127
Norway	8560	6839	-7279	-9398	-14620	-15346	-15698	-22700	-26807
Portugal	4645	6082	7344	8962	9272	8495	9510	9494	9840
Spain	28281	40256	47397	48605	48914	47686	42163	41974	38546
Sweden	30531	28625	25857	28961	25759	21164	19533	17647	14877
Switzerland	13103	14664	13666	13343	13109	11805	11169	12387	11957
Turkey	4374	8661	14251	11536	13281	13350	13754	14972	14908
United Kingdom	103976	113132	41299	18858	1672	-18205	-28029	-43023	-37537
United States	161604	298847	416188	410447	329211	280813	226921	225209	244643
OECD TOTAL	**1012039**	**1314556**	**1311375**	**1316719**	**1131672**	**948221**	**805854**	**752350**	**772487**
OECD EUROPE	625945	741912	629153	638380	575959	482647	441133	399445	394914
NORTH AMERICA	166192	290671	410048	392221	293916	229627	143064	131233	150419
PACIFIC	219902	281973	272174	286118	261797	235947	221657	221672	227154
EU	599383	711070	607901	622250	563613	472281	431386	394298	394363
IEA	1011514	1308147	1327680	1342394	1175158	1008099	888507	836232	855190

	1985	1986	1987	1988	1989	1990	1991	1992	1993
Australia	833	-52	2042	1957	6512	5283	2782	4128	7503
Austria	8595	9322	9594	8926	9162	9887	10234	10127	9968
Belgium	19186	22909	22231	22731	22859	22227	24762	25370	24603
Canada	-16802	-13596	-13104	-19935	-12527	-14074	-19884	-23774	-25490
Denmark	8388	7631	6088	5379	3895	3124	2261	1477	1123
Finland	10847	11764	12659	10409	11442	10423	10273	9534	9395
France	80439	80849	84096	83904	85429	85602	90614	86495	85403
Germany	118013	128642	124247	124374	116341	119579	128074	131552	130408
Greece	10546	12193	11495	12841	13525	14445	14749	16380	16345
Iceland	537	551	612	579	658	729	619	738	723
Ireland	4101	5029	4456	3893	4062	4998	4867	4737	5115
Italy	82691	83353	88731	84815	90582	90361	87069	91246	87714
Japan	207242	211354	213187	226707	242710	252247	253710	258195	256337
Luxembourg	1052	1142	1305	1299	1441	1596	1821	1922	1875
Mexico	-78086	-70457	-71409	-70164	-64740	-66546	-69654	-69550	-70256
Netherlands	24349	29350	26125	30642	30349	30741	32684	33664	32411
New Zealand	2877	1963	2696	2042	2353	2374	2312	2559	2598
Norway	-30108	-32778	-39909	-47790	-65455	-71352	-84629	-97881	-104663
Portugal	8523	9589	9599	9552	12193	12197	12384	13575	12827
Spain	38909	38466	41285	45540	47859	48706	49409	52168	49924
Sweden	16978	19339	15363	15662	14545	14954	14556	14608	15093
Switzerland	12004	13370	11927	12282	12029	12845	12843	12959	11737
Turkey	14974	16700	19398	18860	18248	20270	17097	19436	23591
United Kingdom	-49131	-49738	-48088	-35642	-9367	-10393	-7257	-9625	-15518
United States	224404	279004	301978	333675	361615	361216	338450	359745	393765
OECD TOTAL	**721361**	**815899**	**836604**	**882538**	**955720**	**961439**	**930146**	**949785**	**962531**
OECD EUROPE	380893	407683	401214	408256	419797	420939	422430	418482	398074
NORTH AMERICA	129516	194951	217465	243576	284348	280596	248912	266421	298019
PACIFIC	210952	213265	217925	230706	251575	259904	258804	264882	266438
EU	383486	409840	409186	424325	454317	458447	476500	483230	466686
IEA	798910	885805	907401	952123	1019802	1027256	999181	1018597	1032064

A negative number shows net exports. / *Un chiffre négatif correspond à des exportations nettes.*

INTERNATIONAL ENERGY AGENCY

Final Consumption of Hard Coal (1000 tonnes)
Consommation finale de houille (1000 tonnes)

	1970	1973	1978	1979	1980	1981	1982	1983	1984
Australia	3518	3209	3431	3513	3525	3529	3648	3613	4020
Austria	1013	550	369	436	491	530	404	592	835
Belgium	4871	4155	4297	3251	3484	3091	2608	2138	2420
Canada	4311	2522	1458	1568	1601	1472	1510	1382	1495
Denmark	305	395	707	722	580	488	444	296	543
Finland	801	1151	740	701	870	918	1093	1088	1145
France	14150	9616	6019	5940	6029	6340	6468	5763	6114
Germany	16898	11087	8526	10377	10170	9269	9921	9560	9836
Greece	136	105	137	178	144	144	491	1054	1333
Iceland	1	1	-	10	12	24	25	37	55
Ireland	1108	723	494	1048	949	1263	1267	1446	1444
Italy	1290	482	446	821	828	1336	2170	1731	2223
Japan	6200	3000	3218	3268	7060	11477	11745	9468	10419
Luxembourg	128	305	501	353	331	278	259	144	166
Mexico	-	-	-	-	-	-	-	-	-
Netherlands	1652	570	158	157	175	172	315	347	782
New Zealand	1394	1465	1278	1229	1313	1330	1393	1294	1317
Norway	377	393	357	494	524	579	591	640	682
Portugal	446	101	108	85	93	74	63	144	193
Spain	3372	2245	1099	1828	1310	2909	3773	3740	3715
Sweden	425	333	327	366	399	399	542	604	700
Switzerland	213	124	144	132	292	532	468	427	605
Turkey	1379	1204	810	874	1020	974	1152	1051	1498
United Kingdom	43912	28387	18450	19440	16227	14936	15398	14526	12762
United States	94836	69699	63581	65224	57396	64230	62299	64605	70717
OECD TOTAL	**202736**	**141822**	**116655**	**122015**	**114823**	**126294**	**128047**	**125690**	**135019**
OECD EUROPE	92477	61927	43689	47213	43928	44256	47452	45328	47051
NORTH AMERICA	99147	72221	65039	66792	58997	65702	63809	65987	72212
PACIFIC	11112	7674	7927	8010	11898	16336	16786	14375	15756
EU	90507	60205	42378	45703	42080	42147	45216	43173	44211
IEA	202735	141821	116655	122005	114811	126270	128022	125653	134964

	1985	1986	1987	1988	1989	1990	1991	1992	1993
Australia	4678	4791	4806	4815	5013	5169	5156	5270	5258
Austria	661	633	538	447	397	405	400	436	268
Belgium	2559	2168	2095	2057	2567	2485	2877	2471	2107
Canada	1723	1675	1708	1797	1729	1671	1351	1344	1312
Denmark	684	599	632	662	639	574	650	507	551
Finland	1256	1096	1264	1108	1377	1052	988	820	764
France	7068	6978	7065	7182	7154	7411	7452	7086	5962
Germany	10603	9780	10768	9887	9004	9289	8423	7652	6475
Greece	1443	1408	1364	1396	1276	1380	1478	1388	1355
Iceland	69	74	60	67	71	65	60	50	53
Ireland	1507	1700	1574	1474	1391	1264	1230	683	739
Italy	2783	1455	1935	1202	1302	1912	1799	3083	2799
Japan	10859	9777	11009	12942	14245	15828	14703	16492	13798
Luxembourg	176	181	197	161	195	197	203	278	277
Mexico	-	-	-	-	-	-	-	-	-
Netherlands	833	821	1133	1166	1226	1235	1087	1148	1232
New Zealand	1276	1280	1488	1739	1725	1781	1779	1815	1852
Norway	682	623	660	773	770	754	651	659	749
Portugal	320	575	704	809	839	820	870	789	735
Spain	3585	3452	3247	3379	3306	2762	3423	3227	2020
Sweden	713	724	754	924	960	1008	835	707	747
Switzerland	594	516	505	440	439	462	392	262	218
Turkey	1655	1616	1948	2409	2380	2853	3351	3244	3088
United Kingdom	16120	16448	15054	14567	12520	11199	11873	11682	10764
United States	68386	67682	66224	67549	66063	67300	66044	31514	30347
OECD TOTAL	**140233**	**136052**	**136732**	**138952**	**136588**	**138876**	**137075**	**102607**	**93470**
OECD EUROPE	53311	50847	51497	50110	47813	47127	48042	46172	40903
NORTH AMERICA	70109	69357	67932	69346	67792	68971	67395	32858	31659
PACIFIC	16813	15848	17303	19496	20983	22778	21638	23577	20908
EU	50311	48018	48324	46421	44153	42993	43588	41957	36795
IEA	140164	135978	136672	138885	136517	138811	137015	102557	93417

Final Consumption of Natural Gas (TJ)
Consommation finale de gaz naturel (TJ)

	1970	1973	1978	1979	1980	1981	1982	1983	1984
Australia	31301	98286	180752	201233	233895	256022	268071	279458	288868
Austria	42086	69721	121720	130892	136070	127416	121987	120053	130187
Belgium	106809	214142	309881	335673	329375	312696	287433	287184	306650
Canada	872601	1103917	1464452	1605857	1685597	1660335	1696556	1680396	1811048
Denmark	-	-	-	-	-	-	-	611	2290
Finland	-	-	23811	23852	20758	21018	19004	20553	22893
France	264706	478086	778887	873833	896577	945011	916941	967941	1043320
Germany	380556	842941	1362775	1491174	1544081	1600698	1512338	1577076	1648843
Greece	-	-	-	-	-	-	-	-	-
Iceland	-	-	-	-	-	-	1176	1231	1876
Ireland	-	-	-	12514	16069	17626	21298	18154	23363
Italy	399785	574911	884419	908532	917892	894610	861496	878446	958043
Japan	65574	67664	81768	79164	69312	63715	61511	59041	63405
Luxembourg	477	8244	14913	16597	16630	13783	12636	11883	12824
Mexico	-	383997	545454	621606	678577	782927	818385	868404	766342
Netherlands	500774	897617	1132835	1197220	1128402	1084826	992189	1005050	1044629
New Zealand	2571	5375	13293	12171	14050	21646	25861	35796	62394
Norway	-	-	-	-	-	-	-	-	-
Portugal	-	-	-	-	-	-	-	-	-
Spain	3408	20820	39667	38708	33474	35504	39833	46302	55448
Sweden	-	-	-	-	-	-	-	-	-
Switzerland	226	5066	24037	27420	32940	36460	39300	43850	49970
Turkey	-	-	-	-	-	-	1532	2719	1532
United Kingdom	153341	854977	1570285	1717071	1733113	1741105	1749094	1769156	1800516
United States	16103077	17076328	15025312	15517576	15700836	15421545	14186403	13445970	14425262
OECD TOTAL	**18927292**	**22702092**	**23574261**	**24811093**	**25187648**	**25036943**	**23633044**	**23119274**	**24519703**
OECD EUROPE	1852168	3966525	6263230	6773486	6805381	6830753	6576257	6750209	7102384
NORTH AMERICA	16975678	18564242	17035218	17745039	18065010	17864807	16701344	15994770	17002652
PACIFIC	99446	171325	275813	292568	317257	341383	355443	374295	414667
EU	1851942	3961459	6239193	6746066	6772441	6794293	6535425	6703640	7050882
IEA	18927292	22318095	23028807	24189487	24509071	24254016	22814659	22250870	23753361

	1985	1986	1987	1988	1989	1990	1991	1992	1993
Australia	325855	349390	371291	375791	388588	409366	411148	417817	428562
Austria	137837	132251	132575	130550	135497	142718	152401	151627	159469
Belgium	313214	290680	310598	300492	309632	317260	334546	344114	361014
Canada	1927312	1848008	1846184	1979623	2051503	2008342	2034726	2122999	2228541
Denmark	11663	24842	33007	41867	45319	50990	58329	59903	67497
Finland	22650	24665	34672	34199	46846	58096	62052	64072	61073
France	1082051	1100111	1118938	1080565	1096430	1138395	1280062	1273291	1310440
Germany	1707185	1706232	1824495	1806103	1839243	1817221	1944075	1967987	2104486
Greece	2458	2734	3362	4515	4300	4496	4296	4085	2633
Iceland	-	-	-	-	-	-	-	-	-
Ireland	23928	34194	39084	39491	43184	46559	50351 ·	51270	54296
Italy	1001102	1064683	1175210	1256430	1359584	1414339	1544659	1511243	1531580
Japan	62390	59001	57701	59748	59950	60393	62704	56786	56653
Luxembourg	14059	14043	15181	16256	18261	19533	20377	21223	22070
Mexico	784169	675067	731224	711475	760535	734206	795952	770064	758048
Netherlands	1122029	1087448	1143382	1044693	1043171	1070082	1187288	1119241	1157581
New Zealand	39134	43955	43917	45391	48268	45135	45723	46121	45425
Norway	-	-	-	-	-	-	-	-	-
Portugal	-	-	-	-	-	-	-	-	-
Spain	63793	75300	95509	129498	180381	201194	223897	243444	251096
Sweden	2997	7009	9019	10747	12729	15532	15009	15164	16383
Switzerland	52440	53900	58130	59220	64960	70160	79380	83750	88150
Turkey	1876	1766	2043	7926	19176	33062	51549	75689	96646
United Kingdom	1912911	1937863	2010528	1937123	1906636	1954110	2107239	2027429	2039309
United States	13803595	13153511	13638187	14863372	15589338	15235181	15684016	16210068	17028646
OECD TOTAL	**24414648**	**23686653**	**24694237**	**25935075**	**27023531**	**26846370**	**28149779**	**28637387**	**29869598**
OECD EUROPE	7472193	7557721	8005733	7899675	8125349	8353747	9115510	9013532	9323723
NORTH AMERICA	16515076	15676586	16215595	17554470	18401376	17977729	18514694	19103131	20015235
PACIFIC	427379	452346	472909	480930	496806	514894	519575	520724	530640
EU	7417877	7502055	7945560	7832529	8041213	8250525	8984581	8854093	9138927
IEA	23630479	23011586	23963013	25223600	26262996	26112164	27353827	27867323	29111550

INTERNATIONAL ENERGY AGENCY

Final Consumption of Electricity (GWh)
Consommation finale d'électricité (GWh)

	1970	1973	1978	1979	1980	1981	1982	1983	1984
Australia	42011	52462	71424	75505	79232	83866	86894	87645	93457
Austria	20573	25299	30492	31868	33016	33261	33447	33987	35602
Belgium	26120	34204	41168	43761	43348	43419	43202	44418	46555
Canada	183723	220073	282703	289545	303210	312806	310926	325599	350556
Denmark	12900	15900	20538	21641	21748	22020	22441	22724	23846
Finland	20029	26946	32711	35451	37183	38555	38959	41985	45352
France	119648	148624	193153	203408	209111	210460	214812	226761	236827
Germany	254180	312908	376526	391052	391872	394612	392716	401503	419395
Greece	8420	12709	18145	19059	19903	19920	20146	21551	22991
Iceland	1305	2071	2430	2645	2862	2942	3239	3326	3497
Ireland	4800	6150	7797	8633	8597	8511	8564	8852	9254
Italy	103397	123053	147920	155877	159783	159388	161629	160929	169946
Japan	313000	415141	497139	521883	513269	515544	514960	546630	574161
Luxembourg	2443	2967	3394	3482	3577	3367	3403	3512	3745
Mexico	-	28840	45057	49195	52302	57045	61454	62133	66140
Netherlands	34863	44343	55089	57450	57405	56865	56272	57472	59500
New Zealand	11699	15928	18940	19018	19515	20075	21340	22991	23955
Norway	51398	60776	68986	75270	74821	77789	77803	82812	88738
Portugal	6274	8176	12183	13377	14344	14463	15332	16167	16666
Spain	43623	59032	80268	85694	89770	90879	91290	95601	100093
Sweden	57023	69205	80636	85232	84896	87229	89032	95633	102607
Switzerland	24966	29008	32464	33766	35252	36194	36731	37970	39665
Turkey	6959	9911	18110	18830	19543	21173	22657	23581	26630
United Kingdom	204929	233073	236669	246624	234332	229859	224756	227536	232177
United States	1347462	1667343	1953212	1998637	2025519	2075347	2010450	2073145	2205571
OECD TOTAL	**2901745**	**3624142**	**4327154**	**4486903**	**4534410**	**4615589**	**4562455**	**4724463**	**4996926**
OECD EUROPE	1003850	1224355	1458679	1533120	1541363	1550906	1556431	1606320	1683086
NORTH AMERICA	1531185	1916256	2280972	2337377	2381031	2445198	2382830	2460877	2622267
PACIFIC	366710	483531	587503	616406	612016	619485	623194	657266	691573
EU	919222	1122589	1336689	1402609	1408885	1412808	1416001	1458631	1524556
IEA	2900440	3593231	4279667	4435063	4479246	4555602	4497762	4659004	4927289

	1985	1986	1987	1988	1989	1990	1991	1992	1993
Australia	98070	104238	109068	115783	122658	129214	131716	132965	136758
Austria	37018	37380	38770	40156	41453	43160	44818	44394	44529
Belgium	48303	49328	51822	54083	55988	57984	60516	62583	63481
Canada	366464	383489	390826	409934	418758	416079	420313	423107	431387
Denmark	25358	26717	27691	28051	28769	29268	29702	30208	30621
Finland	48519	49526	52986	55150	56635	58943	59086	59757	62326
France	249392	264299	276089	281721	293092	301912	321055	330019	332298
Germany	432535	439189	450507	457422	464886	455079	455323	450926	446066
Greece	23833	24115	25035	26898	28009	28471	29332	30701	31179
Iceland	3371	3525	3541	3913	3960	3910	3869	3870	4082
Ireland	9762	10201	10590	10724	11279	11868	12464	13206	13549
Italy	174021	179369	188797	198424	207228	214549	219369	223425	224305
Japan	592713	595377	631556	665669	707171	758438	782414	790162	796599
Luxembourg	3793	3812	3893	3983	4068	4127	4220	4250	4376
Mexico	70375	72820	77744	81884	88402	92162	94768	97569	102210
Netherlands	61463	62281	65149	68330	70610	73519	75614	77859	78724
New Zealand	24233	25304	25767	26666	27279	27790	28561	27748	29929
Norway	91415	90109	93187	94194	94421	96808	99005	99383	101750
Portugal	17644	18558	19438	20783	22041	23544	24866	25653	25982
Spain	102828	105036	109215	114160	122434	125799	128637	130769	130683
Sweden	113625	114125	119407	120016	119808	120347	122017	120046	120918
Switzerland	41321	42348	43591	44327	45502	46578	47587	47866	47239
Turkey	28462	30812	35107	38009	41259	44955	47034	51734	56746
United Kingdom	242564	250163	258447	265231	270398	274432	281048	281469	285747
United States	2253015	2274601	2376361	2492363	2565134	2633575	2772927	2775452	2873867
OECD TOTAL	**5160097**	**5256722**	**5484584**	**5717874**	**5911242**	**6072511**	**6296261**	**6335121**	**6475351**
OECD EUROPE	1755227	1800893	1873262	1925575	1981840	2015253	2065562	2088118	2104601
NORTH AMERICA	2689854	2730910	2844931	2984181	3072294	3141816	3288008	3296128	3407464
PACIFIC	715016	724919	766391	808118	857108	915442	942691	950875	963286
EU	1590658	1634099	1697836	1745132	1796698	1823002	1868067	1885265	1894784
IEA	5086351	5180377	5403299	5632077	5818880	5976439	6197624	6233682	6369059

Final Consumption of Oil (1000 tonnes)
Consommation finale de pétrole (1000 tonnes)

	1970	1973	1978	1979	1980	1981	1982	1983	1984
Australia	21510	23943	26348	26700	26708	25678	25575	24041	25146
Austria	7985	10118	9895	10379	9877	9076	8564	8801	8643
Belgium	18484	20597	19174	19471	17022	15510	15358	14431	14393
Canada	65505	75548	77387	79364	78135	74237	65539	62494	62894
Denmark	14088	13986	13037	13300	11809	10538	9190	8851	9012
Finland	8915	11383	10450	10680	10104	9582	9276	8845	8624
France	78490	96978	93732	93737	88348	79435	76542	76394	74318
Germany	114231	136084	134524	138326	124258	113330	107698	107252	108537
Greece	4863	7012	8545	8826	8793	8506	8671	8557	8661
Iceland	480	642	630	613	573	557	524	500	522
Ireland	3009	3792	4041	4388	4037	3960	3586	3432	3474
Italy	61651	71221	64702	68333	65070	61963	59730	60367	60790
Japan	129091	168774	166029	169593	152924	144759	142683	145383	152283
Luxembourg	1279	1525	1348	1249	1051	1013	992	956	964
Mexico	-	24752	34598	37167	41660	46674	47743	44253	46722
Netherlands	20710	23751	21938	22489	20157	18238	16640	17983	18329
New Zealand	3211	3844	3687	3642	3638	3501	3509	3390	3508
Norway	7330	7607	8222	8688	8260	7725	7330	7239	7616
Portugal	3278	4459	5507	5802	6024	6029	6625	6210	6439
Spain	22287	29723	36253	39229	37455	34802	32947	33647	33411
Sweden	24280	24559	21729	22395	20292	19106	17252	15640	14615
Switzerland	11889	13918	12885	12341	12526	11548	10921	11970	11529
Turkey	6062	9597	14042	12389	12698	12527	13310	14156	13918
United Kingdom	72375	78259	70400	71580	62418	59209	58700	58080	58826
United States	595918	669336	732039	720758	666434	640470	620754	606367	632277
OECD TOTAL	**1296921**	**1531408**	**1591142**	**1601439**	**1490271**	**1417973**	**1369659**	**1349239**	**1385451**
OECD EUROPE	481686	565211	551054	564215	520772	482654	463856	463311	462621
NORTH AMERICA	661423	769636	844024	837289	786229	761381	734036	713114	741893
PACIFIC	153812	196561	196064	199935	183270	173938	171767	172814	180937
EU	455925	533447	515275	530184	486715	450297	431771	429446	429036
IEA	1296441	1506014	1555914	1563659	1448038	1370742	1321392	1304486	1338207

	1985	1986	1987	1988	1989	1990	1991	1992	1993
Australia	25373	25769	25927	27469	28635	29242	28547	29106	29962
Austria	8641	9034	9290	9029	8955	9396	10138	9842	9883
Belgium	15280	17362	16977	17446	16851	16781	18194	18940	18396
Canada	62632	63215	65003	67608	69330	67301	64344	65961	67736
Denmark	9350	9287	8870	8329	7867	7749	7894	7728	7608
Finland	8241	9075	9461	9603	9589	9396	9476	9340	8787
France	73551	74371	75363	76111	76462	76712	80756	81732	79991
Germany	111446	117592	114655	115884	108929	113595	120286	121664	123341
Greece	8804	8585	9264	9643	10271	10421	10547	10618	10726
Iceland	520	528	568	596	638	681	653	703	691
Ireland	3486	3561	3636	3519	3708	4038	4159	4274	4379
Italy	59686	59723	61293	62465	63050	62151	61466	62016	60613
Japan	149937	153605	158617	168351	172926	178436	183266	187217	187121
Luxembourg	1027	1105	1275	1297	1439	1580	1835	1877	1872
Mexico	49435	49693	51220	51299	55869	58221	61309	62705	62397
Netherlands	17676	19196	19097	19284	18895	19396	20327	20375	19707
New Zealand	3460	3559	3800	3885	4141	4236	4625	4914	4936
Norway	7886	8254	8974	8097	7902	7710	7409	7218	7388
Portugal	6401	6662	7004	7806	8164	8629	8678	9143	9129
Spain	32960	33052	33937	38258	37925	38941	40891	41766	40592
Sweden	14526	15335	14832	14802	14100	13595	13044	13406	13123
Switzerland	12572	12615	12516	12571	12676	12597	12971	13171	12705
Turkey	14315	15646	18342	18415	18702	20193	19953	20791	23656
United Kingdom	58439	61759	62140	65795	65951	66377	67727	68029	69406
United States	632551	647028	665395	684258	678899	669260	648492	667582	674171
OECD TOTAL	**1388195**	**1425611**	**1457456**	**1501820**	**1501874**	**1506634**	**1506987**	**1540118**	**1548316**
OECD EUROPE	464807	482742	487494	498950	492074	499938	516404	522633	521993
NORTH AMERICA	744618	759936	781618	803165	804098	794782	774145	796248	804304
PACIFIC	178770	182933	188344	199705	205702	211914	216438	221237	222019
EU	429514	445699	447094	459271	452156	458757	475418	480750	477553
IEA	1338240	1375390	1405668	1449925	1445367	1447732	1445025	1476710	1485228

Industry Consumption of Hard Coal (1000 tonnes)
Consommation industrielle de houille (1000 tonnes)

	1970	1973	1978	1979	1980	1981	1982	1983	1984
Australia	3125	3026	3174	3269	3297	3319	3452	3391	3658
Austria	71	46	41	52	67	91	176	324	407
Belgium	680	1421	2660	1639	2151	1931	1377	991	1279
Canada	2680	1921	1412	1510	1524	1365	1422	1300	1404
Denmark	171	319	694	709	548	399	324	193	327
Finland	576	1038	665	623	787	849	1006	1045	1091
France	7152	4890	2910	2980	3349	4040	4417	3568	3939
Germany	7381	4622	5148	6061	6563	6575	7065	7059	7479
Greece	98	80	131	159	139	127	489	1050	1328
Iceland	-	-	-	10	12	24	25	37	55
Ireland	150	50	39	60	137	201	221	304	336
Italy	408	242	312	536	605	1136	1996	1620	2069
Japan	3100	1500	2638	2602	6549	10860	11228	8935	9947
Luxembourg	104	294	496	348	325	272	251	140	164
Mexico	-	-	-	-	-	-	-	-	-
Netherlands	371	112	64	63	76	76	242	280	745
New Zealand	1121	1236	826	786	949	927	985	874	960
Norway	268	367	347	484	514	569	569	617	659
Portugal	200	51	92	75	84	68	59	140	189
Spain	2005	1724	753	992	897	2097	3135	3030	3093
Sweden	365	276	299	330	334	348	483	528	611
Switzerland	166	67	99	126	278	523	450	408	592
Turkey	211	300	334	462	586	573	683	593	914
United Kingdom	19127	11315	6192	6882	5472	4645	5016	4857	4622
United States	79948	47932	44629	42195	44804	49535	47847	48143	54783
OECD TOTAL	**129478**	**82829**	**73955**	**72953**	**80047**	**90550**	**92918**	**89427**	**100651**
OECD EUROPE	39504	27214	21276	22591	22924	24544	27984	26784	29899
NORTH AMERICA	82628	49853	46041	43705	46328	50900	49269	49443	56187
PACIFIC	7346	5762	6638	6657	10795	15106	15665	13200	14565
EU	38859	26480	20496	21509	21534	22855	26257	25129	27679
IEA	129478	82829	73955	72943	80035	90526	92893	89390	100596

	1985	1986	1987	1988	1989	1990	1991	1992	1993
Australia	4333	4453	4450	4477	4660	4846	4836	4969	4966
Austria	385	277	286	254	253	242	265	315	253
Belgium	1180	882	1015	1237	1833	1781	2078	1792	1483
Canada	1506	1389	1472	1558	1503	1411	1135	1148	1105
Denmark	439	344	461	494	527	454	494	387	439
Finland	1210	1057	1231	1097	1368	1043	979	808	756
France	4761	4617	5021	5475	5509	5763	5724	5776	4670
Germany	7947	7306	7960	8178	7653	8262	7229	6568	5572
Greece	1436	1405	1363	1394	1275	1378	1476	1384	1353
Iceland	69	74	60	67	71	65	60	50	53
Ireland	338	449	617	577	541	349	367	198	228
Italy	2623	1335	1825	1137	1302	1853	1735	2772	2519
Japan	10483	9466	10784	12790	14128	15754	14625	16403	13725
Luxembourg	173	178	195	160	194	196	202	278	277
Mexico	-	-	-	-	-	-	-	-	-
Netherlands	731	710	1023	1057	1149	1164	1029	1090	1172
New Zealand	1000	1065	1277	1624	1534	1557	1534	1698	1567
Norway	659	603	641	754	755	742	639	648	744
Portugal	315	569	702	807	837	818	868	788	734
Spain	2902	2834	2798	2856	2804	2253	2716	2427	1383
Sweden	628	643	657	826	868	925	790	686	731
Switzerland	582	505	493	431	430	455	385	256	210
Turkey	969	989	1019	989	965	1459	1865	1630	1507
United Kingdom	5777	6422	6467	7130	6222	5751	5951	6581	5300
United States	55477	55207	54428	55123	54143	53498	52482	28009	27990
OECD TOTAL	**105923**	**102779**	**106245**	**110492**	**110524**	**112019**	**109464**	**86661**	**78737**
OECD EUROPE	33124	31199	33834	34920	34556	34953	34852	34434	29384
NORTH AMERICA	56983	56596	55900	56681	55646	54909	53617	29157	29095
PACIFIC	15816	14984	16511	18891	20322	22157	20995	23070	20258
EU	30845	29028	31621	32679	32335	32232	31903	31850	26870
IEA	105854	102705	106185	110425	110453	111954	109404	86611	78684

Industry Consumption of Brown Coal (1000 tonnes)
Consommation industrielle de lignite (1000 tonnes)

	1970	1973	1978	1979	1980	1981	1982	1983	1984
Australia	361	446	305	354	311	331	301	302	287
Austria	584	205	205	183	155	210	226	182	186
Belgium	-	-	-	8	95	112	92	98	196
Canada	1299	312	288	261	249	278	211	200	212
Denmark	-	-	-	-	-	-	-	-	-
Finland	-	-	-	-	-	-	-	-	-
France	472	251	200	220	163	138	120	129	139
Germany	31197	30063	20548	20392	21769	22671	22509	23451	27662
Greece	155	173	363	523	472	380	427	242	361
Iceland	-	-	-	-	-	-	-	-	-
Ireland	-	-	-	-	-	-	-	-	-
Italy	40	35	35	44	48	45	46	55	74
Japan	100	-	31	24	22	-	-	-	-
Luxembourg	-	-	17	26	28	6	-	-	-
Mexico	-	-	-	-	-	-	-	-	-
Netherlands	-	20	65	179	153	149	127	93	92
New Zealand	50	47	88	141	85	81	103	176	184
Norway	-	-	-	-	-	-	-	-	-
Portugal	-	-	-	-	-	-	-	-	-
Spain	787	407	31	45	52	52	33	60	64
Sweden	-	-	-	-	-	-	-	-	1
Switzerland	-	-	-	-	-	-	-	-	-
Turkey	1013	2476	3633	3344	3485	3695	3658	3801	5486
United Kingdom	-	-	-	-	-	-	-	-	-
United States	1170	2214	2186	3681	2796	2496	2759	2519	3917
OECD TOTAL	**37228**	**36649**	**27995**	**29425**	**29883**	**30644**	**30612**	**31308**	**38861**
OECD EUROPE	34248	33630	25097	24964	26420	27458	27238	28111	34261
NORTH AMERICA	2469	2526	2474	3942	3045	2774	2970	2719	4129
PACIFIC	511	493	424	519	418	412	404	478	471
EU	33235	31154	21464	21620	22935	23763	23580	24310	28775
IEA	37228	36649	27995	29425	29883	30644	30612	31308	38861

	1985	1986	1987	1988	1989	1990	1991	1992	1993
Australia	274	282	257	288	170	73	44	48	51
Austria	280	168	125	122	149	157	231	204	171
Belgium	275	257	258	226	267	276	275	244	226
Canada	171	251	262	270	265	231	212	231	298
Denmark	-	-	-	-	-	-	-	-	-
Finland	-	-	-	-	-	-	-	-	-
France	164	159	144	156	210	230	169	166	156
Germany	30304	28651	28471	27821	27094	20359	11497	7816	4001
Greece	450	443	331	401	596	515	432	379	552
Iceland	-	-	-	-	-	-	-	-	-
Ireland	-	-	-	-	-	-	-	-	-
Italy	143	80	28	24	28	33	32	61	20
Japan	-	-	-	-	-	-	-	-	-
Luxembourg	-	-	12	4	2	9	9	9	8
Mexico	-	-	-	-	-	-	-	-	-
Netherlands	98	73	59	51	49	58	44	30	27
New Zealand	164	108	-	139	93	101	137	116	119
Norway	-	-	-	-	-	-	-	-	-
Portugal	-	-	-	-	-	-	-	-	-
Spain	72	75	72	70	72	75	39	6	10
Sweden	-	-	-	-	6	-	-	-	-
Switzerland	-	-	-	-	-	-	-	-	-
Turkey	5511	4947	6447	7635	8259	8523	8832	7405	7428
United Kingdom	-	-	-	-	-	-	-	-	-
United States	6638	7469	7947	7796	8283	7815	7754	6234	5774
OECD TOTAL	**44544**	**42963**	**44413**	**45003**	**45543**	**38455**	**29707**	**22949**	**18841**
OECD EUROPE	37297	34853	35947	36510	36732	30235	21560	16320	12599
NORTH AMERICA	6809	7720	8209	8066	8548	8046	7966	6465	6072
PACIFIC	438	390	257	427	263	174	181	164	170
EU	31786	29906	29500	28875	28473	21712	12728	8915	5171
IEA	44544	42963	44413	45003	45543	38455	29707	22949	18841

Industry Consumption of Natural Gas (TJ)
Consommation industrielle de gaz naturel (TJ)

	1970	1973	1978	1979	1980	1981	1982	1983	1984
Australia	22609	56874	130368	144485	173739	190536	193115	200386	205241
Austria	39909	56361	81443	86024	85582	81037	76567	74774	79245
Belgium	78992	146642	170352	178923	169054	152781	134075	131753	149951
Canada	417692	552260	716255	750495	862427	803101	747967	770399	849846
Denmark	-	-	-	-	-	-	-	-	602
Finland	-	-	20114	19636	19071	20160	18368	19825	21604
France	162326	263023	391206	441755	438834	469115	437093	454033	492489
Germany	283478	560685	814718	882673	896955	905936	829353	855989	878426
Greece	-	-	-	-	-	-	1176	1231	1876
Iceland	-	-	-	-	-	-	-	-	-
Ireland	-	-	-	12514	16069	17626	21298	18154	22228
Italy	308664	401909	513041	529518	516576	482194	434962	422298	466898
Japan	65574	67634	81048	78360	68412	62886	60745	58217	62595
Luxembourg	477	6486	10655	12017	11430	8093	6867	5812	6372
Mexico	-	363857	523728	597804	654263	759563	792578	845598	734476
Netherlands	221891	378914	422892	441644	391328	400908	383064	379296	399534
New Zealand	561	1507	9797	8152	10228	18108	21785	30452	55311
Norway	-	-	-	-	-	-	-	-	-
Portugal	-	-	-	-	-	-	-	-	-
Spain	3274	18300	34559	33558	28119	30144	33327	39167	47589
Sweden	-	-	-	-	-	-	-	-	-
Switzerland	226	634	12317	13480	16440	17880	18645	19250	22460
Turkey	-	-	-	-	-	-	-	1532	2719	1532
United Kingdom	74843	438228	622947	644810	628033	596141	601492	596442	604063
United States	7454166	8245986	6394232	6528327	7051141	7075805	5695936	5508857	6156371
OECD TOTAL	**9134682**	**11559300**	**10949672**	**11404175**	**12037701**	**12092014**	**10509945**	**10434652**	**11258709**
OECD EUROPE	**1174080**	**2271182**	**3094244**	**3296552**	**3217491**	**3182015**	**2997819**	**3020743**	**3194869**
NORTH AMERICA	**7871858**	**9162103**	**7634215**	**7876626**	**8567831**	**8638469**	**7236481**	**7124854**	**7740693**
PACIFIC	**88744**	**126015**	**221213**	**230997**	**252379**	**271530**	**275645**	**289055**	**323147**
EU	**1173854**	**2270548**	**3081927**	**3283072**	**3201051**	**3164135**	**2977642**	**2998774**	**3170877**
IEA	**9134682**	**11195443**	**10425944**	**10806371**	**11383438**	**11332451**	**9717367**	**9589054**	**10524233**

	1985	1986	1987	1988	1989	1990	1991	1992	1993
Australia	236153	254174	268390	272652	280361	286474	281317	280964	284687
Austria	77671	71386	74808	76814	81166	86237	83204	77910	81940
Belgium	141120	124883	135979	143865	153397	153592	141835	154342	159457
Canada	885752	858558	930329	956859	963822	933220	925672	933529	965210
Denmark	5626	9891	15390	20743	22315	24404	23468	23750	25774
Finland	20670	23765	34622	33446	45132	56143	59574	61684	58505
France	494710	481901	494652	490111	502949	541598	562794	545792	572271
Germany	878929	861376	889788	907425	950828	897913	857039	858877	870132
Greece	2458	2734	3362	4515	4300	4496	4296	4085	2633
Iceland	-	-	-	-	-	-	-	-	-
Ireland	23170	29589	34248	33726	35935	36747	37950	36749	37177
Italy	453573	482701	561919	621096	669169	681431	692571	690287	672671
Japan	61610	58108	56822	56444	56192	56640	59004	53245	53865
Luxembourg	6937	6791	7515	9022	10767	12989	13018	13778	14151
Mexico	751433	638408	695780	674262	722317	692317	751140	723809	708476
Netherlands	390972	366959	403210	391502	393278	408966	419717	414151	424981
New Zealand	27582	30090	30512	32471	34935	34185	34560	34660	33650
Norway	-	-	-	-	-	-	-	-	-
Portugal	-	-	-	-	-	-	-	-	-
Spain	55419	65891	84804	114977	159731	174086	185835	196716	198436
Sweden	2725	5803	6904	8216	9927	11562	10460	10809	11212
Switzerland	23520	23690	23190	22910	25810	27420	31170	33230	36910
Turkey	1876	1766	2043	7920	18908	31172	44381	60504	74509
United Kingdom	610423	551810	588179	539274	552638	556333	541077	483574	478736
United States	5786116	5425553	5753928	6271729	6747995	6895590	7105657	7419450	7815911
OECD TOTAL	**10938445**	**10375827**	**11096374**	**11689979**	**12441872**	**12603515**	**12865739**	**13111895**	**13581294**
OECD EUROPE	**3189799**	**3110936**	**3360613**	**3425562**	**3636250**	**3705089**	**3708389**	**3666238**	**3719495**
NORTH AMERICA	**7423301**	**6922519**	**7380037**	**7902850**	**8434134**	**8521127**	**8782469**	**9076788**	**9489597**
PACIFIC	**325345**	**342372**	**355724**	**361567**	**371488**	**377299**	**374881**	**368869**	**372202**
EU	**3164403**	**3085480**	**3335380**	**3394732**	**3591532**	**3646497**	**3632838**	**3572504**	**3608076**
IEA	**10187012**	**9737419**	**10400594**	**11015717**	**11719555**	**11911198**	**12114599**	**12388086**	**12872818**

Industry Consumption of Electricity (GWh)
Consommation industrielle d'électricité (GWh)

	1970	1973	1978	1979	1980	1981	1982	1983	1984
Australia	26037	23191	29507	31120	32513	34143	34773	34359	38957
Austria	10511	12121	13246	13878	14172	14090	13909	14136	14956
Belgium	17489	22423	23385	25007	23944	23529	22980	23487	24950
Canada	94484	105860	126476	127710	135674	140466	132134	138428	155856
Denmark	3850	4600	5493	5542	5783	6304	6534	6723	7099
Finland	14012	18064	19779	21780	22819	23417	22770	24262	26468
France	72408	83991	91608	95171	95361	92521	91397	92108	94254
Germany	147411	178328	195301	203239	199547	197252	193073	196346	205520
Greece	4949	7367	9637	10249	10498	10155	9986	10629	11209
Iceland	880	1500	1599	1769	1978	2004	2235	2340	2512
Ireland	1605	2199	2936	3256	3210	3124	3066	3171	3439
Italy	67711	77146	88424	92669	94021	90744	88564	86797	91886
Japan	229900	291381	320333	337084	327788	320516	313942	329008	346555
Luxembourg	1995	2365	2413	2437	2466	2249	2252	2338	2523
Mexico	-	18093	26554	28932	30204	33053	34615	35619	38820
Netherlands	17973	22713	27771	29072	28075	27708	26605	26984	27836
New Zealand	2878	5623	7240	7445	7678	7752	8199	9388	9955
Norway	32472	37186	37293	40724	39932	40400	39009	42688	46648
Portugal	3980	5109	7019	7749	8210	7988	8381	9311	9108
Spain	28151	37946	50817	53716	53944	53438	53288	54398	56970
Sweden	34321	39543	39338	41410	40571	40731	39810	42927	46546
Switzerland	10233	11062	11122	11539	11899	12073	12084	12210	12798
Turkey	4427	6436	11583	11703	12153	13350	14268	14692	17023
United Kingdom	83663	91269	93401	96347	87285	83985	79971	79532	83512
United States	526462	645799	744368	769441	746136	753988	668958	698140	767787
OECD TOTAL	**1437802**	**1751315**	**1986643**	**2068989**	**2035861**	**2034980**	**1922803**	**1990021**	**2143187**
OECD EUROPE	558041	661368	732165	767257	755868	745062	730182	745079	785257
NORTH AMERICA	620946	769752	897398	926083	912014	927507	835707	872187	962463
PACIFIC	258815	320195	357080	375649	367979	362411	356914	372755	395467
EU	510029	605184	670568	701522	689906	677235	662586	673149	706276
IEA	1436922	1731722	1958490	2038288	2003679	1999923	1885953	1952062	2101855

	1985	1986	1987	1988	1989	1990	1991	1992	1993
Australia	43068	45709	48005	52166	56747	59184	59481	60168	61786
Austria	15290	15309	15794	16885	17429	18172	18307	17333	16666
Belgium	25565	25846	26991	28763	29594	30523	31081	32212	31269
Canada	166489	171274	172624	173930	169475	166922	169384	167498	172497
Denmark	7523	7968	8235	8451	8636	8730	9033	9194	9073
Finland	27327	27695	29077	30967	31915	32518	31377	31664	33677
France	97133	100494	104451	109072	113119	114666	116946	121052	120648
Germany	210091	212840	215254	224352	229455	216479	214513	211912	202200
Greece	11045	10932	10723	11763	12168	12109	11896	11746	11353
Iceland	2390	2549	2423	2553	2610	2559	2473	2506	2677
Ireland	3593	3793	3905	4035	4332	4485	4626	4879	5054
Italy	92804	94987	98748	104469	109118	110839	110902	111244	109788
Japan	353665	349310	367555	388018	410201	435667	444116	439737	435501
Luxembourg	2510	2479	2520	2582	2621	2617	2609	2588	2638
Mexico	41095	42239	45578	48229	51705	53394	52183	52831	55145
Netherlands	28448	28868	30033	31507	32385	33237	33247	33666	34823
New Zealand	9997	10427	10726	11034	11157	11171	11664	11514	12465
Norway	46025	43451	44504	45212	45643	45810	45286	44808	46260
Portugal	9444	9943	10423	10839	11100	12219	12512	12800	12515
Spain	56649	56411	57232	58828	62930	63279	64707	64876	63253
Sweden	48914	48788	51880	53905	54363	53955	51764	50626	49621
Switzerland	13502	13826	14245	14788	15191	15209	15165	14845	14506
Turkey	18360	19490	22282	23545	25741	27343	26263	29285	31756
United Kingdom	85027	87767	91551	93390	99417	100642	99570	95276	96246
United States	762520	732060	768114	820165	843983	866542	957508	984800	994707
OECD TOTAL	**2178474**	**2164455**	**2252873**	**2369448**	**2451035**	**2498271**	**2596613**	**2619060**	**2626124**
OECD EUROPE	801640	813436	840271	875906	907767	905391	902277	902512	894023
NORTH AMERICA	970104	945573	986316	1042324	1065163	1086858	1179075	1205129	1222349
PACIFIC	406730	405446	426286	451218	478105	506022	515261	511419	509752
EU	721363	734120	756817	789808	818582	814470	813090	811068	798824
IEA	2134989	2119667	2204872	2318666	2396720	2442318	2541957	2563723	2568302

Industry Consumption of Oil (1000 tonnes)
Consommation industrielle de pétrole (1000 tonnes)

	1970	1973	1978	1979	1980	1981	1982	1983	1984
Australia	6357	5885	6119	6086	5761	4928	4294	3462	3660
Austria	2113	2461	1938	1814	1733	1548	1437	1266	1149
Belgium	6803	6963	5119	4813	3656	3249	3845	3433	3243
Canada	11499	16200	15496	16760	15313	14218	11369	10522	11348
Denmark	3214	2893	2269	2262	2119	1723	1484	1354	1456
Finland	3072	4645	3412	3448	3280	3229	3101	2762	2695
France	31071	27793	25790	29175	26578	18533	18036	18700	16307
Germany	35764	42266	36219	37807	31592	26867	24579	24228	21729
Greece	1462	2106	2752	2920	2877	2639	2386	2083	1884
Iceland	64	113	145	148	144	94	93	76	90
Ireland	1292	1486	1307	1537	1437	1359	1155	1092	1143
Italy	24876	26811	19561	21176	19385	17553	15441	16073	14918
Japan	68336	85509	71255	72895	58111	50162	53012	52328	55229
Luxembourg	730	797	473	327	169	150	131	112	116
Mexico	-	3943	7221	7124	6767	8081	8557	9529	10429
Netherlands	6379	8343	8264	8705	7540	5748	5352	6286	5900
New Zealand	616	870	630	669	575	534	466	385	354
Norway	2400	2424	2749	2785	2871	2627	2416	2257	2469
Portugal	1193	1656	2198	2346	2397	2351	2763	2443	2702
Spain	8971	11668	14112	14931	14006	13020	10490	11170	10334
Sweden	7309	7335	6039	6187	5501	4671	4097	3776	3584
Switzerland	2849	3117	2428	2261	2292	2207	1809	2145	1706
Turkey	1236	2250	4096	3541	3874	3873	3993	4224	3919
United Kingdom	31974	32164	23062	23341	16879	15706	14700	13433	12707
United States	96845	110695	119566	143069	129080	119159	114455	93347	99980
OECD TOTAL	**356425**	**410393**	**382220**	**416127**	**363937**	**324229**	**309461**	**286486**	**289051**
OECD EUROPE	172772	187291	161933	169524	148330	127147	117308	116913	108051
NORTH AMERICA	108344	130838	142283	166953	151160	141458	134381	113398	121757
PACIFIC	75309	92264	78004	79650	64447	55624	57772	56175	59243
EU	166223	179387	152515	160789	139149	118346	108997	108211	99867
IEA	356361	406337	374854	408855	357026	316054	300811	276881	278532

	1985	1986	1987	1988	1989	1990	1991	1992	1993
Australia	3257	3080	3014	3300	3544	3793	3553	3568	3780
Austria	1012	1053	1083	1064	963	881	748	761	810
Belgium	3381	4160	3603	3729	3415	3094	3859	3838	3694
Canada	11448	11540	12008	12849	12976	13237	12549	12487	13054
Denmark	1353	1329	1104	1044	875	922	930	864	803
Finland	2023	2253	2043	1933	1943	1834	1899	1585	1373
France	15733	14564	15570	15142	14168	13249	14548	15378	13760
Germany	22369	22683	22159	22969	22501	21860	22376	22629	22376
Greece	1643	1721	1892	1907	1967	1796	1741	1728	1611
Iceland	85	86	78	89	78	71	44	65	73
Ireland	1039	964	1008	850	847	703	714	738	728
Italy	13951	13347	13082	13951	13839	13526	12566	12521	11240
Japan	53619	53566	55544	57454	59554	59951	60000	59490	60356
Luxembourg	135	158	268	267	309	283	298	276	280
Mexico	12167	12250	12984	12855	13870	13057	12215	12577	12365
Netherlands	5759	6895	7186	5783	5674	6216	6098	5641	4603
New Zealand	324	300	310	282	266	225	257	293	263
Norway	2503	2443	2519	2231	2018	1872	1562	1301	1381
Portugal	2607	2671	2644	3135	3267	3451	3151	3214	2948
Spain	9762	9504	9237	10383	9162	8872	8914	8338	8348
Sweden	3449	3456	3278	3102	2735	2728	2582	2595	2579
Switzerland	1777	1578	1246	1084	971	869	859	959	766
Turkey	3774	3902	4929	4882	5118	5185	5091	5612	5457
United Kingdom	12060	13192	12638	13735	12466	11987	13361	12001	12316
United States	92858	95083	95444	93589	89961	87914	80009	85370	82701
OECD TOTAL	**278088**	**281778**	**284871**	**287609**	**282487**	**277576**	**269924**	**273829**	**267665**
OECD EUROPE	104415	105959	105567	107280	102316	99399	101341	100044	95146
NORTH AMERICA	116473	118873	120436	119293	116807	114208	104773	110434	108120
PACIFIC	57200	56946	58868	61036	63364	63969	63810	63351	64399
EU	96276	97950	96795	98994	94131	91402	93785	92107	87469
IEA	265836	269442	271809	274665	268539	264448	257665	261187	255227

Excluding non-energy use, except feedstocks. / *Ne comprend pas l'usage non-énergétique sauf les produits d'alimentation.*

VIII. ELECTRICITY AND HEAT

VIII. ELECTRICITE ET CHALEUR

OECD Total / OCDE Total

Electricity and Heat Production in the Transformation Sector
Production de chaleur et d'élécticité du secteur transformation

	1986	1987	1988	1989	1990	1991	1992	1993

ELECTRICITY / ELECTRICITE (GWh)

	1986	1987	1988	1989	1990	1991	1992	1993
TOTAL ELECTRICITY	6188090	6443814	6703933	7087970	7234741	7426909	7495211	7657454
Thermal								
Hard Coal	2068619	2187811	2260825	2320598	2362216	2392217	1952566	1910765
Lignite and Sub-bit. Coal	390949	393873	403145	424042	413278	411137	865229	934661
Peat	7972	8534	8864	9477	10175	11181	5999	6467
Coke Oven and Blast Fur. Gas	62727	62587	67526	69137	69123	79254	88976	91286
Liquid Fuels/Refinery Gas	570784	572012	622431	709722	679657	686839	643745	580542
Natural Gas/Gas Works Gas	548468	594672	581084	717463	750076	777559	826101	878252
Nuclear	1323592	1407090	1524927	1570505	1633509	1722335	1747074	1813586
Geothermal	19909	21726	21564	26406	28648	29188	30795	31592
Solar *	20	15	11	508	687	784	789	941
Combustible Renewables and Wastes	15456	18299	19079	72718	84154	71788	99479	104530
Solid Biomass and Animal Products	*7758*	*10773*	*10900*	*63963*	*74938*	*62284*	*63078*	*65192*
Gases/Liquids from Biomass	-	-	-	-	-	-	*3281*	*4614*
Industrial Waste	*2943*	*2838*	*3298*	*3594*	*3800*	*3992*	*13756*	*14538*
Municipal Waste	*4755*	*4688*	*4881*	*5161*	*5416*	*5512*	*19364*	*20186*
Non-Thermal								
Hydro	1178832	1176393	1192886	1163800	1199010	1239793	1229390	1299106
of which: pumped storage	*22368*	*38505*	*40047*	*41414*	*40730*	*49172*	*49615*	*48632*
Tide/Wave/Ocean	619	604	588	584	597	616	611	589
Wind	143	198	1003	3010	3611	4216	4126	4764
Other Fuel Sources	-	-	-	-	-	2	331	373

HEAT / CHALEUR (TJ)

	1986	1987	1988	1989	1990	1991	1992	1993
TOTAL HEAT	775899	808481	744218	769304	788837	1055752	1189970	1245069
Hard Coal	-	-	-	-	-	-	311342	318149
Lignite and Sub-bit. Coal	-	-	-	-	-	-	33265	20380
Peat	-	-	-	-	-	-	28597	27182
Coke Oven and Blast Fur. Gas	-	-	-	-	-	-	30029	28219
Liquid Fuels/Refinery Gas	-	-	-	-	-	-	176327	180942
Natural Gas/Gas Works Gas	-	-	-	-	-	-	378198	437037
Nuclear	-	-	-	-	-	-	13368	7657
Geothermal	-	-	-	-	-	-	7594	7142
Solar	-	-	-	-	-	-	-	-
Electricity and Ambient Heat	-	-	-	-	-	-	50630	50245
Heat Pumps	-	-	-	-	-	-	*25013*	*27321*
Electric Boilers	-	-	-	-	-	-	*25617*	*22924*
Combustible Renewables and Wastes	-	-	-	-	-	-	160620	168116
Solid Biomass and Animal Products	-	-	-	-	-	-	*121494*	*111549*
Gases/Liquids from Biomass	-	-	-	-	-	-	*486*	*1062*
Industrial Waste	-	-	-	-	-	-	*1758*	*4379*
Municipal Waste	-	-	-	-	-	-	*36882*	*51126*
Non-specified	-	-	-	-	-	-	-	-

* Figures for electricity generated from photovoltaic systems are not available separately and are included here with electricity produced from solar thermal.
* *Les données sur l'électricité produite à l'aide de systèmes photovoltaïques ne sont pas disponibles séparément et sont montrées ici avec l'électricité produite par l'énergie thermique solaire.*

North America / Amérique du Nord

Electricity and Heat Production in the Transformation Sector
Production de chaleur et d'électricité du secteur transformation

	1986	1987	1988	1989	1990	1991	1992	1993
ELECTRICITY / ELECTRICITE (GWh)								
TOTAL ELECTRICITY	3197700	3325177	3482668	3754595	3793541	3899391	3934443	4065233
Thermal								
Hard Coal	1436205	1526371	1607012	1649813	1646416	1645207	1219888	1205688
Lignite and Sub-bit. Coal	124598	131402	141280	142502	144055	151536	607820	684180
Peat	-	-	-	-	-	-	10	16
Coke Oven and Blast Fur. Gas	90	21	34	-	-	11773	13211	13034
Liquid Fuels/Refinery Gas	203711	193444	230660	255714	208713	203900	184086	195152
Natural Gas/Gas Works Gas	281167	307671	289019	396951	405273	427514	455227	467280
Nuclear	510147	559847	641458	641409	687412	738570	740469	746741
Geothermal	14320	15840	15551	19623	21091	21658	22972	23651
Solar *	18	14	9	492	666	782	786	938
Combustible Renewables and Wastes	3086	3853	4249	56949	68421	56442	69535	72452
Solid Biomass and Animal Products	*3086*	*3853*	*4249*	*56949*	*68421*	*56442*	*44606*	*45784*
Gases/Liquids from Biomass	-	-	-	-	-	-	*3033*	*3304*
Industrial Waste	-	-	-	-	-	-	*9339*	*10349*
Municipal Waste	-	-	-	-	-	-	*12557*	*13015*
Non-Thermal								
Hydro	624325	586680	553374	589283	609217	639371	617462	652988
of which: pumped storage	*62*	*15427*	*16873*	*17573*	*15900*	*21072*	*20635*	*21457*
Tide/Wave/Ocean	33	34	22	26	26	32	33	33
Wind	-	-	-	1833	2251	2606	2944	3080
Other Fuel Sources	-	-	-	-	-	-	-	-
HEAT / CHALEUR (TJ)								
TOTAL HEAT	114003	116937	95866	118824	102315	321007	394008	415656
Hard Coal	-	-	-	-	-	-	55224	57643
Lignite and Sub-bit. Coal	-	-	-	-	-	-	18895	6031
Peat	-	-	-	-	-	-	-	-
Coke Oven and Blast Fur. Gas	-	-	-	-	-	-	23542	21628
Liquid Fuels/Refinery Gas	-	-	-	-	-	-	66718	63620
Natural Gas/Gas Works Gas	-	-	-	-	-	-	171483	221765
Nuclear	-	-	-	-	-	-	12568	6837
Geothermal	-	-	-	-	-	-	-	-
Solar	-	-	-	-	-	-	-	-
Electricity and Ambient Heat	-	-	-	-	-	-	-	-
Heat Pumps	-	-	-	-	-	-	-	-
Electric Boilers	-	-	-	-	-	-	-	-
Combustible Renewables and Wastes	-	-	-	-	-	-	45578	38132
Solid Biomass and Animal Products	-	-	-	-	-	-	*35720*	*27766*
Gases/Liquids from Biomass	-	-	-	-	-	-	*44*	*3*
Industrial Waste	-	-	-	-	-	-	*1222*	*3784*
Municipal Waste	-	-	-	-	-	-	*8592*	*6579*
Non-specified	-	-	-	-	-	-	-	-

* Figures for electricity generated from photovoltaic systems are not available separately and are included here with electricity produced from solar thermal.
* *Les données sur l'électricité produite à l'aide de systèmes photovoltaïques ne sont pas disponibles séparément et sont montrées ici avec l'électricité produite par l'énergie thermique solaire.*

INTERNATIONAL ENERGY AGENCY

Pacific / Pacifique

Electricity and Heat Production in the Transformation Sector
Production de chaleur et d'éléctricité du secteur transformation

	1986	1987	1988	1989	1990	1991	1992	1993
ELECTRICITY / ELECTRICITE (GWh)								
TOTAL ELECTRICITY	830912	880423	922158	977500	1043981	1077664	1086209	1104080
Thermal								
Hard Coal	130529	140565	148024	156478	170185	176415	196023	209707
Lignite and Sub-bit. Coal	26722	31134	30353	32801	31948	34509	34735	33310
Peat	-	-	-	-	-	-	-	-
Coke Oven and Blast Fur. Gas	38280	38443	39993	40765	40526	40367	49413	54089
Liquid Fuels/Refinery Gas	191750	202947	222414	255668	272812	271313	229332	183551
Natural Gas/Gas Works Gas	148934	158846	165379	169666	187631	192128	213755	215323
Nuclear	168305	187758	178659	182869	202272	213460	223259	249256
Geothermal	2558	2591	2595	3293	3951	3979	4059	3936
Solar *	1	1	1	1	1	1	1	-
Combustible Renewables and Wastes	460	470	731	810	600	669	9600	9510
Solid Biomass and Animal Products	*460*	*470*	*731*	*810*	*600*	*669*	*9160*	*9080*
Gases/Liquids from Biomass	-	-	-	-	-	-	-	-
Industrial Waste	-	-	-	-	-	-	-	-
Municipal Waste	-	-	-	-	-	-	*440*	*430*
Non-Thermal								
Hydro	123373	117668	134009	135149	134055	144821	126014	145377
of which: pumped storage	*6268*	*7221*	*6258*	*6790*	*7262*	*8384*	*7490*	*8072*
Tide/Wave/Ocean	-	-	-	-	-	-	-	-
Wind	-	-	-	-	-	-	-	1
Other Fuel Sources	-	-	-	-	-	2	18	20
HEAT / CHALEUR (TJ)								
TOTAL HEAT	9275	9641	9629	10759	10727	11807	13680	14498
Hard Coal	-	-	-	-	-	-	957	1305
Lignite and Sub-bit. Coal	-	-	-	-	-	-	-	-
Peat	-	-	-	-	-	-	-	-
Coke Oven and Blast Fur. Gas	-	-	-	-	-	-	-	-
Liquid Fuels/Refinery Gas	-	-	-	-	-	-	1645	1595
Natural Gas/Gas Works Gas	-	-	-	-	-	-	7933	8554
Nuclear	-	-	-	-	-	-	-	-
Geothermal	-	-	-	-	-	-	-	-
Solar	-	-	-	-	-	-	-	-
Electricity and Ambient Heat	-	-	-	-	-	-	3145	3044
Heat Pumps	-	-	-	-	-	-	-	-
Electric Boilers	-	-	-	-	-	-	*3145*	*3044*
Combustible Renewables and Wastes	-	-	-	-	-	-	-	-
Solid Biomass and Animal Products	-	-	-	-	-	-	-	-
Gases/Liquids from Biomass	-	-	-	-	-	-	-	-
Industrial Waste	-	-	-	-	-	-	-	-
Municipal Waste	-	-	-	-	-	-	-	-
Non-specified	-	-	-	-	-	-	-	-

* Figures for electricity generated from photovoltaic systems are not available separately and are included here with electricity produced from solar thermal.
* *Les données sur l'électricité produite à l'aide de systèmes photovoltaïques ne sont pas disponibles séparément et sont montrées ici avec l'électricité produite par l'énergie thermique solaire.*

OECD Europe / OCDE Europe

Electricity and Heat Production in the Transformation Sector
Production de chaleur et d'éléctricité du secteur transformation

	1986	1987	1988	1989	1990	1991	1992	1993
ELECTRICITY / ELECTRICITE (GWh)								
TOTAL ELECTRICITY	2159478	2238214	2299107	2355875	2397219	2449854	2474559	2488141
Thermal								
Hard Coal	501885	520875	505789	514307	545615	570595	536655	495370
Lignite and Sub-bit. Coal	239629	231337	231512	248739	237275	225092	222674	217171
Peat	7972	8534	8864	9477	10175	11181	5989	6451
Coke Oven and Blast Fur. Gas	24357	24123	27499	28372	28597	27114	26352	24163
Liquid Fuels/Refinery Gas	175323	175621	169357	198340	198132	211626	230327	201839
Natural Gas/Gas Works Gas	118367	128155	126686	150846	157172	157917	157119	195649
Nuclear	645140	659485	704810	746227	743825	770305	783346	817589
Geothermal	3031	3295	3418	3490	3606	3551	3764	4005
Solar *	1	-	1	15	20	1	2	3
Combustible Renewables and Wastes	11910	13976	14099	14959	15133	14677	20344	22568
Solid Biomass and Animal Products	*4212*	*6450*	*5920*	*6204*	*5917*	*5173*	*9312*	*10328*
Gases/Liquids from Biomass	*-*	*-*	*-*	*-*	*-*	*-*	*248*	*1310*
Industrial Waste	*2943*	*2838*	*3298*	*3594*	*3800*	*3992*	*4417*	*4189*
Municipal Waste	*4755*	*4688*	*4881*	*5161*	*5416*	*5512*	*6367*	*6741*
Non-Thermal								
Hydro	431134	472045	505503	439368	455738	455601	485914	500741
of which: pumped storage	*16038*	*15857*	*16916*	*17051*	*17568*	*19716*	*21490*	*19103*
Tide/Wave/Ocean	586	570	566	558	571	584	578	556
Wind	143	198	1003	1177	1360	1610	1182	1683
Other Fuel Sources	-	-	-	-	-	-	313	353
HEAT / CHALEUR (TJ)								
TOTAL HEAT	652621	681903	638723	639721	675795	722938	782282	814915
Hard Coal	-	-	-	-	-	-	255161	259201
Lignite and Sub-bit. Coal	-	-	-	-	-	-	14370	14349
Peat	-	-	-	-	-	-	28597	27182
Coke Oven and Blast Fur. Gas	-	-	-	-	-	-	6487	6591
Liquid Fuels/Refinery Gas	-	-	-	-	-	-	107964	115727
Natural Gas/Gas Works Gas	-	-	-	-	-	-	198782	206718
Nuclear	-	-	-	-	-	-	800	820
Geothermal	-	-	-	-	-	-	7594	7142
Solar	-	-	-	-	-	-	-	-
Electricity and Ambient Heat	-	-	-	-	-	-	47485	47201
Heat Pumps	*-*	*-*	*-*	*-*	*-*	*-*	*25013*	*27321*
Electric Boilers	*-*	*-*	*-*	*-*	*-*	*-*	*22472*	*19880*
Combustible Renewables and Wastes	-	-	-	-	-	-	115042	129984
Solid Biomass and Animal Products	*-*	*-*	*-*	*-*	*-*	*-*	*85774*	*83783*
Gases/Liquids from Biomass	*-*	*-*	*-*	*-*	*-*	*-*	*442*	*1059*
Industrial Waste	*-*	*-*	*-*	*-*	*-*	*-*	*536*	*595*
Municipal Waste	*-*	*-*	*-*	*-*	*-*	*-*	*28290*	*44547*
Non-specified	-	-	-	-	-	-	-	-

* Figures for electricity generated from photovoltaic systems are not available separately and are included here with electricity produced from solar thermal.
* *Les données sur l'électricité produite à l'aide de systèmes photovoltaïques ne sont pas disponibles séparément et sont montrées ici avec l'électricité produite par l'énergie thermique solaire.*

IEA / AIE

Electricity and Heat Production in the Transformation Sector
Production de chaleur et d'éléctricité du secteur transformation

	1986	1987	1988	1989	1990	1991	1992	1993
ELECTRICITY / ELECTRICITE (GWh)								
TOTAL ELECTRICITY	6094593	6343294	6597550	6973370	7115982	7304058	7369012	7526161
Thermal								
Hard Coal	2062282	2180522	2252790	2312708	2354442	2384140	1944248	1900265
Lignite and Sub-bit. Coal	390949	393873	403145	424042	413278	411137	865229	934661
Peat	7972	8534	8864	9477	10175	11181	5999	6467
Coke Oven and Blast Fur. Gas	62727	62587	67526	69137	69123	79254	88976	91286
Liquid Fuels/Refinery Gas	519380	515412	562929	647473	617589	623263	581007	516479
Natural Gas/Gas Works Gas	540091	584864	571994	706779	737062	762262	811316	863287
Nuclear	1323592	1407090	1524927	1570133	1630572	1718093	1743155	1808655
Geothermal	16290	17060	16671	21459	23224	23470	24761	25459
Solar *	20	15	11	508	687	784	789	941
Combustible Renewables and Wastes	15456	18299	19079	72718	84154	71788	99479	104530
Solid Biomass and Animal Products	*7758*	*10773*	*10900*	*63963*	*74938*	*62284*	*63078*	*65192*
Gases/Liquids from Biomass	-	-	-	-	-	-	*3281*	*4614*
Industrial Waste	*2943*	*2838*	*3298*	*3594*	*3800*	*3992*	*13756*	*14538*
Municipal Waste	*4755*	*4688*	*4881*	*5161*	*5416*	*5512*	*19364*	*20186*
Non-Thermal								
Hydro	1155072	1154236	1168023	1135342	1171468	1213852	1198985	1268405
of which: pumped storage	*22368*	*38505*	*40047*	*41414*	*40730*	*49172*	*49615*	*48632*
Tide/Wave/Ocean	619	604	588	584	597	616	611	589
Wind	143	198	1003	3010	3611	4216	4126	4764
Other Fuel Sources	-	-	-	-	-	2	331	373
HEAT / CHALEUR (TJ)								
TOTAL HEAT	772821	805155	740715	765644	783555	1048944	1181771	1237323
Hard Coal	-	-	-	-	-	-	311342	318149
Lignite and Sub-bit. Coal	-	-	-	-	-	-	33265	20380
Peat	-	-	-	-	-	-	28597	27182
Coke Oven and Blast Fur. Gas	-	-	-	-	-	-	30029	28219
Liquid Fuels/Refinery Gas	-	-	-	-	-	-	176327	180926
Natural Gas/Gas Works Gas	-	-	-	-	-	-	378198	437037
Nuclear	-	-	-	-	-	-	13368	7657
Geothermal	-	-	-	-	-	-	-	45
Solar	-	-	-	-	-	-	-	-
Electricity and Ambient Heat	-	-	-	-	-	-	50025	49648
Heat Pumps	-	-	-	-	-	-	*25013*	*27321*
Electric Boilers	-	-	-	-	-	-	*25012*	*22327*
Combustible Renewables and Wastes	-	-	-	-	-	-	160620	168080
Solid Biomass and Animal Products	-	-	-	-	-	-	*121494*	*111549*
Gases/Liquids from Biomass	-	-	-	-	-	-	*486*	*1062*
Industrial Waste	-	-	-	-	-	-	*1758*	*4379*
Municipal Waste	-	-	-	-	-	-	*36882*	*51090*
Non-specified	-	-	-	-	-	-	-	-

* Figures for electricity generated from photovoltaic systems are not available separately and are included here with electricity produced from solar thermal.
* Les données sur l'électricité produite à l'aide de systèmes photovoltaïques ne sont pas disponibles séparément et sont montrées ici avec l'électricité produite par l'énergie thermique solaire.

European Union / Union Européenne

Electricity and Heat Production in the Transformation Sector
Production de chaleur et d'électricité du secteur transformation

	1986	1987	1988	1989	1990	1991	1992	1993

ELECTRICITY / ELECTRICITE (GWh)

	1986	1987	1988	1989	1990	1991	1992	1993
TOTAL ELECTRICITY	1960820	2025478	2075872	2125330	2157522	2216302	2226048	2228532
Thermal								
Hard Coal	500991	520169	505365	513891	544911	569540	534776	493519
Lignite and Sub-bit. Coal	220964	214311	219371	228786	217715	204529	199918	195207
Peat	7972	8534	8864	9477	10175	11181	5989	6451
Coke Oven and Blast Fur. Gas	24357	24123	27499	28372	28422	26977	26214	24014
Liquid Fuels/Refinery Gas	167649	169368	165385	193395	193894	207782	224412	196365
Natural Gas/Gas Works Gas	116802	125360	123183	141058	146677	144987	145951	184475
Nuclear	622559	636482	682018	723391	720189	747352	759898	794238
Geothermal	2762	2989	3089	3155	3226	3187	3464	3671
Solar *	1	-	1	15	20	-	-	-
Combustible Renewables and Wastes	11400	13423	13532	14373	14340	13852	19444	21806
Solid Biomass and Animal Products	*4212*	*6450*	*5920*	*6204*	*5733*	*4954*	*9059*	*10049*
Gases/Liquids from Biomass	-	-	-	-	-	-	*248*	*1310*
Industrial Waste	*2943*	*2838*	*3298*	*3594*	*3800*	*3992*	*4417*	*4189*
Municipal Waste	*4245*	*4135*	*4314*	*4575*	*4807*	*4906*	*5720*	*6258*
Non-Thermal								
Hydro	284634	309951	325996	267682	276022	284721	303912	306197
of which: pumped storage	*14397*	*14282*	*15217*	*15735*	*16144*	*17934*	*19738*	*17831*
Tide/Wave/Ocean	586	570	566	558	571	584	578	556
Wind	143	198	1003	1177	1360	1610	1179	1680
Other Fuel Sources	-	-	-	-	-	-	313	353

HEAT / CHALEUR (TJ)

	1986	1987	1988	1989	1990	1991	1992	1993
TOTAL HEAT	635384	662267	618901	619269	653956	697307	754816	787540
Hard Coal	-	-	-	-	-	-	254526	258561
Lignite and Sub-bit. Coal	-	-	-	-	-	-	14370	14349
Peat	-	-	-	-	-	-	28597	27182
Coke Oven and Blast Fur. Gas	-	-	-	-	-	-	6436	6539
Liquid Fuels/Refinery Gas	-	-	-	-	-	-	104883	114496
Natural Gas/Gas Works Gas	-	-	-	-	-	-	196794	204812
Nuclear	-	-	-	-	-	-	-	-
Geothermal	-	-	-	-	-	-	-	45
Solar	-	-	-	-	-	-	-	-
Electricity and Ambient Heat	-	-	-	-	-	-	45413	45108
Heat Pumps	-	-	-	-	-	-	*24868*	*27173*
Electric Boilers	-	-	-	-	-	-	*20545*	*17935*
Combustible Renewables and Wastes	-	-	-	-	-	-	103797	116448
Solid Biomass and Animal Products	-	-	-	-	-	-	*85672*	*83679*
Gases/Liquids from Biomass	-	-	-	-	-	-	*442*	*1059*
Industrial Waste	-	-	-	-	-	-	*138*	*189*
Municipal Waste	-	-	-	-	-	-	*17545*	*31521*
Non-specified	-	-	-	-	-	-	-	-

* Figures for electricity generated from photovoltaic systems are not available separately and are included here with electricity produced from solar thermal.
* *Les données sur l'électricité produite à l'aide de systèmes photovoltaïques ne sont pas disponibles séparément et sont montrées ici avec l'électricité produite par l'énergie thermique solaire.*

Australia / Australie

Electricity and Heat Production in the Transformation Sector
Production de chaleur et d'électricité du secteur transformation

	1986	1987	1988	1989	1990	1991	1992	1993
ELECTRICITY / ELECTRICITE (GWh)								
TOTAL ELECTRICITY	126383	132670	138959	147788	155077	156851	159649	163751
Thermal								
Hard Coal	65865	69214	75645	80759	87012	88199	91362	95289
Lignite and Sub-bit. Coal	26722	31134	30353	32801	31948	34509	34735	33310
Peat	-	-	-	-	-	-	-	-
Coke Oven and Blast Fur. Gas	270	320	105	105	72	73	73	73
Liquid Fuels/Refinery Gas	3771	2799	2444	3024	4206	4426	3689	3612
Natural Gas/Gas Works Gas	13784	13989	14718	15128	16359	12872	14023	14928
Nuclear	-	-	-	-	-	-	-	-
Geothermal	-	-	-	-	-	-	-	-
Solar *	-	-	-	-	-	-	-	-
Combustible Renewables and Wastes	460	470	731	810	600	669	-	-
Solid Biomass and Animal Products	*460*	*470*	*731*	*810*	*600*	*669*	-	-
Gases/Liquids from Biomass	-	-	-	-	-	-	-	-
Industrial Waste	-	-	-	-	-	-	-	-
Municipal Waste	-	-	-	-	-	-	-	-
Non-Thermal								
Hydro	15511	14744	14963	15161	14880	16103	15767	16539
of which: pumped storage	*1009*	*1147*	*665*	*706*	*732*	*282*	*419*	*414*
Tide/Wave/Ocean	-	-	-	-	-	-	-	-
Wind	-	-	-	-	-	-	-	-
Other Fuel Sources	-	-	-	-	-	-	-	-
HEAT / CHALEUR (TJ)								
TOTAL HEAT	3383	3262	3169	3567	2269	1972	-	-
Hard Coal	-	-	-	-	-	-	-	-
Lignite and Sub-bit. Coal	3383	3262	3169	3567	2269	1972	-	-
Peat	-	-	-	-	-	-	-	-
Coke Oven and Blast Fur. Gas	-	-	-	-	-	-	-	-
Liquid Fuels/Refinery Gas	-	-	-	-	-	-	-	-
Natural Gas/Gas Works Gas	-	-	-	-	-	-	-	-
Nuclear	-	-	-	-	-	-	-	-
Geothermal	-	-	-	-	-	-	-	-
Solar	-	-	-	-	-	-	-	-
Electricity and Ambient Heat	-	-	-	-	-	-	-	-
Heat Pumps	-	-	-	-	-	-	-	-
Electric Boilers	-	-	-	-	-	-	-	-
Combustible Renewables and Wastes	-	-	-	-	-	-	-	-
Solid Biomass and Animal Products	-	-	-	-	-	-	-	-
Gases/Liquids from Biomass	-	-	-	-	-	-	-	-
Industrial Waste	-	-	-	-	-	-	-	-
Municipal Waste	-	-	-	-	-	-	-	-
Non-specified	-	-	-	-	-	-	-	-

* Figures for electricity generated from photovoltaic systems are not available separately and are included here with electricity produced from solar thermal.
* *Les données sur l'électricité produite à l'aide de systèmes photovoltaïques ne sont pas disponibles séparément et sont montrées ici avec l'électricité produite par l'énergie thermique solaire.*

Austria / Autriche

Electricity and Heat Production in the Transformation Sector
Production de chaleur et d'électricité du secteur transformation

	1986	1987	1988	1989	1990	1991	1992	1993
ELECTRICITY / ELECTRICITE (GWh)								
TOTAL ELECTRICITY	44653	50517	49025	50174	50414	51484	51180	52675
Thermal								
Hard Coal	1100	2343	1924	2331	4012	4461	3023	2268
Lignite and Sub-bit. Coal	2063	1934	1811	1792	2468	2667	1308	1190
Peat	-	-	-	-	-	-	-	-
Coke Oven and Blast Fur. Gas	519	601	664	834	815	945	982	986
Liquid Fuels/Refinery Gas	2687	2569	2065	1981	2173	3022	2679	2953
Natural Gas/Gas Works Gas	5631	5444	4973	5985	7338	7339	6760	6903
Nuclear	-	-	-	-	-	-	-	-
Geothermal	-	-	-	-	-	-	-	-
Solar *	-	-	-	-	-	-	-	-
Combustible Renewables and Wastes	973	901	1047	1105	1116	322	346	355
Solid Biomass and Animal Products	*973*	*901*	*1047*	*1105*	*1116*	*322*	*346*	*355*
Gases/Liquids from Biomass	-	-	-	-	-	-	-	-
Industrial Waste	-	-	-	-	-	-	-	-
Municipal Waste	-	-	-	-	-	-	-	-
Non-Thermal								
Hydro	31680	36725	36541	36146	32492	32728	36082	38020
of which: pumped storage	*580*	*712*	*750*	*874*	*998*	*1302*	*1251*	*1317*
Tide/Wave/Ocean	-	-	-	-	-	-	-	-
Wind	-	-	-	-	-	-	-	-
Other Fuel Sources	-	-	-	-	-	-	-	-
HEAT / CHALEUR (TJ)								
TOTAL HEAT	23278	24536	24598	25452	28059	32189	30835	33503
Hard Coal	-	-	-	-	-	-	1515	1097
Lignite and Sub-bit. Coal	-	-	-	-	-	-	405	384
Peat	-	-	-	-	-	-	-	-
Coke Oven and Blast Fur. Gas	-	-	-	-	-	-	565	649
Liquid Fuels/Refinery Gas	-	-	-	-	-	-	17235	19024
Natural Gas/Gas Works Gas	-	-	-	-	-	-	6215	6931
Nuclear	-	-	-	-	-	-	-	-
Geothermal	-	-	-	-	-	-	-	-
Solar	-	-	-	-	-	-	-	-
Electricity and Ambient Heat	-	-	-	-	-	-	-	-
Heat Pumps	-	-	-	-	-	-	-	-
Electric Boilers	-	-	-	-	-	-	-	-
Combustible Renewables and Wastes	-	-	-	-	-	-	4900	5418
Solid Biomass and Animal Products	-	-	-	-	-	-	*1128*	*1397*
Gases/Liquids from Biomass	-	-	-	-	-	-	-	-
Industrial Waste	-	-	-	-	-	-	-	-
Municipal Waste	-	-	-	-	-	-	*3772*	*4021*
Non-specified	23278	24536	24598	25452	28059	32189	-	-

* Figures for electricity generated from photovoltaic systems are not available separately and are included here with electricity produced from solar thermal.
* *Les données sur l'électricité produite à l'aide de systèmes photovoltaïques ne sont pas disponibles séparément et sont montrées ici avec l'électricité produite par l'énergie thermique solaire.*

Belgium / Belgique

Electricity and Heat Production in the Transformation Sector
Production de chaleur et d'éléctricité du secteur transformation

	1986	1987	1988	1989	1990	1991	1992	1993
ELECTRICITY / ELECTRICITE (GWh)								
TOTAL ELECTRICITY	58676	63367	65349	67482	70846	71945	72259	70845
Thermal								
Hard Coal	11549	12688	13342	15009	17095	16511	16010	16297
Lignite and Sub-bit. Coal	-	-	-	-	-	-	-	-
Peat	-	-	-	-	-	-	-	-
Coke Oven and Blast Fur. Gas	2386	2372	2870	2621	2760	2728	2514	2421
Liquid Fuels/Refinery Gas	2499	2239	1717	1703	1314	1826	1543	1475
Natural Gas/Gas Works Gas	973	2094	2549	5374	5405	6216	6668	6812
Nuclear	39394	41967	43102	41217	42722	42861	43456	41927
Geothermal	-	-	-	-	-	-	-	-
Solar *	-	-	-	-	-	-	-	-
Combustible Renewables and Wastes	477	532	594	576	645	816	904	885
Solid Biomass and Animal Products	18	33	54	30	29	114	125	58
Gases/Liquids from Biomass	-	-	-	-	-	-	-	-
Industrial Waste	207	226	224	218	231	272	342	352
Municipal Waste	252	273	316	328	385	430	437	475
Non-Thermal								
Hydro	1398	1469	1167	975	897	979	1156	1020
of which: pumped storage	1055	1040	808	670	631	750	815	766
Tide/Wave/Ocean	-	-	-	-	-	-	-	-
Wind	-	6	8	7	8	8	8	8
Other Fuel Sources	-	-	-	-	-	-	-	-
HEAT / CHALEUR (TJ)								
TOTAL HEAT	9633	9793	9205	9306	9399	9970	9988	9503
Hard Coal	1829	1745	1388	1326	1508	1657	1571	580
Lignite and Sub-bit. Coal	-	-	-	-	-	-	-	-
Peat	-	-	-	-	-	-	-	-
Coke Oven and Blast Fur. Gas	68	60	80	59	71	51	21	28
Liquid Fuels/Refinery Gas	6162	3337	2599	2875	2762	3781	5518	4435
Natural Gas/Gas Works Gas	1502	4627	5085	4963	4990	4390	2740	4372
Nuclear	-	-	-	-	-	-	-	-
Geothermal	-	-	-	-	-	-	-	-
Solar	-	-	-	-	-	-	-	-
Electricity and Ambient Heat								
Heat Pumps	-	-	-	-	-	-	-	-
Electric Boilers	-	-	-	-	-	-	-	-
Combustible Renewables and Wastes	72	24	53	83	68	91	138	88
Solid Biomass and Animal Products	-	-	-	-	-	-	-	-
Gases/Liquids from Biomass	-	-	-	-	-	-	-	-
Industrial Waste	72	24	53	83	68	91	138	88
Municipal Waste	-	-	-	-	-	-	-	-
Non-specified	-	-	-	-	-	-	-	-

* Figures for electricity generated from photovoltaic systems are not available separately and are included here with electricity produced from solar thermal.
* *Les données sur l'électricité produite à l'aide de systèmes photovoltaïques ne sont pas disponibles séparément et sont montrées ici avec l'électricité produite par l'énergie thermique solaire.*

Canada / Canada

Electricity and Heat Production in the Transformation Sector
Production de chaleur et d'éléctricité du secteur transformation

	1986	1987	1988	1989	1990	1991	1992	1993
ELECTRICITY / ELECTRICITE (GWh)								
TOTAL ELECTRICITY	468593	496335	505966	499538	482025	507913	520924	527386
Thermal								
Hard Coal	29960	37603	44655	43214	35032	37237	37474	28320
Lignite and Sub-bit. Coal	41667	46635	47103	48523	48017	51094	53861	50393
Peat	-	-	-	-	-	-	-	-
Coke Oven and Blast Fur. Gas	90	21	34	-	-	-	-	-
Liquid Fuels/Refinery Gas	6166	10061	11842	18174	16002	13252	14845	10785
Natural Gas/Gas Works Gas	6886	6159	9432	14835	10590	9987	13534	15095
Nuclear	71267	77261	82867	79872	72886	84929	80580	94823
Geothermal	-	-	-	-	-	-	-	-
Solar *	-	-	-	-	-	-	37	37
Combustible Renewables and Wastes	1827	2273	2458	3446	2553	2903	4048	4182
Solid Biomass and Animal Products	*1827*	*2273*	*2458*	*3446*	*2553*	*2903*	*4048*	*4182*
Gases/Liquids from Biomass	-	-	-	-	-	-	-	-
Industrial Waste	-	-	-	-	-	-	-	-
Municipal Waste	-	-	-	-	-	-	-	-
Non-Thermal								
Hydro	310697	316288	307553	291448	296919	308479	316484	323690
of which: pumped storage	*62*	*82*	*118*	*98*	*92*	*122*	*123*	*110*
Tide/Wave/Ocean	33	34	22	26	26	32	33	33
Wind	-	-	-	-	-	-	28	28
Other Fuel Sources	-	-	-	-	-	-	-	-
HEAT / CHALEUR (TJ)								
TOTAL HEAT	32235	31794	16392	24432	21007	24816	16880	11022
Hard Coal	-	-	-	-	-	-	-	-
Lignite and Sub-bit. Coal	-	-	504	400	390	-	-	-
Peat	-	-	-	-	-	-	-	-
Coke Oven and Blast Fur. Gas	-	-	-	-	-	-	-	-
Liquid Fuels/Refinery Gas	-	-	1332	1276	2720	2264	2133	1295
Natural Gas/Gas Works Gas	-	-	1628	1285	1868	1967	2179	2890
Nuclear	28069	27616	12928	21471	16029	20585	12568	6837
Geothermal	-	-	-	-	-	-	-	-
Solar	-	-	-	-	-	-	-	-
Electricity and Ambient Heat	-	-	-	-	-	-	-	-
Heat Pumps	-	-	-	-	-	-	-	-
Electric Boilers	-	-	-	-	-	-	-	-
Combustible Renewables and Wastes	-	-	-	-	-	-	-	-
Solid Biomass and Animal Products	-	-	-	-	-	-	-	-
Gases/Liquids from Biomass	-	-	-	-	-	-	-	-
Industrial Waste	-	-	-	-	-	-	-	-
Municipal Waste	-	-	-	-	-	-	-	-
Non-specified	4166	4178	-	-	-	-	-	-

* Figures for electricity generated from photovoltaic systems are not available separately and are included here with electricity produced from solar thermal.

* *Les données sur l'électricité produite à l'aide de systèmes photovoltaïques ne sont pas disponibles séparément et sont montrées ici avec l'électricité produite par l'énergie thermique solaire.*

Denmark / Danemark

Electricity and Heat Production in the Transformation Sector
Production de chaleur et d'éléctricité du secteur transformation

	1986	1987	1988	1989	1990	1991	1992	1993
ELECTRICITY / ELECTRICITE (GWh)								
TOTAL ELECTRICITY	30739	29449	27965	22312	25758	36330	30849	33738
Thermal								
Hard Coal	28398	27905	26104	20003	23320	33723	27805	29552
Lignite and Sub-bit. Coal	-	-	-	-	-	-	-	-
Peat	-	-	-	-	-	-	-	-
Coke Oven and Blast Fur. Gas	-	-	-	-	-	-	-	-
Liquid Fuels/Refinery Gas	1607	1225	1263	1241	1062	1213	1120	1307
Natural Gas/Gas Works Gas	569	107	264	597	660	505	776	1257
Nuclear	-	-	-	-	-	-	-	-
Geothermal	-	-	-	-	-	-	-	-
Solar *	-	-	-	15	20	-	-	-
Combustible Renewables and Wastes	-	-	-	-	59	121	218	567
Solid Biomass and Animal Products	-	-	-	-	*59*	*121*	*218*	*167*
Gases/Liquids from Biomass	-	-	-	-	-	-	-	*43*
Industrial Waste	-	-	-	-	-	-	-	-
Municipal Waste	-	-	-	-	-	-	-	*357*
Non-Thermal								
Hydro	29	29	32	27	27	26	28	27
of which: pumped storage	-	-	-	-	-	-	-	-
Tide/Wave/Ocean	-	-	-	-	-	-	-	-
Wind	136	183	302	429	610	742	902	1028
Other Fuel Sources	-	-	-	-	-	-	-	-
HEAT / CHALEUR (TJ)								
TOTAL HEAT	47734	51980	52912	50422	96178	102650	103718	112162
Hard Coal	44556	45243	44479	46635	54815	59346	56743	62599
Lignite and Sub-bit. Coal	-	-	-	-	-	-	-	-
Peat	-	-	-	-	-	-	-	-
Coke Oven and Blast Fur. Gas	-	-	-	-	-	-	-	-
Liquid Fuels/Refinery Gas	2282	2567	2315	2092	3518	4216	5631	5566
Natural Gas/Gas Works Gas	896	4170	6118	1695	18791	19626	20193	21150
Nuclear	-	-	-	-	-	-	-	-
Geothermal	-	-	-	-	-	-	-	45
Solar	-	-	-	-	-	-	-	-
Electricity and Ambient Heat	-	-	-	-	-	-	-	-
Heat Pumps	-	-	-	-	-	-	-	-
Electric Boilers	-	-	-	-	-	-	-	-
Combustible Renewables and Wastes	-	-	-	-	19054	19462	21151	22802
Solid Biomass and Animal Products	-	-	-	-	*19054*	*19462*	*21151*	*9182*
Gases/Liquids from Biomass	-	-	-	-	-	-	-	*292*
Industrial Waste	-	-	-	-	-	-	-	-
Municipal Waste	-	-	-	-	-	-	-	*13328*
Non-specified	-	-	-	-	-	-	-	-

* Figures for electricity generated from photovoltaic systems are not available separately and are included here with electricity produced from solar thermal.
* Les données sur l'électricité produite à l'aide de systèmes photovoltaïques ne sont pas disponibles séparément et sont montrées ici avec l'électricité produite par l'énergie thermique solaire.

Finland / Finlande

Electricity and Heat Production in the Transformation Sector
Production de chaleur et d'éléctricité du secteur transformation

	1986	1987	1988	1989	1990	1991	1992	1993
ELECTRICITY / ELECTRICITE (GWh)								
TOTAL ELECTRICITY	49266	53402	53878	53817	54377	57985	57722	61172
Thermal								
Hard Coal	7864	9368	9716	8795	9662	9790	7661	9523
Lignite and Sub-bit. Coal	-	-	-	-	-	-	-	-
Peat	6557	6644	6630	7468	7930	9034	3691	4387
Coke Oven and Blast Fur. Gas	330	342	370	357	376	430	483	612
Liquid Fuels/Refinery Gas	1235	1467	1615	1147	1679	1069	1391	1605
Natural Gas/Gas Works Gas	1832	2140	2632	3931	4655	4954	5179	5564
Nuclear	19059	19646	19554	19090	19216	19511	19260	19891
Geothermal	-	-	-	-	-	-	-	-
Solar *	-	-	-	-	-	-	-	-
Combustible Renewables and Wastes	-	-	-	-	-	-	4950	5991
Solid Biomass and Animal Products	-	-	-	-	-	-	*4950*	*5991*
Gases/Liquids from Biomass	-	-	-	-	-	-	-	-
Industrial Waste	-	-	-	-	-	-	-	-
Municipal Waste	-	-	-	-	-	-	-	-
Non-Thermal								
Hydro	12389	13795	13361	13029	10859	13197	15107	13599
of which: pumped storage	-	-	-	-	-	-	-	-
Tide/Wave/Ocean	-	-	-	-	-	-	-	-
Wind	-	-	-	-	-	-	-	-
Other Fuel Sources	-	-	-	-	-	-	-	-
HEAT / CHALEUR (TJ)								
TOTAL HEAT	82811	92430	87242	82116	86832	91800	92042	96012
Hard Coal	35125	39554	40766	35125	36103	38770	35628	33473
Lignite and Sub-bit. Coal	-	-	-	-	-	-	-	-
Peat	17136	19409	19162	17734	21176	22397	18170	17274
Coke Oven and Blast Fur. Gas	-	-	-	-	-	-	-	-
Liquid Fuels/Refinery Gas	24927	21991	16251	12933	12388	12109	12045	15737
Natural Gas/Gas Works Gas	5623	11476	11063	16324	17165	18524	21793	24147
Nuclear	-	-	-	-	-	-	-	-
Geothermal	-	-	-	-	-	-	-	-
Solar	-	-	-	-	-	-	-	-
Electricity and Ambient Heat	-	-	-	-	-	-	-	-
Heat Pumps	-	-	-	-	-	-	-	-
Electric Boilers	-	-	-	-	-	-	-	-
Combustible Renewables and Wastes	-	-	-	-	-	-	4406	5381
Solid Biomass and Animal Products	-	-	-	-	-	-	*3751*	*4749*
Gases/Liquids from Biomass	-	-	-	-	-	-	-	-
Industrial Waste	-	-	-	-	-	-	-	-
Municipal Waste	-	-	-	-	-	-	*655*	*632*
Non-specified	-	-	-	-	-	-	-	-

* Figures for electricity generated from photovoltaic systems are not available separately and are included here with electricity produced from solar thermal.
* Les données sur l'électricité produite à l'aide de systèmes photovoltaïques ne sont pas disponibles séparément et sont montrées ici avec l'électricité produite par l'énergie thermique solaire.

France / France

Electricity and Heat Production in the Transformation Sector
Production de chaleur et d'éléctricité du secteur transformation

	1986	1987	1988	1989	1990	1991	1992	1993
ELECTRICITY / ELECTRICITE (GWh)								
TOTAL ELECTRICITY	362784	378309	391926	406891	420155	454735	462841	472004
Thermal								
Hard Coal	26790	23935	22440	29074	29053	36760	32273	18586
Lignite and Sub-bit. Coal	3790	2996	2073	2727	2420	2850	1961	2365
Peat	-	-	-	-	-	-	-	-
Coke Oven and Blast Fur. Gas	3595	3794	4173	4317	3950	3594	3498	3798
Liquid Fuels/Refinery Gas	5437	5979	5838	11938	8876	14290	9525	6091
Natural Gas/Gas Works Gas	2850	2226	2206	2764	2819	2848	2979	3496
Nuclear	254155	265520	275521	303931	314081	331340	338445	368188
Geothermal	-	-	-	-	-	-	-	-
Solar *	-	-	-	-	-	-	-	-
Combustible Renewables and Wastes	887	924	893	980	1035	991	1060	1030
Solid Biomass and Animal Products	-	-	-	-	-	-	-	-
Gases/Liquids from Biomass	-	-	-	-	-	-	-	-
Industrial Waste	-	-	-	-	-	-	-	-
Municipal Waste	*887*	*924*	*893*	*980*	*1035*	*991*	*1060*	*1030*
Non-Thermal								
Hydro	64694	72365	78216	50602	57350	61478	72522	67894
of which: pumped storage	*2939*	*2899*	*3367*	*3965*	*4002*	*4610*	*4663*	*4182*
Tide/Wave/Ocean	586	570	566	558	571	584	578	556
Wind	-	-	-	-	-	-	-	-
Other Fuel Sources	-	-	-	-	-	-	-	-
HEAT / CHALEUR (TJ)								
TOTAL HEAT	-	-	-	-	-	-	-	-
Hard Coal	-	-	-	-	-	-	-	-
Lignite and Sub-bit. Coal	-	-	-	-	-	-	-	-
Peat	-	-	-	-	-	-	-	-
Coke Oven and Blast Fur. Gas	-	-	-	-	-	-	-	-
Liquid Fuels/Refinery Gas	-	-	-	-	-	-	-	-
Natural Gas/Gas Works Gas	-	-	-	-	-	-	-	-
Nuclear	-	-	-	-	-	-	-	-
Geothermal	-	-	-	-	-	-	-	-
Solar	-	-	-	-	-	-	-	-
Electricity and Ambient Heat	-	-	-	-	-	-	-	-
Heat Pumps	-	-	-	-	-	-	-	-
Electric Boilers	-	-	-	-	-	-	-	-
Combustible Renewables and Wastes	-	-	-	-	-	-	-	-
Solid Biomass and Animal Products	-	-	-	-	-	-	-	-
Gases/Liquids from Biomass	-	-	-	-	-	-	-	-
Industrial Waste	-	-	-	-	-	-	-	-
Municipal Waste	-	-	-	-	-	-	-	-
Non-specified	-	-	-	-	-	-	-	-

* Figures for electricity generated from photovoltaic systems are not available separately and are included here with electricity produced from solar thermal.
* *Les données sur l'électricité produite à l'aide de systèmes photovoltaïques ne sont pas disponibles séparément et sont montrées ici avec l'électricité produite par l'énergie thermique solaire.*

Germany / Allemagne

Electricity and Heat Production in the Transformation Sector
Production de chaleur et d'éléctricité du secteur transformation

	1986	1987	1988	1989	1990	1991	1992	1993

ELECTRICITY / ELECTRICITE (GWh)

	1986	1987	1988	1989	1990	1991	1992	1993
TOTAL ELECTRICITY	523557	532442	549489	559867	549877	539391	537134	525721
Thermal								
Hard Coal	138432	138331	133410	133164	141837	149823	141894	146178
Lignite and Sub-bit. Coal	176960	170261	177119	180125	169387	158363	154525	147481
Peat	-	-	-	-	-	-	-	-
Coke Oven and Blast Fur. Gas	9579	9160	10367	10528	10764	9247	9185	6552
Liquid Fuels/Refinery Gas	13643	13811	11794	10437	10397	14740	13217	10091
Natural Gas/Gas Works Gas	29811	32956	33141	38575	40489	36249	32923	34517
Nuclear	130489	141725	156820	161671	152468	147429	158804	153476
Geothermal	-	-	-	-	-	-	-	-
Solar *	-	-	-	-	-	-	-	-
Combustible Renewables and Wastes	4332	3885	4385	4652	4810	5068	5432	5837
Solid Biomass and Animal Products	-	-	-	-	-	-	-	-
Gases/Liquids from Biomass	-	-	-	-	-	-	-	*403*
Industrial Waste	*1813*	*1693*	*2161*	*2323*	*2373*	*2635*	*2908*	*3028*
Municipal Waste	*2519*	*2192*	*2224*	*2329*	*2437*	*2433*	*2524*	*2406*
Non-Thermal								
Hydro	20311	22313	22451	20713	19722	18460	21115	21465
of which: pumped storage	*1744*	*1975*	*2380*	*2470*	*2365*	*3808*	*3798*	*3789*
Tide/Wave/Ocean	-	-	-	-	-	-	-	-
Wind	-	-	2	2	3	12	39	124
Other Fuel Sources	-	-	-	-	-	-	-	-

HEAT / CHALEUR (TJ)

	1986	1987	1988	1989	1990	1991	1992	1993
TOTAL HEAT	344871	360067	339071	359168	341541	353495	350000	350000
Hard Coal	-	-	-	-	-	-	133315	133315
Lignite and Sub-bit. Coal	-	-	-	-	-	-	13965	13965
Peat	-	-	-	-	-	-	-	-
Coke Oven and Blast Fur. Gas	-	-	-	-	-	-	3150	3150
Liquid Fuels/Refinery Gas	-	-	-	-	-	-	41335	41335
Natural Gas/Gas Works Gas	-	-	-	-	-	-	123760	123760
Nuclear	-	-	-	-	-	-	-	-
Geothermal	-	-	-	-	-	-	-	-
Solar	-	-	-	-	-	-	-	-
Electricity and Ambient Heat	-	-	-	-	-	-	-	-
Heat Pumps	-	-	-	-	-	-	-	-
Electric Boilers	-	-	-	-	-	-	-	-
Combustible Renewables and Wastes	-	-	-	-	-	-	34475	34475
Solid Biomass and Animal Products	-	-	-	-	-	-	*34475*	*34475*
Gases/Liquids from Biomass	-	-	-	-	-	-	-	-
Industrial Waste	-	-	-	-	-	-	-	-
Municipal Waste	-	-	-	-	-	-	-	-
Non-specified	344871	360067	339071	359168	341541	353495	-	-

* Figures for electricity generated from photovoltaic systems are not available separately and are included here with electricity produced from solar thermal.
* *Les données sur l'électricité produite à l'aide de systèmes photovoltaïques ne sont pas disponibles séparément et sont montrées ici avec l'électricité produite par l'énergie thermique solaire.*

Greece / Grèce

Electricity and Heat Production in the Transformation Sector
Production de chaleur et d'élctricité du secteur transformation

	1986	1987	1988	1989	1990	1991	1992	1993
ELECTRICITY / ELECTRICITE (GWh)								
TOTAL ELECTRICITY	28237	30272	33394	34456	35002	35813	37410	38396
Thermal								
Hard Coal	897	361	72	-	-	133	1338	214
Lignite and Sub-bit. Coal	17913	20345	24314	25179	25166	23569	25274	27581
Peat	-	-	-	-	-	-	-	-
Coke Oven and Blast Fur. Gas	-	-	-	-	-	-	-	-
Liquid Fuels/Refinery Gas	6015	6536	6315	7018	7746	8847	8186	7837
Natural Gas/Gas Works Gas	64	63	94	112	92	93	79	84
Nuclear	-	-	-	-	-	-	-	-
Geothermal	-	2	5	-	-	-	-	-
Solar *	-	-	-	-	-	-	-	-
Combustible Renewables and Wastes	-	-	-	-	-	-	136	91
Solid Biomass and Animal Products	-	-	-	-	-	-	-	-
Gases/Liquids from Biomass	-	-	-	-	-	-	-	-
Industrial Waste	-	-	-	-	-	-	*136*	*91*
Municipal Waste	-	-	-	-	-	-	-	-
Non-Thermal								
Hydro	3348	2964	2593	2147	1997	3171	2389	2541
of which: pumped storage	*113*	*184*	*227*	*247*	*228*	*72*	*186*	*259*
Tide/Wave/Ocean	-	-	-	-	-	-	-	-
Wind	-	1	1	-	1	-	8	48
Other Fuel Sources	-	-	-	-	-	-	-	-
HEAT / CHALEUR (TJ)								
TOTAL HEAT	-	-	-	-	-	-	-	-
Hard Coal	-	-	-	-	-	-	-	-
Lignite and Sub-bit. Coal	-	-	-	-	-	-	-	-
Peat	-	-	-	-	-	-	-	-
Coke Oven and Blast Fur. Gas	-	-	-	-	-	-	-	-
Liquid Fuels/Refinery Gas	-	-	-	-	-	-	-	-
Natural Gas/Gas Works Gas	-	-	-	-	-	-	-	-
Nuclear	-	-	-	-	-	-	-	-
Geothermal	-	-	-	-	-	-	-	-
Solar	-	-	-	-	-	-	-	-
Electricity and Ambient Heat	-	-	-	-	-	-	-	-
Heat Pumps	-	-	-	-	-	-	-	-
Electric Boilers	-	-	-	-	-	-	-	-
Combustible Renewables and Wastes	-	-	-	-	-	-	-	-
Solid Biomass and Animal Products	-	-	-	-	-	-	-	-
Gases/Liquids from Biomass	-	-	-	-	-	-	-	-
Industrial Waste	-	-	-	-	-	-	-	-
Municipal Waste	-	-	-	-	-	-	-	-
Non-specified	-	-	-	-	-	-	-	-

* Figures for electricity generated from photovoltaic systems are not available separately and are included here with electricity produced from solar thermal.
* *Les données sur l'électricité produite à l'aide de systèmes photovoltaïques ne sont pas disponibles séparément et sont montrées ici avec l'électricité produite par l'énergie thermique solaire.*

Iceland / Islande

Electricity and Heat Production in the Transformation Sector
Production de chaleur et d'élctricité du secteur transformation

	1986	1987	1988	1989	1990	1991	1992	1993
ELECTRICITY / ELECTRICITE (GWh)								
TOTAL ELECTRICITY	4114	4210	4478	4537	4510	4494	4546	4727
Thermal								
Hard Coal	-	-	-	-	-	-	-	-
Lignite and Sub-bit. Coal	-	-	-	-	-	-	-	-
Peat	-	-	-	-	-	-	-	-
Coke Oven and Blast Fur. Gas	-	-	-	-	-	-	-	-
Liquid Fuels/Refinery Gas	5	5	7	6	6	7	6	5
Natural Gas/Gas Works Gas	-	-	-	-	-	-	-	-
Nuclear	-	-	-	-	-	-	-	-
Geothermal	225	248	260	272	300	283	230	256
Solar *	-	-	-	-	-	-	-	-
Combustible Renewables and Wastes	-	-	-	-	-	-	-	-
Solid Biomass and Animal Products	-	-	-	-	-	-	-	-
Gases/Liquids from Biomass	-	-	-	-	-	-	-	-
Industrial Waste	-	-	-	-	-	-	-	-
Municipal Waste	-	-	-	-	-	-	-	-
Non-Thermal								
Hydro	3884	3957	4211	4259	4204	4204	4310	4466
of which: pumped storage	-	-	-	-	-	-	-	-
Tide/Wave/Ocean	-	-	-	-	-	-	-	-
Wind	-	-	-	-	-	-	-	-
Other Fuel Sources	-	-	-	-	-	-	-	-
HEAT / CHALEUR (TJ)								
TOTAL HEAT	3078	3326	3503	3660	5282	6808	8199	7746
Hard Coal	-	-	-	-	-	-	-	-
Lignite and Sub-bit. Coal	-	-	-	-	-	-	-	-
Peat	-	-	-	-	-	-	-	-
Coke Oven and Blast Fur. Gas	-	-	-	-	-	-	-	-
Liquid Fuels/Refinery Gas	40	40	-	-	-	-	-	16
Natural Gas/Gas Works Gas	-	-	-	-	-	-	-	-
Nuclear	-	-	-	-	-	-	-	-
Geothermal	2789	3037	3139	3232	4819	6309	7594	7097
Solar	-	-	-	-	-	-	-	-
Electricity and Ambient Heat	249	249	364	428	463	499	605	597
Heat Pumps	-	-	-	-	-	-	-	-
Electric Boilers	*249*	*249*	*364*	*428*	*463*	*499*	*605*	*597*
Combustible Renewables and Wastes	-	-	-	-	-	-	-	36
Solid Biomass and Animal Products	-	-	-	-	-	-	-	-
Gases/Liquids from Biomass	-	-	-	-	-	-	-	-
Industrial Waste	-	-	-	-	-	-	-	-
Municipal Waste	-	-	-	-	-	-	-	*36*
Non-specified	-	-	-	-	-	-	-	-

* Figures for electricity generated from photovoltaic systems are not available separately and are included here with electricity produced from solar thermal.
* *Les données sur l'électricité produite à l'aide de systèmes photovoltaïques ne sont pas disponibles séparément et sont montrées ici avec l'électricité produite par l'énergie thermique solaire.*

Ireland / Irlande

Electricity and Heat Production in the Transformation Sector
Production de chaleur et d'éléctricité du secteur transformation

	1986	1987	1988	1989	1990	1991	1992	1993
ELECTRICITY / ELECTRICITE (GWh)								
TOTAL ELECTRICITY	12652	13064	13228	13833	14515	15147	16011	16396
Thermal								
Hard Coal	1828	5057	5291	5944	5918	5852	6658	6614
Lignite and Sub-bit. Coal	-	-	-	-	-	-	-	-
Peat	1415	1890	2234	2009	2245	2147	2180	1875
Coke Oven and Blast Fur. Gas	-	-	-	-	-	-	-	-
Liquid Fuels/Refinery Gas	5378	2692	970	716	1428	2431	2470	2341
Natural Gas/Gas Works Gas	2767	2309	3528	4173	3941	3753	3648	4539
Nuclear	-	-	-	-	-	-	-	-
Geothermal	-	-	-	-	-	-	-	-
Solar *	-	-	-	-	-	-	-	-
Combustible Renewables and Wastes	-	-	-	-	-	-	-	-
Solid Biomass and Animal Products	-	-	-	-	-	-	-	-
Gases/Liquids from Biomass	-	-	-	-	-	-	-	-
Industrial Waste	-	-	-	-	-	-	-	-
Municipal Waste	-	-	-	-	-	-	-	-
Non-Thermal								
Hydro	1264	1116	1205	991	983	964	1050	1012
of which: pumped storage	*345*	*435*	*333*	*299*	*286*	*218*	*233*	*247*
Tide/Wave/Ocean	-	-	-	-	-	-	-	-
Wind	-	-	-	-	-	-	5	15
Other Fuel Sources	-	-	-	-	-	-	-	-
HEAT / CHALEUR (TJ)								
TOTAL HEAT	-	-	-	-	-	-	-	-
Hard Coal	-	-	-	-	-	-	-	-
Lignite and Sub-bit. Coal	-	-	-	-	-	-	-	-
Peat	-	-	-	-	-	-	-	-
Coke Oven and Blast Fur. Gas	-	-	-	-	-	-	-	-
Liquid Fuels/Refinery Gas	-	-	-	-	-	-	-	-
Natural Gas/Gas Works Gas	-	-	-	-	-	-	-	-
Nuclear	-	-	-	-	-	-	-	-
Geothermal	-	-	-	-	-	-	-	-
Solar	-	-	-	-	-	-	-	-
Electricity and Ambient Heat	-	-	-	-	-	-	-	-
Heat Pumps	-	-	-	-	-	-	-	-
Electric Boilers	-	-	-	-	-	-	-	-
Combustible Renewables and Wastes	-	-	-	-	-	-	-	-
Solid Biomass and Animal Products	-	-	-	-	-	-	-	-
Gases/Liquids from Biomass	-	-	-	-	-	-	-	-
Industrial Waste	-	-	-	-	-	-	-	-
Municipal Waste	-	-	-	-	-	-	-	-
Non-specified	-	-	-	-	-	-	-	-

* Figures for electricity generated from photovoltaic systems are not available separately and are included here with electricity produced from solar thermal.
* *Les données sur l'électricité produite à l'aide de systèmes photovoltaïques ne sont pas disponibles séparément et sont montrées ici avec l'électricité produite par l'énergie thermique solaire.*

Italy / Italie

Electricity and Heat Production in the Transformation Sector
Production de chaleur et d'éléctricité du secteur transformation

	1986	1987	1988	1989	1990	1991	1992	1993
ELECTRICITY / ELECTRICITE (GWh)								
TOTAL ELECTRICITY	192330	201372	203561	210750	216891	222041	226243	222788
Thermal								
Hard Coal	26833	29286	29669	27224	30876	27504	20466	15942
Lignite and Sub-bit. Coal	1052	1074	1088	1164	1166	978	848	713
Peat	-	-	-	-	-	-	-	-
Coke Oven and Blast Fur. Gas	3119	2675	3140	3479	3552	3529	3500	3419
Liquid Fuels/Refinery Gas	77483	89941	89702	102784	102718	104287	116020	113919
Natural Gas/Gas Works Gas	26871	31732	32420	34407	39082	35870	35168	39596
Nuclear	8758	174	-	-	-	-	-	-
Geothermal	2760	2986	3082	3155	3222	3182	3459	3667
Solar *	-	-	-	-	-	-	-	-
Combustible Renewables and Wastes	923	919	913	1053	1196	1085	682	696
Solid Biomass and Animal Products	-	-	-	-	-	-	13	25
Gases/Liquids from Biomass	-	-	-	-	-	-	13	12
Industrial Waste	923	919	913	1053	1196	1085	500	489
Municipal Waste	-	-	-	-	-	-	156	170
Non-Thermal								
Hydro	44531	42585	43547	37484	35079	45606	45786	44482
of which: pumped storage	3435	3080	2871	3427	3453	3367	3586	3057
Tide/Wave/Ocean	-	-	-	-	-	-	-	-
Wind	-	-	-	-	-	-	1	1
Other Fuel Sources	-	-	-	-	-	-	313	353
HEAT / CHALEUR (TJ)								
TOTAL HEAT	-	-	-	-	-	-	-	-
Hard Coal	-	-	-	-	-	-	-	-
Lignite and Sub-bit. Coal	-	-	-	-	-	-	-	-
Peat	-	-	-	-	-	-	-	-
Coke Oven and Blast Fur. Gas	-	-	-	-	-	-	-	-
Liquid Fuels/Refinery Gas	-	-	-	-	-	-	-	-
Natural Gas/Gas Works Gas	-	-	-	-	-	-	-	-
Nuclear	-	-	-	-	-	-	-	-
Geothermal	-	-	-	-	-	-	-	-
Solar	-	-	-	-	-	-	-	-
Electricity and Ambient Heat	-	-	-	-	-	-	-	-
Heat Pumps	-	-	-	-	-	-	-	-
Electric Boilers	-	-	-	-	-	-	-	-
Combustible Renewables and Wastes	-	-	-	-	-	-	-	-
Solid Biomass and Animal Products	-	-	-	-	-	-	-	-
Gases/Liquids from Biomass	-	-	-	-	-	-	-	-
Industrial Waste	-	-	-	-	-	-	-	-
Municipal Waste	-	-	-	-	-	-	-	-
Non-specified	-	-	-	-	-	-	-	-

* Figures for electricity generated from photovoltaic systems are not available separately and are included here with electricity produced from solar thermal.
Les données sur l'électricité produite à l'aide de systèmes photovoltaïques ne sont pas disponibles séparément et sont montrées ici avec l'électricité produite par l'énergie thermique solaire.

INTERNATIONAL ENERGY AGENCY

Japan / Japon

Electricity and Heat Production in the Transformation Sector
Production de chaleur et d'éléctricité du secteur transformation

	1986	1987	1988	1989	1990	1991	1992	1993
ELECTRICITY / ELECTRICITE (GWh)								
TOTAL ELECTRICITY	676360	719067	753728	798757	857272	888088	895266	906705
Thermal								
Hard Coal	64197	70768	71877	75266	82798	87473	104241	113854
Lignite and Sub-bit. Coal	-	-	-	-	-	-	-	-
Peat	-	-	-	-	-	-	-	-
Coke Oven and Blast Fur. Gas	38010	38123	39888	40660	40454	40294	49340	54016
Liquid Fuels/Refinery Gas	187968	200148	219956	252622	268585	266844	225531	179868
Natural Gas/Gas Works Gas	130421	140015	146105	148135	165586	172647	191873	192933
Nuclear	168305	187758	178659	182869	202272	213460	223259	249256
Geothermal	1384	1408	1358	1379	1741	1773	1787	1777
Solar *	1	1	1	1	1	1	1	-
Combustible Renewables and Wastes	-	-	-	-	-	-	9600	9510
Solid Biomass and Animal Products	-	-	-	-	-	-	*9160*	*9080*
Gases/Liquids from Biomass	-	-	-	-	-	-	-	-
Industrial Waste	-	-	-	-	-	-	-	-
Municipal Waste	-	-	-	-	-	-	*440*	*430*
Non-Thermal								
Hydro	86074	80846	95884	97825	95835	105594	89616	105470
of which: pumped storage	*5259*	*6074*	*5593*	*6084*	*6530*	*8102*	*7071*	*7658*
Tide/Wave/Ocean	-	-	-	-	-	-	-	-
Wind	-	-	-	-	-	-	-	1
Other Fuel Sources	-	-	-	-	-	2	18	20
HEAT / CHALEUR (TJ)								
TOTAL HEAT	5892	6379	6460	7192	8458	9835	13680	14498
Hard Coal	713	714	678	712	570	531	957	1305
Lignite and Sub-bit. Coal	-	-	-	-	-	-	-	-
Peat	-	-	-	-	-	-	-	-
Coke Oven and Blast Fur. Gas	-	-	-	-	-	-	-	-
Liquid Fuels/Refinery Gas	1143	1161	1169	1158	1176	1277	1645	1595
Natural Gas/Gas Works Gas	2958	3298	3340	3920	4788	5592	7933	8554
Nuclear	-	-	-	-	-	-	-	-
Geothermal	-	-	-	-	-	-	-	-
Solar	-	-	-	-	-	-	-	-
Electricity and Ambient Heat	1078	1206	1273	1402	1924	2435	3145	3044
Heat Pumps	-	-	-	-	-	-	-	-
Electric Boilers	*1078*	*1206*	*1273*	*1402*	*1924*	*2435*	*3145*	*3044*
Combustible Renewables and Wastes	-	-	-	-	-	-	-	-
Solid Biomass and Animal Products	-	-	-	-	-	-	-	-
Gases/Liquids from Biomass	-	-	-	-	-	-	-	-
Industrial Waste	-	-	-	-	-	-	-	-
Municipal Waste	-	-	-	-	-	-	-	-
Non-specified	-	-	-	-	-	-	-	-

* Figures for electricity generated from photovoltaic systems are not available separately and are included here with electricity produced from solar thermal.
* *Les données sur l'électricité produite à l'aide de systèmes photovoltaïques ne sont pas disponibles séparément et sont montrées ici avec l'électricité produite par l'énergie thermique solaire.*

Luxembourg / Luxembourg

Electricity and Heat Production in the Transformation Sector
Production de chaleur et d'éléctricité du secteur transformation

	1986	1987	1988	1989	1990	1991	1992	1993
ELECTRICITY / ELECTRICITE (GWh)								
TOTAL ELECTRICITY	1022	1019	1331	1372	1377	1415	1198	1067
Thermal								
Hard Coal	6	1	6	4	-	-	-	-
Lignite and Sub-bit. Coal	-	-	-	-	-	-	-	-
Peat	-	-	-	-	-	-	-	-
Coke Oven and Blast Fur. Gas	379	347	378	440	477	525	472	503
Liquid Fuels/Refinery Gas	68	14	57	19	9	26	56	38
Natural Gas/Gas Works Gas	1	61	19	46	34	28	30	23
Nuclear	-	-	-	-	-	-	-	-
Geothermal	-	-	-	-	-	-	-	-
Solar *	-	-	-	-	-	-	-	-
Combustible Renewables and Wastes	34	44	46	38	34	38	32	40
Solid Biomass and Animal Products	-	-	-	-	-	-	-	-
Gases/Liquids from Biomass	-	-	-	-	-	-	-	-
Industrial Waste	-	-	-	-	-	-	-	-
Municipal Waste	*34*	*44*	*46*	*38*	*34*	*38*	*32*	*40*
Non-Thermal								
Hydro	534	552	825	825	823	798	608	463
of which: pumped storage	*434*	*441*	*715*	*740*	*753*	*714*	*538*	*396*
Tide/Wave/Ocean	-	-	-	-	-	-	-	-
Wind	-	-	-	-	-	-	-	-
Other Fuel Sources	-	-	-	-	-	-	-	-
HEAT / CHALEUR (TJ)								
TOTAL HEAT	-	-	-	-	-	-	-	-
Hard Coal	-	-	-	-	-	-	-	-
Lignite and Sub-bit. Coal	-	-	-	-	-	-	-	-
Peat	-	-	-	-	-	-	-	-
Coke Oven and Blast Fur. Gas	-	-	-	-	-	-	-	-
Liquid Fuels/Refinery Gas	-	-	-	-	-	-	-	-
Natural Gas/Gas Works Gas	-	-	-	-	-	-	-	-
Nuclear	-	-	-	-	-	-	-	-
Geothermal	-	-	-	-	-	-	-	-
Solar	-	-	-	-	-	-	-	-
Electricity and Ambient Heat	-	-	-	-	-	-	-	-
Heat Pumps	-	-	-	-	-	-	-	-
Electric Boilers	-	-	-	-	-	-	-	-
Combustible Renewables and Wastes	-	-	-	-	-	-	-	-
Solid Biomass and Animal Products	-	-	-	-	-	-	-	-
Gases/Liquids from Biomass	-	-	-	-	-	-	-	-
Industrial Waste	-	-	-	-	-	-	-	-
Municipal Waste	-	-	-	-	-	-	-	-
Non-specified	-	-	-	-	-	-	-	-

* Figures for electricity generated from photovoltaic systems are not available separately and are included here with electricity produced from solar thermal.
* *Les données sur l'électricité produite à l'aide de systèmes photovoltaïques ne sont pas disponibles séparément et sont montrées ici avec l'électricité produite par l'énergie thermique solaire.*

Mexico / Mexique

Electricity and Heat Production in the Transformation Sector
Production de chaleur et d'éléctricité du secteur transformation

	1986	1987	1988	1989	1990	1991	1992	1993
ELECTRICITY / ELECTRICITE (GWh)								
TOTAL ELECTRICITY	89383	96310	101905	110063	114249	118357	121653	126566
Thermal								
Hard Coal	6337	7289	8035	7890	7774	8077	8318	10500
Lignite and Sub-bit. Coal	-	-	-	-	-	-	-	-
Peat	-	-	-	-	-	-	-	-
Coke Oven and Blast Fur. Gas	-	-	-	-	-	-	-	-
Liquid Fuels/Refinery Gas	51399	56595	59495	62243	62062	63569	62732	64058
Natural Gas/Gas Works Gas	8377	9808	9090	10684	13014	15297	14785	14965
Nuclear	-	-	-	372	2937	4242	3919	4931
Geothermal	3394	4418	4633	4675	5124	5435	5804	5877
Solar *	-	-	-	-	-	-	-	-
Combustible Renewables and Wastes	-	-	-	-	-	-	-	-
Solid Biomass and Animal Products	-	-	-	-	-	-	-	-
Gases/Liquids from Biomass	-	-	-	-	-	-	-	-
Industrial Waste	-	-	-	-	-	-	-	-
Municipal Waste	-	-	-	-	-	-	-	-
Non-Thermal								
Hydro	19876	18200	20652	24199	23338	21737	26095	26235
of which: pumped storage	-	-	-	-	-	-	-	-
Tide/Wave/Ocean	-	-	-	-	-	-	-	-
Wind	-	-	-	-	-	-	-	-
Other Fuel Sources	-	-	-	-	-	-	-	-
HEAT / CHALEUR (TJ)								
TOTAL HEAT	-	-	-	-	-	-	-	-
Hard Coal	-	-	-	-	-	-	-	-
Lignite and Sub-bit. Coal	-	-	-	-	-	-	-	-
Peat	-	-	-	-	-	-	-	-
Coke Oven and Blast Fur. Gas	-	-	-	-	-	-	-	-
Liquid Fuels/Refinery Gas	-	-	-	-	-	-	-	-
Natural Gas/Gas Works Gas	-	-	-	-	-	-	-	-
Nuclear	-	-	-	-	-	-	-	-
Geothermal	-	-	-	-	-	-	-	-
Solar	-	-	-	-	-	-	-	-
Electricity and Ambient Heat	-	-	-	-	-	-	-	-
Heat Pumps	-	-	-	-	-	-	-	-
Electric Boilers	-	-	-	-	-	-	-	-
Combustible Renewables and Wastes	-	-	-	-	-	-	-	-
Solid Biomass and Animal Products	-	-	-	-	-	-	-	-
Gases/Liquids from Biomass	-	-	-	-	-	-	-	-
Industrial Waste	-	-	-	-	-	-	-	-
Municipal Waste	-	-	-	-	-	-	-	-
Non-specified	-	-	-	-	-	-	-	-

* Figures for electricity generated from photovoltaic systems are not available separately and are included here with electricity produced from solar thermal.
* *Les données sur l'électricité produite à l'aide de systèmes photovoltaïques ne sont pas disponibles séparément et sont montrées ici avec l'électricité produite par l'énergie thermique solaire.*

Netherlands / Pays-Bas

Electricity and Heat Production in the Transformation Sector
Production de chaleur et d'élécricité du secteur transformation

	1986	1987	1988	1989	1990	1991	1992	1993
ELECTRICITY / ELECTRICITE (GWh)								
TOTAL ELECTRICITY	67158	68419	69611	73050	71866	74252	77202	76992
Thermal								
Hard Coal	15138	16948	22255	22156	25014	22664	22629	21406
Lignite and Sub-bit. Coal	-	-	-	-	-	-	-	-
Peat	-	-	-	-	-	-	-	-
Coke Oven and Blast Fur. Gas	2289	2259	2604	2678	2506	2578	2587	2842
Liquid Fuels/Refinery Gas	3456	3659	3796	3307	3112	3381	3252	3066
Natural Gas/Gas Works Gas	41502	41292	36428	39930	36646	41134	43410	44002
Nuclear	4216	3556	3675	4019	3502	3329	3800	3948
Geothermal	-	-	-	-	-	-	-	-
Solar *	-	-	-	-	-	-	-	-
Combustible Renewables and Wastes	553	702	835	900	916	1014	1257	1458
Solid Biomass and Animal Products	-	-	-	-	-	-	-	-
Gases/Liquids from Biomass	-	-	-	-	-	-	-	*171*
Industrial Waste	-	-	-	-	-	-	-	-
Municipal Waste	*553*	*702*	*835*	*900*	*916*	*1014*	*1257*	*1287*
Non-Thermal								
Hydro	3	1	2	37	120	80	120	92
of which: pumped storage	-	-	-	-	-	-	-	-
Tide/Wave/Ocean	-	-	-	-	-	-	-	-
Wind	1	2	16	23	50	72	147	178
Other Fuel Sources	-	-	-	-	-	-	-	-
HEAT / CHALEUR (TJ)								
TOTAL HEAT	15684	12633	11574	11852	11914	14550	18804	20945
Hard Coal	4015	3592	4744	4429	5606	5864	7309	7690
Lignite and Sub-bit. Coal	-	-	-	-	-	-	-	-
Peat	-	-	-	-	-	-	-	-
Coke Oven and Blast Fur. Gas	511	389	-	-	-	-	-	-
Liquid Fuels/Refinery Gas	832	767	197	75	48	123	70	70
Natural Gas/Gas Works Gas	10326	7885	6633	7348	6260	8563	11415	13165
Nuclear	-	-	-	-	-	-	-	-
Geothermal	-	-	-	-	-	-	-	-
Solar	-	-	-	-	-	-	-	-
Electricity and Ambient Heat	-	-	-	-	-	-	-	-
Heat Pumps	-	-	-	-	-	-	-	-
Electric Boilers	-	-	-	-	-	-	-	-
Combustible Renewables and Wastes	-	-	-	-	-	-	10	20
Solid Biomass and Animal Products	-	-	-	-	-	-	-	-
Gases/Liquids from Biomass	-	-	-	-	-	-	*10*	*20*
Industrial Waste	-	-	-	-	-	-	-	-
Municipal Waste	-	-	-	-	-	-	-	-
Non-specified	-	-	-	-	-	-	-	-

* Figures for electricity generated from photovoltaic systems are not available separately and are included here with electricity produced from solar thermal.
* Les données sur l'électricité produite à l'aide de systèmes photovoltaïques ne sont pas disponibles séparément et sont montrées ici avec l'électricité produite par l'énergie thermique solaire.

New Zealand / Nouvelle-Zélande

Electricity and Heat Production in the Transformation Sector
Production de chaleur et d'éléctricité du secteur transformation

	1986	1987	1988	1989	1990	1991	1992	1993
ELECTRICITY / ELECTRICITE (GWh)								
TOTAL ELECTRICITY	28169	28686	29471	30955	31632	32725	31294	33624
Thermal								
Hard Coal	467	583	502	453	375	743	420	564
Lignite and Sub-bit. Coal	-	-	-	-	-	-	-	-
Peat	-	-	-	-	-	-	-	-
Coke Oven and Blast Fur. Gas	-	-	-	-	-	-	-	-
Liquid Fuels/Refinery Gas	11	-	14	22	21	43	112	71
Natural Gas/Gas Works Gas	4729	4842	4556	6403	5686	6609	7859	7462
Nuclear	-	-	-	-	-	-	-	-
Geothermal	1174	1183	1237	1914	2210	2206	2272	2159
Solar *	-	-	-	-			-	-
Combustible Renewables and Wastes	-	-	-	-	-	-	-	-
Solid Biomass and Animal Products	-	-	-	-	-	-	-	-
Gases/Liquids from Biomass	-	-	-	-	-	-	-	-
Industrial Waste	-	-	-	-	-	-	-	-
Municipal Waste	-	-	-	-	-	-	-	-
Non-Thermal								
Hydro	21788	22078	23162	22163	23340	23124	20631	23368
of which: pumped storage	-	-	-	-	-	-	-	-
Tide/Wave/Ocean	-	-	-	-	-	-	-	-
Wind	-	-	-	-	-	-	-	-
Other Fuel Sources	-	-	-	-	-	-	-	-
HEAT / CHALEUR (TJ)								
TOTAL HEAT	-	-	-	-	-	-	-	-
Hard Coal	-	-	-	-	-	-	-	-
Lignite and Sub-bit. Coal	-	-	-	-	-	-	-	-
Peat	-	-	-	-	-	-	-	-
Coke Oven and Blast Fur. Gas	-	-	-	-	-	-	-	-
Liquid Fuels/Refinery Gas	-	-	-	-	-	-	-	-
Natural Gas/Gas Works Gas	-	-	-	-	-	-	-	-
Nuclear	-	-	-	-	-	-	-	-
Geothermal	-	-	-	-	-	-	-	-
Solar	-	-	-	-	-	-	-	-
Electricity and Ambient Heat	-	-	-	-	-	-	-	-
Heat Pumps	-	-	-	-	-	-	-	-
Electric Boilers	-	-	-	-	-	-	-	-
Combustible Renewables and Wastes	-	-	-	-	-	-	-	-
Solid Biomass and Animal Products	-	-	-	-	-	-	-	-
Gases/Liquids from Biomass	-	-	-	-	-	-	-	-
Industrial Waste	-	-	-	-	-	-	-	-
Municipal Waste	-	-	-	-	-	-	-	-
Non-specified	-	-	-	-	-	-	-	-

* Figures for electricity generated from photovoltaic systems are not available separately and are included here with electricity produced from solar thermal.
* *Les données sur l'électricité produite à l'aide de systèmes photovoltaïques ne sont pas disponibles séparément et sont montrées ici avec l'électricité produite par l'énergie thermique solaire.*

Norway / Norvège

Electricity and Heat Production in the Transformation Sector
Production de chaleur et d'éléctricité du secteur transformation

	1986	1987	1988	1989	1990	1991	1992	1993
ELECTRICITY / ELECTRICITE (GWh)								
TOTAL ELECTRICITY	97284	104283	110019	119197	121848	111009	117506	120004
Thermal								
Hard Coal	42	42	48	49	43	48	55	54
Lignite and Sub-bit. Coal	-	-	-	-	-	-	-	-
Peat	-	-	-	-	-	-	-	-
Coke Oven and Blast Fur. Gas	-	-	-	-	175	137	138	149
Liquid Fuels/Refinery Gas	371	446	373	393	6	7	-	-
Natural Gas/Gas Works Gas	-	-	-	-	-	-	-	-
Nuclear	-	-	-	-	-	-	-	-
Geothermal	-	-	-	-	-	-	-	-
Solar *	-	-	-	-	-	-	-	-
Combustible Renewables and Wastes	52	42	54	57	242	237	248	287
Solid Biomass and Animal Products	-	-	-	-	*184*	*181*	*206*	*223*
Gases/Liquids from Biomass	-	-	-	-	-	-	-	-
Industrial Waste	-	-	-	-	-	-	-	-
Municipal Waste	*52*	*42*	*54*	*57*	*58*	*56*	*42*	*64*
Non-Thermal								
Hydro	96819	103753	109544	118698	121382	110580	117062	119511
of which: pumped storage	*618*	*480*	*687*	*298*	*237*	*446*	*390*	*434*
Tide/Wave/Ocean	-	-	-	-	-	-	-	-
Wind	-	-	-	-	-	-	3	3
Other Fuel Sources	-	-	-	-	-	-	-	-
HEAT / CHALEUR (TJ)								
TOTAL HEAT	3232	3959	4529	4922	5087	5563	6197	6319
Hard Coal	147	147	155	144	108	133	598	610
Lignite and Sub-bit. Coal	-	-	-	-	-	-	-	-
Peat	-	-	-	-	-	-	-	-
Coke Oven and Blast Fur. Gas	-	-	114	36	54	54	51	52
Liquid Fuels/Refinery Gas	-	-	170	134	60	99	51	51
Natural Gas/Gas Works Gas	-	-	-	-	-	-	-	-
Nuclear	-	-	-	-	-	-	-	-
Geothermal	-	-	-	-	-	-	-	-
Solar	-	-	-	-	-	-	-	-
Electricity and Ambient Heat	-	-	-	878	1095	1316	1467	1496
Heat Pumps	-	-	-	*32*	*56*	*71*	*145*	*148*
Electric Boilers	-	-	-	*846*	*1039*	*1245*	*1322*	*1348*
Combustible Renewables and Wastes	3085	3812	4090	3730	3770	3961	4030	4110
Solid Biomass and Animal Products	-	-	*226*	*182*	*174*	*90*	*102*	*104*
Gases/Liquids from Biomass	-	-	-	-	-	-	-	-
Industrial Waste	-	-	-	-	-	-	*398*	*406*
Municipal Waste	*3085*	*3812*	*3864*	*3548*	*3596*	*3871*	*3530*	*3600*
Non-specified	-	-	-	-	-	-	-	-

* Figures for electricity generated from photovoltaic systems are not available separately and are included here with electricity produced from solar thermal.

* Les données sur l'électricité produite à l'aide de systèmes photovoltaïques ne sont pas disponibles séparément et sont montrées ici avec l'électricité produite par l'énergie thermique solaire.

Portugal / Portugal

Electricity and Heat Production in the Transformation Sector
Production de chaleur et d'élécricité du secteur transformation

	1986	1987	1988	1989	1990	1991	1992	1993
ELECTRICITY / ELECTRICITE (GWh)								
TOTAL ELECTRICITY	20355	20135	22489	25808	28500	29871	30087	31205
Thermal								
Hard Coal	3296	5135	5992	7298	9059	9748	10171	11375
Lignite and Sub-bit. Coal	-	-	-	-	-	-	-	-
Peat	-	-	-	-	-	-	-	-
Coke Oven and Blast Fur. Gas	38	42	40	41	45	63	85	83
Liquid Fuels/Refinery Gas	7873	5159	3502	11728	9399	10070	13866	10094
Natural Gas/Gas Works Gas	-	-	-	-	-	-	-	-
Nuclear	-	-	-	-	-	-	-	-
Geothermal	2	1	2	-	4	5	5	4
Solar *	-	-	-	-	-	-	-	-
Combustible Renewables and Wastes	604	613	651	661	689	808	882	901
Solid Biomass and Animal Products	*604*	*613*	*651*	*661*	*689*	*808*	*882*	*901*
Gases/Liquids from Biomass	-	-	-	-	-	-	-	-
Industrial Waste	-	-	-	-	-	-	-	-
Municipal Waste	-	-	-	-	-	-	-	-
Non-Thermal								
Hydro	8542	9185	12302	6079	9303	9176	5074	8737
of which: pumped storage	*28*	*32*	*69*	*260*	*146*	*133*	*428*	*199*
Tide/Wave/Ocean	-	-	-	-	-	-	-	-
Wind	-	-	-	1	1	1	4	11
Other Fuel Sources	-	-	-	-	-	-	-	-
HEAT / CHALEUR (TJ)								
TOTAL HEAT	1348	1398	1264	1411	1188	1182	1318	1437
Hard Coal	-	-	-	-	-	-	-	-
Lignite and Sub-bit. Coal	-	-	-	-	-	-	-	-
Peat	-	-	-	-	-	-	-	-
Coke Oven and Blast Fur. Gas	-	-	-	-	-	-	-	-
Liquid Fuels/Refinery Gas	1348	1398	1264	1411	1188	1182	1318	1437
Natural Gas/Gas Works Gas	-	-	-	-	-	-	-	-
Nuclear	-	-	-	-	-	-	-	-
Geothermal	-	-	-	-	-	-	-	-
Solar	-	-	-	-	-	-	-	-
Electricity and Ambient Heat	-	-	-	-	-	-	-	-
Heat Pumps	-	-	-	-	-	-	-	-
Electric Boilers	-	-	-	-	-	-	-	-
Combustible Renewables and Wastes	-	-	-	-	-	-	-	-
Solid Biomass and Animal Products	-	-	-	-	-	-	-	-
Gases/Liquids from Biomass	-	-	-	-	-	-	-	-
Industrial Waste	-	-	-	-	-	-	-	-
Municipal Waste	-	-	-	-	-	-	-	-
Non-specified	-	-	-	-	-	-	-	-

* Figures for electricity generated from photovoltaic systems are not available separately and are included here with electricity produced from solar thermal.
* *Les données sur l'électricité produite à l'aide de systèmes photovoltaïques ne sont pas disponibles séparément et sont montrées ici avec l'électricité produite par l'énergie thermique solaire.*

Spain / Espagne

Electricity and Heat Production in the Transformation Sector
Production de chaleur et d'éléctricité du secteur transformation

	1986	1987	1988	1989	1990	1991	1992	1993
ELECTRICITY / ELECTRICITE (GWh)								
TOTAL ELECTRICITY	129150	133390	139571	147842	151741	155704	158505	156529
Thermal								
Hard Coal	35622	37023	30105	41823	42629	42694	48220	46536
Lignite and Sub-bit. Coal	19186	17701	12966	17799	17108	16102	16002	15877
Peat	-	-	-	-	-	-	-	-
Coke Oven and Blast Fur. Gas	625	733	826	917	926	919	918	975
Liquid Fuels/Refinery Gas	6187	6436	6937	9138	8604	10156	14329	9544
Natural Gas/Gas Works Gas	2118	1496	1365	1398	1509	1361	1711	1196
Nuclear	37458	41271	50466	56126	54268	55578	55782	56060
Geothermal	-	-	-	-	-	-	-	-
Solar *	-	-	-	-	-	-	-	-
Combustible Renewables and Wastes	538	563	673	594	513	601	609	562
Solid Biomass and Animal Products	*538*	*563*	*673*	*594*	*513*	*601*	*559*	*521*
Gases/Liquids from Biomass	-	-	-	-	-	-	-	-
Industrial Waste	-	-	-	-	-	-	*50*	*41*
Municipal Waste	-	-	-	-	-	-	-	-
Non-Thermal								
Hydro	27416	28167	36233	20047	26184	28293	20934	25779
of which: pumped storage	*922*	*784*	*987*	*698*	*770*	*1011*	*2014*	*1402*
Tide/Wave/Ocean	-	-	-	-	-	-	-	-
Wind	-	-	-	-	-	-	-	-
Other Fuel Sources	-	-	-	-	-	-	-	-
HEAT / CHALEUR (TJ)								
TOTAL HEAT	-	775	679	665	181	160	-	-
Hard Coal	-	-	-	-	-	-	-	-
Lignite and Sub-bit. Coal	-	-	-	-	-	-	-	-
Peat	-	-	-	-	-	-	-	-
Coke Oven and Blast Fur. Gas	-	-	-	-	-	-	-	-
Liquid Fuels/Refinery Gas	-	775	679	665	181	160	-	-
Natural Gas/Gas Works Gas	-	-	-	-	-	-	-	-
Nuclear	-	-	-	-	-	-	-	-
Geothermal	-	-	-	-	-	-	-	-
Solar	-	-	-	-	-	-	-	-
Electricity and Ambient Heat	-	-	-	-	-	-	-	-
Heat Pumps	-	-	-	-	-	-	-	-
Electric Boilers	-	-	-	-	-	-	-	-
Combustible Renewables and Wastes	-	-	-	-	-	-	-	-
Solid Biomass and Animal Products	-	-	-	-	-	-	-	-
Gases/Liquids from Biomass	-	-	-	-	-	-	-	-
Industrial Waste	-	-	-	-	-	-	-	-
Municipal Waste	-	-	-	-	-	-	-	-
Non-specified	-	-	-	-	-	-	-	-

* Figures for electricity generated from photovoltaic systems are not available separately and are included here with electricity produced from solar thermal.
* *Les données sur l'électricité produite à l'aide de systèmes photovoltaïques ne sont pas disponibles séparément et sont montrées ici avec l'électricité produite par l'énergie thermique solaire.*

Sweden / Suède

Electricity and Heat Production in the Transformation Sector
Production de chaleur et d'électricité du secteur transformation

ELECTRICITY / ELECTRICITE (GWh)

	1986	1987	1988	1989	1990	1991	1992	1993
TOTAL ELECTRICITY	138651	146571	146230	143091	146508	147384	146444	145975
Thermal								
Hard Coal	1877	1864	1727	1205	1267	1961	1805	2100
Lignite and Sub-bit. Coal	-	-	-	-	-	-	-	-
Peat	-	-	-	-	-	-	118	189
Coke Oven and Blast Fur. Gas	328	253	308	306	477	491	754	729
Liquid Fuels/Refinery Gas	2846	2452	2018	1445	1201	2079	2625	3076
Natural Gas/Gas Works Gas	70	108	141	217	396	505	654	916
Nuclear	69951	67385	69424	65603	68185	76761	63544	61395
Geothermal	-	-	-	-	-	-	-	-
Solar *	-	-	-	-	-	-	-	-
Combustible Renewables and Wastes	2079	2061	2140	2389	1943	1912	2052	2142
Solid Biomass and Animal Products	*2079*	*2061*	*2140*	*2389*	*1943*	*1912*	*1960*	*2018*
Gases/Liquids from Biomass	-	-	-	-	-	-	*8*	*15*
Industrial Waste	-	-	-	-	-	-	*84*	*109*
Municipal Waste	-	-	-	-	-	-	-	-
Non-Thermal								
Hydro	61494	72442	70467	71921	73033	63662	74861	75380
of which: pumped storage	*567*	*594*	*589*	*175*	*530*	*426*	*529*	*780*
Tide/Wave/Ocean	-	-	-	-	-	-	-	-
Wind	6	6	5	5	6	13	31	48
Other Fuel Sources	-	-	-	-	-	-	-	-

HEAT / CHALEUR (TJ)

	1986	1987	1988	1989	1990	1991	1992	1993
TOTAL HEAT	109451	108090	91872	78358	78134	91022	148111	157944
Hard Coal	23120	37519	34532	24808	23176	22187	18445	17942
Lignite and Sub-bit. Coal	-	-	-	-	-	-	-	-
Peat	-	-	-	-	-	-	10427	9908
Coke Oven and Blast Fur. Gas	1817	1502	3045	4060	2584	2618	2700	2712
Liquid Fuels/Refinery Gas	18706	37034	23476	16412	13100	18377	21731	24500
Natural Gas/Gas Works Gas	134	1911	2752	4721	6356	7848	10678	9689
Nuclear	-	-	-	-	-	-	-	-
Geothermal	-	-	-	-	-	-	-	-
Solar	-	-	-	-	-	-	-	-
Electricity and Ambient Heat	-	-	-	-	-	-	45413	45108
Heat Pumps	-	-	-	-	-	-	*24868*	*27173*
Electric Boilers	-	-	-	-	-	-	*20545*	*17935*
Combustible Renewables and Wastes	6364	30124	28067	28357	32918	39992	38717	48085
Solid Biomass and Animal Products	*6364*	*30124*	*28067*	*28357*	*32918*	*39992*	*25167*	*33876*
Gases/Liquids from Biomass	-	-	-	-	-	-	*432*	*705*
Industrial Waste	-	-	-	-	-	-	-	-
Municipal Waste	-	-	-	-	-	-	*13118*	*13504*
Non-specified	59310	-	-	-	-	-	-	-

* Figures for electricity generated from photovoltaic systems are not available separately and are included here with electricity produced from solar thermal.
* *Les données sur l'électricité produite à l'aide de systèmes photovoltaïques ne sont pas disponibles séparément et sont montrées ici avec l'électricité produite par l'énergie thermique solaire.*

Switzerland / Suisse

Electricity and Heat Production in the Transformation Sector
Production de chaleur et d'éléctricité du secteur transformation

	1986	1987	1988	1989	1990	1991	1992	1993
ELECTRICITY / ELECTRICITE (GWh)								
TOTAL ELECTRICITY	57564	59890	60690	54767	55796	57803	59117	61070
Thermal								
Hard Coal	79	37	31	50	40	9	9	1
Lignite and Sub-bit. Coal	-	-	-	-	-	-	-	-
Peat	-	-	-	-	-	-	-	-
Coke Oven and Blast Fur. Gas	-	-	-	-	-	-	-	-
Liquid Fuels/Refinery Gas	297	306	288	298	284	536	636	294
Natural Gas/Gas Works Gas	224	267	263	264	303	341	355	386
Nuclear	22581	23003	22792	22836	23636	22953	23448	23351
Geothermal	-	-	-	-	-	-	-	-
Solar *	-	-	-	-	-	1	2	3
Combustible Renewables and Wastes	458	511	513	529	551	550	605	419
Solid Biomass and Animal Products	-	-	-	-	-	-	-	-
Gases/Liquids from Biomass	-	-	-	-	-	-	-	-
Industrial Waste	-	-	-	-	-	-	-	-
Municipal Waste	*458*	*511*	*513*	*529*	*551*	*550*	*605*	*419*
Non-Thermal								
Hydro	33925	35766	36803	30790	30982	33413	34062	36616
of which: pumped storage	*1023*	*1095*	*1012*	*1018*	*1187*	*1336*	*1362*	*838*
Tide/Wave/Ocean	-	-	-	-	-	-	-	-
Wind	-	-	-	-	-	-	-	-
Other Fuel Sources	-	-	-	-	-	-	-	-
HEAT / CHALEUR (TJ)								
TOTAL HEAT	10927	12351	11790	11870	11470	13260	13070	13310
Hard Coal	247	138	116	331	198	40	37	30
Lignite and Sub-bit. Coal	-	-	-	-	-	-	-	-
Peat	-	-	-	-	-	-	-	-
Coke Oven and Blast Fur. Gas	-	-	-	-	-	-	-	-
Liquid Fuels/Refinery Gas	1938	2173	1802	1714	1508	2513	3030	1164
Natural Gas/Gas Works Gas	1553	1918	1800	1685	1728	2043	1988	1906
Nuclear	779	858	830	890	890	910	800	820
Geothermal	-	-	-	-	-	-	-	-
Solar	-	-	-	-	-	-	-	-
Electricity and Ambient Heat								
Heat Pumps	-	-	-	-	-	-	-	-
Electric Boilers	-	-	-	-	-	-	-	-
Combustible Renewables and Wastes	6410	7264	7242	7250	7146	7754	7215	9390
Solid Biomass and Animal Products	-	-	-	-	-	-	-	-
Gases/Liquids from Biomass	-	-	-	-	-	-	-	-
Industrial Waste	-	-	-	-	-	-	-	-
Municipal Waste	*6410*	*7264*	*7242*	*7250*	*7146*	*7754*	*7215*	*9390*
Non-specified	-	-	-	-	-	-	-	-

* Figures for electricity generated from photovoltaic systems are not available separately and are included here with electricity produced from solar thermal.

* *Les données sur l'électricité produite à l'aide de systèmes photovoltaïques ne sont pas disponibles séparément et sont montrées ici avec l'électricité produite par l'énergie thermique solaire.*

Turkey / Turquie

Electricity and Heat Production in the Transformation Sector
Production de chaleur et d'éléctricité du secteur transformation

	1986	1987	1988	1989	1990	1991	1992	1993
ELECTRICITY / ELECTRICITE (GWh)								
TOTAL ELECTRICITY	39696	44353	48048	52044	57543	60246	67342	73808
Thermal								
Hard Coal	773	627	345	317	621	998	1815	1796
Lignite and Sub-bit. Coal	18665	17026	12141	19953	19560	20563	22756	21964
Peat	-	-	-	-	-	-	-	-
Coke Oven and Blast Fur. Gas	-	-	-	-	-	-	-	-
Liquid Fuels/Refinery Gas	7001	5496	3304	4248	3942	3294	5273	5175
Natural Gas/Gas Works Gas	1341	2528	3240	9524	10192	12589	10813	10788
Nuclear	-	-	-	-	-	-	-	-
Geothermal	44	58	69	63	80	81	70	78
Solar *	-	-	-	-	-	-	-	-
Combustible Renewables and Wastes	-	-	-	-	-	38	47	56
Solid Biomass and Animal Products	-	-	-	-	-	38	47	56
Gases/Liquids from Biomass	-	-	-	-	-	-	-	-
Industrial Waste	-	-	-	-	-	-	-	-
Municipal Waste	-	-	-	-	-	-	-	-
Non-Thermal								
Hydro	11872	18618	28949	17939	23148	22683	26568	33951
of which: pumped storage	-	-	-	-	-	-	-	-
Tide/Wave/Ocean	-	-	-	-	-	-	-	-
Wind	-	-	-	-	-	-	-	-
Other Fuel Sources	-	-	-	-	-	-	-	-
HEAT / CHALEUR (TJ)								
TOTAL HEAT	-	-	-	-	-	-	-	-
Hard Coal	-	-	-	-	-	-	-	-
Lignite and Sub-bit. Coal	-	-	-	-	-	-	-	-
Peat	-	-	-	-	-	-	-	-
Coke Oven and Blast Fur. Gas	-	-	-	-	-	-	-	-
Liquid Fuels/Refinery Gas	-	-	-	-	-	-	-	-
Natural Gas/Gas Works Gas	-	-	-	-	-	-	-	-
Nuclear	-	-	-	-	-	-	-	-
Geothermal	-	-	-	-	-	-	-	-
Solar	-	-	-	-	-	-	-	-
Electricity and Ambient Heat	-	-	-	-	-	-	-	-
Heat Pumps	-	-	-	-	-	-	-	-
Electric Boilers	-	-	-	-	-	-	-	-
Combustible Renewables and Wastes	-	-	-	-	-	-	-	-
Solid Biomass and Animal Products	-	-	-	-	-	-	-	-
Gases/Liquids from Biomass	-	-	-	-	-	-	-	-
Industrial Waste	-	-	-	-	-	-	-	-
Municipal Waste	-	-	-	-	-	-	-	-
Non-specified	-	-	-	-	-	-	-	-

* Figures for electricity generated from photovoltaic systems are not available separately and are included here with electricity produced from solar thermal.
* *Les données sur l'électricité produite à l'aide de systèmes photovoltaïques ne sont pas disponibles séparément et sont montrées ici avec l'électricité produite par l'énergie thermique solaire.*

United Kingdom / Royaume-Uni

Electricity and Heat Production in the Transformation Sector
Production de chaleur et d'éléctricité du secteur transformation

	1986	1987	1988	1989	1990	1991	1992	1993
ELECTRICITY / ELECTRICITE (GWh)								
TOTAL ELECTRICITY	301590	303750	308825	314585	319695	322805	320963	323029
Thermal								
Hard Coal	201361	209924	203312	199861	205169	207916	194823	166928
Lignite and Sub-bit. Coal	-	-	-	-	-	-	-	-
Peat	-	-	-	-	-	-	-	-
Coke Oven and Blast Fur. Gas	1170	1545	1759	1854	1774	1928	1236	1094
Liquid Fuels/Refinery Gas	31235	25189	27796	28793	34176	30345	34133	22928
Natural Gas/Gas Works Gas	1743	3332	3423	3549	3611	4132	5966	35570
Nuclear	59079	55238	63456	71734	65747	70543	76807	89353
Geothermal	-	-	-	-	-	-	-	-
Solar *	1	-	1	-	-	-	-	-
Combustible Renewables and Wastes	-	2279	1355	1425	1384	1076	884	1251
Solid Biomass and Animal Products	-	*2279*	*1355*	*1425*	*1384*	*1076*	*6*	*13*
Gases/Liquids from Biomass	-	-	-	-	-	-	*227*	*666*
Industrial Waste	-	-	-	-	-	-	*481*	*188*
Municipal Waste	-	-	-	-	-	-	*170*	*384*
Non-Thermal								
Hydro	7001	6243	7054	6659	7153	6103	7080	5686
of which: pumped storage	*2235*	*2106*	*2121*	*1910*	*1982*	*1523*	*1697*	*1437*
Tide/Wave/Ocean	-	-	-	-	-	-	-	-
Wind	-	-	669	710	681	762	34	219
Other Fuel Sources	-	-	-	-	-	-	-	-
HEAT / CHALEUR (TJ)								
TOTAL HEAT	574	565	484	519	530	289	-	6034
Hard Coal	-	-	-	-	-	-	-	1865
Lignite and Sub-bit. Coal	-	-	-	-	-	-	-	-
Peat	-	-	-	-	-	-	-	-
Coke Oven and Blast Fur. Gas	-	-	-	-	-	-	-	-
Liquid Fuels/Refinery Gas	574	565	484	519	483	289	-	2392
Natural Gas/Gas Works Gas	-	-	-	-	47	-	-	1598
Nuclear	-	-	-	-	-	-	-	-
Geothermal	-	-	-	-	-	-	-	-
Solar	-	-	-	-	-	-	-	-
Electricity and Ambient Heat	-	-	-	-	-	-	-	-
Heat Pumps	-	-	-	-	-	-	-	-
Electric Boilers	-	-	-	-	-	-	-	-
Combustible Renewables and Wastes	-	-	-	-	-	-	-	179
Solid Biomass and Animal Products	-	-	-	-	-	-	-	-
Gases/Liquids from Biomass	-	-	-	-	-	-	-	*42*
Industrial Waste	-	-	-	-	-	-	-	*101*
Municipal Waste	-	-	-	-	-	-	-	*36*
Non-specified	-	-	-	-	-	-	-	-

* Figures for electricity generated from photovoltaic systems are not available separately and are included here with electricity produced from solar thermal.
* Les données sur l'électricité produite à l'aide de systèmes photovoltaïques ne sont pas disponibles séparément et sont montrées ici avec l'électricité produite par l'énergie thermique solaire.

United States / Etats-Unis

Electricity and Heat Production in the Transformation Sector
Production de chaleur et d'élctricité du secteur transformation

	1986	1987	1988	1989	1990	1991	1992	1993
ELECTRICITY / ELECTRICITE (GWh)								
TOTAL ELECTRICITY	2639724	2732532	2874797	3144994	3197267	3273121	3291866	3411281
Thermal								
Hard Coal	1399908	1481479	1554322	1598709	1603610	1599893	1174096	1166868
Lignite and Sub-bit. Coal	82931	84767	94177	93979	96038	100442	553959	633787
Peat	-	-	-	-	-	-	10	16
Coke Oven and Blast Fur. Gas	-	-	-	-	-	11773	13211	13034
Liquid Fuels/Refinery Gas	146146	126788	159323	175297	130649	127079	106509	120309
Natural Gas/Gas Works Gas	265904	291704	270497	371432	381669	402230	426908	437220
Nuclear	438880	482586	558591	561165	611589	649399	655970	646987
Geothermal	10926	11422	10918	14948	15967	16223	17168	17774
Solar *	18	14	9	492	666	782	749	901
Combustible Renewables and Wastes	1259	1580	1791	53503	65868	53539	65487	68270
Solid Biomass and Animal Products	*1259*	*1580*	*1791*	*53503*	*65868*	*53539*	*40558*	*41602*
Gases/Liquids from Biomass	-	-	-	-	-	-	*3033*	*3304*
Industrial Waste	-	-	-	-	-	-	*9339*	*10349*
Municipal Waste	-	-	-	-	-	-	*12557*	*13015*
Non-Thermal								
Hydro	293752	252192	225169	273636	288960	309155	274883	303063
of which: pumped storage	-	*15345*	*16755*	*17475*	*15808*	*20950*	*20512*	*21347*
Tide/Wave/Ocean	-	-	-	-	-	-	-	-
Wind	-	-	-	1833	2251	2606	2916	3052
Other Fuel Sources	-	-	-	-	-	-	-	-
HEAT / CHALEUR (TJ)								
TOTAL HEAT	81768	85143	79474	94392	81308	296191	377128	404634
Hard Coal	-	-	-	-	-	39527	55224	57643
Lignite and Sub-bit. Coal	-	-	-	-	-	-	18895	6031
Peat	-	-	-	-	-	-	-	-
Coke Oven and Blast Fur. Gas	-	-	-	-	-	23729	23542	21628
Liquid Fuels/Refinery Gas	-	-	-	-	-	32847	64585	62325
Natural Gas/Gas Works Gas	-	-	-	-	-	140916	169304	218875
Nuclear	-	-	-	-	-	-	-	-
Geothermal	-	-	-	-	-	-	-	-
Solar	-	-	-	-	-	-	-	-
Electricity and Ambient Heat	-	-	-	-	-	-	-	-
Heat Pumps	-	-	-	-	-	-	-	-
Electric Boilers	-	-	-	-	-	-	-	-
Combustible Renewables and Wastes	-	-	-	-	-	59172	45578	38132
Solid Biomass and Animal Products	-	-	-	-	-	*59172*	*35720*	*27766*
Gases/Liquids from Biomass	-	-	-	-	-	-	*44*	*3*
Industrial Waste	-	-	-	-	-	-	*1222*	*3784*
Municipal Waste	-	-	-	-	-	-	*8592*	*6579*
Non-specified	81768	85143	79474	94392	81308	-	-	-

* Figures for electricity generated from photovoltaic systems are not available separately and are included here with electricity produced from solar thermal.
* Les données sur l'électricité produite à l'aide de systèmes photovoltaïques ne sont pas disponibles séparément et sont montrées ici avec l'électricité produite par l'énergie thermique solaire.

INTERNATIONAL ENERGY AGENCY
ENERGY STATISTICS DIVISION
POSSIBLE STAFF VACANCIES

The Division is responsible for statistical support and advice to the policy and operational Divisions of the International Energy Agency. It also produces a wide range of annual and quarterly publications complemented by a data service on microcomputer diskettes. For these purposes, the Division maintains, on a central computer and an expanding network of microcomputers, extensive international databases covering most aspects of energy supply and use.

Vacancies for statistical assistants occur from time to time. Typically their work includes:

● Gathering and vetting data from questionnaires and publications, discussions on data issues with respondents to questionnaires in national administrations and fuel companies.

● Managing energy databases on a mainframe computer and microcomputers in order to maintain accuracy and timeliness of output.

● Preparing computer procedures for the production of tables, reports and analyses. Seasonal adjustment of data and analysis of trends and market movements.

● Preparing studies on an ad-hoc basis as required by other Divisions of the International Energy Agency.

Nationals of any OECD Member Country are eligible for appointment. Basic salaries range from 14 790 to 19 000 French francs per month, depending on qualifications. The possibilities for advancement are good for candidates with appropriate qualifications and experience. Tentative enquiries about future vacancies are welcomed from men and women with relevant qualifications and experience. Applications in French or English, specifying the reference "ENERSTAT" and enclosing a curriculum vitae, should be sent to:

Human Resources Management Division
Organisation for Economic
Co-operation and Development
2, rue André-Pascal, 75775 Paris CEDEX 16, France

AGENCE INTERNATIONALE DE L'ENERGIE
DIVISION DES STATISTIQUES DE L'ENERGIE
VACANCES D'EMPLOI EVENTUELLES

Cette Division est chargée de fournir une aide et des conseils dans le domaine statistique aux Divisions administratives et opérationnelles de l'Agence internationale de l'énergie. En outre, elle diffuse une large gamme de publications annuelles et trimestrielles complétées par un service de données sur disquettes pour micro-ordinateur. A cet effet, la Division tient à jour, sur un ordinateur central et un réseau de plus en plus étendu de micro-ordinateurs, de vastes bases de données internationales portant sur la plupart des aspects de l'offre et de la consommation d'énergie.

Des postes d'assistant statisticien sont susceptibles de se libérer de temps à autre. Les fonctions dévolues aux titulaires de ces postes sont notamment les suivantes :

● Rassembler et valider les données tirées de questionnaires et de publications, ainsi que d'échanges de vues sur les données avec les répondants aux questionnaires qui appartiennent à des administrations nationales ou à des entreprises du secteur des combustibles.

● Gérer des bases de données relatives à l'énergie sur un ordinateur central et des micro-ordinateurs en vue de s'assurer de l'exactitude et de l'actualité des données de sortie.

● Mettre au point des procédures informatiques pour l'établissement de tableaux, rapports et analyses. Procéder à l'ajustement saisonnier des données et analyses relatives aux tendances et aux fluctuations du marché.

● Etablir des études en fonction des besoins des autres Divisions de l'Agence internationale de l'énergie.

Ces postes sont ouverts aux candidats ressortissants des pays Membres de l'OCDE. Les traitements de base sont compris entre 14 790 et 19 000 francs français par mois, suivant les qualifications. Les candidats possédant les qualifications et l'expérience appropriées se verront offrir des perspectives de promotion. Les demandes de renseignements sur les postes susceptibles de se libérer qui émanent de personnes dotées des qualifications et de l'expérience voulues seront les bienvenues. Les candidatures, rédigées en français ou en anglais et accompagnées d'un curriculum vitae, doivent être envoyées, sous la référence "ENERSTAT", à l'adresse suivante :

Division de la Gestion des Ressources Humaines
Organisation de coopération et de
développement économiques
2, rue André-Pascal, 75775 Paris CEDEX 16, France

MULTILINGUAL PULLOUT

MULTILINGUAL PULLOUT

MAIN SALES OUTLETS OF OECD PUBLICATIONS
PRINCIPAUX POINTS DE VENTE DES PUBLICATIONS DE L'OCDE

ARGENTINA – ARGENTINE
Carlos Hirsch S.R.L.
Galería Güemes, Florida 165, 4° Piso
1333 Buenos Aires   Tel. (1) 331.1787 y 331.2391
Telefax: (1) 331.1787

AUSTRALIA – AUSTRALIE
D.A. Information Services
648 Whitehorse Road, P.O.B 163
Mitcham, Victoria 3132   Tel. (03) 873.4411
Telefax: (03) 873.5679

AUSTRIA – AUTRICHE
Gerold & Co.
Graben 31
Wien I   Tel. (0222) 533.50.14

BELGIUM – BELGIQUE
Jean De Lannoy
Avenue du Roi 202
B-1060 Bruxelles   Tel. (02) 538.51.69/538.08.41
Telefax: (02) 538.08.41

CANADA
Renouf Publishing Company Ltd.
1294 Algoma Road
Ottawa, ON K1B 3W8   Tel. (613) 741.4333
Telefax: (613) 741.5439
Stores:
61 Sparks Street
Ottawa, ON K1P 5R1   Tel. (613) 238.8985
211 Yonge Street
Toronto, ON M5B 1M4   Tel. (416) 363.3171
Telefax: (416)363.59.63

Les Éditions La Liberté Inc.
3020 Chemin Sainte-Foy
Sainte-Foy, PQ G1X 3V6   Tel. (418) 658.3763
Telefax: (418) 658.3763

Federal Publications Inc.
165 University Avenue, Suite 701
Toronto, ON M5H 3B8   Tel. (416) 860.1611
Telefax: (416) 860.1608

Les Publications Fédérales
1185 Université
Montréal, QC H3B 3A7   Tel. (514) 954.1633
Telefax : (514) 954.1635

CHINA – CHINE
China National Publications Import
Export Corporation (CNPIEC)
16 Gongti E. Road, Chaoyang District
P.O. Box 88 or 50
Beijing 100704 PR   Tel. (01) 506.6688
Telefax: (01) 506.3101

DENMARK – DANEMARK
Munksgaard Book and Subscription Service
35, Nørre Søgade, P.O. Box 2148
DK-1016 København K   Tel. (33) 12.85.70
Telefax: (33) 12.93.87

FINLAND – FINLANDE
Akateeminen Kirjakauppa
Keskuskatu 1, P.O. Box 128
00100 Helsinki

Subscription Services/Agence d'abonnements :
P.O. Box 23
00371 Helsinki   Tel. (358 0) 12141
Telefax: (358 0) 121.4450

FRANCE
OECD/OCDE
Mail Orders/Commandes par correspondance:
2, rue André-Pascal
75775 Paris Cedex 16   Tel. (33-1) 45.24.82.00
Telefax: (33-1) 49.10.42.76
Telex: 640048 OCDE
Orders via Minitel, France only/
Commandes par Minitel, France exclusivement :
36 15 OCDE
OECD Bookshop/Librairie de l'OCDE :
33, rue Octave-Feuillet
75016 Paris   Tel. (33-1) 45.24.81.67
(33-1) 45.24.81.81
Documentation Française
29, quai Voltaire
75007 Paris   Tel. 40.15.70.00
Gibert Jeune (Droit-Économie)
6, place Saint-Michel
75006 Paris   Tel. 43.25.91.19
Librairie du Commerce International
10, avenue d'Iéna
75016 Paris   Tel. 40.73.34.60
Librairie Dunod
Université Paris-Dauphine
Place du Maréchal de Lattre de Tassigny
75016 Paris   Tel. (1) 44.05.40.13
Librairie Lavoisier
11, rue Lavoisier
75008 Paris   Tel. 42.65.39.95
Librairie L.G.D.J. - Montchrestien
20, rue Soufflot
75005 Paris   Tel. 46.33.89.85
Librairie des Sciences Politiques
30, rue Saint-Guillaume
75007 Paris   Tel. 45.48.36.02
P.U.F.
49, boulevard Saint-Michel
75005 Paris   Tel. 43.25.83.40
Librairie de l'Université
12a, rue Nazareth
13100 Aix-en-Provence   Tel. (16) 42.26.18.08
Documentation Française
165, rue Garibaldi
69003 Lyon   Tel. (16) 78.63.32.23
Librairie Decitre
29, place Bellecour
69002 Lyon   Tel. (16) 72.40.54.54

GERMANY – ALLEMAGNE
OECD Publications and Information Centre
August-Bebel-Allee 6
D-53175 Bonn   Tel. (0228) 959.120
Telefax: (0228) 959.12.17

GREECE – GRÈCE
Librairie Kauffmann
Mavrokordatou 9
106 78 Athens   Tel. (01) 32.55.321
Telefax: (01) 36.33.967

HONG-KONG
Swindon Book Co. Ltd.
13–15 Lock Road
Kowloon, Hong Kong   Tel. 366.80.31
Telefax: 739.49.75

HUNGARY – HONGRIE
Euro Info Service
Margitsziget, Európa Ház
1138 Budapest   Tel. (1) 111.62.16
Telefax : (1) 111.60.61

ICELAND – ISLANDE
Mál Mog Menning
Laugavegi 18, Pósthólf 392
121 Reykjavik   Tel. 162.35.23

INDIA – INDE
Oxford Book and Stationery Co.
Scindia House
New Delhi 110001   Tel.(11) 331.5896/5308
Telefax: (11) 332.5993
17 Park Street
Calcutta 700016   Tel. 240832

INDONESIA – INDONÉSIE
Pdii-Lipi
P.O. Box 269/JKSMG/88
Jakarta 12790   Tel. 583467
Telex: 62 875

ISRAEL
Praedicta
5 Shatner Street
P.O. Box 34030
Jerusalem 91430   Tel. (2) 52.84.90/1/2
Telefax: (2) 52.84.93
R.O.Y.
P.O. Box 13056
Tel Aviv 61130   Tél. (3) 49.61.08
Telefax (3) 544.60.39

ITALY – ITALIE
Libreria Commissionaria Sansoni
Via Duca di Calabria 1/1
50125 Firenze   Tel. (055) 64.54.15
Telefax: (055) 64.12.57
Via Bartolini 29
20155 Milano   Tel. (02) 36.50.83
Editrice e Libreria Herder
Piazza Montecitorio 120
00186 Roma   Tel. 679.46.28
Telefax: 678.47.51
Libreria Hoepli
Via Hoepli 5
20121 Milano   Tel. (02) 86.54.46
Telefax: (02) 805.28.86
Libreria Scientifica
Dott. Lucio de Biasio 'Aeiou'
Via Coronelli, 6
20146 Milano   Tel. (02) 48.95.45.52
Telefax: (02) 48.95.45.48

JAPAN – JAPON
OECD Publications and Information Centre
Landic Akasaka Building
2-3-4 Akasaka, Minato-ku
Tokyo 107   Tel. (81.3) 3586.2016
Telefax: (81.3) 3584.7929

KOREA – CORÉE
Kyobo Book Centre Co. Ltd.
P.O. Box 1658, Kwang Hwa Moon
Seoul   Tel. 730.78.91
Telefax: 735.00.30

MALAYSIA – MALAISIE
Co-operative Bookshop Ltd.
University of Malaya
P.O. Box 1127, Jalan Pantai Baru
59700 Kuala Lumpur
Malaysia   Tel. 756.5000/756.5425
Telefax: 757.3661

MEXICO – MEXIQUE
Revistas y Periodicos Internacionales S.A. de C.V.
Florencia 57 - 1004
Mexico, D.F. 06600   Tel. 207.81.00
Telefax : 208.39.79

NETHERLANDS – PAYS-BAS
SDU Uitgeverij Plantijnstraat
Externe Fondsen
Postbus 20014
2500 EA's-Gravenhage   Tel. (070) 37.89.880
Voor bestellingen: Telefax: (070) 34.75.778

OECD PUBLICATIONS, 2, rue André-Pascal, 75775 PARIS CEDEX 16
PRINTED IN FRANCE
(61 95 16 3) ISBN 92-64-04457-4 – N° 47951 1995